Solutions Manual to Accompany

Frederick S. Hillier
Professor of Operations Research
Stanford University

Gerald J. Lieberman
Professor Emeritus of Operations Research and Statistics
Stanford University

INTRODUCTION TO OPERATIONS RESEARCH

Sixth Edition

Prepared by:
Kenichi Futamura, Herbert Hackney and Qing Wu
with the assistance of
Ann Hillier and Sumana Sur

McGraw-Hill, Inc.
New York St. Louis San Francisco Auckland Bogotá
Caracas Lisbon London Madrid Mexico City Milan Montreal
New Delhi San Juan Singapore Sydney Tokyo Toronto

This book is printed on recycled, acid-free paper containing a minimum of 50% recycled de-inked fiber.

Solutions Manual to Accompany
INTRODUCTION TO OPERATIONS RESEARCH
Sixth Edition

ISBN 0-07-028957-3

234567890 BKM BKM 909876

Instructor's Manual

Introduction to Operations Research

TABLE OF CONTENTS

Note to Instructors:

Introduction to Operations Research, Sixth Edition comes packaged with OR Courseware formatted for either IBM PC or Macintosh computers. If you would like to obtain one or the other alternative form of the OR Courseware, please contact your local McGraw-Hill sales representative or Marketing Manager for Engineering, College Division, 27th Floor, 1221 Avenue of the Americas, New York, NY 10020, (212) 512-3500, who will be happy to arrange for you to receive it.

RECOMMENDED USE OF THE SOFTWARE ACCOMPANYING THE BOOK

Prepared by Frederick S. Hillier and Gerald J. Lieberman

We begin by highlighting the special features of the book's software. (Most of this information also is available to students in Appendix 1 of the book.) Section 2 then provides a road map that outlines our recommendations for where to use the various routines of the software in parallel with coverage of the book.

1. Special Features of the Software

The book's software, called OR Courseware, is quite different from the usual software now widely available for running the algorithms of operations research (OR) on microcomputers, and so should be used differently. First and foremost, it is *tutorial software*, designed specifically to be a *teaching supplement* to the book as a *personal tutor* for the student. Its most important tools are *demonstration examples* and *interactive routines* for learning and understanding the algorithms. In addition, it does include some of the usual automatic routines for solving the textbook-size problems found in the book. (Key changes for this edition include making some of the automatic routines more powerful and adding a considerable number of new routines of all three types.)

The *demonstration examples* (demos) supplement the examples in the book in ways that cannot be duplicated on the printed page. Each one vividly demonstrates one of the algorithms or concepts of OR in action. Most combine an *algebraic description* of each step with a *geometric display* of what is happening. Some of these geometric displays become quite dynamic, with moving points or moving lines, to demonstrate the evolution of the algorithm. The demos also are integrated with the book, using the same notation and terminology, with references to material in the book, etc. Students find them an enjoyable and effective learning aid.

Each demo should be assigned as soon as coverage of the corresponding topic begins. After gaining basic insights from the initial viewing, students then are likely to return to the demo for reinforcement while doing homework, etc. In Sec. 2, we shall cite all of the available demos and where they arise relative to the sections of the book.

Interactive routines also are a key tutorial feature of this software. Each one enables the student to *interactively execute* one of the algorithms of OR. While viewing all relevant information on the computer screen, the student makes the decision on how the next step of the algorithm should be performed, and then the computer does all of the necessary number crunching to execute that step. A Help file always is available to guide the student through the computer mechanics. When uncertain about the logic of the algorithm for how to perform the next algorithm step, the student can switch temporarily to reviewing the corresponding demonstration example and then switch back to the same point in the interactive routine. When a previous mistake is discovered, the routine allows the student to quickly backtrack to undo the mistake. To get the student started properly, the computer points out any mistake made on the *first iteration* (where possible). When done, the student prints out all the work performed to turn in for homework.

In our judgment, these interactive routines provide the "right way" in this computer age for students to do homework designed to help them learn the algorithms of OR. They enable focusing on concepts rather than mindless number crunching, thereby making the learning process far more efficient and effective, as well as far more stimulating. They also point the student in the right direction, including organizing the work to be done. However, they do not do the thinking for the student. Like any good homework assignment, the student is allowed to make mistakes (and to learn from those mistakes), so that hard thinking will be done to try to stay on the right path. We have been careful in designing the division of labor between the computer and the student to provide both an efficient and complete learning process for the student. In certain cases, the computer will take over a relatively routine task after the student has demonstrated the ability to perform it correctly on the first iteration.

The software also includes a considerable number of *automatic routines* to provide number crunching help to students. Many are for stochastic modeling problems involving complicated formulas. Several others are for algorithms that are not well suited for interactive execution. In some cases, an algorithm will have both kinds of routines available. In these cases, the automatic routine will only show and print the original problem and the final result.

Except for the two introductory chapters, relevant routines are available for every chapter. These routines are listed by type just in front of the chapter's problems. A code is used next to the problem numbers to instruct the student as to when a routine of each type can or should be used.

All the routines are designed only for dealing with problems of the size found in this book. (Some of the automatic routines have been made more powerful for this edition so that they can handle the new large case problems that have been added at the end of some chapters, and can also handle student projects of similar size.) Each routine includes an introduction (found under the Help menu) that spells out limits on problem size, etc. It should be made clear to students that realistic problems often are vastly larger, and that powerful software packages are available for such problems. Some instructors may even want to give their students hands-on experience with one such package.

The OR Courseware is divided into two programs:

1. MathProg (short for "Mathematical Programming"),
2. ProbMod (short for "Probabilistic Models"),

that correspond roughly to Chapters 3-13 and Chapters 14-21, respectively, of the book. (MathProg now combines the LinProg and MathProg programs from the preceding edition of the book.) Both programs are included on the one diskette packaged with the book.

Two versions of the book are available, one containing a diskette for an IBM-compatible personal computer with a graphics card and the other containing a diskette for a Macintosh computer. We also have included with this *Instructor's Guide* both types of diskettes. These extra diskettes are both for your convenience and for copying by any of your students who did not obtain the desired type of diskette with their book. Please announce that you have both types available.

The programs are menu driven, with detailed instructions available from the Help file for students without much computer experience.

2. *A Road Map for the Use of the Software*

The students are first introduced to the OR Courseware in Section 1.4 of the book. Problem 1.4-1 then takes them on a guided tour through the software, and we strongly recommend that this problem be assigned. Appendix 1 provides documentation for the OR Courseware. Most of the routines are mentioned in the book at the point where they first become relevant, and then listed at the end of the chapter.

For each of the two programs, we next give a table whose fourth column lists all the routines contained in that program. (Those given in parentheses are preliminary routines that must precede the one given below.) The third column identifies the area of the software in which the routine is found. The second column indicates whether that routine is a demo (demonstration example), an interactive routine, or an automatic routine. The first column gives the section in the book where the routine first becomes relevant. In the case of a demo, we recommend that it be assigned concurrently with coverage of that section. In the case of an interactive or automatic routine, we recommend that the students generally be instructed to use this routine for doing homework problems assigned from that section (and perhaps some subsequent sections) as prescribed by the code given next to the problem number. Many of the solutions given in this *Instructor's Guide* are actual printouts from one of these routines.

Table 1. Routines Available in MathProg

Sec.	Type	Area	Name of Routine	Comment
3.1	Demo	General LP	Graphical Method	
3.1	Interactive	General LP	(Enter or Revise a General LP Model) Solve Interactively by the Graphical Method	
3.4	Automatic	General LP	Solve Automatically by the Simplex Method	
4.2	Demo	General LP	Interpretation of the Slack Variables	
4.3	Demo	General LP	Simplex Method — Algebraic Form	
4.3	Interactive	General LP	(Set up for the (interactive) Simplex Method) Solve Interactively by the Simplex Method	Choose Algebraic Form from the Option menu
4.4	Demo	General LP	Simplex Method — Tabular Form	
4.4	Interactive	General LP	Solve Interactively by the Simplex Method	Choose Tabular Form from the Option Menu
4.6	Interactive	General LP	Set Up for the (interactive) Simplex Method Solve Interactively by the Simplex Method	Have choice of Big M or Two-Phase method
4.9	Automatic	General LP	Solve Automatically by the Interior-Point Algorithm	
5.3	Demo	General LP	Fundamental Insight	
6.6	Demo	General LP	Sensitivity Analysis	
6.7	Interactive	General LP	Sensitivity Analysis	
7.4	Automatic	General LP	Solve Automatically by the Interior-Point Algorithm	Choose $\alpha = 0.5$ or $\alpha = 0.9$ from the Option menu
8.1	Automatic	Transp. Problem	(Enter or Revise a Transportation Problem) Solve Automatically by the Transportation Simplex Method	
8.2	Demo	Transp. Problem	The Transportation Problem	
8.2	Interactive	Transp. Problem	(Find Initial Basic Feasible Solution) Solve Interactively by the Transportation Simplex Method	Use the Option Menu to choose the criterion for finding the initial basic feasible solution
8.3	Automatic	Transp. Problem	(Enter or Revise an Assignment Problem) Solve Automatically by the Assignment Problem Algorithm	
9.7	Demo	Network Analysis	Network Simplex Method	
9.7	Interactive	Network Analysis	Network Simplex Method - Interactive	Fits Probs. 9.7-2 to 9.7-8 only
9.7	Automatic	Network Analysis	Network Simplex Method - Automatic	
9.8	Automatic	Network Analysis	CPM Method of Time-Cost Trade-offs — Automatic	

Table 1 continued on next page.

Sec.	Type	Area	Name of Routine	Comment
10.3	Demo	Dynamic Progr.	Deterministic Dynamic Programming Alg.	
10.3	Interactive	Dynamic Progr.	Interactive Deterministic Dynamic Programming Algorithm	
12.5	Demo	Integer Progr.	Binary Integer Programming Branch-and-Bound Algorithm	
12.5	Interactive	Integer Progr.	(Enter or Revise an IP Model) Solve Binary Integer Program Interactively	
12.5	Automatic	Integer Progr.	Solve Binary Integer Program Automatically	
12.6	Demo	Integer Progr.	Mixed Integer Programming Branch-and-Bound Algorithm	
12.6	Interactive	Integer Progr.	Solve Mixed Integer Program Interactively	
12.6	Automatic	Integer Progr.	Solve Mixed Integer Program Automatically	
13.4	Interactive	Nonlinear Progr.	Interactive One-Dimensional Search Procedure	
13.4	Automatic	Nonlinear Progr.	Automatic One-Dimensional Search Procedure	
13.5	Demo	Nonlinear Progr.	Gradient Search Procedure	
13.5	Interactive	Nonlinear Progr.	Interactive Gradient Search Procedure	
13.5	Automatic	Nonlinear Progr.	Automatic Gradient Search Procedure	
13.7	Interactive	Nonlinear Progr. General LP	(Interactive Modified Simplex Method) Modified Simplex Method	
13.7	Automatic	Nonlinear Progr.	Solve Quadratic Programming Model Automatically	
13.9	Demo	Nonlinear Progr.	Frank-Wolfe Algorithm	
13.9	Interactive	Nonlinear Progr.	Interactive Frank-Wolfe Algorithm	
13.10	Demo	Nonlinear Progr.	SUMT	
13.10	Automatic	Nonlinear Progr.	Sequential Unconstrained Minimization Algorithm (SUMT)	

Table 2. Routines Available in ProbMod

Sec.	Type	Area	Name of Routine	Comments
14.3	Automatic	Markov Chains	(Enter Transition Matrix) Chapman-Kolmogorov Equations	
14.6	Automatic	Markov Chains	Steady State Probabilities	
15.6	Automatic	Queueing Theory	The M/M/s Model	
15.6	Automatic	Queueing Theory	The Finite Queue Variation of the M/M/s Model	
15.6	Automatic	Queueing Theory	The Finite Calling Population Variation of the M/M/s Model	
15.8	Automatic	Queueing Theory	Nonpreemptive Priorities Model	
15.8	Automatic	Queueing Theory	Preemptive Priorities Model	
15.9	Automatic	Queueing Theory	Jackson Network	
17.4	Automatic	Inventory Theory	Single Period Model, No Setup	Use the Option Menu to choose either a uniform distribution or an exponential distribution for the demand distribution.
17.4	Automatic	Inventory Theory	Single Period Model, With Setup	
17.4	Automatic	Inventory Theory	Two-Period Model, No Setup	
17.4	Automatic	Inventory Theory	Infinite-Period Model, No Setup	
17.4	Automatic	Inventory Theory	Continuous Review Model, With Fixed Delivery Lag - Backlogging	
17.4	Automatic	Inventory Theory	Continuous Review Model, With Fixed Delivery Lag - No Backlogging	
18.3	Automatic	Forecasting	Exponential Smoothing Forecasting Procedure	
18.4	Automatic	Forecasting	Exponential Smoothing With Linear Trend Forecasting Procedure	
18.5	Automatic	Forecasting	Exponential Smoothing With Seasonal Effects Forecasting Procedure	
18.8	Automatic	Forecasting	Method of Least Squares	
19.4	Demo	Markov Decision Processes	Policy Improvement Algorithm — Average Cost Case	
19.4	Interactive	Markov Decision Processes	(Enter Markov Decision Model) Interactive Policy Improvement Algorithm — Average Cost	
19.5	Interactive	Markov Decision Processes	Interactive Policy Improvement Algorithm — Discounted Cost	
19.5	Interactive	Markov Decision Processes	Interactive Method of Successive Approximations	
20.3	Automatic	Decision Analysis	(Enter Prior Distribution) Solve for Posterior Distribution	
21.1	Demo	Simulation	Simulating a Basic Queueing Model	
21.1	Demo	Simulation	Simulating a Queueing Model with Priorities	
21.1	Interactive	Simulation	(Enter Queueing Problem) Interactively Simulate Queueing Problem	
21.1	Automatic	Simulation	Automatically Simulate Queueing Problem	

Chapter 2

2.1-1

(a) San Francisco Police Department has a total police force of 1900, with 850 officers on patrol. The total budget of SFPD in 1986 was $176 million with patrol coverage cost of $79 million. This brings out the importance of the problem.

Like most police departments, SFPD was also operated with manually designed schedules. It was impossible to know if the manual schedules were optimal in serving residents' needs. It was difficult to evaluate alternative policies for scheduling and deploying officers. There was also the problem of poor response time and low productivity, pressure of increasing demands for service with decreasing budgets. The scheduling system was facing the problem of providing the highest possible correlation between the number of officers needed and the number actually on duty during each hour. All these problems led the Task Force to search for a new system and thus undertake this study.

(b) After reviewing the manual system, the Task Force decided to search for a new system. The criteria it specified included the following six directives :

-- the system must use the CAD (computer aided dispatching) system, which provides a large and rich data base on resident calls for service. The CAD system was used to dispatch patrol officers to call for service and to maintain operating statistics such as call types, waiting times, travel time and total time consumed in servicing calls. The directive was to use this data on calls for service and consumed times to establish work load by day of week and hour of day

-- it must generate optimal and realistic integer schedules that meet management policy guidelines using a micro-computer

-- it must allow easy adjustment of optimal schedules to accommodate human considerations without sacrificing productivity

-- it must create schedules in less than 30 minutes and make changes in less than 60 seconds

-- it must be able to perform both tactical scheduling and strategic policy testing in one integrated system

-- the user interface must be flexible and easy, allowing the users (captains) to decide the sequence of functions to be executed instead of forcing them to follow a restrictive sequence.

(c) The computer aided dispatching (CAD) system also is used to gather hourly data on historical patrol activity. For each of the 168 hours of the week, data are gathered on call types, consumed times by call type, and percent of each call type requiring two or more officers. Other operating statistics maintained include waiting times and travel times. When needed for forecasting purposes, the call and consumed time data are downloaded from the mainframe to a microcomputer. The other needed data are input by the captains and stored in a file for reuse. (See Figures 1 and 2 of the article for further information.)

(d) A list of the various tangible and intangible benefits are as follows :

-- total savings of $11 million per year
-- finding 4/10 plan (4 day 10 hour shift) is superior to 5/8 plan (5 day 8 hour shift) which leads to a saving of 5.8 million
-- added 176,000 productive hours to the patrol staff every year --> a saving of $5.2 million per year
-- response times dropped an average of 20 percent which led to potential crime reduction
-- an approximate 50 percent reduction in shortages and surpluses of police officers
-- resulted in a 32 percent increase in traffic citation --> a $3 million increase in citation revenues
-- a cost benefit analysis of the scheduling aspects shows a one-time cost of $50,000 and benefits of $5.2 million per year
-- a 36 percent decrease in days lost due to sick leave
-- a 21 percent increase in self-initiated office activities
-- an improved morale of the officers revealed by a survey by an approval rating of 96 percent
-- it allowed management to adjust schedules easily and quickly to meet seasonal changes in pattern of crime.

2.1.2

(a) Taking all the statistics of AIDS cases into account it was inferred that just one-third of all cases nation-wide involved some aspect of Injection Drug Use(IDU). But in contrast to this national picture, over 60% of 500 cases reported in New Haven , Connecticut was traced to drug use. Though it was realized previously , by 1987 it was clear that the dominant mode of HIV transmission in New Haven was the practice of needle sharing for drug injection.

This was the background of the study and in 1987 a street outreach program was implemented which included a survey of drug addicts with partial intent to determine why IDUs continued to share needles given the threat of HIV infection and AIDS. It was claimed by the survey respondents that IDUs shared needles since they were scared and feared arrest for possessing a syringe without prescription which was forbidden by law in Connecticut. Respondents also pointed out difficulties involved in entering drug treatment program. The officials recognized that logical intervention was needle exchange whereby IDUs exchanged their used needles for clean ones. This would remove infectious drug injection equipment from circulation and also ease access to clean needles. Further, contacts made as a result of needle exchange might lead some active IDUs to consider counseling or enter drug treatment. After a lot of lobbying finally the bill for the first legal needle exchange program became effective on July 1, 1990.

(b) The design for the needle exchange program was achieved over the summer of 1980. The relevant committee decided that IDUs would be treated with respect and so no identification information was asked of program clients. The program began operating on November 13, 1990.

The needle exchange operate on an outreach basis. A van donated by Yale university visits neighborhoods with high concentration of IDUs. Outreach staff members try to educate the clients over there by different means like distributing literature documenting risks of HIV infection, dispensing condoms , clean packets, etc.

The primary goal of needle exchange is to reduce incidence of new HIV infection among IDUs. While studies showed consistent self-reported reductions in risky behavior among IDUs participating in needle exchange programs the studies were not convincing. So the mechanics of needle exchange require that the behavior of needles must change. What was required was to reduce the time needles spend circulating in the population. As needles circulate for shorter period of time, needles share fewer people which lower the number of infected needles in the pool of circulating needles which in effect lowers chances of an IDU becoming infected being injected with a previously infected needle. To use this theory required invention of new data collection system which is as follows.

A syringe tracking and testing is a system developed to interview the needles returned to the program. All clients participating in the needle exchange are given unique code names and every needle distributed receives a code. Everytime a client exchanges needles, an outreach worker records the date and location of exchange. He also records the code name of the client receiving the needles alongside the codes of the needles. The client then places the returned needles in a canister to which the worker puts a label with the date and location of exchange and code name of client.

All returned needles are brought to a laboratory at Yale University where a technician collates the information on the canister labels with the tracking numbers on the returned needles. For non-program or street needles returned to needle exchange , the location, date, and client code are recorded. A sample of the returned needles are tested for HIV.

(c) The initial results from this system were both shocking and decisive. At the start of the program, the IDUs presented the needles in their possession for clear needles. These street needles are representative of risk faced by an IDU prior to operation of needle exchange which showed a prevalence level of 67.5 percent which tested HIV positive. As of middle of March 1991, 50.3 percent of the program needles tested positive. Since March 1991, additional program needles have been tested of which 40.5 percent tested positive. This gave further support to the protection offered by needle exchange program.

Though these results are encouraging, they do not link operations of needle exchange to changes in the rate of new HIV infections . To achieve this required a development of a mathematical model describing HIV transmission among IDUs via needle sharing. The syringe tracking and testing system in concert with limited observation obtained from surveying program clients provided data required to estimate parameters for this model. Though the model developed was conservative, the results were interesting. It estimated that in absence of behavioral changes on part of IDUs in the program, rate of new HIV infections among needle exchange clients would drop. It estimates a 33 percent reduction in new HIV infections.

(d) To understand the impact of this study requires both a local and national perspective. In the local aspect, it is possible to construct a conservative estimate of the actual number of infections averted. As many clients who joined the needle exchange apparently dropped out, the conservative impact of the program can be estimated by multiplying the cumulative number of person years spent in the program over all clients by the incidence reduction of 2 HIV infections per 100 client years. This assumes all those who apparently dropped out of the program are truly recidivists, an assumption that may be patently false. Calculations have shown that between $1 million and $2 million dollar in public health care expenditure have been avoided over the first two years of the program.

This only hints at the true impact of this work. Needle exchange has been returned to the menu of legitimate AIDS intervention in major American cities in large part due to the evaluation of New Haven. In some calculations made as to how much public health care costs could be avoided only the annual reduction in HIV incidence among needle exchange program clients is considered, as opposed to changes in lifetime probability of acquiring HIV infection. While decrease in lifetime risk will be less than decrease in annual incidence the effect of placing clients in drug treatment via needle exchange has been ignored. If this point is considered impact of needle exchange on probability of their acquiring HIV could be substantial.

2.2-1

(a) The Dutch Government has been facing problems regarding its water management the past it was too much water but now it is the scarcity of fresh water and pollution due to increased industrialization and a growing population with high standard of living. Some features of the Dutch landscape exaggerate the problem.

Netherlands , one of the densely populated countries of the world and the seventh largest wealthiest nation derives a huge amount of wealth from crops grown in irrigated land. Since agriculture is the largest user of fresh water in Netherlands water shortages can cause large economic losses. The Rhine river is Netherlands major source of surface water for agriculture, irrigation and other purposes. Along with other rivers and canals it is a major artery for the inland shipping fleet of Western Europe. Low water levels in rivers and canals can cause shipping delays and economic losses too because only partially laden ships can navigate the inland waterways. Besides this mines and industries along the Rhine discharge into the water different type of pollutants which also contribute to the rivers increasing level of salinity which in turn damage crops and threaten environment and personal health. Power plants on the banks can degrade quality of water by discharging excess heat into streams. which may in turn endanger the ecological balance in the neighborhood. Besides salinity, the most important water quality problem is eutrophication heavy growth of algae in relatively stagnant water of storage reservoirs and lakes which cause the water to smell and taste foul.

Though in mid 1970s supply met the demand of fresh surface water except in dry years, it was predicted not to be true for late 1980s. But ground water sources were already facing scarcity. Rapid increases in ground water extraction recently have resulted in drop of its level in many areas. This in turn can cause agricultural and environmental damage in areas where water level was higher. Facing such water management problem the Netherlands Government agency responsible for water control and public works, Rijkswaterstaat commissioned an analysis on which to base a new national water management policy. which resulted in PAWN , the Policy Analysis for the Water Management of the Netherlands in April, 1977.

(b) The purpose of the five mathematical models are as follows:

The Water Distribution Model is the heart of the analytic method. The infrastructure of the surface water system consists of rivers and canals that transport water, lakes and reservoirs that store water, weirs, locks and lock bypasses , sluices and pumping stations that are used to control the transport of water throughout the country. The model simulates the major components of this system in detail and contains aggregated representations of the other components. The model provides information on the water management system, including flows, level of water, extractions, discharges, depth of shipping and concentration of pollutants. It provides information on different costs, including investment and operating for technical and managerial tactics and irrigation, as well as shortage and salinity losses for agriculture, low water shipping loss and shipping delay losses. This information is provided for each 10-day period and is given in a summary of totals on averages for the entire year.

The Industry Response Simulation Model : When water becomes more expensive or less available, firms respond by modifying their production process to consume less water; usually with an accompanying increase in costs, part or all which may be passed on to their customers. To find out these responses and their costs, PAWN developed and used this model. The model simulates the behavior of industrial firms in response to a change in ground water extractions or an increase in the price of drinking water. In determining behavior, the model assumes that each firm will choose the least costly alternative available.

Although the model was developed to investigate the effect of ground water charges on industry it is also used to examine effect of imposing quotas that restrict ground water extractions.

Electric Power Reallocation and Cost Model : The Water Distribution Model provides an excess temperature table that shows rise in temperature at one node resulting from a reference heat discharge by a power plant at another node. To obtain the excess temperatures created by heat of power plant discharges other than the reference, this model scales the correct entries in the table by the ratio of the new to reference discharge.

The model calculates the optimal generating schedule for two basic conditions: one in which the thermal standards are relaxed and the other in which it is imposed. The difference is the cost attributable to the thermal standards, the thermal penalty cost. The model repeats this process for each 10-day period in the year and calculates the total thermal penalty annually as well as some other statistics.

The Nutrient Model : Eutrophication, a heavy growth of algae called an algae bloom occurs in the still water of lakes and reservoirs. This model estimates the amounts of nutrients , phosphates, nitrogen and silicon available to algae, given the nutrient flows entering the lake. The model calculates the composition of a column of water 1 square meter in area and as deep as the lake under investigation , in contact with the air and with the bottom sedimentations. The important nutrient processes include the inflow and outflow of nutrient bearing water, the flux of nutrients from the bottom, and the flux of nutrient to and from algae.

The Algae Bloom Model : PAWN used this model to analyze the effect on algae blooms of circumstances, including introducing control tactics. It predicts weekly size and species composition of the algae bloom, given amounts of nutrients and solar energy available to the algae.

(c) PAWN compares policies in terms of their impacts. In choosing impact measures, primary criterion was that they are sufficient to span quite a number of objectives. It includes both national and general water management as well as specific objectives mentioned by different interest groups. The objectives also had to reflect both equity and efficiency.

Impacts on water management system include investment and operating cost of technical and managerial tactics, as well as flood risk in the Ijssal lake.

Direct impact on users include change in profit, expenditure, revenue for each user group like agriculture, shipping, electric power generation, industries, drinking water supply companies.

Environmental impacts include violation of water quality standards, damage to nature areas caused by construction of new facilities and total amount of ground water extracted.

Impact on entire nation include net monetary benefit to nation after deducting transfer payments, total economic effects-- both Government revenues and charges-- in production , employment and imports-- that occurs in both industries directly involved in construction of major new facilities and interrelated industries and effects on public health.

PAWN also pays attention to distributional effects that show uneven distribution of monetary benefit and costs among producers, consumers, Government and uneven distribution of other impacts among different groups and locations.

(d) The several tangible benefits are:

-- the building of Brielse Mier pipeline which will yield $38 million investment savings and $15 million annual net benefit in decreased salinity damage to agriculture.

-- rejection of plan to build the second dike to separate Markermeer from an adjacent saline lake-- saving more than $95 million in investment costs, 0.2% of Dutch domestic product.

-- implementation of new flushing policy for Markermeer is expected to yield net benefits between $1.2 million and $5.4 million per year.

-- adoption of a more stringent thermal standard of an increase of 3 degree Celsius for canals by Dutch since PAWN showed it was practical and not costly. This led to a decrease in locally harmful ecological effects of power plant heat discharges.

The intangible benefits are:

-- drastic changes in Dutch approach to eutrophication, their most serious water quality problem

-- implementation of all recommendations by PAWN would lead to an expected profit between $53 million and $128 million per year

-- to deal with ground water extraction problem, priority had to be given to industry and drinking water companies. If practical methods to replenish the ground water cannot be devised, regulatory measures will show growth of ground water sprinkling.

-- comprehensive methodology developed by PAWN has been adopted by the Government, other departments, laboratories and used in several major studies.

-- PAWN provides method to educate decision makers and train analysts in analyses of complex natural resource and environmental questions.

-- the general approach and some of the techniques have potentially wide applicability.

2.2-2

(a) The author's example of a model in natural sciences is Newton's Law of Universal Gravitation. Tough he says it is one of the most important models in Physics this does not account for all details. For example, it is only approximate if the particles are objects with non-spherical shapes and model ignores relativity.

The model in OR identified by him is the Economic Order Quantity (EOQ) model. Like Newton's Law in Physics, this model too is simple and highlights important features of the real world. It identifies some critical relationships and also shows that a single model can be used for all types of orders. This model too ignores details of the real world which might be considered important. But just like Newton's law, EOQ model is one of the most important one in MS/OR.

(b) The MS/OR profession is often compared to natural sciences. Basic precepts in natural sciences can be used to guide research in MS/OR. The author believes a greater understanding of these precepts can provide needed focus form the profession and help resolve some recent debates.

To be useful, an MS/OR model must possess some qualities as models in natural science. The most important of them are :

-- understandibility
-- verifiability
-- reproducibility

The extent to which a model can be understood depends on tools available for evaluation. But models have inherent values which can be interpreted on inspection. In 1960s many MS/OR professionals tried to model the behavior of automobile traffic. The most successful models examined traffic from macro point of view and found similarities between traffic flow and fluid flow. Less successful models examined behavior of individual drivers with complicated queuing expressions. The latter models though more accurate have less value. They are too difficult to interpret.

A model should be verifiable and based on observable phenomena. It must capture the essence of a problem faced by MS/OR practitioners. It must include important parameters, decision variables, aims and objectives and their relationships.

As a criterion for publication, the phenomena underlying the model must be reproducible. To have a broader appeal the model must be sufficiently general.

2.3-1

(a) The role of evaluating a model is to extract information from it. It entails two, often simultaneous activities -- identifying alternatives and calculating objectives.

The most known technique for identifying alternatives is optimization. The process yields a single solution which maximizes or minimizes a single objective function. The most prevalent technique used for identifying multiple alternatives is sensitivity analysis. The process can show how the optimum changes when model parameters change or can provide near-optimal alternative solutions.

The author views that optimization should not be the sole goal, not just because models are abstractions of real world but because does not provide adequate information for making decisions. Its objective is to find only one solution. But the decision maker probably would prefer information on several alternatives. Though sensitivity analysis increases effectiveness of optimization , it is deficient. It only yields alternative solution near optimum. The decision maker rather needs unique solutions which offer distinct alternatives.

So the author opines that research should be devoted to identify multiple alternatives. One may begin in the solution process itself. Each solution is a feasible alternative, which the decision maker may choose over the optimum. New algorithms may be designed to identify distinct alternatives.

The second step of evaluation should involve calculating quantifiable objective for each alternative.

Thus summarizing, the author views that although optimization has dominated research in MS/OR it is but one technique for addressing one part of MS/OR process. It is deficient since does not provide adequate information for making important decisions/ Complex decisions rather require information on many alternatives and also an understanding of basic trade-offs and principles. Optimization alone cannot provide this information.

(b) The key to MS/OR is not only possessing knowledge. Though different practitioners take different approaches -- three key steps being

-- modeling
-- evaluating
-- deciding , which are all complementary.

In MS/OR systematized knowledge is reflected in better decisions. The key to good decisions is knowledge and judgment. Modeling and evaluation form a systematized way for acquiring knowledge; judgment is acquired through experience.

The problems which do not require judgment are the ones which can be formulated with well-defined objective functions and solved automatically with algorithms which are pretty efficient; an example being the shortest path algorithm. On the other hand, there are problems which are easy to formulate but difficult to solve, example a carpet store owner would not argue with the objective of the cutting stock problem but may not be happy with solutions provided by available software. He would benefit from models that offer help in cutting the carpet. Combining knowledge from modeling with judgment of store owner would give best result.

Generally, important questions facing management are not well-defined as shortest path or cutting stock problem. Neither there are related well-defined problems which can be optimized, example the facilities layout problem.

Thus the roles are all complementary. Most depend on both judgment of decision maker and knowledge gained from modeling and evaluating.

2.4-1

The credibility of analyses and therefore the probability that policies based upon them will be implemented depends on the perceived validity of the models.

The process of model validation though is a burden helps to learn lessons which may not lead to just improvements in the model but also to changes in the scientific theory and public policy. This happened in PAWN with the Nutrient model and eutrophication. When PAWN was started, the Dutch eutrophication control strategy was to decrease phosphate discharges into surface water from point sources mostly sewerage treatment plants.

To find out how effective this strategy is the Algae Bloom model was applied to some major Dutch lakes. It was revealed that in most cases this required enormous percentage decrease in phosphate concentrations.

Next question was what was to be done to achieve a particular percentage decrease in phosphate concentration. The Dutch strategy was based on the fact that large amount of phosphates and other nutrients accumulated in bottom of the lakes was bound permanently to the bottom and hence unavailable to support algae blooms. This was contradicted both in the Nutrient Model calibration process and validation process.

Studies taken convinced that nutrients particularly phosphate can be liberated from bottom sediments both in normal steady mode and explosive mode. This conclusion was widely accepted in the scientific community.

But the conclusion implied that use of a phosphate reduction program as the only way to limit algae bloom would have hardly any immediate success. But analysis with the Algae Bloom model suggests other tactics which could be effective and combination of tactics should be tailored to individual lakes.

2.4-2 The author feels that observation and experimentation are not emphasized in the MS/OR literature or in the training of its workers as much as experience would lead one to believe. As examples he has given some experiences with the US AirForce in early '50s which strengthens his belief.

He opines that observing actual operations as part of analysis process provides a required base for understanding what is going on in a problem situation. They can help to point out difficulties being encountered, suggest hypothesis and theories that may account for problems and offer evidence regarding the validity of the models built as part of problem solving process.

If a problem is in regard to a non-existing system or an operating system fulfills an important function that must continue, so that controlled experiments with are not possible-- one can build a theory about relevant phenomena and analyze the theory but numerical results obtained in this way clearly can be viewed with suspicion. Alternatively if a similar system exists, one can extrapolate from results with it to make estimates about the prospective system. Infact, administrative emergencies or an executive desire to try something new may cause the behavior of a system already in existence to change. The analyst may then be able to collect data useful for analyzing how the system would operate under changed circumstances or for identifying problems that might crop up under different operating regimes.

From his personal experiences he gives evidence to give substance to these remarks of his.

If data was used from one system to predict performance of another he believes that the parameter values form observing another similar system can be useful, and incorporating such estimates in a crude study can be better than not doing a study at all. Parameter values from one context to another cannot be expected to support detailed findings, but even crude findings are enough to provide indispensable information on which to base policy.

He has also analyzed the results of a continent wide Air Defense exercise. He says here that analysis must be carefully planned, and planning must begin early. Early work serves to put attention on the structure of the work and issues to be faced as well as other responsibilities.

Thus, in nutshell, the author views that skills involved in observation and experimentation are enumerous and should be part of the tool kit of many MS/OR analysts. He views that discriminating observation and carefully planned experimentation and analysis are central to MS/OR.

Observing actual operations and collection of data allow us to discern problems, develop hypotheses and validate models needing skill.

Similarly, accurate and complete data are required to estimate validity. Program evaluation brings together many of the issues of observation and experimentation.

Thus issues of scientific and professional craft related to observation and experimentation should occur important places in experience, literature and training of MS/OR workers.

2.4-3

(a) The author views that analysts do not believe that a model can be completely validated. He further opines that policy models can at best be invalidated. Thus the objective of validation or invalidation attempts is to increase the degree of confidence that the events obtained from the model will take place under conditions assumed. After trying all invalidation procedures, one will have a good understanding of strengths and weaknesses of the model and will be able to meet criticisms of omissions. Knowing the limitations of the model will enable one to express proper confidence on its results.

(b) Model Validity deals with correspondence of the model to the real world and related to pointing out all stated and implied assumptions, identification and inclusion of all decision variables and hypothesized relations among variables. Different assumptions are made and the analyst compares each assumption and hypothesis to the internal and external problem environments viewed by the decision maker and comments on the extent of divergence.

Data validity deals with raw and structured data, where structured data is manipulated raw data. Raw data validity is concerned with measurement problems and determining if the data is accurate, impartial and representative. Structured data validity needs review of each step of the manipulation and is a part of model verification.

Logical/mathematical validity deals with translating the model form into a numerical, computer process that produces solutions. There is no standard method to determine this. Approaches include comparing model outcomes with expected or historical results and a close scrutiny of the model form and its numerical representation on a flow chart.

Predictive validity is analyzing errors between actual and predicted outcomes for a model's components and relationships. Here one looks for errors and their magnitudes, why they exist and if how they can be corrected.

Operational validity attempts to assess the importance of errors found under technical validity. It must find out if the use of the model is appropriate for the observed and expected errors. It also deals with the fact whether the model can produce unacceptable answers for proper ranges of parameter values.

Dynamic validity is concerned with determining how the model will be maintained during its life cycle so it will continue to be an accepted representation of the real system. The two areas of interest thus are update and review.

(c) Sensitivity analysis plays an important role in testing the operational validity of a model. In this, values of model parameters are varied over some range of interest to determine if and how the recommended solution changes. If the solution is sensitive to certain parameter changes, the decision maker may want the model analysts to explore further or justify in detail values of these parameters. Sensitivity analysis also involves the relationship between small changes in parameter values and magnitude of related changes in outputs.

(d) Validating a model tests the agreement between behavior of the model and the real world system being modeled. Models of a non-existing system are the difficult to validate. Three concepts apply here : face validity or expert opinion, variable -parameter validity and sensitivity analysis and hypothesis validity. Though these concepts are applicable to all models, models of real systems can be subjected to further tests. Validity is measured by how well the real-system compares with model-generated data.The model is replicatively valid if it matches data acquired from the real system. It is predictively valid when it matches data before getting the data from the real system. A model is structurally valid if it reproduces the observed real system behavior as well as reflects the way in which real system works to produce this.

The author views that there is no validation methodology appropriate for all models. He says that a decision-aiding model can never be completely validated as there are never real data about the alternatives not implemented. Thus, analysts must be careful in devising, implementing, interpreting and reporting validation tests for their models.

(e) Basic validation steps have been cited in page 616 of the article.

2.5-1

(a) In late 1970s oil companies began to experience downward pressure on profitability due to rapid and continuing changes in external environment. Partially in response to these pressures Texaco's Computer Information Systems department developed an improved on-line interactive gasoline blending system called OMEGA. It was first installed in 1983 and is now used in all seven Texaco US refineries and in two foreign plants.

(b) Simple interactive user interface makes OMEGA easy to use. All input data can be entered by hand. OMEGA can interface with refinery data acquisition system. The user can access stock qualities, stock availabilities, blend specification and requirements, starting values and limits, optimization options, automatic stock selection, automatic blend specification and several other options.

Several features aid the user in performing planning functions. By choosing appropriate options user can obtain optimization options. User also has other options.

Each refinery uses different set of features depending on its availability of blending stocks. These vary depending on the configuration of the refinery and particular crudes being refined. Availability and easy use of OMEGA features has provided engineers and blenders with powerful and easy tool.

(c) OMEGA is constantly being updated and extended. It had to be modified to take into account EPA's regulation for a lead phase down for regular-leaded gasoline so that now OMEGA could be more accurate for these lower lead levels.

OMEGA is continuously modified to reflect changes in refinery operations. Differences in refineries required changes to the system.

When Texaco began installing OMEGA in their foreign refineries, additional changes had to be made to handle different requirements of different countries.

Improvements to OMEGA are needed to enable it to answer the new and unanticipated what-if questions often asked by refinery engineers.

(d) Each refinery uses OMEGA in varying degrees and for various purposes depending on their needs, complexity and configuration. Below the typical usage of the system is pointed out.

On a monthly basis, refineries use OMEGA to develop a gasoline blending plan for the month. The refinery planning model's projected blending stock volumes are input to OMEGA. The blending planner calculates 3 to 8 blends in a single OMEGA run. The refinery planning model's blend compositions are input into OMEGA as initial values. Once a reasonable blend is developed, the marketing department is contacted to discuss resulting grade splits. After marketing department does their job a finalized blending plan is developed for the month. The scheduler determines when each of the grades will be blended. All these work are done by using OMEGA.

(e) OMEGA contributes to overall profitability. To measure actual benefit, a method tried was comparing blend composition that blenders used with and without OMEGA. Here OMEGA achieved as much as 30 percent increase in profit. Average increase in profit is approximately 5 percent of gross gasoline revenue. If OMEGA is used to calculate blending recipes fewer blends fail to meet their quality specification. OMEGA's more reliable gasoline grade-split estimates provide significant aid to those developing marketing strategies and refinery production targets. OMEGA is used for what-if case studies performed for example for economic analysis of refinery improvement projects and analysis of how proposed Government regulations would affect Texaco. OMEGA's features have enabled Texaco with capacity to do things not possible with previous blending system, for example, to deal with mix stocks, consider new grades of gasoline, more control on inventory, etc. OMEGA's features make it easy and quick to explore new avenues of profitability for a refinery.

2.5-2

(a) Yellow Freight System, Inc. was founded in 1926 as a regional motor carrier serving the Mid-West. Today it is one of the largest motor carriers in the country. From a mixed operations in 1970s, Yellow now predominantly serves the less-than-truckload (LTL) portion of the freight market. The '80s were a difficult decade for the motor carrier industry. Deregulation made the way for tremendous opportunity for growth but also presented management with new and difficult challenges to manage these larger operations more efficiently than before. After 1980, motor carriers were forced to compete on price, which led to a lot of pressure to cut costs. The result was decrease in transportation rates. Between 1980 to 1990, transportation rates translated to a drop in real terms of 29%. In addition to real rate decreases, the shipping community in response to intense international competition, started to increase their expectation in service. For many shippers, Yellow Freight is a full partner in their total quality management programs. Another important component of the logistics system is timely delivery of freight. Service reliability is also critical. This heightened emphasis on service was a problem for some long-standing operating practices used by national LTL carriers. The effect of these pressures can be seen in the tremendous attrition the industry suffered. Out of top 20 revenue producing LTL carriers in 1979, only 6 are there today. In this period, Yellow Freight grew from 248 to 630 terminals. This growth has had the effect of creating an extremely large and complex operation. The large network also needs a greater degree of coordination.

In 1986, Yellow initiated a project to improve its ability to manage a complex system. Yellow was interested in using modern network method to simulate and optimize a large network. The project had a main goal-- improved service and service reliability through better management control of the network. This goal was supplemented by broader management objectives. There was also an expectation that improved planning would lead to higher productivity level and lower costs. Consequently, a project team was formed.

(b) The development effort at Yellow started with an existing model as a base and then were modified. The result of this effort was SYSNET. SYSNET is more than 80,000 lines of FORTRAN code for performing sophisticated optimizations using modern network tools. They developed an innovative, interactive optimization technology that puts human beings in the loop, placing sophisticated, up-to-date optimization methods in their hands. These methods were required in the development of a system that would handle the entire network without resorting to heuristic methods to decrease the size of the problem. As a result , user is able to analyze impacts of changes in the whole network in a simple but interactive fashion. Projects can be completed earlier new with greater precision. Decisions on shipment consolidations are now optimized taking into account the system effect of each decision.

Yellow uses SYSNET for two sets of applications:

-- main use is tactical load planning, which involves monthly planning and revision of set of instructions that govern handling and consolidation of shipments through the network.

-- the second set of applications involve longer range planning of the network itself. These problems cover the location and sizing of new facilities, and long range decisions that govern the flow of freight between terminals.

At Yellow SYSNET is more than just a piece of code. It embodies an entire planning methodology adopted by all levels of the company. From strategic planning studies communicated to high-level management to network routing instructions sent right to the field, SYSNET has become a comprehensive planning process that has allowed management to maintain control of a large complex operation. In addition, Yellow uses SYSNET as the central tool in the design and evaluation of projects of over $10 million in annual savings.

(c) The interactive aspects of the code proved important in two respects:

-- the user was needed to guide the search for changes in the network. For example, user may know that freight levels are in the rise in the Midwest or a particular breakbulk is facing problems with capacity. In other cases, user may know that current solution is a local minimum and a major change in the network is needed to achieve an overall improvement. A human being can easily point out these spatial patterns and test for promising configurations.

-- the second use proved critical to the adoption of the system and was the user's capability to accept and reject suggestions made by the computer. SYSNET displays suggested changes and allows the user to evaluate each one in terms of difficult to quantify factors. Also local factors, such as work rules or special operating practices that are not incorporated into the model can be accounted for by a knowledgeable user.

(d) For strategic planning, the outputs from SYSNET are a set of reports used to prepare management summaries on different options. SYSNET is also used on a operational basis to perform load planning. In this role, SYSNET is used to maintain a file that determines the actual routing of shipments through the service network. This file, which contains the load planning, is accessed directly by systems that are used by every terminal manager in the field. SYSNET'S control of load planning and its capability to communicate these instructions to the field is the most important accomplishment of the project.

(e) SYSNET's effect can be seen in four areas :

-- quality of planning practices and management culture

-- cost savings resulting directly from improvement in load planning

-- in analyzing projects
-- improved service to customers from more reliable transportation

Qualitative changes includes the following :

-- management had more control over network operations. SYSNET now allows managers to have direct control. The new load pattern closely controls the loading of directs and management can quickly change the load pattern in response to changing needs.

-- it could set realistic performance standards. SYSNET allowed Yellow to set direct loading standards based on anticipated freight levels, creating more realistic performance expectations.

-- planners can better understand the total system now. Yellow can now evaluate new projects and ideas based on their impact on the entire system

-- SYSNET allows managers to analyze projects formally before making decisions

-- with SYSNET managers can analyze new options quickly in response to changing situations

-- Analysts can now try new ideas on computers which ultimately leads to new ideas in the field

-- because of SYSNET, Yellow is more open now to use of new information technologies

-- the new system has reduced claims. SYSNET has had a substantial impact on management culture at Yellow

Performance improvement due to better load planning include :

A study was undertaken to estimate savings that could be attributed to SYSNET. Total cost savings for the system were estimated at over \$7.3 million annually. Savings in breakbulk handling costs also increased.

Besides this, reducing shipments handled in the long run may bring down investments in fixed facilities.

SYSNET brought down the cost of routing trailers in part by identifying directs with lower transportation costs-- savings due to better routing of trailers were estimated to be \$1 million annually.

Ongoing projects include :

Operations planning uses SYSNET to scrutinize various projects with a wide range from relocating breakbulks to realigning satellites with breakbulks. Using SYSNET, operational planning now completes over 200 projects per year, mostly on an informal, exploratory basis. SYSNET'S speed in evaluating different ideas is critical to this process.

In 1990, Yellow used SYSNET to identify over $10 million in annual savings from different projects. SYSNET improved the speed with which such analyses could be completed and expanded the scope of each project thus allowing Yellow to study system impacts with more precision than before. SYSNET thus has played a main role in identification, design and evaluation of these projects.

Improved service includes :

Savings from SYSNET are substantial compared to the cost of its development and implementation. Following the implementation of SYSNET management can be better focused on improved service.

Yellow continues to use SYSNET for a number of planning projects and to continuously monitor and improve the load planning system which is now used directly within linehaul operations group responsible for day-to-day management of flows through the system. In addition, Yellow is using SYSNET as a foundation to expand the use of optimization methods for the other aspects of its operations.

SYSNET is now very popular within the company for its capability to carry out accurate, comprehensive network planning projects.

2.6-1

(a) Implementing this major change in operations needed involvement and support of all levels of the company. Process started with acceptance of system with operation planning department. Operation planning was responsible for guiding the project and managing with close cooperation from the information services department and all aspects of the implementation. The systems acceptance was ma lot due to use of interactive optimization which gave users the support needed to optimize such a large network while simultaneously keeping them in close control of the entire process. Users could also analyze suggested changes to the network based on changes in flows and costs, which could be compared against actual field totals.

The next step was to validate the cost model. They were able to compare both total system costs and different subcategories against actual cost summaries for these categories. The individual cost categories within SYSNET consistently match corporate statistics within a few percent and total costs often match with 1 or 2 percent.

The validation of the cost model, both in totality and individual components, played a vital role in gaining upper management's acceptance. The interactive reports and features that convinced operations planning also played a strong role in winning support of top management. They ran sessions for upper management to demonstrate how SYSNET made suggestions and generated supporting reports to back-up the numbers. They also demonstrated how standard operating practices could be detrimental and why coordinating the entire network was important. By taking all these efforts, they gained the needed confidence of upper management required to support a field implementation.

(b) With the support of upper management, they were able to develop an implementation strategy. The controlled direct program changed operating philosophy so drastically that a single corporate-wide transition was viewed as not safe. In implementing SYSNET, Yellow made a systematic change in the way it loaded directs. SYSNET encourages a greater proportion of directs to be loaded onto breakbulks. It was not possible to change this operation methods so easily over the whole network. It was also difficult to do it in a piecemeal fashion. To deal with this problem, they developed a phased implementation strategy that started with smallest breakbulks in the system and went up to larger ones. Careful planning made sure that no breakbulk would be over capacity during the intermediate stages of the process. The entire implementation was so planned as to ensure that no breakbulk would find itself over capacity during the transition period.

(c) To communicate the new concept to terminal managers in the field involved three steps :

-- designing new support tools so that SYSNET routing instructions were easy to follow

-- training terminal managers and dock personnel to use these new system and most important

-- convincing terminal managers that the new approach was a good idea.

They developed two new support tools to assist field operations :

-- first was a set of reports that managers or dock supervisors could access from their local computer terminals which would give them immediate access to SYSNET load pattern.

-- second, was a revised shipment movement bill. This provides a very high level of control over the routing of individual shipments.

The Operations Planning department handled training by organizing series of visits to all 25 breakbulks. During each visit, the staff members explained the principles behind the controlled direct program, new reports and use of new routing directions. Follow-up was done by phone calls.

The most important task was to convince terminal managers of the logic behind the new operations strategy. Terminal managers needed to understand that they had to follow the load planning since it was designed to coordinate different parts of the system. They used examples to illustrate the effect their decisions could have on other terminals. Generally, people in the field accepted the principle that their decisions should be coordinated with those in the rest of the system

(d) Following the implementation of SYSNET, they developed a target that represented the expected number of directs that they should be loading based on the SYSNET plan. Yellow then measured terminal manager's performance based on how close they were to this target. After some period, it deemed compliance with the plan so good that it now measures terminal managers performance on other activities and Yellow continues to monitor compliance with the load plan informally. It then contacts managers that appear to be not in compliance to determine the reasons. In short, SYSNET has changed load planning from a decentralized process that depended on local management incentives to a centralized process that relies on monitoring and enforcement.

2.6-2

(a) The information processing industry has experienced several decades of sustained profitable growth. Recently, competition has intensified leading to quick advances in computer technology. This in turn leads to proliferation of both-end products and services. These trends are especially relevant for after-sales service. Maintaining a service parts logistic system to support products installed in the field is essential to competing in this industry.

Growth in both sales and scope of products offered has dramatically increased the number of spare parts that must be maintained. For IBM, the number of installed machines and the annual usage of spare parts have both increased. This growth has increased the dollar value of service inventories, which are used to maintain the very high levels of service expected by IBM's customers. IBM has developed an extensive multiple-echelon logistic structure to provide ready service for the large population of installed machines, which are distributed through the United States.

IBM developed a large and sophisticated inventory management system to provide customers with prompt and reliable service. A fast changing business environment and pressures to decrease investment in inventory led IBM to look for improvements in its control system.

In response to these new needs, IBM initiated the development of a new planning and control system for management of service parts. The result of this was the creation and implementation of a system called Optimizer.

(b) The complicating factors faced by the OR team are as follows :

-- there are more than 15 million part-location combinations

-- there are more than 50000 product-location combinations

-- frequent updating (weekly) of system control parameters was a requirement in response to changes in the service environment and installed base

-- success of the system is important to IBM's daily operations and so can have a major impact on its future sales and revenues

-- employees could be expected to protest against any change since the existing control system was working and sophisticated and overall parts logistics problem was complex.

(c) The system developed in this phase had minimum interface to provide data inputs and multi-echelon algorithm without any improvements. Most of the big changes from the original design was in this phase.

They discovered that the echelon structure was in reality more complex than the one used in the analytic model. Consequently, they had to develop extensions to the demand pass-up methodology and incorporate them into the model.

The test was conducted in early 1986 and led to the finding that the value of the total inventory generated by the new system was smaller than expected. It was discovered that the problem was due to differences in criticality of parts. The algorithm made extensive use of inexpensive, non-functional parts to meet product-service objective. Another problem found out at this stage was the churn (instability) in the recommended stock levels every week. Although stock levels are expected to change periodically in response to changing failure rates and to changes in the installed base, it is desirable to keep the stock levels quasi-static in order to avoid logistic and supply problems. They developed control procedures and changed the model to take care of this problem.

(d) In this phase, they completed all functions required for implementation and developed a measurement system to monitor the field implementation test. After being done with the system coding for this phase, they conducted an extensive user acceptance test. Every program module was tested individually and jointly. Finally, a field implementation test went live on 7 machine types in early 1987. The working of the system fulfilled expectations. Scope of the field test was slowly expanded. Results were monitored on a weekly and then monthly basis by the measurement system.

(e) In this phase, they completed the development and installation of all the functions currently in place in Optimizer. The system was able to provide the specified service performance for all parts and locations. Improvements were made. User acceptance testing and integration of final system went smoothly. The project staging helped to sustain support for the project by demonstrating concrete progress throughout the implementation process. It also helped to eradicate problems in formulation and algorithm and programming bugs early. So very few problems occurred when the system went live in a national basis. The final Optimizer system for national implementation consisted of four major modules :

-- a forecasting system module
-- a data delivery system module
-- a decision system that solves multi-echelon stock control problem
-- the PIMS interface system

(f) The implementation of Optimizer yielded a variety of benefits :

-- a decrease in investment on inventory
-- improved services
-- enhanced flexibility in responding to changing service requirements
-- provision of a planning capability
-- improved understanding of the impact of parts operations
-- increased responsive of the control system
-- increased efficiency of NSD human resources
-- identifying the role of functional parts in providing product service is an example of benefits derived from implementation of Optimizer
-- ability to run Optimizer a weekly basis has increased responsiveness of entire parts inventory system
-- for machines controlled by Optimizer, inventory analysts no longer have to specify parts stocking lists for each echelon in order to make sure that service objectives are attained. They can now focus on other critical management issues.

Optimizer thus has proved to be an extremely valuable planning and operating control tool.

2.7-1

The 13 detailed phases of an OR study according to this reference are : Initiation(Embryonic), Feasibility, Formulation, Data, Design, Verification(Software Development), Validation, Training and Education, Installation, Implementation, Maintenance and Update, Evaluation and Review, Documentation and Dissemination.

Following are the 6 broader phases given in the chapter and in parentheses are given the detailed phases of the article that fall partially or primarily within the broader phase :
Define the problem of interest and gather relevant data (initiation, feasibility, data),
formulate a mathematical model to represent the problem (formulation),
develop a computer-based procedure for deriving solutions for the problem from the model(design, verification that is software development),
test the model and refine it as needed(validation),
prepare for ongoing application of the model as prescribed by management(training and education, installation),
implementation(implementation, maintenance and update, evaluation and review, documentation and dissemination).

Chapter 3: Introduction to Linear Programming

1-1.

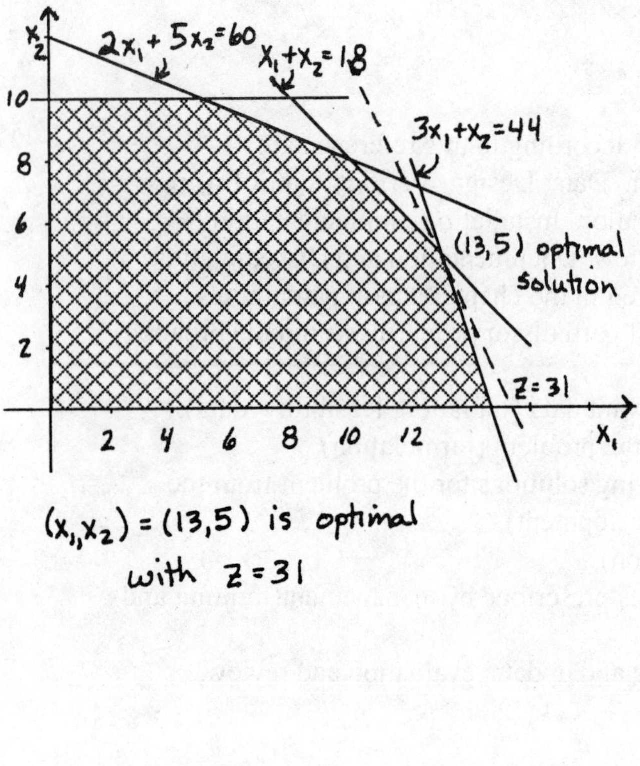

$(x_1, x_2) = (13, 5)$ is optimal with $Z = 31$

3.1-2.

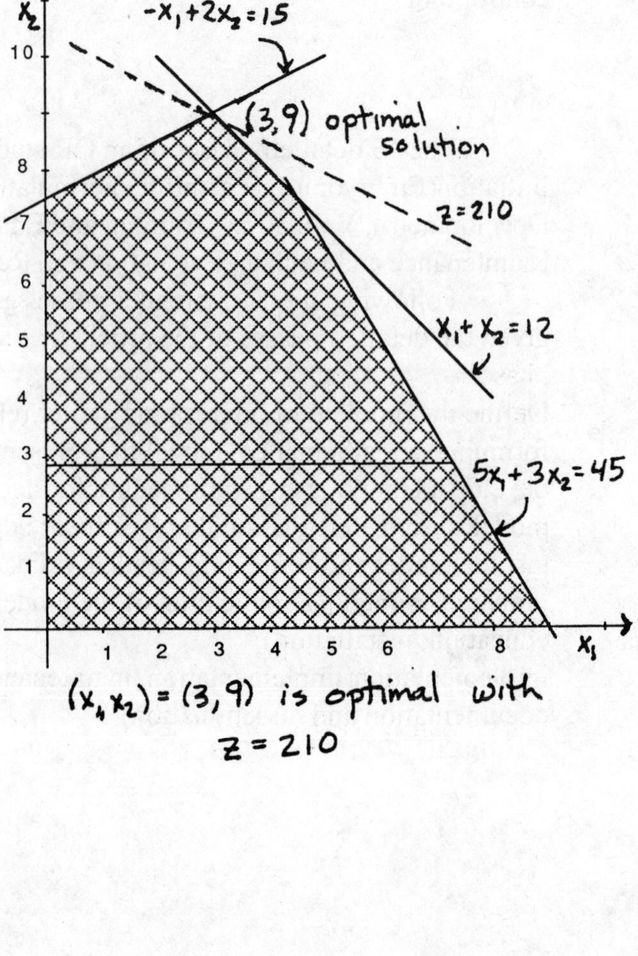

$(x_1, x_2) = (3, 9)$ is optimal with $Z = 210$

3.1-3a) Let x_1 = number of units of product 1 produced
x_2 = number of units of product 2 produced
x_3 = number of units of product 3 produced.

Maximize $z = 50x_1 + 20x_2 + 25x_3$

subject to

$$9x_1 + 3x_2 + 5x_3 \le 500$$
$$5x_1 + 4x_2 \le 350$$
$$3x_1 + 2x_3 \le 150$$
$$x_3 \le 20$$
$$x_1 \ge 0 \quad x_2 \ge 0 \quad x_3 \ge 0$$

b)

Solve Automatically by the Simplex Method:

Optimal Solution

Value of the
Objective Function: Z = 2904.7619

Variable	Value
X_1	26.1905
X_2	54.7619
X_3	20

Constraint	Slack or Surplus	Shadow Price
1	0	4.7619
2	0	1.42857
3	31.4286	0
4	0	1.19048

Sensitivity Analysis

Objective Function Coefficient

Current Value	Allowable Range To Stay Optimal Minimum	Maximum
50	25	51.25
20	19	40
25	23.8095	$+\infty$

Right Hand Sides

Current Value	Allowable Range To Stay Feasible Minimum	Maximum
500	362.5	555
350	276.667	533.333
150	118.571	$+\infty$
20	0	47.5

3.1-4 a) X_1 = # of 27" TV sets to be produced per month

X_2 = # of 20" " " " " " "

Maximize $Z = 120X_1 + 80X_2$

subject to

$$20X_1 + 10X_2 \le 500$$
$$X_1 \le 40$$
$$X_2 \le 10$$
$$X_1 \ge 0,\ X_2 \ge 0$$

b)

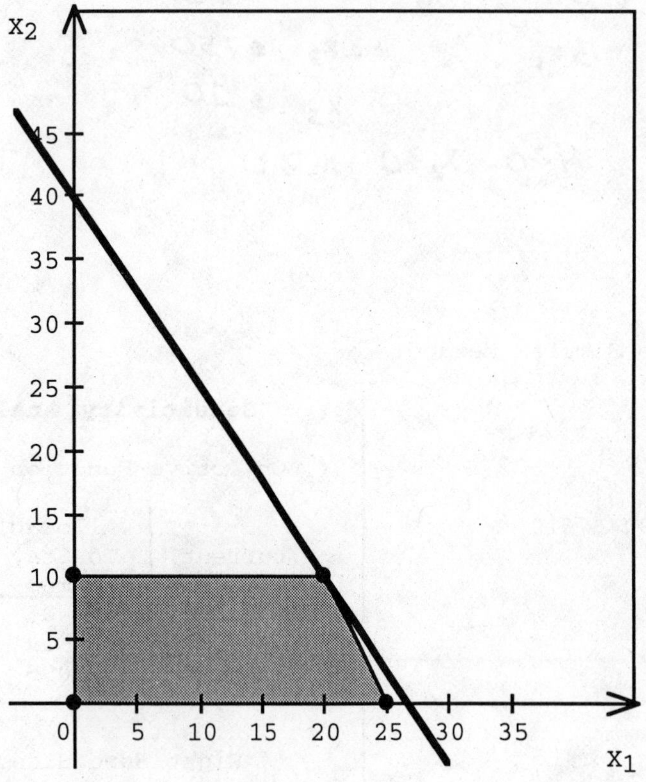

Corner Points		Z
(20,	10)	3200*
(25,	0)	3000
(0,	10)	800
(0,	0)	0

Optimal value of Z: 3200

Optimal solution: (20, 10)

c)

Optimal Solution

Value of the Objective Function: Z = 3200

Variable	Value
X1	20
X2	10

Constraint	Slack or Surplus	Shadow Price
1	0	6
2	20	0
3	0	20

Sensitivity Analysis

Objective Function Coefficient

Current Value	Allowable Range To Stay Optimal Minimum	Maximum
120	0	160
80	60	$+\infty$

Right Hand Sides

Current Value	Allowable Range To Stay Feasible Minimum	Maximum
500	100	900
40	20	$+\infty$
10	0	50

3.1-5. a) Let x_1 = # units of product 1 to produce
x_2 = # units of product 2 to produce

Maximize $Z = x_1 + 2x_2$

subject to

$$x_1 + 3x_2 \leq 200$$
$$2x_1 + 2x_2 \leq 300$$
$$x_2 \leq 60$$
$$x_1 \geq 0,\ x_2 \geq 0$$

b)

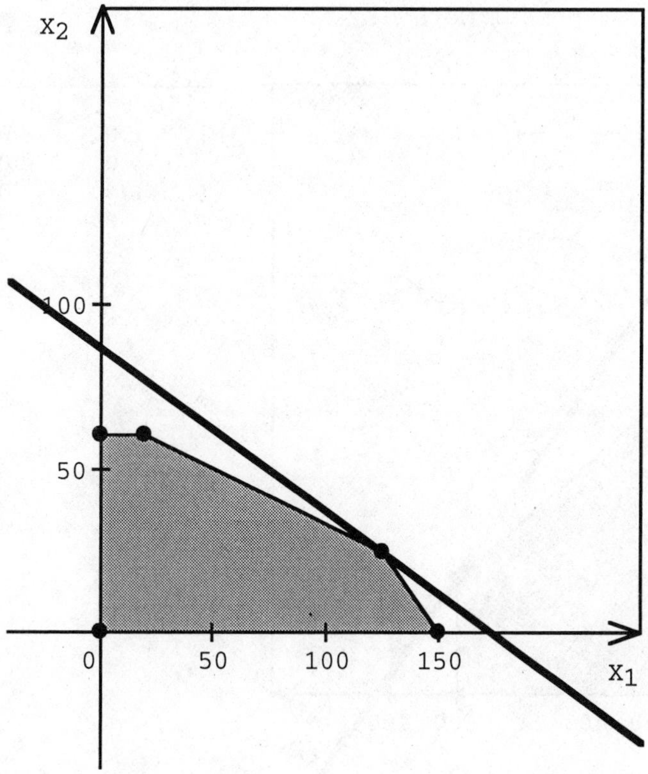

Corner Points		Z
(125,	25)	175*
(20,	60)	140
(150,	0)	150
(0,	60)	120
(0,	0)	0

Optimal value of Z: 175

Optimal solution: (125, 25)

c) **Optimal Solution**

Value of the
Objective Function: Z = 175

Variable	Value
X_1	125
X_2	25

Constraint	Slack or Surplus	Shadow Price
1	0	0.5
2	0	0.25
3	35	0

Sensitivity Analysis

Objective Function Coefficient

Current Value	Allowable Range To Stay Optimal Minimum	Maximum
1	0.66667	2
2	1	3

Right Hand Sides

Current Value	Allowable Range To Stay Feasible Minimum	Maximum
200	150	270
300	160	400
60	25	$+\infty$

3.1-6a) Let x_1 = # units on special risk insurance
x_2 = # " " mortgages

Maximize $Z = 5x_1 + 2x_2$

subject to

$$3x_1 + 2x_2 \leq 2400$$
$$x_2 \leq 800$$
$$2x_1 \leq 1200$$
$$x_1 \geq 0,\ x_2 \geq 0$$

b) Solve Interactively by the Graphical Method:

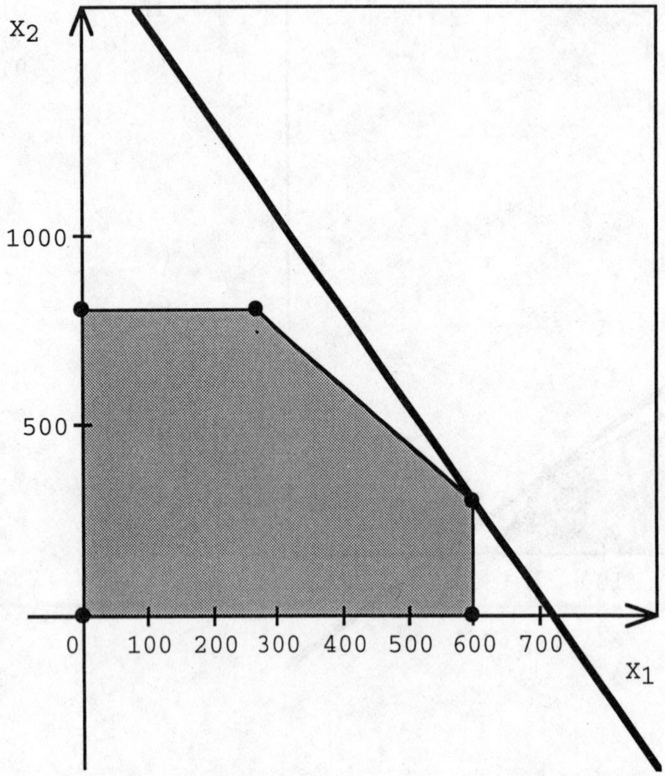

Corner Points		Z
(266.67,	800)	2933.3
(600,	300)	3600*
(0,	800)	1600
(600,	0)	3000
(0,	0)	0

Optimal value of Z: 3600

Optimal solution: (600, 300)

3.1-7.a)
Let x_1 = # of units of part A to produce per month
x_2 = # " " " " B " " "
x_3 = # " " " " C " " "

Maximize $Z = 50x_1 + 40x_2 + 30x_3$

subject to

$$0.02x_1 + 0.03x_2 + 0.05x_3 \leq 40$$
$$0.05x_1 + 0.02x_2 + 0.04x_3 \leq 40$$
$$x_1 \geq 0,\ x_2 \geq 0,\ x_3 \geq 0$$

3.1-7. b)

Solve Automatically by the Simplex Method:

Optimal Solution

Value of the
Objective Function: Z = 61818.1818

Variable	Value
X_1	363.636
X_2	1090.91
X_3	0

Constraint	Slack or Surplus	Shadow Price
1	0	909.091
2	0	636.364

Sensitivity Analysis

Objective Function Coefficient

Current Value	Allowable Range To Stay Optimal Minimum	Maximum
50	26.6667	100
40	20	75
30	$-\infty$	70.9091

Right Hand Sides

Current Value	Allowable Range To Stay Feasible Minimum	Maximum
40	16	60
40	26.6667	100

3.1-8.

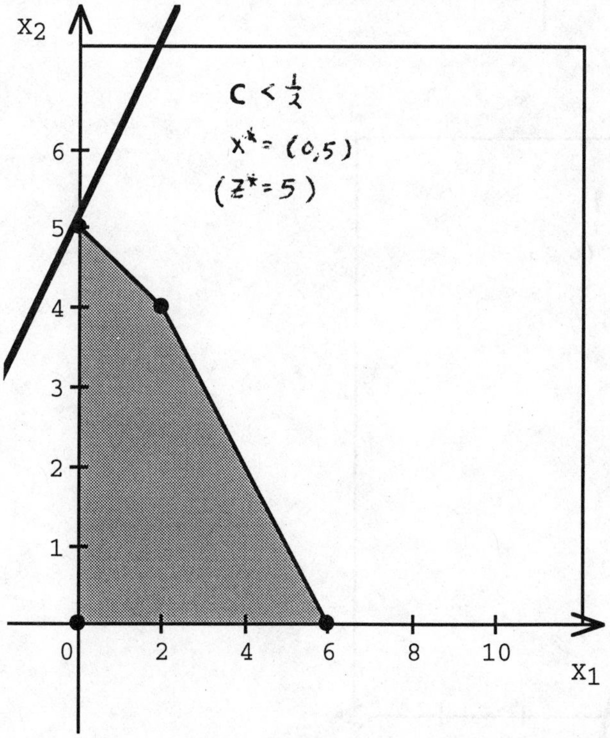

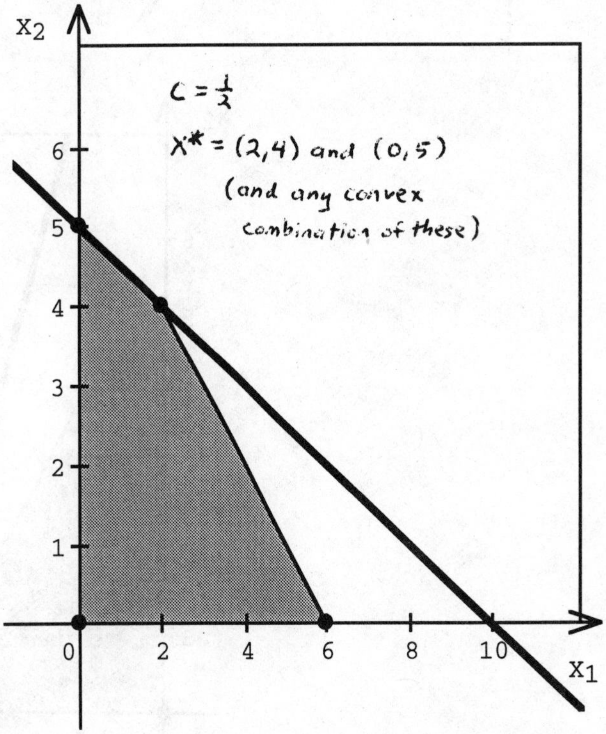

3.1-8. (con't)

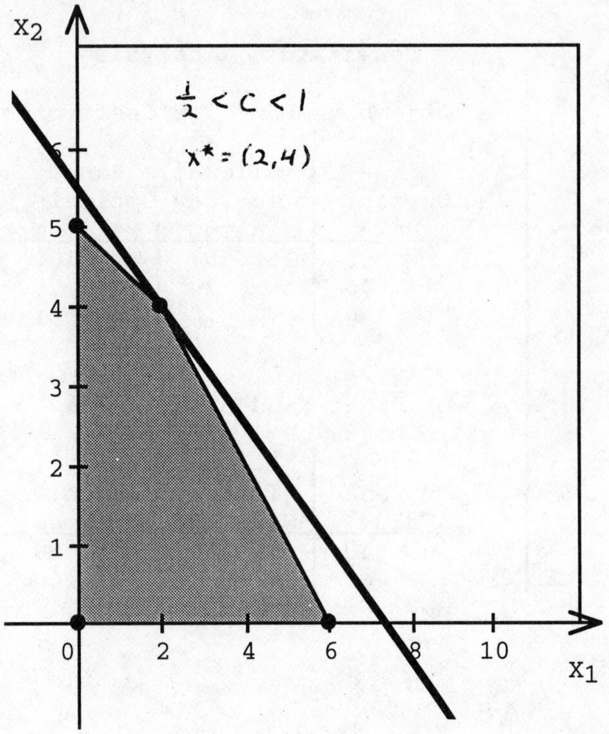
x2
1/2 < c < 1
x* = (2,4)
6
5
4
3
2
1
0
2
4
6
8
10
x1

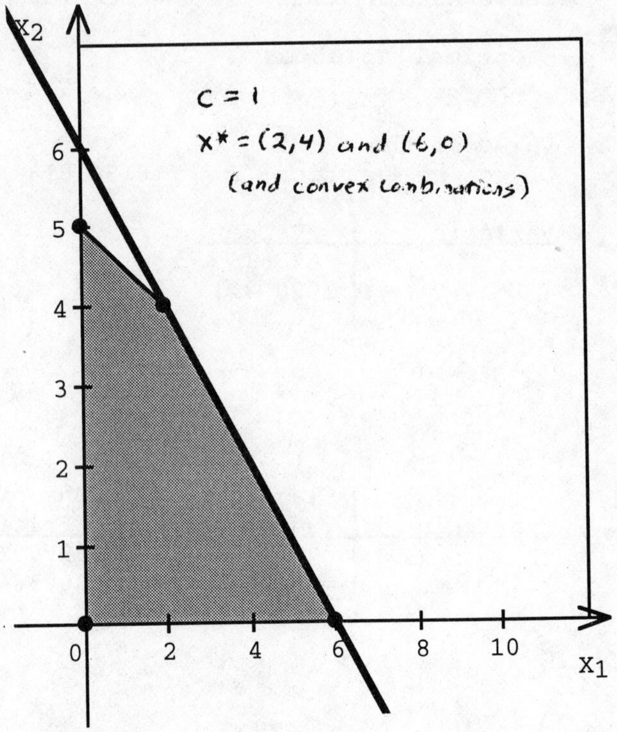
x2
c = 1
x* = (2,4) and (6,0)
(and convex combinations)
6
5
4
3
2
1
0
2
4
6
8
10
x1

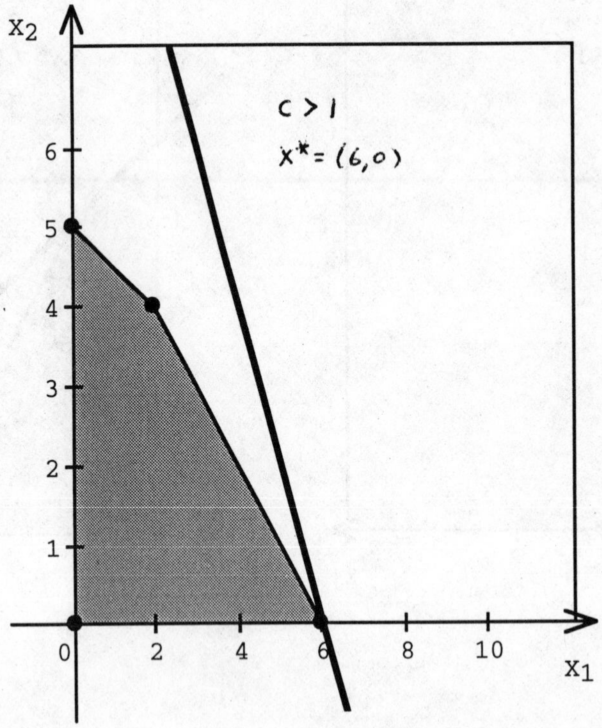
x2
c > 1
x* = (6,0)
6
5
4
3
2
1
0
2
4
6
8
10
x1

3.1-9. First note that (2,3) always satisfies the 3 constraints. (i.e. (2,3) is always feasible)

In fact since $kx_1 + x_2 = 2k+3$ at (2,3) for any k, the third constraint is always binding.

We only need to check if (2,3) is optimal.

Since the line $kx_1 + x_2 = 2k+3$ always passes through the point (2,3), changing k simply rotates the line. Rewriting: $x_2 = -kx_1 + (2k+3)$, we see that the slope of the line is $-k$, and, therefore, the slope ranges from 0 to $-\infty$.

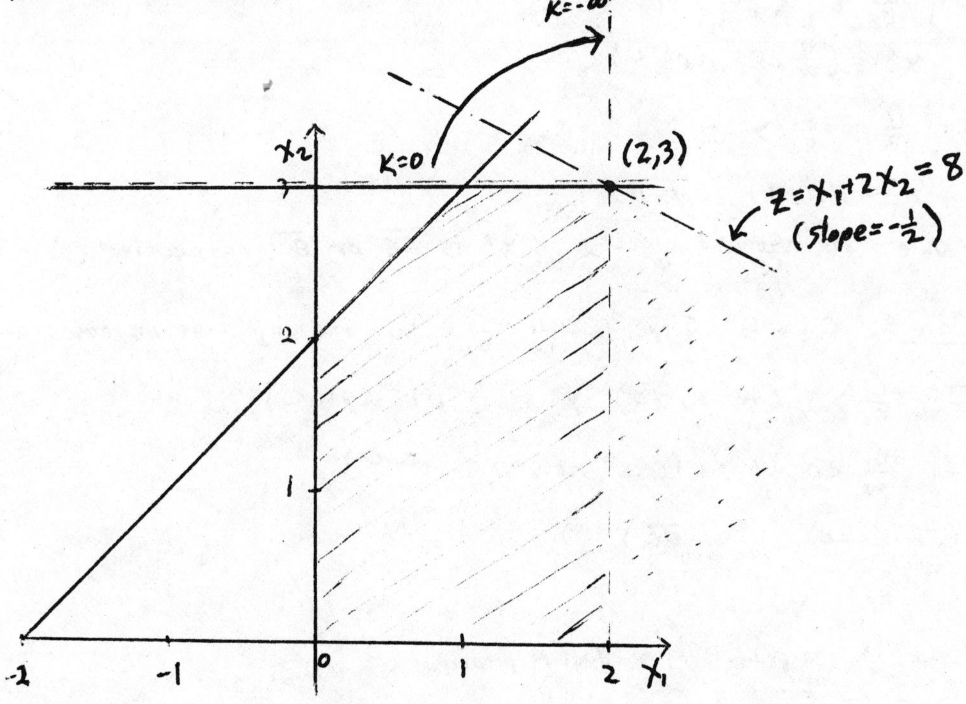

As we can see, (2,3) is optimal as long as the slope of the 3rd constraint line is less than $-\frac{1}{2}$ (the slope of the objective line). If $k < \frac{1}{2}$, then we can increase the objective by traveling along the 3rd constraint to point $(2+\frac{3}{k}, 0)$ which has an objective value of $2 + \frac{3}{k} > 8$ if $k < \frac{1}{2}$.

Therefore, (2,3) is optimal for $k \geq \frac{1}{2}$.

3.1-10. Case 1: $c_2 = 0$ (Objective line is vertical)

If $c_1 > 0$, objective increases as x_1 increases,

so $x^* = (\frac{11}{2}, 0)$ (pt. C)

If $c_1 < 0$, opposite is true,

so $x^* = (0,0)$ and $(0,1)$ (line $\overline{OA}$)

(Note if $c_1 = 0$, every feasible point gives "optimal" of $0x_1 + 0x_2 = 0$)

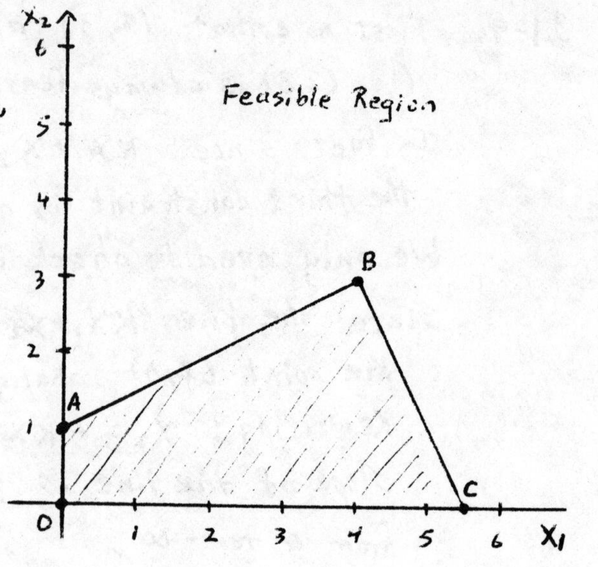

Case 2: $c_2 > 0$ (Slope of obj. is $-\frac{c_1}{c_2}$)

If $-\frac{c_1}{c_2} > \frac{1}{2}$ (or equivalently, $\frac{c_1}{c_2} < -\frac{1}{2}$),

$x^* = (0,1)$ (pt. A)

If $-\frac{c_1}{c_2} < -2$,

$x^* = (\frac{11}{2}, 0)$ (pt. C)

If $\frac{1}{2} > -\frac{c_1}{c_2} > -2$,

$x^* = (4,3)$ (pt. B)

(Note, if $-\frac{c_1}{c_2} = \frac{1}{2}$ or -2, x^* is $\overline{AB}$ or $\overline{BC}$, respectively)

Case 3: $c_2 < 0$ (Slope is still $-\frac{c_1}{c_2}$, but the objective increases as the line is shifted down)

If $-\frac{c_1}{c_2} > 0$ (i.e. $c_1 > 0$), $x^* = (\frac{11}{2}, 0)$ (pt. C)

If $-\frac{c_1}{c_2} < 0$ ($c_1 < 0$), $x^* = (0,0)$ (pt. O)

(If $c_1 = 0$, x^* is $\overline{OC}$)

3.2-1. a) Let x_1 = # of units of product A produced

x_2 = # " " " B "

Maximize $Z = 3x_1 + 2x_2$

subject to

$2x_1 + x_2 \le 2$

$x_1 + 2x_2 \le 2$

$3x_1 + 3x_2 \le 4$ (*)

$x_1 \ge 0, x_2 \ge 0$

Note that the third constraint (marked (*)) is redundant

32-1.b) X_3, X_4, X_5 slack variables

Solve Interactively by the Simplex Method:

Bas Var	Eq No	Z	X_1	X_2	X_3	X_4	X_5	Right Side
Z	0	1	-3	-2	0	0	0	0
X_3	1	0	2	1	1	0	0	2
X_4	2	0	1	2	0	1	0	2
X_5	3	0	3	3	0	0	1	4

Bas Var	Eq No	Z	X_1	X_2	X_3	X_4	X_5	Right Side
Z	0	1	0	-0.5	1.5	0	0	3
X_1	1	0	1	0.5	0.5	0	0	1
X_4	2	0	0	1.5	-0.5	1	0	1
X_5	3	0	0	1.5	-1.5	0	1	1

Bas Var	Eq No	Z	X_1	X_2	X_3	X_4	X_5	Right Side
Z	0	1	0	0	1.3333	0.3333	0	3.33333
X_1	1	0	1	0	0.6667	-0.333	0	0.66667
X_2	2	0	0	1	-0.333	0.6667	0	0.66667
X_5	3	0	0	0	-1	-1	1	0

$(x_1^*, x_2^*) = (\frac{2}{3}, \frac{2}{3})$

$z^* = 3\frac{1}{3}$

32-2.

a) True. (Ex. Max $z = -x_1 + 4x_2$)

b) True. (Ex. Max $z = -x_1 + 3x_2$)

c) False. (Ex. Max $z = -x_1 - x_2$)

3.2-3.a) As in the Wyndor Glass Co. problem, one wants to find optimal levels of two activities that compete for limited resources. We want to find the optimal mix of the two activities.

Let x_1 be the fraction purchased of Activity 1., partnership in the first friend's venture. Let x_2 be the fraction purchased of Activity 2, the second friend's venture.

The data for the problem is given by the following table:

Resource	Resource Usage per Unit of Activity 1	Resource Usage per Unit of Activity 2	Amount of Resource Available
Fraction of partnership in first friend's venture	1	0	1
Fraction of partnership in second friend's venture	0	1	1
Money	5000	4000	6000
Summer Work Hours	400	500	600
ΔZ per unit of activity level	4500	4500	

b) Maximize $Z = 4500x_1 + 4500x_2$

subject to

$$x_1 \le 1$$
$$x_2 \le 1$$
$$5000x_1 + 4000x_2 \le 6000$$
$$400x_1 + 500x_2 \le 600$$
$$x_1 \ge 0 \quad x_2 \ge 0$$

c)

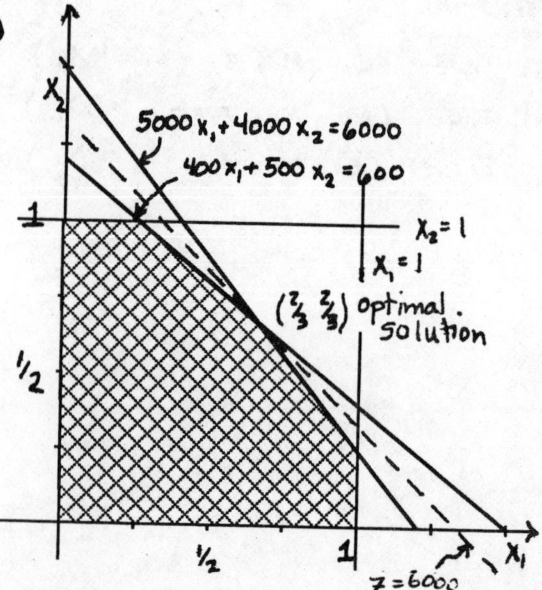

$(x_1, x_2) = (2/3, 2/3)$ is optimal with $Z = 6000$

3.3-1.

Proportionality: It is fair to assume the amount of work and money spent and the profit earned are directly proportional to the fraction of partnership purchased in either venture.

Additivity: The profit as well as time and money requirements for one venture should not affect the profit or time and money requirements of the other venture. This assumption is reasonably satisfied.

Divisibility: Because both friends will allow purchase of any fraction of a full partnership, divisibility is a reasonable assumption.

Certainty: Because we don't know how accurate the friends' profit estimates are, this is a more doubtful assumption. We should conduct sensitivity analysis after finding the optimal solutions for the current values of the profits.

3.3-2.

Proportionality: OK, since if either variable is fixed, the objective value grows in proportion to the increase in the other variable.

Additivity: Not OK, since activities interact. For example, the objective value with $(x_1, x_2) = (1,1)$ isn't equal to the objective value with $(x_1, x_2) = (1,0)$ plus the objective value with $(x_1, x_2) = (0,1)$.

Divisibility: Not OK, since activity levels are not allowed to be fractional.

Certainty: OK, since data is given as accurate.

3.4-1.a) Proportionality: OK, since beam effects on tissue types are proportional to beam strength.

Additivity: OK, since it was stated that effects from multiple beams are additive.

Divisibility: OK, since beam strength can be any fractional level.

Certainty: Due to the complicated analysis required to estimate the data on radiation absorbtion in different tissue types, sensitivity analysis should be used.

b) Proportionality: OK, as long as there is no set up cost associated with planting a crop.

Additivity: OK, as long as crops do not interact.

Divisibility: OK, since acres are divisible.

Certainty: OK, since data can be accurately determined.

c) Proportionality: OK, since set up costs were considered.

Additivity: OK, since it was stated that there is no interaction.

Divisibility: OK, since methods can be used at fractional levels

Certainty: Data is hard to estimate so it could easily be stochastic. Sensitivity analysis should be used.

3.4-2.*a*) Reclaiming solid wastes

Proportionality: The amalgamation & treatment processes are unlikely to be proportional. There are bound to be set up costs. (Treating 1,000 lbs. of material will not cost the same as treating 10 lbs. of material 100 ties.)

Additivity: Probably O.K., though it is possible that there is some interaction between treatments of materials (e.g., if *A* is treated after *B*, the machines do not need to be cleaned out . . .)

Divisibility: Probably O.K., unless selling/buying materials can only be done in batches (of 100 lbs., say).

Certainty: Selling/buying prices may change; costs of treatment & amalgamation are, most likely, crude estimates and may also change.

3.4-2. *b*) Personnel Scheduling

Proportionality: O.K. It is possible that *some* costs are not proportional to # of agents hired (e.g., benefits, working space, . . .), but for the most part, this assumption is satisfied.

Additivity: O.K. Same, pretty much, as proportionality.

Divisibility: Clearly, one cannot hire a fraction of an agent.

Certainty: The "min. # of agents needed" is suspect. Perhaps 45 agents will suffice instead of 48, for example, for a nominal fee. Also, does an agent in one shift do the same amount of work as one from another (or even the same) shift?

(*c*) Distribution goods through a distribution network

Proportionality: As in (*a*), there is probably a "set-up" cost for delivery (i.e., delivering 50 units one at a time will cost much more than delivering all 50 at the same time).

Additivity: Probably O.K., but it is possible that 2 routes may be "combined" to lower costs (e.g., if $x_{F2\text{-}OC} = x_{OC\text{-}W2} = 50$, the truck *may* be able to deliver 50 units directly from F2 to W2, without stopping at DC, saving some money). Another question is whether F1 and F2 produce equivalent units.

Divisibility: It seems that one cannot deliver a fraction of a unit.

Certainty: Shipping costs are probably approximations and are subject to change, as are amounts produced. Even the capacities may depend on available daily trucking force, weather, etc. As in any problem, sensitivity analysis should be done.

3.4-3.

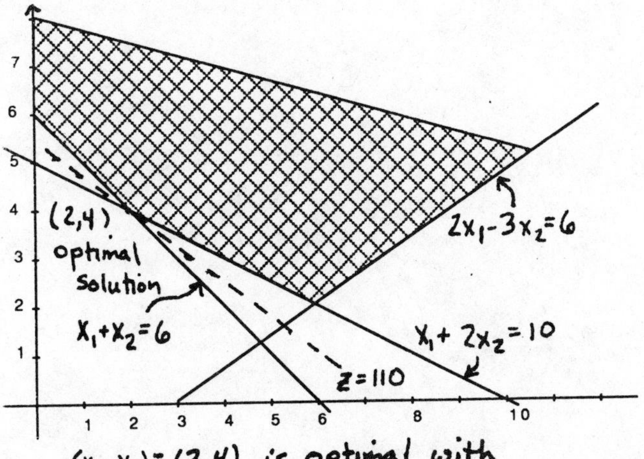

$(x_1, x_2) = (2,4)$ is optimal with $z = 110$

3.4-4.

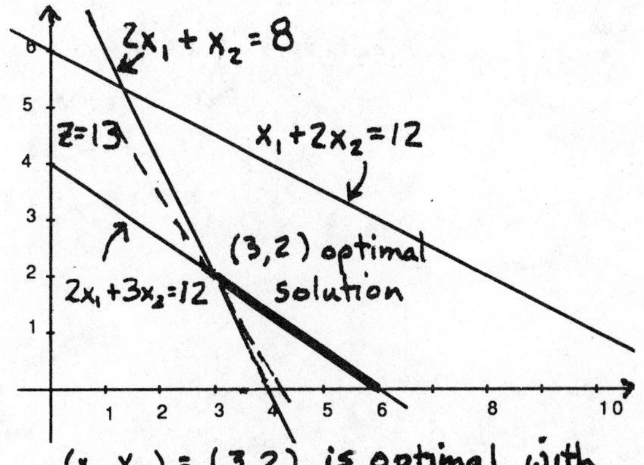

$(x_1, x_2) = (3,2)$ is optimal with $z = 13$

3.4-5. Feasible region:

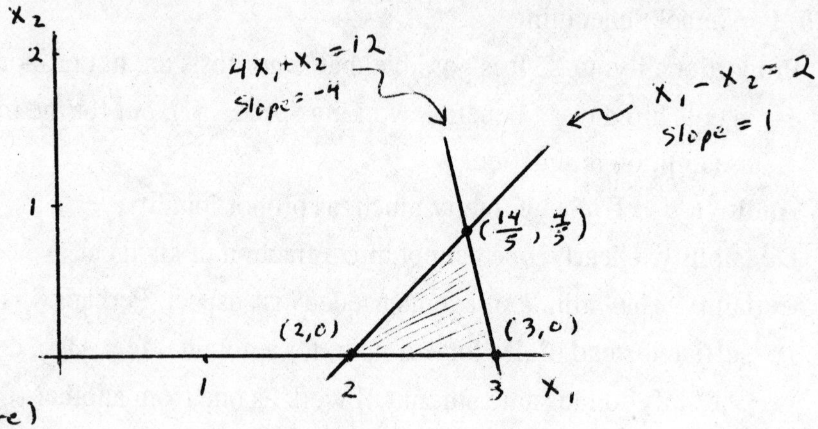

Since $c_2 > 0$ ($c_2 = 2$, here)

If slope of objective $= -\frac{c_1}{c_2} > 1$, then (2,0) is optimal

or $c_1 < -2 \Rightarrow (x_1^*, x_2^*) = (2,0)$

If $1 > \frac{-c_1}{c_2} > -12$, then $(\frac{14}{5}, \frac{4}{5})$ is optimal

or $-2 < c_1 < 24 \Rightarrow (x_1^*, x_2^*) = (\frac{14}{5}, \frac{4}{5})$

If $\frac{-c_1}{c_2} < -12$ (or $c_1 > 24$), then (3,0) is optimal

Of course, if $c_1 = -2$, then both (2,0) and $(\frac{14}{5}, \frac{4}{5})$ are optimal (as are all convex combinations of these),

and if $c_1 = 24$, $(\frac{14}{5}, \frac{4}{5})$, (3,0), and all convex combinations are optimal

3.4-6.

a) Let x_1 = # of daily servings of steak

x_2 = # " " " " potatoes

Minimize $Z = 4x_1 + 2x_2$

subject to
$$5x_1 + 15x_2 \geq 50$$
$$20x_1 + 5x_2 \geq 40$$
$$15x_1 + 2x_2 \leq 60$$
$$x_1 \geq 0, \ x_2 \geq 0$$

3.4-6.6) Solve Interactively by the Graphical Method:

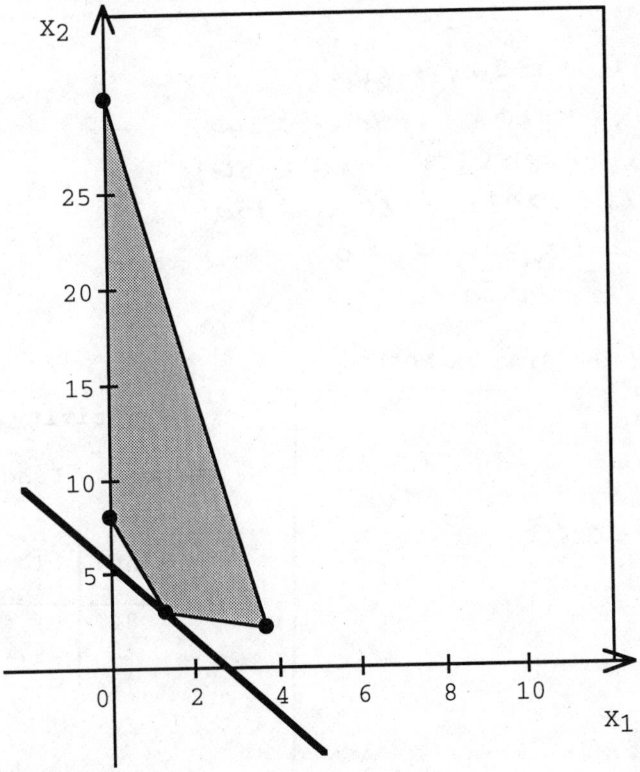

Corner Points	Z
(1.2727, 2.9091)	10.909*
(3.7209, 2.093)	19.07
(0, 8)	16
(0, 30)	60

Optimal value of Z: 10.909

Optimal solution: (1.2727, 2.9091)

c) Solve Automatically by the Simplex Method:

Optimal Solution

Value of the
Objective Function: Z = 10.9090909

Variable	Value
X_1	1.27273
X_2	2.90909

Constraint	Slack or Surplus	Shadow Price
1	0	-0.0727
2	0	-0.1818
3	35.0909	0

Sensitivity Analysis

Objective Function Coefficient

Current Value	Allowable Range To Stay Optimal Minimum	Maximum
4	0.66667	8
2	1	12

Right Hand Sides

Current Value	Allowable Range To Stay Feasible Minimum	Maximum
50	10	120
40	16.6667	84.8837
60	24.9091	$+\infty$

3.4-7. Let X_1, X_2, X_3 denote the # of kilograms of corn, tankage and alfalfa,
a) respectively.

$$\text{Minimize } Z = 84X_1 + 72X_2 + 60X_3$$

subject to
$$90X_1 + 20X_2 + 40X_3 \geq 200$$
$$30X_1 + 80X_2 + 60X_3 \geq 180$$
$$10X_1 + 20X_2 + 60X_3 \geq 150$$
$$X_1 \geq 0,\ X_2 \geq 0,\ X_3 \geq 0$$

b) Solve Automatically by the Simplex Method:

Optimal Solution

Value of the
Objective Function: Z = 241.714286

Variable	Value
X_1	1.14286
X_2	0
X_3	2.42857

Constraint	Slack or Surplus	Shadow Price
1	0	-0.7714
2	0	-0.4857
3	7.14286	0

Sensitivity Analysis

Objective Function Coefficient

Current Value	Allowable Range To Stay Optimal Minimum	Maximum
84	46.8	135
72	54.2857	+∞
60	37.3333	71.2727

Right Hand Sides

Current Value	Allowable Range To Stay Feasible Minimum	Maximum
200	120	225
180	174	300
150	-∞	157.143

3.4-8.
a)

Let x_{ij} be the number of units of product size j ($j = L, M, S$) produced at plant i ($i = 1, 2, 3$).

$$\text{Maximize } Z = 420\sum_{i=1}^{3} x_{iL} + 360\sum_{i=1}^{3} x_{iM} + 300\sum_{i=1}^{3} x_{iS}$$

subject to:
$$x_{1L} + x_{1M} + x_{1S} \leq 750$$
$$x_{2L} + x_{2M} + x_{2S} \leq 900$$
$$x_{3L} + x_{3M} + x_{3S} \leq 450$$

(con't)

3.4-8. a) (cont')

$$20x_{1L} + 15x_{1M} + 12x_{1S} \le 13000$$
$$20x_{2L} + 15x_{2M} + 12x_{2S} \le 12000$$
$$20x_{3L} + 15x_{3M} + 12x_{3S} \le 5000$$
$$x_{1L} + x_{2L} + x_{3L} \le 900$$
$$x_{1M} + x_{2M} + x_{3M} \le 1200$$
$$x_{1S} + x_{2S} + x_{3S} \le 750$$
$$900(x_{1L} + x_{1M} + x_{1S}) - 750(x_{2L} + x_{2M} + x_{2S}) = 0$$
$$450(x_{2L} + x_{2M} + x_{2S}) - 900(x_{3L} + x_{3M} + x_{3S}) = 0$$
$$x_{ij} \ge 0 \text{ for } i = 1,2,3,\ j = L, M, S$$

b) **Optimal Solution**

Value of the
Objective Function: Z = 696000

Variable	Value
X_1	516.667
X_2	0
X_3	0
X_4	177.778
X_5	666.667
X_6	0
X_7	0
X_8	166.667
X_9	416.667

Constraint	Slack or Surplus	Shadow Price
1	55.5556	0
2	66.6667	0
3	450	0
4	0	12
5	0	20
6	0	60
7	383.333	0
8	355.556	0
9	166.667	0
10	0	0.2
11	0	0.46667

Sensitivity Analysis

Objective Function Coefficient

Current Value	Allowable Range To Stay Optimal Minimum	Maximum
420	360	460
420	$-\infty$	460
420	$-\infty$	780
360	345	420
360	345	420
360	$-\infty$	480
300	$-\infty$	324
300	252	324
300	204	$+\infty$

Right Hand Sides

Current Value	Allowable Range To Stay Feasible Minimum	Maximum
750	694.444	$+\infty$
900	833.333	$+\infty$
450	0	$+\infty$
13000	11222.2	13888.9
12000	11500	12500
5000	4800	5181.82
900	516.667	$+\infty$
1200	844.444	$+\infty$
750	583.333	$+\infty$
0	-40000	50000
0	-15000	15000

Here, $X_1 = X_{1L}$, $X_2 = X_{2L}$, $X_3 = X_{3L}$, $X_4 = X_{1M}$, $X_5 = X_{2M}$, etc

3.4-9 a) Let x_{ij} denote the number of tons of cargo type i $(i=1,2,3,4)$ stowed in compartment j $(j=1,2,3)$ with 1, 2, 3 being front, center and back, respectively.

$$\text{Maximize } Z = 320\sum_{j=1}^{3} x_{1j} + 400\sum_{j=1}^{3} x_{2j} + 360\sum_{j=1}^{3} x_{3j} + 290\sum_{j=1}^{3} x_{4j}$$

subject to:

$$\sum_{j=1}^{3} x_{ij} \le \begin{cases} 20 & \text{for } i=1 \\ 16 & \text{for } i=2 \\ 25 & \text{for } i=3 \\ 13 & \text{for } i=4 \end{cases}$$

$$\sum_{i=1}^{4} x_{ij} \le \begin{cases} 12 & \text{for } j=1 \\ 18 & \text{for } j=2 \\ 10 & \text{for } j=3 \end{cases}$$

$$\frac{\sum_{i=1}^{4} x_{i1}}{12} = \frac{\sum_{i=1}^{4} x_{i2}}{18} = \frac{\sum_{i=1}^{4} x_{i3}}{10}$$

$$500x_{1j} + 700x_{2j} + 600x_{3j} + 400x_{4j} \le \begin{cases} 7000 & \text{for } j=1 \\ 9000 & \text{for } j=2 \\ 5000 & \text{for } j=3 \end{cases}$$

$$x_{ij} \ge 0 \text{ for } i=1,2,3,4; \; j=1,2,3.$$

b) Letting $x_1 = x_{11}$, $x_2 = x_{12}$, $x_3 = x_{13}$, $x_4 = x_{21}$, $x_5 = x_{22}$, etc.

Optimal Solution

Value of the Objective Function: Z = 13330

Variable	Value
X_1	7
X_2	6
X_3	0
X_4	5
X_5	4
X_6	5e-18
X_7	0
X_8	0
X_9	5
X_{10}	0
X_{11}	8
X_{12}	5

Sensitivity Analysis

Objective Function Coefficient

Current Value	Allowable Range To Stay Optimal Minimum	Maximum
320	320	400
320	320	320
320	$-\infty$	320
400	400	400
400	400	400
400	384.444	406.667
360	$-\infty$	360
360	$-\infty$	360
360	360	369.767
290	$-\infty$	290
290	290	290
290	290	303.333

3.4-9. b) (cont')

Constraint	Slack or Surplus	Shadow Price
1	7	0
2	7	0
3	20	0
4	0	10
5	0	120
6	-3e-19	0
7	0	336
8	0	-7e-16
9	0	12
10	0	0.4
11	0	0.4
12	0	0.4

Right Hand Sides

Current Value	Allowable Range To Stay Feasible Minimum	Maximum
20	13	+∞
16	9	+∞
25	5	+∞
13	8.33333	17
12	11.8148	12
18	18	+∞
10	10	10
0	-5e-18	3.33333
0	-4e-18	0
7000	6000	8400
9000	8200	10200
5000	4066.67	5800

3.4-10. a) Let x_i = # of asset i purchased, $i = 1, 2, 3$.

Then we want to:

$$\text{Minimize } Z = 100x_1 + 100x_2 + 100x_3$$

subject to

$$200x_1 + 100x_2 + 50x_3 \geq 4000$$
$$50x_1 + 50x_2 + 100x_3 \geq 0 \quad \leftarrow \text{redundant}$$
$$150x_2 + 200x_3 \geq 3000$$
$$x_1 \geq 0,\ x_2 \geq 0,\ x_3 \geq 0$$

b)

Optimal Solution

Value of the Objective Function: Z = 3000

Variable	Value
X_1	10
X_2	20
X_3	0

Constraint	Slack or Surplus	Shadow Price
1	0	-0.5
2	1500	0
3	0	-0.3333

Sensitivity Analysis

Objective Function Coefficient

Current Value	Allowable Range To Stay Optimal Minimum	Maximum
100	80	200
100	50	106.25
100	91.6667	+∞

Right Hand Sides

Current Value	Allowable Range To Stay Feasible Minimum	Maximum
4000	2000	+∞
0	-∞	1500
3000	0	6000

3.4-11 a) Let X_{ij} = amount invested in activity j at the beginning of year i.
(j = A, B, C, D ; i = 1, 2, 3, 4, 5)

L_i = amount money not invested in year i (thus carried over to year $i+1$) i = 1, 2, 3, 4, 5, 6

So we want to max L_6 (i.e. amount of money at start of year 6)
subject to:

$$L_1 + X_{1A} + X_{1B} = 60000$$

$$L_2 + X_{2A} + X_{2B} + X_{2C} = L_1$$

$$L_3 + X_{3A} + X_{3B} = L_2 + 1.4\,X_{1A}$$

$$L_4 + X_{4A} + X_{4B} = L_3 + 1.4\,X_{2A} + 1.7\,X_{1B}$$

$$L_5 + X_{5A} + X_{5B} + X_{5D} = L_4 + 1.4\,X_{3A} + 1.7\,X_{2B}$$

$$L_6 = L_5 + 1.4\,X_{4A} + 1.7\,X_{3B} + 1.9\,X_{2C} + 1.3\,X_{5D}$$

Note that clearly $X_{4B} = X_{5B} = X_{5A} = L_5 = 0$ at optimal
(It doesn't make sense to invest in something that doesn't realize a return until after the end of year 5.)

b) **Optimal Solution**

Value of the Objective Function: Z = 152880

Variable	Value
X_1 (X_{1A})	60000
X_2 (X_{2A})	0
X_3 (X_{3A})	84000
X_4 (X_{4A})	0
X_5 (X_{5A})	0
X_6 (X_{1B})	0
X_7 (X_{2B})	0
X_8 (X_{3B})	0
X_9 (X_{4B})	0
X_{10} (X_{5B})	0
X_{11} (L_1)	0
X_{12} (L_2)	0
X_{13} (L_3)	0
X_{14} (L_4)	0
X_{15} (L_5)	0
X_{16} (X_{2C})	0
X_{17} (X_{5D})	117600

Sensitivity Analysis

Objective Function Coefficient

Current Value	Allowable Range To Stay Optimal Minimum	Maximum
0	-0.168	0.13557
0	-∞	0.11165
0	-0.12	0.09684
1.4	-∞	1.49882
0	-∞	1.3
0	-0.1356	0.168
0	-0.1116	0.338
1.7	-∞	1.82
0	-∞	1.49882
0	-∞	1.3
0	-∞	0.338
0	-∞	0.39
0	-∞	0.32118
0	-∞	0.19882
1	-∞	1.3
1.9	-∞	2.21
1.3	1.21429	+∞

3.4-12. a) Let x_i = proportion of alloy i used in new alloy ($i=1,2,3,4,5$)

$$\text{Minimize } Z = 22x_1 + 20x_2 + 25x_3 + 24x_4 + 27x_5$$

subject to

$$60x_1 + 25x_2 + 45x_3 + 20x_4 + 50x_5 = 40$$
$$10x_1 + 15x_2 + 45x_3 + 50x_4 + 40x_5 = 35$$
$$30x_1 + 60x_2 + 10x_3 + 30x_4 + 10x_5 = 25$$
$$x_1 \geq 0,\ x_2 \geq 0,\ x_3 \geq 0,\ x_4 \geq 0,\ x_5 \geq 0$$

(Note that $x_1 + x_2 + x_3 + x_4 + x_5 = 1$ is not needed here since it is redundant.)

b)

Optimal Solution

Value of the Objective Function: Z = 23.4565217

Variable	Value
X_1	0.04348
X_2	0.28261
X_3	0.67391
X_4	0
X_5	0

Constraint	Slack or Surplus	Shadow Price
1	0	-0.2378
2	0	-0.2813
3	0	-0.1639

Sensitivity Analysis

Objective Function Coefficient

Current Value	Allowable Range To Stay Optimal Minimum	Maximum
22	21.6471	32.2
20	-5.5	20.375
25	$-\infty$	25.25
24	23.7391	$+\infty$
27	24.7826	$+\infty$

Right Hand Sides

Current Value	Allowable Range To Stay Feasible Minimum	Maximum
40	38.0392	66
35	7.80702	37.0408
25	10.5556	36.1111

3.4-13. a) Let x_{ij} = # hours operator i is assigned to work of day j

(i = KC, DH, HB, SC, KS, NK ; j = M, T, W, Th, F)

$$\text{Minimize } Z = 10(x_{KC,M} + x_{KC,W} + x_{KC,F}) + 10.1(x_{DH,T} + x_{DH,Th})$$
$$+ 9.9(x_{HB,M} + x_{HB,T} + x_{HB,W} + x_{HB,F})$$
$$+ 9.8(x_{SC,M} + x_{SC,T} + x_{SC,W} + x_{SC,F})$$
$$+ 10.8(x_{KS,M} + x_{KS,W} + x_{KS,Th}) + 11.3(x_{NK,Th} + x_{NK,F})$$

subject to

$x_{KC,M} \le 6$	$x_{DH,M} \le 6$	$x_{HB,M} \le 4$
$x_{KC,W} \le 6$	$x_{DH,Th} \le 6$	$x_{HB,T} \le 8$
$x_{KC,F} \le 6$		$x_{HB,W} \le 4$
		$x_{HB,F} \le 4$
$x_{SC,M} \le 5$	$x_{KS,M} \le 3$	$x_{NK,Th} \le 6$
$x_{SC,T} \le 5$	$x_{KS,W} \le 3$	$x_{NK,F} \le 2$
$x_{SC,W} \le 5$	$x_{KS,Th} \le 8$	
$x_{SC,F} \le 5$		

$$x_{KC,M} + x_{KC,W} + x_{KC,F} \ge 8$$
$$x_{DH,T} + x_{DH,Th} \ge 8$$
$$x_{HB,M} + x_{HB,T} + x_{HB,W} + x_{HB,F} \ge 8$$
$$x_{SC,M} + x_{SC,T} + x_{SC,W} + x_{SC,F} \ge 8$$
$$x_{KS,M} + x_{KS,W} + x_{KS,Th} \ge 7$$
$$x_{NK,Th} + x_{NK,F} \ge 7$$

$$x_{KC,M} + x_{HB,M} + x_{SC,M} + x_{KS,M} = 14$$
$$x_{DH,T} + x_{HB,T} + x_{SC,T} = 14$$
$$x_{KC,W} + x_{HB,W} + x_{SC,W} + x_{KS,W} = 14$$
$$x_{DH,Th} + x_{KS,Th} + x_{NK,Th} = 14$$
$$x_{KC,F} + x_{HB,F} + x_{SC,F} + x_{NK,F} = 14$$

$$x_{ij} \ge 0 \quad \forall i, j$$

3.4-13.b)

Optimal Solution

Value of the
Objective Function: Z = 709.6

Variable	Value
X_1 ($X_{KC,m}$)	2
X_2 ($X_{KC,w}$)	3
X_3 ($X_{KC,F}$)	4
X_4 ($X_{DH,T}$)	2
X_5 ($X_{DH,Th}$)	6
X_6 ($X_{HB,m}$)	4
X_7 ($X_{HB,T}$)	7
X_8 ($X_{HB,w}$)	4
X_9 ($X_{HB,F}$)	4
X_{10} ($X_{SC,m}$)	5
X_{11} ($X_{SC,T}$)	5
X_{12} ($X_{SC,w}$)	5
X_{13} ($X_{SC,F}$)	5
X_{14} ($X_{KS,m}$)	3
X_{15} ($X_{KS,w}$)	2
X_{16} ($X_{KS,Th}$)	2
X_{17} ($X_{NK,Th}$)	6
X_{18} ($X_{NK,F}$)	1

Sensitivity Analysis

Objective Function Coefficient

Current Value	Allowable Range To Stay Optimal Minimum	Maximum
10	10	+∞
10	10	10
10	9.9	10
10.1	10	+∞
10.1	−∞	10.2
9.9	−∞	10
9.9	9.8	10
9.9	−∞	10
9.9	−∞	10
9.8	−∞	10
9.8	−∞	9.9
9.8	−∞	10
9.8	−∞	10
10.8	−∞	10.8
10.8	10.8	10.8
10.8	10.8	+∞
11.3	−∞	11.3
11.3	11.3	+∞

3.4-14. a) Let x_{ij} = amt of space leased in month i for a period of j months.

$(i = 1, 2, 3, 4, 5 \; ; \; j = 1, \ldots, 6-i)$

The formulation is:

Minimize $Z = 650(x_{11}+x_{21}+x_{31}+x_{41}+x_{51}) + 1000(x_{12}+x_{22}+x_{32}+x_{42}) + 1350(x_{13}+x_{23}+x_{33}) + 1600(x_{14}+x_{24}) + 1900x_{15}$

subject to

$$x_{11}+x_{12}+x_{13}+x_{14}+x_{15} \geq 30$$
$$x_{12}+x_{13}+x_{14}+x_{15}+x_{21}+x_{22}+x_{23}+x_{24} \geq 20$$
$$x_{13}+x_{14}+x_{15}+x_{22}+x_{23}+x_{24}+x_{31}+x_{32}+x_{33} \geq 40$$
$$x_{14}+x_{15}+x_{23}+x_{24}+x_{32}+x_{33}+x_{41}+x_{42} \geq 10$$
$$x_{15}+x_{24}+x_{33}+x_{42}+x_{51} \geq 50$$
$$x_{ij} \geq 0 \quad i = 1, \ldots, 5 \; ; \; j = 1, \ldots, 6-i$$

b) **Optimal Solution**

Value of the
Objective Function: Z = 76500

Variable	Value
X1 (x_{11})	0
X2 (x_{12})	0
X3 (x_{13})	0
X4 (x_{14})	0
X5 (x_{15})	30
X6 (x_{21})	0
X7 (x_{22})	0
X8 (x_{23})	0
X9 (x_{24})	0
X10 (x_{31})	10
X11 (x_{32})	0
X12 (x_{33})	0
X13 (x_{41})	0
X14 (x_{42})	0
X15 (x_{51})	20

Constraint	Slack or Surplus	Shadow Price
1	0	-600
2	10	0
3	0	-650
4	20	0
5	0	-650

Sensitivity Analysis

Objective Function Coefficient

Current Value	Allowable Range To Stay Optimal Minimum	Maximum
650	600	+∞
1000	600	+∞
1350	1250	+∞
1600	1250	+∞
1900	1300	1950
650	0	+∞
1000	650	+∞
1350	650	+∞
1600	1300	+∞
650	600	700
1000	650	+∞
1350	1300	+∞
650	0	+∞
1000	650	+∞
650	600	700

Right Hand Sides

Current Value	Allowable Range To Stay Feasible Minimum	Maximum
30	20	40
20	-∞	30
40	30	+∞
10	-∞	30
50	30	+∞

34-15.

Let t_{ijk} = # of units of paper type k shipped from paper mill i to customer j.

Y_{ikl} = # of units of paper type k produced on machine type l at mill i.

We want to:

$$\text{minimize} \quad \sum_i \sum_j \sum_k T_{ijk} t_{ijk} + \sum_i \sum_k \sum_l P_{ikl} Y_{ikl}$$

subject to:

$$\sum_i t_{ijk} \geq D_{jk} \quad \forall j,k \quad \text{(demand met)}$$

$$\sum_l Y_{ikl} = \sum_j t_{ijk} \quad \forall i,k \quad \text{(amt produced of paper type k, at mill i = amt shipped)}$$

$$\sum_k \sum_l Y_{ikl} r_{klm} \leq R_{im} \quad \forall i,m \quad \text{(raw material available)}$$

$$\sum_k C_{kl} Y_{ikl} \leq C_{il} \quad \forall i,l \quad \text{(machine capacity)}$$

$$t_{ijk} \geq 0 \quad \forall i,j,k$$

$$Y_{ikl} \geq 0 \quad \forall i,k,l$$

3. 5-1. a) The two factors which often hinder the use of optimization models by managers are cultural differences and response time. Cultural differences cause managers and model developers to often have a hard time understanding each other. Response time is often slow due to the time to translate, formulate and solve the manager's problem using optimization systems.

b) As stated in the article, "[b]ased on unit profits, the company in the past emphasized the manufacture of thicker plywoods (TYPEA), but the optimization procedure showed that in fact thinner plywoods (TYPEB) were more profitable. This product mix change has increased the overall profitability of the company by 20%." (p. 30)

c) The chapter before "Conclusions" describes this: "With the success of this application, management is now eager to use optimization for other problems, too. Since Ponderosa uses timber for products other than plywood, they intend to explore the optimum allocation of this raw material between different products. Raw material and inventory management is another potential area of application. Also, the conversion of the optimization model into the financial planning language will now facilitate the integration of financial models with production models." (p. 31)

d) The Xerox of the appendices:

APPENDIX A. MATHEMATICAL FORMULATION OF THE PROBLEM

X_{it} = Amount of product i in period t $(i = 1, \ldots, n)$, $(t = 1, \ldots, T)$
C_{it} = Contribution margin of product i in period t
Y_{jt} = Amount of veneer sheet type j produced in period t $(j = 1, \ldots, n_1)$
Z_{kt} = Amount of green veneer type k produced in period t $(k = 1, \ldots, n_2)$
C_{pt} = Consumption of log type p in period t $(p = 1, \ldots, n_3)$
F_{pt} = Final inventory of log type p in period t
S_{pt} = Supply of log type p in period t
P_i = Pressing hours required per unit of product i
G_i = Polishing hours required per unit of product i
A_t = Total polishing hours available in period t
B_t = Total pressing hours available in period t
D_{ij} = Amount of type j veneer sheet required per unit of product i
E_{pT} = Final inventory requirement coefficients for log type p in period T
Q_{kp} = Green veneer type k yield per unit of log type p
H_{kj} = Green veneer type k required per unit of veneer sheet of type j
U_{it} = Upper limit on market demand for product i in period t
L_{it} = Lower limit on market demand for product i in period t

Objective

$$\text{Maximize} \sum_{i,t} C_{it} X_{it}.$$

Constraints

Polishing capacity limited:

$$\sum_i G_i X_{it} \leqslant A_t, \quad t = 1, \ldots, T$$

Pressing capacity limited:

$$\sum_i P_i X_{it} \leqslant B_t, \quad t = 1, \ldots, T$$

Veneer sheet required:

$$\sum_i D_{ij} X_{it} = Y_{jt}, \quad j = 1, \ldots, n_1, \quad t = 1, \ldots, T$$

Material balance on log:

$$C_{pt} + F_{pt} - F_{pt-1} = S_{pt}, \quad p = 1, \ldots, n_3, \quad t = 1, \ldots, T$$

Final inventory composition requirement:

$$\sum_p E_{pT} F_{pT} = 0$$

Green veneer yield from logs:

$$\sum_p Q_{kp} C_{pt} = Z_{kt}, \quad k = 1, \ldots, n_2, \quad t = 1, \ldots, T$$

Green veneers required:

$$\sum_j H_{kj} Y_{jt} = Z_{kt}, \quad k = 1, \ldots, n_2, \quad t = 1, \ldots, T$$

Market constraints:

$$L_{it} \leqslant X_{it} \leqslant U_{it}.$$

35-1. d) (con't)

APPENDIX B. STRUCTURE OF THE LP MODEL

Vector Rows	Products by Grade and Thickness	Veneer Sheet Production	Green Veneer Production	Log Consumption	Final Log Inventory	Right Hand Side
Market Constraints	1					≤ Limits Forecast by Sales
Veneer Requirements	X1	−1				=0
Pressing & Polishing Constraints	X2					≤ Production Capacity
Green Veneer Requirement		X3	−1 +1			=0
Green Veneer Generated			−1	X4		=0
Material Balance				1	1	= Initial Inventory + Log Supply
Final Inventory Composition Requirements					X5	=0
Objective Function	Unit Contribution Margin					= Maximize Contribution Margin

3. 5-2. a) The shift schedules at airports and reservations offices were done by hand prior to this study. (see paragraph 2, col 2, p. 42)

b) The project requirements (see bottom of col. 1, p. 42) were:
i) to determine the needs for increased manpower,
ii) to identify excess manpower for reallocation,
iii) to reduce the time required for preparing schedules,
iv) to make manpower allocation more day- and time-sensitve, and
v) to quantify the cost associated with scheduling.

c) United Airlines dealt with the integrality problem by using "[a] heuristic rounding algorithm similar to that described in Henderson and Berry [1979, see article for reference] ... incorporated in the Report Module ... and serv[ing] to covert the Schduling Module's fractionated LP solution into a workable shift schedule." (see p. 45)

d) Flexibility was necessary to "[satisfy] the group culture at each office [which was] essential in garnering field support. As a result, office-specified input variables, such as the number of start times, the preferred shift lengths, the length of breaks, preferred days off combinations, and so forth, became an intergral part of SMPS. This versatility gave office managers the luxury of evaluating schedules incorporating different input parameters but identical manpower requirements." (p. 47)

e) Benefits included: (p.48)
i) significant labor cost savings,
ii) improved customer service,
iii) improved emplyee schedules,
iv) quantified manpower planning and evaluation,
(pp. 48-49 describes these in more detail)

3. 5-3. a) During the years preceding this OR study, "the price of crude oil increased tenfold ... as the short-term interest rates more than tripled ... This meant that the cost associated with financing the working capital employed in the refining and marketing industry increased more than 30 fold during that time ... Con-sequently, it [became] vastly more important to maintain tight control over required working capital." (p. 2)

b) "Citgo's distribution network of pipelines, tankers, and barges span[ned] the eastern two-third of the United States. The addition of the Southland 7-Eleven store increase[d] their marketing and distribution network to all of the 48 contiguous United States." (p. 4)

c) An 11-week planning horizon, partitioned into 6 one-week periods and 1 five-week period, was used. Also, "the model [was] partitioned into time zones, and replications of the model [were] employed to represent the multiple time periods." (p. 6)

d) Citgo used "a medium-sized computer, an IBM 4381 and mod." Typical run times for "model generation, solution and reports [were] respectively two minutes, half a minute, and seven minutes."

3.5-3. e) The four types of model users were the product managers, the pricing manager, the product traders, and the budget manager. "Product manager compare[d] the model recommendations to the actual operational decisions to determine the existence and cause of discrepancies. They also use[d] the model's what-if capabilities to generate economically viable alternatives to current and forecasted operations ... The pricing manager use[d] the model in several ways. He use[d] one set of reports to set ranges for terminal prices for each product ... In addition, the pricing manager use[d] the wholesale report to help set prices and reommended volumes for bulk sales made to reduce excess inventories ... [Product] traders use[d] the Volume Summary Report and the Infeasibility Report to determine which side of the trading board they should be on for each product ... They [could] also use the model's what-if capabilities to determine the sensitivity of spot prices to the required purchases or sales volumes as prices fluctuate[d] during the week ... [T] he budget manager use[d] the Financial Summary Report to generate various components of the monthly and quarterly budgets." (p. 9)

f) The major reports generated by the SDM system are listed on page 8 of the article. They are:

i) Infeasibility report,
ii) In-transit, Terminal, Exchange, Inventory reports,
iii) Spot Recommendation report,
iv) Purchases, Sales, Trades reports,
v) Wholesale report,
vi) Volume Summary report,
vii) Financial Summary report.

g) "The education of the users was a challenge because both organizational responsibilities and people within the organizations flucutuated." (p. 10) "Another major implementation challenge concerned the collection, validation and correction of input data for the model." (p. 11) "A third implementation challenge concerned the forecasting sales volumes and wholesales prices. Citgo forcasted only total volumes for monthly and quarterly budgets. The SDM systems, on the other hand, required volume and price forecasts to be detailed by terminal, by product, by line of business, and by week." (p. 11)

h) "The major benefit realized from the SDM Model was the reduction in Citgo's product inventory with no drop in service levels ... Another direct benefit of implementing the model was the improvement in operational decision making: improvements in coordination, pricing and purchasing decisions, as well as the incorporation of the 'new concepts' into the decision process itself ... In addition to the direct benefits, several indirect benefits result[ed] from the modeling process and implementation ... One such indirect benefit [was] the establishment of a corporate data base which provide[d] common, up-to-date, on-line operational information for current decision support. Another such benefit [was] the utilization of a single forcast throughout the different departments, thus keeping the entire organization focused and traveling down a single path. A third benefit [was] the closed-loop planning process fostered by the continual feedback provided by the product manager when comparing actual decision to model-recommended decision ... A fourth benefit [was] the increased interdepartmental communication the model's use has fostered at Citgo ... A final benefit [was] the insight gained from the modeling process itself." (pp. 15-16)

CP 3-1. a)

Let X_{ij} = number of students from area i going to school j. ($i=1,\dots,6$; $j=1,2,3$)

Since "—" indicates infeasible assignments, we need: $X_{21}=X_{43}=X_{52}=0$.

(We could also simply leave these variables out.)

Constants:

Let S_i = # students in area i.

BC_{ij} = Bussing cost (per student) of bussing from area i to school j

P_{ik} = % of students in area i falling into grade category k ($k=6,7,8$)

SC_j = School capacity of school j

So S_1 = # students in area 1 = 450

$S_2 = 600$, etc

$BC_{11} = \$300$, $BC_{12} = \$0$, $BC_{13} = \$700$, $BC_{21} = \infty$ (or any number),

$P_{16} = 32$, $P_{17} = 38$, $P_{18} = 30$, etc.

$SC_1 = 900$, $SC_2 = 1100$, $SC_3 = 1000$

Then the formulation is:

$$\text{Minimize } Z = \sum_{i=1}^{6}\sum_{j=1}^{3} BC_{ij} X_{ij}$$

subject to

$$\sum_{j=1}^{3} X_{ij} = S_i \quad i=1,2,3,4,5,6 \quad \text{(must assign all students)}$$

$$\sum_{i=1}^{6} X_{ij} \le SC_j \quad j=1,2,3 \quad \text{(can't exceed school capacity)}$$

$$(*)\left[\begin{array}{ll} \sum_{i=1}^{6}(P_{ik}-30)X_{ij} \ge 0 & j=1,2,3,\ k=6,7,8 \\ \sum_{i=1}^{6}(35-P_{ik})X_{ij} \ge 0 & j=1,2,3;\ k=6,7,8 \end{array}\right\} \text{(30-35\% restriction)}$$

$$X_{ij} \ge 0 \quad i=1,\dots,6,\ j=1,2,3 \quad (X_{21}=X_{43}=X_{52}=0)$$

We get (*) from:

$$30 \le \frac{\sum_{i=1}^{6} P_{ik} X_{ij}}{\sum_{i=1}^{6} X_{ij}} \le 35 \qquad j=1,2,3;\ k=6,7,8$$

(this term represents % of students at school j in grade categ. k.)

By multiplying "both" sides by $\sum_{i=1}^{6} X_{ij}$ and simplifying, we get the desired result.

CP3-1. b) *Proportionality*: Bussing cost is probably not proportional to # students riding (set up costs).

Additivity: Fine, unless students from different areas are somehow inherently different or bussing 2 areas can be combined.

Divisibility: Obviously, we cannot (realistically) assign a fraction of a student...

Certainty: Not OK probably. Costs change, students may move, % restrictions are probably relaxable, etc.

c) The computer output is:

Optimal Solution

Value of the
Objective Function: Z = 644444.444

Variable		Value
X_1	(X_{11})	0
X_2	(X_{12})	450
X_3	(X_{13})	0
X_4	(X_{21})	-3e-18 = 0 ← Note that X_{21}, X_{43} and X_{52} are set equal to zero
X_5	(X_{22})	577.778
X_6	(X_{23})	22.2222
X_7	(X_{31})	0
X_8	(X_{32})	72.2222
X_9	(X_{33})	477.778
X_{10}	(X_{41})	350
X_{11}	(X_{42})	0
X_{12}	(X_{43})	0 ←
X_{13}	(X_{51})	233.333
X_{14}	(X_{52})	0 ←
X_{15}	(X_{53})	266.667
X_{16}	(X_{61})	216.667
X_{17}	(X_{62})	0
X_{18}	(X_{63})	233.333

(which is why in the sensit. anal. the "allowable range to stay optimal" for the coefficient is $-\infty$ to $+\infty$)

Sensitivity Analysis

Objective Function Coefficient

Current Value	Allowable Range To Stay Optimal: Minimum	Maximum
300	122.222	$+\infty$
0	$-\infty$	177.778
700	433.333	$+\infty$
99999 (arbitrary #'s)	$-\infty$	$+\infty$
400	395.455	432.203
500	467.797	504.545
600	588.889	$+\infty$
300	267.797	304.545
200	192.308	232.203
200	$-\infty$	566.667
500	133.333	$+\infty$
9999 (arbitrary #'s)	$-\infty$	$+\infty$
0	-90.476	16.6667
9999 (arbitrary #'s)	$-\infty$	$+\infty$
400	383.333	490.476
500	333.333	533.333
300	100	$+\infty$
0	-33.333	166.667

Since # students must be integer, a more realistic solution would be:

$Z^* = \$644,700$

School \ Area	1	2	3	4	5	6	Total
1	0	0	0	350	233	217	800
2	450	578	72	0	0	0	1100
3	0	22	478	0	267	233	1000
Total	450	600	550	350	500	450	2900

CP3-1. d) This <u>could</u> be solved through "Integer Programming" (Chapter 12), but we can get a good approximate by "rounding off." For areas 1 and 4, there is no need. Areas 2 and 3 are pretty clear as to which school they should be assigned to. Finally, areas 5 and 6 must be split between schools 1 and 3. Both the costs associated with bussing students from areas 5 (6) to school 1 (3), and the restriction that school 3 has a capacity of 1000, leads us to assign students from area 5 to school 1 and area 6 to school 3:

School \ Area	1	2	3	4	5	6	Total
1	0	0	0	350	500	0	850
2	450	600	0	0	0	0	1050
3	0	0	550	0	0	450	1000
Total	450	600	550	350	500	450	2900

Total Cost = $420,000

Note that the cost is <u>lower</u> than the "optimal." This is because we are violating one of the constraints (actually, more than one)

	% 6th grade	% 7th grade	% 8th grade
School 1	34.5	36.5*	29.1*
School 2	34.9	32.3	32.9
School 3	31.8	30.2	38.0*

*Violation of 30-35% restriction

As it turns out, it is not possible to "keep each neighborhood together" and satisfy all constraints at the same time.

CP3-1. e) The formulation stays exactly the same. The only thing that changes are the constants: ~~T33~~

$BC_{33} = \$0$ (from \$200)
$BC_{41} = \$0$ (from \$200)

The solution (again, rounding to the nearest student) is:

School \ Area	1	2	3	4	5	6	Total
1	0	0	0	350	227	223	800
2	450	600	50	0	0	0	1100
3	0	0	500	0	273	227	1000
Total	450	600	550	350	500	450	2900

$Z^* = \$475,700$ (computer gives \$475,454.54 if fraction of students are allowed)

We "save" about \$169,000.

f) Again, the formulation is the same except that:

$BC_{33} = \$0$ }
$BC_{41} = \$0$ } from \$200

$BC_{11} = \$0$ }
$BC_{32} = \$0$ } from \$300
$BC_{62} = \$0$ }

Solution (this time, there was no need for rounding – optimal is integral):

School \ Area	1	2	3	4	5	6	Total
1	0	0	0	329	392	179	900
2	450	96	262	21	0	271	1100
3	0	504	288	0	108	0	900
Total	450	600	550	350	500	450	2900

$Z^* = \$433,600$, "saving" \$211,100.

CP 3-1. g) The following table summarizes the key information:

Option	Cost	# students walking more than 1 mile	# students walking more than 1.5 miles
current	$644,700	0	0
1	$475,700	850	0
2	$433,600	1150 *	533

*includes 533 walking more than 1.5 miles.

h) By taking option 1, we save about $170K, but requires 850 students to walk 1 to 1.5 miles.

Taking option 2 saves an additional $40K, but requires an additional 300 students to walk more than 1 mile and a total of 533 students to walk 1.5+ miles to school.

Since the school board expressed concerns about students walking >1.5 miles to school, it seems that the benefit of option 2 is small compared to the risk compared to option 1.

It seems that option 1 would be the best compromise, though some may opt for the "current" plan.

Chapter 4: Solving Linear Programming Problems: The Simplex Method.

4.1-1. a), b)

	CP sol'n	Feasible?	Value
A	$(0, \frac{3}{2})$	Infeas.	6750
B	$(0, \frac{6}{5})$	Infeas.	5400
C	$(0, 1)$	Feas.	4500
D	$(\frac{1}{4}, 1)$	F	5625
E	$(\frac{2}{5}, 1)$	I	6300
F	$(1, 1)$	I	9000
G	$(\frac{2}{3}, \frac{2}{3})$	F	6000*
H	$(1, \frac{2}{5})$	I	6300
I	$(1, \frac{1}{4})$	F	5625
J	$(1, 0)$	F	4500
K	$(\frac{6}{5}, 0)$	I	5400
L	$(\frac{3}{2}, 0)$	I	6750
M	$(0, 0)$	F	0

*optimal

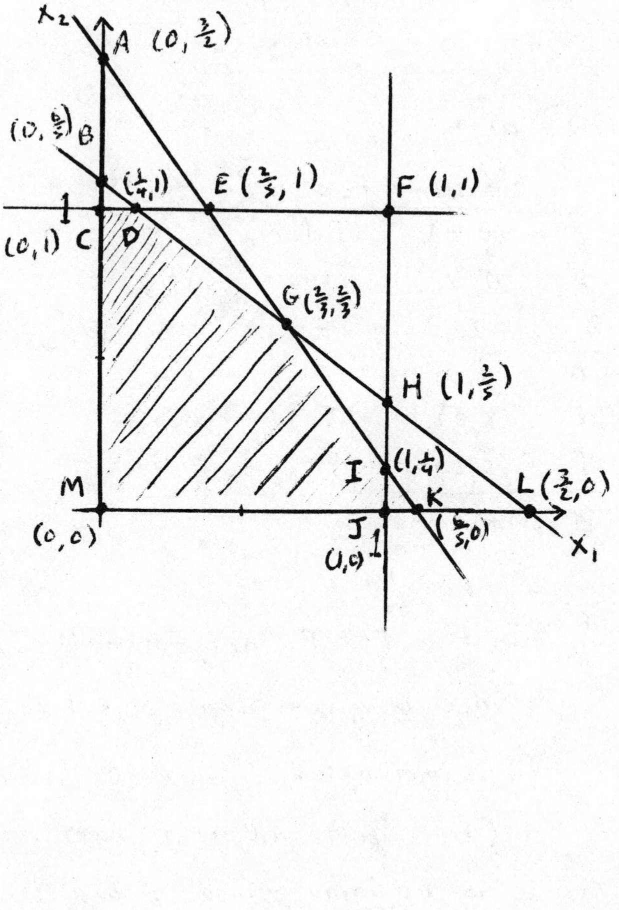

4.1-1. c)

Initial Pt M [(0,0)] ⟶ Not optimal since C and J [(0,1) and (1,0)] are better.

Since C and J give same objective value, either can be chosen.
We will choose C.

C is not optimal since D [($\frac{1}{4}$,1)] is adjacent and better. Move to D.
(Note that B is CP soln but not feasible)

D is not optimal since G [($\frac{2}{3}$, $\frac{2}{3}$)] is adjacent and better. Move to G.
(Note that G is the only better adjacent CPF soln. D is CPF, but worse.)

G is optimal since CPF's D and I give objective values 5625 < 6000.

Note: If J is chosen at first step, the path will be: M-J-I-G (with the same arguments as above).

4.1-2. a), b)

	CP soln	Feasible?	Value	
A	(0,4)	Infeas.	8	
B	(0, 8/3)	Feas	$5\frac{1}{3}$	
C	(2,2)	F	6	*
D	(4,0)	F	4	
E	(8,0)	I	8	
F	(0,0)	F	0	

* optimal

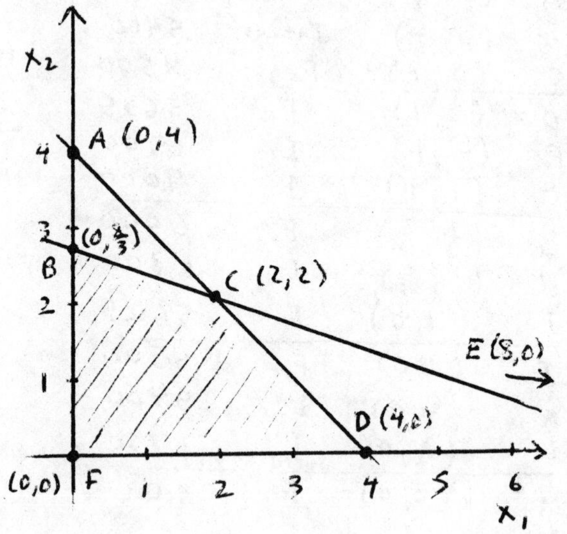

c) Initial Pt F, not optimal since B and D are better than F.
Since B gives higher objective value than B, chose B.

B is not optimal since C is adjacent and better. Move to C.
(Note A is adjacent, but not feasible)

C is optimal since B and D are only adjacent CPF solns and C is better than either.

4.1-3. a), b)

	CP sol'n	Feasible?	Value	
A	(0,5)	Feas.	10	
B	(0,10)	Infeas	20	
C	(3,4)	F	17	*
D	(4, 4/3)	I	$19\frac{1}{3}$	
E	(4,2)	F	16	
F	(4,0)	F	12	
G	(5,0)	I	15	
H	(15,0)	I	45	
I	(0,0)	F	0	

* optimal

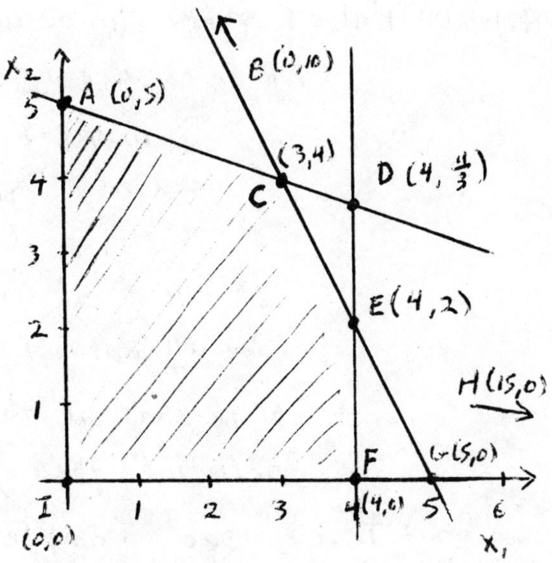

c)

Initial pt I, not optimal since A (value 10) and F (value 12) are adjacent and better than I (value 0). Chose F (since 12 > 10).

F is not optimal since E is adjacent and better (value 16). Move to E.

E is not optimal since C (value 17) is adjacent and better.

C is optimal since A (value 10) and E (value 16) are the only adjacent CPF sol'ns and 17 > 16 > 10.

4.1-4. a) True: Use optimality test — here, "better" means smaller. To see this, note that $\min Z = -\max(-Z)$

4.1-4.b) False: There can be an infinite number of optimal solutions. CPF sol'ns are not the only possible optimal solutions (e.g.

$$\max Z = X_1 + X_2$$
$$\text{s.t.} \quad X_1 + X_2 \le 10$$
$$X_1 \ge 0,\ X_2 \ge 0$$

$Z^* = 10$, $X_1^* = k$, $X_2^* = 10 - k$ k ranging from 0 to 10 are all optimal solutions.)

Note that if there are, in fact, more than one optimal solution, then there must be an infinite number.

c) True: See example in (b). (0,10) and (10,0) are both optimal and adjacent. If we replace the word "may" with "must" in the problem, the statement is still true.

4.2-1.

a) augmented form:

$$\text{Max } 4500X_1 + 4500X_2$$

s.t.

$$X_1 + X_3 = 1$$
$$X_2 + X_4 = 1$$
$$5000X_1 + 4000X_2 + X_5 = 6000$$
$$400X_1 + 500X_2 + X_6 = 600$$
$$X_1 \ge 0,\ X_2 \ge 0,\ X_3 \ge 0,\ X_4 \ge 0,\ X_5 \ge 0,\ X_6 \ge 0$$

b)

	CPF Sol'n	BF Sol'n	Nonbasic Var's	Basic Var's
A	(0, 1)	(0, 1, 1, 0, 2000, 100)	X_1, X_4	X_2, X_3, X_5, X_6
B	$(\frac{1}{4}, 1)$	$(\frac{1}{4}, 1, \frac{3}{4}, 0, 250, 0)$	X_4, X_6	X_1, X_2, X_3, X_5
C	$(\frac{2}{3}, \frac{2}{3})$	$(\frac{2}{3}, \frac{2}{3}, \frac{1}{3}, \frac{1}{3}, 0, 0)$	X_5, X_6	X_1, X_2, X_3, X_4
D	$(1, \frac{1}{4})$	$(1, \frac{1}{4}, 0, \frac{3}{4}, 0, 75)$	X_3, X_5	X_1, X_2, X_4, X_6
E	(1, 0)	(1, 0, 0, 1, 1000, 200)	X_2, X_3	X_1, X_4, X_5, X_6
F	(0, 0)	(0, 0, 1, 1, 6000, 600)	X_1, X_2	X_3, X_4, X_5, X_6

4.2-1, c)

BF Sol'n	Set Non-basic Var's to Zero	Solve	
A	$x_1 = x_4 = 0$	$x_3 = 1$ $x_2 = 1$ $4000x_2 + x_5 = 6000$ $500x_2 + x_6 = 600$	$x_5 = 6000 - 4000 = 2000$ $x_6 = 600 - 500 = 100$
B	$x_4 = x_6 = 0$	$x_1 + x_3 = 1$ $x_2 = 1$ $5000x_1 + 4000x_2 + x_5 = 6000$ $400x_1 + 500x_2 = 600$	$400x_1 = 600 - 500 = 100$ $\Rightarrow x_1 = \frac{1}{4}$ $x_3 = 1 - \frac{1}{4} = \frac{3}{4}$ $x_5 = 6000 - 4000 - 5000(\frac{1}{4})$ $= 750$
C	$x_5 = x_6 = 0$	$x_1 + x_3 = 1$ $x_2 + x_4 = 1$ $5000x_1 + 4000x_2 = 6000$ $400x_1 + 500x_2 = 600$	$5x_1 + 4x_2 = 6$ $4x_1 + 5x_2 = 6$ $x_1 - x_2 = 0$ $\Rightarrow x_1 = x_2 = \frac{2}{3}$ $x_3 = 1 - \frac{2}{3} = \frac{1}{3}$ $x_4 = 1 - \frac{2}{3} = \frac{1}{3}$
D	$x_3 = x_5 = 0$	$x_1 = 1$ $x_2 + x_4 = 1$ $5000x_1 + 4000x_2 = 6000$ $400x_1 + 500x_2 + x_6 = 600$	$4000x_2 = 6000 - 5000 = 1000$ $\Rightarrow x_2 = \frac{1}{4}$ $x_4 = 1 - \frac{1}{4} = \frac{3}{4}$ $x_6 = 600 - 400 - 500(\frac{1}{4}) = 75$
E	$x_2 = x_3 = 0$	$x_1 = 1,\ x_4 = 1$ $5000x_1 + x_5 = 6000$ $400x_1 + x_6 = 600$	$x_5 = 6000 - 5000 = 1000$ $x_6 = 600 - 400 = 200$
F	$x_1 = x_2 = 0$	$x_3 = 1,\ x_4 = 1$ $x_5 = 6000$ $x_6 = 600$	

4.2-2. a) augmented form:

$$\max \; x_1 + 2x_2$$
$$\text{s.t.} \; x_1 + 3x_2 + x_3 = 8$$
$$x_1 + x_2 + x_4 = 4$$
$$x_1 \ge 0,\; x_2 \ge 0,\; x_3 \ge 0,\; x_4 \ge 0$$

b)

	CPF soln	BF soln	Non-basic Var's	Basic Var's
A	(0,0)	(0,0,8,4)	x_1, x_2	x_3, x_4
B	$(0,\frac{8}{3})$	$(0, 8/3, 0, 4/3)$	x_1, x_3	x_2, x_4
C	(2,2)	(2,2,0,0)	x_3, x_4	x_1, x_2
D	(4,0)	(4,0,4,0)	x_2, x_4	x_1, x_3

c)

BF Sol'n	Set Non-basic Var's to Zero	Solve:
A	$x_1 = x_2 = 0$	$x_3 = 8$, $x_4 = 4$
B	$x_1 = x_3 = 0$	$3x_2 = 8$, $x_2 + x_4 = 4$ } $x_2 = 8/3$, $x_4 = 4 - 8/3 = 4/3$
C	$x_3 = x_4 = 0$	$x_1 + 3x_2 = 8$, $x_1 + x_2 = 4$, $2x_2 = 4$ } $x_2 = 2$, $x_1 = 8 - 3(2) = 2$
D	$x_2 = x_4 = 0$	$x_1 + x_3 = 8$, $x_1 = 4$ } $x_3 = 8 - 4 = 4$

d)

	CP Infeas Sol'n	Basic Infeas Sol'n	Nonbasic Var's	Basic Var's
E	(0,4)	(0,4,−4,0)	x_1, x_4	x_2, x_3
F	(8,0)	(8,0,0,−4)	x_2, x_3	x_1, x_4

e)

Basic Infeas Sol'n	Set Non-basic Var's to Zero	Solve:
E	$x_1 = x_4 = 0$	$3x_2 + x_3 = 8$, $x_2 = 4$ } $x_3 = 8 - 3(4) = -4$
F	$x_2 = x_3 = 0$	$x_1 = 8$, $x_1 + x_4 = 4$ } $x_4 = 4 - 8 = -4$

4.2-3. a) augmented form:

$$\text{Max } 3x_1 + 2x_2$$

$$\begin{aligned} \text{s.t.} \quad & x_1 \qquad\quad + x_3 \qquad\qquad = 4 \\ & x_1 + 3x_2 \qquad + x_4 \qquad = 15 \\ & 2x_1 + x_2 \qquad\qquad + x_5 = 10 \\ & x_1 \geq 0, x_2 \geq 0, x_3 \geq 0, x_4 \geq 0, x_5 \geq 0 \end{aligned}$$

b)

	CPF Sol'n	BF Sol'n	Non-basic Var's	Basic Var's
A	(0,0)	(0,0,4,15,10)	x_1, x_2	x_3, x_4, x_5
B	(0,5)	(0,5,4,0,5)	x_1, x_4	x_2, x_3, x_5
C	(3,4)	(3,4,1,0,0)	x_4, x_5	x_1, x_2, x_3
D	(4,2)	(4,2,0,5,0)	x_3, x_5	x_1, x_2, x_4
E	(4,0)	(4,0,0,11,2)	x_2, x_3	x_1, x_4, x_5

c)

BF Sol'n	Set Non-basic Vars to zero	Solve:	
A	$x_1 = x_2 = 0$	$x_3 = 4,\ x_4 = 15,\ x_5 = 10$	
B	$x_1 = x_4 = 0$	$x_3 = 4$ $3x_2 = 15$ $x_2 + x_5 = 10$	$x_2 = 5$ $x_5 = 10 - 5 = 5$
C	$x_4 = x_5 = 0$	$x_1 + x_3 = 4$ $x_1 + 3x_2 = 15$ $2x_1 + x_2 = 10$ $2x_1 + 6x_2 = 30$ $2x_1 + x_2 = 10$ $5x_2 = 20$	$x_2 = 4$ $x_1 = 3$ $x_3 = 4 - 3 = 1$
D	$x_3 = x_5 = 0$	$x_1 = 4$ $x_1 + 3x_2 + x_4 = 15$ $2x_1 + x_2 = 10$	$x_2 = 10 - 2(4) = 2$ $x_4 = 15 - 4 - 3(2) = 5$
E	$x_2 = x_3 = 0$	$x_1 = 4$ $x_1 + x_4 = 15$ $2x_1 + x_5 = 10$	$x_4 = 15 - 4 = 11$ $x_5 = 10 - 2(4) = 2$

4.3-1.

Input: Max Z = 4500 X_1 + 4500 X_2

subject to

1)   1 X_1 +   0 X_2 ≤ 1

2)   0 X_1 +   1 X_2 ≤ 1

3)   5000 X_1 + 4000 X_2 ≤ 6000

4)   400 X_1 + 500 X_2 ≤ 600

and

X_1 ≥ 0, X_2 ≥ 0.

Solve Interactively by the Simplex Method:

```
0) Z-4500 X1-4500 X2+    0 X3+    0 X4+    0 X5+    0 X6 = 0
1)       1 X1+    0 X2+    1 X3+    0 X4+    0 X5+    0 X6 = 1
2)       0 X1+    1 X2+    0 X3+    1 X4+    0 X5+    0 X6 = 1
3)    5000 X1+4000 X2+    0 X3+    0 X4+    1 X5+    0 X6 = 6000
4)     400 X1+ 500 X2+    0 X3+    0 X4+    0 X5+    1 X6 = 600
```

X_1 ≥ 0, X_2 ≥ 0, X_3 ≥ 0, X_4 ≥ 0, X_5 ≥ 0, X_6 ≥ 0.

```
0) Z+    0 X1-4500 X2+4500 X3+    0 X4+    0 X5+    0 X6 = 4500
1)       1 X1+    0 X2+    1 X3+    0 X4+    0 X5+    0 X6 = 1
2)       0 X1+    1 X2+    0 X3+    1 X4+    0 X5+    0 X6 = 1
3)       0 X1+4000 X2-5000 X3+    0 X4+    1 X5+    0 X6 = 1000
4)       0 X1+ 500 X2- 400 X3+    0 X4+    0 X5+    1 X6 = 200
```

X_1 ≥ 0, X_2 ≥ 0, X_3 ≥ 0, X_4 ≥ 0, X_5 ≥ 0, X_6 ≥ 0.

```
0) Z+    0 X1+    0 X2-1125 X3+    0 X4+1.12 X5+    0 X6 = 5625
1)       1 X1+    0 X2+    1 X3+    0 X4+    0 X5+    0 X6 = 1
2)       0 X1+    0 X2+1.25 X3+    1 X4-2e-4 X5+    0 X6 = 0.75
3)       0 X1+    1 X2-1.25 X3+    0 X4+2e-4 X5+    0 X6 = 0.25
4)       0 X1+    0 X2+ 225 X3+    0 X4-0.12 X5+    1 X6 = 75
```

X_1 ≥ 0, X_2 ≥ 0, X_3 ≥ 0, X_4 ≥ 0, X_5 ≥ 0, X_6 ≥ 0.

```
0) Z+    0 X1+    0 X2+    0 X3+    0 X4+ 0.5 X5+    5 X6 = 6000
1)       1 X1+    0 X2+    0 X3+    0 X4+6e-4 X5-4e-3 X6 = 0.66667
2)       0 X1+    0 X2+    0 X3+    1 X4+4e-4 X5-6e-3 X6 = 0.33333
3)       0 X1+    1 X2+    0 X3+    0 X4-4e-4 X5+6e-3 X6 = 0.66667
4)       0 X1+    0 X2+    1 X3+    0 X4-6e-4 X5+4e-3 X6 = 0.33333
```

X_1 ≥ 0, X_2 ≥ 0, X_3 ≥ 0, X_4 ≥ 0, X_5 ≥ 0, X_6 ≥ 0.

Solution: $(X_1^*, X_2^*) = \left(\frac{2}{3}, \frac{2}{3}\right)$, $Z^* = 6000$

4.3-2.a) $\text{Max } Z = x_1 + 2x_2$

s.t. $x_1 + 3x_2 + x_3 = 8$

$x_1 + x_2 + x_4 = 4$

$x_1 \geq 0, x_2 \geq 0, x_3 \geq 0, x_4 \geq 0$

Initialization : $x_1 = x_2 = 0 \Rightarrow x_3 = 8, x_4 = 4$

$Z = x_1 + 2x_2 \Rightarrow Z = 0$, not optimal since improvement rates > 0

Increase x_2 (rate of improvement $= 2$)
↑ "entering basic variable for iteration 1"

$x_1 = 0$, so $x_3 = 8 - 3x_2 \geq 0 \Rightarrow x_2 \leq 8/3$ ← min

$x_4 = 4 - x_2 \geq 0 \Rightarrow x_2 \leq 4$

Thus, x_2 can be increased to $8/3 \Rightarrow x_3 = 0$
↑ "leaving basic variable for iteration 1"

Using Gaussian elimination, we get:

$Z = \frac{1}{3}x_1 - \frac{2}{3}x_3 + \frac{16}{3}$

$\frac{1}{3}x_1 + x_2 + \frac{1}{3}x_3 = \frac{8}{3}$

$\frac{2}{3}x_1 - \frac{1}{3}x_3 + x_4 = \frac{4}{3}$ $(x_1, x_2, x_3, x_4 \geq 0)$

Again $(0, 8/3, 0, 4/3)$ is not optimal since rate of improvement for x_1 is > 0.

Increase x_1, $(x_3 = 0)$

$x_2 = \frac{8}{3} - \frac{1}{3}x_1 \geq 0 \Rightarrow x_1 \leq 8$

$x_4 = \frac{4}{3} - \frac{2}{3}x_1 \geq 0 \Rightarrow x_1 \leq 2$ ← min

x_1 can be increased to $2 \Rightarrow x_4 = 0$

4.3-2. a) (cont')

Again, using Gaussian elimination:

$$Z = -\frac{1}{2}x_3 - \frac{1}{2}x_4 + 6$$

$$x_2 + \frac{1}{2}x_3 + \frac{1}{2}x_4 = 2$$

$$x_1 \quad - \frac{1}{2}x_3 + \frac{3}{2}x_4 = 2 \quad (x_1, x_2, x_3, x_4 \geq 0)$$

Now, we are <u>optimal</u> since increasing x_3 or x_4 would <u>decrease</u> Z.

$x^* = (2, 2, 0, 0)$, $Z^* = 6$ (i.e. $x_1^* = 2$, $x_2^* = 2$)

b) Computer output:

Solve Interactively by the Simplex Method:

```
0) Z-   1 X1-   2 X2+   0 X3+   0 X4  = 0
1)      1 X1+   3 X2+   1 X3+   0 X4  = 8
2)      1 X1+   1 X2+   0 X3+   1 X4  = 4
```

$X_1 \geq 0$, $X_2 \geq 0$, $X_3 \geq 0$, $X_4 \geq 0$.

```
0) Z-0.33 X1+    0 X2+0.67 X3+    0 X4  = 5.33333
1) 0.333 X1+    1 X2+0.33 X3+    0 X4  = 2.66667
2) 0.667 X1+    0 X2-0.33 X3+    1 X4  = 1.33333
```

$X_1 \geq 0$, $X_2 \geq 0$, $X_3 \geq 0$, $X_4 \geq 0$.

```
0) Z+   0 X1+   0 X2+ 0.5 X3+ 0.5 X4  = 6
1)      0 X1+   1 X2+ 0.5 X3- 0.5 X4  = 2
2)      1 X1+   0 X2- 0.5 X3+ 1.5 X4  = 2
```

$X_1 \geq 0$, $X_2 \geq 0$, $X_3 \geq 0$, $X_4 \geq 0$.

$x_1^* = x_2^* = 2$, $Z^* = 6$

c) Again, you get the same solution:

Optimal Solution

Value of the
Objective Function: Z = 6

Variable	Value
X_1	2
X_2	2

Sensitivity Analysis

Objective Function Coefficient

Current Value	Allowable Range To Stay Optimal: Minimum	Maximum
1	0.66667	2
2	1	3

4.3-3. a) Max $Z = 3x_1 + 2x_2$

s.t.

$$x_1 + x_3 = 4$$
$$x_1 + 3x_2 + x_4 = 15$$
$$2x_1 + x_2 + x_5 = 10$$
$$x_1 \geq 0, x_2 \geq 0, x_3 \geq 0, x_4 \geq 0, x_5 \geq 0$$

Iter 1: $x_1 = x_2 = 0 \Rightarrow x_3 = 4, x_4 = 15, x_5 = 10$, not optimal

Increase x_1 (rate improvement = 3), $x_2 = 0$

$x_3 = 4 - x_1 \geq 0 \Rightarrow x_1 \leq 4$ ← min.

$x_4 = 15 - x_1 \geq 0 \Rightarrow x_1 \leq 15$

$x_5 = 10 - 2x_1 \geq 0 \Rightarrow x_1 \leq 5$

Increase x_1 to 4, $x_3 \to 0$

Now, $Z = 2x_2 - 3x_3 + 12$

$$x_1 + x_3 = 4$$
$$3x_2 - x_3 + x_4 = 11$$
$$x_2 - 2x_3 + x_5 = 2$$

Iter 2: (4, 0, 0, 11, 2) is not optimal

Increase x_2, $(x_3 = 0)$

$x_1 = 4 \geq 0$

$x_4 = 11 - 3x_2 \geq 0 \Rightarrow x_2 \leq \frac{11}{3}$

$x_5 = 2 - x_2 \geq 0 \Rightarrow x_2 \leq 2$ ← min

Increase x_2 to 2, $x_5 \to 0$

Now, $Z = x_3 - 2x_5 + 16$

$$x_1 + x_3 = 4$$
$$5x_3 + x_4 - 3x_5 = 5$$
$$x_2 - 2x_3 + x_5 = 2$$
$$(x_1, x_2, x_3, x_4, x_5 \geq 0)$$

4.3-3. a) (cont')

Iter 3: $(4, 2, 0, 5, 0)$ is not optimal

Increase x_3, $(x_5 = 0)$

$$x_1 = 4 - x_3 \geq 0 \Rightarrow x_3 \leq 4$$

$$x_4 = 5 - 5x_3 \geq 0 \Rightarrow x_3 \leq 1 \longleftarrow \text{min}$$

$$x_5 = 2 + 2x_3 \geq 0 \Rightarrow \text{no bound on } x_3$$

Increase x_3 to 1, $x_4 \to 0$

Now
$$Z = -\tfrac{1}{5}x_4 - \tfrac{7}{5}x_5 + 17$$

$$\begin{aligned} x_1 \quad\quad & -\tfrac{1}{5}x_4 + \tfrac{3}{5}x_5 = 3 \\ x_3 & + \tfrac{1}{5}x_4 - \tfrac{3}{5}x_5 = 1 \quad (x_1, x_2, x_3, x_4, x_5 \geq 0) \\ x_2 \quad\quad & + \tfrac{2}{5}x_4 - \tfrac{1}{5}x_5 = 4 \end{aligned}$$

Since all rates of improvement are ≤ 0, this is optimal

$x_1^* = 3$, $x_2^* = 4$, $Z^* = 17$

b) Computer output:

Solve Interactively by the Simplex Method:

0)	Z-	3 X_1-	2 X_2+	0 X_3+	0 X_4+	0 X_5	= 0
1)		1 X_1+	0 X_2+	1 X_3+	0 X_4+	0 X_5	= 4
2)		1 X_1+	3 X_2+	0 X_3+	1 X_4+	0 X_5	= 15
3)		2 X_1+	1 X_2+	0 X_3+	0 X_4+	1 X_5	= 10

$X_1 \geq 0$, $X_2 \geq 0$, $X_3 \geq 0$, $X_4 \geq 0$, $X_5 \geq 0$.

0)	Z+	0 X_1-	2 X_2+	3 X_3+	0 X_4+	0 X_5	= 12
1)		1 X_1+	0 X_2+	1 X_3+	0 X_4+	0 X_5	= 4
2)		0 X_1+	3 X_2-	1 X_3+	1 X_4+	0 X_5	= 11
3)		0 X_1+	1 X_2-	2 X_3+	0 X_4+	1 X_5	= 2

$X_1 \geq 0$, $X_2 \geq 0$, $X_3 \geq 0$, $X_4 \geq 0$, $X_5 \geq 0$.

0)	Z+	0 X_1+	0 X_2-	1 X_3+	0 X_4+	2 X_5	= 16
1)		1 X_1+	0 X_2+	1 X_3+	0 X_4+	0 X_5	= 4
2)		0 X_1+	0 X_2+	5 X_3+	1 X_4-	3 X_5	= 5
3)		0 X_1+	1 X_2-	2 X_3+	0 X_4+	1 X_5	= 2

$X_1 \geq 0$, $X_2 \geq 0$, $X_3 \geq 0$, $X_4 \geq 0$, $X_5 \geq 0$.

4.3-3. b) (cont')

```
0) Z+    0 X1+    0 X2+    0 X3+ 0.2 X4+ 1.4 X5 = 17
1)       1 X1+    0 X2+    0 X3- 0.2 X4+ 0.6 X5 = 3
2)       0 X1+    0 X2+    1 X3+ 0.2 X4- 0.6 X5 = 1
3)       0 X1+    1 X2+    0 X3+ 0.4 X4- 0.2 X5 = 4
```

$X_1 \geq 0,\ X_2 \geq 0,\ X_3 \geq 0,\ X_4 \geq 0,\ X_5 \geq 0.$

Optimal Solution: $x_1^* = 3,\ x_2^* = 4,\ Z^* = 17$.

c) Again, we get same solution!

Optimal Solution

Value of the Objective Function: Z = 17

Variable	Value
X_1	3
X_2	4

Sensitivity Analysis

Objective Function Coefficient

Current Value	Allowable Range To Stay Optimal Minimum	Maximum
3	0.66667	4
2	1.5	9

4.3-4.

(0)

Bas Var	Eq No	Z	X_1	X_2	X_3	X_4	X_5	Right Side
Z	0	1	-4	-3	-6	0	0	0
X_4	1	0	3	1	3	1	0	30
X_5	2	0	2	2	3	0	1	40

(1)

Bas Var	Eq No	Z	X_1	X_2	X_3	X_4	X_5	Right Side
Z	0	1	2	-1	0	2	0	60
X_3	1	0	1	0.3333	1	0.3333	0	10
X_5	2	0	-1	1	0	-1	1	10

(2)

Bas Var	Eq No	Z	X_1	X_2	X_3	X_4	X_5	Right Side
Z	0	1	1	0	0	1	1	70
X_3	1	0	1.3333	0	1	0.6667	-0.333	6.66667
X_2	2	0	-1	1	0	-1	1	10

$(x_1^*, x_2^*, x_3^*) = (0, 10, 6\frac{2}{3})$ is optimal with $Z^* = 70$

43-5. Output:

Solve Interactively by the Simplex Method:

$$\begin{array}{llllllll}
0) & Z - 1X_1 - & 2X_2 - & 4X_3 + & 0X_4 + & 0X_5 + & 0X_6 = & 0 \\
1) & 3X_1 + & 1X_2 + & 5X_3 + & 1X_4 + & 0X_5 + & 0X_6 = & 10 \\
2) & 1X_1 + & 4X_2 + & 1X_3 + & 0X_4 + & 1X_5 + & 0X_6 = & 8 \\
3) & 2X_1 + & 0X_2 + & 2X_3 + & 0X_4 + & 0X_5 + & 1X_6 = & 7
\end{array}$$

$X_1 \geq 0,\ X_2 \geq 0,\ X_3 \geq 0,\ X_4 \geq 0,\ X_5 \geq 0,\ X_6 \geq 0.$

$$\begin{array}{llllllll}
0) & Z + 1.4X_1 - & 1.2X_2 + & 0X_3 + & 0.8X_4 + & 0X_5 + & 0X_6 = & 8 \\
1) & 0.6X_1 + & 0.2X_2 + & 1X_3 + & 0.2X_4 + & 0X_5 + & 0X_6 = & 2 \\
2) & 0.4X_1 + & 3.8X_2 + & 0X_3 - & 0.2X_4 + & 1X_5 + & 0X_6 = & 6 \\
3) & 0.8X_1 - & 0.4X_2 + & 0X_3 - & 0.4X_4 + & 0X_5 + & 1X_6 = & 3
\end{array}$$

$X_1 \geq 0,\ X_2 \geq 0,\ X_3 \geq 0,\ X_4 \geq 0,\ X_5 \geq 0,\ X_6 \geq 0.$

$$\begin{array}{llllllll}
0) & Z + 1.53X_1 + & 0X_2 + & 0X_3 + & 0.74X_4 + & 0.32X_5 + & 0X_6 = & 9.89474 \\
1) & 0.579X_1 + & 0X_2 + & 1X_3 + & 0.21X_4 - & 0.05X_5 + & 0X_6 = & 1.68421 \\
2) & 0.105X_1 + & 1X_2 + & 0X_3 - & 0.05X_4 + & 0.26X_5 + & 0X_6 = & 1.57895 \\
3) & 0.842X_1 + & 0X_2 + & 0X_3 - & 0.42X_4 + & 0.11X_5 + & 1X_6 = & 3.63158
\end{array}$$

$X_1 \geq 0,\ X_2 \geq 0,\ X_3 \geq 0,\ X_4 \geq 0,\ X_5 \geq 0,\ X_6 \geq 0.$

Optimal solution is: $(0, 30/19, 32/19) = (x_1^*, x_2^*, x_3^*)$, $z^* = 9\frac{17}{19}$

43-6. Output:

$$\begin{array}{llllllll}
0) & Z - 1X_1 - & 2X_2 - & 2X_3 + & 0X_4 + & 0X_5 + & 0X_6 = & 0 \\
1) & 5X_1 + & 2X_2 + & 3X_3 + & 1X_4 + & 0X_5 + & 0X_6 = & 15 \\
2) & 1X_1 + & 4X_2 + & 2X_3 + & 0X_4 + & 1X_5 + & 0X_6 = & 12 \\
3) & 2X_1 + & 0X_2 + & 1X_3 + & 0X_4 + & 0X_5 + & 1X_6 = & 8
\end{array}$$

$X_1 \geq 0,\ X_2 \geq 0,\ X_3 \geq 0,\ X_4 \geq 0,\ X_5 \geq 0,\ X_6 \geq 0.$

$$\begin{array}{llllllll}
0) & Z - 0.5X_1 + & 0X_2 - & 1X_3 + & 0X_4 + & 0.5X_5 + & 0X_6 = & 6 \\
1) & 4.5X_1 + & 0X_2 + & 2X_3 + & 1X_4 - & 0.5X_5 + & 0X_6 = & 9 \\
2) & 0.25X_1 + & 1X_2 + & 0.5X_3 + & 0X_4 + & 0.25X_5 + & 0X_6 = & 3 \\
3) & 2X_1 + & 0X_2 + & 1X_3 + & 0X_4 + & 0X_5 + & 1X_6 = & 8
\end{array}$$

$X_1 \geq 0,\ X_2 \geq 0,\ X_3 \geq 0,\ X_4 \geq 0,\ X_5 \geq 0,\ X_6 \geq 0.$

$$\begin{array}{llllllll}
0) & Z + 1.75X_1 + & 0X_2 + & 0X_3 + & 0.5X_4 + & 0.25X_5 + & 0X_6 = & 10.5 \\
1) & 2.25X_1 + & 0X_2 + & 1X_3 + & 0.5X_4 - & 0.25X_5 + & 0X_6 = & 4.5 \\
2) & -0.88X_1 + & 1X_2 + & 0X_3 - & 0.25X_4 + & 0.38X_5 + & 0X_6 = & 0.75 \\
3) & -0.25X_1 + & 0X_2 + & 0X_3 - & 0.5X_4 + & 0.25X_5 + & 1X_6 = & 3.5
\end{array}$$

$X_1 \geq 0,\ X_2 \geq 0,\ X_3 \geq 0,\ X_4 \geq 0,\ X_5 \geq 0,\ X_6 \geq 0.$

Optimal solution: $(x_1^*, x_2^*, x_3^*) = (0, \frac{3}{4}, 4\frac{1}{2})$, $z^* = 10\frac{1}{2}$

4.3-7. a) The simplest adaptation is to force x_2 and x_3 into the basis (entering basic variable) at the earliest opportunity. (In fact, since we know Gaussian elimination, we can simply solve for the optimal solution directly).

b) $Z = 5x_1 + 3x_2 + 4x_3$

$$2x_1 + x_2 + x_3 + x_4 = 20$$
$$3x_1 + x_2 + 2x_3 + x_5 = 30$$
$$(x_1, x_2, x_3, x_4, x_5 \geq 0)$$

(i) Increase x_2 (force it into basis — we could do x_3 first, but it doesn't really matter...)

$(x_1 = x_3 = 0)$

$x_4 = 20 - x_2 \geq 0 \Rightarrow x_2 \leq 20$ ← min

$x_5 = 30 - x_2 \geq 0 \Rightarrow x_2 \leq 30$

Increase x_2 to 20, $x_4 \to 0$

$$Z = -x_1 + x_3 - 3x_4 + 60$$
$$2x_1 + x_2 + x_3 + x_4 = 20$$
$$x_1 + x_3 - x_4 + x_5 = 10$$
$$(x_1, x_2, x_3, x_4, x_5 \geq 0)$$

(ii) Increase x_3 (as it turns out, this is what we would normally do anyway)

$(x_1 = x_4 = 0)$

$x_2 = 20 - x_3 \geq 0 \Rightarrow x_3 \leq 20$

$x_5 = 10 - x_3 \geq 0 \Rightarrow x_3 \leq 10$ ← min

So increase x_3 to 10 $\Rightarrow x_5 \to 0$

$$Z = -2x_1 - 2x_4 - x_5 + 70$$
$$x_1 + x_2 + 2x_4 - x_5 = 10$$
$$x_1 + x_3 - x_4 + x_5 = 10$$
$$(x_1, x_2, x_3, x_4, x_5 \geq 0)$$

This is, indeed, optimal.

$(x_1^*, x_2^*, x_3^*) = (0, 10, 10)$, $Z^* = 70$

4.3-8. (a) Because $x_2 = 0$ in the optimal solution, we need only solve the linear program:

Maximize $Z = 2x_1 + 3x_3$

subject to:

$$x_1 + 2x_3 \le 30$$
$$x_1 + x_3 \le 24$$
$$3x_1 + 3x_3 \le 60$$
$$x_1 \ge 0,\ x_3 \ge 0.$$

or, equivalently,

Maximize $Z = 2x_1 + 3x_3$

subject to:

$$x_1 + 2x_3 \le 30$$
$$x_1 + x_3 \le 20$$
$$x_1 \ge 0 \quad x_3 \ge 0.$$

Since $x_1 > 0$ and $x_3 > 0$ in the optimal solution, they must be basic variables in the optimal solution. Choosing x_1 and x_3 as the first two entering variables will lead directly to the optimal solution. Leaving variables must still be determined by a minimum ratio test.

(b)

	Bas Var	Eq No	Z	X1	X3	X4	X5	Right side
(0)	Z	0	1	-2	-3	0	0	0
	X4	1	0	1	2*	1	0	30
	X5	2	0	1	1	0	1	20

	Bas Var	Eq No	Z	X1	X3	X4	X5	Right side
(1)	Z	0	1	-0.5	0	1.5	0	45
	X3	1	0	0.5	1	0.5	0	15
	X5	2	0	0.5*	0	-0.5	1	5

	Bas Var	Eq No	Z	X1	X3	X4	X5	Right side
(2)	Z	0	1	0	0	1	1	50
	X3	1	0	0	1	1	-1	10
	X1	2	0	1	0	-1	2	10

$(x_1, x_2, x_3) = (10, 0, 10)$ is optimal with $Z = 50$

4.3-9.

a) False. The simplex method's rule for choosing the entering basic variable is used because it will increase Z at the fastest rate, because it has the best rate of improvement.

b) True. Simplex method's rule for choosing the leaving basic variable determines which basic variable drops to zero first as the entering basic variable is increased. Thus, choosing any other would normally cause this variable to become negative (infeasible).

c) False. When the simplex method solves for the next BF solution, elementary algebraic operations are used to eliminate each basic variable from all but one equation (its equation) and to give it a coefficient of +1 in that one equation

4.4-1. Computer output (Tabular form):

Solve Interactively by the Simplex Method:

(0)

Bas Var	Eq No	Z	X_1	X_2	X_3	X_4	X_5	X_6	Right Side
Z	0	1	-4500	-4500	0	0	0	0	0
X_3	1	0	1	0	1	0	0	0	1
X_4	2	0	0	1	0	1	0	0	1
X_5	3	0	5000	4000	0	0	1	0	6000
X_6	4	0	400	500	0	0	0	1	600

(1)

Bas Var	Eq No	Z	X_1	X_2	X_3	X_4	X_5	X_6	Right Side
Z	0	1	0	-4500	4500	0	0	0	4500
X_1	1	0	1	0	1	0	0	0	1
X_4	2	0	0	1	0	1	0	0	1
X_5	3	0	0	4000	-5000	0	1	0	1000
X_6	4	0	0	500	-400	0	0	1	200

(2)

Bas Var	Eq No	Z	X_1	X_2	X_3	X_4	X_5	X_6	Right Side
Z	0	1	0	0	-1125	0	1.125	0	5625
X_1	1	0	1	0	1	0	0	0	1
X_4	2	0	0	0	1.25	1	-2e-4	0	0.75
X_2	3	0	0	1	-1.25	0	0.0002	0	0.25
X_6	4	0	0	0	225	0	-0.125	1	75

(3)

Bas Var	Eq No	Z	X_1	X_2	X_3	X_4	X_5	X_6	Right Side
Z	0	1	0	0	0	0	0.5	5	6000
X_1	1	0	1	0	0	0	0.0006	-0.004	0.66667
X_4	2	0	0	0	0	1	0.0004	-0.006	0.33333
X_2	3	0	0	1	0	0	-4e-4	0.0056	0.66667
X_3	4	0	0	0	1	0	-6e-4	0.0044	0.33333

Solution: $x_1^* = x_2^* = 2/3$, $Z^* = 6000$

4.4-2.

(0)

Bas Var	Eq No	Z	X_1	X_2	X_3	X_4	Right Side
Z	0	1	-1	-2	0	0	0
X_3	1	0	1	3	1	0	8
X_4	2	0	1	1	0	1	4

(1)

Bas Var	Eq No	Z	X_1	X_2	X_3	X_4	Right Side
Z	0	1	-0.333	0	0.6667	0	5.33333
X_2	1	0	0.3333	1	0.3333	0	2.66667
X_4	2	0	0.6667	0	-0.333	1	1.33333

4.4-2. (cont')

(2)

Bas Var	Eq No	Z	X_1	X_2	X_3	X_4	Right Side
Z	0	1	0	0	0.5	0.5	6
X_2	1	0	0	1	0.5	-0.5	2
X_1	2	0	1	0	-0.5	1.5	2

Solution: $x_1^* = x_2^* = 2$, $Z^* = 6$

4.4-3.

Bas Var	Eq No	Z	X_1	X_2	X_3	X_4	X_5	Right Side
Z	0	1	-3	-2	0	0	0	0
X_3	1	0	1	0	1	0	0	4
X_4	2	0	1	3	0	1	0	15
X_5	3	0	2	1	0	0	1	10

Bas Var	Eq No	Z	X_1	X_2	X_3	X_4	X_5	Right Side
Z	0	1	0	-2	3	0	0	12
X_1	1	0	1	0	1	0	0	4
X_4	2	0	0	3	-1	1	0	11
X_5	3	0	0	1	-2	0	1	2

Bas Var	Eq No	Z	X_1	X_2	X_3	X_4	X_5	Right Side
Z	0	1	0	0	-1	0	2	16
X_1	1	0	1	0	1	0	0	4
X_4	2	0	0	0	5	1	-3	5
X_2	3	0	0	1	-2	0	1	2

Bas Var	Eq No	Z	X_1	X_2	X_3	X_4	X_5	Right Side
Z	0	1	0	0	0	0.2	1.4	17
X_1	1	0	1	0	0	-0.2	0.6	3
X_3	2	0	0	0	1	0.2	-0.6	1
X_2	3	0	0	1	0	0.4	-0.2	4

(Optimal) solution: $x_1^* = 3$, $x_2^* = 4$, $Z^* = 17$.

4.4-4. a)

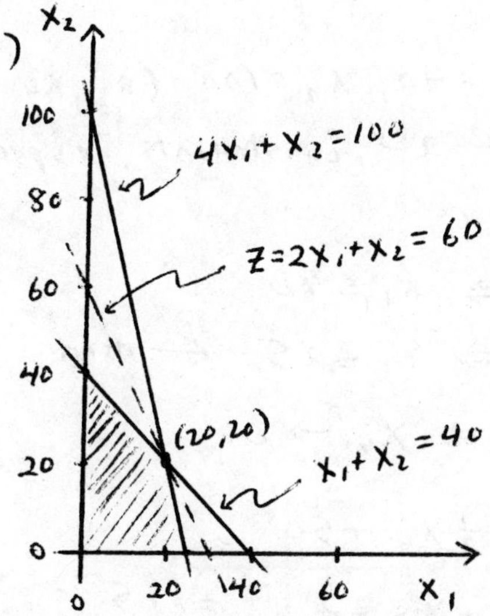

$Z^*=60$, $x^*=(20, 20)$

b)

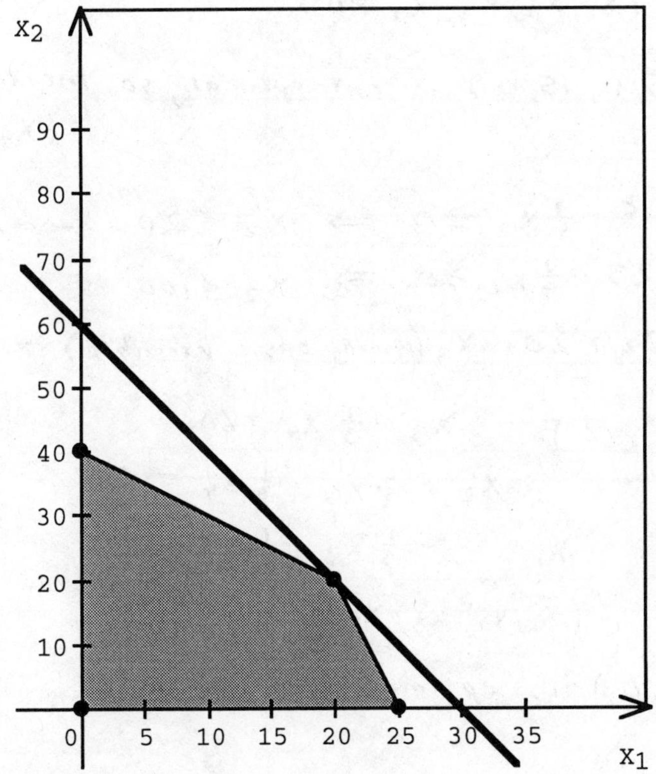

Corner Points		Z
(20,	20)	60*
(0,	40)	40
(25,	0)	50
(0,	0)	0

Optimal value of Z: 60

Optimal solution: (20, 20)

4.4-4. c) <u>Iter 1</u>: $x_1 = x_2 = 0 \Rightarrow x_3 = 40,\ x_4 = 100$ (x_3, x_4 are slack variables for 1st, 2nd constraints, respectively)

Increase x_1, x_2 set to 0.

$$x_3 = 40 - x_1 \geq 0 \Rightarrow x_1 \leq 40$$

$$x_4 = 100 - 4x_1 \geq 0 \Rightarrow x_1 \leq 25 \quad \leftarrow \text{min}$$

Can increase x_1 to 25 $\Rightarrow x_4 \to 0$.

Next, $$Z = \tfrac{1}{2}x_2 - \tfrac{1}{2}x_4 + 50$$

$$\tfrac{3}{4}x_2 + x_3 - \tfrac{1}{4}x_4 = 15$$

$$x_1 + \tfrac{1}{4}x_2 \qquad + \tfrac{1}{4}x_4 = 25$$

$$(x_1, x_2, x_3, x_4 \geq 0)$$

<u>Iter 2</u>: $(25, 0, 15, 0)$ is not optimal, so increase x_2. ($x_4 = 0$)

$$x_3 = 15 - \tfrac{3}{4}x_2 \geq 0 \Rightarrow x_2 \leq 20 \quad \leftarrow \text{min}$$

$$x_1 = 25 - \tfrac{1}{4}x_2 \geq 0 \Rightarrow x_2 \leq 100$$

Increase x_2 to 20, x_3 (leaving basic variable) $\to 0$

So now, $$Z = -\tfrac{2}{3}x_3 - \tfrac{1}{3}x_4 + 60$$

$$x_2 + \tfrac{4}{3}x_3 - \tfrac{1}{3}x_4 = 20$$

$$x_1 \qquad - \tfrac{1}{3}x_3 + \tfrac{1}{3}x_4 = 20$$

$$(x_1, x_2, x_3, x_4 \geq 0)$$

$(2, 2, 0, 0)$ is optimal, $Z^* = 60$

4.4-4. d)

Solve Interactively by the Simplex Method:

(0)

0) $Z - 2X_1 - 1X_2 + 0X_3 + 0X_4 = 0$
1) $1X_1 + 1X_2 + 1X_3 + 0X_4 = 40$
2) $4X_1 + 1X_2 + 0X_3 + 1X_4 = 100$

$X_1 \geq 0,\ X_2 \geq 0,\ X_3 \geq 0,\ X_4 \geq 0.$

(1)

0) $Z + 0X_1 - 0.5X_2 + 0X_3 + 0.5X_4 = 50$
1) $0X_1 + 0.75X_2 + 1X_3 - 0.25X_4 = 15$
2) $1X_1 + 0.25X_2 + 0X_3 + 0.25X_4 = 25$

$X_1 \geq 0,\ X_2 \geq 0,\ X_3 \geq 0,\ X_4 \geq 0.$

(2)

0) $Z + 0X_1 + 0X_2 + 0.67X_3 + 0.33X_4 = 60$
1) $0X_1 + 1X_2 + 1.33X_3 - 0.33X_4 = 20$
2) $1X_1 + 0X_2 - 0.33X_3 + 0.33X_4 = 20$

$X_1 \geq 0,\ X_2 \geq 0,\ X_3 \geq 0,\ X_4 \geq 0.$

Solution: $X_1^* = 20, X_2^* = 20$, $Z^* = 60$

e), f)

Solve Interactively by the Simplex Method:

Bas Var	Eq No	Z	X_1	X_2	X_3	X_4	Right Side
Z	0	1	-2	-1	0	0	0
X_3	1	0	1	1	1	0	40
X_4	2	0	4	1	0	1	100

Coefficients for X_1 and X_2 are <0 so not optimal.
X_1 is entering basic variable (largest absolute value), col 1 is the "pivot column"
Ratio test:
X_3: $\frac{40}{1} = 40$
X_4: $\frac{100}{4} = 25$ ← min
So X_4 is pivot row.

Bas Var	Eq No	Z	X_1	X_2	X_3	X_4	Right Side
Z	0	1	0	-0.5	0	0.5	50
X_3	1	0	0	0.75	1	-0.25	15
X_1	2	0	1	0.25	0	0.25	25

Coefficient for X_2 is <0 so not optimal.
X_2 is pivot column,
Ratio test:
X_3: $\frac{15}{.75} = 20$ ← min
X_1: $\frac{25}{.25} = 100$
X_3 is pivot row

Bas Var	Eq No	Z	X_1	X_2	X_3	X_4	Right Side
Z	0	1	0	0	0.6667	0.3333	60
X_2	1	0	0	1	1.3333	-0.333	20
X_1	2	0	1	0	-0.333	0.3333	20

All coefficients in objective row are ≥0 so we are at optimum.

Solution: $(x_1^*, x_2^*) = (20, 20)$, $Z^* = 60$

4.4-5. a)

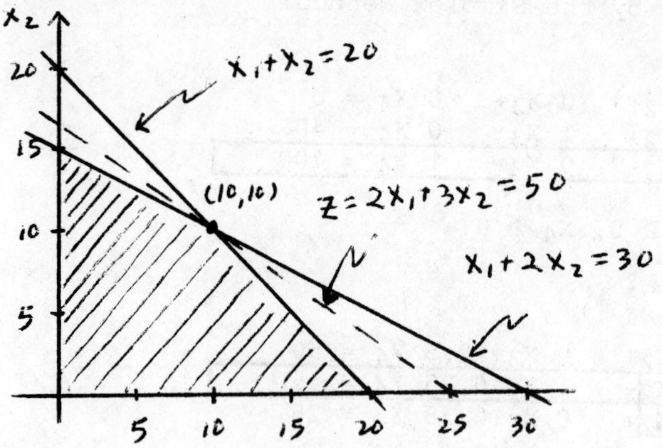

$Z^* = 50, \; x^* = (10, 10)$

b)

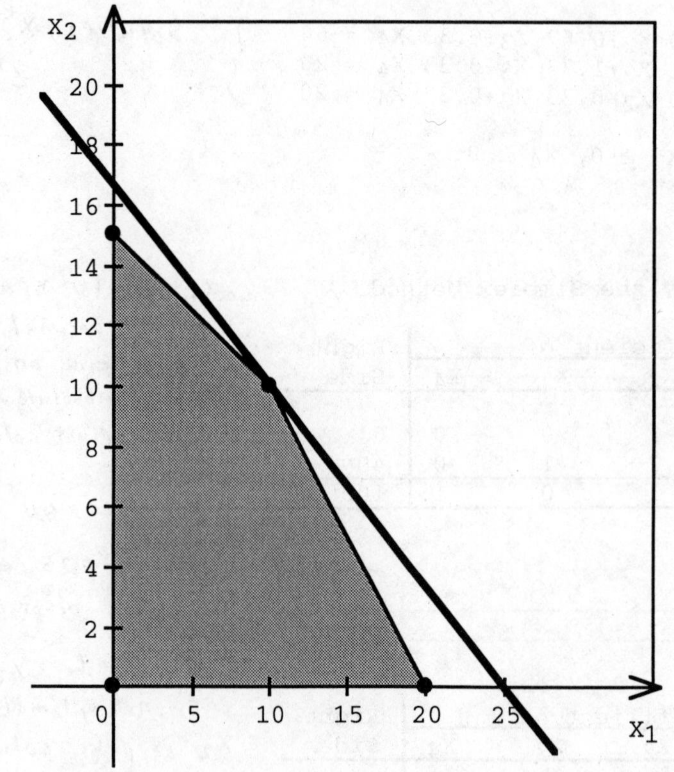

Corner Points		Z
(10,	10)	50*
(0,	15)	45
(20,	0)	40
(0,	0)	0

Optimal value of Z: 50

Optimal solution: (10, 10)

c) Iter 1: $x_1 = x_2 = 0 \Rightarrow x_3 = 30, \; x_4 = 20$ (x_3, x_4 slack variables)

Entering basic variable: x_2 ($X_1 = 0$)

$x_3 = 30 - 2x_2 \geq 0 \Rightarrow x_2 \leq 15 \leftarrow$ min

$x_4 = 20 - x_2 \geq 0 \Rightarrow x_2 \leq 20$

Increase x_2 to 15, x_3 goes to 0 (leaving basic variable)

4.4-5. c) (cont')

$$Z = \tfrac{1}{2}x_1 - \tfrac{3}{2}x_3 + 45$$

$$\tfrac{1}{2}x_1 + x_2 + \tfrac{1}{2}x_3 = 15$$

$$\tfrac{1}{2}x_1 - \tfrac{1}{2}x_3 + x_4 = 5$$

$$(x_1, x_2, x_3, x_4 \geq 0)$$

Iter 2: $(0, 15, 0, 5)$ is not optimal. Increase x_1. ($x_3 = 0$)

$$x_2 = 15 - \tfrac{1}{2}x_1 \geq 0 \Rightarrow x_1 \leq 30$$

$$x_4 = 5 - \tfrac{1}{2}x_1 \geq 0 \Rightarrow x_1 \leq 10 \quad \leftarrow \text{min}$$

Increase x_1 to 10, $x_4 \to 0$.

$$Z = -x_3 - x_4 + 50$$

$$x_2 + x_3 - x_4 = 10$$

$$x_1 - x_3 + 2x_4 = 10$$

$$(x_1, x_2, x_3, x_4 \geq 0)$$

This is optimal: $(x_1^*, x_2^*) = (10, 10)$, $Z^* = 50$

d) Solve Interactively by the Simplex Method:

(0)

```
0) Z-   2 X1-   3 X2+   0 X3+   0 X4 = 0
1)      1 X1+   2 X2+   1 X3+   0 X4 = 30
2)      1 X1+   1 X2+   0 X3+   1 X4 = 20
```

$X_1 \geq 0,\ X_2 \geq 0,\ X_3 \geq 0,\ X_4 \geq 0.$

(1)

```
0) Z- 0.5 X1+   0 X2+ 1.5 X3+   0 X4 = 45
1)    0.5 X1+   1 X2+ 0.5 X3+   0 X4 = 15
2)    0.5 X1+   0 X2- 0.5 X3+   1 X4 = 5
```

$X_1 \geq 0,\ X_2 \geq 0,\ X_3 \geq 0,\ X_4 \geq 0.$

(2)

```
0) Z+   0 X1+   0 X2+   1 X3+   1 X4 = 50
1)      0 X1+   1 X2+   1 X3-   1 X4 = 10
2)      1 X1+   0 X2-   1 X3+   2 X4 = 10
```

$X_1 \geq 0,\ X_2 \geq 0,\ X_3 \geq 0,\ X_4 \geq 0.$

Solution: $x_1^* = 10$, $x_2^* = 10$, $Z^* = 50$

4.4-5, e), f)

Solve Interactively by the Simplex Method:

(0)

Bas Var	Eq No	Z	X_1	X_2	X_3	X_4	Right Side
Z	0	1	-2	-3	0	0	0
X_3	1	0	1	2	1	0	30
X_4	2	0	1	1	0	1	20

Coefficients < 0 ⇒ not optimal.
X_2 is entering basic variable
Pivot col = X_2
Ratio test: X_3: $\frac{30}{2} = 15$ ← min
X_4: $\frac{20}{1} = 20$
So X_3 is pivot row,
Gaussian elim...

(1)

Bas Var	Eq No	Z	X_1	X_2	X_3	X_4	Right Side
Z	0	1	-0.5	0	1.5	0	45
X_2	1	0	0.5	1	0.5	0	15
X_4	2	0	0.5	0	-0.5	1	5

X_1 coefficient < 0 ⇒ not optim.
X_1 is pivot col.
Ratio test: X_2: $\frac{15}{.5} = 30$
X_4: $\frac{5}{.5} = 10$ ← min
So X_4 is pivot row.

(2)

Bas Var	Eq No	Z	X_1	X_2	X_3	X_4	Right Side
Z	0	1	0	0	1	1	50
X_2	1	0	0	1	1	-1	10
X_1	2	0	1	0	-1	2	10

All coefficients ≥ 0, so optimal

$Z^* = 50$, $X_1^* = 10$, $X_2^* = 10$

4.4-6. a)

(0)

0) $Z - 2X_1 - 4X_2 - 3X_3 + 0X_4 + 0X_5 + 0X_6 = 0$
1) $3X_1 + 4X_2 + 2X_3 + 1X_4 + 0X_5 + 0X_6 = 60$
2) $2X_1 + 1X_2 + 2X_3 + 0X_4 + 1X_5 + 0X_6 = 40$
3) $1X_1 + 3X_2 + 2X_3 + 0X_4 + 0X_5 + 1X_6 = 80$

$X_1 \geq 0,\ X_2 \geq 0,\ X_3 \geq 0,\ X_4 \geq 0,\ X_5 \geq 0,\ X_6 \geq 0.$

(1)

0) $Z + 1X_1 + 0X_2 - 1X_3 + 1X_4 + 0X_5 + 0X_6 = 60$
1) $0.75X_1 + 1X_2 + 0.5X_3 + 0.25X_4 + 0X_5 + 0X_6 = 15$
2) $1.25X_1 + 0X_2 + 1.5X_3 - 0.25X_4 + 1X_5 + 0X_6 = 25$
3) $-1.25X_1 + 0X_2 + 0.5X_3 - 0.75X_4 + 0X_5 + 1X_6 = 35$

$X_1 \geq 0,\ X_2 \geq 0,\ X_3 \geq 0,\ X_4 \geq 0,\ X_5 \geq 0,\ X_6 \geq 0.$

(2)

0) $Z + 1.83X_1 + 0X_2 + 0X_3 + 0.83X_4 + 0.67X_5 + 0X_6 = 76.6667$
1) $0.333X_1 + 1X_2 + 0X_3 + 0.33X_4 - 0.33X_5 + 0X_6 = 6.66667$
2) $0.833X_1 + 0X_2 + 1X_3 - 0.17X_4 + 0.67X_5 + 0X_6 = 16.6667$
3) $-1.67X_1 + 0X_2 + 0X_3 - 0.67X_4 - 0.33X_5 + 1X_6 = 26.6667$

$X_1 \geq 0,\ X_2 \geq 0,\ X_3 \geq 0,\ X_4 \geq 0,\ X_5 \geq 0,\ X_6 \geq 0.$

Optimal solution: $(X_1^*, X_2^*, X_3^*) = (0, 6\frac{2}{3}, 16\frac{2}{3})$, $Z^* = 76\frac{2}{3}$

4.4-6, b)

(0)

Bas Var	Eq No	Z	X_1	X_2	X_3	X_4	X_5	X_6	Right Side
Z	0	1	-2	-4	-3	0	0	0	0
X_4	1	0	3	4	2	1	0	0	60
X_5	2	0	2	1	2	0	1	0	40
X_6	3	0	1	3	2	0	0	1	80

(1)

Bas Var	Eq No	Z	X_1	X_2	X_3	X_4	X_5	X_6	Right Side
Z	0	1	1	0	-1	1	0	0	60
X_2	1	0	0.75	1	0.5	0.25	0	0	15
X_5	2	0	1.25	0	1.5	-0.25	1	0	25
X_6	3	0	-1.25	0	0.5	-0.75	0	1	35

(2)

Bas Var	Eq No	Z	X_1	X_2	X_3	X_4	X_5	X_6	Right Side
Z	0	1	1.8333	0	0	0.8333	0.6667	0	76.6667
X_2	1	0	0.3333	1	0	0.3333	-0.333	0	6.66667
X_3	2	0	0.8333	0	1	-0.167	0.6667	0	16.6667
X_6	3	0	-1.667	0	0	-0.667	-0.333	1	26.6667

Optimal solution: $x_1^* = 0,\ x_2^* = 6\frac{2}{3},\ x_3^* = 16\frac{2}{3},\ Z^* = 76\frac{2}{3}$

4.4-7, a)

(0)

0) Z- 3 X_1- 5 X_2- 6 X_3+ 0 X_4+ 0 X_5+ 0 X_6+ 0 X_7 = 0
1) 2 X_1+ 1 X_2+ 1 X_3+ 1 X_4+ 0 X_5+ 0 X_6+ 0 X_7 = 4
2) 1 X_1+ 2 X_2+ 1 X_3+ 0 X_4+ 1 X_5+ 0 X_6+ 0 X_7 = 4
3) 1 X_1+ 1 X_2+ 2 X_3+ 0 X_4+ 0 X_5+ 1 X_6+ 0 X_7 = 4
4) 1 X_1+ 1 X_2+ 1 X_3+ 0 X_4+ 0 X_5+ 0 X_6+ 1 X_7 = 3

$X_1 \geq 0,\ X_2 \geq 0,\ X_3 \geq 0,\ X_4 \geq 0,\ X_5 \geq 0,\ X_6 \geq 0,\ X_7 \geq 0.$

(1)

0) Z+ 0 X_1- 2 X_2+ 0 X_3+ 0 X_4+ 0 X_5+ 3 X_6+ 0 X_7 = 12
1) 1.5 X_1+ 0.5 X_2+ 0 X_3+ 1 X_4+ 0 X_5- 0.5 X_6+ 0 X_7 = 2
2) 0.5 X_1+ 1.5 X_2+ 0 X_3+ 0 X_4+ 1 X_5- 0.5 X_6+ 0 X_7 = 2
3) 0.5 X_1+ 0.5 X_2+ 1 X_3+ 0 X_4+ 0 X_5+ 0.5 X_6+ 0 X_7 = 2
4) 0.5 X_1+ 0.5 X_2+ 0 X_3+ 0 X_4+ 0 X_5- 0.5 X_6+ 1 X_7 = 1

$X_1 \geq 0,\ X_2 \geq 0,\ X_3 \geq 0,\ X_4 \geq 0,\ X_5 \geq 0,\ X_6 \geq 0,\ X_7 \geq 0.$

(2)

0) Z+0.67 X_1+ 0 X_2+ 0 X_3+ 0 X_4+1.33 X_5+2.33 X_6+ 0 X_7 = 14.6667
1) 1.333 X_1+ 0 X_2+ 0 X_3+ 1 X_4-0.33 X_5-0.33 X_6+ 0 X_7 = 1.33333
2) 0.333 X_1+ 1 X_2+ 0 X_3+ 0 X_4+0.67 X_5-0.33 X_6+ 0 X_7 = 1.33333
3) 0.333 X_1+ 0 X_2+ 1 X_3+ 0 X_4-0.33 X_5+0.67 X_6+ 0 X_7 = 1.33333
4) 0.333 X_1+ 0 X_2+ 0 X_3+ 0 X_4-0.33 X_5-0.33 X_6+ 1 X_7 = 0.33333

$X_1 \geq 0,\ X_2 \geq 0,\ X_3 \geq 0,\ X_4 \geq 0,\ X_5 \geq 0,\ X_6 \geq 0,\ X_7 \geq 0.$

Optimal Solution: $(x_1^*, x_2^*, x_3^*) = (0, \frac{4}{3}, \frac{4}{3}),\ Z^* = 14\frac{2}{3}$

4.4-7. b)

Bas Var	Eq No	Z	X_1	X_2	X_3	X_4	X_5	X_6	X_7	Right Side
Z	0	1	-3	-5	-6	0	0	0	0	0
X_4	1	0	2	1	1	1	0	0	0	4
X_5	2	0	1	2	1	0	1	0	0	4
X_6	3	0	1	1	2	0	0	1	0	4
X_7	4	0	1	1	1	0	0	0	1	3

Bas Var	Eq No	Z	X_1	X_2	X_3	X_4	X_5	X_6	X_7	Right Side
Z	0	1	0	-2	0	0	0	3	0	12
X_4	1	0	1.5	0.5	0	1	0	-0.5	0	2
X_5	2	0	0.5	1.5	0	0	1	-0.5	0	2
X_3	3	0	0.5	0.5	1	0	0	0.5	0	2
X_7	4	0	0.5	0.5	0	0	0	-0.5	1	1

Bas Var	Eq No	Z	X_1	X_2	X_3	X_4	X_5	X_6	X_7	Right Side
Z	0	1	0.6667	0	0	0	1.3333	2.3333	0	14.6667
X_4	1	0	1.3333	0	0	1	-0.333	-0.333	0	1.33333
X_2	2	0	0.3333	1	0	0	0.6667	-0.333	0	1.33333
X_3	3	0	0.3333	0	1	0	-0.333	0.6667	0	1.33333
X_7	4	0	0.3333	0	0	0	-0.333	-0.333	1	0.33333

Solution $x_1^* = 0$, $x_2^* = 1\frac{1}{3}$, $x_3^* = 1\frac{1}{3}$, $Z^* = 14\frac{2}{3}$

4.4-8. a)

(0)

0) $Z - 2X_1 + 1X_2 - 1X_3 + 0X_4 + 0X_5 + 0X_6 = 0$
1) $1X_1 - 1X_2 + 3X_3 + 1X_4 + 0X_5 + 0X_6 = 4$
2) $2X_1 + 1X_2 + 0X_3 + 0X_4 + 1X_5 + 0X_6 = 10$
3) $1X_1 - 1X_2 - 1X_3 + 0X_4 + 0X_5 + 1X_6 = 7$

$X_1 \geq 0,\ X_2 \geq 0,\ X_3 \geq 0,\ X_4 \geq 0,\ X_5 \geq 0,\ X_6 \geq 0.$

(1)

0) $Z + 0X_1 - 1X_2 + 5X_3 + 2X_4 + 0X_5 + 0X_6 = 8$
1) $1X_1 - 1X_2 + 3X_3 + 1X_4 + 0X_5 + 0X_6 = 4$
2) $0X_1 + 3X_2 - 6X_3 - 2X_4 + 1X_5 + 0X_6 = 2$
3) $0X_1 + 0X_2 - 4X_3 - 1X_4 + 0X_5 + 1X_6 = 3$

$X_1 \geq 0,\ X_2 \geq 0,\ X_3 \geq 0,\ X_4 \geq 0,\ X_5 \geq 0,\ X_6 \geq 0.$

(2)

0) $Z + 0X_1 + 0X_2 + 3X_3 + 1.33X_4 + 0.33X_5 + 0X_6 = 8.66667$
1) $1X_1 + 0X_2 + 1X_3 + 0.33X_4 + 0.33X_5 + 0X_6 = 4.66667$
2) $0X_1 + 1X_2 - 2X_3 - 0.67X_4 + 0.33X_5 + 0X_6 = 0.66667$
3) $0X_1 + 0X_2 - 4X_3 - 1X_4 + 0X_5 + 1X_6 = 3$

$X_1 \geq 0,\ X_2 \geq 0,\ X_3 \geq 0,\ X_4 \geq 0,\ X_5 \geq 0,\ X_6 \geq 0.$

Optimal Solution: $(X_1^*, X_2^*, X_3^*) = (4\frac{2}{3}, \frac{2}{3}, 0)$, $Z^* = 8\frac{2}{3}$

4.4-8. b)

(0)

Bas Var	Eq No	Z	X_1	X_2	X_3	X_4	X_5	X_6	Right Side
Z	0	1	-2	1	-1	0	0	0	0
X_4	1	0	1	-1	3	1	0	0	4
X_5	2	0	2	1	0	0	1	0	10
X_6	3	0	1	-1	-1	0	0	1	7

(1)

Bas Var	Eq No	Z	X_1	X_2	X_3	X_4	X_5	X_6	Right Side
Z	0	1	0	-1	5	2	0	0	8
X_1	1	0	1	-1	3	1	0	0	4
X_5	2	0	0	3	-6	-2	1	0	2
X_6	3	0	0	0	-4	-1	0	1	3

(2)

Bas Var	Eq No	Z	X_1	X_2	X_3	X_4	X_5	X_6	Right Side
Z	0	1	0	0	3	1.3333	0.3333	0	8.66667
X_1	1	0	1	0	1	0.3333	0.3333	0	4.66667
X_2	2	0	0	1	-2	-0.667	0.3333	0	0.66667
X_6	3	0	0	0	-4	-1	0	1	3

Optimal Solution: $x_1^* = 4\frac{2}{3}$, $x_2^* = \frac{2}{3}$, $x_3^* = 0$, $Z^* = 8\frac{2}{3}$

4.4-9.

(0)

Bas Var	Eq No	Z	X_1	X_2	X_3	X_4	X_5	X_6	Right Side
Z	0	1	-2	1	-1	0	0	0	0
X_4	1	0	3	1	1	1	0	0	6
X_5	2	0	1	-1	2	0	1	0	1
X_6	3	0	1	1	-1	0	0	1	2

(1)

Bas Var	Eq No	Z	X_1	X_2	X_3	X_4	X_5	X_6	Right Side
Z	0	1	0	-1	3	0	2	0	2
X_4	1	0	0	4	-5	1	-3	0	3
X_1	2	0	1	-1	2	0	1	0	1
X_6	3	0	0	2	-3	0	-1	1	1

(2)

Bas Var	Eq No	Z	X_1	X_2	X_3	X_4	X_5	X_6	Right Side
Z	0	1	0	0	1.5	0	1.5	0.5	2.5
X_4	1	0	0	0	1	1	-1	-2	1
X_1	2	0	1	0	0.5	0	0.5	0.5	1.5
X_2	3	0	0	1	-1.5	0	-0.5	0.5	0.5

Optimal: $Z^* = 2.5$, $(x_1^*, x_2^*, x_3^*) = (1.5, 0.5, 0)$

4.4-10.

(0)

Bas Var	Eq No	Z	X_1	X_2	X_3	X_4	X_5	X_6	Right Side
Z	0	1	1	-1	-2	0	0	0	0
X_4	1	0	1	2	-1	1	0	0	20
X_5	2	0	-2	4	2	0	1	0	60
X_6	3	0	2	3	1	0	0	1	50

(1)

Bas Var	Eq No	Z	X_1	X_2	X_3	X_4	X_5	X_6	Right Side
Z	0	1	-1	3	0	0	1	0	60
X_4	1	0	0	4	0	1	0.5	0	50
X_3	2	0	-1	2	1	0	0.5	0	30
X_6	3	0	3	1	0	0	-0.5	1	20

(2)

Bas Var	Eq No	Z	X_1	X_2	X_3	X_4	X_5	X_6	Right Side
Z	0	1	0	3.3333	0	0	0.8333	0.3333	66.6667
X_4	1	0	0	4	0	1	0.5	0	50
X_3	2	0	0	2.3333	1	0	0.3333	0.3333	36.6667
X_1	3	0	1	0.3333	0	0	-0.167	0.3333	6.66667

Optimal Sol'n: $x_1^* = 6\frac{2}{3}$, $x_2^* = 0$, $x_3^* = 36\frac{2}{3}$ and $Z^* = 66\frac{2}{3}$

4.5-1. a) True. The Ratio test tells us how far we can increase the entering basic variable before one of the current basic variables goes to zero. If two variables "tie" for which should be the leaving variable, then both variables go to zero at the same value of the entering basic variable. Since only one variable can become non-basic in any iteration, the other will be basic and zero.

b) False. If there is no leaving basic variable, then the solution is unbounded. (Can increase the entering basic variable indefinitely)

c) True, usually. If we pivot on the column with the zero coefficient, then we will get another optimal solution (remember that the objective value will not change since the "rate of improvement" is zero. The exception occurs when the problem is also degenerate. If the basic variable (which has a coefficient of zero) is itself equal to zero (ie. degenerate), then pivotting on that column will not change the optimal solution.

d) False. Examples: (i) Max $x_1 - x_2$

$$x_1 - x_2 \le 1$$
$$x_1 \ge 0, x_2 \ge 0$$

Clearly, $Z^* = 1$ (optimal) but $x_1^* = k+1$, $x_2^* = k$ $k \in [0, \infty)$

(ii) Max $-x_1$

$$x_1 + x_2 \ge -1$$
$$x_1 \ge 0, x_2 \ge 0$$

This is a trivial example. $x_1^* = 0$, $x_2^* \ge 0$, $Z^* = 0$

4.5-2.

(0)

Bas Var	Eq No	Z	X_1	X_2	X_3	X_4	X_5	X_6	X_7	Right Side
Z	0	1	-5	-1	-3	-4	0	0	0	0
X_5	1	0	1	-2	4	3	1	0	0	20
X_6	2	0	-4	6	5	-4	0	1	0	40
X_7	3	0	2	-3	3	8	0	0	1	50

(1)

Bas Var	Eq No	Z	X_1	X_2	X_3	X_4	X_5	X_6	X_7	Right Side
Z	0	1	0	-11	17	11	5	0	0	100
X_1	1	0	1	-2	4	3	1	0	0	20
X_6	2	0	0	-2	21	8	4	1	0	120
X_7	3	0	0	1	-5	2	-2	0	1	10

(2)

Bas Var	Eq No	Z	X_1	X_2	X_3	X_4	X_5	X_6	X_7	Right Side
Z	0	1	0	0	-38	33	-17	0	11	210
X_1	1	0	1	0	-6	7	-3	0	2	40
X_6	2	0	0	0	11	12	0	1	2	140
X_2	3	0	0	1	-5	2	-2	0	1	10

(3)

Bas Var	Eq No	Z	X_1	X_2	X_3	X_4	X_5	X_6	X_7	Right Side
Z	0	1	0	0	0	74.455	-17	3.4545	17.909	693.636
X_1	1	0	1	0	0	13.545	-3	0.5455	3.0909	116.364
X_3	2	0	0	0	1	1.0909	0	0.0909	0.1818	12.7273
X_2	3	0	0	1	0	7.4545	-2	0.4545	1.9091	73.6364

We can see from either the second or the third iteration that, because all of the constraint coefficients of x_5 are non-positive, it can increase without forcing a basic variable to zero. From iteration three, $(x_1, x_2, x_3, x_4) = (116.4+3\theta, 73.64+2\theta, 12.73, 0)$ is feasible for all $\theta \geq 0$ and $Z = 693.6 + 17\theta$ is unbounded.

4.5-3. a) The constraints of any LP problem can be expressed in matrix notation as:

$$Ax = b \ , \ x \geq 0$$

If $x^1, x^2, \ldots, x^N$ are feasible solutions and

$$x = \sum_{k=1}^{N} \alpha_k x^k \quad \text{with} \quad \sum_{k=1}^{N} \alpha_k = 1 \ , \ \alpha_k \geq 0 \ (k=1,\ldots,N)$$

then $Ax = A\left(\sum_{k=1}^{N} \alpha_k x^k\right) = \sum_{k=1}^{N} \alpha_k A x^k = \sum_{k=1}^{N} \alpha_k b = b \sum_{k=1}^{N} \alpha_k = b$

So x is also a feasible solution.

b) Since basic feasible solutions are feasible solutions, the argument in part (a) shows any weighted average of them is also feasible.

4.5-4. (a) If z^0 is the value of the objective function for an optimal solution, and $x^1, x^2, \ldots, x^N$ is the set of optimal basic feasible solutions, then for $x = \sum_{k=1}^{N} \alpha_k x^k$ with $\sum_{k=1}^{N} \alpha_k = 1$, $\alpha_k \geq 0$ for $k = 1, 2, \ldots, N$, problem 4.13 shows x is feasible. The objective function is of the form $c^T w$ so for the feasible solution x we have

$$c^T x = c^T\left(\sum_{k=1}^{N} \alpha_k x^k\right) = \sum_{k=1}^{N} \alpha_k c^T x^k$$

$$= \sum_{k=1}^{N} \alpha_k z^0 = z^0 \sum_{k=1}^{N} \alpha_k = z^0$$

so x is also an optimal solution.

(b) Let x be a feasible solution which is not a weighted average of the set of optimal basic feasible solutions, $x^1, x^2, \ldots, x^N$. x must be a weighted average of basic feasible solutions, not all of which are optimal. If $\bar{x}^1, \bar{x}^2, \ldots, \bar{x}^L$ are the basic feasible solutions which are not optimal, we can express x as:

$$x = \sum_{k=1}^{N} \alpha_k x^k + \sum_{i=1}^{L} \beta_i \bar{x}^i \quad \text{with}$$

$$\sum_{k=1}^{N} \alpha_k + \sum_{i=1}^{L} \beta_i = 1, \quad \alpha_k \geq 0 \text{ for } k = 1, 2, \ldots, N$$

$$\beta_i \geq 0 \text{ for } i = 1, 2, \ldots, L \text{ and some } \beta_i \neq 0.$$

We can conclude,

$$c^T x = c^T\left(\sum_{k=1}^{N} \alpha_k x^k + \sum_{i=1}^{L} \beta_i \bar{x}^i\right)$$

$$= \sum_{k=1}^{N} \alpha_k c^T x^k + \sum_{i=1}^{L} \beta_i c^T \bar{x}^i$$

$$< z^0\left(\sum_{k=1}^{N} \alpha_k + \sum_{i=1}^{L} \beta_i\right) = z^0$$

so x is not an optimal solution.

4.5-5.

(0)

Bas Var	Eq No	Z	X_1	X_2	X_3	X_4	X_5	X_6	Right Side
Z	0	1	−1	−1	−1	−1	0	0	0
X_5	1	0	1	1	0	0	1	0	3
X_6	2	0	0	0	1	1	0	1	2

(1)

Bas Var	Eq No	Z	X_1	X_2	X_3	X_4	X_5	X_6	Right Side
Z	0	1	0	0	−1	−1	1	0	3
X_1	1	0	1	1	0	0	1	0	3
X_6	2	0	0	0	1	1	0	1	2

(2)

Bas Var	Eq No	Z	X_1	X_2	X_3	X_4	X_5	X_6	Right Side
Z	0	1	0	0	0	0	1	1	5
X_1	1	0	1	1	0	0	1	0	3
X_3	2	0	0	0	1	1	0	1	2

Since cost coefficients (row Z) for X_1, X_2, X_3 are 0, we can pivot to get other optimal BF sol'ns.

4.5-5. (cont')

(3)

Bas Var	Eq No	Z	X_1	X_2	X_3	X_4	X_5	X_6	Right Side
Z	0	1	0	0	0	0	1	1	5
X_2	1	0	1	1	0	0	1	0	3
X_3	2	0	0	0	1	1	0	1	2

(4)

Bas Var	Eq No	Z	X_1	X_2	X_3	X_4	X_5	X_6	Right Side
Z	0	1	0	0	0	0	1	1	5
X_2	1	0	1	1	0	0	1	0	3
X_4	2	0	0	0	1	1	0	1	2

(5)

Bas Var	Eq No	Z	X_1	X_2	X_3	X_4	X_5	X_6	Right Side
Z	0	1	0	0	0	0	1	1	5
X_1	1	0	1	1	0	0	1	0	3
X_4	2	0	0	0	1	1	0	1	2

Tableaux (2) – (5) show the set of optimal solutions:

(2) $(x_1, x_2, x_3, x_4) = (3, 0, 2, 0)$

(3) $(x_1, x_2, x_3, x_4) = (0, 3, 2, 0)$

(4) $(x_1, x_2, x_3, x_4) = (0, 3, 0, 2)$

(5) $(x_1, x_2, x_3, x_4) = (3, 0, 0, 2)$

all with $Z = 5$.

4.6-1.

(a)

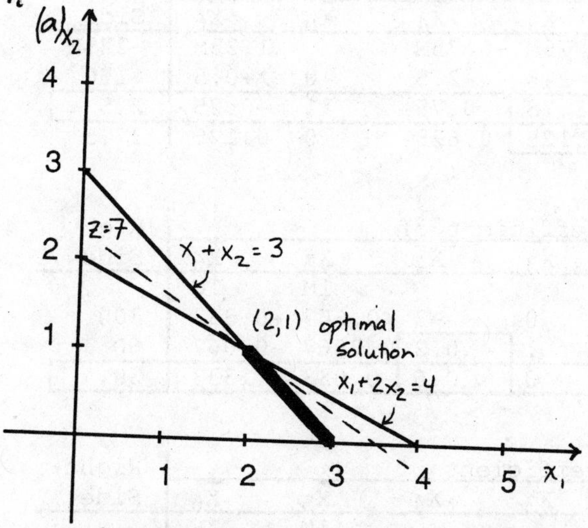

$(x_1, x_2) = (2, 1)$ is optimal with $Z = 7$

4.6-1. b)

(0)

Bas Var	Eq No	Z	X_1	X_2	X_3	$\bar{X}_4$	Right Side
			-1M	-1M			
Z	0	1	-2	-3	0	0	-3M
X_3	1	0	1	2	1	0	4
$\bar{X}_4$	2	0	1	1	0	1	3

The initial artificial basic feasible solution is $(x_1, x_2, x_3, \bar{x}_4) = (0, 0, 4, 3)$.

c)

(1)

Bas Var	Eq No	Z	X_1	X_2	X_3	$\bar{X}_4$	Right Side
			-0.5M		0.5M		-1M
Z	0	1	-0.5	0	+1.5	0	+6
X_2	1	0	0.5	1	0.5	0	2
$\bar{X}_4$	2	0	0.5	0	-0.5	1	1

(2)

Bas Var	Eq No	Z	X_1	X_2	X_3	$\bar{X}_4$	Right Side
						1M	
Z	0	1	0	0	1	+1	7
X_2	1	0	0	1	1	-1	1
X_1	2	0	1	0	-1	2	2

Optimal: $(x_1^*, x_2^*) = (2, 1)$, $Z^* = 7$

4.6-2. a), b)

(0)

Bas Var	Eq No	Z	X_1	X_2	X_3	X_4	$\bar{X}_5$	$\bar{X}_6$	Right Side
			-10M	-4M	-5M	-7M			
Z	0	1	-4	-2	-3	-5	0	0	-600M
$\bar{X}_5$	1	0	2	3	4	2	1	0	300
$\bar{X}_6$	2	0	8	1	1	5	0	1	300

Initial artificial BF sol'n is (0, 0, 0, 0, 300, 300)

(1)

Bas Var	Eq No	Z	X_1	X_2	X_3	X_4	$\bar{X}_5$	$\bar{X}_6$	Right Side
				-2.75M	-3.75M	-0.75M		1.25M	-225M
Z	0	1	0	-1.5	-2.5	-2.5	0	+0.5	+150
$\bar{X}_5$	1	0	0	2.75	3.75	0.75	1	-0.25	225
X_1	2	0	1	0.125	0.125	0.625	0	0.125	37.5

(2)

Bas Var	Eq No	Z	X_1	X_2	X_3	X_4	$\bar{X}_5$	$\bar{X}_6$	Right Side
							1M	1M	
Z	0	1	0	0.3333	0	-2	+0.667	+0.333	300
X_3	1	0	0	0.7333	1	0.2	0.2667	-0.067	60
X_1	2	0	1	0.0333	0	0.6	-0.033	0.1333	30

(3)

Bas Var	Eq No	Z	X_1	X_2	X_3	X_4	$\bar{X}_5$	$\bar{X}_6$	Right Side
							1M	1M	
Z	0	1	3.3333	0.4444	0	0	+0.556	+0.778	400
X_3	1	0	-0.333	0.7222	1	0	0.2778	-0.111	50
X_4	2	0	1.6667	0.0556	0	1	-0.056	0.2222	50

Optimal: $(x_1^*, x_2^*, x_3^*, x_4^*) = (0, 0, 50, 50)$, $Z^* = 400$

4.6-2, c) - f) Phase 1:

(0)

Bas Var	Eq No	Z	X_1	X_2	X_3	X_4	$\bar{X}_5$	$\bar{X}_6$	Right Side
Z	0	1	-10	-4	-5	-7	0	0	-600
$\bar{X}_5$	1	0	2	3	4	2	1	0	300
$\bar{X}_6$	2	0	8	1	1	5	0	1	300

Initial artificial BF Sol'n is (0,0,0,0,300,300)

(1)

Bas Var	Eq No	Z	X_1	X_2	X_3	X_4	$\bar{X}_5$	$\bar{X}_6$	Right Side
Z	0	1	0	-2.75	-3.75	-0.75	0	1.25	-225
X_5	1	0	0	2.75	3.75	0.75	1	-0.25	225
X_1	2	0	1	0.125	0.125	0.625	0	0.125	37.5

(2)

Bas Var	Eq No	Z	X_1	X_2	X_3	X_4	$\bar{X}_5$	$\bar{X}_6$	Right Side
Z	0	1	0	0	0	0	1	1	0
X_3	1	0	0	0.7333	1	0.2	0.2667	-0.067	60
X_1	2	0	1	0.0333	0	0.6	-0.033	0.1333	30

Phase 2:

(2)

Bas Var	Eq No	Z	X_1	X_2	X_3	X_4	Right Side
Z	0	1	0	0.3333	0	-2	300
X_3	1	0	0	0.7333	1	0.2	60
X_1	2	0	1	0.0333	0	0.6	30

(3)

Bas Var	Eq No	Z	X_1	X_2	X_3	X_4	Right Side
Z	0	1	3.3333	0.4444	0	0	400
X_3	1	0	-0.333	0.7222	1	0	50
X_4	2	0	1.6667	0.0556	0	1	50

Optimal Sol'n: $(x_1^*, x_2^*, x_3^*, x_4^*) = (0, 0, 50, 50)$, $Z^* = 400$

(g) The basic solutions of the two methods coincide. They are artificial basic feasible solutions for the revised problem until both artificial variables x_5 and x_6 are driven out of the basis, which in the Two Phase Method is the end of Phase 1.

4.6-3. a)

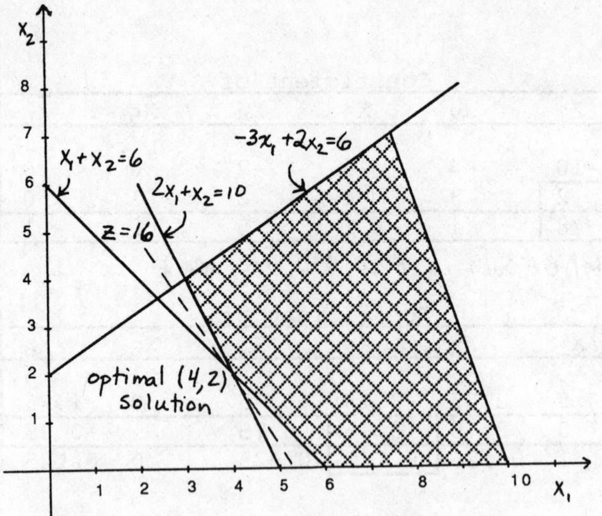

$(x_1, x_2) = (4,2)$ is optimal with $Z = 16$

b), c)

(0)

Bas Var	Eq No	Z	x_1	x_2	x_3	x_4	$\bar{x}_5$	x_6	$\bar{x}_7$	Right Side
Z	0	1	-3M +3	-2M +2	1M	1M	0	0	0	-16M
$\bar{x}_5$	1	0	2	1	-1	0	1	0	0	10
x_6	2	0	-3	2	0	0	0	1	0	6
$\bar{x}_7$	3	0	1	1	0	-1	0	0	1	6

The initial artificial BF solution is (0,0,0,0,10,6,6).

(1)

Bas Var	Eq No	Z	x_1	x_2	x_3	x_4	$\bar{x}_5$	x_6	$\bar{x}_7$	Right Side
Z	0	1	0	-0.5M +0.5	-0.5M +1.5	1M	1.5M -1.5	0	0	-1M -15
x_1	1	0	1	0.5	-0.5	0	0.5	0	0	5
x_6	2	0	0	3.5	-1.5	0	1.5	1	0	21
$\bar{x}_7$	3	0	0	0.5	0.5	-1	-0.5	0	1	1

(2)

Bas Var	Eq No	Z	x_1	x_2	x_3	x_4	$\bar{x}_5$	x_6	$\bar{x}_7$	Right Side
Z	0	1	0	0	1	1	1M -1	0	1M -1	-16
x_1	1	0	1	0	-1	1	1	0	-1	4
x_6	2	0	0	0	-5	7	5	1	-7	14
x_2	3	0	0	1	1	-2	-1	0	2	2

Optimal Solution is $(x_1^*, x_2^*) = (4,2)$, $Z^* = 16$.

4.6-4. a)

Maximize $(-Z) = -2x_1 - 3x_2 - x_3$

subject to:

$$-x_1 - 4x_2 - 2x_3 \le -8$$

$$-3x_1 - 2x_2 \le -6$$

$$x_1 \ge 0,\quad x_2 \ge 0,\quad x_3 \ge 0.$$

b)

(0)

Bas Var	Eq No	Z	X_1	X_2	X_3	X_4	X_5	$\bar{X}_6$	$\bar{X}_7$	Right Side
Z	0	1	-4M +2	-6M +3	-2M +1	1M	1M	0	0	-14M
$\bar{X}_6$	1	0	1	4	2	-1	0	1	0	8
$\bar{X}_7$	2	0	3	2	0	0	-1	0	1	6

(1)

Bas Var	Eq No	Z	X_1	X_2	X_3	X_4	X_5	$\bar{X}_6$	$\bar{X}_7$	Right Side
Z	0	1	-2.5M +1.25	0	1M -0.5	-0.5M +0.75	1M	1.5M -0.75	0	-2M -6
X_2	1	0	0.25	1	0.5	-0.25	0	0.25	0	2
$\bar{X}_7$	2	0	2.5	0	-1	0.5	-1	-0.5	1	2

(2)

Bas Var	Eq No	Z	X_1	X_2	X_3	X_4	X_5	$\bar{X}_6$	$\bar{X}_7$	Right Side
Z	0	1	0	0	0	0.5	0.5	1M -0.5	1M -0.5	-7
X_2	1	0	0	1	0.6	-0.3	0.1	0.3	-0.1	1.8
X_1	2	0	1	0	-0.4	0.2	-0.4	-0.2	0.4	0.8

Optimal: $(x_1^*, x_2^*, x_3^*) = (0.8, 1.8, 0)$, $Z^* = 7$ (Pivoting x_3 into the basis for x_2 provides the alternate optimal solution $(2, 0, 3)$.

c)

Phase 1:

(0)

Bas Var	Eq No	Z	X_1	X_2	X_3	X_4	X_5	$\bar{X}_6$	$\bar{X}_7$	Right Side
Z	0	1	-4	-6	-2	1	1	0	0	-14
$\bar{X}_6$	1	0	1	4	2	-1	0	1	0	8
$\bar{X}_7$	2	0	3	2	0	0	-1	0	1	6

(1)

Bas Var	Eq No	Z	X_1	X_2	X_3	X_4	X_5	$\bar{X}_6$	$\bar{X}_7$	Right Side
Z	0	1	-2.5	0	1	-0.5	1	1.5	0	-2
X_2	1	0	0.25	1	0.5	-0.25	0	0.25	0	2
$\bar{X}_7$	2	0	2.5	0	-1	0.5	-1	-0.5	1	2

4.6-4. c) (cont')

Bas Var	Eq No	Z	X_1	X_2	X_3	X_4	X_5	$\bar{X}_6$	$\bar{X}_7$	Right Side
(2) Z	0	1	0	0	0	0	0	1	1	0
X_2	1	0	0	1	0.6	-0.3	0.1	0.3	-0.1	1.8
X_1	2	0	1	0	-0.4	0.2	-0.4	-0.2	0.4	0.8

Phase 2:

Bas Var	Eq No	Z	X_1	X_2	X_3	X_4	X_5	Right Side
(2) Z	0	1	0	0	-5e-20 (≈ 0)	0.5	0.5	-7
X_2	1	0	0	1	0.6	-0.3	0.1	1.8
X_1	2	0	1	0	-0.4	0.2	-0.4	0.8

Again, optimal is $(x_1^*, x_2^*, x_3^*) = (0.8, 1.8, 0)$, $Z^* = 7$ with the alternate optimal (by pivoting X_3 into the basis for X_2) of $(2, 0, 3)$.

(d) The basic solutions of the two methods coincide. They are artificial basic feasible solutions for the revised problem until both artificial variables x_6 and x_7 are driven out of the basis, which in the Two Phase Method is the end of Phase 1.

4.6-5. Once all artificial variables are driven from the basis in a maximization (minimization) problem, choosing an artificial variable to re-enter the basis can only lower (raise) the objective value by an arbitrarily large amount depending on M.

4.6-6. a)

Bas Var	Eq No	Z	X_1	X_2	X_3	X_4	$\bar{X}_5$	$\bar{X}_6$	Right Side
(0) Z	0	1	-3M -2	-2M -5	-2M -3	1M	0	0	-70M
$\bar{X}_5$	1	0	1	-2	1	-1	1	0	20
$\bar{X}_6$	2	0	2	4	1	0	0	1	50

Initial artificial BF Sol'n is (0,0,0,0,20,50)

4.6-6. b)

(1)

Bas Var	Eq No	Z	X_1	X_2	X_3	X_4	$\bar{X}_5$	$\bar{X}_6$	Right Side
				-8M	1M	-2M	3M		-10M
Z	0	1	0	-9	-1	-2	+2	0	+40
X_1	1	0	1	-2	1	-1	1	0	20
$\bar{X}_6$	2	0	0	8	-1	2	-2	1	10

(2)

Bas Var	Eq No	Z	X_1	X_2	X_3	X_4	$\bar{X}_5$	$\bar{X}_6$	Right Side
							1M	1M	
Z	0	1	0	0	-2.125	0.25	-0.25	+1.125	51.25
X_1	1	0	1	0	0.75	-0.5	0.5	0.25	22.5
X_2	2	0	0	1	-0.125	0.25	-0.25	0.125	1.25

(3)

Bas Var	Eq No	Z	X_1	X_2	X_3	X_4	$\bar{X}_5$	$\bar{X}_6$	Right Side
							1M	1M	
Z	0	1	2.8333	0	0	-1.167	+1.167	+1.833	115
X_3	1	0	1.3333	0	1	-0.667	0.6667	0.3333	30
X_2	2	0	0.1667	1	0	0.1667	-0.167	0.1667	5

(4)

Bas Var	Eq No	Z	X_1	X_2	X_3	X_4	$\bar{X}_5$	$\bar{X}_6$	Right Side
								1M	
Z	0	1	4	7	0	0	1M	+3	150
X_3	1	0	2	4	1	0	0	1	50
X_4	2	0	1	6	0	1	-1	1	30

Optimal Solution: $(x_1^*, x_2^*, x_3^*) = (0, 0, 50)$, $z^* = 150$

c) Phase 1:

(0)

Bas Var	Eq No	Z	X_1	X_2	X_3	X_4	$\bar{X}_5$	$\bar{X}_6$	Right Side
Z	0	1	-3	-2	-2	1	0	0	-70
$\bar{X}_5$	1	0	1	-2	1	-1	1	0	20
$\bar{X}_6$	2	0	2	4	1	0	0	1	50

Initial (artificial) BF Sol'n is (0, 0, 0, 0, 20, 50).

d)

(1)

Bas Var	Eq No	Z	X_1	X_2	X_3	X_4	$\bar{X}_5$	$\bar{X}_6$	Right Side
Z	0	1	0	-8	1	-2	3	0	-10
X_1	1	0	1	-2	1	-1	1	0	20
$\bar{X}_6$	2	0	0	8	-1	2	-2	1	10

(2)

Bas Var	Eq No	Z	X_1	X_2	X_3	X_4	$\bar{X}_5$	$\bar{X}_6$	Right Side
Z	0	1	0	0	0	0	1	1	0
X_1	1	0	1	0	0.75	-0.5	0.5	0.25	22.5
X_2	2	0	0	1	-0.125	0.25	-0.25	0.125	1.25

4.6-6. e), f) Phase 2:

(2)

Bas Var	Eq No	Z	X_1	X_2	X_3	X_4	Right Side
Z	0	1	0	0	-2.125	0.25	51.25
X_1	1	0	1	0	0.75	-0.5	22.5
X_2	2	0	0	1	-0.125	0.25	1.25

(3)

Bas Var	Eq No	Z	X_1	X_2	X_3	X_4	Right Side
Z	0	1	2.8333	0	0	-1.167	115
X_3	1	0	1.3333	0	1	-0.667	30
X_2	2	0	0.1667	1	0	0.1667	5

(4)

Bas Var	Eq No	Z	X_1	X_2	X_3	X_4	Right Side
Z	0	1	4	7	0	0	150
X_3	1	0	2	4	1	0	50
X_4	2	0	1	6	0	1	30

Optimal: $(x_1^*, x_2^*, x_3^*) = (0, 0, 50)$, $Z^* = 150$

(g) The basic solutions of the two methods coincide. They are artificial basic feasible solutions for the revised problem until both artificial variables x_5 and x_6 are driven out of the basis, which in the Two Phase Method is the end of Phase 1.

4.6-7. Phase 1:

(0)

Bas Var	Eq No	Z	X_1	X_2	X_3	X_4	$\bar{X}_5$	$\bar{X}_6$	Right Side
Z	0	1	-8	-4	-12	1	0	0	-700
$\bar{X}_5$	1	0	5	2	7	0	1	0	420
$\bar{X}_6$	2	0	3	2	5	-1	0	1	280

(1)

Bas Var	Eq No	Z	X_1	X_2	X_3	X_4	$\bar{X}_5$	$\bar{X}_6$	Right Side
Z	0	1	-0.8	0.8	0	-1.4	0	2.4	-28
$\bar{X}_5$	1	0	0.8	-0.8	0	1.4	1	-1.4	28
X_3	2	0	0.6	0.4	1	-0.2	0	0.2	56

4.6-7. (cont')

(2)

Bas Var	Eq No	Z	X_1	X_2	X_3	X_4	$\bar{X}_5$	$\bar{X}_6$	Right Side
Z	0	1	5e-20	1e-19	0	0	1	1	2e-18
X_4	1	0	0.5714	-0.571	0	1	0.7143	-1	20
X_3	2	0	0.7143	0.2857	1	0	0.1429	0	60

Phase 2:

(2)

Bas Var	Eq No	Z	X_1	X_2	X_3	X_4	Right Side
Z	0	1	-0.143	0.1429	0	0	-180
X_4	1	0	0.5714	-0.571	0	1	20
X_3	2	0	0.7143	0.2857	1	0	60

(3)

Bas Var	Eq No	Z	X_1	X_2	X_3	X_4	Right Side
Z	0	1	-1e-20 (=0)	8e-20 (=0)	0	0.25	-175
X_1	1	0	1	-1	0	1.75	35
X_3	2	0	0	1	1	-1.25	35

Optimal Solution: $(x_1^*, x_2^*, x_3^*) = (35, 0, 35)$, $Z^* = 175$

Pivoting x_2 into the basis for x_3 provides the alternative optimal solution $(70, 35, 0)$

4.6-8. a)

(0)

Bas Var	Eq No	Z	X_1	X_2	X_3	X_4	$\bar{X}_5$	$\bar{X}_6$	Right Side
Z	0	1	-5M +3	-4M +2	-8M +4	1M	0	0	-180M
$\bar{X}_5$	1	0	2	1	3	0	1	0	60
$\bar{X}_6$	2	0	3	3	5	-1	0	1	120

(1)

Bas Var	Eq No	Z	X_1	X_2	X_3	X_4	$\bar{X}_5$	$\bar{X}_6$	Right Side
Z	0	1	0.333M +0.333	-1.33M +0.667	0	1M	2.667M -1.333	0	-20M -80
X_3	1	0	0.6667	0.3333	1	0	0.3333	0	20
$\bar{X}_6$	2	0	-0.333	1.3333	0	-1	-1.667	1	20

(2)

Bas Var	Eq No	Z	X_1	X_2	X_3	X_4	$\bar{X}_5$	$\bar{X}_6$	Right Side
Z	0	1	0.5	0	0	0.5	1M -0.5	1M -0.5	-90
X_3	1	0	0.75	0	1	0.25	0.75	-0.25	15
X_2	2	0	-0.25	1	0	-0.75	-1.25	0.75	15

Optimal is $x_1^* = 0$, $x_2^* = 15$, $x_3^* = 15$, $Z^* = 90$

4.6-8. b) Phase 1:

(0)

Bas Var	Eq No	Z	X_1	X_2	X_3	X_4	$\bar{X}_5$	$\bar{X}_6$	Right Side
Z	0	1	-5	-4	-8	1	0	0	-180
$\bar{X}_5$	1	0	2	1	3	0	1	0	60
$\bar{X}_6$	2	0	3	3	5	-1	0	1	120

(1)

Bas Var	Eq No	Z	X_1	X_2	X_3	X_4	$\bar{X}_5$	$\bar{X}_6$	Right Side
Z	0	1	0.3333	-1.333	0	1	2.6667	0	-20
X_3	1	0	0.6667	0.3333	1	0	0.3333	0	20
$\bar{X}_6$	2	0	-0.333	1.3333	0	-1	-1.667	1	20

(2)

Bas Var	Eq No	Z	X_1	X_2	X_3	X_4	$\bar{X}_5$	$\bar{X}_6$	Right Side
Z	0	1	-3e-20	0	0	0	1	1	0
X_3	1	0	0.75	0	1	0.25	0.75	-0.25	15
X_2	2	0	-0.25	1	0	-0.75	-1.25	0.75	15

Phase 2:

(2)

Bas Var	Eq No	Z	X_1	X_2	X_3	X_4	Right Side
Z	0	1	0.5	0	0	0.5	-90
X_3	1	0	0.75	0	1	0.25	15
X_2	2	0	-0.25	1	0	-0.75	15

Optimal : $(x_1^*, x_2^*, x_3^*) = (0, 15, 15)$, $Z^* = 90$

(c) In both the Big-M method and Two Phase Method only the final tableau (2) represents a feasible solution for the real problem.

4.6-9. a)

(0)

Bas Var	Eq No	Z	X_1	X_2	X_3	X_4	$\bar{X}_5$	$\bar{X}_6$	Right Side
			-1M		-1M				
Z	0	1	+3	2	+7	1M	0	0	-20M
$\bar{X}_5$	1	0	-1	1	0	0	1	0	10
$\bar{X}_6$	2	0	2	-1	1	-1	0	1	10

(1)

Bas Var	Eq No	Z	X_1	X_2	X_3	X_4	$\bar{X}_5$	$\bar{X}_6$	Right Side
				-0.5M	-0.5M	0.5M		0.5M	-15M
Z	0	1	0	+3.5	+5.5	+1.5	0	-1.5	-15
$\bar{X}_5$	1	0	0	0.5	0.5	-0.5	1	0.5	15
X_1	2	0	1	-0.5	0.5	-0.5	0	0.5	5

4.6-9. a) (con't)

(2)

Bas Var	Eq No	Z	X_1	X_2	X_3	X_4	$\bar{X}_5$	$\bar{X}_6$	Right Side
Z	0	1	0	0	2	5	1M -7	1M -5	-120
X_2	1	0	0	1	1	-1	2	1	30
X_1	2	0	1	0	1	-1	1	1	20

Optimal: $(x_1^*, x_2^*, x_3^*) = (20, 30, 0)$, $Z^* = 120$

b) Phase 1:

(0)

Bas Var	Eq No	Z	X_1	X_2	X_3	X_4	$\bar{X}_5$	$\bar{X}_6$	Right Side
$\underline{Z}$	0	1	-1	0	-1	1	0	0	-20
$\bar{X}_5$	1	0	-1	1	0	0	1	0	10
$\bar{X}_6$	2	0	2	-1	1	-1	0	1	10

(1)

Bas Var	Eq No	Z	X_1	X_2	X_3	X_4	$\bar{X}_5$	$\bar{X}_6$	Right Side
$\underline{Z}$	0	1	0	-0.5	-0.5	0.5	0	0.5	-15
$\bar{X}_5$	1	0	0	0.5	0.5	-0.5	1	0.5	15
X_1	2	0	1	-0.5	0.5	-0.5	0	0.5	5

(2)

Bas Var	Eq No	Z	X_1	X_2	X_3	X_4	$\bar{X}_5$	$\bar{X}_6$	Right Side
Z	0	1	0	0	0	0	1	1	0
X_2	1	0	0	1	1	-1	2	1	30
X_1	2	0	1	0	1	-1	1	1	20

Phase 2:

(2)

Bas Var	Eq No	Z	X_1	X_2	X_3	X_4	Right Side
Z	0	1	0	0	2	5	-120
X_2	1	0	0	1	1	-1	30
X_1	2	0	1	0	1	-1	20

Optimal: $(x_1^*, x_2^*, x_3^*) = (20, 30, 0)$, $Z^* = 120$

c) Only the final tableau for the Big-M method and 2-phase method represent feasible solutions to the real problem. The BF solutions for the 2 methods are the same.

4.6-10. a)

(0)

Bas Var	Eq No	Z	x_1	x_2	x_3	x_4	$\bar{x}_5$	$\bar{x}_6$	Right Side
Z	0	1	-4M +3	-2M +2	-1M +1	1M	0	0	-17M
$\bar{x}_5$	1	0	1	1	0	0	1	0	7
$\bar{x}_6$	2	0	3	1	1	-1	0	1	10

(1)

Bas Var	Eq No	Z	x_1	x_2	x_3	x_4	$\bar{x}_5$	$\bar{x}_6$	Right Side
Z	0	1	0	-0.67M +1	0.333M	-0.33M +1	0	1.333M -1	-3.667M -10
$\bar{x}_5$	1	0	0	0.6667	-0.333	0.3333	1	-0.333	3.66667
x_1	2	0	1	0.3333	0.3333	-0.333	0	0.3333	3.33333

(2)

Bas Var	Eq No	Z	x_1	x_2	x_3	x_4	$\bar{x}_5$	$\bar{x}_6$	Right Side
Z	0	1	0	0	0.5	0.5	1M -1.5	1M -0.5	-15.5
x_2	1	0	0	1	-0.5	0.5	1.5	-0.5	5.5
x_1	2	0	1	0	0.5	-0.5	-0.5	0.5	1.5

Optimal: $(x_1^*, x_2^*, x_3^*) = (1.5, 5.5, 0)$, $Z^* = 15.5$

b) Phase 1:

(0)

Bas Var	Eq No	Z	x_1	x_2	x_3	x_4	$\bar{x}_5$	$\bar{x}_6$	Right Side
Z	0	1	-4	-2	-1	1	0	0	-17
$\bar{x}_5$	1	0	1	1	0	0	1	0	7
$\bar{x}_6$	2	0	3	1	1	-1	0	1	10

(1)

Bas Var	Eq No	Z	x_1	x_2	x_3	x_4	$\bar{x}_5$	$\bar{x}_6$	Right Side
Z	0	1	0	-0.667	0.3333	-0.333	0	1.3333	-3.6667
$\bar{x}_5$	1	0	0	0.6667	-0.333	0.3333	1	-0.333	3.66667
x_1	2	0	1	0.3333	0.3333	-0.333	0	0.3333	3.33333

(2)

Bas Var	Eq No	Z	x_1	x_2	x_3	x_4	$\bar{x}_5$	$\bar{x}_6$	Right Side
Z	0	1	0	0	3e-20	-3e-20	1	1	-2e-19
x_2	1	0	0	1	-0.5	0.5	1.5	-0.5	5.5
x_1	2	0	1	0	0.5	-0.5	-0.5	0.5	1.5

Phase 2:

(2)

Bas Var	Eq No	Z	x_1	x_2	x_3	x_4	Right Side
Z	0	1	0	0	0.5	0.5	-15.5
x_2	1	0	0	1	-0.5	0.5	5.5
x_1	2	0	1	0	0.5	-0.5	1.5

Optimal: $(x_1^*, x_2^*, x_3^*) = (1.5, 5.5, 0)$, $Z^* = 15.5$

4.6-10. c) The BF solutions for the 2 methods coincide. Only the final tableau for the Big-m method and 2-phase method represent feasible solutions to the real problem.

4.6-11. a) False. The initial basic solution for the artificial model is not feasible for the original model.

b) False. The reverse is true: if at least one of the artificial variables is not zero, then the real problem has no feasible solutions

c) False. The two methods are basically (no pun intended) equivalent — they should take the same # of iterations

4.6-12. a) Substitute $x_1^+ - x_1^-$ for x_1:

$$\text{Maximize } Z = x_1^+ - x_1^- + 4x_2 + 2x_3$$

$$4x_1^+ - 4x_1^- + x_2 + x_3 \le 5$$

$$-x_1^+ + x_1^- + x_2 + 2x_3 \le 10$$

$$x_1^+ \ge 0,\ x_1^- \ge 0,\ x_2 \ge 0,\ x_3 \ge 0$$

b)

Bas Var	Eq No	Z	X_1	X_2	X_3	X_4	X_5	X_6	Right Side
Z	0	1	-1	1	-4	-2	0	0	0
X_5	1	0	4	-4	1	1	1	0	5
X_6	2	0	-1	1	1	2	0	1	10

Bas Var	Eq No	Z	X_1	X_2	X_3	X_4	X_5	X_6	Right Side
Z	0	1	15	-15	0	2	4	0	20
X_3	1	0	4	-4	1	1	1	0	5
X_6	2	0	-5	5	0	1	-1	1	5

Bas Var	Eq No	Z	X_1	X_2	X_3	X_4	X_5	X_6	Right Side
Z	0	1	0	0	0	5	1	3	35
X_3	1	0	0	0	1	1.8	0.2	0.8	9
X_2	2	0	-1	1	0	0.2	-0.2	0.2	1

Optimal Solution (to the original problem):

$(x_1^*, x_2^*, x_3^*) = (-1, 9, 0)$, $Z^* = 35$ $(x_1^{*+} = 0, x_1^{*-} = 1)$

4.6-13. a)

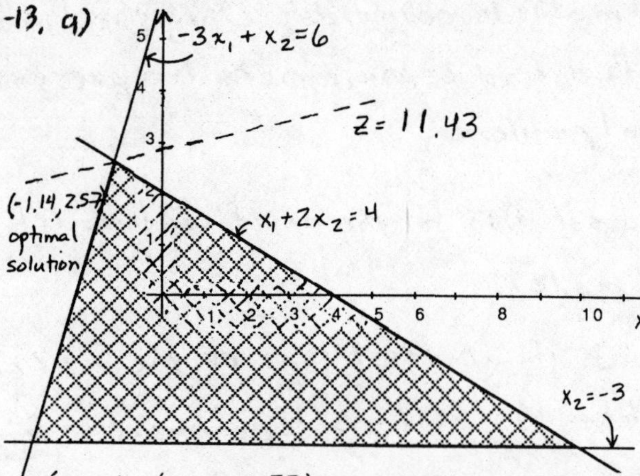

$(x_1, x_2) = (-1.14, 2.57)$ is optimal with $Z = 11.43$

(b) If we let $x_{1\,OLD} = x_1 - x_2$ and $x_{2\,OLD} + 3 = x_3$, we get

Maximize $-x_1 + x_2 + 4x_3 - 12$

subject to: $-3x_1 + 3x_2 + x_3 \le 9$

$x_1 - x_2 + 2x_3 \le 10$

$x_1 \ge 0 \quad x_2 \ge 0 \quad x_3 \ge 0.$

c)

(0)

Bas Var	Eq No	Z	X1	X2	X3	X4	X5	Right Side
Z	0	1	1	-1	-4	0	0	0
X4	1	0	-3	3	1	1	0	9
X5	2	0	1	-1	2	0	1	10

(1)

Bas Var	Eq No	Z	X1	X2	X3	X4	X5	Right Side
Z	0	1	3	-3	0	0	2	20
X4	1	0	-3.5	3.5	0	1	-0.5	4
X3	2	0	0.5	-0.5	1	0	0.5	5

(2)

Bas Var	Eq No	Z	X1	X2	X3	X4	X5	Right Side
Z	0	1	0	0	0	0.8571	1.5714	23.4286
X2	1	0	-1	1	0	0.2857	-0.143	1.14286
X3	2	0	0	0	1	0.1429	0.4286	5.57143

Optimal for original problem is:

$(x_1^*, x_2^*) = (-1.14, 2.57)$, $Z^* = 11.43$

(For revised problem: $(0, 1.14, 5.57)$ with $Z = 23.43$)

4.6-14. a) Let $x_{1\,OLD} = x_1 - x_2$, $x_{2\,OLD} = x_3 - x_4$ and $x_{3\,OLD} = x_5 - x_6$

The equivalent linear program with nonnegativity constraints is:

Maximize $Z = -x_1 + x_2 + 2x_3 - 2x_4 + x_5 - x_6$

subject to:

$$3x_3 - 3x_4 + x_5 - x_6 \le 120$$

$$x_1 - x_2 - x_3 + x_4 - 4x_5 + 4x_6 \le 80$$

$$-3x_1 + 3x_2 + x_3 - x_4 + 2x_5 - 2x_6 \le 100$$

$$x_i \ge 0 \quad \text{for } i = 1, 2, \ldots, 6.$$

4.6-14. b)

(0)

Bas Var	Eq No	Z	X_1	X_2	X_3	X_4	X_5	X_6	X_7	X_8	X_9	Right Side
Z	0	1	1	-1	-2	2	-1	1	0	0	0	0
X_7	1	0	0	0	3	-3	1	-1	1	0	0	120
X_8	2	0	1	-1	-1	1	-4	4	0	1	0	80
X_9	3	0	-3	3	1	-1	2	-2	0	0	1	100

(1)

Bas Var	Eq No	Z	X_1	X_2	X_3	X_4	X_5	X_6	X_7	X_8	X_9	Right Side
Z	0	1	1	-1	0	0	-0.33	0.333	0.667	0	0	80
X_3	1	0	0	0	1	-1	0.333	-0.33	0.333	0	0	40
X_8	2	0	1	-1	0	0	-3.67	3.667	0.333	1	0	120
X_9	3	0	-3	3	0	0	1.667	-1.67	-0.33	0	1	60

(2)

Bas Var	Eq No	Z	X_1	X_2	X_3	X_4	X_5	X_6	X_7	X_8	X_9	Right Side
Z	0	1	0	0	0	0	0.222	-0.22	0.556	0	0.333	100
X_3	1	0	0	0	1	-1	0.333	-0.33	0.333	0	0	40
X_8	2	0	0	0	0	0	-3.11	3.111	0.222	1	0.333	140
X_2	3	0	-1	1	0	0	0.556	-0.56	-0.11	0	0.333	20

(3)

Bas Var	Eq No	Z	X_1	X_2	X_3	X_4	X_5	X_6	X_7	X_8	X_9	Right Side
Z	0	1	0	0	0	0	0, 0	0	0.571	0.071	0.357	110
X_3	1	0	0	0	1	-1	3e-20	-3e-2	0.357	0.107	0.036	55
X_6	2	0	0	0	0	0	-1	1	0.071	0.321	0.107	45
X_2	3	0	-1	1	0	0	0	0	-0.07	0.179	0.393	45

Optimal for revised problem is (0,45,55,0,0,45) so optimal for the original problem is: $(x_1^*, x_2^*, x_3^*) = (-45, 55, -45)$ with $Z^* = 110$.

4.6-15. a) If we wish to decrease the objective value in the Simplex Method, we will choose as entering variable the nonbasic variable that has the largest positive coefficient in the objective row of the tableau. We will need the same minimum ratio test to determine the leaving variable, however.

b)

(0)

Bas Var	Eq No	Z	X1	X2	X3	X4	X5	X6	X7	Right side
			3M	8M	6M	-1M	-1M			140 M
Z	0	1	-3	-8	5	0	0	0	0	0
X6	1	0	0	3	4	-1	0	1	0	70
X7	2	0	3	5*	2	0	-1	0	1	70

4.6-15. b) (cont')

(1)

Bas Var	Eq No	Z	X1	X2	X3	X4	X5	X6	X7	Right side
			-1.8M		2.8M	-1M	0.6M		-1.6M	28 M
Z	0	1	1.8	0	-1.8	0	-1.6	0	1.6	112
X6	1	0	-1.8	0	2.8*	-1	0.6	1	-0.6	28
X2	2	0	0.6	1	0.4	0	-0.2	0	0.2	14

(2)

Bas Var	Eq No	Z	X1	X2	X3	X4	X5	X6	X7	Right side
								-1M	-1M	
Z	0	1	0.64	0	0	-0.643	-1.214	0.64	1.21	130
X3	1	0	-0.64	0	1	-0.36	0.214	0.357	-0.21	10
X2	2	0	0.857*	1	0	0.143	-0.29	-0.14	0.286	10

(3)

Bas Var	Eq No	Z	X1	X2	X3	X4	X5	X6	X7	Right side
								-1M	-1M	
Z	0	1	0	-0.75	0	-0.75	1	0.75	1	122
X3	1	0	0	0.75	1	-0.25	0	0.25	0	17.5
X1	2	0	1	1.167	0	0.167	-0.33	-0.17	0.333	11.67

$(x_1, x_2, x_3) = (11.67, 0, 17.5)$ is optimal with $z = 122$.

4.6-16. a)

Maximize $z = -2x_1 + 2x_2 + x_3 - 4x_4 + 3x_5$

subject to:

$x_1 - x_2 + x_3 + 3x_4 + 2x_5 \le 4$

$-x_1 + x_2 + x_4 - x_5 \le 1$

$2x_1 - 2x_2 + x_3 \le 2$

$x_1 - x_2 + 2x_3 + x_4 + 2x_5 = 2$

$x_i \ge 0$ for $i = 1, 2, \ldots, 5$

(b)

Bas Var	Eq No	Z	X1	X2	X3	X4	X5	X6	X7	X8	X9	Right side
			-1M	1M	-2M	-1M	-2M					-2 M
Z	0	1	2	-2	-1	4	-3	0	0	0	0	0
X6	1	0	1	-1	1	3	2	1	0	0	0	4
X7	2	0	-1	1	0	1	-1	0	1	0	0	1
X8	3	0	2	-2	1	0	0	0	0	1	0	2
X9	4	0	1	-1	2	1	2*	0	0	0	1	2

(c)

Bas Var	Eq No	Z	X1	X2	X3	X4	X5	X6	X7	X8	X9	Right side
Z	0	1	-1	1	-2	-1	-2	0	0	0	0	-2

d) **Optimal Solution**

Value of the Objective Function: Z = 17

Variable	Value
X1	0
X2	4
X3	0
X4	0
X5	3

Sensitivity Analysis

Objective Function Coefficient

Current Value	Allowable Range To Stay Optimal: Minimum	Maximum
-2	$-\infty$	-2
2	-1.5	2
1	$-\infty$	10
-4	$-\infty$	12
3	-1.5	$+\infty$

4.6-17. Reformulation:

Maximize

$$x_1 + x_2 + 2x_3 - x_4 + \bar{x}_7 = 20$$
$$15x_1 + 6x_2 - 5x_3 + x_5 = 50$$
$$x_1 + 3x_2 + 5x_3 + x_6 = 30$$
$$x_1, x_2, x_3, x_4, x_5, x_6, \bar{x}_7 \geq 0$$

Solution: Phase 1:

Bas Var	Eq No	Z	X1	X2	X3	X4	X5	X6	$\bar{X}_7$	Right Side
Z	0	1	-1	-1	-2	1	0	0	0	-20
$\bar{X}_7$	1	0	1	1	2	-1	0	0	1	20
X5	2	0	15	6	-5	0	1	0	0	50
X6	3	0	1	3	5	0	0	1	0	30

Bas Var	Eq No	Z	X1	X2	X3	X4	X5	X6	$\bar{X}_7$	Right Side
Z	0	1	-0.6	0.2	0	1	0	0.4	0	-8
$\bar{X}_7$	1	0	0.6	-0.2	0	-1	0	-0.4	1	8
X5	2	0	16	9	0	0	1	1	0	80
X3	3	0	0.2	0.6	1	0	0	0.2	0	6

Bas Var	Eq No	Z	X1	X2	X3	X4	X5	X6	$\bar{X}_7$	Right Side
Z	0	1	0	0.5375	0	1	0.0375	0.4375	0	-5
$\bar{X}_7$	1	0	0	-0.538	0	-1	-0.038	-0.438	1	5
X1	2	0	1	0.5625	0	0	0.0625	0.0625	0	5
X3	3	0	0	0.4875	1	0	-0.013	0.1875	0	5

Since this is the optimal for Phase 1 and the artificial variable $x_7 = 5 > 0$, this problem does not have a feasible solution.

4.7-1.

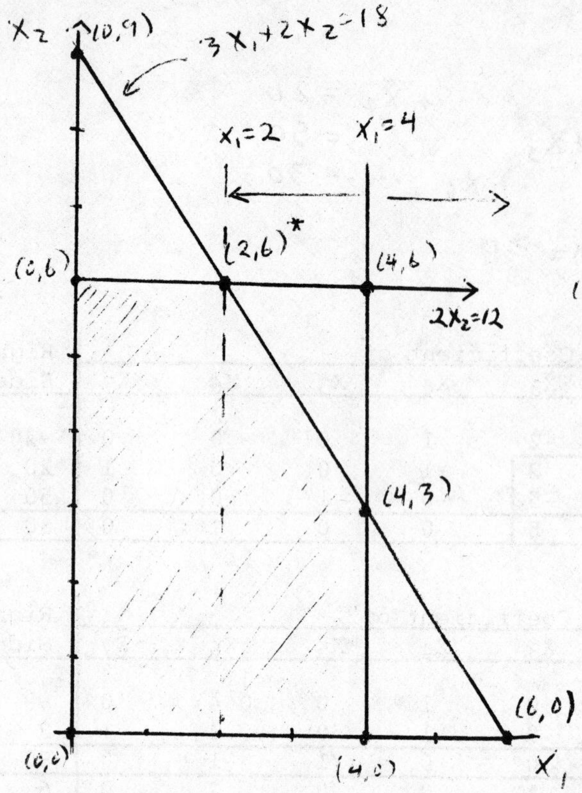

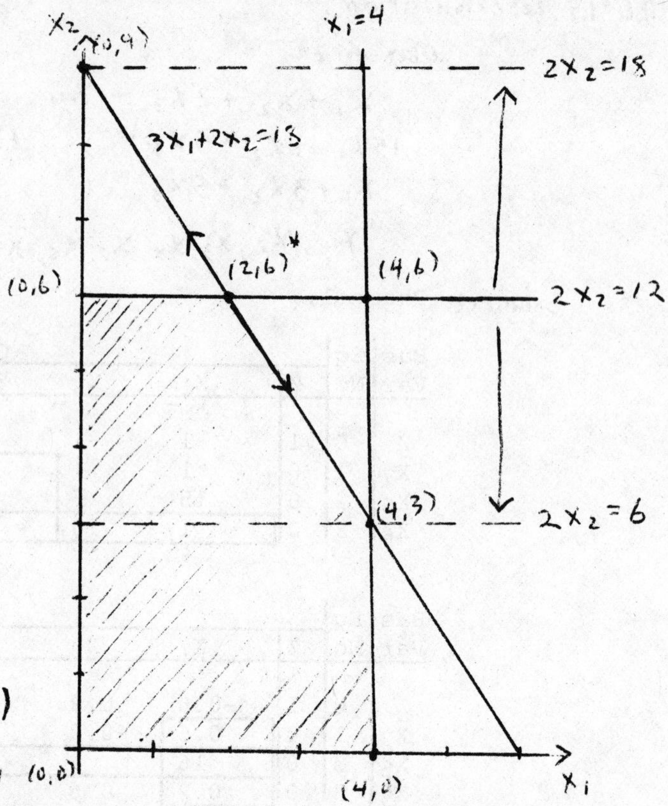

[The CP Sol'n (2,6) remains feasible for $x_1 = k$ $2 \le k < \infty$. For $k < 2$, that CP Sol'n become infeasible. *(2,6) is, of course, the optimal.]

[The CP Sol'n $\left(\frac{18-k}{3}, \frac{k}{2}\right)$ remains feasible for $2x_2 = k$ $6 \le k \le 18$ only.]

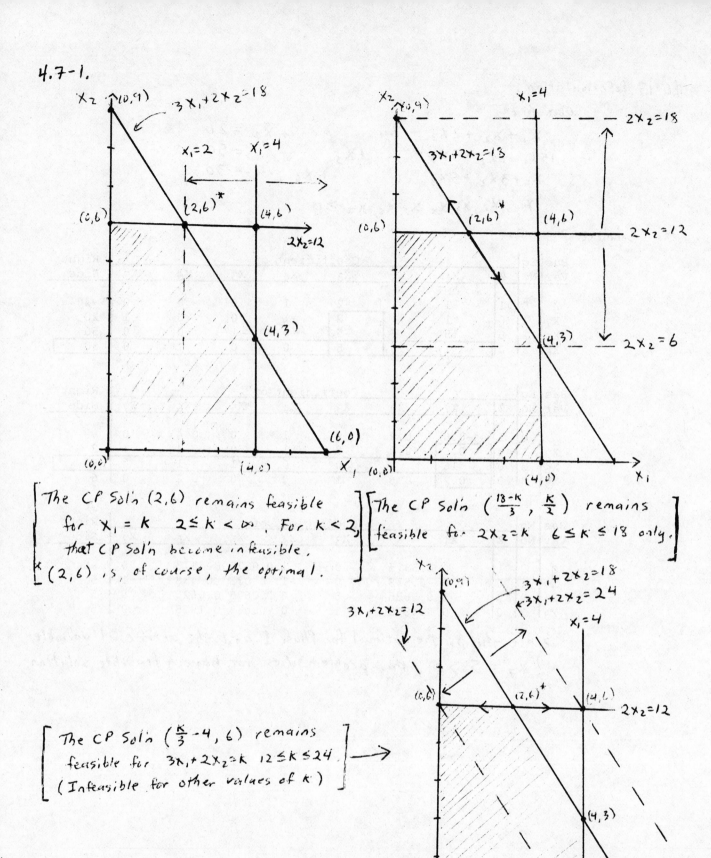

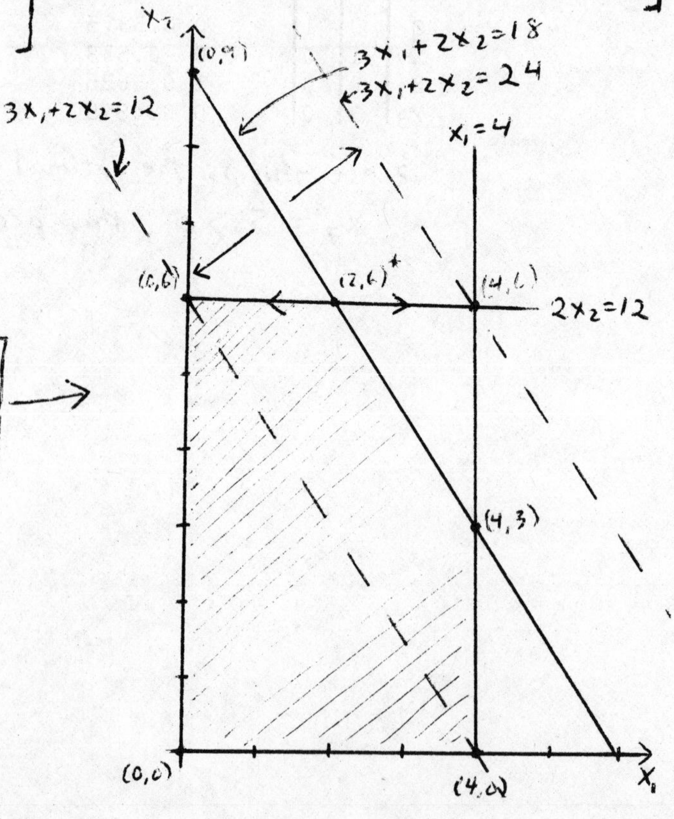

[The CP Sol'n $\left(\frac{k}{3}-4, 6\right)$ remains feasible for $3x_1+2x_2=k$ $12 \le k \le 24$ (Infeasible for other values of k)] →

4.7-2. a)

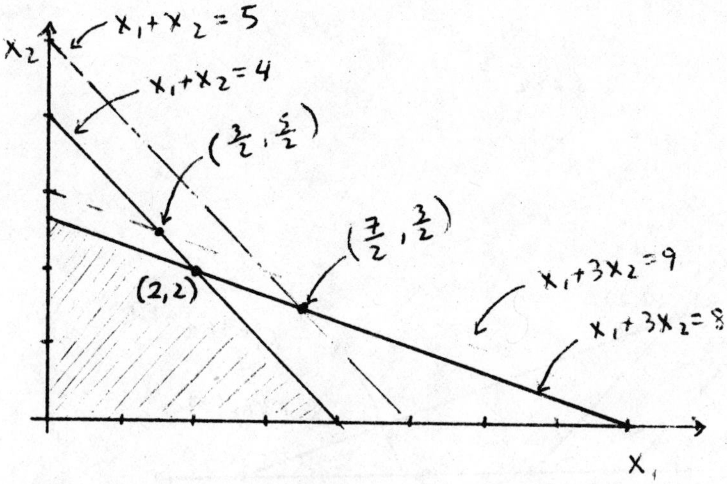

Constraint 1 ("- - -" line):

$$\left.\begin{array}{l} x_1+3x_2=8 \rightarrow Z=(2)+2(2)=6 \\ x_1+3x_2=9 \rightarrow Z=(\frac{3}{2})+2(\frac{5}{2})=\frac{13}{2} \end{array}\right\} \Delta Z=\frac{1}{2}=y_1^*$$

Constraint 2 ("—·—·—" line)

$$\left.\begin{array}{l} x_1+x_2=4 \rightarrow Z=(2)+2(2)=6 \\ x_1+x_2=5 \rightarrow Z=(\frac{7}{2})+2(\frac{3}{2})=\frac{13}{2} \end{array}\right\} \Delta Z=\frac{1}{2}=y_2^*$$

b) From (a), we see that $b_1=8$, $b_2=4$ are sensitive parameters. As will be seen in part (c), $c_1=1, c_2=2$ are not sensitive parameters. As can be seen in the figure in part (a), both constraints are active or binding, so all coefficients $a_{11}=1, a_{12}=3, a_{21}=1, a_{22}=1$ are sensitive parameters.

c)

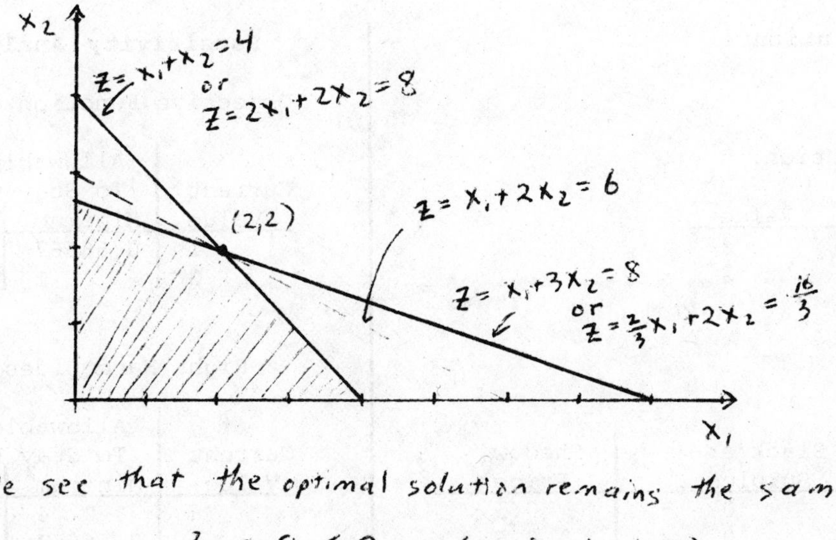

We see that the optimal solution remains the same for:

$$\frac{2}{3} \le c_1 \le 2 \quad (c_2 \text{ fixed at } 2)$$

$$\text{and } 1 \le c_2 \le 3 \quad (c_1 \text{ fixed at } 1)$$

4.7-2. d)

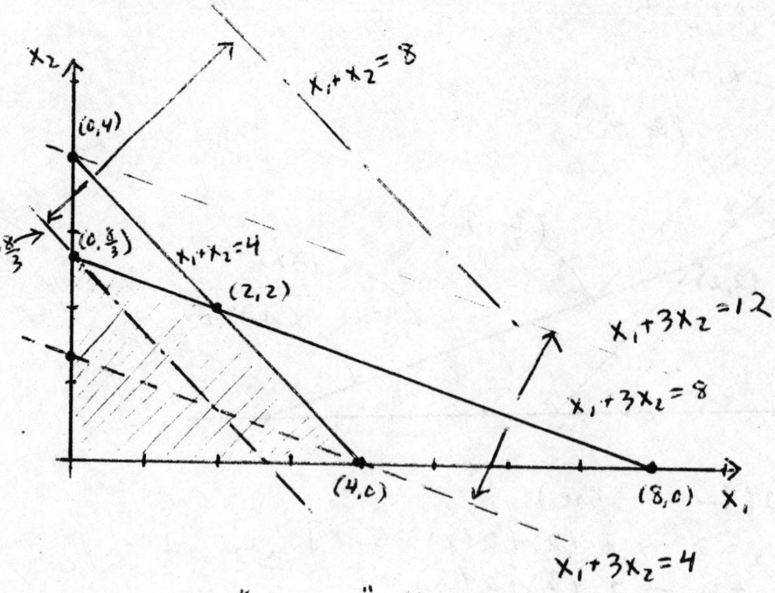

Looking at the "– – –" lines, the CP Sol'n ranges from (4,0) to (0,4) as b_1 ranges from 4 to 12. The CP Sol'n becomes infeasible for values of b_1 outside of this range.

Similarly, looking at the "–·–·–" lines, the CP Sol'n ranges from $(0, \frac{8}{3})$ to $(8,0)$ as b_2 ranges from $\frac{8}{3}$ to 8.

The allowable ranges are, therefore,

$$4 \le b_1 \le 12$$

and $\frac{8}{3} \le b_2 \le 8$

e) **Optimal Solution**

Value of the Objective Function: Z = 6

Variable	Value
X_1	2
X_2	2

Constraint	Slack or Surplus	Shadow Price
1	0	0.5
2	0	0.5

Sensitivity Analysis

Objective Function Coefficient

Current Value	Allowable Range To Stay Optimal Minimum	Maximum
1	0.66667	2
2	1	3

Right Hand Sides

Current Value	Allowable Range To Stay Feasible Minimum	Maximum
8	4	12
4	2.66667	8

4.7-3. a)

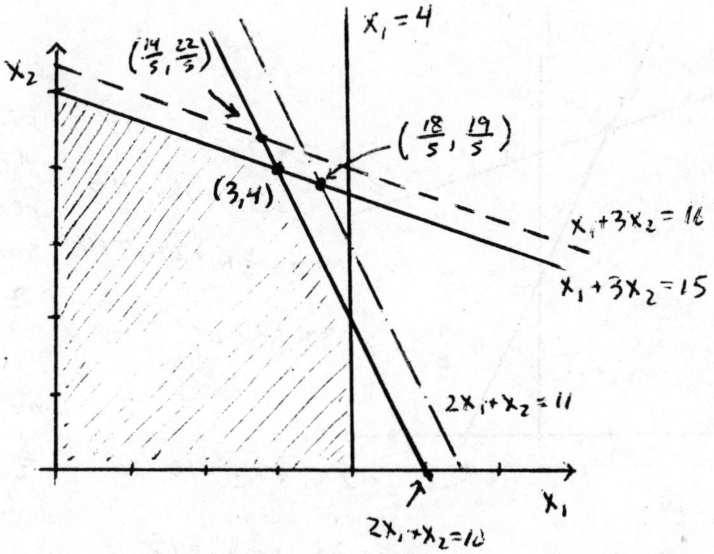

Constraint 1 is not binding changes (small) in $b_1 = 4$ do not change the optimal Z, so $y_1^* = 0$.

Constraint 2 ("– – – –" line):

$$\left.\begin{array}{l} x_1 + 3x_2 = 15 \rightarrow Z = 3(3) + 2(4) = 17 \\ x_1 + 3x_2 = 16 \rightarrow Z = 3(\frac{14}{5}) + 2(\frac{22}{5}) = \frac{86}{5} = 17.2 \end{array}\right\} \Delta Z = 0.2 = y_2^*$$

Constraint 3 ("—·—·—·" line):

$$\left.\begin{array}{l} 2x_1 + x_2 = 10 \rightarrow Z = 3(3) + 2(4) = 17 \\ 2x_1 + x_2 = 11 \rightarrow Z = 3(\frac{18}{5}) + 2(\frac{19}{5}) = \frac{92}{5} = 18.4 \end{array}\right\} \Delta Z = 1.4 = y_3^*$$

b) From (a) we see that b_1 is not a sensitive parameter while b_2 and b_3 are sensitive. As will be seen in part (c), c_1, c_2 are not sensitive parameters. Finally, since constraints 2 and 3 are binding, coefficients of these constraints ($a_{21}, a_{22}, a_{31}, a_{32}$) are sensitive parameters while coefficients of the non-binding constraint 1 (a_{11}, a_{12}) are not sensitive.

4.7-3. c)

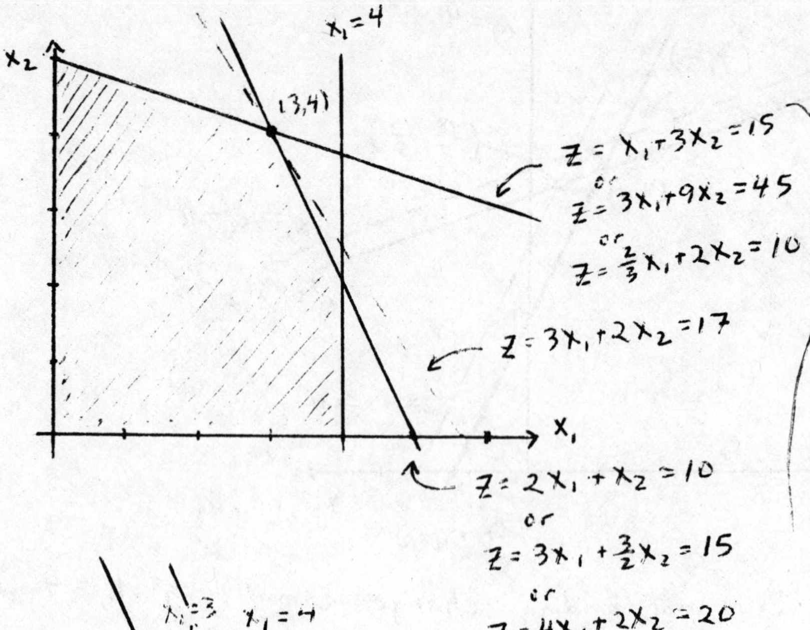

We see that the optimal Sol'n remains the same for

$\frac{2}{3} \le c_1 \le 4$

(c_2 fixed at 2)

and for

$\frac{3}{2} \le c_2 \le 9$

(c_1 fixed at 3)

d)

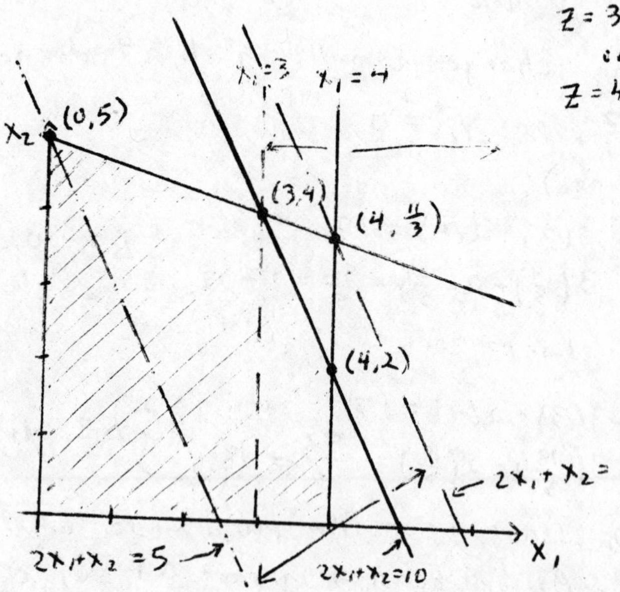

For constraint 1 ("— — — —" line), the CP Sol'n remains (3,4) (since the constraint is not binding) for $3 \le b_1 < \infty$.

For constraint 2 (not shown — off the page), the CP Sol'n ranges from (4,2) (when $x_1 + 3x_2 = b_2 = 10$) to (0,10) (when $x_1 + 3x_2 = b_2 = 30$). Thus, b_2 ranges from 10 to 30 (allowable range to be feasible).

For constraint 3 ("-——-——-" lines) the CP Sol'n ranges from (0,5) (when $2x_1 + x_2 = b_3 = 5$) to $(4, \frac{11}{3})$ (when $2x_1 + x_2 = b_3 = 11\frac{2}{3}$). Thus the allowable range to be feasible for b_3 is: $5 \le b_3 \le 11\frac{2}{3}$.

4.7-3. e)

Optimal Solution

Value of the Objective Function: Z = 17

Variable	Value
X_1	3
X_2	4

Constraint	Slack or Surplus	Shadow Price
1	1	0
2	0	0.2
3	0	1.4

Sensitivity Analysis

Objective Function Coefficient

Current Value	Allowable Range To Stay Optimal Minimum	Maximum
3	0.66667	4
2	1.5	9

Right Hand Sides

Current Value	Allowable Range To Stay Feasible Minimum	Maximum
4	3	+∞
15	10	30
10	5	11.6667

4.7-4. a)

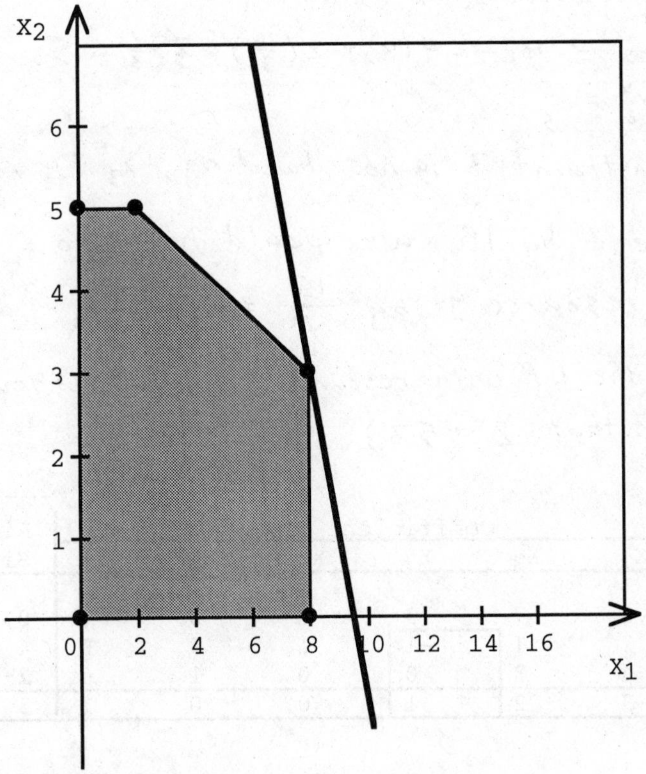

Corner Points		Z
(8,	3)	38*
(8,	0)	32
(2,	5)	18
(0,	5)	10
(0,	0)	0

Optimal value of Z: 38

Optimal solution: (8, 3)

4.7-4. b)

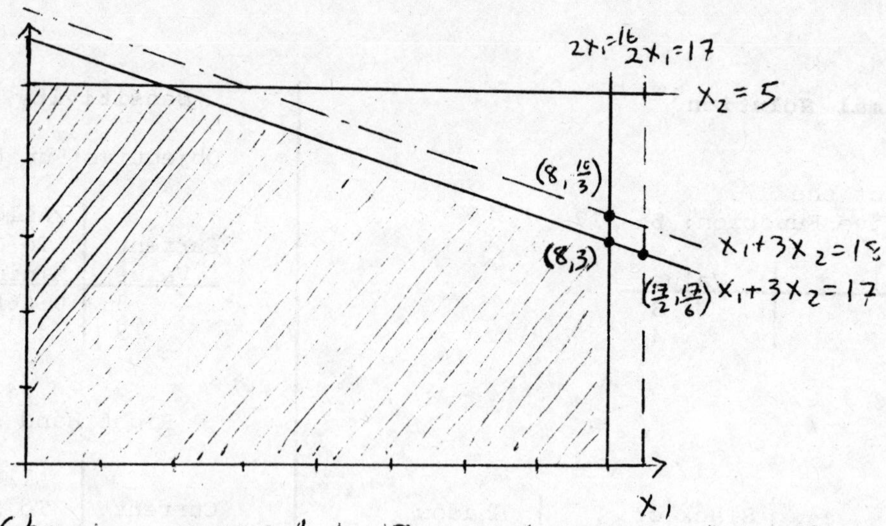

Changing resource 1 to 17 units ("— — —" line)

causes Z to increase to $Z = 4(\frac{17}{2}) + 2(\frac{17}{6}) = 39\frac{2}{3}$

So $\Delta Z = y_1^* = 1\frac{2}{3}$.

Increasing resource 2 to 18 units ("—·—·—" line)

increases Z to $Z = 4(8) + 2(\frac{10}{3}) = 38\frac{2}{3}$. So

$\Delta Z = y_2^* = \frac{2}{3}$.

Since constraint 3 is not binding, $y_3^* = 0$.

c) To increase Z by 15, we would need to

increase resource 1 by $\frac{15}{y_1^*} = \frac{15}{\frac{5}{3}} = 9$.

(Solving the LP with resource 1 set to 16+9=25

confirms that $Z^* = 53$).

4.7-5. a)

(0)

Bas Var	Eq No	Z	X_1	X_2	X_3	X_4	X_5	X_6	Right Side
Z	0	1	-1	7	-3	0	0	0	0
X_4	1	0	2	1	-1	1	0	0	4
X_5	2	0	4	-3	0	0	1	0	2
X_6	3	0	-3	2	1	0	0	1	3

(1)

Bas Var	Eq No	Z	X_1	X_2	X_3	X_4	X_5	X_6	Right Side
Z	0	1	-10	13	0	0	0	3	9
X_4	1	0	-1	3	0	1	0	1	7
X_5	2	0	4	-3	0	0	1	0	2
X_3	3	0	-3	2	1	0	0	1	3

4.7-5. a) (cont')

(2)

Bas Var	Eq No	Z	X_1	X_2	X_3	X_4	X_5	X_6	Right Side
Z	0	1	0	5.5	0	0	2.5	3	14
X_4	1	0	0	2.25	0	1	0.25	1	7.5
X_1	2	0	1	-0.75	0	0	0.25	0	0.5
X_3	3	0	0	-0.25	1	0	0.75	1	4.5

Optimal: $(x_1^*, x_2^*, x_3^*) = (0.5, 0, 4.5)$, $Z^* = 14$.

b) The shadow prices for the three resources are given by the reduced costs (in the objective function) for the corresponding slack variables (circled above). The shadow prices for resources 1, 2, and 3 are 0, 2.5, and 3, resp. These represent the rate at which Z (the objective value) increases as the corresponding resource is increased. For example, increasing resource 2 by 1 unit should increase Z by 2.5 (assuming no other constraints cause trouble...)

4.7-6. a)

(0)

Bas Var	Eq No	Z	X_1	X_2	X_3	X_4	X_5	X_6	Right Side
Z	0	1	-2	2	-3	0	0	0	0
X_4	1	0	-1	1	1	1	0	0	4
X_5	2	0	2	-1	1	0	1	0	2
X_6	3	0	1	1	3	0	0	1	12

(1)

Bas Var	Eq No	Z	X_1	X_2	X_3	X_4	X_5	X_6	Right Side
Z	0	1	4	-1	0	0	3	0	6
X_4	1	0	-3	2	0	1	-1	0	2
X_3	2	0	2	-1	1	0	1	0	2
X_6	3	0	-5	4	0	0	-3	1	6

(2)

Bas Var	Eq No	Z	X_1	X_2	X_3	X_4	X_5	X_6	Right Side
Z	0	1	2.5	0	0	0.5	2.5	0	7
X_2	1	0	-1.5	1	0	0.5	-0.5	0	1
X_3	2	0	0.5	0	1	0.5	0.5	0	3
X_6	3	0	1	0	0	-2	-1	1	2

Optimal: $(x_1^*, x_2^*, x_3^*) = (0, 1, 3)$, $Z^* = 7$

b) The shadow prices are:

$y_1^* = \frac{1}{2}$, $y_2^* = \frac{5}{2}$, $y_3^* = 0$

They are the marginal values of resources 1, 2 and 3, respectively.

4.7-7. a)

(0)

Bas Var	Eq No	Z	x_1	x_2	x_3	x_4	x_5	x_6	Right Side
Z	0	1	-2	-4	1	0	0	0	0
x_4	1	0	0	3	-1	1	0	0	30
x_5	2	0	2	-1	1	0	1	0	10
x_6	3	0	4	2	-2	0	0	1	40

(1)

Bas Var	Eq No	Z	x_1	x_2	x_3	x_4	x_5	x_6	Right Side
Z	0	1	-2	0	-0.333	1.3333	0	0	40
x_2	1	0	0	1	-0.333	0.3333	0	0	10
x_5	2	0	2	0	0.6667	0.3333	1	0	20
x_6	3	0	4	0	-1.333	-0.667	0	1	20

(2)

Bas Var	Eq No	Z	x_1	x_2	x_3	x_4	x_5	x_6	Right Side
Z	0	1	0	0	-1	1	0	0.5	50
x_2	1	0	0	1	-0.333	0.3333	0	0	10
x_5	2	0	0	0	1.3333	0.6667	1	-0.5	10
x_1	3	0	1	0	-0.333	-0.167	0	0.25	5

(3)

Bas Var	Eq No	Z	x_1	x_2	x_3	x_4	x_5	x_6	Right Side
Z	0	1	0	0	0	1.5	0.75	0.125	57.5
x_2	1	0	0	1	0	0.5	0.25	-0.125	12.5
x_3	2	0	0	0	1	0.5	0.75	-0.375	7.5
x_1	3	0	1	0	0	0	0.25	0.125	7.5

Optimal: $(x_1^*, x_2^*, x_3^*) = (7.5, 12.5, 7.5)$, $Z^* = 57.5$

b) The shadow prices are:

$y_1^* = 1.5$, $y_2^* = 0.75$, $y_3^* = 0.125$

They are the marginal values of resources 1, 2 and 3, respectively.

4.7-8. a)

(0)

Bas Var	Eq No	Z	x_1	x_2	x_3	x_4	x_5	x_6	Right Side
Z	0	1	-5	-2	1	-3	0	0	0
x_5	1	0	3	2	-3	1	1	0	24
x_6	2	0	3	3	1	3	0	1	36

(1)

Bas Var	Eq No	Z	x_1	x_2	x_3	x_4	x_5	x_6	Right Side
Z	0	1	0	1.3333	-4	-1.333	1.6667	0	40
x_1	1	0	1	0.6667	-1	0.3333	0.3333	0	8
x_6	2	0	0	1	4	2	-1	1	12

4.7-8. a) (cont')

Bas Var	Eq No	Z	X_1	X_2	X_3	X_4	X_5	X_6	Right Side
(2) Z	0	1	0	2.3333	0	0.6667	0.6667	1	52
X_1	1	0	1	0.9167	0	0.8333	0.0833	0.25	11
X_3	2	0	0	0.25	1	0.5	−0.25	0.25	3

Optimal ; $(x_1, x_2, x_3, x_4) = (11, 0, 3, 0)$, $Z^* = 52$

b) The shadow prices are $y_1^* = 2/3$ and $y_2^* = 1$. They are the marginal values of resources 1 and 2, respectively.

4.8-1. a) Instead of storing every coefficient in a matrix, say, store only the non-zero elements and their positions (variable column and equation row). There are many ways to do this, but the easiest (though not most efficient) way would be to have three columns: Row #, Column #, and Value of Coefficient.

b) Hard code coefficients that are not basic raw data that requires manual input. For example, it is not necessary to manually input the 1's on the left hand side of $\sum_i e_{ijk} \geq D_{jk} \ \forall j,k$. One could generate these in the code itself.

4.9-1. The points generated are :

It.	X_1	X_2	Z
0	0.1	0.4	2250
1	0.12711	0.7	3722
2	0.16	0.85	4545.01
3	0.22951	0.90539	5107.06
4	0.29209	0.91083	5413.13
5	0.33622	0.90327	5577.73
6	0.38555	0.87769	5684.56
7	0.49463	0.79736	5813.95
8	0.58617	0.72511	5900.76
9	0.6315	0.68954	5944.67
10	0.65298	0.67323	5967.95
11	0.66213	0.66707	5981.38
12	0.66523	0.66582	5989.75
13	0.66607	0.66609	5994.74
14	0.66637	0.66637	5997.36
15	0.66652	0.66652	5998.68

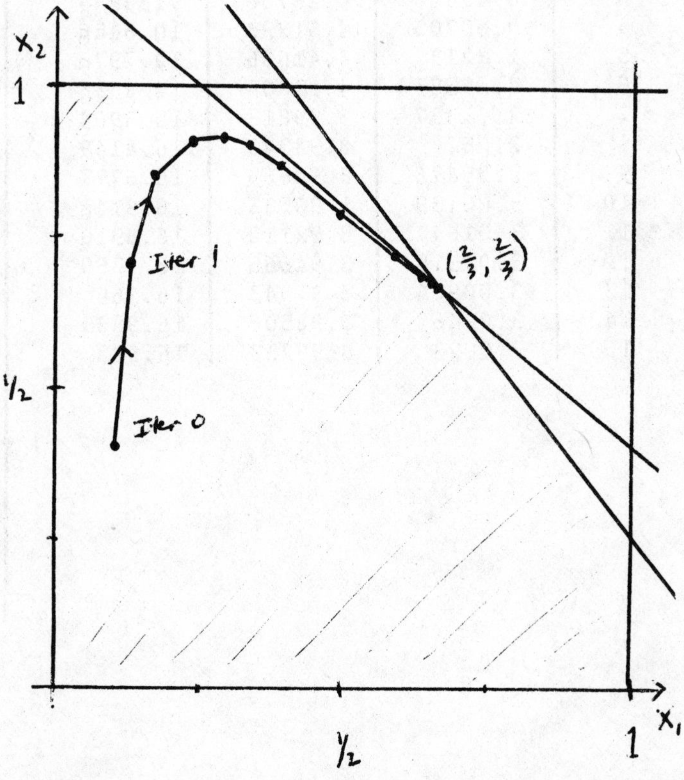

4.9-2. The points generated are:

It.	x_1	x_2	Z
0	0.1	0.4	0.9
1	0.13445	1.50518	3.14482
2	0.13711	2.06263	4.26237
3	0.13972	2.34093	4.82157
4	0.14518	2.47869	5.10256
5	0.15744	2.54439	5.24623
6	0.18669	2.56954	5.32577
7	0.26908	2.55952	5.38813
8	0.60813	2.45523	5.51859
9	1.30911	2.22257	5.75425
10	1.65995	2.10589	5.87173
11	1.835	2.04792	5.93084
12	1.92183	2.01963	5.96109
13	1.96414	2.00659	5.97732
14	1.98388	2.00148	5.98685
15	1.99253	2.00015	5.99283

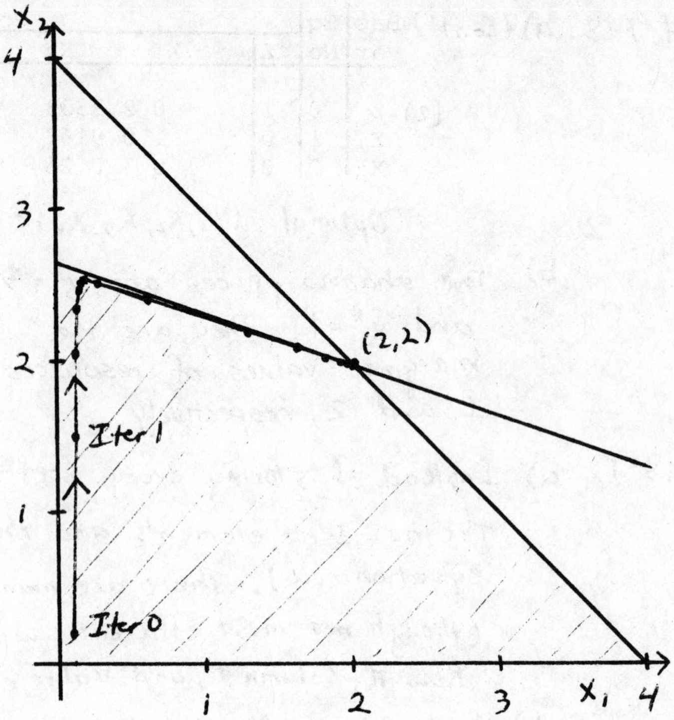

4.9-3. Generated output of points:

It.	x_1	x_2	Z
0	0.1	0.4	1.1
1	0.30854	2.61382	6.15325
2	0.35481	3.74006	8.54455
3	0.42446	4.28768	9.84874
4	0.60705	4.51223	10.8456
5	1.3213	4.41686	12.7976
6	2.19583	4.13808	14.8636
7	2.63337	3.99813	15.8964
8	2.85	3.93243	16.4149
9	2.95476	3.90669	16.6777
10	3.00139	3.90533	16.8148
11	3.01647	3.92112	16.8916
12	3.01519	3.94665	16.9389
13	3.00904	3.97043	16.968
14	3.0046	3.98506	16.9839
15	3.0023	3.99253	16.992

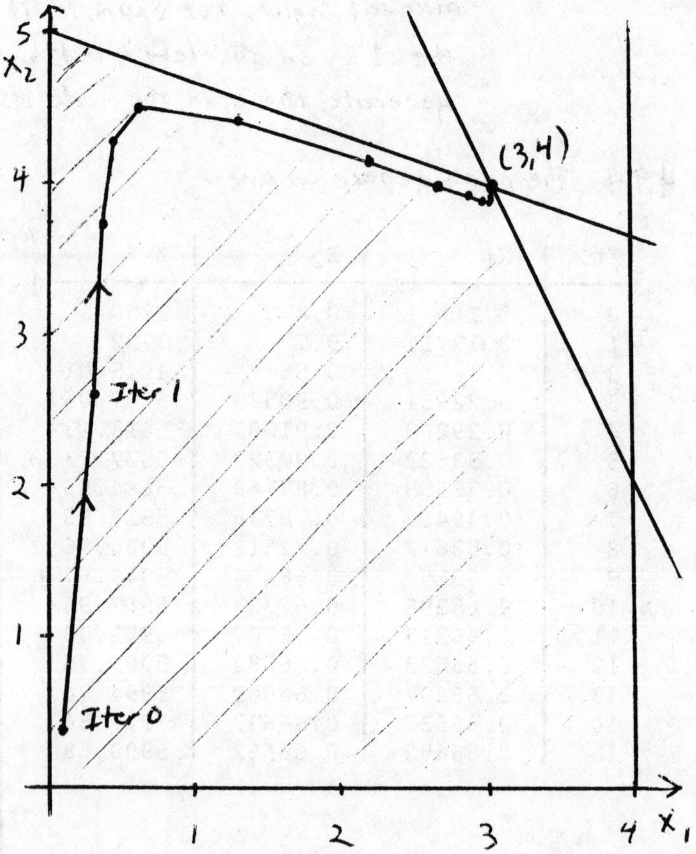

CP 4-1, a) Let X_i = # of acres of crop i planted for the coming year

i = soybean, corn, wheat (s, c, w)

l_i = # of livestock i to <u>buy</u> (in addition to those currently on the farm) for the coming year

i = cows, hens (c, h)

For convenience, we let

N_l = Net income from livestock for the coming year

N_c = Net value of the crops for the coming year

I = Investment fund remaining (not used)

V_l = Value of livestock at end of the coming year

L_{ws} = # person-hours of labor <u>not</u> used in winter/spring months

L_{SF} = # person-hrs of labor <u>not</u> used in summer/fall months.

Note that these 3 <u>may</u> be < 0.

The objective is to:

$$\text{Maximize } Z = N_l + N_c + I + V_l - 40{,}000 + 5L_{ws} + 5.5L_{SF}$$

(at beginning of problem, this is stated. Perhaps could be included in net value of crops)

Constraints are:

(acreage) $2(l_c + 30) + X_s + X_c + X_w \le 640$

(barn space) $l_c + 30 \le 42$

(chicken house) $l_h + 2000 \le 5000$

(winter-spring person-hrs labor) $X_s + (.9)X_c + (.6)X_w + 60^*(l_c + 30) + (.3^*)(l_h + 2000) + L_{ws} = 4000$

(S-F person hrs) $(1.4)X_s + (1.2)X_c + (.7)X_w + 60^*(l_c + 30) + (.3^*)(l_h + 2000) + L_{SF} = 4500$

(Investment fund) $1500l_c + 3l_h + I = 20{,}000$

* We assume 6 months during winter-spring and summer-fall.

(Feed for cows) $X_c \ge l_c + 30$

(Feed for chickens) $X_w \ge (.05)(l_h + 2000)$

(Net value of crops) $N_c = 70X_s + 60X_c + 40X_w$

(Net income-livestock) $N_l = 850(l_c + 30) + (4.25)(l_h + 2000)$

(Value of livestock at year end) $V_l = (.9)(35000 + 1500l_c) + (.75)(5000 + 3l_h)$

$X_i \ge 0,\ l_j \ge 0,\ I \ge 0,\ L_{ws} \ge 0,\ L_{SF} \ge 0 \quad (i = s, c, w;\ j = c, h)$

Taking out N_c, N_e & V_e and simplifying, we get:

$$\text{Max } Z = 2200 l_c + 6.5 l_h + 70 X_s + 60 X_c + 40 X_w + I + 5 L_{ws} + 5.5 L_{SF} + 29250$$

subject to

$$2 l_c + X_s + X_c + X_w \le 580$$

$$l_c \le 12$$

$$l_h \le 3000$$

$$60 l_c + 0.3 l_h + X_s + 0.9 X_c + 0.6 X_w + L_{ws} = 1600$$

$$60 l_c + 0.3 l_h + 1.4 X_s + 1.2 X_c + 0.7 X_w + L_{SF} = 2100$$

$$1500 l_c + 3 l_h + I = 20000$$

$$-l_c + X_c \ge 30$$

$$-0.05 l_h + X_w \ge 100$$

$$l_c \ge 0,\ l_h \ge 0,\ X_s \ge 0,\ X_c \ge 0,\ X_w \ge 0,\ I \ge 0,\ L_{ws} \ge 0,\ L_{SF} \ge 0$$

b) Solving this, we get the solution:

Optimal Solution

Value of the
Objective Function: Z = 70117 (+29250 = 99367)

Variable		Value
X1	(l_c)	0
X2	(l_h)	0
X3	(X_s)	450
X4	(X_c)	30
X5	(X_w)	100
X6	(I)	20000
X7	(L_{ws})	1063
X8	(L_{SF})	1364

Constraint	Slack or Surplus	Shadow Price
1	0	57.3
2	12	0
3	3000	0
4	0	5
5	0	5.5
6	0	1
7	0	-8.4
8	0	-24.15

Sensitivity Analysis

Objective Function Coefficient

Current Value	Allowable Range To Stay Optimal Minimum	Maximum
2200	-∞	2253
6.5	-∞	7.3575
70	61.6	+∞
60	-∞	68.4
40	-∞	57.15
1	0.96467	+∞
5	4.08463	62.3
5.5	4.57018	40

Right Hand Sides

Current Value	Allowable Range To Stay Feasible Minimum	Maximum
580	130	1554.29
12	0	+∞
3000	0	+∞
1600	537	+∞
2100	736	+∞
20000	0	+∞
30	0	480
100	0	550

Optimal is to buy no more livestock and grow as much soybean as possible.

c) To formulate for the new conditions, we need only change the coefficients for X_s, X_c & X_w in the objective function. The constraints remain the same. For example, for the "Drought" scenario, the objective should be:

$$\text{Max } Z = 2200\,l_c + 6.5\,l_h \underbrace{-\,10X_s - 15X_c + 0X_w}_{\text{changed...}} + \overbrace{I + 5L_{ws} + 5.5L_{SF}}^{\text{not actually decision var's}} + 29250$$

<u>Results:</u>

Scenario	Z^*	l_c^*	l_h^*	X_s^*	X_c^*	X_w^*	I^*	L_{ws}^*	L_{SF}^*
Drought	67,864	12	666.7	0	42	133.3	0	562.2	1036.3
Flood	74,055	12	666.7	0	422.7	133.3	0	219.6	579.5
Early Frost	88,767	0	0	450	30	100	20,000	1063	1364
Drought & Early Frost	66,649	12	0	0	42	100	2000	782.2	1259.6
Flood & Early Frost	69,860	7.33	3000	0	37.33	250	0	76.4	540.2

d) Plugging the solutions for each scenario into the objective function for each of the scenarios gives the actual family's monetary worth if that scenario occured:

Optimal Solution Used	Family's monetary worth at year's end if what actually occurred was scenario: Good weather	Drought	Flood	Early Frost	Drought & Early Frost	Flood & Early Frost
Good Weather	99,367	57,117	70,417	88,767	53,717	67,367
Drought	76,348	67,864	70,668	74,174	66,321	69,581
Flood	94,962	57,929	74,055	85,175	54,482	69,162
Early Frost	99,367	57,117	70,417	88,767	53,717	67,367
Drought & Early Frost	75,009	67,859	70,329	73,169	66,649	69,409
Flood & Early Frost	80,476	67,676	71,483	77,230	64,990	69,860

If you are conservative the "Flood & Early Frost" solution looks pretty good — it does better than the "Drought" and "Drought & Early Frost" solutions in most cases and seems like a good compromise. If you are more risk-taking, the "Flood" solution may work well, though the "Good weather" solution is too risky.

e) The average net value for each of the crops are:

Soybean: $\sum p_i NV_i = (.4)(70) + (.2)(-10) + (.1)(15) + (.15)(50) + (.1)(-15) + (.05)(10) = 34$

Corn: $(.4)(60) + (.2)(-15) + (.1)(20) + (.15)(40) + (.1)(-20) + (.05)(10) = 27.5$

Wheat: $(.4)(40) + (.2)(0) + (.1)(10) + (.15)(30) + (.1)(-10) + (.05)(5) = 20.75$

So the objective becomes:

$$\text{Max } Z = 2200 l_c + 6.5 l_h + 34 X_s + 27.5 X_c + 20.75 X_w + I + 5 L_{ws} + 5.5 L_{sp} + 29250$$

Since the family's <u>current</u> monetary worth is:

$35,000 + $5000 + $20,000 = $60,000
(cows) (hens) (investment fund)

$10,000 less than current. ↓

We need to add the constraints:

$$2200 l_c + 6.5 l_h + NV_s X_s + NV_c X_c + NV_w X_w + I + 5 L_{ws} + 5.5 L_{sf} + 29250 \geq 50000$$

for each set (NV_s, NV_c, NV_w) (net value of crops) represented by each possible scenario (There will be 6 extra constraints — one corresponding with each scenario — $(NV_s, NV_c, NV_w) = (70, 60, 40), (-10, -15, 0), (15, 20, 10), (50, 40, 30), (-15, -20, -10), (10, 10, 5)$.)

f) Solving this, we get:

Optimal Solution

Value of the Objective Function: Z = 51287

Variable	Value
X_1	12
X_2	0
X_3	414
X_4	42
X_5	100
X_6	2000
X_7	368.2
X_8	680

Sensitivity Analysis

Objective Function Coefficient

Current Value	Allowable Range To Stay Optimal Minimum	Maximum
2200	2177.5	$+\infty$
6.5	$-\infty$	6.52
34	33.6	41.5
27.5	5	32.4
20.75	$-\infty$	21.15
1	0.99333	1.015
5	4.92857	5.3886
5.5	5.42453	5.89474

g) The shadow prices for the problem in (f) are given below:

Constraint	Slack or Surplus	Shadow Price	Right Hand Sides: Current Value	Allowable Range To Stay Feasible: Minimum	Maximum
1	0	21.3	580	166	767.04
2	0	22.5	12	0	13.3333
3	3000	0	3000	-7e-16	+∞
4	0	5	1600	1231.8	+∞
5	0	5.5	2100	1420	+∞
6	0	1	20000	18000	+∞
7	0	-4.9	30	-12	444
8	0	-7.4	100	2e-17	514
9	48731	0	20750	-∞	69481
10	8461	0	20750	-∞	29211
11	21281	0	20750	-∞	42031
12	38611	0	20750	-∞	59361
13	5181	0	20750	-∞	25931
14	18291	0	20750	-∞	39041

Constraint 7 corresponds to the investment fund constraint. Since the shadow price for the investment fund is 1, this means that one expects a \$1 increase in the objective for every \$1 added to the investment fund. (This is clear since at optimal, $I^* = 2000$ = amount of investment fund not used is greater than 0). If the shadow price were ≥ 1.1, then we would be willing to obtain a bank loan.

h) Looking back at (f), we see that most of the coefficients have little latitude for change. The coefficients for l_c and l_h seem to be the most "important", though the avg. net values for soybeans and wheat also need to be estimated very carefully.

i) There are many examples of this type of problem. Some include: Finding the best portfolio of stocks and bonds given certain risk and return restrictions – deciding how much (what mix of) stocks/bonds to invest in. Selling insurance — deciding what rates to charge, who to sell to; of course, the uncertain future lies in the # of claims filed, say. Global warming – deciding how much prevention/research to do in face of uncertainty of how the earth's atmosphere reacts to different conditions. Buying insurance, deciding how much money to save for emergencies, etc.

Chapter 5: The Theory of the Simplex Method

5.1-1.

(a)

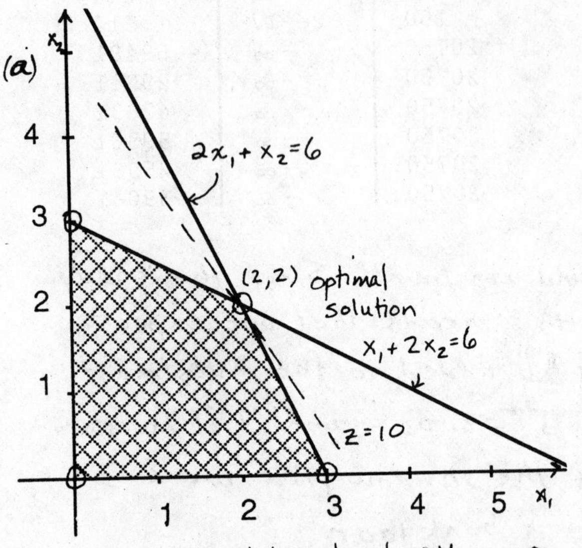

$(x_1, x_2) = (2,2)$ is optimal with $z=10$

(c) Maximize $Z = 3x_1 + 2x_2$

subject to: $2x_1 + x_2 + x_3 = 6$

$x_1 + 2x_2 + x_4 = 6$

$x_i \geq 0$ for $i = 1, 2, 3, 4$.

b) – d)

Defining Equations	CP	Feasible?	Basic Solution	Indicating Var's	Equations
$x_1=0$ $x_2=0$	(0,0)	Yes	(0,0,6,6)	x_1 x_2	$x_3=6$ $x_4=6$
$x_1=0$ $x_1+2x_2=6$	(0,3)	Yes	(0,3,3,0)	x_1 x_4	$x_2+x_3=6$ $2x_2=6$
$x_1=0$ $2x_1+x_2=6$	(0,6)	No	(0,6,0,−6)	x_1 x_3	$x_2=6$ $2x_2+x_4=6$
$x_2=0$ $x_1+2x_2=6$	(6,0)	No	(6,0,−6,0)	x_2 x_4	$2x_1+x_3=6$ $x_1=6$
$x_2=0$ $2x_1+x_2=6$	(3,0)	Yes	(3,0,0,3)	x_2 x_3	$2x_1=6$ $x_1+x_4=6$
$2x_1+x_2=6$ $x_1+2x_2=6$	(2,2)	Yes	(2,2,0,0)	x_3 x_4	$2x_1+x_2=6$ $x_1+2x_2=6$

5.1-1. e)

Step #	CPF Sol'n	Deleted Defining Eqn.	Added Defining Eqn	Deleted Ind. Var.	Added Ind. Var
1	(0, 0)	$x_1 = 0$	$2x_1 + x_2 = 6$	x_1	x_3
2	(3, 0)	$x_2 = 0$	$x_1 + 2x_2 = 6$	x_2	x_4
3	(2, 2)	Optimal			

5.1-2.

a)

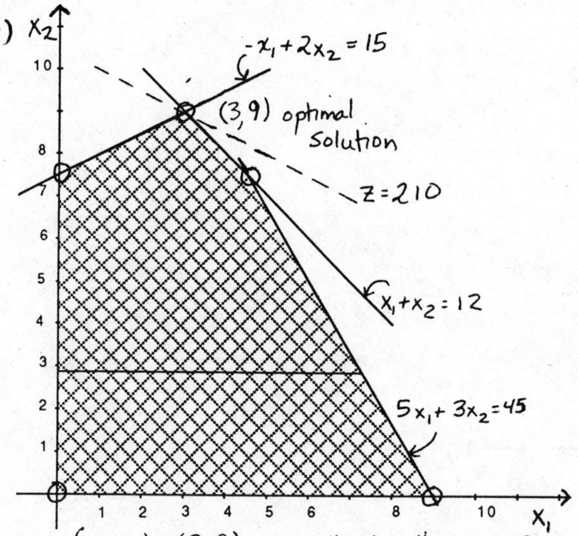

$(x_1, x_2) = (3, 9)$ is optimal with $Z = 210$

(c) Maximize $Z = 10x_1 + 20x_2$

subject to:

$$-x_1 + 2x_2 + x_3 = 15$$
$$x_1 + x_2 + x_4 = 12$$
$$5x_1 + 3x_2 + x_5 = 45$$

$x_i \geq 0$ for $i = 1, 2, 3, 4, 5$.

b)-d)

Defining Eqns	CP	Feasible?	Basic Sol'n	Ind. Variables	Equations
$x_1 = 0$, $x_2 = 0$	(0,0)	Yes	(0,0,15,12,45)	x_1, x_2	$x_3 = 15$, $x_4 = 12$, $x_5 = 45$
$x_1 = 0$, $-x_1 + 2x_2 = 15$	(0, 7.5)	Yes	(0, 7.5, 0, 4.5, 22.5)	x_1, x_3	$2x_2 = 15$, $x_2 + x_4 = 12$, $3x_2 + x_5 = 45$
$x_1 = 0$, $x_1 + x_2 = 15$	(0, 12)	No	(0, 12, -9, 0, 9)	x_1, x_4	$2x_2 + x_3 = 15$, $x_2 = 12$, $3x_2 + x_5 = 45$
$x_1 = 0$, $5x_1 + 3x_2 = 45$	(0, 15)	No	(0, 15, -15, -3, 0)	x_1, x_5	$2x_2 + x_3 = 15$, $x_2 + x_4 = 12$, $3x_2 = 45$
$x_2 = 0$, $-x_1 + 2x_2 = 15$	(-15, 0)	No	(-15, 0, 0, 3, 120)	x_2, x_3	$-x_1 = 15$, $x_1 + x_4 = 12$, $5x_1 + x_5 = 45$
$x_2 = 0$, $x_1 + x_2 = 12$	(12, 0)	No	(12, 0, 27, 0, -15)	x_2, x_4	$-x_1 + x_3 = 15$, $x_1 = 12$, $5x_1 + x_5 = 45$
$x_2 = 0$, $5x_1 + 3x_2 = 45$	(9, 0)	Yes	(9, 0, 24, 3, 0)	x_2, x_5	$-x_1 + x_3 = 15$, $x_1 + x_4 = 12$, $5x_1 = 45$
$-x_1 + 2x_2 = 15$, $x_1 + x_2 = 12$	(3, 9)	Yes	(3, 9, 0, 0, 3)	x_3, x_4	$-x_1 + 2x_2 = 15$, $x_1 + x_2 = 12$, $5x_1 + 3x_2 + x_5 = 45$
$-x_1 + 2x_2 = 15$, $5x_1 + 3x_2 = 45$	$(\frac{45}{13}, \frac{120}{13})$	No	$(\frac{45}{13}, \frac{120}{13}, 0, -\frac{9}{13}, 0)$	x_3, x_5	$-x_1 + 2x_2 = 15$, $x_1 + x_2 + x_4 = 12$, $5x_1 + 3x_2 = 45$
$x_1 + x_2 = 12$, $5x_1 + 3x_2 = 45$	(4.5, 7.5)	Yes	(4.5, 7.5, 3.5, 0, 0)	x_4, x_5	$-x_1 + 2x_2 + x_3 = 15$, $x_1 + x_2 = 12$, $5x_1 + 3x_2 = 45$

5.1-2, e)

Step #	CPF Sol'n	Deleted Defining Eqn.	Added Defining Eqn.	Deleted Ind. Var.	Added Ind. Var
1	(0,0)	$x_2=0$	$-x_1+2x_2=15$	x_2	x_3
2	(0,7.5)	$x_1=0$	$x_1+x_2=12$	x_1	x_4
3	(3,9)	Optimal			

5.1-3. a)

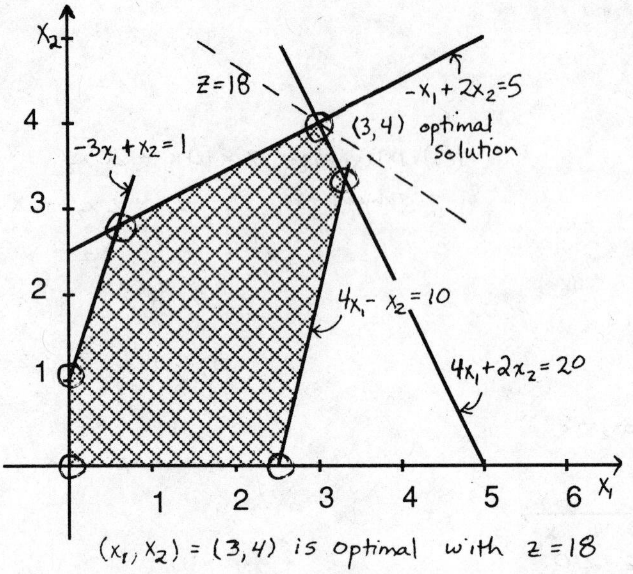

$(x_1, x_2) = (3,4)$ is optimal with $Z=18$

b)

CPF Sol'ns	Defining Eqns	BF Solutions	Non-basic var's	Z
(0,0)	$x_1=0$ $x_2=0$	(0, 0, 1, 20, 10, 5)	x_1 & x_2	0
(0,1)	$x_1=0$ $-3x_1+x_2=1$	(0, 1, 0, 18, 11, 3)	x_1 & x_3	3
(0.6, 2.8)	$-3x_1+x_2=1$ $-x_1+2x_2=5$	(0.6, 2.8, 0, 12, 10.4, 0)	x_3 & x_6	9.6
(3, 4) *	$-x_1+2x_2=5$ $4x_1+2x_2=20$	(3, 4, 6, 0, 2, 0)	x_4 & x_6	18 *
(3.33, 3.33)	$4x_1+2x_2=20$ $4x_1-x_2=10$	(3.33, 3.33, 7.67, 0, 0, 1.67)	x_4 & x_5	16.67
(2.5, 0)	$4x_1-x_2=10$ $x_2=0$	(2.5, 0, 8.5, 10, 0, 7.5)	x_2 & x_5	5

* Optimal

5.1-3. c)

CP Infeas Sol'ns	Defining Eqns	B Infeas Sol'ns	Non-basic Var's
$(-1/3, 0)$	$-3x_1 + x_2 = 1$ $x_2 = 0$	$(-\frac{1}{3}, 0, 0, 21\frac{1}{3}, 11\frac{1}{3}, 4\frac{2}{3})$	x_3 x_2
$(-5, 0)$	$-x_1 + 2x_2 = 5$ $x_2 = 0$	$(-5, 0, -14, 40, 30, 0)$	x_6 x_2
$(0, 10)$	$4x_1 + 2x_2 = 20$ $x_1 = 0$	$(0, 10, -9, 0, 20, -15)$	x_4 x_1
$(0, \frac{5}{2})$	$-x_1 + 2x_2 = 5$ $x_1 = 0$	$(0, \frac{5}{2}, -\frac{3}{2}, 15, 12\frac{1}{2}, 0)$	x_6 x_1
$(\frac{9}{5}, \frac{32}{5})$	$4x_1 + 2x_2 = 20$ $-3x_1 + x_2 = 1$	$(\frac{9}{5}, \frac{32}{5}, 0, 0, \frac{46}{5}, -6)$	x_4 x_3
$(11, 34)$	$-3x_1 + x_2 = 1$ $4x_1 - x_2 = 10$	$(11, 34, 0, -92, 0, -52)$	x_3 x_5
$(\frac{25}{7}, \frac{30}{7})$	$4x_1 - x_2 = 10$ $-x_1 + 2x_2 = 5$	$(\frac{25}{7}, \frac{30}{7}, \frac{52}{7}, \frac{-20}{7}, 0, 0)$	x_5 x_6
$(5, 0)$	$4x_1 + 2x_2 = 20$ $x_2 = 0$	$(5, 0, 16, 0, -10, 10)$	x_4 x_2
$(0, -10)$	$4x_1 - x_2 = 10$ $x_1 = 0$	$(0, -10, 11, 40, 0, 25)$	x_5 x_1

All sets yield a solution.

5.1-4. a) $(x_1, x_2, x_3) = (10, 0, 0)$

b) $x_2 = 0$

$x_3 = 0$

$x_1 - x_2 + 2x_3 = 10$

5.1-5. (a)

Corner Point Feasible Solution	Defining Equations
(0,0,0)	$x_1=0$, $x_2=0$, $x_3=0$
(4,0,0)	$x_1=4$, $x_2=0$, $x_3=0$
(4,2,0)	$x_1=4$, $x_1+x_2=6$, $x_3=0$
(2,4,0)	$x_2=4$, $x_1+x_2=6$, $x_3=0$
(0,4,0)	$x_1=0$, $x_2=4$, $x_3=0$
(0,4,2)	$x_1=0$, $x_2=4$, $-x_1+2x_3=4$
(2,4,3)	$x_1+x_2=6$, $x_2=4$, $-x_1+2x_3=4$
(4,2,4)	$x_1+x_2=6$, $x_1=4$, $-x_1+2x_3=4$
(4,0,4)	$x_2=0$, $x_1=4$, $-x_1+2x_3=4$
(0,0,2)	$x_2=0$, $x_1=0$, $-x_1+2x_3=4$

(b)

$x_1+x_2=6$

$x_2=0$

$-x_1+2x_3=4$

(c)

$x_1=4$

$x_1=0$ The system is inconsistent.

$x_2=0$

5.1-6. (a) & (b)

Defining Equations	Corner Point	Feasible?	Basic Solution $(y_1, y_2, y_3, y_4, y_5)$	Nonbasic Variables
$y_1=0$, $y_2=0$, $y_3=0$	(0,0,0)	No	(0,0,0,-3,-5)	y_1, y_2, y_3
$y_1=0$, $y_2=0$, $y_1+3y_3=3$	(0,0,1)	No	(0,0,1,0,-3)	y_1, y_2, y_4
$y_1=0$, $y_2=0$, $2y_2+2y_3=5$	(0,0,2.5)	Yes	(0,0,2.5,4.5,0)	y_1, y_2, y_5
$y_1=0$, $y_1+3y_3=3$, $y_3=0$	No Solution			y_1, y_3, y_4
$y_1=0$, $2y_2+2y_3=5$, $y_3=0$	(0,2.5,0)	No	(0,2.5,0,-3,0)	y_1, y_3, y_5
$y_2=0$, $y_1+3y_3=3$, $y_3=0$	(3,0,0)	No	(3,0,0,0,-5)	y_2, y_3, y_4
$y_2=0$, $2y_2+2y_3=5$, $y_3=0$	No Solution			y_2, y_3, y_5
$y_2=0$, $y_1+3y_3=3$, $2y_2+2y_3=5$	(-4.5,0,2.5)	No	(-4.5,0,2.5,0,0)	y_2, y_4, y_5
$y_3=0$, $y_1+3y_3=3$, $2y_2+2y_3=5$	(3,2.5,0)	Yes	(3,2.5,0,0,0)	y_3, y_4, y_5
$y_1=0$, $y_1+3y_3=3$, $2y_2+2y_3=5$	(0,1.5,1)	Yes	(0,1.5,1,0,0)	y_1, y_4, y_5

5.1- 7.(a)

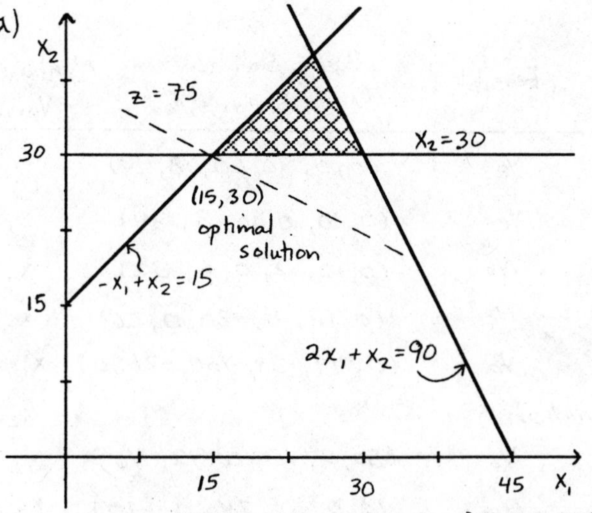

$(x_1, x_2) = (15, 30)$ is optimal with $z = 75$

(b)

Corner Point	Defining Equations	Basic Feasible Solution $(x_1, x_2, x_3, x_4, x_5)$	Nonbasic Variables
(15, 30)	$x_2 = 30$, $-x_1 + x_2 = 15$	(15, 30, 0, 30, 0)	x_3 and x_5
(30, 30)	$x_2 = 30$, $2x_1 + x_2 = 90$	(30, 30, 15, 0, 0)	x_4 and x_5
(25, 40)	$-x_1 + x_2 = 15$, $2x_1 + x_2 = 90$	(25, 40, 0, 0, 10)	x_3 and x_4

5.1- 8. (a) and (b)

Defining Equations	Corner Point	Feasible?	Basic Solution $(x_1, x_2, x_3, x_4, x_5)$	Nonbasic Variables
$x_1 = 0$, $x_2 = 0$	(0,0)	No	(0, 0, -10, 6, -6)	x_1 and x_2
$x_1 = 0$, $2x_1 + x_2 = 10$	(0, 10)	No	(0, 10, 0, -14, 4)	x_1 and x_3
$x_1 = 0$, $-3x_1 + 2x_2 = 6$	(0, 3)	No	(0, 3, -7, 0, -3)	x_1 and x_4
$x_1 = 0$, $x_1 + x_2 = 6$	(0, 6)	No	(0, 6, -4, -6, 0)	x_1 and x_5
$x_2 = 0$, $2x_1 + x_2 = 10$	(5, 0)	No	(5, 0, 0, 21, -11)	x_2 and x_3
$x_2 = 0$, $-3x_1 + 2x_2 = 6$	(-2, 0)	No	(-2, 0, -14, 0, -8)	x_2 and x_4
$x_2 = 0$, $x_1 + x_2 = 6$	(6, 0)	Yes	(6, 0, 2, 24, 0)	x_2 and x_5
$2x_1 + x_2 = 10$, $-3x_1 + 2x_2 = 6$	(2, 6)	Yes	(2, 6, 0, 0, 8)	x_3 and x_4
$2x_1 + x_2 = 10$, $x_1 + x_2 = 6$	(4, 2)	Yes	(4, 2, 0, 14, 0)	x_3 and x_5
$-3x_1 + 2x_2 = 6$, $x_1 + x_2 = 6$	(1.2, 4.8)	No	(1.2, 4.8, -2.8, 0, 0)	x_4 and x_5

5.1-9. (a) and (b)

Defining Equations	Corner Point	Feasible?	Basic Solution $(x_1, x_2, x_3, x_4, x_5, x_6)$	Nonbasic Variables
$x_1=0$, $x_2=0$	(0,0)	Yes	(0, 0, 10, 60, 18, 44)	x_1 and x_2
$x_1=0$, $x_2=10$	(0,10)	Yes	(0, 10, 0, 10, 8, 34)	x_1 and x_3
$x_1=0$, $2x_1+5x_2=60$	(0,12)	No	(0, 12, -2, 0, 6, 32)	x_1 and x_4
$x_1=0$, $x_1+x_2=18$	(0,18)	No	(0, 18, -8, -30, 0, 26)	x_1 and x_5
$x_1=0$, $3x_1+x_2=44$	(0,44)	No	(0, 44, -34, -160, -26, 0)	x_1 and x_6
$x_2=0$, $x_2=10$	No Solution			x_2 and x_3
$x_2=0$, $2x_1+5x_2=60$	(30,0)	No	(30, 0, 10, 0, -12, -46)	x_2 and x_4
$x_2=0$, $x_1+x_2=18$	(18,0)	No	(18, 0, 10, 24, 0, -10)	x_2 and x_5
$x_2=0$, $3x_1+x_2=44$	(14.67,0)	Yes	(14.67, 0, 10, 30.67, 3.33, 0)	x_2 and x_6
$x_2=10$, $2x_1+5x_2=60$	(5,10)	Yes	(5, 10, 0, 0, 3, 19)	x_3 and x_4
$x_2=10$, $x_1+x_2=18$	(8,10)	No	(8, 10, 0, -6, 0, 10)	x_3 and x_5
$x_3=10$, $3x_1+x_2=44$	(11.33,10)	No	(11.33, 10, 0, -12.67, -3.33, 0)	x_3 and x_6
$2x_1+5x_2=60$, $x_1+x_2=18$	(10,8)	Yes	(10, 8, 2, 0, 0, 6)	x_4 and x_5
$2x_1+5x_2=60$, $3x_1+x_2=44$	(12.31,7.08)	No	(12.31, 7.08, 2.92, 0, -1.38, 0)	x_4 and x_6
$x_1+x_2=18$, $3x_1+x_2=44$	(13,5)	Yes	(13, 5, 5, 9, 0, 0)	x_5 and x_6

5.1-10. a) False, (p. 5-10) Property 1: (a) If there is exactly one optimal solution, then it must be a CPF. (b) If there are multiple optimal solutions, then at least 2 must be adjacent CPF Sol'ns. We can take a convex combination of 2 optimal CPF Soln's to get a non-CPF optimal solution, for example.

b) False, the number of CPF solutions is at most $\frac{(m+n)!}{m!\,n!} = \binom{m+n}{n}$ (p. 5-12).

c) False, Property 3 (p. 5-13). If this statement were true, it would mean no matter which CPF we started on, it or one of its adjacent CPF solutions would be optimal! (which, of course, is not the case)

5.1-11. (*a*) True. By property 1(*a*), there must be multiple solutions (since this optimal solution is not a CPF). This then means there are an infinite number of optimal solutions since any convex combination of optimal solutions is also optimal.
(*b*) True. The points on the line segment connecting x^* and x^{**} can be represented by $x = \alpha Z^* + (1 - \alpha)x^{**}$, α ranging from 0 to 1. Let $Z^* = Z^{**}$ represent the objective function values for x^* and x^{**}. Then the objective function value at x would be (by linearity) $Z = \alpha Z^* + (1 - \alpha)Z^{**} = \alpha Z^* + (1 - \alpha) Z^* = Z^*$. So the objective function value is the same at all these points. Furthermore, since the feasible region is convex, all these points must be feasible.
(*c*) False. The simultaneous solution of any set of n constraint boundary equations may be infeasible, or it may not even exist (e.g., $x_1 = 2, x_1 = 4$).

5.1-12. (*a*). True. If there are *no* optimal solutions, then the problem must have no feasible solutions *or* the objective value can be increased indefinitely (Chap. 3). The former is not the case (assumed in the problem) and the latter cannot be true since the feasible region is *bounded.* Thus, there must be at least one optimal solution.
(*b*) False. If a solution is optimal, it need not be a BF solution. A convex combination of BF solutions can give an optimal but not Basic (i.e. CP) solution. However, it is true that if optimal solutions exist, then at least one of them must be a BF solution. This follows straight from Property 1 (since BF solutions $\Rightarrow$ CPF solutions).
(*c*) True. Since BF solutions correspond to CPF solutions, this follows directly from Property 2.

5.1-13. $x_1 = 0$

$2x_1 + x_2 + 3x_3 = 60$

$3x_1 + 3x_2 + 5x_3 = 120$

This system has solution $(x_1, x_2, x_3) = (0, 15, 15)$

5.1-14. Since $x_2 > 0$ and $x_3 > 0$, $x_2 = 0$ and $x_3 = 0$ cannot be part of the three boundary equations. Therefore, the boundary equations are:

$$x_1 = 0$$
$$2x_1 + x_2 + x_3 = 20$$
$$3x_1 + x_2 + 2x_3 = 30$$

The solution to this set of equation (and, therefore, the optimal) is: $(x_1, x_2, x_3) = (0, 10, 10)$

5.1-15. Since $x_1 > 0$ and $x_3 > 0$, $x_1 = 0$ and $x_3 = 0$ can't be part of the three boundary equations. If $x_2 = 0$, then $x_1 + x_3 \le 24$ and $3x_1 + 3x_3 \le 60$ or, equivalently, $x_1 + x_3 \le 24$ and $x_1 + x_3 \le 20$. This implies the second constraint must have some slack and can't be a boundary equation. Therefore, the boundary equations are: $x_2 = 0$

$$x_1 + 3x_2 + 2x_3 = 30$$
$$3x_1 + 5x_2 + 3x_3 = 60.$$

The optimal solution is $(x_1, x_2, x_3) = (10, 0, 10)$

5.1-16. a)

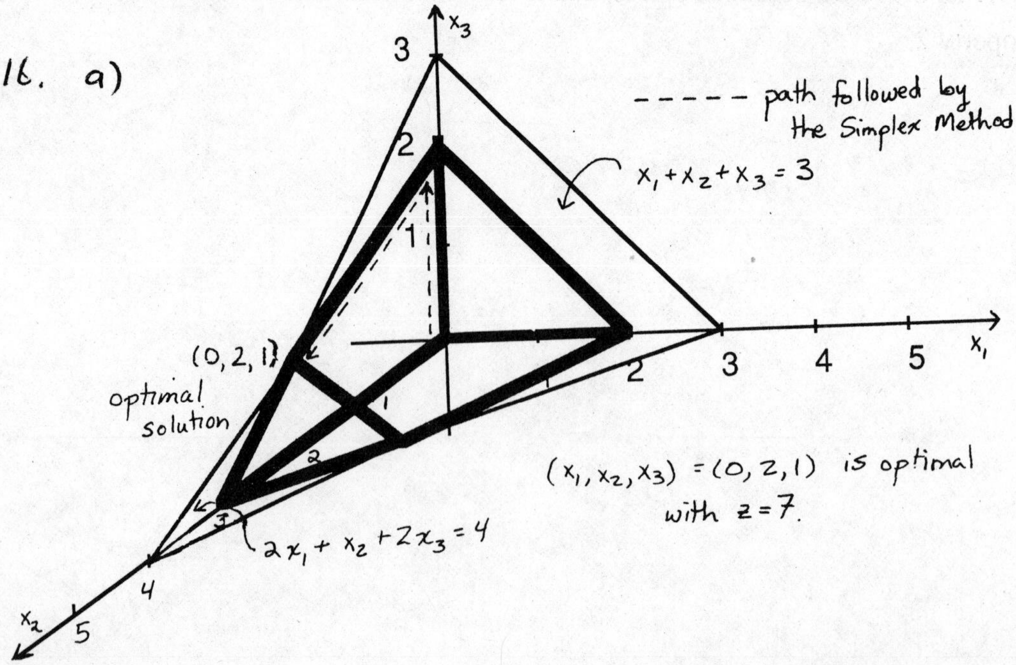

$(x_1, x_2, x_3) = (0, 2, 1)$ is optimal with $z = 7$.

5.1-16.

(b) The path is chosen because moving along the edges chosen provides the greatest increase in the objective value for a unit move in the chosen direction for any possible edge at each vertex/decision point.

(c)

Edge	Constraint Boundary Equations	End Points	Additional Constraint
1	$x_2=0$, $x_1=0$	(0, 0, 0) (0, 0, 2)	$x_3=0$ $2x_1+x_2+2x_3=4$
2	$2x_1+x_2+2x_3=4$, $x_1=0$	(0, 0, 2) (0, 2, 1)	$x_2=0$ $x_1+x_2+x_3=3$

(d) and (e)

Corner Point	Defining Equations	Basic Feasible Solution $(x_1, x_2, x_3, x_4, x_5)$	Nonbasic Variables
(0, 0, 0)	$x_1=0$, $x_2=0$, $x_3=0$	(0, 0, 0, 4, 3)	x_1, x_2, x_3
(0, 0, 2)	$x_1=0$, $x_2=0$, $2x_1+x_2+2x_3=4$	(0, 0, 2, 0, 1)	x_1, x_2, x_4
(0, 2, 1)	$x_1=0$, $2x_1+x_2+2x_3=4$, $x_1+x_2+x_3=3$	(0, 0, 2, 0, 1)	x_1, x_4, x_5

The nonbasic variables, having value zero, are equivalent to indicating variables. They indicate that their associated inequality constraints are actually equalities. These associated equalities are the defining equations.

5.1-17. a)

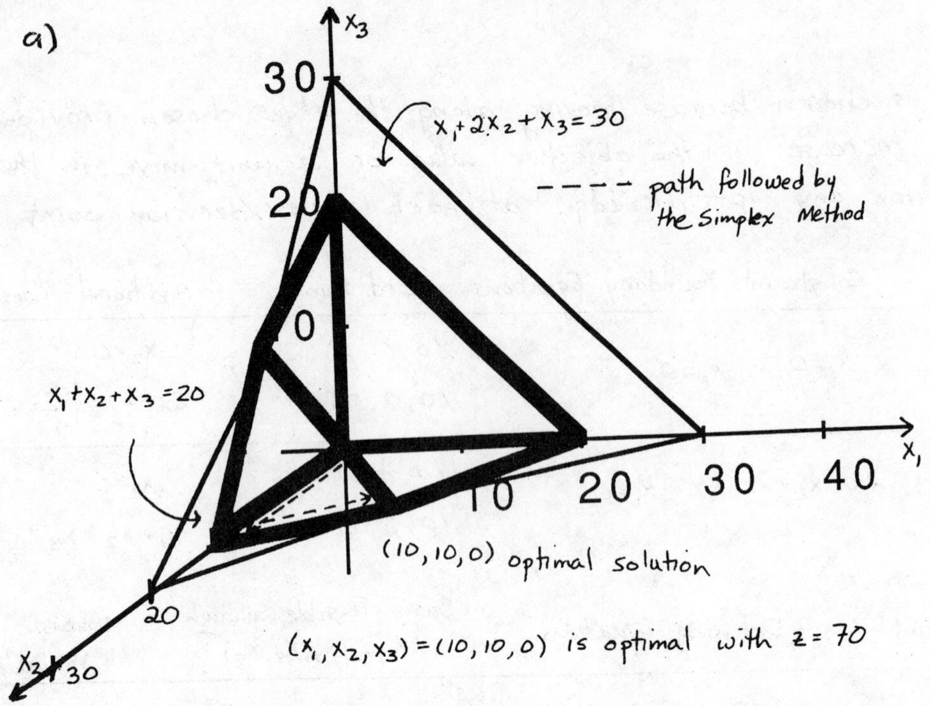

$(x_1, x_2, x_3) = (10, 10, 0)$ is optimal with $z = 70$

(b) The path is chosen because moving along these edges provides the greatest increase in the objective value for a unit move in the chosen direction for any possible edge at each vertex / decision point.

(c)

Edge	Constraint Boundary Equations	End Points	Additional Constraint
1	$x_1 = 0$, $x_3 = 0$	(0,0,0) (0,15,0)	$x_2 = 0$ $x_1 + 2x_2 + x_3 = 30$
2	$x_3 = 0$, $x_1 + 2x_2 + x_3 = 30$	(0,15,0) (10,10,0)	$x_1 = 0$ $x_1 + x_2 + x_3 = 20$

(d) and (e)

Corner Point	Defining Equations	Basic Feasible Solution $(x_1, x_2, x_3, x_4, x_5)$	Nonbasic Variables
(0,0,0)	$x_1 = 0$, $x_2 = 0$, $x_3 = 0$	(0,0,0,20,30)	x_1, x_2, x_3
(0,15,0)	$x_1 = 0$, $x_3 = 0$, $x_1 + 2x_2 + x_3 = 30$	(0, 15, 0, 5, 0)	x_1, x_3, x_5
(10,10,0)	$x_3 = 0$, $x_1 + 2x_2 + x_3 = 30$, $x_1 + x_2 + x_3 = 20$	(10, 10, 0, 0, 0)	x_3, x_4, x_5

The nonbasic variables, having value zero, are equivalent to indicating variables. They indicate that their associated inequality constraints are actually equalities. These associated equalities are the defining equations.

5.1-18. (a) For the objective function Maximize $z = x_3$, both corner points $(4,2,4)$ and $(4,0,4)$ provide the maximum value $z = 4$

(b) For the objective function Maximize $z = -x_1 + 2x_3$, all the corner points, $(0,0,2)$, $(4,0,4)$, $(4,2,4)$, $(2,4,3)$ and $(0,4,2)$ provide the maximum value $z = 4$

5.1-19. (a) Geometrically each constraint is a plane and the points feasible for a given (inequality) constraint form a half-space. The line segment defined by any two feasible points must lie entirely on the feasible side of the plane and, therefore, all points on the line segment are feasible implying that the set of solutions for any one constraint is a convex set.

(b) Because the points in the feasible region of the linear program satisfy all constraints simultaneously, it must be the case that for any two feasible points the points on the line segment joining them must also satisfy each constraint (from part (a)). Therefore, the set of solutions that satisfy all constraints simultaneously is a convex set.

5.1-20. For the objective function Maximize $z = 3x_1 + 4x_2 + 3x_3$, starting at the point $(0,0,0)$ the first edge chosen would be that connecting to $(0,4,0)$ because moving along that edge increases z faster than any other edge.

From $(0,4,0)$ the edge that increases z fastest connects to either $(0,4,2)$ or $(2,4,0)$. From either of these the edge with fastest increase connects to $(2,4,3)$. From $(2,4,3)$ the only edge that will provide an increase in z connects to the optimal solution $(4,2,4)$

5.1-21. (a)

Original Constraint	Boundary Equation	Indicating Variable.
$x_1 \geq 0$	$x_1 = 0$	x_1
$x_2 \geq 0$	$x_2 = 0$	x_2
$x_3 \geq 0$	$x_3 = 0$	x_3
$x_1 + x_4 = 4$	$x_1 = 4$	x_4
$x_2 + x_5 = 4$	$x_2 = 4$	x_5
$x_1 + x_2 + x_6 = 6$	$x_1 + x_2 = 6$	x_6
$-x_1 + 2x_3 + x_7 = 4$	$-x_1 + 2x_3 = 4$	x_7

(b)

Corner Point Feasible Solution	Defining Equations	Basic Feasible Solutions $(x_1, x_2, x_3, x_4, x_5, x_6, x_7)$	Nonbasic Variables
(2, 4, 3)	$x_1 + x_2 = 6$, $x_2 = 4$, $-x_1 + 2x_3 = 4$	(2, 4, 3, 2, 0, 0, 0)	x_5, x_6, x_7
(4, 2, 4)	$x_1 + x_2 = 6$, $-x_1 + 2x_3 = 4$, $x_1 = 4$	(4, 2, 4, 0, 2, 0, 0)	x_4, x_6, x_7
(0, 4, 2)	$x_1 = 0$, $x_2 = 4$, $-x_1 + 2x_3 = 4$	(0, 4, 2, 4, 0, 2, 0)	x_1, x_5, x_7
(2, 4, 0)	$x_3 = 0$, $x_1 + x_2 = 6$, $x_2 = 4$	(2, 4, 0, 2, 0, 0, 6)	x_3, x_5, x_6

(c) Because the sets of defining equations of (4, 2, 4), (0, 4, 2) and (2, 4, 0) differ from the set of defining equations of (2, 4, 3) by only one equation, they are adjacent to (2, 4, 3). Since the sets of defining equations of (4, 2, 4), (0, 4, 2) and (2, 4, 0) differ by more than one equation they are not adjacent.

If we substitute "nonbasic variables" for "defining equations" and "variable" for "equation," we see the same statement is true.

5.1-22. (a) x_5 enters

(b) x_4 leaves

(c) (4, 2, 4, 0, 2, 0, 0)

5.1-23.

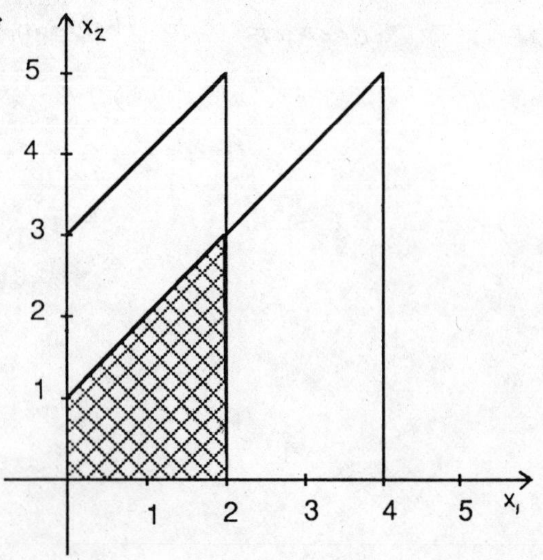

(a) The optimal solution is:

$$\begin{pmatrix} x_3 \\ x_1 \\ x_5 \end{pmatrix} = B^{-1}b = \frac{1}{27}\begin{pmatrix} 11 & -3 & 1 \\ -6 & 9 & -3 \\ 2 & -3 & 10 \end{pmatrix}\begin{pmatrix} 180 \\ 270 \\ 180 \end{pmatrix} = \begin{pmatrix} 50 \\ 30 \\ 50 \end{pmatrix}$$

$$z = c^T x = (8, 4, 6, 3, 9)\begin{pmatrix} 30 \\ 0 \\ 50 \\ 0 \\ 50 \end{pmatrix} = 990$$

(b) The shadow prices are:

$$c_B B^{-1} = \frac{1}{27}(6, 8, 9)\begin{pmatrix} 11 & -3 & 1 \\ -6 & 9 & -3 \\ 2 & -3 & 10 \end{pmatrix} = \begin{pmatrix} 1.33 \\ 1 \\ 2.67 \end{pmatrix}$$

5.2-1 (a) The optimal solution is:

$$\begin{pmatrix} x_3 \\ x_1 \\ x_5 \end{pmatrix} = B^{-1} b = \frac{1}{27} \begin{pmatrix} 11 & -3 & 1 \\ -6 & 9 & -3 \\ 2 & -3 & 10 \end{pmatrix} \begin{pmatrix} 180 \\ 270 \\ 180 \end{pmatrix} = \begin{pmatrix} 50 \\ 30 \\ 50 \end{pmatrix}$$

$$z = c^T x = (8, 4, 6, 3, 9) \begin{pmatrix} 30 \\ 0 \\ 50 \\ 0 \\ 50 \end{pmatrix} = 990$$

(b) The shadow prices are:

$$c_B B^{-1} = \frac{1}{27} (6, 8, 9) \begin{pmatrix} 11 & -3 & 1 \\ -6 & 9 & -3 \\ 2 & -3 & 10 \end{pmatrix} = \begin{pmatrix} 1.33 \\ 1 \\ 2.67 \end{pmatrix}$$

Note: In early printings the first and third constraints are incorrect. However, working from the given information following the constraints gives the above answers.

5.2-2. $c = (5, 8, 7, 4, 6, 0, 0)$, $A = \begin{pmatrix} 2 & 3 & 3 & 2 & 2 & 1 & 0 \\ 3 & 5 & 4 & 2 & 4 & 0 & 1 \end{pmatrix}$, $b = \begin{pmatrix} 20 \\ 30 \end{pmatrix}$

Iteration 0: $B = B^{-1} = \begin{pmatrix} 1 & 0 \\ 0 & 1 \end{pmatrix}$ $x_B = \begin{pmatrix} x_6 \\ x_7 \end{pmatrix} = \begin{pmatrix} 1 & 0 \\ 0 & 1 \end{pmatrix}\begin{pmatrix} 20 \\ 30 \end{pmatrix} = \begin{pmatrix} 20 \\ 30 \end{pmatrix}$

$c_B = (0,0)$ $-c = (-5, -8, -7, -4, -6, 0, 0)$ so x_2 enters

Revised x_2 coefficients: $\begin{pmatrix} 1 & 0 \\ 0 & 1 \end{pmatrix}\begin{pmatrix} 3 \\ 5 \end{pmatrix} = \begin{pmatrix} 3 \\ 5 \end{pmatrix}$ so x_7 leaves the basis

Iteration 1: $\eta = \begin{pmatrix} -3/5 \\ 1/5 \end{pmatrix}$ $B^{-1}_{NEW} = \begin{pmatrix} 1 & -3/5 \\ 0 & 1/5 \end{pmatrix}$ $x_B = \begin{pmatrix} x_6 \\ x_2 \end{pmatrix} = \begin{pmatrix} 1 & -3/5 \\ 0 & 1/5 \end{pmatrix}\begin{pmatrix} 20 \\ 30 \end{pmatrix} = \begin{pmatrix} 2 \\ 6 \end{pmatrix}$

$c_B = (0,8)$ Revised Row 0: $(0, \tfrac{8}{5})\begin{pmatrix} 2 & 3 & 3 & 2 & 2 & 1 & 0 \\ 3 & 5 & 4 & 2 & 4 & 0 & 1 \end{pmatrix} - (5,8,7,4,6,0,0)$

$= (-\tfrac{1}{5}, 0, -\tfrac{3}{5}, -\tfrac{4}{5}, \tfrac{2}{5}, 0, \tfrac{8}{5})$

so x_4 enters the basis

Revised x_4 coefficients: $\begin{pmatrix} 1 & -3/5 \\ 0 & 1/5 \end{pmatrix}\begin{pmatrix} 2 \\ 2 \end{pmatrix} = \begin{pmatrix} 4/5 \\ 2/5 \end{pmatrix}$ so x_6 leaves the basis

Iteration 2: $\eta = \begin{pmatrix} 5/4 \\ -1/2 \end{pmatrix}$ $B^{-1}_{NEW} = \begin{pmatrix} 5/4 & -3/4 \\ -1/2 & 1/2 \end{pmatrix}$ $x_B = \begin{pmatrix} x_4 \\ x_2 \end{pmatrix} = \begin{pmatrix} 5/4 & -3/4 \\ -1/2 & 1/2 \end{pmatrix}\begin{pmatrix} 20 \\ 30 \end{pmatrix} = \begin{pmatrix} 5/2 \\ 5 \end{pmatrix}$

$c_B = (4,8)$ Revised Row 0: $(1,1)\begin{pmatrix} 2 & 3 & 3 & 2 & 2 & 1 & 0 \\ 3 & 5 & 4 & 2 & 4 & 0 & 1 \end{pmatrix} - (5,8,7,4,6,0,0)$

$= (0,0,0,0,0,1,1)$

Current Solution is optimal

$(x_1, x_2, x_3, x_4, x_5) = (0, 5, 0, \tfrac{5}{2}, 0)$ $Z = 8 \cdot 5 + 4 \cdot \tfrac{5}{2} = 50$

5.2-3. $c = (4, 3, 6, 0, 0)$, $A = \begin{pmatrix} 3 & 1 & 3 & 1 & 0 \\ 2 & 2 & 3 & 0 & 1 \end{pmatrix}$, $b = \begin{pmatrix} 30 \\ 40 \end{pmatrix}$

Iteration 0: $B = B^{-1} = \begin{pmatrix} 1 & 0 \\ 0 & 1 \end{pmatrix}$ $x_B = \begin{pmatrix} x_4 \\ x_5 \end{pmatrix} = \begin{pmatrix} 1 & 0 \\ 0 & 1 \end{pmatrix}\begin{pmatrix} 30 \\ 40 \end{pmatrix} = \begin{pmatrix} 30 \\ 40 \end{pmatrix}$

$c_B = (0,0)$ $-c = (-4, -3, -6, 0, 0)$ so x_3 enters the basis

Revised x_3 coefficients: $\begin{pmatrix} 1 & 0 \\ 0 & 1 \end{pmatrix}\begin{pmatrix} 3 \\ 3 \end{pmatrix} = \begin{pmatrix} 3 \\ 3 \end{pmatrix}$ so x_4 leaves the basis

Iteration 1: $\eta = \begin{pmatrix} 1/3 \\ -1 \end{pmatrix}$ $B^{-1}_{NEW} = \begin{pmatrix} 1/3 & 0 \\ -1 & 1 \end{pmatrix}$ $x_B = \begin{pmatrix} x_3 \\ x_5 \end{pmatrix} = \begin{pmatrix} 1/3 & 0 \\ -1 & 1 \end{pmatrix}\begin{pmatrix} 30 \\ 40 \end{pmatrix} = \begin{pmatrix} 10 \\ 10 \end{pmatrix}$

5.2-3. (cont')

$c_B = (6, 0)$ Revised Row 0 : $(2,0)\begin{pmatrix} 3 & 1 & 3 & 1 & 0 \\ 2 & 2 & 3 & 0 & 1 \end{pmatrix} - (4,3,6,0,0)$

$= (2,-1,0,2,0)$ so x_2 enters the basis.

Revised x_2 coefficients : $\begin{pmatrix} 1/3 & 0 \\ -1 & 1 \end{pmatrix}\begin{pmatrix} 1 \\ 2 \end{pmatrix} = \begin{pmatrix} 1/3 \\ 1 \end{pmatrix}$ so x_5 leaves the basis.

Iteration 2 : $\eta = \begin{pmatrix} -\frac{1}{2} \\ \frac{1}{2} \end{pmatrix}$ $B^{-1}_{NEW} = \begin{pmatrix} 2/3 & -1/3 \\ -1 & 1 \end{pmatrix}$ $x_B = \begin{pmatrix} x_3 \\ x_2 \end{pmatrix} = \begin{pmatrix} 2/3 & -1/3 \\ -1 & 1 \end{pmatrix}\begin{pmatrix} 30 \\ 40 \end{pmatrix} = \begin{pmatrix} 20/3 \\ 10 \end{pmatrix}$

$c_B = (6, 3)$ Revised Row 0 : $(1,1)\begin{pmatrix} 3 & 1 & 3 & 1 & 0 \\ 2 & 2 & 3 & 0 & 1 \end{pmatrix} - (4,3,6,0,0)$

$= (1, 0, 0, 1, 1)$

Current Solution is optimal.

$(x_1, x_2, x_3) = (0, 10, \frac{20}{3})$ $z = 10 \cdot 3 + \frac{20}{3} \cdot 6 = 70.$

5.2-4. For Corner Point $(0,0)$: $x_B = \begin{pmatrix} x_3 \\ x_4 \end{pmatrix}$ $B = \begin{pmatrix} 1 & 0 \\ 0 & 1 \end{pmatrix} = B^{-1}$

$x_B = \begin{pmatrix} 1 & 0 \\ 0 & 1 \end{pmatrix}\begin{pmatrix} 6 \\ 6 \end{pmatrix} = \begin{pmatrix} 6 \\ 6 \end{pmatrix}$ Row 0 $= (-3, -2, 0, 0)$

For Corner Point $(3,0)$: $x_B = \begin{pmatrix} x_1 \\ x_4 \end{pmatrix}$ $B = \begin{pmatrix} 2 & 0 \\ 1 & 1 \end{pmatrix}$ $B^{-1} = \begin{pmatrix} \frac{1}{2} & 0 \\ -\frac{1}{2} & 1 \end{pmatrix}$

$x_B = \begin{pmatrix} \frac{1}{2} & 0 \\ -\frac{1}{2} & 1 \end{pmatrix}\begin{pmatrix} 6 \\ 6 \end{pmatrix} = \begin{pmatrix} 3 \\ 3 \end{pmatrix}$ $c_B = (3, 0)$

Row 0 $= (\frac{3}{2}, 0)\begin{pmatrix} 2 & 1 & 1 & 0 \\ 1 & 2 & 0 & 1 \end{pmatrix} - (3,2,0,0) = (0, -\frac{1}{2}, \frac{3}{2}, 0)$

For Corner Point $(2,2)$: $x_B = \begin{pmatrix} x_1 \\ x_2 \end{pmatrix}$ $B = \begin{pmatrix} 2 & 1 \\ 1 & 2 \end{pmatrix}$ $B^{-1} = \begin{pmatrix} 2/3 & -1/3 \\ -1/3 & 2/3 \end{pmatrix}$

$x_B = \begin{pmatrix} 2/3 & -1/3 \\ -1/3 & 2/3 \end{pmatrix}\begin{pmatrix} 6 \\ 6 \end{pmatrix} = \begin{pmatrix} 2 \\ 2 \end{pmatrix}$ $c_B = (3, 2)$

Row 0 : $(3,2)\begin{pmatrix} 2 & 1 & 1 & 0 \\ 1 & 2 & 0 & 1 \end{pmatrix} - (3,2,0,0) = (0, 0, 1/3, 1/3)$

$(x_1, x_2) = (2, 2)$ is optimal with $z = 3 \cdot 2 + 2 \cdot 2 = 10$

5.2-5. $c = (1, 2, 0, 0)$ $\quad A = \begin{pmatrix} 1 & 3 & 1 & 0 \\ 1 & 1 & 0 & 1 \end{pmatrix}$ $\quad b = \begin{pmatrix} 8 \\ 4 \end{pmatrix}$

Iteration 0: $B = B^{-1} = \begin{pmatrix} 1 & 0 \\ 0 & 1 \end{pmatrix}$ $\quad x_B = \begin{pmatrix} x_3 \\ x_4 \end{pmatrix} = \begin{pmatrix} 1 & 0 \\ 0 & 1 \end{pmatrix}\begin{pmatrix} 8 \\ 4 \end{pmatrix} = \begin{pmatrix} 8 \\ 4 \end{pmatrix}$

$c_B = (0, 0)$ $\quad -c = (-1, -2, 0, 0)$ so x_2 enters the basis

Revised x_2 coefficients : $\begin{pmatrix} 1 & 0 \\ 0 & 1 \end{pmatrix}\begin{pmatrix} 3 \\ 1 \end{pmatrix} = \begin{pmatrix} 3 \\ 1 \end{pmatrix}$ so x_3 leaves the basis

Iteration 1: $\eta = \begin{pmatrix} 1/3 \\ -1/3 \end{pmatrix}$ $\quad B_{NEW}^{-1} = \begin{pmatrix} 1/3 & 0 \\ -1/3 & 1 \end{pmatrix}$ $\quad x_B = \begin{pmatrix} x_2 \\ x_4 \end{pmatrix} = \begin{pmatrix} 1/3 & 0 \\ -1/3 & 1 \end{pmatrix}\begin{pmatrix} 8 \\ 4 \end{pmatrix} = \begin{pmatrix} 8/3 \\ 4/3 \end{pmatrix}$

$c_B = (2, 0)$ $\quad$ Revised Row 0: $(2/3, 0)\begin{pmatrix} 1 & 3 & 1 & 0 \\ 1 & 1 & 0 & 1 \end{pmatrix} - (1, 2, 0, 0)$

$= (-1/3, 0, 2/3, 0)$ $\quad x_1$ enters the basis

Revised x_1 coefficients : $\begin{pmatrix} 1/3 & 0 \\ -1/3 & 1 \end{pmatrix}\begin{pmatrix} 1 \\ 1 \end{pmatrix} = \begin{pmatrix} 1/3 \\ 2/3 \end{pmatrix}$ $\quad x_4$ leaves the basis

Iteration 2: $\eta = \begin{pmatrix} -1/2 \\ 3/2 \end{pmatrix}$ $\quad B_{NEW}^{-1} = \begin{pmatrix} 1/2 & -1/2 \\ -1/2 & 3/2 \end{pmatrix}$ $\quad x_B = \begin{pmatrix} x_2 \\ x_1 \end{pmatrix} = \begin{pmatrix} 1/2 & -1/2 \\ -1/2 & 3/2 \end{pmatrix}\begin{pmatrix} 8 \\ 4 \end{pmatrix} = \begin{pmatrix} 2 \\ 2 \end{pmatrix}$

$c_B = (2, 1)$ $\quad$ Revised Row 0 : $(1/2, 1/2)\begin{pmatrix} 1 & 3 & 1 & 0 \\ 1 & 1 & 0 & 1 \end{pmatrix} - (1, 2, 0, 0)$

$= (0, 0, 1/2, 1/2)$

Current Solution is optimal

$(x_1, x_2) = (2, 2)$ $\quad z = 2 \cdot 1 + 2 \cdot 2 = 6$

5.2-6. $c = (2, -2, 3, 0, 0, 0)$ $\quad A = \begin{pmatrix} -1 & 1 & 1 & 1 & 0 & 0 \\ 2 & -1 & 1 & 0 & 1 & 0 \\ 1 & 1 & 3 & 0 & 0 & 1 \end{pmatrix}$ $\quad b = \begin{pmatrix} 4 \\ 2 \\ 12 \end{pmatrix}$

Iteration 0: $B = B^{-1} = \begin{pmatrix} 1 & 0 & 0 \\ 0 & 1 & 0 \\ 0 & 0 & 1 \end{pmatrix}$ $\quad x_B = \begin{pmatrix} x_4 \\ x_5 \\ x_6 \end{pmatrix} = \begin{pmatrix} 1 & 0 & 0 \\ 0 & 1 & 0 \\ 0 & 0 & 1 \end{pmatrix}\begin{pmatrix} 4 \\ 2 \\ 12 \end{pmatrix} = \begin{pmatrix} 4 \\ 2 \\ 12 \end{pmatrix}$

$c_B = (0, 0, 0)$ $\quad -c = (-2, 2, -3, 0, 0, 0)$ $\quad x_3$ enters the basis

Revised x_3 coefficients : $\begin{pmatrix} 1 & 0 & 0 \\ 0 & 1 & 0 \\ 0 & 0 & 1 \end{pmatrix}\begin{pmatrix} 1 \\ 1 \\ 3 \end{pmatrix} = \begin{pmatrix} 1 \\ 1 \\ 3 \end{pmatrix}$ $\quad x_5$ leaves the basis.

Iteration 1: $\eta = \begin{pmatrix} -1 \\ 1 \\ -3 \end{pmatrix}$ $\quad B_{NEW}^{-1} = \begin{pmatrix} 1 & -1 & 0 \\ 0 & 1 & 0 \\ 0 & -3 & 1 \end{pmatrix}$ $\quad x_B = \begin{pmatrix} x_4 \\ x_3 \\ x_6 \end{pmatrix} = \begin{pmatrix} 1 & -1 & 0 \\ 0 & 1 & 0 \\ 0 & -3 & 1 \end{pmatrix}\begin{pmatrix} 4 \\ 2 \\ 12 \end{pmatrix} = \begin{pmatrix} 2 \\ 2 \\ 6 \end{pmatrix}$

$c_B = (0, 3, 0)$ $\quad$ Revised Row 0: $(0, 3, 0)\begin{pmatrix} -1 & 1 & 1 & 1 & 0 & 0 \\ 2 & -1 & 1 & 0 & 1 & 0 \\ 1 & 1 & 3 & 0 & 0 & 1 \end{pmatrix} - (2, -2, 3, 0, 0, 0)$

$= (4, -1, 0, 0, 3, 0)$ $\quad x_2$ enters the basis

5.2-6. (cont')

Revised x_2 coefficients: $\begin{pmatrix} 1 & -1 & 0 \\ 0 & 1 & 0 \\ 0 & -3 & 1 \end{pmatrix}\begin{pmatrix} 1 \\ -1 \\ 1 \end{pmatrix} = \begin{pmatrix} 2 \\ -1 \\ 4 \end{pmatrix}$ x_4 leaves the basis.

Iteration 2: $\eta = \begin{pmatrix} 1/2 \\ 1/2 \\ -2 \end{pmatrix}$ $B_{NEW}^{-1} = \begin{pmatrix} 1/2 & -1/2 & 0 \\ 1/2 & 1/2 & 0 \\ -2 & -1 & 1 \end{pmatrix}$ $x_B = \begin{pmatrix} x_2 \\ x_3 \\ x_6 \end{pmatrix} = \begin{pmatrix} \frac{1}{2} & -\frac{1}{2} & 0 \\ \frac{1}{2} & \frac{1}{2} & 0 \\ -2 & -1 & 1 \end{pmatrix}\begin{pmatrix} 4 \\ 2 \\ 12 \end{pmatrix} = \begin{pmatrix} 1 \\ 3 \\ 2 \end{pmatrix}$

$c_B = (-2, 3, 0)$ Revised Row 0: $(\frac{1}{2}, \frac{5}{2}, 0)\begin{pmatrix} -1 & 1 & 1 & 1 & 0 & 0 \\ 2 & -1 & 1 & 0 & 1 & 0 \\ 1 & 1 & 3 & 0 & 0 & 1 \end{pmatrix} - (2, -2, 3, 0, 0, 0)$

$= (\frac{5}{2}, 0, 0, \frac{1}{2}, \frac{5}{2}, 0)$

Current Solution is optimal

$(x_1, x_2, x_3) = (0, 1, 3)$ $z = -2 \cdot 1 + 3 \cdot 3 = 7$

5.2-7.a) $c = (10, 20, 0, 0, 0)$ $A = \begin{pmatrix} -1 & 2 & 1 & 0 & 0 \\ 1 & 1 & 0 & 1 & 0 \\ 5 & 3 & 0 & 0 & 1 \end{pmatrix}$ $b = \begin{pmatrix} 15 \\ 12 \\ 45 \end{pmatrix}$

Iteration 0: $B = B^{-1} = \begin{pmatrix} 1 & 0 & 0 \\ 0 & 1 & 0 \\ 0 & 0 & 1 \end{pmatrix}$ $x_B = \begin{pmatrix} x_3 \\ x_4 \\ x_5 \end{pmatrix} = \begin{pmatrix} 1 & 0 & 0 \\ 0 & 1 & 0 \\ 0 & 0 & 1 \end{pmatrix}\begin{pmatrix} 15 \\ 12 \\ 45 \end{pmatrix} = \begin{pmatrix} 15 \\ 12 \\ 45 \end{pmatrix}$

$c_B = (0, 0, 0)$ $-c = (-10, -20, 0, 0, 0)$ x_2 enters the basis

Revised x_2 coefficients: $\begin{pmatrix} 1 & 0 & 0 \\ 0 & 1 & 0 \\ 0 & 0 & 1 \end{pmatrix}\begin{pmatrix} 2 \\ 1 \\ 3 \end{pmatrix} = \begin{pmatrix} 2 \\ 1 \\ 3 \end{pmatrix}$ x_3 leaves the basis

Iteration 1: $\eta = \begin{pmatrix} 1/2 \\ -1/2 \\ -3/2 \end{pmatrix}$ $B_{NEW}^{-1} = \begin{pmatrix} \frac{1}{2} & 0 & 0 \\ -1/2 & 1 & 0 \\ -3/2 & 0 & 1 \end{pmatrix}$ $x_B = \begin{pmatrix} x_2 \\ x_4 \\ x_5 \end{pmatrix} = \begin{pmatrix} \frac{1}{2} & 0 & 0 \\ -\frac{1}{2} & 1 & 0 \\ -3/2 & 0 & 1 \end{pmatrix}\begin{pmatrix} 15 \\ 12 \\ 45 \end{pmatrix} = \begin{pmatrix} 15/2 \\ 9/2 \\ 45/2 \end{pmatrix}$

$c_B = (20, 0, 0)$ Revised Row 0: $(10, 0, 0)\begin{pmatrix} -1 & 2 & 1 & 0 & 0 \\ 1 & 1 & 0 & 1 & 0 \\ 5 & 3 & 0 & 0 & 1 \end{pmatrix} - (10, 20, 0, 0, 0)$

$= (-20, 0, 10, 0, 0)$ x_1 enters the basis

Revised x_1 coefficients: $\begin{pmatrix} 1/2 & 0 & 0 \\ -1/2 & 1 & 0 \\ -3/2 & 0 & 1 \end{pmatrix}\begin{pmatrix} -1 \\ 1 \\ 5 \end{pmatrix} = \begin{pmatrix} -1/2 \\ 3/2 \\ 13/2 \end{pmatrix}$ x_4 leaves the basis.

Iteration 2: $\eta = \begin{pmatrix} 1/3 \\ 2/3 \\ -13/3 \end{pmatrix}$ $B_{NEW}^{-1} = \begin{pmatrix} 1/3 & 1/3 & 0 \\ -1/3 & 2/3 & 0 \\ 2/3 & -13/3 & 1 \end{pmatrix}$ $x_B = \begin{pmatrix} x_2 \\ x_1 \\ x_5 \end{pmatrix} = \begin{pmatrix} \frac{1}{3} & 1/3 & 0 \\ -1/3 & 2/3 & 0 \\ 2/3 & -13/3 & 1 \end{pmatrix}\begin{pmatrix} 15 \\ 12 \\ 45 \end{pmatrix} = \begin{pmatrix} 9 \\ 3 \\ 3 \end{pmatrix}$

$c_B = (20, 10, 0)$ Revised Row 0: $(10/3, 40/3, 0)\begin{pmatrix} -1 & 2 & 1 & 0 & 0 \\ 1 & 1 & 0 & 1 & 0 \\ 5 & 3 & 0 & 0 & 1 \end{pmatrix} - (10, 20, 0, 0, 0)$

$= (0, 0, 10/3, 40/3, 0)$

Current Solution is optimal

$(x_1, x_2) = (3, 9)$ $z = 10 \cdot 3 + 20 \cdot 9 = 210$

5.2-7. (b) $c = (5, 4, -1, 3, 0, 0)$ $A = \begin{pmatrix} 3 & 2 & -3 & 1 & 1 & 0 \\ 3 & 3 & 1 & 3 & 0 & 1 \end{pmatrix}$ $b = \begin{pmatrix} 24 \\ 36 \end{pmatrix}$

Iteration 0: $B = B^{-1} = \begin{pmatrix} 1 & 0 \\ 0 & 1 \end{pmatrix}$ $x_B = \begin{pmatrix} x_5 \\ x_6 \end{pmatrix} = \begin{pmatrix} 1 & 0 \\ 0 & 1 \end{pmatrix}\begin{pmatrix} 24 \\ 36 \end{pmatrix} = \begin{pmatrix} 24 \\ 36 \end{pmatrix}$

$c_B = (0, 0)$ $-c = (-5, -4, 1, -3, 0, 0)$ x_1 enters the basis.

Revised x_1 coefficients: $\begin{pmatrix} 1 & 0 \\ 0 & 1 \end{pmatrix}\begin{pmatrix} 3 \\ 3 \end{pmatrix} = \begin{pmatrix} 3 \\ 3 \end{pmatrix}$ x_5 leaves the basis.

Iteration 1: $\eta = \begin{pmatrix} 1/3 \\ -1 \end{pmatrix}$ $B^{-1}_{New} = \begin{pmatrix} 1/3 & 0 \\ -1 & 1 \end{pmatrix}$ $x_B = \begin{pmatrix} x_1 \\ x_6 \end{pmatrix} = \begin{pmatrix} 1/3 & 0 \\ -1 & 1 \end{pmatrix}\begin{pmatrix} 24 \\ 36 \end{pmatrix} = \begin{pmatrix} 8 \\ 12 \end{pmatrix}$

$c_B = (5, 0)$ Revised Row 0: $(5/3, 0)\begin{pmatrix} 3 & 2 & -3 & 1 & 1 & 0 \\ 3 & 3 & 1 & 3 & 0 & 1 \end{pmatrix} - (5, 4, -1, 3, 0, 0)$

$= (0, -2/3, -4, -4/3, 5/3, 0)$ x_3 enters

Revised x_3 coefficients: $\begin{pmatrix} 1/3 & 0 \\ -1 & 1 \end{pmatrix}\begin{pmatrix} -3 \\ 1 \end{pmatrix} = \begin{pmatrix} -1 \\ 4 \end{pmatrix}$ x_6 leaves the basis.

Iteration 2: $\eta = \begin{pmatrix} 1/4 \\ 1/4 \end{pmatrix}$ $B^{-1}_{NEW} = \begin{pmatrix} \frac{1}{12} & \frac{1}{4} \\ -1/4 & \frac{1}{4} \end{pmatrix}$ $x_B = \begin{pmatrix} x_1 \\ x_3 \end{pmatrix} = \begin{pmatrix} 1/12 & 1/4 \\ -1/4 & 1/4 \end{pmatrix}\begin{pmatrix} 24 \\ 36 \end{pmatrix} = \begin{pmatrix} 11 \\ 3 \end{pmatrix}$

$c_B = (5, -1)$ Revised Row 0: $(2/3, 1)\begin{pmatrix} 3 & 2 & -3 & 1 & 1 & 0 \\ 3 & 3 & 1 & 3 & 0 & 1 \end{pmatrix} - (5, 4, -1, 3, 0, 0)$

$= (0, 1/3, 0, 2/3, 2/3, 1)$

Current Solution is optimal

$(x_1, x_2, x_3, x_4) = (11, 0, 3, 0)$ $Z = 11 \cdot 5 + 3 \cdot (-1) = 52$

5.3-1. (a) $B^{-1} = \begin{pmatrix} 1 & 3 & 0 \\ 0 & 1 & 1 \\ 1 & 2 & 0 \end{pmatrix}$. The final constraint columns for (x_1, x_2, x_3) will be

$$B^{-1}\begin{pmatrix} 2 & -2 & 3 \\ 1 & 1 & -1 \\ 1 & -1 & 1 \end{pmatrix} = \begin{pmatrix} 5 & 1 & 0 \\ 2 & 0 & 0 \\ 4 & 0 & 1 \end{pmatrix}$$

$C_B = (-1, 0, 2)$. The final objective coefficients for (x_1, x_2, x_3) will be

$$(-1, 0, 2)\begin{pmatrix} 5 & 1 & 0 \\ 2 & 0 & 0 \\ 4 & 0 & 1 \end{pmatrix} - (1, -1, 2) = (2, 0, 0)$$

The right-hand side is $B^{-1}b = \begin{pmatrix} 1 & 3 & 0 \\ 0 & 1 & 1 \\ 1 & 2 & 0 \end{pmatrix}\begin{pmatrix} 5 \\ 3 \\ 2 \end{pmatrix} = \begin{pmatrix} 14 \\ 5 \\ 11 \end{pmatrix}$. $Z = (-1, 0, 2)\begin{pmatrix} 14 \\ 5 \\ 11 \end{pmatrix} = 8$

Final Tableau becomes:

Bas Var	Eq No	Z	X1	X2	X3	X4	X5	X6	Right side
Z	0	1	2	0	0	1	1	0	8
X2	1	0	5	1	0	1	3	0	14
X6	2	0	2	0	0	0	1	1	5
X3	3	0	4	0	1	1	2	0	11

(Coefficient of: X1 … X6)

(b) The Defining Equations are:

$$2x_1 - 2x_2 + 3x_3 = 5$$
$$x_1 + x_2 - x_3 = 3$$
$$x_1 = 0$$

5.3-2. (a) The final constraint columns for (x_1, x_2, x_3, x_4) will be:

$$B^{-1}\begin{pmatrix} 4 & 2 & 1 & 1 \\ 3 & 1 & 2 & 1 \end{pmatrix} = \begin{pmatrix} 1 & -1 \\ -1 & 2 \end{pmatrix}\begin{pmatrix} 4 & 2 & 1 & 1 \\ 3 & 1 & 2 & 1 \end{pmatrix} = \begin{pmatrix} 1 & 1 & -1 & 0 \\ 2 & 0 & 3 & 1 \end{pmatrix}$$

The final objective coefficients for (x_1, x_2, x_3, x_4) will be:

$$-c + c_B B^{-1} A = -(4,3,1,2) + (3,2)\begin{pmatrix} 1 & 1 & -1 & 0 \\ 2 & 0 & 3 & 1 \end{pmatrix} = (3,0,2,0)$$

The right-hand side is $B^{-1}b = \begin{pmatrix} 1 & -1 \\ -1 & 2 \end{pmatrix}\begin{pmatrix} 5 \\ 4 \end{pmatrix} = \begin{pmatrix} 1 \\ 3 \end{pmatrix}$. $\quad Z = (3,2)\begin{pmatrix} 1 \\ 3 \end{pmatrix} = 9$

The final tableau becomes:

Bas Var	Eq No	Z	X1	X2	X3	X4	X5	X6	Right side
Z	0	1	3	0	2	0	1	1	9
X2	1	0	1	1	-1	0	1	-1	1
X4	2	0	2	0	3	1	-1	2	3

(b) The Defining Equations are:

$$4x_1 + 2x_2 + x_3 + x_4 = 5$$
$$3x_1 + x_2 + 2x_3 + x_4 = 4$$
$$x_1 = 0$$
$$x_3 = 0$$

5.3-3. The final constraint columns for (x_1, x_2, x_3) will be:

$$B^{-1}\begin{pmatrix} 2 & 2 & \frac{1}{2} \\ -4 & -2 & -\frac{3}{2} \\ 1 & 2 & \frac{1}{2} \end{pmatrix} = \begin{pmatrix} 1 & 1 & 2 \\ -2 & 0 & 4 \\ 1 & 0 & -1 \end{pmatrix}\begin{pmatrix} 2 & 2 & \frac{1}{2} \\ -4 & -2 & -\frac{3}{2} \\ 1 & 2 & \frac{1}{2} \end{pmatrix} = \begin{pmatrix} 0 & 4 & 0 \\ 0 & 4 & 1 \\ 1 & 0 & 0 \end{pmatrix}$$

The final objective coefficients for (x_1, x_2, x_3) will be:

$$-(6,1,2) + (0,2,6)\begin{pmatrix} 0 & 4 & 0 \\ 0 & 4 & 1 \\ 1 & 0 & 0 \end{pmatrix} = (0,7,0)$$

The right-hand side will be $B^{-1}b = \begin{pmatrix} 1 & 1 & 2 \\ -2 & 0 & 4 \\ 1 & 0 & -1 \end{pmatrix}\begin{pmatrix} 2 \\ 3 \\ 1 \end{pmatrix} = \begin{pmatrix} 7 \\ 0 \\ 1 \end{pmatrix}$

$$Z = (0,2,6)\begin{pmatrix} 7 \\ 0 \\ 1 \end{pmatrix} = 6$$

The final tableau becomes:

Bas Var	Eq No	Z	X1	X2	X3	X4	X5	X6	Right side
Z	0	1	0	7	0	2	0	2	6
X5	1	0	0	4	0	1	1	2	7
X3	2	0	0	4	1	-2	0	4	0
X1	3	0	1	0	0	1	0	-1	1

5.3-4. (a) The final constraint coefficients for (x_1, x_2, x_3) will be:

$$B^{-1}\begin{pmatrix} 1 & 1 & 3 \\ 2 & -1 & 1 \\ -1 & 1 & 1 \end{pmatrix} = \begin{pmatrix} 1 & -1 & -2 \\ 0 & \frac{1}{2} & \frac{1}{2} \\ 0 & -\frac{1}{2} & \frac{1}{2} \end{pmatrix}\begin{pmatrix} 1 & 1 & 3 \\ 2 & -1 & 1 \\ -1 & 1 & 1 \end{pmatrix} = \begin{pmatrix} 1 & 0 & 0 \\ \frac{1}{2} & 0 & 1 \\ -\frac{3}{2} & 1 & 0 \end{pmatrix}.$$

The final objective coefficients will be:

$$-(1,-1,2) + (0,2,-1)\begin{pmatrix} 1 & 0 & 0 \\ \frac{1}{2} & 0 & 1 \\ -\frac{3}{2} & 1 & 0 \end{pmatrix} = (\tfrac{3}{2}, 0, 0).$$

The right-hand side will be: $B^{-1}b = \begin{pmatrix} 1 & -1 & -2 \\ 0 & \frac{1}{2} & \frac{1}{2} \\ 0 & -\frac{1}{2} & \frac{1}{2} \end{pmatrix}\begin{pmatrix} 15 \\ 2 \\ 4 \end{pmatrix} = \begin{pmatrix} 5 \\ 3 \\ 1 \end{pmatrix}$

$$Z = (0,2,-1)\begin{pmatrix} 5 \\ 3 \\ 1 \end{pmatrix} = 5$$

The final tableau becomes:

Bas Var	Eq No	Z	X1	X2	X3	X4	X5	X6	Right side
Z	0	1	1.5	0	0	0	1.5	0.5	5
X4	1	0	1	0	0	1	-1	-2	5
X3	2	0	0.5	0	1	0	0.5	0.5	3
X2	3	0	-1.5	1	0	0	-0.5	0.5	1

(b) The Defining Equations are:

$$2x_1 - x_2 + x_3 = 2$$
$$-x_1 + x_2 + x_3 = 4$$
$$x_1 = 0$$

5.3-5. (a) The constraint coefficients for (x_1, x_2, x_3) will be:

$$B^{-1}\begin{pmatrix} 8 & 2 & 3 \\ 4 & 3 & 0 \\ 2 & 0 & 1 \\ 0 & 0 & 1 \end{pmatrix} = \begin{pmatrix} \frac{3}{16} & -\frac{1}{8} & 0 & 0 \\ -\frac{1}{4} & \frac{1}{2} & 0 & 0 \\ -\frac{3}{8} & \frac{1}{4} & 1 & 0 \\ 0 & 0 & 0 & 1 \end{pmatrix}\begin{pmatrix} 8 & 2 & 3 \\ 4 & 3 & 0 \\ 2 & 0 & 1 \\ 0 & 0 & 1 \end{pmatrix} = \begin{pmatrix} 1 & 0 & \frac{9}{16} \\ 0 & 1 & -\frac{3}{4} \\ 0 & 0 & -\frac{1}{8} \\ 0 & 0 & 1 \end{pmatrix}$$

The objective coefficients for (x_1, x_2, x_3) will be:

$$-(20,6,8) + (20,6,0,0)\begin{pmatrix} 1 & 0 & \frac{9}{16} \\ 0 & 1 & -\frac{3}{4} \\ 0 & 0 & -\frac{1}{8} \\ 0 & 0 & 1 \end{pmatrix} = (0, 0, -\tfrac{5}{4})$$

The right-hand side is: $B^{-1}b = \begin{pmatrix} \frac{3}{16} & -\frac{1}{8} & 0 & 0 \\ -\frac{1}{4} & \frac{1}{2} & 0 & 0 \\ -\frac{3}{8} & \frac{1}{4} & 1 & 0 \\ 0 & 0 & 0 & 1 \end{pmatrix}\begin{pmatrix} 200 \\ 100 \\ 50 \\ 20 \end{pmatrix} = \begin{pmatrix} 25 \\ 0 \\ 0 \\ 20 \end{pmatrix}$

$$Z = c_B^T x_B = (20,6,0,0)\begin{pmatrix} 25 \\ 0 \\ 0 \\ 20 \end{pmatrix} = 500$$

5.3-5. a) (cont')

The tableau is:

Bas Var	Eq No	Z	X1	X2	X3	X4	X5	X6	X7	Right side
Z	0	1	0	0	-1.25	2.25	0.5	0	0	500
X1	1	0	1	0	0.563	0.188	-0.13	0	0	25
X2	2	0	0	1	-0.75	-0.25	0.5	0	0	0
X6	3	0	0	0	-0.13	-0.38	0.25	1	0	0
X7	4	0	0	0	1	0	0	0	1	20

(b) The Revised Simplex Method would generate the reduced costs for Row 0 and then the revised column for x_3

(c) The Defining Equations are:

$$8x_1 + 2x_2 + 3x_3 = 200$$
$$4x_1 + 3x_2 = 100$$
$$x_3 = 0$$

$2x_1 + x_3 = 50$ is also a "tight" constraint.

5.3-6. $B^{-1} = \begin{pmatrix} \frac{1}{12} & \frac{1}{4} \\ -\frac{1}{4} & \frac{1}{4} \end{pmatrix}$ The final right-hand side will be:

$$B^{-1}b = \begin{pmatrix} \frac{1}{12} & \frac{1}{4} \\ -\frac{1}{4} & \frac{1}{4} \end{pmatrix}\begin{pmatrix} 120 \\ 180 \end{pmatrix} = \begin{pmatrix} 55 \\ 15 \end{pmatrix}$$

$$Z^* = (6, 5, -1, 4)\begin{pmatrix} 55 \\ 0 \\ 15 \\ 0 \end{pmatrix} = 315$$

Also Z^* can be calculated by the reduced objective coefficients:

$$Z^* = \left(\frac{3}{4}, \frac{5}{4}\right)\begin{pmatrix} 120 \\ 180 \end{pmatrix} = 315$$

$b_1^* = 55$, $b_2^* = 15$, $Z^* = 315$

5.3-7. a) $[-c_1, -c_2, -c_3 \mid 0 \ 0 \mid 0] + \left[\frac{3}{5}, \frac{4}{5}\right]\left[\begin{array}{ccccc|c} 1 & 2 & 1 & 1 & 0 & b \\ 2 & 1 & 3 & 0 & 1 & 2b \end{array}\right] = \left[\frac{7}{10}, 0, 0, \frac{3}{5}, \frac{4}{5}, Z^*\right]$

Or:

$$[-c_1, -c_2, -c_3 \mid 0 \ 0 \mid 0] + \left[\frac{11}{5}, 2, 3, \frac{3}{5}, \frac{4}{5}, \frac{11}{5}b\right] = \left[\frac{7}{10}, 0, 0, \frac{3}{5}, \frac{4}{5}, Z^*\right]$$

So $c_1 = \frac{11}{5} - \frac{7}{10} = \frac{3}{2}$

$c_2 = 2$

$c_3 = 3$

b) $B^{-1} = \begin{pmatrix} 3/5 & -1/5 \\ -1/5 & 2/5 \end{pmatrix}$

$$B^{-1}b = b^* \Leftrightarrow \begin{pmatrix} 3/5 & -1/5 \\ -1/5 & 2/5 \end{pmatrix}\begin{pmatrix} b \\ 2b \end{pmatrix} = \begin{pmatrix} 1 \\ 3 \end{pmatrix}$$

$$\Rightarrow \begin{pmatrix} 1/5 \\ 3/5 \end{pmatrix} b = \begin{pmatrix} 1 \\ 3 \end{pmatrix} \Rightarrow b = 5.$$

5.3-7. c) Using (a), $Z^* = c_B b^* = (c_2, c_3)\begin{pmatrix}1\\3\end{pmatrix} = (2,3)\begin{pmatrix}1\\3\end{pmatrix} = 11.$

Using (b), $Z^* = \tilde{c}_B b = \left(\frac{3}{5}, \frac{4}{5}\right)\begin{pmatrix}b\\2b\end{pmatrix} = \left(\frac{3}{5}, \frac{4}{5}\right)\begin{pmatrix}5\\10\end{pmatrix} = 11.$

5.3-8. First iteration: $\frac{5}{2}$ of row 2 is added to row 0

(i.e. premultiply $A_0 = \left[\begin{array}{cc:ccc:c} 1 & 0 & 1 & 0 & 0 & 4 \\ 0 & 2 & 0 & 1 & 0 & 12 \\ 3 & 2 & 0 & 0 & 1 & 18 \end{array}\right]$ by $[0, \frac{5}{2}, 0]$

and add to row 0)

Second iteration: row 3 is added to row 0

(i.e. premultiply $A_1 = \left[\begin{array}{cc:ccc:c} 1 & 0 & 1 & 0 & 0 & 4 \\ 0 & 1 & 0 & \frac{1}{2} & 0 & 6 \\ 3 & 0 & 0 & -1 & 1 & 6 \end{array}\right] = \begin{bmatrix} 1 & 0 & 0 \\ 0 & \frac{1}{2} & 0 \\ 0 & -1 & 1 \end{bmatrix} A_0$

by $[0, 0, 1]$ and add to row 0)

Therefore, the final row 0 is:

$$\text{Init row } 0 + [0, \tfrac{5}{2}, 0]A_0 + [0,0,1]\begin{bmatrix} 1 & 0 & 0 \\ 0 & \frac{1}{2} & 0 \\ 0 & -1 & 1 \end{bmatrix} A_0$$

$$\text{Final row } 0 = [-3, -5 \,\vdots\, 0, 0, 0 \,\vdots\, 0] + [0, \tfrac{3}{2}, 1]\, A_0 \quad \text{as desired}$$

$$\left([0, \tfrac{5}{2}, 0] + [0,0,1]\begin{bmatrix} 1 & 0 & 0 \\ 0 & \frac{1}{2} & 0 \\ 0 & -1 & 1 \end{bmatrix} = [0, \tfrac{3}{2}, 1] \right)$$

5.3-9. a) Use the columns corresponding to artificial variables in exactly the same way a slack column would have been used.

Note: The shadow price of this column may be positive or negative.

b) For the reversed inequalities, use the negative of the column corresponding to the slack variable (the artificial column may be discarded) in exactly the same formulae.

c) Same as (b)

d) No change, use slack and artificial variables as above.

5.3-10. For the tableau see the solution to problem 18 in chapter 4. The columns that will contain S^* are those corresponding to x_5 and x_6 since those columns contain the identity in the initial tableau.

5.3-11.

(a) The final constraint columns for $(x_1, x_2, x_3, x_4, x_6)$ are:

$$B^{-1}\begin{pmatrix} 1 & 4 & 2 & -1 & 0 \\ 3 & 2 & 0 & 0 & -1 \end{pmatrix} = \begin{pmatrix} 3/10 & -1/10 \\ -2/10 & 2/5 \end{pmatrix}\begin{pmatrix} 1 & 4 & 2 & -1 & 0 \\ 3 & 2 & 0 & 0 & -1 \end{pmatrix} = \begin{pmatrix} 0 & 1 & 3/5 & -3/10 & 1/10 \\ 1 & 0 & -2/5 & 2/10 & -2/5 \end{pmatrix}$$

The final objective coefficients for $(x_1, x_2, x_3, x_4, x_6)$ are:

$$(-4M+2, -6M+3, -2M+2, M, M) - (-6M+3, -4M+2)\begin{pmatrix} 0 & 1 & 3/5 & -3/10 & 1/10 \\ 1 & 0 & -2/5 & 2/10 & -2/5 \end{pmatrix}$$

$$= (0, 0, 1, \tfrac{1}{2}, \tfrac{1}{2})$$

The right-hand side is: $B^{-1}b = \begin{pmatrix} 3/10 & -1/10 \\ -2/10 & 2/5 \end{pmatrix}\begin{pmatrix} 8 \\ 6 \end{pmatrix} = \begin{pmatrix} 9/5 \\ 4/5 \end{pmatrix}$

$$Z = -14M + c_B^T x_B = -14M + (-6M+3, -4M+2)\begin{pmatrix} 9/5 \\ 4/5 \end{pmatrix} = 7$$

The final tableau is:

Bas Var	Eq No	Z	X1	X2	X3	X4	X_6	$\bar{X}5$	$\bar{X}7$	Right side
								1M	1M	
Z	0	-1	0	0	1	0.5	0.5	-0.5	-0.5	-7
X2	1	0	0	1	0.6	-0.3	0.1	0.3	-0.1	1.8
X1	2	0	1	0	-0.4	0.2	-0.4	-0.2	0.4	0.8

b) The constraints in the original tableau are $(A \mid I \mid I \mid b)$ with the second identity matrix corresponding to the artificial variables. When we pre-multiply by M, we get:

$$(A^* \mid S^* \mid L^* \mid b^*) = M(A \mid I \mid I \mid b) = (MA \mid M \mid M \mid Mb)$$

and we have $M = S^* = L^*$. For this problem $M = \begin{pmatrix} 3/10 & -1/10 \\ -1/5 & 2/5 \end{pmatrix}$

The original Row 0 $t = (c + e^T AM \mid Me^T \mid 0 \mid -Me^T b)$

and in the final tableau

$$t^* = t + vT = (z^* + c \mid -y^* \mid Me^T - y^* \mid Z^*)$$

$$= (c + e^T AM \mid Me^T \mid 0 \mid -Me^T b) + v^T(A \mid I \mid I \mid b)$$

5.3-11. b) (cont')

$$t^* = (c + e^T A M + v^T A \mid Me^T + v \mid v \mid -Me^T b + vb)$$

We can see $v = -y^* + Me^T$

For this problem $v = \left(-\frac{1}{2} + M, -\frac{1}{2} + M\right)$

(c) If $t = (2, 3, 2, 0, M, 0, M, 0)$, then in matrix notation

$$t = (c \mid 0 \mid Me^T \mid Me^T b).$$

$$t^* = t + v^T T = (z^* + c \mid y^* \mid Me^T - y^* \mid Z^*)$$

$$= (c \mid 0 \mid Me^T \mid Me^T b) + v^T (A \mid I \mid I \mid b)$$

$$= c + v^T A \mid v \mid Me^T + v \mid Me^T b + v^T b).$$

We conclude $v = -y^*$. For this problem $v = \left(-\frac{1}{2}, -\frac{1}{2}\right)$

(d) The defining equations are $x = M b$ or $M^{-1} x = b$.

– or –

$$x_1 + 4x_2 + 2x_3 = 8$$
$$3x_1 + 2x_2 = 6$$
$$x_3 = 0.$$

5.3-12. (a) The final constraint columns for (x_1, x_2, x_3) are:

$$B^{-1}\begin{pmatrix} 1 & 3 & 2 \\ 1 & 5 & 0 \end{pmatrix} = \begin{pmatrix} 1 & 0 \\ 1 & -1 \end{pmatrix}\begin{pmatrix} 1 & 3 & 2 \\ 1 & 5 & 0 \end{pmatrix} = \begin{pmatrix} 1 & 3 & 2 \\ 0 & -2 & 2 \end{pmatrix}$$

The final objective coefficients for (x_1, x_2, x_3) are:

$$-(2, 4, 3) + (2, 0)\begin{pmatrix} 1 & 3 & 2 \\ 0 & -2 & 2 \end{pmatrix} = (0, 2, 1)$$

The right-hand side is $B^{-1}b = \begin{pmatrix} 1 & 0 \\ 1 & -1 \end{pmatrix}\begin{pmatrix} 20 \\ 10 \end{pmatrix} = \begin{pmatrix} 20 \\ 10 \end{pmatrix}$. $z = c_B^T x_B = (2, 0)\begin{pmatrix} 20 \\ 10 \end{pmatrix} = 40$

The final tableau is:

Bas Var	Eq No	Z	X1	X2	X3	X_5	$\bar{X}4$	X6	Right side
							1M	1M	
Z	0	1	0	2	1	0	2	0	40
X1	1	0	1	3	2	0	1	0	20
X5	2	0	0	-2	2	1	1	-1	10

(b) The Defining Equations are:

$$x_1 + 3x_2 + 2x_3 = 20$$
$$x_2 = 0$$
$$x_3 = 0$$

5.3-13. (a)

$$-2x_1 + 2x_2 + x_3 + x_4 = 10$$
$$3x_1 + x_2 - x_3 + x_5 = 20$$

$$x_1 - x_2 - \tfrac{1}{2}x_3 - \tfrac{1}{2}x_4 = -5$$
$$4x_2 + \tfrac{1}{2}x_3 + \tfrac{3}{2}x_4 + x_5 = 35$$

$$x_1 + 3x_2 + x_4 + x_5 = 30$$
$$8x_2 + x_3 + 3x_4 + 2x_5 = 70$$

$(x_1, x_2, x_3) = (30, 0, 70)$ is optimal

$z = 30 \cdot 3 + 70 \cdot 2 = 230$

(b) If we add (-3) of the 1st row from the result in (a) and (-2) of the 2nd row from the result in (a) to our original objective, we get:

$$3x_1 + 7x_2 + 2x_3$$
$$-3x_1 - 9x_2 \quad -3x_4 - 3x_5$$
$$-16x_2 - 2x_3 - 6x_4 - 4x_5$$

$$-18x_2 \quad -9x_4 - 7x_5$$

The shadow prices are 9 and 7

(c) The Defining Equations are:

$$-2x_1 + 2x_2 + x_3 = 10$$
$$3x_1 + x_2 - x_3 = 20$$
$$x_2 = 0$$

(d) $B = \begin{pmatrix} -2 & 1 \\ 3 & -1 \end{pmatrix}$ $\quad B^{-1} = \begin{pmatrix} 1 & 1 \\ 3 & 2 \end{pmatrix}$. $\quad x_B = \begin{pmatrix} 1 & 1 \\ 3 & 2 \end{pmatrix}\begin{pmatrix} 10 \\ 20 \end{pmatrix} = \begin{pmatrix} 30 \\ 70 \end{pmatrix}$

$y^* = (3, 2)\begin{pmatrix} 1 & 1 \\ 3 & 2 \end{pmatrix} = (9, 7)$

Revised Row 0 $= (9, 7)\begin{pmatrix} -2 & 2 & 1 & 1 & 0 \\ 3 & 1 & -1 & 0 & 1 \end{pmatrix} - (3, 7, 2, 0, 0) = (0, 18, 0, 9, 7)$

so, the current solution is optimal.

(e) The final tableau is:

Bas Var	Eq No	Z	X1	X2	X3	X4	X5	Right side
Z	0	1	0	18	0	9	7	230
X1	1	0	1	3	0	1	1	30
X3	2	0	0	8	1	3	2	70

Chapter 6: Duality Theory and Sensitivity Analysis

6.1-1 (a)

	x_1	x_2	
y_1	1	0	≤ 4
y_2	1	3	≤ 15
y_3	2	1	≤ 10
	IV	IV	
	3	2	

Dual: Minimize $4y_1 + 15y_2 + 10y_3$

subject to: $y_1 + y_2 + 2y_3 \geq 3$

$3y_2 + y_3 \geq 2$

$y_i \geq 0$ for $i = 1, 2, 3$

(b)

	x_1	x_2	x_3	x_4	
y_1	3	2	-3	1	≤ 24
y_2	3	3	1	3	≤ 36
	IV	IV	IV	IV	
	5	4	-1	3	

Dual: Minimize $24y_1 + 36y_2$

subject to: $3y_1 + 3y_2 \geq 5$

$2y_1 + 3y_2 \geq 4$

$-3y_1 + y_2 \geq -1$

$y_1 + 3y_2 \geq 3$

$y_1 \geq 0, y_2 \geq 0$

6.1-2 (a) Minimize $15y_1 + 12y_2 + 45y_3$

subject to: $-y_1 + y_2 + 5y_3 \geq 10$

$2y_1 + y_2 + 3y_3 \geq 20$

$y_i \geq 0$ for $i = 1, 2, 3$

(b) Minimize $4y_1 + 2y_2 + 12y_3$

subject to: $-y_1 + 2y_2 + y_3 \geq 2$

$y_1 - y_2 + y_3 \geq -2$

$y_1 + y_2 + 3y_3 \geq 3$

$y_i \geq 0$ for $i = 1, 2, 3$.

6.1-3. (a)

	x_1	x_2	x_3	x_4	
y_1	1	-2	4	3	≤ 20
y_2	-4	6	5	-4	≤ 40
y_3	2	-3	3	8	≤ 50
	IV	IV	IV	IV	
	5	1	3	4	

Dual: Minimize $20y_1 + 40y_2 + 50y_3$

subject to
$$y_1 - 4y_2 + 2y_3 \ge 5$$
$$-2y_1 + 6y_2 - 3y_3 \ge 1$$
$$4y_1 + 5y_2 + 3y_3 \ge 3$$
$$3y_1 - 4y_2 + 8y_3 \ge 4$$
$y_i \ge 0$ for $i = 1, 2, 3$.

(b) The dual problem has no feasible solutions.

6.1-4. (a) Apply the simplex method to the dual of the problem, since the dual has fewer constraints (not including nonnegativity constraints). We expect the simplex method will pass through fewer basic feasible solutions

(b) Apply the simplex method to the primal problem, since it has fewer constraints (not including nonnegativity constraints). We expect the simplex method will pass through fewer basic feasible solutions.

6.1-5. (a) Dual is Minimize $12y_1 + y_2$

subject to:
$$y_1 + 2y_2 \ge -1$$
$$y_1 \ge -2$$
$$2y_1 - y_2 \ge -1$$
$$y_1 \ge 0, \; y_2 \ge 0$$

(b) It is clear from the dual problem that $(y_1, y_2) = (0, 0)$ is the optimal dual solution. By strong duality $z = 0 \le 0$.

6.1-6. a) Dual is

Minimize $w = 3y_1 + 5y_2$

subject to
$$y_1 \ge 2$$
$$y_2 \ge 6$$
$$y_1 + 2y_2 \ge 9$$
$$y_1 \ge 0, \; y_2 \ge 0$$

b)

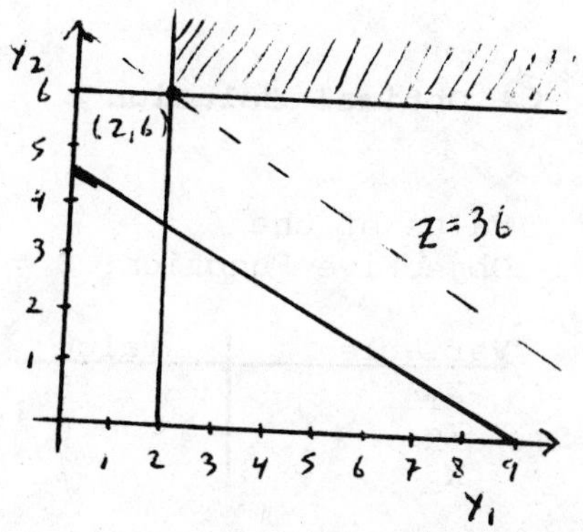

Optimal. $(y_1^*, y_2^*) = (2, 6)$

So shadow prices for resource 1 and 2 are $y_1^* = 2$, $y_2^* = 6$.

6.1-6. c)

Optimal Solution

Value of the
Objective Function: Z = 36

Variable	Value
X_1	3
X_2	5
X_3	0

Constraint	Slack or Surplus	Shadow Price
1	0	2
2	0	6

Sensitivity Analysis

Objective Function Coefficient

Current Value	Allowable Range To Stay Optimal Minimum	Maximum
2	0	$+\infty$
6	3.5	$+\infty$
9	$-\infty$	14

Right Hand Sides

Current Value	Allowable Range To Stay Feasible Minimum	Maximum
3	0	$+\infty$
5	0	$+\infty$

6.1-7. a) Dual is

Minimize $w = 6y_1 + 4y_2$

subject to

$$2y_1 \geq 1$$
$$2y_1 - y_2 \geq -3$$
$$-2y_1 + 2y_2 \geq 2$$
$$y_1 \geq 0,\ y_2 \geq 0$$

b)

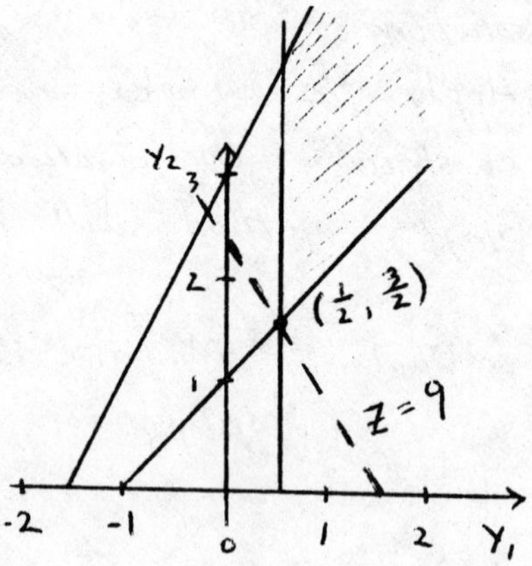

Optimal: $(y_1^*, y_2^*) = (\frac{1}{2}, \frac{3}{2})$

Shadow prices for resources 1 and 2 are $y_1^* = \frac{1}{2}$, $y_2^* = \frac{3}{2}$ resp.

c) **Optimal Solution**

Value of the
Objective Function: Z = 9

Variable	Value
X_1	5
X_2	0
X_3	2

Constraint	Slack or Surplus	Shadow Price
1	0	0.5
2	0	1.5

Sensitivity Analysis

Objective Function Coefficient

Current Value	Allowable Range To Stay Optimal Minimum	Maximum
1	0	$+\infty$
-3	$-\infty$	-0.5
2	-1	7

Right Hand Sides

Current Value	Allowable Range To Stay Feasible Minimum	Maximum
6	-4	$+\infty$
4	0	$+\infty$

6.1-8. a)

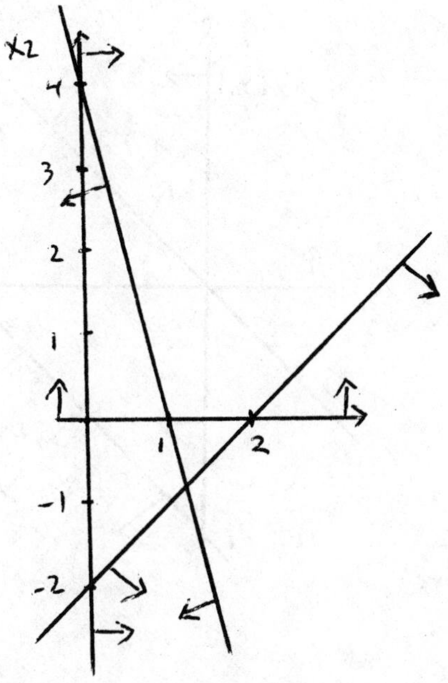

There is no feasible region

b) Dual is

Minimize $w = -2y_1 + 4y_2$

subject to $-y_1 + 4y_2 \ge 1$

$y_1 + y_2 \ge 2$

$y_1 \ge 0, \ y_2 \ge 0$

c)

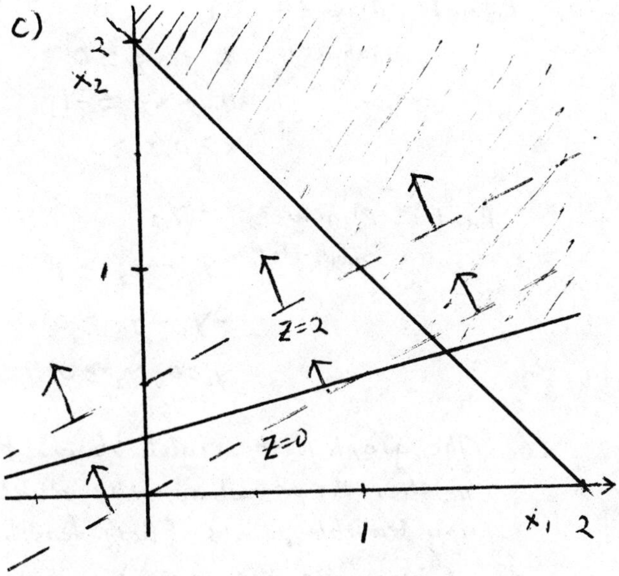

We see that Z can be increased infinitely

One possible solution : $(0, y_2)$ let $y_2 \to \infty$.

6.1-9. Primal : Max $Z = x_1 + x_2$

subject to : $-x_1 + x_2 \le 1$

$x_1 - x_2 \le 0$

$x_1 \ge 0, x_2 \ge 0$

(Let $x_1 = x_2 = c$ and $c \to \infty$
$Z = 2c$ is unbounded)

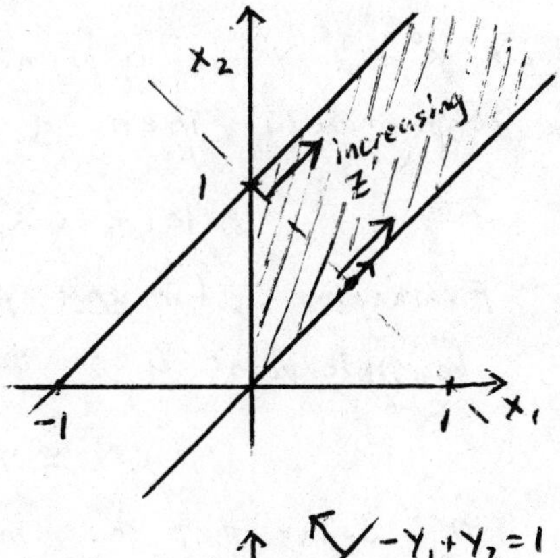

Dual : Min $w = y_1$

subject to : $-y_1 + y_2 \ge 1$

$y_1 - y_2 \ge 1$

$y_1 \ge 0, y_2 \ge 0$

(No feasible points)

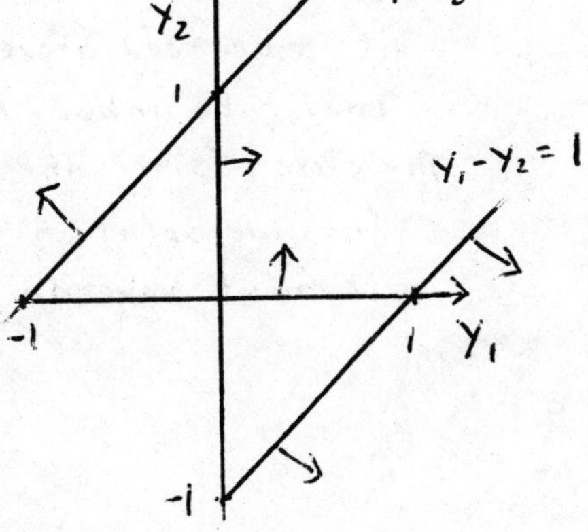

6.1-10. Primal: Max $Z = x_1$

subject to: $x_1 - x_2 \le 0$

$-x_1 + x_2 \le -1$

$x_1 \ge 0, x_2 \ge 0$

Dual: Min $w = -y_2$

subject to: $y_1 - y_2 \ge 1$

$-y_1 + y_2 \ge 0$

$y_1 \ge 0, y_2 \ge 0$

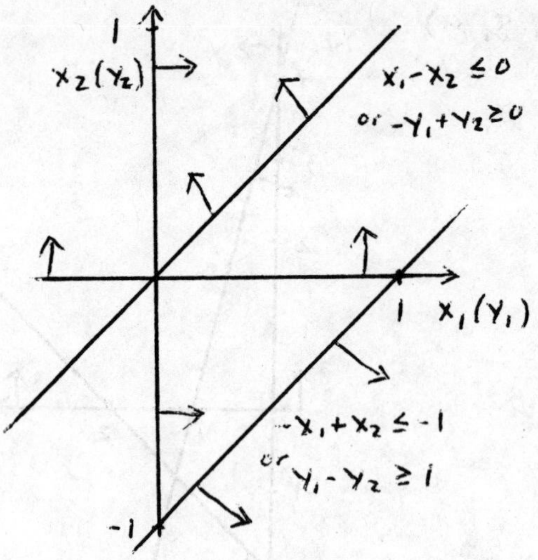

The graph to the right shows that neither the primal nor the dual have any feasible points. (Both feasible regions are the same)

6.1-11. Primal: Max $Z = x_1 + x_2$

subject to: $x_1 \le -1$

$x_1 + x_2 \le 0$

$x_1 \ge 0, x_2 \ge 0$

Clearly infeasible (what is x_1 ?)

Dual: Min $w = -y_1$

subject to: $y_1 + y_2 \ge 1$

$y_2 \ge 1$

$y_1 \ge 0, y_2 \ge 0$

Clearly, $(c, 1)$, $c \to \infty$ is feasible, unbounded

6.1-12. Let x^0 and y^0 be a primal feasible point and a dual feasible point, respectively. Then by weak duality,

$$-\infty < cx^0 \le y^0 b < \infty$$

Furthermore, for <u>any</u> primal feasible point x and <u>any</u> dual feasible point y,

$$cx \le y^0 b \quad \text{and} \quad cx^0 \le yb$$

This means that the primal problem <u>cannot</u> be unbounded (since it is bounded above by $y^0 b$), and, similarly, the dual problem cannot be unbounded (since it is bounded below by cx^0). Therefore, since the primal problem (and the dual problem) has feasible solution and the objective is not unbounded, it must have an optimal solution.

6.1-13. a) From primal, $Ax \le b, x \ge 0$, and from dual, $y^T A \ge c, y \ge 0$. Thus,

$$y^T A - c^T \ge 0, \quad x \ge 0, \quad \text{so } (y^T A - c^T)x \ge 0$$

$$b - Ax \ge 0, \quad y \ge 0, \quad \text{so } y^T(b - Ax) \ge 0$$

In other words,

$$y^T A x \ge c^T x \quad \text{and} \quad y^T b \ge y^T A x$$

So

$$y^T b \ge y^T A x \ge c^T x,$$

which is weak duality.

b) There are many ways to prove this. The simplest is by contradiction: Assume primal Z can be increased indefinitely and the dual problem <u>does</u> have a feasible solution. By above argument, we see than $c^T x \le \tilde{y}^T b$ for all primal feasible x, given $\tilde{y}$ is a dual feasible solution. But this means Z is bounded above (contradiction). Thus, if Z is unbounded (can be increased indefinitely), then dual must not have any feasible solutions.

6.1-14. Primal: Max $Z = cx$ subject to $Ax \le b$, $x \ge 0$ Dual: Min $v = yb$ subject to $yA \ge c$, $y \ge 0$

Since changing b to $\bar{b}$ keeps the dual feasible region unchanged, y^* must be feasible for the new problem. Let $\bar{y}$ be the optimal solution for the new dual. Then clearly $\bar{y}\bar{b} \le y^*\bar{b}$ since $\bar{y}$ is optimal. Further, by strong duality, we know that $c\bar{x} = \bar{y}\bar{b}$. Thus, $c\bar{x} = \bar{y}\bar{b} \le y^*\bar{b}$.

6.1-15. a) True. If A is an $n \times m$ matrix (n rows, m columns), then, in standard form, the number of functional constraints for the primal is n, for the dual is m. The number of variables in the primal is m, in the dual is n. So for both the sum is $m+n$.

b) False. This cannot be true since the weak and strong duality theorems imply that the primal and dual objective function values are the same <u>only</u> at optimality.

c) False. If the primal problem has an unbounded objective function, the dual problem must be infeasible (since by weak duality, if the dual has a feasible point, $\tilde{y}$, the objective value of the primal $Z = cx \le \tilde{y}b$.)

6.2-1. a) Iter 0: Since all coefficients are zero, at the current solution (0,0), the 3 resources (production time per week at plant 1, 2 & 3) are "free goods." That is, having more doesn't increase our objective.

Iter 1: $[0, \frac{5}{2}, 0]$ Now resource 2 has been entirely used up and contributes $\frac{5}{2}$ to profit per unit of resource. Since this is positive it is worthwhile to continue fully using this resource.

Iter 2: $[0, \frac{3}{2}, 1]$ Resources 2 & 3 are used up and contributes a positive unit to profit. Resource 1 is a free good while resources 2 & 3 contribute $\frac{3}{2}$ and 1 per unit of resource, resp.

b) Iter 0: $[-3, -5]$ Both activities 1 & 2 (# batches of product 1 & 2 produced per week) can be initiated to give a more profitable allocation of the resources. That is, the current contribution to profits of the resources required to produce 1 batch of product 1 or 2 is smaller than the unit profit per batch of product 1 or 2, resp.

Iter 1: $[-3, 0]$ Again activity 1 can be initiated to give a more profitable use of resources, but activity 2 is already being produced (or the resources are being used just as well in other activities).

Iter 2: $[0, 0]$ Both activities are being produced (or the resources are being used just as profitably elsewhere).

c) Iter 1: Since activities 1 & 2 can be initiated to increase profit (given same amount of resources), we choose to increase one of these. We choose activity 2 as the entering activity (basic variable) since it increases the profit by 5 for every unit of product 2 produced (as opposed to 3 for product 1).

Iter 2: Only activity 1 can be initiated for more profit, so we do so.

Iter 3: Both activity 1 & 2 are being used. Furthermore, since the coefficients for x_3, x_4, x_5 are non-negative, it is not worthwhile to cut back on the use of any of the resources. Thus, we must be at the optimal solution.

6.3-1. (a) Minimize $v = 20y_1 + 10y_2$

subject to:

$$5y_1 + y_2 \geq 6$$
$$2y_1 + 2y_2 \geq 8$$
$$y_1 \geq 0,\ y_2 \geq 0$$

6.3-1. (b) Primal

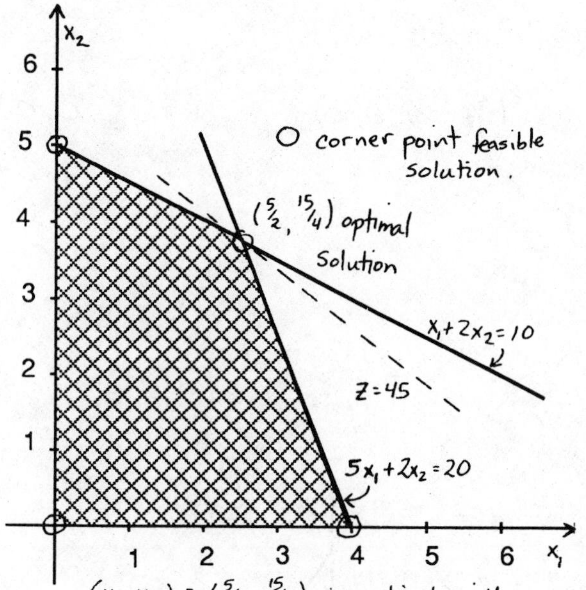

$(x_1, x_2) = (5/2, 15/4)$ is optimal with $Z = 45$

Corner Point infeasible solutions are: (0,10) and (10,0).

Dual

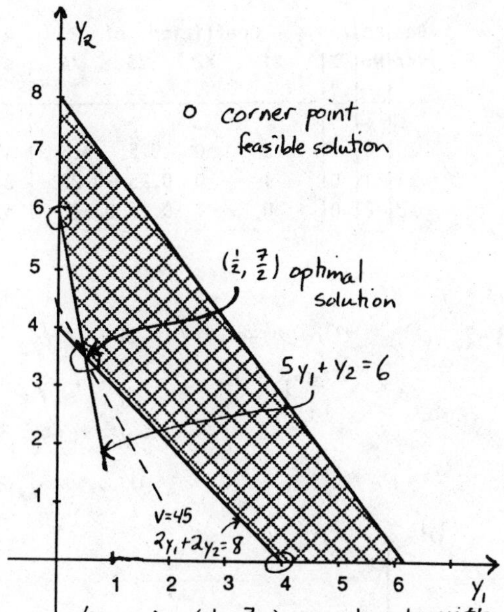

$(y_1, y_2) = (\frac{1}{2}, 7/2)$ is optimal with $V = 45$

Corner Point infeasible solutions are: (0,4), (0,0), (6/5, 0).

(c)

Primal Basic Solution (x_1, x_2, x_3, x_4)	Feasible?	Z	Dual Basic Solution (y_1, y_2, y_3, y_4)	Feasible?
(0, 5, 10, 0)	Yes	40	(0, 4, -2, 0)	No
(0, 0, 20, 10)	Yes	0	(0, 0, -6, -8)	No
(4, 0, 0, 6)	Yes	24	(6/5, 0, 0, -28/5)	No
(5/2, 15/4, 0, 0)	Yes	45	(1/2, 7/2, 0, 0)	Yes
(0, 10, 0, -10)	No	80	(4, 0, 14, 0)	Yes
(10, 0, -30, 0)	No	60	(0, 6, 0, 4)	Yes

(d)

Iteration 0

Bas Var	Eq No	Z	X1	X2	X3	X4	Right side
Z	0	1	-6	-8	0	0	0
X3	1	0	5	2	1	0	20
X4	2	0	1	2*	0	1	10

Solutions: Primal (0, 0, 20, 10); Dual (0, 0, -6, -8)

Iteration 1

Bas Var	Eq No	Z	X1	X2	X3	X4	Right side
Z	0	1	-2	0	0	4	40
X3	1	0	4*	0	1	-1	10
X2	2	0	0.5	1	0	0.5	5

Solutions: Primal (0, 5, 10, 0); Dual (0, 4, -2, 0)

6.3-1. d) (cont')

Bas Var	Eq No	Z	Coefficient of X1	X2	X3	X4	Right side
Z	0	1	0	0	0.5	3.5	45
X1	1	0	1	0	0.25	-0.25	2.5
X2	2	0	0	1	-0.13	0.625	3.75

2

$(5/2, 15/4, 0, 0)$ $(\frac{1}{2}, 7/2, 0, 0)$

6.3-2. (a) Minimize $v = 8y_1 + 4y_2$

subject to:

$y_1 + y_2 \geq 1$

$3y_1 + y_2 \geq 2$

$y_1 \geq 0 \quad y_2 \geq 0$

(b) Primal

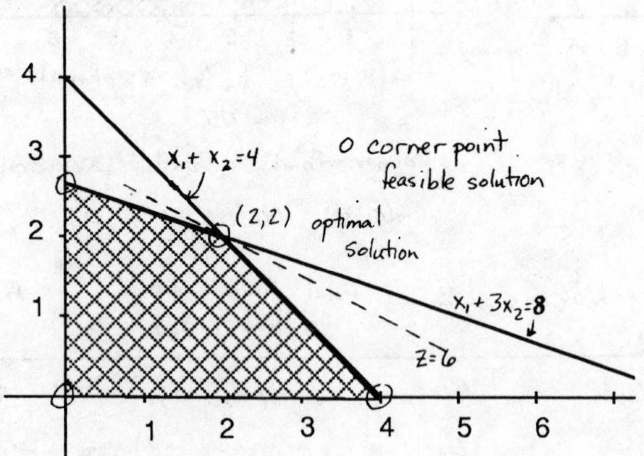

$(x_1, x_2) = (2,2)$ is optimal with $z = 6$

Corner Point infeasible solutions are: (8,0) and (0,4)

Dual

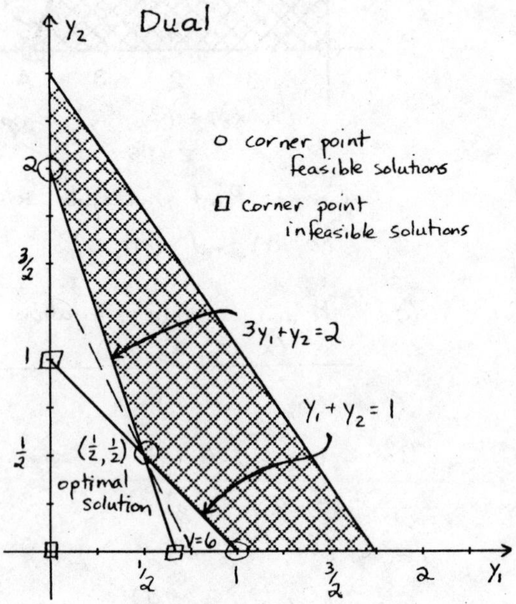

$(y_1, y_2) = (\frac{1}{2}, \frac{1}{2})$ is optimal with $v = 6$

(c)

Primal Basic Solution (x_1, x_2, x_3, x_4)	Feasible?	Z	Dual Basic Solution (y_1, y_2, y_3, y_4)	Feasible?
(4, 0, 4, 0)	Yes	4	$(0, 1, 0, -1/3)$	No
(0, 0, 8, 4)	Yes	0	(0, 0, -1, -2)	No
$(0, 8/3, 0, 4/3)$	Yes	$16/3$	$(2/3, 0, -1/3, 0)$	No
(2, 2, 0, 0)	Yes	6	$(1/2, 1/2, 0, 0)$	Yes
(0, 4, -2, 0)	No	8	(0, 2, -1, 0)	Yes
(8, 0, 0, -4)	No	8	(1, 0, 0, 1)	Yes

6.3-2. d)

Bas Var	Eq No	Z	X1	X2	X3	X4	Right side
Z	0	1	-1	-2	0	0	0
X3	1	0	1	3*	1	0	8
X4	2	0	1	1	0	1	4

O

Solutions

Primal	Dual
$(0, 0, 8, 4)$	$(0, 0, -1, -2)$

Bas Var	Eq No	Z	X1	X2	X3	X4	Right side
Z	0	1	-0.33	0	0.667	0	5.333
X2	1	0	0.333	1	0.333	0	2.667
X4	2	0	0.667*	0	-0.33	1	1.333

1

$(0, \frac{8}{3}, 0, \frac{4}{3})$ $(\frac{2}{3}, 0, -\frac{1}{3}, 0)$

Bas Var	Eq No	Z	X1	X2	X3	X4	Right side
Z	0	1	0	0	0.5	0.5	6
X2	1	0	0	1	0.5	-0.5	2
X1	2	0	1	0	-0.5	1.5	2

2

$(2, 2, 0, 0)$ $(\frac{1}{2}, \frac{1}{2}, 0, 0)$

6.3-3.

Nonbasic Primal Variables	Associated Dual Variables	Nonbasic Dual Variables
x_1, x_2	y_4, y_5	y_1, y_2, y_3
x_1, x_4	y_4, y_2	y_1, y_3, y_5
x_4, x_5	y_2, y_3	y_1, y_4, y_5
x_3, x_5	y_1, y_3	y_2, y_4, y_5
x_2, x_3	y_5, y_1	y_2, y_3, y_4
x_1, x_5	y_4, y_3	y_1, y_2, y_5
x_3, x_4	y_1, y_2	y_3, y_4, y_5
x_2, x_5	y_5, y_3	y_1, y_2, y_4

In all cases Complementary Slackness holds: $x_1 y_4 = 0$, $x_2 y_5 = 0$, $x_3 y_1 = 0$,

$x_4 y_2 = 0$, $x_5 y_3 = 0$.

6.3-4.   If either the primal or the dual has a degenerate optimal basic feasible solution, then the other may have multiple solutions.

For example, in the problem Maximize $3x_1$

subject to: $a_{11} x_1 + x_2 = 0$

$-2x_1 + x_3 = 1$

$x_1 \geq 0, \; x_2 \geq 0, \; x_3 \geq 0$

If $a_{11} > 0$, we can pivot and get an alternative optimal solution to the dual problem.

If $a_{11} \leq 0$, we cannot.

6.3-4. (cont) The converse is true, however. If a problem has multiple optimal solutions, then two of them must be adjacent corner points. To move from the tableau of one solution to that of the other requires exactly one pivot. Let's say x_j enters and x_k leaves. A partial tableau is below:

$$\begin{array}{c|ccc|c} & & x_j & & \text{RHS} \\ & & \bar{c}_j & & \\ x_k & & \bar{a}_{kj} & & \bar{b}_k \end{array}$$

$\bar{a}_{kj}$ must be positive and $\bar{b}_k \geq 0$.

If $\bar{b}_k > 0$, then $\bar{c}_j = 0$ or z would change value with the pivot.

If $\bar{b}_k = 0$, then x_j pivots in at value zero and the resulting tableau represents the same corner point, contradicting the assumption that the two optimal solutions are distinct.

6.3-5. a) Minimize $v = y_1$

subject to:

$y_1 \geq 2$

$-y_1 \geq -4$

$y_1 \geq 0$

The optimal solution is $v = y_1 = 2$

(b) $(y_1, y_2, y_3) = (2, 0, 2)$ is the optimal basic feasible solution for the dual. By Complementary Slackness, $y_1 x_3 = y_2 x_1 = y_3 x_2 = 0$, so $x_2 = x_3 = 0$. Since $x_1 - x_2 + x_3 = 1$, $(x_1, x_2, x_3) = (1, 0, 0)$ is optimal for the primal

(c) For $c_1 > 4$ the dual will have no feasible solution. Therefore, the primal objective function will be unbounded.

6.3-6. a) Minimize $w = 10y_1 + 10y_2$

subject to:

$y_1 + 3y_2 \geq 2$

$2y_1 + 3y_2 \geq 7$

$y_1 + 2y_2 \geq 4$

$y_1 \geq 0,\ y_2 \geq 0$

(b) $(0, \frac{5}{2})$ is feasible for the dual problem. Using Weak Duality, $w = 10 \cdot 0 + 10 \cdot \frac{5}{2} = 25 \geq z$ so the optimal primal objective value is less than 25.

6.3-6.

(c)

Bas Var	Eq No	Z	X1	X2	X3	X4	X5	Right side
Z	0	1	-2	-7	-4	0	0	0
X4	1	0	1	2	1	1	0	10
X5	2	0	3	3*	2	0	1	10

Bas Var	Eq No	Z	X1	X2	X3	X4	X5	Right side
Z	0	1	5	0	0.667	0	2.333	23.33
X4	1	0	-1	0	-0.33*	1	-0.67	3.333
X2	2	0	1	1	0.667	0	0.333	3.333

Bas Var	Eq No	Z	X1	X2	X3	X4	X5	Right side
Z	0	1	3	0	0	2	1	30
X3	1	0	3	0	1	-3	2	-10
X2	2	0	-1	1	0	2	-1	10

The primal basic solution is $(x_1, x_2, x_3, x_4, x_5) = (0, 10, -10, 0, 0)$ which is not feasible. The dual basic solution is $(y_1, y_2, z_1 - c_1, z_2 - c_2, z_3 - c_3) = (2, 1, 3, 0, 0)$

(d)

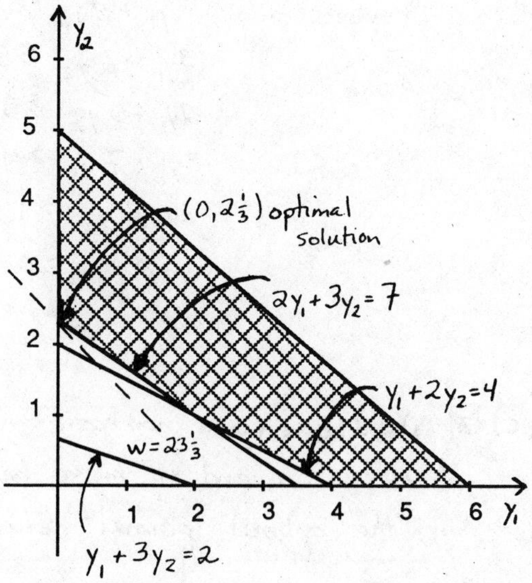

$(y_1, y_2) = (0, 2\frac{1}{3})$ is optimal with $w = 23\frac{1}{3}$.

From the dual solution y_2, y_3 and y_5 are basic, therefore, x_3, x_5 and x_1 are nonbasic primal variables. x_2 and x_4 are basic.

Bas Var	Eq No	Z	X1	X2	X3	X4	X5	Right side
Z	0	1	-2	-7	-4	0	0	0
X4	1	0	1	2	1	1	0	10
X5	2	0	3	3*	2	0	1	10

Bas Var	Eq No	Z	X1	X2	X3	X4	X5	Right side
Z	0	1	5	0	0.667	0	2.333	23.33
X4	1	0	-1	0	-0.33*	1	-0.67	3.333
X2	2	0	1	1	0.667	0	0.333	3.333

$(x_1, x_2, x_3, x_4, x_5) = (0, 3\frac{1}{3}, 0, 3\frac{1}{3}, 0)$ is the primal optimal basic solution with $Z = 23\frac{1}{3}$

6.3-7. a) Minimize $w = 6y_1 + 15y_2$

subject to:

$$y_1 + 4y_2 \geq 2$$
$$3y_1 + 6y_2 \geq 5$$
$$2y_1 + 5y_2 \geq 3$$
$$3y_1 + 7y_2 \geq 4$$
$$y_1 + y_2 \geq 1$$
$$y_1 \geq 0,\ y_2 \geq 0$$

(b)

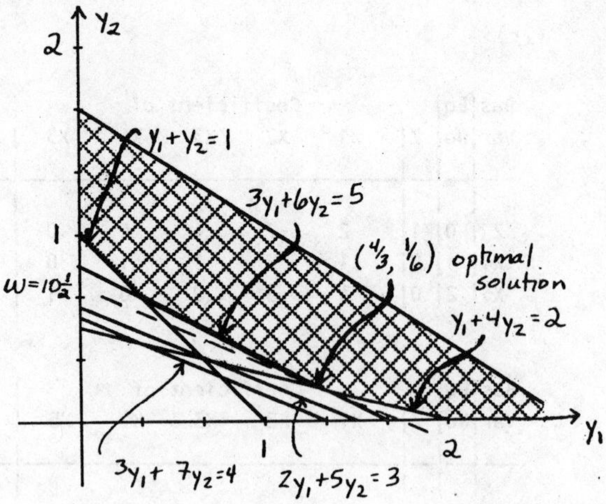

$(y_1, y_2) = (4/3, 1/6)$ is optimal with $w = 10\frac{1}{2}$.

(c) $(z_1 - c_1)$ and $(z_2 - c_2)$ are nonbasic in the dual, so x_1 and x_2 must be basic in the optimal primal solution.

(d)

Bas Var	Eq No	Z	X1	X2	X3	X4	X5	X6	X7	Right side
Z	0	1	-2	-5	-3	-4	-1	0	0	0
X6	1	0	1	3*	2	3	1	1	0	6
X7	2	0	4	6	5	7	1	0	1	15

Bas Var	Eq No	Z	X1	X2	X3	X4	X5	X6	X7	Right side
Z	0	1	-0.33	0	0.333	1	0.667	1.667	0	10
X2	1	0	0.333	1	0.667	1	0.333	0.333	0	2
X7	2	0	2*	0	1	1	-1	-2	1	3

Bas Var	Eq No	Z	X1	X2	X3	X4	X5	X6	X7	Right side
Z	0	1	0	0	0.5	1.167	0.5	1.333	0.167	10.5
X2	1	0	0	1	0.5	0.833	0.5	0.667	-0.17	1.5
X1	2	0	1	0	0.5	0.5	-0.5	-1	0.5	1.5

$(x_1, x_2) = (3/2, 3/2)$ is optimal with $z = 10\frac{1}{2}$.

(e) The Defining Equations are:

$$x_1 + 3x_2 + 2x_3 + 3x_4 + x_5 = 6$$
$$4x_1 + 6x_2 + 5x_3 + 7x_4 + x_5 = 15$$
$$x_3 = 0$$
$$x_4 = 0$$
$$x_5 = 0$$

Which have solution

$$(x_1, x_2, x_3, x_4, x_5) = (3/2, 3/2, 0, 0, 0)$$

6.3-8. a) Minimize $V = 10y_1 + 20y_2$

subject to:

$$-2y_1 + 3y_2 \geq 3$$
$$2y_1 + y_2 \geq 7$$
$$y_1 - y_2 \geq 2$$
$$y_1 \geq 0, \quad y_2 \geq 0$$

(b) Because x_2, x_4 and x_5 are nonbasic in the optimal primal solution, y_1, y_2 and y_4 will be basic in the optimal dual solution.

(c) The Defining Equations are:

$$-2y_1 + 3y_2 - y_3 = 3$$
$$2y_1 + y_2 - y_4 = 7$$
$$y_1 - y_2 - y_5 = 2$$
$$y_3 = 0$$
$$y_5 = 0$$

which have solution

$$(y_1, y_2, y_3, y_4, y_5) = (9, 7, 0, 18, 0)$$

(d)

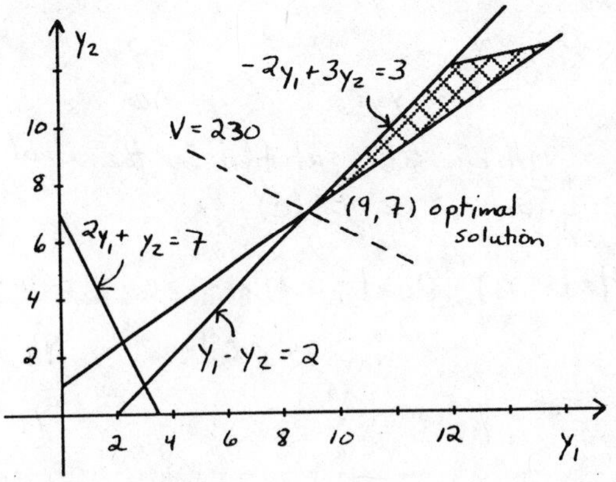

$(y_1, y_2) = (9, 7)$ is optimal with $V = 230$

6.3-9 a) Minimize $V = 10y_1 + 60y_2 + 18y_3 + 44y_4$

subject to:

$$2y_2 + y_3 + 3y_4 \geq 2$$
$$y_1 + 5y_2 + y_3 + y_4 \geq 1$$
$$y_i \geq 0 \text{ for } i = 1,2,3,4$$

(b) The Defining Equations for $(x_1, x_2) = (13, 5)$ are:

$$x_1 + x_2 = 18$$
$$3x_1 + x_2 = 44$$

We conclude y_3 and y_4 must be basic for the optimal dual solution and y_1, y_2, y_5 and y_6 nonbasic.

(c) The basic variables for the primal optimal solution are x_1, x_2, x_3 and x_4. We can procede by introducing x_1 and x_2 into the basis from the initial tableau.

Bas Var	Eq No	Z	X1	X2	X3	X4	X5	X6	Right side
Z	0	1	-2	-1	0	0	0	0	0
X3	1	0	0	1	1	0	0	0	10
X4	2	0	2	5	0	1	0	0	60
X5	3	0	1	1	0	0	1	0	18
X6	4	0	3*	1	0	0	0	1	44

Bas Var	Eq No	Z	X1	X2	X3	X4	X5	X6	Right side
Z	0	1	0	-0.33	0	0	0	0.667	29.33
X3	1	0	0	1	1	0	0	0	10
X4	2	0	0	4.333	0	1	0	-0.67	30.67
X5	3	0	0	0.667*	0	0	1	-0.33	3.333
X1	4	0	1	0.333	0	0	0	0.333	14.67

Bas Var	Eq No	Z	X1	X2	X3	X4	X5	X6	Right side
Z	0	1	0	0	0	0	0.5	0.5	31
X3	1	0	0	0	1	0	-1.5	0.5	5
X4	2	0	0	0	0	1	-6.5	1.5	9
X2	3	0	0	1	0	0	1.5	-0.5	5
X1	4	0	1	0	0	0	-0.5	0.5	13

$(x_1, x_2, x_3, x_4, x_5, x_6) = (13, 5, 5, 9, 0, 0)$ is optimal with $Z = 31$.

The basic dual solution is:

$$(y_1, y_2, y_3, y_4, y_5, y_6) = (0, 0, \tfrac{1}{2}, \tfrac{1}{2}, 0, 0)$$

6.3-9. (d) The Defining Equations for the optimal solution are:

$$2y_2 + y_3 + 3y_4 = 2$$
$$y_1 + 5y_2 + y_3 + y_4 = 1$$
$$y_1 = 0$$
$$y_2 = 0$$

which are satisfied by the dual solution given in part (c).

3-10. (a) The optimal solution for the dual will correspond to the revised row 0 computed by the Revised Simplex Method to determine optimality.

(b) The complementary basic solution corresponds to the revised row 0 as well.

6.4-1. a) Dual: Minimize $Y_0 = 10y_1 + 2y_2$

subject to:

$$y_1 + 2y_2 = 1$$
$$2y_1 + y_2 \geq 1$$
$$y_2 \leq 0 \quad (y_1 \text{ unconstrained in sign})$$

b) Standard form: Maximize $Z = x_1^+ - x_1^- + x_2$

subject to:

$$x_1^+ - x_1^- + 2x_2 \leq 10$$
$$-x_1^+ + x_1^- - 2x_2 \leq -10$$
$$-2x_1^+ + 2x_1^- - x_2 \leq -2$$
$$x_1^+ \geq 0,\ x_1^- \geq 0,\ x_2 \geq 0$$

Dual of Standard form:

Minimize $Y_0 = 10y_1 - 10y_2 - 2y_3$

subject to:

$$\left.\begin{aligned} y_1 - y_2 - 2y_3 &\geq 1 \\ -y_1 + y_2 + 2y_3 &\geq -1 \end{aligned}\right\} \Leftrightarrow y_1 - y_2 - 2y_3 = 1$$
$$2y_1 - 2y_2 - y_3 \geq 1$$
$$y_1 \geq 0,\ y_2 \geq 0,\ y_3 \geq 0$$

Let $y_1' = y_1 - y_2$ (so y_1' is unrestricted in sign)

and $y_2' = -y_3$ (so $y_2' \leq 0$)

Then the dual is: Min $Y_0 = 10y_1' + 2y_2'$

subject to

$$y_1' + 2y_2' = 1$$
$$2y_1' + y_2' \geq 1$$
$$y_2' \leq 0 \quad (y_1' \text{ unrestricted in sign})$$

as given in (a)

6.4-2. a) Since $\{Ax = b\}$ is equivalent to $\left\{\begin{bmatrix} A \\ -A \end{bmatrix} x \le \begin{bmatrix} b \\ -b \end{bmatrix}\right\}$, changing the primal functional constraints from $Ax \le b$ to $Ax = b$ changes the dual to:

$$\text{Minimize } Y_0 = [\tilde{y}^T, \tilde{w}^T]\begin{bmatrix} b \\ -b \end{bmatrix}$$

$$\text{subject to: } [\tilde{y}^T, \tilde{w}^T]\begin{bmatrix} A \\ -A \end{bmatrix} \ge c$$

$$\tilde{y}, \tilde{w} \ge 0$$

where $\tilde{y}, \tilde{w}$ are simply the first and last halfs of the vector normally called y

This is equivalent to:

$$\text{Min } Y_0 = (\tilde{y} - \tilde{w})^T b$$

$$\text{subject to: } (\tilde{y} - \tilde{w})^T A \ge c$$

$$\tilde{y}, \tilde{w} \ge 0$$

Now, letting $y = \tilde{y} - \tilde{w}$, so y is unrestricted in sign.

The dual is: $\text{Min } Y_0 = yb$

subject to: $yA \ge c$

(y unrestricted in sign)

So the only difference is that the non-negativity constraints $Y \ge 0$ have been deleted.

b) Similarly (as in (a)), $\{Ax \ge b\}$ is equivalent to $\{-Ax \le -b\}$

So the dual of

$$\text{Max } Z = cx \quad \text{s.t. } Ax \ge b, \quad x \ge 0$$

is

Dual: $\text{Min } Y_0 = \tilde{y}(-b)$ s.t. $\tilde{y}(-A) \ge c$, $\tilde{y} \ge 0$

Letting $y = -\tilde{y}$,

Dual: $\text{Min } Y_0 = yb$ s.t. $yA \ge c$, $y \le 0$

So $Y \ge 0$ is replaced with $Y \le 0$ in dual.

c) Primal: $\text{Max } Z = cx$ s.t. $Ax \le b$ (x unrestr.) $\Leftrightarrow$ Primal: $\text{Max } Z = cx^+ - cx^-$ s.t. $Ax^+ - Ax^- \le b$, $x^+ \ge 0, x^- \ge 0$ $\Leftrightarrow$ Dual: $\text{Min } Y_0 = yb$ s.t. $yA \ge c$, $y(-A) \ge -c$, $y \ge 0$ $\Leftrightarrow$ Dual: $\text{Min } Y_0 = yb$ s.t. $yA = c$, $y \ge 0$

So $yA \ge c$ is simply replaced by $yA = c$.

6.4-3. Dual is: Maximize $V = 8y_1 + 6y_2$

subject to:

$$y_1 + 3y_2 \le 2$$
$$4y_1 + 2y_2 \le 3$$
$$2y_1 \le 1$$
$$y_1 \ge 0,\ y_2 \ge 0$$

6.4-4. a) Dual is: maximize $V = y_1 + y_2$

subject to:

$$-2y_1 + y_2 \le 1$$
$$y_1 - 2y_2 \le 2$$
$$y_1 \ge 0,\ y_2 \ge 0$$

b)

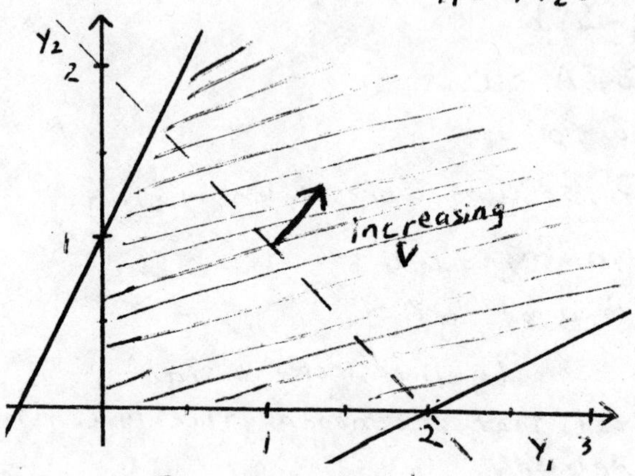

Since V can be increased indefinitely, the primal problem cannot have any feasible solutions. (This can be shown by weak duality, keeping in mind that the primal and dual are "reversed" in this problem)

6.4-5.

$$\text{Min } y_0 = 2.7y_1 + 6y_2 + 6y_3'$$

s.t.

$$0.3y_1 + 0.5y_2 + 0.6y_3 \ge -0.4$$
$$0.1y_1 + 0.5y_2 + 0.4y_3' \ge -0.5$$
$$y_1 \ge 0,\ y_3' \le 0 \text{ (}y_2\text{ unconstrained in sign)}$$

is equivalent to:

$$\text{Max } -y_0 = -2.7y_1 - 6y_2 - 6y_3'$$

Min $Z \Leftrightarrow$ Max $(-Z)$

s.t.

$$0.3y_1 + 0.5y_2 + 0.6y_3' \ge -0.4$$
$$0.1y_1 + 0.5y_2 + 0.4y_3' \ge -0.5$$
$$y_1 \ge 0,\ y_3' \le 0 \text{ (}y_2\text{ unconstrained)}$$

which is equivalent to:

$$\text{Max } y_0' = 2.7y_1' + 6y_2' + 6y_3$$

Let $y_1' = -y_1$, $y_2' = -y_2$, $y_3 = -y_3'$

s.t.

$$-0.3y_1' - 0.5y_2' - 0.6y_3 \ge -0.4$$
$$-0.1y_1' - 0.5y_2' - 0.4y_3 \ge -0.5$$
$$y_1' \le 0,\ y_3 \ge 0 \text{ (}y_2'\text{ unconstrained)}$$

which is equivalent to:

$$\text{Max } y_0' = 2.7y_1' + 6y_2' + 6y_3$$

s.t.

$$0.3y_1' + 0.5y_2' + 0.6y_3 \le 0.4$$
$$0.1y_1' + 0.5y_2' + 0.4y_3 \le 0.5$$
$$y_1' \le 0,\ y_3 \ge 0 \text{ (}y_2'\text{ unconstrained)}$$

$$\sum_{j=1}^{n} a_{ij}x_j \ge b_i \Leftrightarrow -\sum_{j=1}^{n} a_{ij}x_j \le -b_i$$

as desired.

6.4-6. a) Minimize $Z = 3x_1 + 2x_2$

subject to:

$$2x_1 + x_2 \geq 10$$
$$-3x_1 + 2x_2 \leq 6$$
$$x_1 + x_2 \geq 6$$
$$x_1 \geq 0,\ x_2 \geq 0$$

Dual: Maximize $V = 10y_1 + 6y_2 + 6y_3$

subject to:

$$2y_1 - 3y_2 + y_3 \leq 3$$
$$y_1 + 2y_2 + y_3 \leq 2$$
$$y_1 \geq 0,\ y_2 \leq 0,\ y_3 \geq 0$$

b) Maximize $Z = 2x_1 + 5x_2 + 3x_3$

subject to:

$$x_1 - 2x_2 + x_3 \geq 20$$
$$2x_1 + 4x_2 + x_3 = 50$$
$$x_1 \geq 0,\ x_2 \geq 0,\ x_3 \geq 0$$

Dual: Minimize $V = 20y_1 + 50y_2$

subject to:

$$y_1 + 2y_2 \geq 2$$
$$-2y_1 + 4y_2 \geq 5$$
$$y_1 + y_2 \geq 3$$
$$y_1 \leq 0 \ (y_2 \text{ unconstrained})$$

c) Max $Z = -2x_1 + x_2 - 4x_3 + 3x_4$

s.t.

$$x_1 + x_2 + 3x_3 + 2x_4 \leq 4$$
$$x_1 - x_3 + x_4 \geq -1$$
$$2x_1 + x_2 \leq 2$$
$$x_1 + 2x_2 + x_3 + 2x_4 = 2$$
$$x_2 \geq 0,\ x_3 \geq 0,\ x_4 \geq 0$$

(x_1 unconstrained in sign)

Dual: Min $V = 4y_1 - y_2 + 2y_3 + 2y_4$

s.t.

$$y_1 + y_2 + 2y_3 + y_4 = -2$$
$$y_1 + y_3 + 2y_4 \geq 1$$
$$3y_1 - y_2 + y_4 \geq -4$$
$$2y_1 + y_2 + 2y_4 \geq 3$$
$$y_1 \geq 0,\ y_2 \geq 0,\ y_3 \geq 0$$

(y_4 unconstrained in sign)

6.4-7. a) Dual: Minimize $V = 300y_1 + 300y_2$

subject to:

$$2y_1 + 8y_2 \geq 4$$
$$3y_1 + y_2 \geq 2$$
$$4y_1 + y_2 \geq 3$$
$$2y_1 + 5y_2 \geq 5$$

(y_1, y_2 unrestricted in sign)

b) Max $Z = 4x_1 + 2x_2 + 3x_3 + 5x_4$

s.t.

$$2x_1 + 3x_2 + 4x_3 + 2x_4 = 300$$
$$8x_1 + x_2 + x_3 + 5x_4 = 300$$
$$x_1 \geq 0,\ x_2 \geq 0,\ x_3 \geq 0,\ x_4 \geq 0$$

(To standard form) →

Max $Z = 4x_1 + 2x_2 + 3x_3 + 5x_4$

s.t.

$$2x_1 + 3x_2 + 4x_3 + 2x_4 \leq 300$$
$$-2x_1 - 3x_2 - 4x_3 - 2x_4 \leq -300$$
$$8x_1 + x_2 + x_3 + 5x_4 \leq 300$$
$$-8x_1 - x_2 - x_3 - 5x_4 \leq -300$$
$$x_1 \geq 0,\ x_2 \geq 0,\ x_3 \geq 0,\ x_4 \geq 0$$

↓ Finding Dual

Dual:

Min $V = 300y_1 - 300y_2 + 300y_3 - 300y_4$

s.t.

$$2y_1 - 2y_2 + 8y_3 - 8y_4 \geq 4$$
$$3y_1 - 3y_2 + y_3 - y_4 \geq 2$$
$$4y_1 - 4y_2 + y_3 - y_4 \geq 3$$
$$2y_1 - 2y_2 + 5y_3 - 5y_4 \geq 5$$
$$y_1 \geq 0,\ y_2 \geq 0,\ y_3 \geq 0,\ y_4 \geq 0$$

← Let $y_1' = y_1 - y_2$, $y_2' = y_3 - y_4$

Dual:

Min $V = 300y_1' + 300y_2'$

s.t.

$$2y_1' + 8y_2' \geq 4$$
$$3y_1' + y_2' \geq 2$$
$$4y_1' + y_2' \geq 3$$
$$2y_1' + 5y_2' \geq 5$$

(y_1', y_2' unrestricted in sign)

↗ same as in (a)

6.4-8, (a) Minimize $v = 120y_1 + 80y_2 + 100y_3$

subject to:

$$y_2 - 3y_3 = -1$$
$$3y_1 - y_2 + y_3 = 2$$
$$y_1 - 4y_2 + 2y_3 = 1$$
$$y_1 \geq 0,\ y_2 \geq 0,\ y_3 \geq 0.$$

(b) Standard form for the primal is:

Maximize $Z = -x_1' + x_1'' + 2x_2' - 2x_2'' + x_3' - x_3''$

subject to:

$$3x_2' - 3x_2'' + x_3' - x_3'' \leq 120$$
$$x_1' - x_1'' - x_2' + x_2'' - 4x_3' + 4x_3'' \leq 80$$
$$-3x_1' + 3x_1'' + x_2' - x_2'' + 2x_3' - 2x_3'' \leq 100$$
$$x_1' \geq 0,\ x_1'' \geq 0,\ x_2' \geq 0,\ x_2'' \geq 0,$$
$$x_3' \geq 0,\ x_3'' \geq 0.$$

The dual is: Minimize $v = 120y_1 + 80y_2 + 100y_3$

subject to:

$$y_2 - 3y_3 \geq -1$$
$$-y_2 + 3y_3 \geq 1$$
$$3y_1 - y_2 + y_3 \geq 2$$
$$-3y_1 + y_2 - y_3 \geq -2$$
$$y_1 - 4y_2 + 2y_3 \geq 1$$
$$-y_1 + 4y_2 - 2y_3 \geq -1$$
$$y_1 \geq 0,\ y_2 \geq 0,\ y_3 \geq 0$$

By combining constraints 1 and 2, 3 and 4 and 5 and 6 we get the form in part (a).

6.4-9. The Wyndor dual in standard form is:

Maximize $(-v) = -4y_1 - 12y_2 - 18y_3$

subject to:

$$-y_1 \quad - 3y_3 \leq -3$$
$$-2y_2 - 2y_3 \leq -5$$
$$y_1 \geq 0,\ y_2 \geq 0,\ y_3 \geq 0$$

The dual of this dual is:

Minimize $(-Z) = -3x_1 - 5x_2$

subject to:

$$-x_1 \geq -4$$
$$-2x_2 \geq -12$$
$$-3x_1 - 2x_2 \geq -18$$
$$x_1 \geq 0,\ x_2 \geq 0$$

This is equivalent to the primal:

Maximize $Z = 3x_1 + 5x_2$

subject to:

$$x_1 \leq 4$$
$$2x_2 \leq 12$$
$$3x_1 + 2x_2 \leq 18$$
$$x_1 \geq 0,\ x_2 \geq 0$$

6.4-10. a)

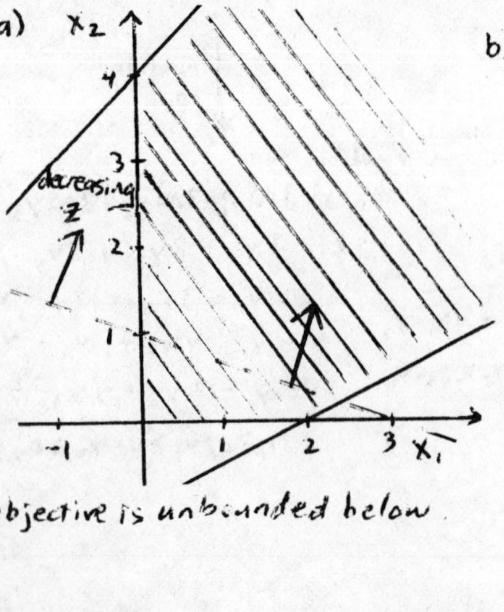

Objective is unbounded below.

b) Dual:

Maximize $2y_1 + 4y_2$

subject to:

$$y_1 - y_2 \leq -1$$
$$-2y_1 + y_2 \leq -3$$
$$y_1 \leq 0,\ y_2 \leq 0$$

c)

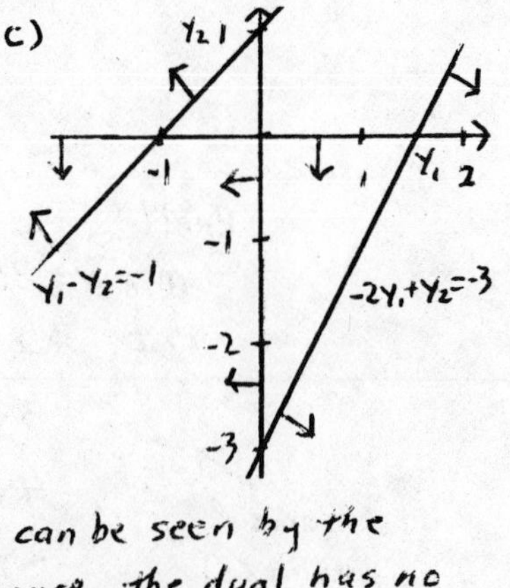

As can be seen by the figure, the dual has no feasible solutions.

6.5-1. a) Since X_1 was non-basic, changing the coefficients of X_1 does not affect feasibility. To check optimality, we check dual feasibility:

The first dual constraint becomes

$$0Y_1 + 5Y_2 \geq -2$$

which clearly must be true ($Y_2 \geq 0$).

Therefore, the current basic solution remains optimal.

b) Adding a new variable does not affect primal feasibility (if we let $X_6 = 0$). To check for optimality, we check dual feasibility:

The constraint (corresponding to X_6) in the dual is:

$$3Y_1 + 5Y_2 \geq 10$$

(Note: we are assuming that $X_6 \geq 0$. If one assumes X_6 is unrestricted, the constraint would become $3Y_1 + 5Y_2 = 10$.)

$Y_1 = 5, Y_2 = 0$. So $3(5) + 5(0) = 15 \geq 10$

and the current basic solution (with $X_6 = 0$) remains optimal.

6.5-2. a) Since X_3 was non-basic, changing the coefficients of X_3 does not affect primal feasibility. To check optimality, we see if the dual solution is still feasible:

The third dual constraint becomes

$$3Y_1 + Y_2 - 2Y_3 \geq 2$$

$Y_1 = 0, Y_2 = 3/2, Y_3 = 1/2$, So $3(0) + \frac{3}{2} - 2(\frac{1}{2}) = \frac{1}{2} \not\geq 2$.

Thus, the current basic solution though feasible, is not optimal.

b) If we let $X_8 = 0$, adding the new variable does not affect primal feasibility. We check dual feasibility:

The dual constraint (corresponding to X_8) is

$$-2Y_1 + Y_2 + 2Y_3 \geq -1$$

or $-2(0) + \frac{3}{2} + 2(\frac{1}{2}) = \frac{5}{2} \geq -1$

So the current basic solution (with $X_8 = 0$) remains optimal.

6.5-3. a) Since X_3 is non-basic, primal feasibility still holds. To check for optimality, we look at the dual constraint (corresponding to X_3):

$$3Y_1 - 2Y_2 \geq -2 \quad (Y_1 = 0, Y_2 = 2 \Rightarrow 3(0) - 2(2) = -4 \not\geq -2)$$

Since this constraint does not hold, the current basic solution is not optimal.

6.5-3. b) If we let $X_6 = 0$, primal feasibility still holds. We need only check to see that the dual contraint corresponding to X_6 still holds:

$$Y_1 + 2Y_2 \geq 3$$

or $$0 + 2(2) = 4 \geq 3$$

So, since dual feasibility holds, the current basic solution remains feasible and optimal.

6.5-4. Since X_3 was non-basic, changing the coefficients of X_3 does not affect primal feasibility. To check for optimality, we must see if the complementary basic solution for the dual problem remains feasible:

The third dual constraint becomes

$$3Y_1 + 2Y_2 + Y_3 \geq 4 \quad (Y_1 = 1,\ Y_2 = 1,\ Y_3 = 0)$$

or $$3(1) + 2(1) + 0 = 5 \geq 4$$

So the current basic solution remains optimal.

6.6-1. (a) $(x_1, x_2, x_3) = (5/3, 0, 3)$. $z = 17$

(b) Minimize $v = 25y_1 + 20y_2$

subject to:

$$6y_1 + 3y_2 \geq 3$$
$$3y_1 + 4y_2 \geq 1$$
$$5y_1 + 5y_2 \geq 4$$
$$y_1 \geq 0,\ y_2 \geq 0.$$

(c)

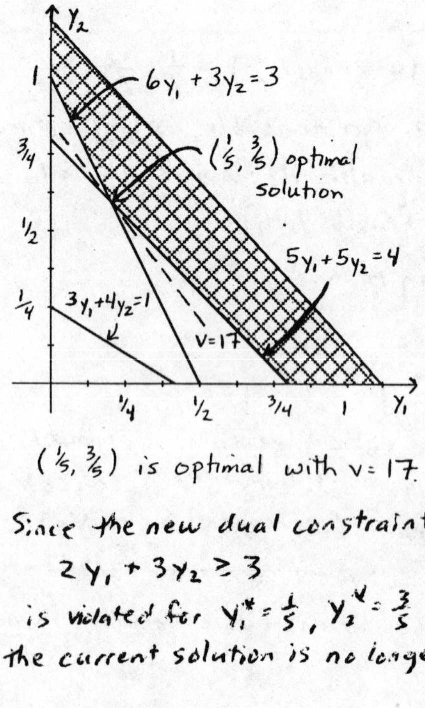

$(\frac{1}{5}, \frac{3}{5})$ is optimal with $v = 17$.

(d) Since the new dual constraint

$$2y_1 + 3y_2 \geq 3$$

is violated for $Y_1^* = \frac{1}{5}$, $Y_2^* = \frac{3}{5}$

the current solution is no longer optimal.

(e) New x_2 column is:

$$\begin{pmatrix} 1/3 & -1/3 \\ -1/5 & 2/5 \end{pmatrix} \begin{pmatrix} 2 \\ 3 \end{pmatrix} = \begin{pmatrix} -1/3 \\ 4/5 \end{pmatrix}$$

(f) The new primal variable adds a constraint to the dual,

$3y_1 + 2y_2 \geq 2$, which is not satisfied by $(y_1, y_2) = (\frac{1}{5}, \frac{3}{5})$. Therefore, the previous solution is no longer optimal.

(g) $\bar{c}_{NEW} = (\frac{1}{5}, \frac{3}{5})\begin{pmatrix} 3 \\ 2 \end{pmatrix} - 2 = -\frac{1}{5}$

New column $= \begin{pmatrix} 1/3 & -1/3 \\ -1/5 & 2/5 \end{pmatrix} \begin{pmatrix} 3 \\ 2 \end{pmatrix} = \begin{pmatrix} 1/3 \\ 1/5 \end{pmatrix}$.

6.6-2. (a) $\Delta b_1 = -10$, $\Delta b_2 = 0$ $\Big\}$ $\Delta Z = \left(\frac{1}{5}, \frac{3}{5}\right)\begin{pmatrix}-10\\0\end{pmatrix} = -2$

$\Delta b_1^* = \left(\frac{1}{3}, -\frac{1}{3}\right)\begin{pmatrix}-10\\0\end{pmatrix} = -\frac{10}{3}$

$\Delta b_2^* = \left(-\frac{1}{5}, \frac{2}{5}\right)\begin{pmatrix}-10\\0\end{pmatrix} = 2$

New Tableau:

Bas Var	Eq No	Z	X1	X2	X3	X4	X5	Right side
Z	0	1	0	2	0	0.2	0.6	15
X1	1	0	1	-0.33	0	0.333	-0.33	-1.67
X3	2	0	0	1	1	-0.2	0.4	5

The current basic solution $(-5/3, 0, 5, 0, 0)$ is infeasible and super optimal.

(b) $\Delta b_1 = 0$, $\Delta b_2 = -15$ $\Big\}$ $\Delta Z = \left(\frac{1}{5}, \frac{3}{5}\right)\begin{pmatrix}0\\-15\end{pmatrix} = -9$

$\Delta b_1^* = \left(\frac{1}{3}, -\frac{1}{3}\right)\begin{pmatrix}0\\-15\end{pmatrix} = 5$

$\Delta b_2^* = \left(-\frac{1}{5}, \frac{2}{5}\right)\begin{pmatrix}0\\-15\end{pmatrix} = -6$

New Tableau:

Bas Var	Eq No	Z	X1	X2	X3	X4	X5	Right side
Z	0	1	0	2	0	0.2	0.6	8
X1	1	0	1	-0.33	0	0.333	-0.33	6.667
X3	2	0	0	1	1	-0.2	0.4	-3

The current basic solution $(20/3, 0, -3, 0, 0)$ is infeasible and superoptimal.

(c) $\Delta c_2 = 3$ $\}$ $\Delta(z_2^* - c_2) = -3$

New Tableau:

Bas Var	Eq No	Z	X1	X2	X3	X4	X5	Right side
Z	0	1	0	-1	0	0.2	0.6	17
X1	1	0	1	-0.33	0	0.333	-0.33	1.667
X3	2	0	0	1	1	-0.2	0.4	3

The current basic solution $(5/3, 0, 3, 0, 0)$ is feasible, but not optimal.

(d) $\Delta c_3 = -1$ $\}$ $\Delta(z_3^* - c_3) = 1$

New Tableau:

Bas Var	Eq No	Z	X1	X2	X3	X4	X5	Right side
Z	0	1	0	2	1	1/5	3/5	17
X1	1	0	1	-1/3	0	1/3	-1/3	5/3
X_3	2	0	0	1	1	-1/5	2/5	3

Proper Form:

Bas Var	Eq No	Z	X1	X2	X3	X4	X5	Right side
Z	0	1	0	1	0	2/5	1/5	14
X1	1	0	1	-1/3	0	1/3	-1/3	5/3
X3	2	0	0	1	1	-1/5	2/5	3

The current basic solution $(5/3, 0, 3, 0, 0)$ is feasible and optimal.

(e) $\Delta a_{22} = -3 \Rightarrow \Delta(z_2^* - c_2) = \left(\frac{1}{5}\ \frac{3}{5}\right)\begin{pmatrix}0\\-3\end{pmatrix} = -\frac{9}{5}$

$\Delta a_{12}^* = \left(\frac{1}{3}, -\frac{1}{3}\right)\begin{pmatrix}0\\-3\end{pmatrix} = 1$

$\Delta a_{22}^* = \left(-\frac{1}{5}, \frac{2}{5}\right)\begin{pmatrix}0\\-3\end{pmatrix} = -\frac{6}{5}$

New Tableau:

Bas Var	Eq No	Z	X1	X2	X3	X4	X5	Right side
Z	0	1	0	0.2	0	0.2	0.6	17
X1	1	0	1	0.667	0	0.333	-0.33	1.667
X3	2	0	0	-0.2	1	-0.2	0.4	3

The current basic solution $(5/3, 0, 3, 0, 0)$ is feasible and optimal.

(f) $\Delta a_{11} = 4 \Rightarrow \Delta(z_1^* - c_1) = \left(\frac{1}{5}, \frac{3}{5}\right)\begin{pmatrix}4\\0\end{pmatrix} = \frac{4}{5}$

$\Delta a_{11}^* = \left(\frac{1}{3}, -\frac{1}{3}\right)\begin{pmatrix}4\\0\end{pmatrix} = \frac{4}{3}$

$\Delta a_{21}^* = \left(-\frac{1}{5}, \frac{2}{5}\right)\begin{pmatrix}4\\0\end{pmatrix} = -\frac{4}{5}$

New Tableau:

Bas Var	Eq No	Z	X1	X2	X3	X4	X5	Right side
Z	0	1	4/5	2	0	1/5	3/5	17
X1	1	0	7/3	-1/3	0	1/3	-1/3	5/3
X3	2	0	-4/5	1	1	-1/5	2/5	3

6.6-2. (f) (cont.)

Tableau in Proper Form:

Bas Var	Eq No	Z	X1	X2	X3	X4	X5	Right side
Z	0	1	0	2.11	0	0.09	0.71	16.43
X1	1	0	1	0.14	0	0.14	-0.14	0.71
X3	2	0	0	0.89	1	-0.09	0.29	3.57

The current basic solution (0.71, 0, 3.57, 0, 0) is feasible and optimal.

6.6-3. (a) In the dual problem,

$$\left.\begin{array}{l}\Delta b_1 = -2 \\ \Delta b_2 = 1\end{array}\right\} \quad \Delta z^* = (1,1)\begin{pmatrix}-2\\1\end{pmatrix} = -1$$

$$\Delta b_1^* = (1,-1)\begin{pmatrix}-2\\1\end{pmatrix} = -3$$

$$\Delta b_2^* = (-1,2)\begin{pmatrix}-2\\1\end{pmatrix} = 4$$

New Tableau:

Bas Var	Eq No	Z	X1	X2	X3	X4	X5	X6	Right side
Z	0	1	3	0	2	0	1	1	8
X2	1	0	1	1	-1	0	1	-1	-2
X4	2	0	2	0	3	1	-1	2	7

From the tableau we can see the primal basic solution is feasible, but not optimal.

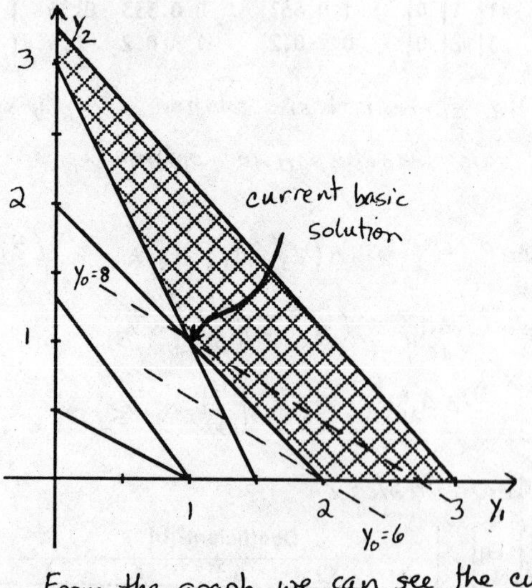

From the graph we can see the current basic solution is feasible, but not optimal

6-3. (b)

In the dual problem:

$$\Delta c_1 = -1 \Rightarrow \Delta(z_1^* - c_1) = 1$$

$$\Delta c_2 = 2 \Rightarrow \Delta(z_2^* - c_2) = -2$$

$$\Delta c_3 = 1 \Rightarrow \Delta(z_3^* - c_3) = -1$$

$$\Delta c_4 = 1 \Rightarrow \Delta(z_4^* - c_4) = -1$$

New Tableau:

Bas Var	Eq No	Z	X1	X2	X3	X4	X5	X6	Right side
Z	0	1	4	-2	1	-1	1	1	9
X2	1	0	1	1	-1	0	1	-1	1
X4	2	0	2	0	3	1	-1	2	3

Proper Form:

Bas Var	Eq No	Z	X1	X2	X3	X4	X5	X6	Right side
Z	0	1	8	0	2	0	2	1	14
X2	1	0	1	1	-1	0	1	-1	1
X4	2	0	2	0	3	1	-1	2	3

The primal basic solution is both feasible and optimal.

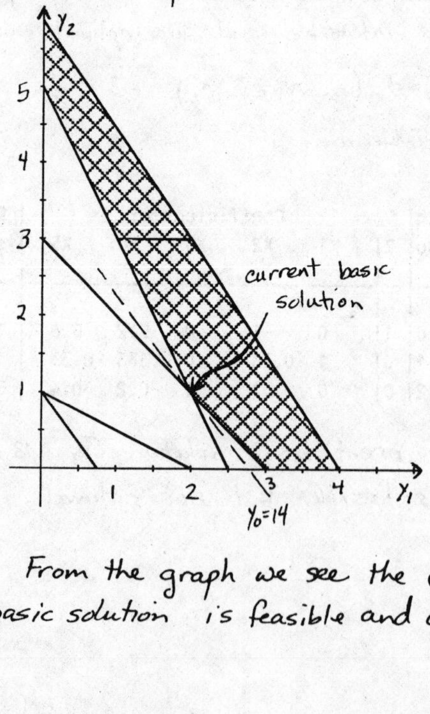

From the graph we see the current basic solution is feasible and optimal.

6.6-3. (c) In the dual problem:

$$\left.\begin{array}{l}\Delta c_1 = 3 \\ \Delta a_{11} = -2 \\ \Delta a_{21} = 1\end{array}\right\} \quad \begin{array}{l}\Delta(z_1^* - c_1) = -3 + (1,1)\begin{pmatrix}-2\\1\end{pmatrix} = -4 \\ \Delta a_{11}^* = (1,-1)\begin{pmatrix}-2\\1\end{pmatrix} = -3 \\ \Delta a_{21}^* = (-1,2)\begin{pmatrix}-2\\1\end{pmatrix} = 4\end{array}$$

New Tableau:

Bas Var	Eq No	Z	X1	X2	X3	X4	X5	X6	Right side
Z	0	1	-1	0	2	0	1	1	9
X2	1	0	-2	1	-1	0	1	-1	1
X4	2	0	6	0	3	1	-1	2	3

The primal basic solution is infeasible, but satisfies optimality criterion.

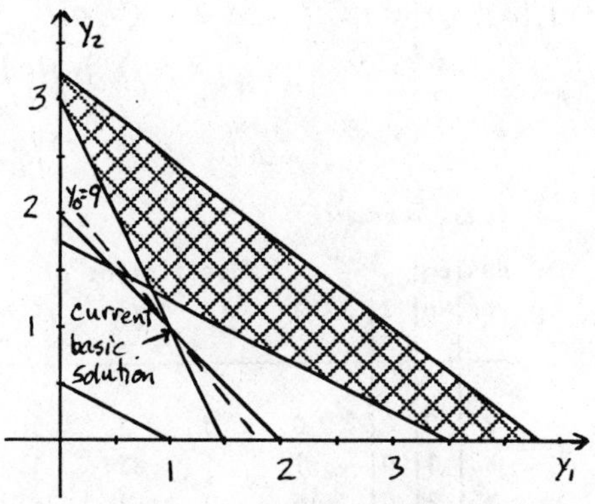

From the graph, the current basic solution is infeasible and superoptimal.

(d) In the dual problem,

$$\left.\begin{array}{l}\Delta c_2 = 7 \\ \Delta a_{12} = 3 \\ \Delta a_{22} = 1\end{array}\right\} \quad \begin{array}{l}\Delta(z_2^* - c_2) = -7 + (1,1)\begin{pmatrix}3\\1\end{pmatrix} = -3 \\ \Delta a_{12}^* = (1,-1)\begin{pmatrix}3\\1\end{pmatrix} = 2 \\ \Delta a_{22}^* = (-1,2)\begin{pmatrix}3\\1\end{pmatrix} = -1\end{array}$$

New Tableau:

Bas Var	Eq No	Z	X1	X2	X3	X4	X5	X6	Right side
Z	0	1	3	-3	2	0	1	1	9
X2	1	0	1	3	-1	0	1	-1	1
X4	2	0	2	-1	3	1	-1	2	3

Proper Form:

Bas Var	Eq No	Z	X1	X2	X3	X4	X5	X6	Right side
Z	0	1	4	0	1	0	2	0	10
X2	1	0	0.333	1	-0.33	0	0.333	-0.33	0.333
X4	2	0	2.333	0	2.667	1	-0.67	1.667	3.333

The primal basic solution is feasible and optimal.

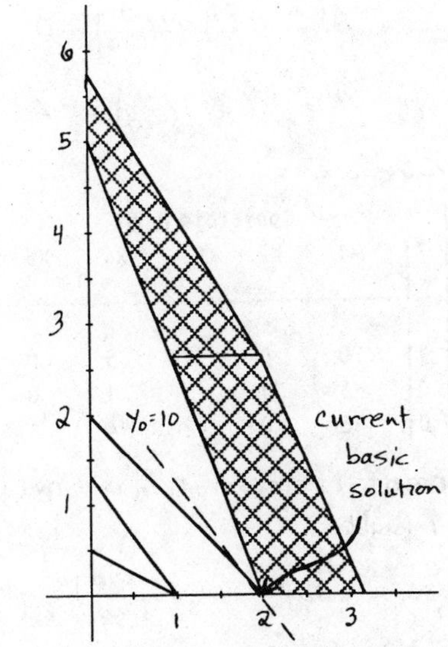

From the graph the current basic solution is feasible and optimal.

6.7-1.(a) $\left.\begin{array}{l}\Delta b_1=10\\ \Delta b_2=0\end{array}\right\}$ $\Delta z^*=(5,0)\begin{pmatrix}10\\0\end{pmatrix}=50$

$\Delta b_1^*=(1,0)\begin{pmatrix}10\\0\end{pmatrix}=10$

$\Delta b_2^*=(-4,1)\begin{pmatrix}10\\0\end{pmatrix}=-40$

New Tableau:

Bas Var	Eq No	Z	X1	X2	X3	X4	X5	Right side
Z	0	1	0	0	2	5	0	150
X2	1	0	-1	1	3	1	0	30
X5	2	0	16	0	-2	-4	1	-30

The current basic solution is superoptimal, but infeasible.

(b) $\left.\begin{array}{l}\Delta b_1=0\\ \Delta b_2=-20\end{array}\right\}$ $\Delta z^*=(5,0)\begin{pmatrix}0\\-20\end{pmatrix}=0$

$\Delta b_1^*=(1,0)\begin{pmatrix}0\\-20\end{pmatrix}=0$

$\Delta b_2^*=(-4,1)\begin{pmatrix}0\\-20\end{pmatrix}=-20$

New Tableau:

Bas Var	Eq No	Z	X1	X2	X3	X4	X5	Right side
Z	0	1	0	0	2	5	0	100
X2	1	0	-1	1	3	1	0	20
X5	2	0	16	0	-2	-4	1	-10

The current basic solution is superoptimal, but infeasible

(c) $\left.\begin{array}{l}\Delta b_1=-10\\ \Delta b_2=10\end{array}\right\}$ $\Delta b_1^*=(1,0)\begin{pmatrix}-10\\10\end{pmatrix}=-10$

$\Delta b_2^*=(-4,1)\begin{pmatrix}-10\\10\end{pmatrix}=50$

New Tableau: $\Delta Z^*=(5,0)\begin{pmatrix}-10\\10\end{pmatrix}=-50$

Bas Var	Eq No	Z	X1	X2	X3	X4	X5	Right side
Z	0	1	0	0	2	5	0	50
X2	1	0	-1	1	3	1	0	10
X5	2	0	16	0	-2	-4	1	60

The current basic solution is feasible and optimal.

(d) $\Delta c_3=-5 \Rightarrow \Delta(z_3^*-c_3)=5$

New Tableau:

Bas Var	Eq No	Z	X1	X2	X3	X4	X5	Right side
Z	0	1	0	0	7	5	0	100
X2	1	0	-1	1	3	1	0	20
X5	2	0	16	0	-2	-4	1	10

The current basic solution is feasible and optimal.

(e) $\left.\begin{array}{l}\Delta c_1=3\\ \Delta a_{11}=1\\ \Delta a_{21}=-7\end{array}\right\}$ $\Delta(z_1^*-c_1)=-3+(5,0)\begin{pmatrix}1\\-7\end{pmatrix}=2$

$\Delta a_{11}^*=(1,0)\begin{pmatrix}1\\-7\end{pmatrix}=1$

$\Delta a_{21}^*=(-4,1)\begin{pmatrix}1\\-7\end{pmatrix}=-11$

New Tableau:

Bas Var	Eq No	Z	X1	X2	X3	X4	X5	Right side
Z	0	1	2	0	2	5	0	100
X2	1	0	0	1	3	1	0	20
X5	2	0	5	0	-2	-4	1	10

The current basic solution is feasible and optimal.

(f) $\left.\begin{array}{l}\Delta c_2=1\\ \Delta a_{12}=1\\ \Delta a_{22}=1\end{array}\right\}$ $\Delta(z_2^*-c_2)=-1+(5,0)\begin{pmatrix}1\\1\end{pmatrix}=4$

$\Delta a_{12}^*=(1,0)\begin{pmatrix}1\\1\end{pmatrix}=1$

$\Delta a_{22}^*=(-4,1)\begin{pmatrix}1\\1\end{pmatrix}=-3$

New Tableau:

Bas Var	Eq No	Z	X1	X2	X3	X4	X5	Right side
Z	0	1	0	4	2	5	0	100
X2	1	0	-1	2	3	1	0	20
X5	2	0	16	-3	-2	-4	1	10

Proper Form:

Bas Var	Eq No	Z	X1	X2	X3	X4	X5	Right side
Z	0	1	2	0	-4	3	0	60
X2	1	0	-0.5	1	1.5	0.5	0	10
X5	2	0	14.5	0	2.5	-2.5	1	40

The current basic solution is feasible, but not optimal.

6.7-1. (g) $\Delta c_6 = 10$, $\Delta a_{16} = 3$, $\Delta a_{26} = 5$

$$\Delta(z_6^* - c_6) = -10 + (5,0)\begin{pmatrix}3\\5\end{pmatrix} = 5$$

$$\Delta a_{16}^* = (1,0)\begin{pmatrix}3\\5\end{pmatrix} = 3$$

$$\Delta a_{26}^* = (-4,1)\begin{pmatrix}3\\5\end{pmatrix} = -7$$

New Tableau:

Bas Var	Eq No	Z	X1	X2	X3	X4	X5	X6	Right side
Z	0	1	0	0	2	5	0	5	100
X2	1	0	-1	1	3	1	0	3	20
X5	2	0	16	0	-2	-4	1	-7	10

The current basic solution is feasible and optimal

(h) New Tableau and Reduction to Proper Form:

Bas Var	Eq No	Z	X1	X2	X3	X4	X5	X6	Right side
Z	0	1	0	0	2	5	0	0	100
X2	1	0	-1	1	3	1	0	0	20
X5	2	0	16	0	-2	-4	1	0	10
X6	3	0	2	3	5	0	0	1	50

Bas Var	Eq No	Z	X1	X2	X3	X4	X5	X6	Right side
Z	0	1	0	0	2	5	0	0	100
X2	1	0	-1	1	3	1	0	0	20
X5	2	0	16	0	-2	-4	1	0	10
X6	3	0	5	0	-4	-3	0	1	-10

The current basic solution is superoptimal, but infeasible.

(i) $\Delta c_1 = 0$, $\Delta a_{11} = 0$, $\Delta a_{21} = -2$

$$\Delta(z_1^* - c_1) = 0 + (5,0)\begin{pmatrix}0\\-2\end{pmatrix} = 0$$

$$\Delta a_{11}^* = (1,0)\begin{pmatrix}0\\-2\end{pmatrix} = 0$$

$$\Delta a_{21}^* = (-4,1)\begin{pmatrix}0\\-2\end{pmatrix} = -2$$

$\Delta c_2 = 0$, $\Delta a_{12} = 0$, $\Delta a_{22} = 1$

$$\Delta(z_2^* - c_2) = 0 + (5,0)\begin{pmatrix}0\\1\end{pmatrix} = 0$$

$$\Delta a_{12}^* = (1,0)\begin{pmatrix}0\\1\end{pmatrix} = 0$$

$$\Delta a_{22}^* = (-4,1)\begin{pmatrix}0\\1\end{pmatrix} = 1$$

$\Delta b_1 = 0$, $\Delta b_2 = 10$

$$\Delta Z^* = (5,0)\begin{pmatrix}0\\10\end{pmatrix} = 0$$

$$\Delta b_1^* = (1,0)\begin{pmatrix}0\\10\end{pmatrix} = 0$$

$$\Delta b_2^* = (-4,1)\begin{pmatrix}0\\10\end{pmatrix} = 10$$

New tableau:

Bas Var	Eq No	Z	X1	X2	X3	X4	X5	Right side
Z	0	1	0	0	2	5	0	100
X2	1	0	-1	1	3	1	0	20
X5	2	0	14	1	-2	-4	1	20

Proper Form:

Bas Var	Eq No	Z	X1	X2	X3	X4	X5	Right side
Z	0	1	0	0	2	5	0	100
X2	1	0	-1	1	3	1	0	20
X5	2	0	15	0	-5	-5	1	0

6.7-2. $\Delta b_1 = 2\theta$, $\Delta b_2 = -\theta$

$$\Delta Z^* = (5,0)\begin{pmatrix}2\theta\\-\theta\end{pmatrix} = 10\theta$$

$$\Delta b_1^* = (1,0)\begin{pmatrix}2\theta\\-\theta\end{pmatrix} = 2\theta$$

$$\Delta b_2^* = (-4,1)\begin{pmatrix}2\theta\\-\theta\end{pmatrix} = -9\theta$$

Therefore, $Z = 100 + 10\theta$.

We need $b_1^* \geq 0$ and $b_2^* \geq 0$

so

$$\left.\begin{array}{l}20 + 2\theta \geq 0\\ 10 - 9\theta \geq 0\end{array}\right\} -10 \leq \theta \leq 10/9$$

6.7-3. (a) $\Delta b_1 = 10$, $\Delta b_2 = 10$, $\Delta b_3 = -10$

$$\Delta Z^* = (0, \tfrac{3}{2}, \tfrac{1}{2})\begin{pmatrix}10\\10\\-10\end{pmatrix} = 10$$

$$\Delta b_1^* = (1, -1, -2)\begin{pmatrix}10\\10\\-10\end{pmatrix} = 20$$

$$\Delta b_2 = (0, \tfrac{1}{2}, \tfrac{1}{2})\begin{pmatrix}10\\10\\-10\end{pmatrix} = 0$$

$$\Delta b_3 = (0, -\tfrac{1}{2}, \tfrac{1}{2})\begin{pmatrix}10\\10\\-10\end{pmatrix} = -10$$

New Tableau:

Bas Var	Eq No	Z	X1	X2	X3	X4	X5	X6	Right side
Z	0	1	0	0	1.5	0	1.5	0.5	35
X4	1	0	0	0	1	1	-1	-2	30
X1	2	0	1	0	0.5	0	0.5	0.5	15
X2	3	0	0	1	-1.5	0	-0.5	0.5	-5

The current basic solution is superoptimal, but infeasible

(b) $\Delta a_{11} = -1$, $\Delta a_{21} = 1$, $\Delta a_{31} = -1$, $\Delta c_1 = -1$

$$\Delta a_{11}^* = (1, -1, -2)\begin{pmatrix}-1\\1\\-1\end{pmatrix} = 0$$

$$\Delta a_{21}^* = (0, \tfrac{1}{2}, \tfrac{1}{2})\begin{pmatrix}-1\\1\\-1\end{pmatrix} = 0$$

$$\Delta a_{31}^* = (0, -\tfrac{1}{2}, \tfrac{1}{2})\begin{pmatrix}-1\\1\\-1\end{pmatrix} = -1$$

$$\Delta(z_1^* - c_1) = 1 + (0, \tfrac{3}{2}, \tfrac{1}{2})\begin{pmatrix}-1\\1\\-1\end{pmatrix} = 2$$

New Tableau:

Bas Var	Eq No	Z	X1	X2	X3	X4	X5	X6	Right side
Z	0	1	2	0	1.5	0	1.5	0.5	25
X4	1	0	0	0	1	1	-1	-2	10
X1	2	0	1	0	0.5	0	0.5	0.5	15
X2	3	0	-1	1	-1.5	0	-0.5	0.5	5

Proper Form:

Bas Var	Eq No	Z	X1	X2	X3	X4	X5	X6	Right side
Z	0	1	0	0	0.5	0	0.5	-0.5	-5
X4	1	0	0	0	1	1	-1	-2	10
X1	2	0	1	0	0.5	0	0.5	0.5	15
X2	3	0	0	1	-1	0	0	1	20

The current basic solution is feasible, but not optimal.

(c) $\Delta c_3 = 1$, $\Delta a_{13} = 2$, $\Delta a_{23} = -1$, $\Delta a_{33} = -1$

$$\Delta(z_3^* - c_3) = -1 + (0, \tfrac{3}{2}, \tfrac{1}{2})\begin{pmatrix}2\\-1\\-1\end{pmatrix} = -3$$

$$\Delta a_{13}^* = (1, -1, -2)\begin{pmatrix}2\\-1\\-1\end{pmatrix} = 5$$

$$\Delta a_{23}^* = (0, \tfrac{1}{2}, \tfrac{1}{2})\begin{pmatrix}2\\-1\\-1\end{pmatrix} = -1$$

$$\Delta a_{33}^* = (0, -\tfrac{1}{2}, +\tfrac{1}{2})\begin{pmatrix}2\\-1\\-1\end{pmatrix} = 0$$

(c) (cont.)

New Tableau:

Bas Var	Eq No	Z	X1	X2	X3	X4	X5	X6	Right side
Z	0	1	0	0	-1.5	0	1.5	0.5	25
X4	1	0	0	0	6	1	-1	-2	10
X1	2	0	1	0	-0.5	0	0.5	0.5	15
X2	3	0	0	1	-1.5	0	-0.5	0.5	5

The current basic solution is feasible, but not optimal.

(d) $\Delta c_1 = 1$, $\Delta c_2 = -1$, $\Delta c_3 = 2$

$$\Delta(z_1^* - c_1) = -1$$

$$\Delta(z_2^* - c_2) = 1$$

$$\Delta(z_3^* - c_3) = -2$$

New Tableau:

Bas Var	Eq No	Z	X1	X2	X3	X4	X5	X6	Right side
Z	0	1	-1	1	-0.5	0	1.5	0.5	25
X4	1	0	0	0	1	1	-1	-2	10
X1	2	0	1	0	0.5	0	0.5	0.5	15
X2	3	0	0	1	-1.5	0	-0.5	0.5	5

Proper Form:

Bas Var	Eq No	Z	X1	X2	X3	X4	X5	X6	Right side
Z	0	1	0	0	1.5	0	2.5	0.5	35
X4	1	0	0	0	1	1	-1	-2	10
X1	2	0	1	0	0.5	0	0.5	0.5	15
X2	3	0	0	1	-1.5	0	-0.5	0.5	5

The current basic solution is feasible and optimal.

(e) New Tableau:

Bas Var	Eq No	Z	X1	X2	X3	X4	X5	X6	X7	Right side
Z	0	1	0	0	3/2	0	3/2	1/2	0	25
X4	1	0	0	0	1	1	-1	-2	0	10
X1	2	0	1	0	1/2	0	1/2	1/2	0	15
X2	3	0	0	1	-3/2	0	-1/2	1/2	0	5
X7	4	0	3	-2	1	0	0	0	1	30

Proper Form:

Bas Var	Eq No	Z	X1	X2	X3	X4	X5	X6	X7	Right side
Z	0	1	0	0	3/2	0	3/2	1/2	0	25
X4	1	0	0	0	1	1	-1	-2	0	10
X1	2	0	1	0	1/2	0	1/2	1/2	0	15
X2	3	0	0	1	-3/2	0	-1/2	1/2	0	5
X7	4	0	0	0	-7/2	0	-5/2	-1/2	1	-5

The current basic solution is superoptimal, but infeasible.

6.7-3. f) $\Delta c_8 = -1$, $\Delta a_{18} = -2$, $\Delta a_{28} = 1$, $\Delta a_{38} = 2$

$$\Delta(z_8^* - c_8) = 1 + (0, \tfrac{3}{2}, \tfrac{1}{2})\begin{pmatrix}-2\\1\\2\end{pmatrix} = \tfrac{7}{2}$$

$$\Delta a_{18}^* = (1,-1,-2)\begin{pmatrix}-2\\1\\2\end{pmatrix} = -7$$

$$\Delta a_{28}^* = (0, \tfrac{1}{2}, \tfrac{1}{2})\begin{pmatrix}-2\\1\\2\end{pmatrix} = \tfrac{3}{2}$$

$$\Delta a_{38}^* = (0, -\tfrac{1}{2}, \tfrac{1}{2})\begin{pmatrix}-2\\1\\2\end{pmatrix} = \tfrac{1}{2}$$

New Tableau:

Bas Var	Eq No	Z	X1	X2	X3	X4	X5	X6	X8	Right side
Z	0	1	0	0	3/2	0	3/2	1/2	7/2	25
X4	1	0	0	0	1	1	-1	-2	-7	10
X1	2	0	1	0	1/2	0	1/2	1/2	3/2	15
X2	3	0	0	1	-3/2	0	-1/2	1/2	1/2	5

The current basic solution remains feasible and optimal.

6.7-4. (a) $\Delta b_1 = -10$, $\Delta b_2 = 20$

$$\Delta z^* = (0,2)\begin{pmatrix}-10\\20\end{pmatrix} = 40$$

$$\Delta b_1^* = (1,-1)\begin{pmatrix}-10\\20\end{pmatrix} = -30$$

$$\Delta b_2^* = (0,1)\begin{pmatrix}-10\\20\end{pmatrix} = 20$$

New Tableau:

Bas Var	Eq No	Z	X1	X2	X3	X4	X5	Right side
Z	0	1	0	1	1	0	2	60
X4	1	0	0	-1	5	1	-1	-10
X1	2	0	1	4	-1	0	1	30

The current basic solution is superoptimal, but infeasible.

(b) $\Delta c_3 = 1$, $\Delta a_{13} = -1$, $\Delta a_{23} = -1$

$$\Delta(z_3^* - c_3) = -1 + (0,2)\begin{pmatrix}-1\\-1\end{pmatrix} = -3$$

$$\Delta a_{13}^* = (1,-1)\begin{pmatrix}-1\\-1\end{pmatrix} = 0$$

$$\Delta a_{23}^* = (0,1)\begin{pmatrix}-1\\-1\end{pmatrix} = -1$$

New Tableau:

Bas Var	Eq No	Z	X1	X2	X3	X4	X5	Right side
Z	0	1	0	1	-2	0	2	20
X4	1	0	0	-1	5	1	-1	20
X1	2	0	1	4	-2	0	1	10

The current basic solution is feasible, but not optimal.

7-4. (c) $\Delta c_1 = 2$, $\Delta a_{11} = 2$, $\Delta a_{21} = 1$

$$\Delta(z_1^* - c_1) = -2 + (0,2)\begin{pmatrix}2\\1\end{pmatrix} = 0$$

$$\Delta a_{11}^* = (1,-1)\begin{pmatrix}2\\1\end{pmatrix} = 1$$

$$\Delta a_{21}^* = (0,1)\begin{pmatrix}2\\1\end{pmatrix} = 1$$

New Tableau:

Bas Var	Eq No	Z	X1	X2	X3	X4	X5	Right side
Z	0	1	0	1	1	0	2	20
X4	1	0	1	-1	5	1	-1	20
X1	2	0	2	4	-1	0	1	10

Proper Form:

Bas Var	Eq No	Z	X1	X2	X3	X4	X5	Right side
Z	0	1	0	1	1	0	2	20
X4	1	0	0	-3	5.5	1	-1.5	15
X1	2	0	1	2	-0.5	0	0.5	5

The current basic solution is feasible and optimal.

(d) $\Delta c_6 = 3$, $\Delta a_{16} = 1$, $\Delta a_{26} = 2$

$$\Delta(z_6^* - c_6) = -3 + (0,2)\begin{pmatrix}1\\2\end{pmatrix} = 1$$

$$\Delta a_{16}^* = (1,-1)\begin{pmatrix}1\\2\end{pmatrix} = -1$$

$$\Delta a_{26}^* = (0,1)\begin{pmatrix}1\\2\end{pmatrix} = 2$$

New Tableau:

Bas Var	Eq No	Z	X1	X2	X3	X4	X5	X6	Right side
Z	0	1	0	1	1	0	2	1	20
X4	1	0	0	-1	5	1	-1	-1	20
X1	2	0	1	4	-1	0	1	2	10

The current basic solution is feasible and optimal

(e) $\Delta c_1 = -1$, $\Delta c_2 = -2$, $\Delta c_3 = 1$

$$\Delta(z_1^* - c_1) = 1$$

$$\Delta(z_2^* - c_2) = 2$$

$$\Delta(z_3^* - c_3) = -1$$

New Tableau:

Bas Var	Eq No	Z	X1	X2	X3	X4	X5	Right side
Z	0	1	1	3	0	0	2	20
X4	1	0	0	-1	5	1	-1	20
X1	2	0	1	4	-1	0	1	10

6.7-4. (e) (cont.) Proper Form:

Bas Var	Eq No	Z	X1	X2	X3	X4	X5	Right side
Z	0	1	0	-1	1	0	1	10
X4	1	0	0	-1	5	1	-1	20
X1	2	0	1	4	-1	0	1	10

The current basic solution is feasible, but not optimal

(f) New Tableau:

Bas Var	Eq No	Z	X1	X2	X3	X4	X5	X6	Right side
Z	0	1	0	1	1	0	2	0	20
X4	1	0	0	-1	5	1	-1	0	20
X1	2	0	1	4	-1	0	1	0	10
X6	3	0	3	2	3	0	0	1	25

Proper Form:

Bas Var	Eq No	Z	X1	X2	X3	X4	X5	X6	Right side
Z	0	1	0	1	1	0	2	0	20
X4	1	0	0	-1	5	1	-1	0	20
X1	2	0	1	4	-1	0	1	0	10
X6	3	0	0	-10	6	0	-3	1	-5

The current basic solution is superoptimal, but infeasible.

(g) $\left.\begin{array}{l}\Delta a_{22} = -2 \\ \Delta a_{23} = 3\end{array}\right\}$ $\Delta(z_2^* - c_2) = (0,2)\binom{0}{-2} = -4$

$\Delta a_{12}^* = (1,-1)\binom{0}{-2} = 2$

$\Delta a_{22}^* = (0,1)\binom{0}{-2} = -2$

$\Delta(z_3^* - c_3) = (0,2)\binom{0}{3} = 6$

$\Delta a_{13}^* = (1,-1)\binom{0}{3} = -3$

$\Delta a_{23}^* = (0,1)\binom{0}{3} = 3$

$\Delta b_2 = 25$ $\Delta z^* = (0,2)\binom{0}{25} = 50$

$\Delta b_1^* = (1,-1)\binom{0}{25} = -25$

$\Delta b_2^* = (0,1)\binom{0}{25} = 25$

New Tableau:

Bas Var	Eq No	Z	X1	X2	X3	X4	X5	Right side
Z	0	1	0	-3	7	0	2	70
X4	1	0	0	1	2	1	-1	-5
X1	2	0	1	2	2	0	1	35

The current basic solution is neither feasible nor optimal.

6.7-5. $\left.\begin{array}{l}\Delta b_1 = 3\theta \\ \Delta b_2 = -\theta\end{array}\right\}$ $\Delta z^* = (0,2)\binom{3\theta}{-\theta} = -2\theta$

$\Delta b_1^* = (1,-1)\binom{3\theta}{-\theta} = 4\theta$

$\Delta b_2^* = (0,1)\binom{3\theta}{-\theta} = -\theta$

$z^*(\theta) = 20 - 2\theta$

$(x_1, x_2, x_3, x_4, x_5) = (10-\theta, 0, 0, 20+4\theta, 0)$

which is feasible if

$-5 \le \theta \le 10$

6.7-6. (a) $\left.\begin{array}{l}\Delta b_1 = -5 \\ \Delta b_2 = 1 \\ \Delta b_3 = -2\end{array}\right\}$ $\Delta z^* = (1,1,0)\begin{pmatrix}-5\\1\\-2\end{pmatrix} = -4$

$\Delta b_1^* = (1,3,0)\begin{pmatrix}-5\\1\\-2\end{pmatrix} = -2$

$\Delta b_2^* = (0,1,1)\begin{pmatrix}-5\\1\\-2\end{pmatrix} = -1$

$\Delta b_3^* = (1,2,0)\begin{pmatrix}-5\\1\\-2\end{pmatrix} = -3$

New Tableau:

Bas Var	Eq No	Z	X1	X2	X3	X4	X5	X6	Right side
Z	0	1	0	0	2	1	1	0	14
X2	1	0	0	1	5	1	3	0	22
X6	2	0	0	0	2	0	1	1	6
X1	3	0	1	0	4	1	2	0	18

The current basic solution is feasible and optimal.

(b) $\Delta c_3 = 1 \Rightarrow \Delta(z_3^* - c_3) = -1$

New Tableau:

Bas Var	Eq No	Z	X1	X2	X3	X4	X5	X6	Right side
Z	0	1	0	0	1	1	1	0	18
X2	1	0	0	1	5	1	3	0	24
X6	2	0	0	0	2	0	1	1	7
X1	3	0	1	0	4	1	2	0	21

The current basic solution remains feasible and optimal.

6.7-6. c) $\Delta c_1 = 3 \Rightarrow \Delta(z_1^* - c_1) = -3$

New tableau:

Bas Var	Eq No	Z	X1	X2	X3	X4	X5	X6	Right side
Z	0	1	-1	0	2	1	1	0	18
X2	1	0	0	1	5	1	3	0	24
X6	2	0	0	0	2	0	1	1	7
X1	3	0	1	0	4	1	2	0	21

Proper Form:

Bas Var	Eq No	Z	X1	X2	X3	X4	X5	X6	Right side
Z	0	1	0	0	6	2	3	0	39
X2	1	0	0	1	5	1	3	0	24
X6	2	0	0	0	2	0	1	1	7
X1	3	0	1	0	4	1	2	0	21

The current basic solution is feasible and optimal.

(d) $\Delta c_3 = 3$, $\Delta a_{13} = 1$, $\Delta a_{23} = 1$, $\Delta a_{33} = 0$

$$\Delta(z_3^* - c_3) = -3 + (1,1,0)\begin{pmatrix}1\\1\\0\end{pmatrix} = -1$$

$$\Delta a_{13}^* = (1,3,0)\begin{pmatrix}1\\1\\0\end{pmatrix} = 4$$

$$\Delta a_{23}^* = (0,1,1)\begin{pmatrix}1\\1\\0\end{pmatrix} = 1$$

$$\Delta a_{33}^* = (1,2,0)\begin{pmatrix}1\\1\\0\end{pmatrix} = 3$$

New Tableau:

Bas Var	Eq No	Z	X1	X2	X3	X4	X5	X6	Right side
Z	0	1	0	0	1	1	1	0	18
X2	1	0	0	1	9	1	3	0	24
X6	2	0	0	0	3	0	1	1	7
X1	3	0	1	0	7	1	2	0	21

The current basic solution remains feasible and optimal.

(e) $\Delta c_1 = -1$, $\Delta a_{11} = -2$, $\Delta a_{21} = -1$, $\Delta a_{31} = 2$

$$\Delta(z_1^* - c_1) = 1 + (1,1,0)\begin{pmatrix}-2\\-1\\2\end{pmatrix} = -2$$

$$\Delta a_{11}^* = (1,3,0)\begin{pmatrix}-2\\-1\\2\end{pmatrix} = -5$$

$$\Delta a_{21}^* = (0,1,1)\begin{pmatrix}-2\\-1\\2\end{pmatrix} = 1$$

$$\Delta a_{31}^* = (1,2,0)\begin{pmatrix}-2\\-1\\2\end{pmatrix} = -4$$

$\Delta c_2 = -1$, $\Delta a_{12} = 1$, $\Delta a_{22} = 2$, $\Delta a_{32} = 3$

$$\Delta(z_2^* - c_2) = 1 + (1,1,0)\begin{pmatrix}1\\2\\3\end{pmatrix} = 4$$

$$\Delta a_{12}^* = (1,3,0)\begin{pmatrix}1\\2\\3\end{pmatrix} = 7$$

$$\Delta a_{22}^* = (0,1,1)\begin{pmatrix}1\\2\\3\end{pmatrix} = 5$$

$$\Delta a_{32}^* = (1,2,0)\begin{pmatrix}1\\2\\3\end{pmatrix} = 5.$$

(e) (cont.)

New Tableau:

Bas Var	Eq No	Z	X1	X2	X3	X4	X5	X6	Right side
Z	0	1	0	4	2	1	1	0	18
X2	1	0	-5	8	5	1	3	0	24
X6	2	0	1	5	2	0	1	1	7
X1	3	0	-3	5	4	1	2	0	21

Proper Form:

Bas Var	Eq No	Z	X1	X2	X3	X4	X5	X6	Right side
Z	0	1	0	0	-18	-7	-3	0	-114
X2	1	0	0	1	5	2	1	0	33
X6	2	0	0	0	-30	-13	-5	1	-206
X1	3	0	1	0	7	3	1	0	48

The current basic solution is neither feasible nor optimal.

(f) $\Delta c_1 = 3$, $\Delta c_2 = 2$, $\Delta c_3 = 2$

$\Delta(z_1^* - c_1) = -3$

$\Delta(z_2^* - c_2) = -2$

$\Delta(z_3^* - c_3) = -2$

New Tableau:

Bas Var	Eq No	Z	X1	X2	X3	X4	X5	X6	Right side
Z	0	1	-3	-2	0	1	1	0	18
X2	1	0	0	1	5	1	3	0	24
X6	2	0	0	0	2	0	1	1	7
X1	3	0	1	0	4	1	2	0	21

Proper Form:

Bas Var	Eq No	Z	X1	X2	X3	X4	X5	X6	Right side
Z	0	1	0	0	22	6	13	0	129
X2	1	0	0	1	5	1	3	0	24
X6	2	0	0	0	2	0	1	1	7
X1	3	0	1	0	4	1	2	0	21

The current basic solution is feasible and optimal.

(g) $\Delta a_{11} = -1 \Rightarrow \Delta(z_1^* - c_1) = (1,1,0)\begin{pmatrix}-1\\0\\0\end{pmatrix} = -1$

$$\Delta a_{11}^* = (1,3,0)\begin{pmatrix}-1\\0\\0\end{pmatrix} = -1$$

$$\Delta a_{21}^* = (0,1,1)\begin{pmatrix}-1\\0\\0\end{pmatrix} = 0$$

$$\Delta a_{31}^* = (1,2,0)\begin{pmatrix}-1\\0\\0\end{pmatrix} = -1$$

6.7-6. g) (cont')

$\Delta a_{12} = 1 \Rightarrow \Delta(z_2^* - c_2) = (1,1,0)\begin{pmatrix}1\\0\\0\end{pmatrix} = 1$

$\Delta a_{12}^* = (1,3,0)\begin{pmatrix}1\\0\\0\end{pmatrix} = 1$

$\Delta a_{22}^* = (0,1,1)\begin{pmatrix}1\\0\\0\end{pmatrix} = 0$

$\Delta a_{32}^* = (1,2,0)\begin{pmatrix}1\\0\\0\end{pmatrix} = 1$

$\Delta a_{13} = 2 \Rightarrow \Delta(z_3^* - c_3) = (1,1,0)\begin{pmatrix}2\\0\\0\end{pmatrix} = 2$

$\Delta a_{13}^* = (1,3,0)\begin{pmatrix}2\\0\\0\end{pmatrix} = 2$

$\Delta a_{23}^* = (0,1,1)\begin{pmatrix}2\\0\\0\end{pmatrix} = 0$

$\Delta a_{33}^* = (1,2,0)\begin{pmatrix}2\\0\\0\end{pmatrix} = 2$

$\Delta b_1 = -3 \Rightarrow \Delta Z^* = (1,1,0)\begin{pmatrix}-3\\0\\0\end{pmatrix} = -3$

$\Delta b_1^* = (1,3,0)\begin{pmatrix}-3\\0\\0\end{pmatrix} = -3$

$\Delta b_2^* = (0,1,1)\begin{pmatrix}-3\\0\\0\end{pmatrix} = 0$

$\Delta b_3^* = (1,2,0)\begin{pmatrix}-3\\0\\0\end{pmatrix} = -3$

New Tableau:

Bas Var	Eq No	Z	X1	X2	X3	X4	X5	X6	Right side
Z	0	1	-1	1	4	1	1	0	15
X2	1	0	-1	2	7	1	3	0	21
X6	2	0	0	0	2	0	1	1	7
X1	3	0	0	1	6	1	2	0	18

Proper Form:

Bas Var	Eq No	Z	X1	X2	X3	X4	X5	X6	Right side
Z	0	1	0	0	3	1	0	0	12
X2	1	0	0	1	6	1	2	0	18
X6	2	0	0	0	2	0	1	1	7
X1	3	0	1	0	5	1	1	0	15

The current basic solution is feasible and optimal.

(h) New Tableau

Bas Var	Eq No	Z	X1	X2	X3	X4	X5	X6	X7	Right side
Z	0	1	0	0	2	1	1	0	0	18
X2	1	0	0	1	5	1	3	0	0	24
X6	2	0	0	0	2	0	1	1	0	7
X1	3	0	1	0	4	1	2	0	0	21
X7	4	0	2	-1	3	0	0	0	1	60

Proper Form:

Bas Var	Eq No	Z	X1	X2	X3	X4	X5	X6	X7	Right side
Z	0	1	0	0	2	1	1	0	0	18
X_2	1	0	0	1	5	1	3	0	0	24
X6	2	0	0	0	2	0	1	1	0	7
X1	3	0	1	0	4	1	2	0	0	21
X7	4	0	0	0	0	1	1	0	1	42

The current basic solution is feasible and optimal.

6.7-7. a)

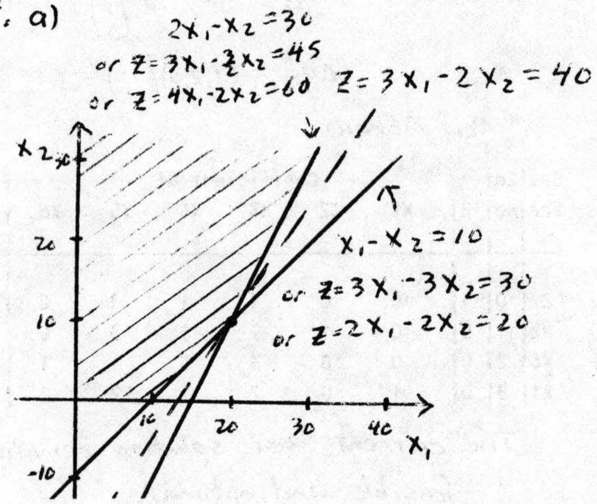

The allowable range to stay optimal for c_1 is $2 \le c_1 \le 4$, for c_2 is $-3 \le c_2 \le -\frac{3}{2}$.

6.7-7.b) Increment c_1 by Δc_1 (so $c_1 = 3 + \Delta c_1$). This causes the coefficient of x_1 in row 0 of the final tableau to become $-\Delta c_1$. Adding Δc_1 times row 2 to row 0 will make this 0:

$$[-\Delta c_1, 0, 1, 1] + \Delta c_1 [1, 0, 1, -1] = [0, 0, 1+\Delta c_1, 1-\Delta c_1]$$

In order for this to stay optimal, we need $1+\Delta c_1 \geq 0$ and $1-\Delta c_1 \geq 0$ or $-1 \leq \Delta c_1 \leq 1$. Thus, the allowable range to stay optimal for c_1 is $3-1 \leq c_1 \leq 3+1$ or $2 \leq c_1 \leq 4$.

Similarly, incrementing c_2 by Δc_2 and adding Δc_2 times row 1 to the row 0 of the final tableau gives:

$$[0, -\Delta c_2, 1, 1] + \Delta c_2 [0, 1, 1, -2] = [0, 0, 1+\Delta c_2, 1-2\Delta c_2]$$

So to stay optimal, we need $-1 \leq \Delta c_2 \leq \frac{1}{2}$ or $-3 \leq c_2 \leq \frac{-3}{2}$.

c)

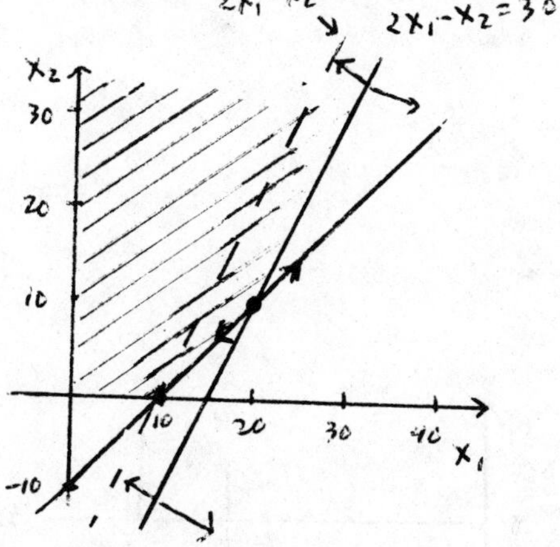

The allowable range to stay feasible for b_1 is

$$20 \leq b_1$$

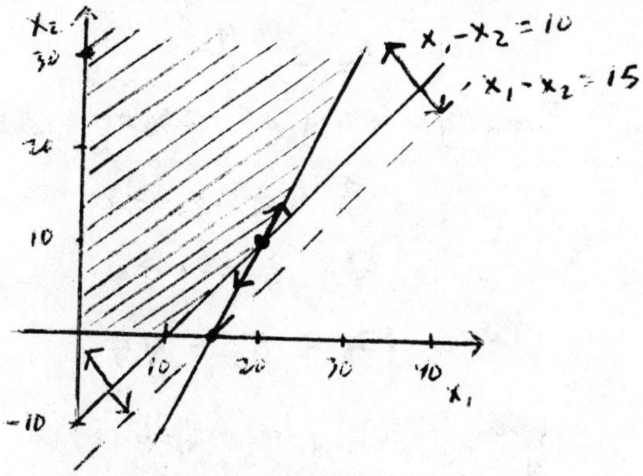

The allowable range to stay feasible for b_2 is

$$b_2 \leq 15$$

d) Increment b_1 by Δb_1. The final right side will be

$$S^* \bar{b} = \begin{pmatrix} 1 & -2 \\ 1 & -1 \end{pmatrix} \begin{pmatrix} 30+\Delta b_1 \\ 10 \end{pmatrix} = \begin{pmatrix} 10 \\ 20 \end{pmatrix} + \begin{pmatrix} \Delta b_1 \\ \Delta b_1 \end{pmatrix}$$

Thus, in order to be feasible, $\Delta b_1 \geq -10$

So the allowable range to feasible for b_1 is $b_1 \geq 20$.

Similarly incrementing b_2 by Δb_2, we get the final right side:

$$S^* \bar{b} = \begin{pmatrix} 1 & -2 \\ 1 & -1 \end{pmatrix} \begin{pmatrix} 30 \\ 10+\Delta b_2 \end{pmatrix} = \begin{pmatrix} 10 \\ 20 \end{pmatrix} + \begin{pmatrix} -2 \\ -1 \end{pmatrix} \Delta b_2$$

So $\Delta b_2 \leq 5$ to stay feasible, or, in otherwords, the allowable range to stay feasible for b_2 is $b_2 \leq 15$.

6.7-8. We increment b_i by Δb_i and check for feasibility for each i.

We can look at all three b_i's simultaneously:

$$b^* = S^*\bar{b} = \begin{pmatrix} 1 & 0 & 0 \\ -3/4 & 0 & 1/4 \\ 9/4 & 1 & -3/4 \end{pmatrix} \begin{pmatrix} 4+\Delta b_1 \\ 24+\Delta b_2 \\ 18+\Delta b_3 \end{pmatrix} = \begin{pmatrix} 4 \\ 3/2 \\ 39/2 \end{pmatrix} + \begin{pmatrix} 1 \\ -3/4 \\ 9/4 \end{pmatrix}\Delta b_1 + \begin{pmatrix} 0 \\ 0 \\ 1 \end{pmatrix}\Delta b_2 + \begin{pmatrix} 0 \\ 1/4 \\ -3/4 \end{pmatrix}\Delta b_3$$

to remain feasible Δb_1 must satisfy (keeping $\Delta b_2 = \Delta b_3 = 0$)

$4 + \Delta b_1 \geq 0 \qquad \Delta b_1 \geq -4$

$3/2 - 3/4\,\Delta b_1 \geq 0 \qquad \Delta b_1 \leq 2$

$\frac{39}{2} + \frac{9}{4}\Delta b \geq 0 \qquad \Delta b_i \geq -\frac{78}{9}$

or $-4 \leq \Delta b_1 \leq 2 \implies 0 \leq b_1 \leq 6$

Similarly, keeping $\Delta b_1 = \Delta b_3 = 0$, Δb_2 must satisfy

$\frac{39}{2} + \Delta b_2 \geq 0 \implies \Delta b_2 \geq -\frac{39}{2}$

or $b_2 \geq \frac{9}{2}$

Finally, letting $\Delta b_1 = \Delta b_2 = 0$, Δb_3 must satisfy

$\frac{3}{2} + \frac{1}{4}\Delta b_3 \geq 0 \qquad \Delta b_3 \geq -6$

$\frac{39}{2} - \frac{3}{4}\Delta b_3 \geq 0 \qquad \Delta b_3 \leq 26$

or $12 \leq b_3 \leq 44$

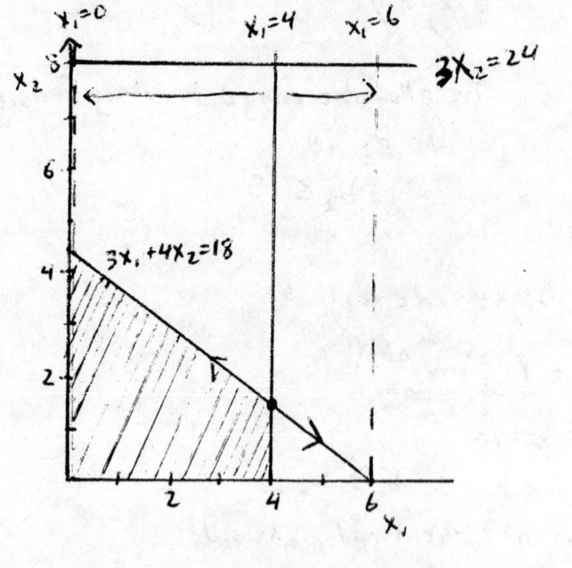

The allowable range to stay feasible for b_1 is

$0 \leq b_1 \leq 6$

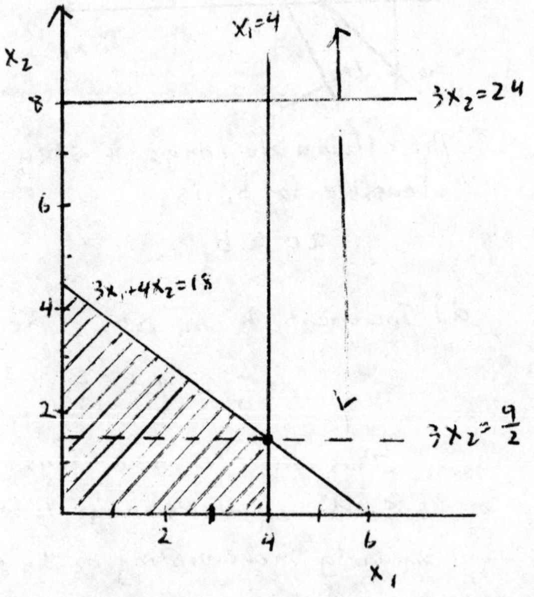

The allowable range to stay feasible for b_2 is

$\frac{9}{2} \leq b_2$

6.7-8. (cont')

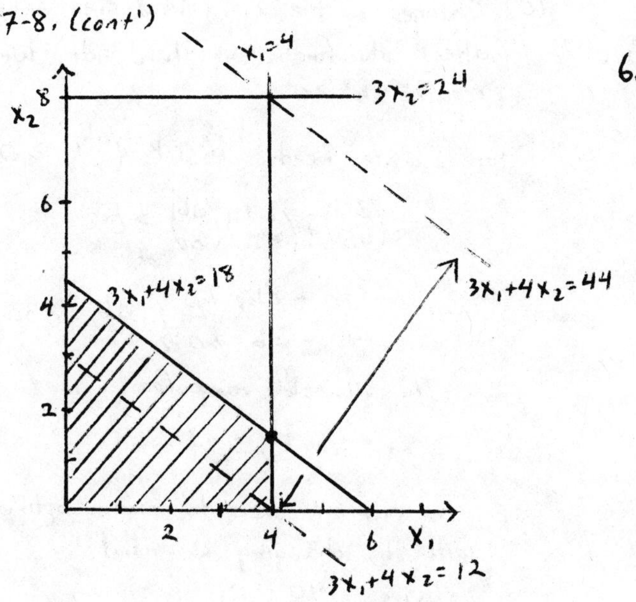

The allowable range to stay feasible for b_3 is

$$12 \le b_3 \le 44$$

6.7-10. (a) If b_1 or b_2 is changed,

$$(b_1^*, b_2^*) = \begin{pmatrix} 1 & 1 \\ 1 & 2 \end{pmatrix}\begin{pmatrix} \Delta b_1 \\ \Delta b_2 \end{pmatrix} = \begin{pmatrix} \Delta b_1 + \Delta b_2 \\ \Delta b_1 + 2\Delta b_2 \end{pmatrix},$$

so both are sensitive parameters.

If c_1 changes, $\bar{c}_{1\,new} = \bar{c}_1 - \Delta c_1 = 8 - \Delta c_1$. c_1 is not sensitive, since small changes in c_1 will not affect the optimal solution.

If c_2 or c_3 changes, $\bar{c}_{2\,new} = 0 - \Delta c_2$ and $\bar{c}_{3\,new} = 0 - \Delta c_3$ so the optimal objective value will change.

If a_{11} or a_{21} changes, it will only affect a_{11}^*, a_{22}^* and $\bar{c}_1$ so small changes won't affect the optimal solution. These parameters are not sensitive.

Changes in a_{12}, a_{13}, a_{22} and a_{23} will change B and also $B^{-1}b$. The optimal solution will change so these parameters are sensitive.

6.7-9. Algebraically: Increment c_1 by Δc_1 (so $c_1 = 3 + \Delta c_1$). Then the coefficient of x_1 in row 0 of the final tableau is $-\Delta c_1$. Adding Δc_1 times row 1 to row 0, we get:

$$\text{Final row } 0 = [-\Delta c_1, 0, \tfrac{3}{4}, 0, \tfrac{3}{4}] + \Delta c_1[1, 0, 1, 0, 0] = [0, 0, \tfrac{3}{4} + \Delta c_1, 0, \tfrac{3}{4}]$$

In order for this to stay optimal, we need $\frac{3}{4} + \Delta c_1 \ge 0$ or $\Delta c_1 \ge -\frac{3}{4}$. Thus, the allowable range to stay optimal for c_1 is $c_1 \ge \frac{9}{4}$.

Graphically:

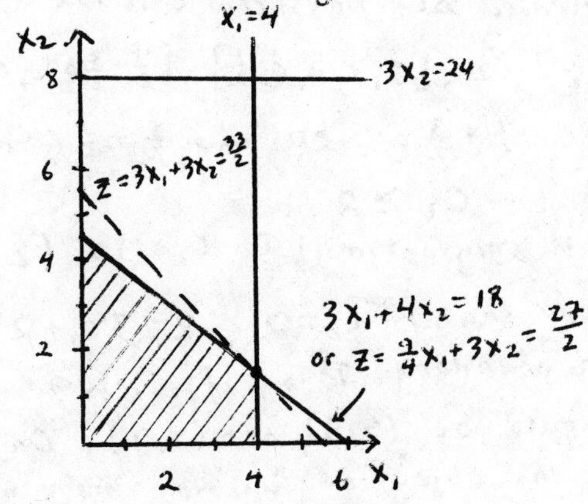

The allowable range to stay optimal for c_1 is $c_1 \ge \frac{9}{4}$. (Note that no matter how large c_1 gets, $(4, \frac{3}{2})$ will be optimal as long as $c_1 \ge \frac{9}{4}$)

6.7-10. (b) We've seen in (a) that changes in c_1 only affect $\bar{c}_1$. $\bar{c}_{1,new} = \bar{c}_1 - \Delta c_1 = 8 - \Delta c_1$. If $\Delta c_1 \le 8$, the current solution is optimal. The allowable range for c_1 is:

$$c_1 \le 11.$$

For changes in c_2, the current basis remains optimal (although the objective value may change) if:

Row 0 + Δc_2 Row 2 ≥ 0

This is equivalent to:

$$\left.\begin{aligned} 8 + 5\Delta c_2 &\ge 0 \\ 3 + \Delta c_2 &\ge 0 \\ 4 + 2\Delta c_2 &\ge 0 \end{aligned}\right\} \quad \Delta c_2 \ge -8/5$$

The allowable range for c_2 is

$$c_2 \ge -3/5$$

For changes in c_3, the current basis remains optimal (although the objective value may change) if:

Row 0 + Δc_3 Row 1 ≥ 0

Equivalently:

$$\left.\begin{aligned} 8 + 3\Delta c_3 &\ge 0 \\ 3 + \Delta c_3 &\ge 0 \\ 4 + \Delta c_3 &\ge 0 \end{aligned}\right\} \quad \Delta c_3 \ge -8/3$$

The allowable range for c_3 is:

$$c_3 \ge -2/3.$$

(c) Changes in the right-hand side only affect the final right-hand side. We require $b^* \ge 0$.

For b_1 we need: $b^* + B^{-1}\begin{pmatrix}\Delta b_1 \\ 0\end{pmatrix} \ge 0$

$$\text{-or-} \quad \begin{pmatrix}30 \\ 40\end{pmatrix} + \begin{pmatrix}1 & 1 \\ 1 & 2\end{pmatrix}\begin{pmatrix}\Delta b_1 \\ 0\end{pmatrix} \ge 0$$

$$\text{-or-} \quad \left.\begin{aligned} 30 + \Delta b_1 &\ge 0 \\ 40 + \Delta b_1 &\ge 0 \end{aligned}\right\} \quad \Delta b_1 \ge -30$$

The allowable range for b_1 is

$$b_1 \ge -10.$$

For the current basis to remain optimal with b_2 changing we need:

$$b^* + B^{-1}\begin{pmatrix}0 \\ \Delta b_2\end{pmatrix} \ge 0$$

$$\text{-or-} \quad \begin{pmatrix}30 \\ 40\end{pmatrix} + \begin{pmatrix}1 & 1 \\ 1 & 2\end{pmatrix}\begin{pmatrix}0 \\ \Delta b_2\end{pmatrix} \ge 0$$

$$\text{-or-} \quad \left.\begin{aligned} 30 + \Delta b_2 &\ge 0 \\ 40 + 2\Delta b_2 &\ge 0 \end{aligned}\right\} \quad \Delta b_2 \ge -20$$

The allowable range for b_2 is:

$$b_2 \ge -10.$$

6.7-11. Increment c_2 by Δc_2 (so $c_2 = 5 + \Delta c_2$). The resulting coefficient in the final tableau (for x_2 in row 0) is $-\Delta c_2$. Adding Δc_2 times row 2 to row 0, we get:

$$\text{Final row } 0 = \left[\tfrac{9}{2}, -\Delta c_2, 0, 0, \tfrac{5}{2}\right] + \Delta c_2\left[\tfrac{3}{2}, 1, 0, 0, \tfrac{1}{2}\right] = \left[\tfrac{9}{2} + \tfrac{3}{2}\Delta c_2, 0, 0, \tfrac{5}{2} + \tfrac{1}{2}\Delta c_2\right]$$

Thus, to stay optimal, we need $\frac{9}{2} + \frac{3}{2}\Delta c_2 \ge 0$ and $\frac{5}{2} + \frac{1}{2}\Delta c_2 \ge 0$

In other words, $\Delta c_2 \ge -3$ or $c_2 \ge 2$.

So, the allowable range to stay optimal for c_2 is $c_2 \ge 2$.

Looking at figure 6.3, we see that if $c_2 = 2$, $Z = 3x_1 + 2x_2 = 18$ lies exactly on the constraint boundary. Thus, if c_2 were decreased any more, the optimal would be $(4,3)$, not $(0,9)$. On the other hand, increasing c_2 only makes the objective function "more horizontal" approaching $Z = x_2 = 9$, so for any $c_2 \ge 2$, the optimal remains $(0,9)$.

6.7-12.

(a) We need $b^* + \begin{pmatrix} 1 & 1/3 & -1/3 \\ 0 & 1/2 & 0 \\ 0 & -1/3 & 1/3 \end{pmatrix} \begin{pmatrix} \Delta b_1 \\ 0 \\ 0 \end{pmatrix} \geq 0$

-or- $(2,6,2) + (\Delta b_1, 0, 0) \geq 0$

So, $\Delta b_1 \geq -2$ and $b_1 \geq 2$.

For b_2 we require $b^* + \begin{pmatrix} 1 & 1/3 & -1/3 \\ 0 & 1/2 & 0 \\ 0 & -1/3 & 1/3 \end{pmatrix} \begin{pmatrix} 0 \\ \Delta b_2 \\ 0 \end{pmatrix} \geq 0$

-or- $(2,6,2) + (\frac{1}{3}\Delta b_2, \frac{1}{2}\Delta b_2, -\frac{1}{3}\Delta b_2) \geq 0$

So, $-6 \leq \Delta b_2 \leq 6$. The allowable range for b_2 is: $6 \leq b_2 \leq 18$

For b_3 we need $b^* + \begin{pmatrix} 1 & 1/3 & -1/3 \\ 0 & 1/2 & 0 \\ 0 & -1/3 & 1/3 \end{pmatrix} \begin{pmatrix} 0 \\ 0 \\ \Delta b_3 \end{pmatrix} \geq 0$

-or- $(2,6,2) + (-\frac{1}{3}\Delta b_3, 0, \frac{1}{3}\Delta b_3) \geq 0$

So, $-6 \leq \Delta b_3 \leq 6$. The allowable range for b_3 is: $12 \leq b_3 \leq 24$.

(b) For changes in c_1 we need:

Row 0 + Δc_1 Row 3 ≥ 0

-or- $\frac{3}{2} - \frac{1}{3}\Delta c_1 \geq 0$

$1 + \frac{1}{3}\Delta c_1 \geq 0$

This implies $-3 \leq \Delta c_1 \leq 9/2$. The allowable range for c_1 is: $0 \leq c_1 \leq 15/2$.

For changes in c_2 we require:

Row 0 + Δc_2 Row 2 ≥ 0

-or- $\frac{3}{2} + \frac{1}{2}\Delta c_2 \geq 0$

This implies $-3 \leq \Delta c_2$. The allowable range for c_2 is: $2 \leq c_2$.

6.7-13. a) Increment b_1 by Δb_1 and calculate the new right side:

$$b^* = S^* \bar{b} = \begin{pmatrix} 1 & 0 & 0 & 0 \\ 0 & 0 & 0 & 1/3 \\ 0 & 1 & 0 & -2/3 \\ 0 & 0 & 1 & -2/3 \end{pmatrix} \begin{pmatrix} 4+\Delta b_1 \\ 24 \\ 18 \\ 24 \end{pmatrix} = \begin{pmatrix} 4 \\ 8 \\ 8 \\ 2 \end{pmatrix} + \begin{pmatrix} 1 \\ 0 \\ 0 \\ 0 \end{pmatrix} \Delta b_1$$

To stay feasible, $\Delta b_1 \geq -4$ or $b_1 \geq 0$.

Similarly, incrementing b_2, b_3, b_4 by $\Delta b_2, \Delta b_3, \Delta b_4$ respectively, we get:

b_2: $b^* = \begin{pmatrix} 4 \\ 8 \\ 8 \\ 2 \end{pmatrix} + \begin{pmatrix} 0 \\ 0 \\ 1 \\ 0 \end{pmatrix} \Delta b_2 \geq 0 \Rightarrow \Delta b_2 \geq -8$

b_3: $b^* = \begin{pmatrix} 4 \\ 8 \\ 8 \\ 2 \end{pmatrix} + \begin{pmatrix} 0 \\ 0 \\ 0 \\ 1 \end{pmatrix} \Delta b_3 \geq 0 \Rightarrow \Delta b_3 \geq -2$

b_4: $b^* = \begin{pmatrix} 4 \\ 8 \\ 8 \\ 2 \end{pmatrix} + \begin{pmatrix} 0 \\ 1/3 \\ -2/3 \\ -2/3 \end{pmatrix} \Delta b_4 \geq 0 \Rightarrow \begin{matrix} \Delta b_4 \geq -24 \\ \Delta b_4 \leq 12 \\ \Delta b_4 \leq 3 \end{matrix}$

So the allowable range to stay feasible for:

b_1 is $b_1 \geq 0$

b_2 is $b_2 \geq 16$

b_3 is $b_3 \geq 16$

b_4 is $0 \leq b_4 \leq 27$

6.7-13. b)

Incrementing c_1 by Δc_1, the x_1 coefficient in row 0 of the final tableau becomes $\frac{1}{3} - \Delta c_1$. In order for this to remain optimal, $\frac{1}{3} - \Delta c_1 \geq 0$ or $\Delta c_1 \leq \frac{1}{3}$. Thus, the allowable range to stay optimal for c_1 is $c_1 \leq 3 + \frac{1}{3} = \frac{10}{3}$.

Incrementing c_2 by Δc_2, the x_2 coefficient in row 0 of the final tableau becomes $-\Delta c_2$. Using row 2 to eliminate this coefficient, we get:

$$\text{Final row } 0 = \left[\tfrac{1}{3}, -\Delta c_2, 0, 0, 0, \tfrac{5}{3}\right] + \Delta c_2\left[\tfrac{2}{3}, 1, 0, 0, 0, \tfrac{1}{3}\right] = \left[\tfrac{1}{3} + \tfrac{2}{3}\Delta c_2, 0, 0, 0, 0, \tfrac{5}{3} + \tfrac{1}{3}\Delta c_1\right]$$

In order to remain optimal, we need $\frac{1}{3} + \frac{2}{3}\Delta c_2 \geq 0$ and $\frac{5}{3} + \frac{1}{3}\Delta c_1 \geq 0$. This means $\Delta c_2 \geq -\frac{1}{2}$ or $c_2 \geq \frac{9}{2}$.

6.7-14. (a)

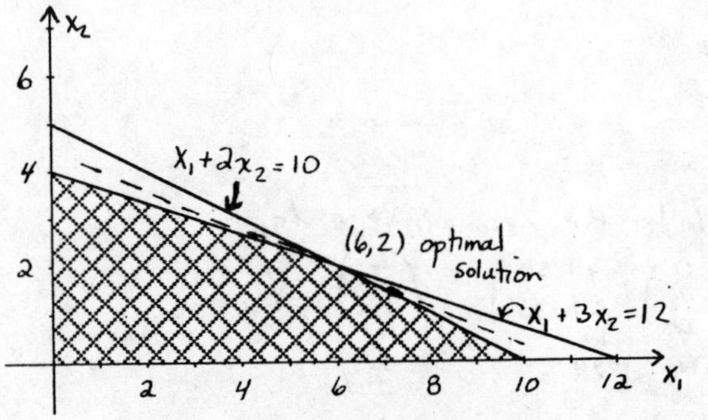

Parameter	Allowable Range	Likely, but not Allowable Range(s)
b_1	[8, 12]	[5, 8) and (12, 15]
b_2	[10, 15]	[6, 10) and (15, 18]
c_1	$[1\frac{2}{3}, 2\frac{1}{2}]$	$[1, 1\frac{2}{3})$ and $(2\frac{1}{2}, 3]$
c_2	[4, 6]	$[2\frac{1}{2}, 4)$ and $(6, 7\frac{1}{2}]$

(b) For b_1 the current basis is optimal if

$$b^* + B^{-1}\begin{pmatrix}\Delta b_1 \\ 0\end{pmatrix} \geq 0$$

-or- $\begin{pmatrix}6 \\ 2\end{pmatrix} + \begin{pmatrix}3 & -2 \\ -1 & 1\end{pmatrix}\begin{pmatrix}\Delta b_1 \\ 0\end{pmatrix} \geq 0$

-or- $\left.\begin{array}{l} 6 + 3\Delta b_1 \geq 0 \\ 2 - \Delta b_1 \geq 0 \end{array}\right\} -2 \leq \Delta b_1 \leq 2$

The allowable range for b_1 is

$$8 \leq b_1 \leq 12.$$

For c_1 the current basis is optimal if Row 0 + Δc_1 Row 1 ≥ 0

-or- $\left.\begin{array}{l} 1 + 3\Delta c_1 \geq 0 \\ 1 - 2\Delta c_1 \geq 0 \end{array}\right\} -\frac{1}{3} \leq \Delta c_1 \leq \frac{1}{2}$

The allowable range for c_1 is:

$$1\tfrac{2}{3} \leq c_1 \leq 2\tfrac{1}{2}.$$

(c) For b_2 the current basis is optimal if $b^* + B^{-1}\begin{pmatrix}0 \\ \Delta b_2\end{pmatrix} \geq 0$

-or- $\begin{pmatrix}6 \\ 2\end{pmatrix} + \begin{pmatrix}3 & -2 \\ -1 & 1\end{pmatrix}\begin{pmatrix}0 \\ \Delta b_2\end{pmatrix} \geq 0$

-or- $\left.\begin{array}{l} 6 - 2\Delta b_2 \geq 0 \\ 2 + \Delta b_2 \geq 0 \end{array}\right\} -2 \leq \Delta b_2 \leq 3$

The allowable range for b_2 is

$$10 \leq b_2 \leq 15$$

(d) For c_2 the current basis remains optimal if Row 0 + Δc_2 Row 2 ≥ 0

-or- $\left.\begin{array}{l} 1 - \Delta c_2 \geq 0 \\ 1 + \Delta c_2 \geq 0 \end{array}\right\} -1 \leq \Delta c_2 \leq 1$

The allowable range for c_2 is:

$$4 \leq c_2 \leq 6$$

6.7-15. (a) For b_2 the current basis remains optimal if $b^* + B^{-1}\begin{pmatrix}0\\ \Delta b_2\end{pmatrix} \geq 0$

-or- $\begin{pmatrix}2\\1\end{pmatrix} + \begin{pmatrix}3 & -5\\ -1 & 2\end{pmatrix}\begin{pmatrix}0\\ \Delta b_2\end{pmatrix} \geq 0$

-or- $\left.\begin{array}{l} 2 - 5\Delta b_2 \geq 0 \\ 1 + 2\Delta b_2 \geq 0 \end{array}\right\} -\frac{1}{2} \leq \Delta b_2 \leq \frac{2}{5}$

The allowable range for b_2 is

$4\frac{1}{2} \leq b_2 \leq 5\frac{2}{5}$

(b) For c_2 the current basis is optimal if

$\bar{c}_{2new} = \bar{c}_2 - \Delta c_2 = 1 - \Delta c_2 \geq 0$

-or- $\Delta c_2 \leq 1$

The allowable range for c_2 is

$c_2 \leq 5$

(c) For a_{22} the current basis remains optimal if $\bar{c}_{2new} = \bar{c}_2 + (1,1)\begin{pmatrix}0\\ \Delta a_{22}\end{pmatrix} \geq 0$

-or- $1 + \Delta a_{22} \geq 0 \Rightarrow \Delta a_{22} \geq -1$

The allowable range for a_{22} is

$a_{22} \geq 1$

(d) For c_3 the current basis is optimal if Row 0 + Δc_3 Row 2 ≥ 0

-or- $\left.\begin{array}{l} 1 + \Delta c_3 \geq 0 \\ 1 - \Delta c_3 \geq 0 \\ 1 + 2\Delta c_3 \geq 0 \end{array}\right\} -\frac{1}{2} \leq \Delta c_3 \leq 1$

The allowable range for c_3 is

$7\frac{1}{2} \leq c_3 \leq 9$

(e) For a_{12} the current basis is optimal if $\bar{c}_{2new} = \bar{c}_2 + (1,1)\begin{pmatrix}\Delta a_{12}\\ 0\end{pmatrix} \geq 0$

-or- $1 + \Delta a_{12} \geq 0 \Rightarrow \Delta a_{12} \geq -1$

The allowable range for a_{12} is

$a_{12} \geq 2$

(f) For b_1 the current basis remains optimal if $b^* + B^{-1}\begin{pmatrix}\Delta b_1\\ 0\end{pmatrix} \geq 0$

-or- $\begin{pmatrix}2\\1\end{pmatrix} + \begin{pmatrix}3 & -5\\ -1 & 2\end{pmatrix}\begin{pmatrix}\Delta b_1\\ 0\end{pmatrix} \geq 0$

-or- $\left.\begin{array}{l} 2 + 3\Delta b_1 \geq 0 \\ 1 - \Delta b_1 \geq 0 \end{array}\right\} -\frac{2}{3} \leq \Delta b_1 \leq 1$

The allowable range for b_1 is

$8\frac{1}{3} \leq b_1 \leq 10$

The results of (a)-(f) are summarized below:

Parameter	Allowable Range	Likely, but not Allowable Range(s)
b_2	$[4\frac{1}{2}, 5\frac{2}{5}]$	$[2\frac{1}{2}, 4\frac{1}{2})$ and $(5\frac{2}{5}, 7\frac{1}{2}]$
c_2	$(-\infty, 5]$	$(5, 6]$
a_{22}	$[1, \infty)$	none
c_3	$[7\frac{1}{2}, 9]$	$[4, 7\frac{1}{2})$ and $(9, 12]$
a_{12}	$[2, \infty)$	$[1\frac{1}{2}, 2)$
b_1	$[8\frac{1}{3}, 10]$	$[4\frac{1}{2}, 8\frac{1}{3})$ and $(10, 13\frac{1}{2}]$

6.7-16:

$\Delta c_1 = \theta \Rightarrow \Delta(z_1^* - c_1) = -\theta$

$\Delta c_2 = 2\theta \Rightarrow \Delta(z_2^* - c_2) = -2\theta$

Revised Final Tableau:

Bas Var	Eq No	Z	Coefficient of X1	X2	X3	X4	X5	Right side
Z(θ)	0	1	$-\theta$	-2θ	3/4	0	3/4	33/2
X1	1	0	1	0	1	0	0	4
X2	2	0	0	1	-3/4	0	1/4	3/2
X4	3	0	0	0	9/4	1	-3/4	39/2

Proper Form:

Bas Var	Eq No	Z	Coefficient of X1	X2	X3			Right side
Z(θ)	0	1	0	0	$\frac{3}{4} - \frac{\theta}{2}$	0	$\frac{3}{4} + \frac{\theta}{2}$	$\frac{33}{2} + 7\theta$
X1	1	0	1	0	1	0	0	4
X2	2	0	0	1	-3/4	0	1/4	3/2
X4	3	0	0	0	9/4	1	-3/4	39/2

This basic solution is optimal if;

$\left.\begin{array}{l} \frac{3}{4} - \frac{\theta}{2} \geq 0 \\ \frac{3}{4} + \frac{\theta}{2} \geq 0 \end{array}\right\} -\frac{3}{2} \leq \theta \leq \frac{3}{2}$

6.7-17. $\Delta c_1 = \theta \Rightarrow \Delta(z_1^* - c_1) = -\theta$

$\Delta c_2 = -\theta \Rightarrow \Delta(z_2^* - c_2) = \theta$

New Tableau:

Bas Var	Eq No	Z	X1	X2	X3	X4	X5	X6	Right side
Z	0	1	$-\theta$	θ	2	1	1	0	18
X2	1	0	0	1	5	1	3	0	24
X6	2	0	0	0	2	0	1	1	7
X1	3	0	1	0	4	1	2	0	21

Proper Form:

Bas Var	Eq No	Z	X1	X2	X3	X4	X5	X6	Right side
Z	0	1	0	0	$2-\theta$	1	$1-\theta$	0	$18-3\theta$
X2	1	0	0	1	5	1	3	0	24
X6	2	0	0	0	2	0	1	1	7
X1	3	0	1	0	4	1	2	0	21

The current basic solution is optimal if,

$$\left.\begin{array}{l} 2-\theta \geq 0 \\ 1-\theta \geq 0 \end{array}\right\} \quad \theta \leq 1$$

Clearly $Z(\theta) = 18 - 3\theta$ is maximized when θ is as small as possible. θ is restricted to be nonnegative so $\theta = 0$ is optimal.

6.7-18. a) Row 0 of the final tableau will look like this: $[4\theta, \theta, 3-\theta, 2, 2 \,|\, 24]$

Eliminating the X_1 and X_2 coefficients using row 1 and 2, resp. we get:

Final row 0 $= [4\theta, \theta, 3-\theta, 2, 2 \,|\, 24] - 4\theta[1, 0, -1, 1, -1 \,|\, 2] - \theta[0, 1, 5, -2, 3 \,|\, 1]$

$= [0, 0, 3-2\theta, 2-2\theta, 2+\theta \,|\, 24-9\theta]$

To remain optimal, therefore, we need:

$$3-2\theta \geq 0 \Rightarrow \theta \leq 3/2$$
$$2-2\theta \geq 0 \Rightarrow \theta \leq 1$$
$$2+\theta \geq 0 \Rightarrow \theta \geq -2$$

So the range of values over which this BF stays optimal is

$$-2 \leq \theta \leq 1$$

Since $Z - 9\theta$ is decreasing in θ, the best choice of θ is -2.

$(\theta = -2 \Rightarrow Z = 42)$

b) Adding Δb_1 (Δb_2) to b_1 (b_2), we get

b_1: $b^* = S^* \bar{b} = \begin{pmatrix} 1 & -1 \\ -2 & 3 \end{pmatrix} \begin{pmatrix} 7+\Delta b_1 \\ 5 \end{pmatrix} = \begin{pmatrix} 2 \\ 1 \end{pmatrix} + \begin{pmatrix} 1 \\ -2 \end{pmatrix} \Delta b_1$

b_2: $b^* = S^* \bar{b} = \begin{pmatrix} 1 & -1 \\ -2 & 3 \end{pmatrix} \begin{pmatrix} 7 \\ 5+\Delta b_2 \end{pmatrix} = \begin{pmatrix} 2 \\ 1 \end{pmatrix} + \begin{pmatrix} -1 \\ 3 \end{pmatrix} \Delta b_2$

So the allowable range to stay feasible is:

b_1: $\left.\begin{array}{l} 2+\Delta b_1 \geq 0 \\ 1-2\Delta b_1 \geq 0 \end{array}\right\} \Rightarrow -2 \leq \Delta b_1 \leq \frac{1}{2} \Rightarrow 5 \leq b_1 \leq \frac{15}{2}$

b_2: $\left.\begin{array}{l} 2-\Delta b_2 \geq 0 \\ 1+3\Delta b_2 \geq 0 \end{array}\right\} \Rightarrow -\frac{1}{3} \leq \Delta b_2 \leq 2 \Rightarrow \frac{14}{3} \leq b_2 \leq 7$

c) From the final row 0 in part (a), we get $y_1^* = 2-2\theta$, $y_2^* = 2+\theta$

Decreasing resource 1 (b_1) by 1 and increasing resource 2 (b_2) by 1 gives us a new objective value $\tilde{Z} = Z - (2-2\theta) + (2+\theta) = Z + \theta$

Z would increase by θ

6.7-18. d) Dual: Minimize $V(\theta) = 7y_1 + 5y_2$

subject to
$$3y_1 + 2y_2 \ge 10 - 4\theta$$
$$y_1 + y_2 \ge 4 - \theta$$
$$2y_1 + 3y_2 \ge 7 + \theta$$
$$y_1 \ge 0,\ y_2 \ge 0$$

at $\theta = 0$, graphically:

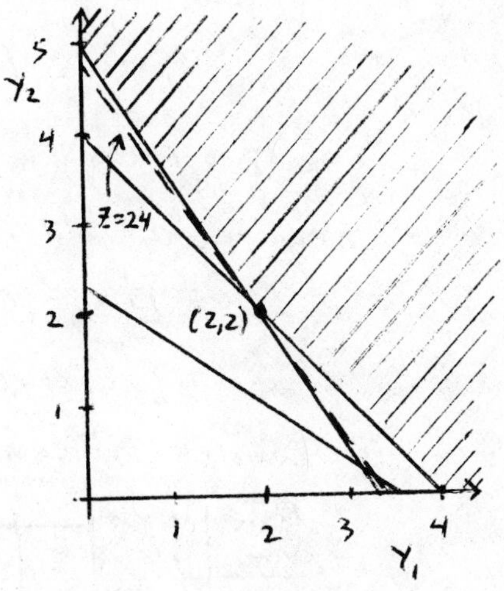

Optimal at $(y_1^*, y_2^*) = (2, 2)$

Starting with tableau:

-7	-5	0	0	0	0
-3	-2	1	0	0	$-10+4\theta$
-1	-1	0	1	0	$-4+\theta$
-2	-3	0	0	1	$-7-\theta$

We force y_1, y_2 into basis and y_3, y_4 out of basis, we get:

0	0	-2	-1	0	$24-9\theta$
0	1	1	-3	0	$2+\theta$
1	0	-1	2	0	$2-2\theta$
0	0	1	-5	1	$3-2\theta$

With shadow prices
$(y_1^*, y_2^*) = (2-2\theta, 2+\theta)$ as in (c).

6.7-19. a) Using $b^* = S^* \bar{b}$, we get

$$b^* = \begin{pmatrix} 3 & -2 \\ -1 & 1 \end{pmatrix}\begin{pmatrix} 5+\theta \\ 6+2\theta \end{pmatrix} = \begin{pmatrix} 3 \\ 1 \end{pmatrix} + \begin{pmatrix} -1 \\ 1 \end{pmatrix}\theta \Rightarrow \text{BF is } (3-\theta, 0, 1+\theta, 0, 0)$$

Thus, to be feasible, we need $3-\theta \ge 0$, $1+\theta \ge 0$ or $-1 \le \theta \le 3$.

The new Z becomes $(1\ 1)\begin{pmatrix} 5+\theta \\ 6+2\theta \end{pmatrix} = 11 + 3\theta$ (increasing in θ)

So the best choice of θ would be $\theta = 3$ ($Z = 20$)

b) Incrementing c_1 by Δc_1, then adding Δc_1 times row 1 to row 0, we get:

Final row 0 $= [-\Delta c_1, 1, 0, 1, 1 \,|\, 11+3\theta] + \Delta c_1 [1, 5, 0, 3, -2, 3-\theta]$

$= [0, 1+5\Delta c_1, 0, 1+3\Delta c_1, 1-2\Delta c_1, 11+3\Delta c_1 + (3-\Delta c_1)\theta]$

In order to stay optimal, we need

$$\left.\begin{array}{lll} 1+5\Delta c_1 \ge 0 & \Rightarrow & \Delta c_1 \ge -\frac{1}{5} \\ 1+3\Delta c_1 \ge 0 & \Rightarrow & \Delta c_1 \ge -\frac{1}{3} \\ 1-2\Delta c_1 \ge 0 & \Rightarrow & \Delta c_1 \le \frac{1}{2} \end{array}\right\} -\frac{1}{5} \le \Delta c_1 \le \frac{1}{2}$$

Thus, the allowable range to stay optimal for c_1 is

$$\frac{9}{5} \le c_1 \le \frac{5}{2}$$

6.7-20.a)-c) $B^{-1} = \begin{pmatrix} 0 & 1 \\ -1 & 1 \end{pmatrix}$. So new right hand side is

$$\text{new RHS} = \begin{pmatrix} 0 & 1 \\ -1 & 1 \end{pmatrix}\begin{pmatrix} 5+5\theta \\ 10-10\theta \end{pmatrix} = \begin{pmatrix} 10-10\theta \\ 5-15\theta \end{pmatrix}$$

new $Z = (2-\theta)(10-10\theta) = 20-30\theta+10\theta^2$

new row 0 = old row 0 $- \theta$(row 1)

$= [1-2\theta, \theta, 1-\theta, 0, M, M+2] - \theta[3, 1, 2, 0, 0, 1]$

$= [1-5\theta, 0, 1-3\theta, 0, M, M+2-\theta]$

The complete tableau is:

Basic Var	Eq. No	Coefficient of Z	x_1	x_2	x_3	x_4	$\bar{x}_5$	$\bar{\bar{x}}_6$	Right Side
Z	0	1	$1-5\theta$	0	$1-3\theta$	0	M	$M+2-\theta$	$20-30\theta+10\theta^2$
x_2	1	0	3	1	2	0	0	1	$10-10\theta$
x_4	2	0	-1	0	2	1	-1	1	$5-15\theta$

(b) To be feasible, $10-10\theta \geq 0$, $5-15\theta \geq 0$ $\Rightarrow 0 \leq \theta \leq \frac{1}{3}$

To be optimal, $1-5\theta \geq 0$, $1-3\theta \geq 0$ $\Rightarrow 0 \leq \theta \leq \frac{1}{5}$

(c) Or $0 \leq \theta \leq \frac{1}{5}$ to be feasible and optimal.

So the solution is:

$(x_1^*, x_2^*) = (0, 10-10\theta)$, $Z^*(\theta) = 20-30\theta+10\theta^2$

for $0 \leq \theta \leq \frac{1}{5}$

The best choice for θ is the one that maximizes $Z^*(\theta) = 20-30\theta+10\theta^2$ over $0 \leq \theta \leq \frac{1}{5}$.

Since $Z^*(\theta)$ is convex in θ, we need only look at the end points.

$Z^*(0) = 20$

$Z^*(\frac{1}{5}) = 20 - 30(\frac{1}{5}) + 10(\frac{1}{25}) = 14\frac{2}{5}$

So $\theta = 0$ is the best choice of θ.

6.7-21. (a) $\left.\begin{array}{l}\Delta c_1 = -2\theta \\ \Delta a_{11} = 1\end{array}\right\}$ $\Delta(z_1^* - c_1) = 2\theta + (2,2)\binom{1}{0} = 2\theta + 2$

$\Delta a_{11}^* = (-2,3)\binom{1}{0} = -2$

$\Delta a_{21}^* = (1,-1)\binom{1}{0} = 1$

$\Delta c_2 = \theta \Rightarrow \Delta(z_2^* - c_2) = -\theta$

$\Delta b_1 = 10 \Rightarrow \Delta Z^* = (2,2)\binom{10}{0} = 20$

$\Delta b_1^* = (-2,3)\binom{10}{0} = -20$

$\Delta b_2^* = (1,-1)\binom{10}{0} = 10$

New Tableau:

Bas Var	Eq No	Z	Coefficient of X1	X2	X3	X4	Right side
Z	0	1	$2\theta+2$	$-\theta$	2	2	130
X2	1	0	-2	1	-2	3	-5
X1	2	0	2	0	1	-1	15

Proper Form:

Bas Var	Eq No	Z	Coefficient of X1	X2	X3	X4	Right side
Z	0	1	0	0	$-3\theta+1$	$4\theta+3$	$-20\theta+115$
X2	1	0	0	1	-1	2	10
X1	2	0	1	0	$\frac{1}{2}$	$-\frac{1}{2}$	$\frac{15}{2}$

For θ near 0, the optimal solution is $(x_1, x_2, x_3, x_4) = (15/2, 10, 0, 0)$ with $Z = -20\theta + 115$.

(b) The solution above remains optimal, if

$\left.\begin{array}{l}-3\theta+1 \geq 0 \\ 4\theta+3 \geq 0\end{array}\right\} \Rightarrow -\frac{3}{4} \leq \theta \leq \frac{1}{3}$

(c) $Z(\theta) = -20\theta + 115$ is largest when θ is smallest. $\theta = 0$ gives the largest objective function value.

6.7-22. (a) $\left.\begin{array}{l}\Delta c_1 = 9 \\ \Delta a_{11} = 1 \\ \Delta a_{21} = 1\end{array}\right\}$ $\Delta(z_1^* - c_1) = -9 + (2,1)\binom{1}{1} = -6$

$\Delta a_{11}^* = (3,-1)\binom{1}{1} = 2$

$\Delta a_{21}^* = (-5,2)\binom{1}{1} = -3$

New Tableau:

Bas Var	Eq No	Z	Coefficient of X1	X2	X3	X4	X5	Right side
Z	0	1	-6	2	0	2	1	19
X1	1	0	3	5	0	3	-1	1
X3	2	0	-3	-7	1	-5	2	2

6.7-22. (a) (cont')

Proper Form:

Bas Var	Eq No	Z	Coefficient of X1	X2	X3	X4	X5	Right side
Z	0	1	0	12	0	8	-1	21
X1	1	0	1	5/3	0	1	-1/3	1/3
X3	2	0	0	-2	1	-2	1*	3

Optimal Tableau:

Bas Var	Eq No	Z	Coefficient of X1	X2	X3	X4	X5	Right side
Z	0	1	0	10	1	6	0	24
X1	1	0	1	1	1/3	1/3	0	4/3
X5	2	0	0	-2	1	2	1	3

With the new technology, $(x_1, x_2, x_3, x_4, x_5) = (4/3, 0, 0, 0, 3)$ is optimal with $Z = 24$.

(b) Changes to $(z_1^* - c_1)$, a_{11}^*, a_{21}^* will be θ times the results in (a)

New Tableau:

Bas Var	Eq No	Z	Coefficient of X1	X2	X3	X4	X5	Right side
Z	0	1	-6θ	2	0	2	1	19
X1	1	0	$1+2\theta$	5	0	3	-1	1
X3	2	0	-3θ	7	1	-5	2	2

Proper Form:

Bas Var	Eq No	Z	Coefficient of X1	X2	X3	X4	X5	Right side
Z	0	1	0	$\frac{34\theta+2}{2\theta+1}$	0	$\frac{22\theta+2}{2\theta+1}$	$\frac{-4\theta+1}{2\theta+1}$	$\frac{44\theta+19}{2\theta+1}$
X1	1	0	1	$\frac{5}{2\theta+1}$	0	$\frac{3}{2\theta+1}$	$\frac{-1}{2\theta+1}$	$\frac{1}{2\theta+1}$
X3	2	0	0	$\frac{29\theta+7}{2\theta+1}$	1	$\frac{19\theta+5}{2\theta+1}$	$\frac{\theta+2}{2\theta+1}$	$\frac{7\theta+2}{2\theta+1}$

Since $2\theta+1 > 0$ for all choices of θ between 0 and 1, the right-hand side will always be positive. The current basic solution is feasible for all choices of $\theta \in [0,1]$.

For optimality we require:

$\left.\begin{array}{l}34\theta + 2 \geq 0 \\ 22\theta + 2 \geq 0 \\ -4\theta + 1 \geq 0\end{array}\right\}$ $\theta \leq 1/4$

The current basis is optimal for $\theta \in [0, 1/4]$. $Z(\theta)$ is maximized when $\theta = 1/4$ on the range $0 \leq \theta \leq 1/4$.

6.7-23. $\Delta c_1 = 2\theta \Rightarrow \Delta(z_1^* - c_1) = -2\theta$

$\Delta c_2 = \theta \Rightarrow \Delta(z_2^* - c_2) = -\theta$

$\Delta c_3 = -\theta \Rightarrow \Delta(z_3^* - c_3) = \theta$

$\left.\begin{array}{l}\Delta b_1 = 6\theta \\ \Delta b_2 = -8\theta\end{array}\right\}$ $\Delta z^* = (9,7)\begin{pmatrix}6\theta \\ -8\theta\end{pmatrix} = -2\theta$

$\Delta b_1^* = (1,1)\begin{pmatrix}6\theta \\ -8\theta\end{pmatrix} = -2\theta$

$\Delta b_2^* = (3,2)\begin{pmatrix}6\theta \\ -8\theta\end{pmatrix} = 2\theta$

New Tableau:

Bas Var	Eq No	Z	X1	X2	X3	X4	X5	Right side
Z	0	1	-2θ	$20-\theta$	θ	9	7	$115-2\theta$
X1	1	0	1	3	0	1	1	$15-2\theta$
X3	2	0	0	8	1	3	2	$35+2\theta$

Proper Form:

Bas Var	Eq No	Z	X1	X2	X3	X4	X5	Right side
Z	0	1	0	$20-3\theta$	0	$9-\theta$	7	$115-7\theta-8\theta^2$
X1	1	0	1	3	0	1	1	$15-2\theta$
3	2	0	0	8	1	3	2	$35+2\theta$

For $\theta \geq 0$ the current basic solution is feasible if $\left.\begin{array}{l}15-2\theta \geq 0 \\ 35+2\theta \geq 0\end{array}\right\}$ $\theta \leq 15/2$

For $\theta \geq 0$ the current basic solution is optimal if $\left.\begin{array}{l}20-3\theta \geq 0 \\ 9-\theta \geq 0\end{array}\right\}$ $\theta \leq 20/3$

The current basic solution is both feasible and optimal if $\theta \leq 20/3$.

For $0 \leq \theta \leq 20/3$, $Z(\theta) = 15 - 7\theta - 8\theta^2$ is maximized with $\theta = 0$.

6.7-24. a) $B^{-1} = \begin{pmatrix} 1 & 1/3 & 1/3 \\ 0 & 1/2 & 0 \\ 0 & -1/3 & 1/3 \end{pmatrix}$, New $b = \begin{pmatrix} 1 & 1/3 & 1/3 \\ 0 & 1/2 & 0 \\ 0 & -1/3 & 1/3 \end{pmatrix}\begin{pmatrix} 4-\theta \\ 12-4\theta \\ 18-3\theta \end{pmatrix} = \begin{pmatrix} 2 \\ 6 \\ 2 \end{pmatrix} - \begin{pmatrix} 4/3 \\ 2 \\ -1/3 \end{pmatrix}\theta$

$Z = 3(2+\frac{1}{3}\theta) + 5(6-2\theta) = 36 - 9\theta$

To remain feasible, we need $2 - \frac{4}{3}\theta \geq 0,\ 6 - 2\theta \geq 0,\ 2 + \frac{1}{3}\theta \geq 0$

or $-6 \leq \theta \leq \frac{3}{2}$

So for $-6 \leq \theta \leq \frac{3}{2}$,

$(x_1^*, x_2^*) = (2+\frac{1}{3}\theta, 6-2\theta)$, $Z^*(\theta) = 36 - 9\theta$

b) Since $Z^*(\theta) = 36 - 9\theta$, every unit of change (increase) in the production of the old product results in a change (decrease) in the profit (of the optimal product mix of the two new products) of 9 (which represents \$9000 per batch). Thus, if unit profit for the old product is more than this, θ should be > 0. If less, then θ should be < 0.

Break even point is \$9000 per batch of old product.

c) As shown in (a), to remain feasible, $\theta \leq \frac{3}{2}$, so old product's production rate cannot be increased more than $\frac{3}{2}$ units without changing BF soln.

d) Similarly, the old product's production rate cannot decreased more than 6 units without changing the BF solution.

6.7-25. $\Delta c_2 = 4 \Rightarrow \Delta(z_2^* - c_2) = -4$

$\Delta c_3 = 1 \Rightarrow \Delta(z_3^* - c_3) = -1$

$\Delta b_3 = -1 \Rightarrow \Delta Z^* = (2, 0, 1)\begin{pmatrix}0\\0\\1\end{pmatrix} = -1$

$\Delta b_1^* = (1, 0, -1)\begin{pmatrix}0\\0\\-1\end{pmatrix} = 1$

$\Delta b_2^* = (1, -1, 0)\begin{pmatrix}0\\0\\-1\end{pmatrix} = 0$

$\Delta b_3^* = (0, 0, 1)\begin{pmatrix}0\\0\\-1\end{pmatrix} = -1$

New Tableau

Bas Var	Eq No	Z	X1	X2	X3	$\bar{X}4$	X5	$\bar{X}6$	X7	Right side
			Coefficient of							
Z	0	1	0	1	-1	M+2	0	M	1	7
X1	1	0	1	-1	0	1	0	0	-1	2
X5	2	0	0	3	0	1	1	-1	0	2
X3	3	0	0	2	1	0	0	0	1	1

Proper Form:

Bas Var	Eq No	Z	X1	X2	X3	$\bar{X}4$	X5	$\bar{X}6$	X7	Right side
			Coefficient of							
Z	0	1	0	3	0	M+2	0	M	2	8
X1	1	0	1	-1	0	1	0	0	-1	2
X5	2	0	0	3	0	1	1	-1	0	2
X3	3	0	0	2	1	0	0	0	1	1

The current basic solution is feasible and optimal.

CP6-1. a) The formulation is given in Sec. 3.4 (The order of the constraints and variables were kept the same). The results were:

Optimal Solution

Value of the
Objective Function: Z = 32.1546313

Variable	Value
X_1	1
X_2	0.6227
X_3	0.34348
X_4	1
X_5	0.04757
X_6	1

Constraint	Slack or Surplus	Shadow Price
1	0	-0.111
2	0	-0.1268
3	0	-0.0693
4	0	0.33621
5	0.3773	0
6	0.65652	0
7	0	1.81609
8	0.95243	0
9	0	0.04416

Sensitivity Analysis

Objective Function Coefficient

Current Value	Allowable Range To Stay Optimal Minimum	Maximum
8	$-\infty$	8.33621
10	9.33304	10.4294
7	4.98854	7.38163
6	$-\infty$	7.81609
11	10.9554	13.9752
9	$-\infty$	9.04416

Right Hand Sides

Current Value	Allowable Range To Stay Feasible Minimum	Maximum
60	52.52	74.2971
150	148.31	170.453
125	103.308	127.042
1	0.25152	1.24623
1	0.6227	$+\infty$
1	0.34348	$+\infty$
1	0	1.11061
1	0.04757	$+\infty$
1	0.03729	1.04809

CP6-1. b) Since the shadow prices for the first 3 constraints are non-zero, all the b_i's (required reductions in emission rates) are sensitive (as one would expect...). Similarly, since all 3 constraints are tight (binding), all the coefficients (a_{ij}) of these constraints are also sensitive. Finally, since each c_i has an allowable range to stay optimal around it, so that the optimal solution is insensitive to small changes in c_i, all the c_i's are insensitive. But note that most c_i's don't have much leeway to stay optimal, so that a modest change in c_5, for example, from 11 to 10.9 results in a different optimum.

Since the shadow price of constraint 2 is largest in absolute value, and the fact that b_2, being a larger number, is probably more uncertain (so a 10% change in b_2 has a larger effect than a 10% change in b_1) b_2 should be estimated more closely (So, also, should the coefficients of that constraints, though these are not as critical). Even though c_i's are not sensitive, it seems that these should also be estimated more closely since many are close to the end of their allowable ranges to stay optimal. c_5 and c_6 are most critical (meaning closest to "non-optimality") here.

c) If cost parameters are changed, would the optimal solution change? Here is a table:

True value is:	c_1	c_2	c_3	c_4	c_5	c_6
10% less	N	Y	N	N	Y	N
10% more	Y	Y	Y	N	N	Y

than estimated

This suggests that c_2 should estimated more closely, since it affects the optimal solution in both directions.

CP6-1.d) Dual of the OR Courseware converted (to maximization) problem;

$$\text{Minimize } V = 60y_1 + 150y_2 + 125y_3 + y_4 + y_5 + y_6 + y_7 + y_8 + y_9$$

subject to

$$12y_1 + 35y_2 + 37y_3 + y_4 \geq -8$$
$$9y_1 + 42y_2 + 53y_3 + y_5 \geq -10$$
$$25y_1 + 18y_2 + 28y_3 + y_6 \geq -7$$
$$20y_1 + 31y_2 + 24y_3 + y_7 \geq -6$$
$$17y_1 + 56y_2 + 29y_3 + y_8 \geq -11$$
$$13y_1 + 49y_2 + 20y_3 + y_9 \geq -9$$
$$y_1 \leq 0,\ y_2 \leq 0,\ y_3 \leq 0;\ y_4 \geq 0, y_5 \geq 0, y_6 \geq 0, y_7 \geq 0, y_8 \geq 0, y_9 \geq 0$$

Looking at the shadow prices of the constraints to get dual solution:

$y_1^* = -0.111$ $\quad y_4^* = 0.33621$ $\quad y_7^* = 1.8161$

$y_2^* = -0.1268$ $\quad y_5^* = 0$ $\quad y_8^* = 0$

$y_3^* = -0.0693$ $\quad y_6^* = 0$ $\quad y_9^* = 0.04416$

If the primal had been left in minimization form, the dual would change as follows: ① the right side would be positive (not negative)
② objective would be maximized (not minimized)
③ the signs of all the variable will be reversed.

Of course, the optimal dual solution would be exactly the same, except that the signs are reversed (+ → − and − → +)

e) The numbers of interest here are y_1^*, y_2^* and y_3^* which represent the rate at which the objective value changes as the values of b_1, b_2 and b_3 (respectively) change. So, for example, an increase of b_1 by 1 unit increases the optimal cost by 0.111 units (for small changes).
The amount that b_1, b_2, b_3 can be changed without affecting the rate of change in the total cost is simply the "allowable range to stay feasible."
In summary:

pollutant	Current req. reduction	Rate that Z changes with change in b_i	Lowest value before rate changes	Highest value before rate changes
Particulates	60	+0.111	52.52	74.297
Sulfur oxides	150	+0.1268	148.31	170.453
Hydrocarbons	125	+0.0693	103.308	127.042

CP6-1. f) To keep optimal solution total cost unchanged, the rates of change must "cancel out." That is, for particulates, a unit change in the policy standard results in +0.111 units of change in Z. To counteract this, we need −0.111 units of change in Z due to changes in sulfur oxides. Thus, we would change the policy standard for sulfur oxides by $\frac{-0.111}{0.1268}$ = −0.875 units. Similarly for every unit change for particulates policy standard, we must change that of hydrocarbons by $\frac{-0.111}{0.0693}$ = −1.602 units. If both sulfur oxides and hydrocarbons are simultaneously used, the change required is $\frac{-0.111}{0.1268+0.0693}$ = −0.566 units. (Here negative signs means "change in the opposite direction").

g) Formulation of simultaneous proportional increases:

Let θ = % increase (so θ = 1 means 1% increase, not 100%)

The problem remains exactly the same as before, except that the right side changes from

$$\begin{bmatrix} 60 \\ 150 \\ 125 \\ \vdots \end{bmatrix} \text{ to } \begin{bmatrix} 60+.6\theta \\ 150+1.5\theta \\ 125+1.25\theta \\ \vdots \end{bmatrix}$$

The costs, other coefficients, inequalities, etc. stay the same.

The rate at which the optimal increases with increase in θ would be .6(0.111) + 1.5(0.1268) + 1.25(0.0693) = 0.3434 units per unit change in θ.

h) The optimal solutions and objective value are:

θ	x_1	x_2	x_3	x_4	x_5	x_6	Z	Z − .35θ (tax incentives)
0	1	0.6227	0.3435	1	0.0476	1	32.155	32.155
10	1	0.7188	0.4360	1	0.2136	1	35.590	32.090
20	1	0.8150	0.5285	1	0.3796	1	39.025	32.025
30	1	0.9111	0.6210	1	0.5456	1	42.460	31.960
40	1	1	0.7053	1	0.7816	0.9293	45.898	31.898 *
50	1	1	0.9491	1	1	0.8963	49.710	32.210

Subtracting 3.5 for each 10% (due to tax incentives) for optimal Z, we see that, to minimize total costs of pollution abatement and taxes, θ = 40 should be chosen.

CP61. i) Looking at the output for the case $\Theta = 40$:

Optimal Solution

Value of the
Objective Function: Z = 45.8981883

Variable	Value
X_1	1
X_2	1
X_3	0.70528
X_4	1
X_5	0.78158
X_6	0.92932

Constraint	Slack or Surplus	Shadow Price
1	0	-0.0993
2	0	-0.124
3	0	-0.0817
4	0	0.55269
5	0	0.42945
6	0.29472	0
7	0	1.78923
8	0.21842	0
9	0.07068	0

Sensitivity Analysis

Objective Function Coefficient

Current Value	Allowable Range To Stay Optimal Minimum	Maximum
8	-∞	8.55269
10	-∞	10.4294
7	5.70764	7.38163
6	-∞	7.78923
11	10.9554	11.3844
9	8.62811	9.04416

Right Hand Sides

Current Value	Allowable Range To Stay Feasible Minimum	Maximum
84	83.1542	84.2648
210	203.706	211.112
175	174.747	175.864
1	0.95669	1.01442
1	0.9773	1.00727
1	0.70528	+∞
1	0.88376	2.17467
1	0.78158	+∞
1	0.92932	+∞

From this, we follow the same steps as in e) and f) to get the desired rates and values:

Pollutant	Current req. reduction	Rate that Z changes with change in b.	Lowest value 'til rate changes	Highest value 'til rate changes
Particulates	84	0.0993	83.154	84.265
Sulfur oxides	210	0.124	203.706	211.112
Hydrocarbons	175	0.0817	174.747	175.864

To keep Z unchanged, for every unit of change of particulate policy standard we need to change the policy standard(s) for:

sulfur oxides by $\frac{-0.0993}{0.124} = -0.801$ units

hydrocarbons by $\frac{-0.0993}{0.0817} = -1.215$ units

both simultaneously by $\frac{-0.0993}{0.124 + 0.0817} = -0.483$ units each.

Chapter 7
Other Algorithms for Linear Programming

7.1-1

(a) and (c)

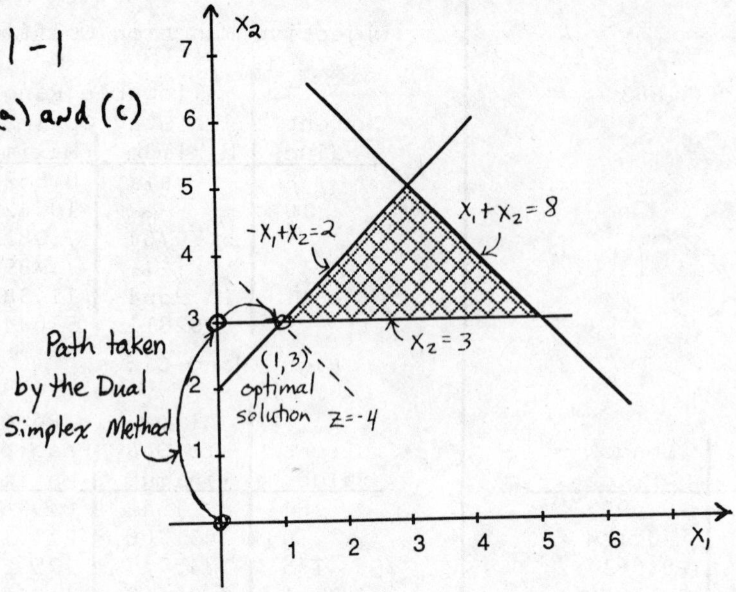

(b)

	BV	Eq. #	Z	x_1	x_2	x_3	x_4	x_5	RHS
(0)	Z	0	1	1	1	0	0	0	0
	x_3	1	0	1	1	1	0	0	8
	x_4	2	0	0	-1*	0	1	0	-3
	x_5	3	0	-1	1	0	0	1	2
(1)	Z	0	1	1	0	0	1	0	-3
	x_3	1	0	1	0	1	1	0	5
	x_2	2	0	0	1	0	-1	0	3
	x_5	3	0	-1*	0	0	1	1	-1
(2)	Z	0	1	0	0	0	2	1	-4
	x_3	1	0	0	0	1	2	1	4
	x_2	2	0	0	1	0	-1	0	3
	x_1	3	0	1	0	0	-1	-1	1

So $(x_1, x_2) = (1, 3)$ with $Z = -4$ is optimal

7.1-2

(a)

	BV	Eq. #	Z	x_1	x_2	x_3	x_4	x_5	RHS
(0)	Z	0	-1	3	2	0	0	0	0
	x_3	1	0	-2*	-1	1	0	0	-10
	x_4	2	0	-3	2	0	1	0	6
	x_5	3	0	-1	-1	0	0	1	-6
(1)	Z	0	-1	0	1/2	3/2	0	0	-15
	x_1	1	0	1	1/2	-1/2	0	0	5
	x_4	2	0	0	7/2	-3/2	1	0	21
	x_5	3	0	0	-1/2*	-1/2	0	1	-1
(2)	Z	0	-1	0	0	1	0	1	-16
	x_1	1	0	1	0	-1	0	1	4
	x_4	2	0	0	0	-5	1	7	14
	x_2	3	0	0	1	1	0	2	2

$(x_1, x_2) = (4, 2)$ is optimal with $Z = 16$

7.1-2 (b)

	BV	Eq. #	z	x_1	x_2	x_3	x_4	x_5	RHS
(0)	Z	0	-1	2	3	1	0	0	0
	x_4	1	0	-1	-4	-2*	1	0	-8
	x_5	2	0	-3	-2	0	0	1	-6
(1)	Z	0	-1	3/2	1	0	1/2	0	-4
	x_3	1	0	1/2	2	1	-1/2	0	4
	x_5	2	0	-3*	-2	0	0	1	6
(2)	Z	0	-1	0	0	0	1/2	1/2	-7
	x_3	1	0	0	5/3	1	-1/2	1/6	3
	x_1	2	0	1	2/3	0	0	-1/3	2

So $(x_1, x_2, x_3) = (2, 0, 3)$ with $z = 7$ is optimal.
Note that $(x_1, x_2, x_3) = (4/5, 9/5, 0)$ is also optimal

7.1-3

	BV	Eq. #	z	x_1	x_2	x_3	x_4	x_5	RHS
(0)	Z	0	-1	5	2	4	0	0	0
	x_4	1	0	-3	-1	-2	1	0	-4
	x_5	2	0	-6	-3*	-5	0	1	-10
(1)	Z	0	-1	1	0	2/3	0	2/3	-20/3
	x_4	1	0	-1*	0	-1/3	1	-1/3	-2/3
	x_2	2	0	2	1	5/3	0	-1/3	10/3
(2)	Z	0	-1	0	0	1/3	1	1/3	-22/3
	x_1	1	0	1	0	1/3	-1	1/3	2/3
	x_2	2	0	0	1	1	2	-1	2

So $(x_1, x_2, x_3) = (2/3, 2, 0)$ with $z = 7\,1/3$ is optimal.

7.1-4

	BV	Eq. #	z	x_1	x_2	x_3	x_4	x_5	x_6	x_7	RHS
(0)	Z	0	-1	7	2	5	4	0	0	0	0
	x_5	1	0	-2	-4	-7	-1	1	0	0	-5
	x_6	2	0	8	-4*	-6	-4	0	1	0	-8
	x_7	3	0	-3	-8	-1	-4	0	0	1	-4
(1)	Z	0	-1	3	0	2	2	0	1/2	0	-4
	x_5	1	0	6	0	-1	3	1	-1	0	3
	x_2	2	0	2	1	3/2	1	0	-1/4	0	2
	x_7	3	0	13	0	11	4	0	-2	1	12

So $(x_1, x_2, x_3, x_4) = (0, 2, 0, 0)$ with $z = 4$ is optimal.

7.1-5 (a)

	BV	Eq. #	z	x_1	x_2	x_3	x_4	x_5	RHS	Primal Solution	Dual Solution
(0)	Z	0	1	-3	-2	0	0	0	0		
	x_3	1	0	3*	1	1	0	0	12	(0, 0, 12, 6, 27)	(0, 0, 0, -3, -2)
	x_4	2	0	1	1	0	1	0	6		
	x_5	3	0	5	3	0	0	1	27		
(1)	Z	0	1	0	-1	1	0	0	12		
	x_1	1	0	1	1/3	1/3	0	0	4	(4, 0, 0, 2, 7)	(1, 0, 0, 0, -1)
	x_4	2	0	0	2/3*	-1/3	1	0	2		
	x_5	3	0	0	4/3	-5/3	0	1	7		
(2)	Z	0	1	0	0	1/2	3/2	0	15		
	x_1	1	0	1	0	1/2	-1/2	0	3	(3, 3, 0, 0, 3)	(1/2, 3/2, 0, 0, 0)
	x_2	2	0	0	1	-1/2	3/2	0	3		
	x_5	3	0	0	0	-1	-2	1	3		

So $(x_1, x_2) = (3, 3)$ with $z = 15$ is optimal

7.1-5 (b) The dual is minimize $12y_1 + 6y_2 + 27y_3$

subject to

$$3y_1 + y_2 + 5y_3 \geq 3$$
$$y_1 + y_2 + 3y_3 \geq 2$$
$$y_1 \geq 0,\ y_2 \geq 0,\ y_3 \geq 0$$

	BV	Eq. #	w	y_1	y_2	y_3	y_4	y_5	RHS	Primal Solution	Dual Solution
(0)	z	0	-1	12	6	27	0	0	0	(0,0,12,6,27)	(0,0,0,-3,-2)
	y_4	1	0	-3*	-1	-5	1	0	-3		
	y_5	2	0	-1	-1	-3	0	1	-2		
(1)	z	0	-1	0	2	7	4	0	12	(4,0,0,2,7)	(1,0,0,0,-1)
	y_1	1	0	1	1/3	5/3	-1/3	0	1		
	y_5	2	0	0	-2/3*	-4/3	-1/3	1	-1		
(2)	z	0	-1	0	0	3	3	3	15		
	y_1	1	0	1	0	1	-1/2	1/2	1/2	(3,3,0,0,3)	(1/2,3/2,0,0,0)
	y_2	2	0	0	1	2	-2	-3/2	3/2		

The dual optimal solution is $(y_1, y_2, y_3) = (1/2, 3/2, 0)$ with $z = 15$.

The sequence of basic solutions and complementary basic solutions is identical to that in part (a).

7.1-6

	BV	Eq. #	z	x_1	x_2	x_3	x_4	x_5	RHS
(0)	z	0	1	0	0	0	3/2	1	54
	x_3	1	0	0	0	1	1/3	-1/3	6
	x_2	2	0	0	1	0	1/2	0	12
	x_1	3	0	1	0	0	-1/3*	1/3	-2
(1)	z	0	1	9/2	0	0	0	5/2	45
	x_3	1	0	1	0	1	0	0	4
	x_2	2	0	3/2	1	0	0	1/2	9
	x_4	3	0	-3	0	0	1	-1	6

So the new optimal solution is $(x_1, x_2, x_3, x_4, x_5) = (0, 9, 4, 6, 0)$ with $z = 45$

7.1-7 (a)

	BV	Eq. #	z	x_1	x_2	x_3	x_4	x_5	RHS
(0)	z	0	1	0	0	2	5	0	150
	x_2	1	0	-1	1	3	1	0	30
	x_5	2	0	16	0	-2*	-4	1	-30
(1)	z	0	1	16	0	0	1	1	120
	x_2	1	0	23	1	0	-5*	3/2	-15
	x_3	2	0	-8	0	1	2	-1/2	15
(2)	z	0	1	103/5	1/5	0	0	13/10	117
	x_4	1	0	23/5	-1/5	0	1	-3/10	3
	x_3	2	0	6/5	2/5	1	0	1/10	9

So $(x_1, x_2, x_3, x_4, x_5) =$ (–, –, 9, 3, 0) with $z = 117$ is optimal.

(b)

	BV	Eq. #	z	x_1	x_2	x_3	x_4	x_5	RHS
(0)	z	0	1	0	0	2	5	0	100
	x_2	1	0	-1	1	3	1	0	20
	x_5	2	0	16	0	-2*	-4	1	-10
(1)	z	0	1	16	0	0	1	1	90
	x_2	1	0	23	1	0	-5	3/2	5
	x_3	2	0	-8	0	1	2	-1/2	5

So $(x_1, x_2, x_3, x_4, x_5) = (0, 5, 5, 0, 0)$ with $z = 90$ is optimal

7.2-1 (a)

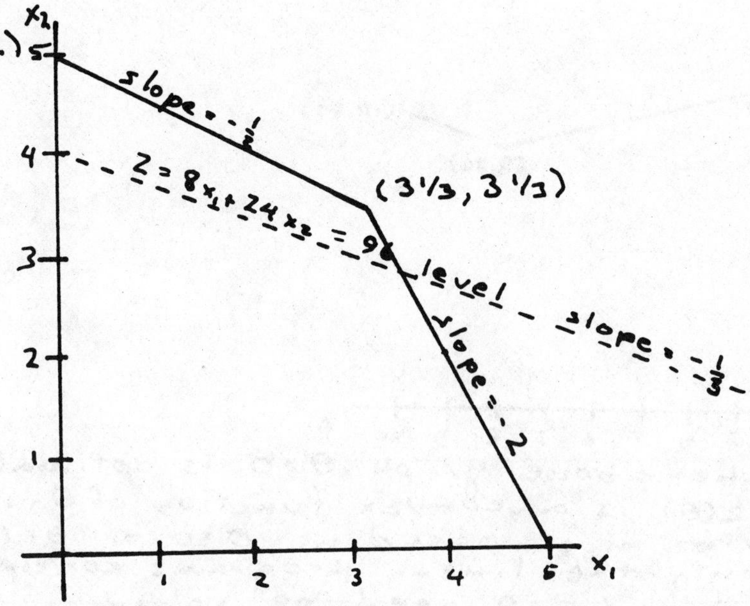

⇒ $(0,5)$ with $Z = 120$ is optimum.

$(0,5)$ will remain optimal until

$$-\frac{(8+\theta)}{(24-2\theta)} = -\frac{1}{2} \quad \text{or} \quad \theta = 2$$

at which point $(10/3, 10/3)$ will be optimal.
In turn, $(10/3, 10/3)$ will remain optimal until

$$-\frac{(8+\theta)}{(24-2\theta)} = -2 \quad \text{or} \quad \theta = 8$$

at which point $(5,0)$ will be optimal

Summarizing:

θ	(x_1^*, x_2^*)	$Z^*(\theta)$
$0 \le \theta \le 2$	$(0, 5)$	$120 - 10\theta$
$2 \le \theta \le 8$	$(10/3, 10/3)$	$(320 - 10\theta)/3$
$8 \le \theta \le 10$	$(5, 0)$	$40 + 5\theta$

(b)

BV	Eq.#	Z	x_1	x_2	x_3	x_4	RHS	Optimal for:
Z	0	1	$-8-\theta$	$-24+2\theta$	0	0	0	
x_3	1	0	1	2*	1	0	10	
x_4	2	0	2	1	0	1	10	
Z	0	1	$4-2\theta$	0	$12-\theta$	0	$120-10\theta$	$0 \le \theta \le 2$
x_2	1	0	1/2	1	1/2	0	5	
x_4	2	0	3/2*	0	-1/2	1	5	
Z	0	1	0	0	$(40-5\theta)/3$	$(-8+4\theta)/3$	$(320-10\theta)/3$	$2 \le \theta \le 8$
x_2	1	0	0	1	2/3*	-1/3	10/3	
x_1	2	0	1	0	-1/3	2/3	10/3	
Z	0	1	0	$(-40+5\theta)/2$	0	$(8+\theta)/2$	$40+5\theta$	$8 \le \theta \le 10$
x_3	1	0	0	3/2	1	-1/2	5	
x_1	2	0	1	1/2	0	1/2	5	

7.2-1 (b) cont.

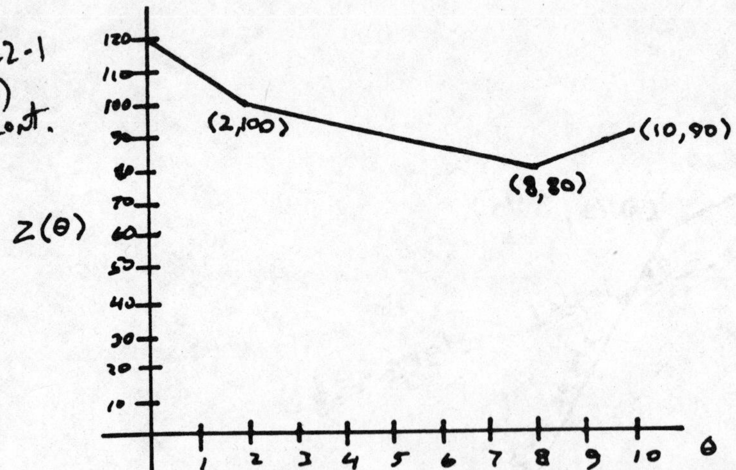

(c) From the above graph $\theta = 0$ is optimal. Since $z(\theta)$ is a convex function of θ, its maximum must occur at $\theta = 0$ or $\theta = 10$. Thus, only the linear programs corresponding to $\theta = 10$ and $\theta = 0$ need be solved.

7.2-2

BV	Eq.#	Z	x_1	x_2	x_3	x_4	x_5	x_6	RHS	optimal solution
Z	0	1	$-20-4\theta$	$-30+3\theta$	-5	0	0	0	0	
x_4	1	0	3	3^*	1	1	0	0	30	
x_5	2	0	8	6	4	0	1	0	75	
x_6	3	0	6	1	1	0	0	1	45	
Z	0	1	$10-7\theta$	0	$5-\theta$	$10-\theta$	0	0	$300-30\theta$	
x_2	1	0	1	1	1/3	1/3	0	0	10	For $0 \le \theta \le 10/7$
x_5	2	0	2	0	2	-2	1	0	15	$x^* = (0,10,0)$
x_6	3	0	5^*	0	2/3	$-1/3$	0	1	35	$Z = 300-30\theta$
Z	0	1	0	0	$2/3 - \theta/15$	$32/3 - \frac{22}{15}\theta$	0	$-2+7/5\,\theta$	$230+19\theta$	
									3	For $10/7 \le \theta \le 80/11$
x_2	1	0	0	1	1/5	$2/5^*$	0	$-1/5$		
x_5	2	0	0	0	26/15	$-28/15$	1	$-2/5$	1	$x^* = (7,3,0)$
x_1	3	0	1	0	2/15	$-1/15$	0	1/5	7	$Z = 230+19\theta$
Z	0	1	0	$-80/3+11/3\,\theta$	$-14/3+2/3\,\theta$	0	0	$10/3 + \frac{2}{3}\theta$	$150+30\theta$	
x_4	1	0	0	5/2	1/2	1	0	$-1/2$	15/2	For $80/11 \le \theta$
x_5	2	0	0	14/3	8/3	0	1	$-4/3$	15	$x^* = (15/2,0,0)$
x_1	3	0	1	1/6	1/6	0	0	1/6	15/2	$Z = 150+30\theta$

7.2-3

(a) Starting with the optimal tableau for $\theta = 0$ obtained after two iterations:

BV	Eq.#	Z	x_1	x_2	x_3	x_4	x_5	RHS	optimal solution
Z	0	1	0	0	$5-\theta$	$2+2\theta$	$8-3\theta$	220	For $0 \le \theta \le 8/3$
x_2	1	0	0	1	1	1	-1	10	$x^* = (10,10,0)$
x_1	2	0	1	0	0	-1	2^*	10	$Z = 220$
Z	0	1	$\frac{-8+3\theta}{2}$	0	$5-\theta$	$\frac{12+\theta}{2}$	0	$180+15\theta$	For $8/3 \le \theta \le 5$
x_2	1	0	1/2	1	1^*	1/2	0	15	$x^* = (0,15,0)$
x_5	2	0	1/2	0	0	$-1/2$	1	5	$Z = 180+15\theta$
Z	0	1	$\frac{-13+4\theta}{2}$	$-5+\theta$	0	$\frac{7+2\theta}{2}$	0	$105+30\theta$	For $\theta \ge 5$
x	1	0	1/2	1	1	1/2	0	15	$x^* = (0,0,15)$
x_5	2	0	1/2	0	0	$-1/2$	1	5	$Z = 105+30\theta$

7.2-3 (b) The dual is minimize $30y_1 + 20y_2$

subject to

$$y_1 + y_2 \geq 10 - \theta$$
$$2y_1 + y_2 \geq 12 + \theta$$
$$2y_1 + y_2 \geq 7 + 2\theta$$
$$y_1 \geq 0,\ y_2 \geq 0$$

Starting with the optimal tableau for $\theta = 0$ obtained after two iterations:

BV	Eq #	w	y_1	y_2	y_3	y_4	y_5	RHS	optimal solution
w	0	−1	0	0	10	10	0	−220	For $0 \leq \theta \leq 8/3$
y_2	1	0	0	1	-2^*	1	0	$8-3\theta$	$y^* = (2+2\theta, 8-3\theta)$
y_1	2	0	1	0	1	−1	0	$2+2\theta$	and $w^* = 220$
y_5	3	0	0	0	0	−1	1	$5-\theta$	
w	0	−1	0	5	0	15	0	$-180-15\theta$	For $8/3 \leq \theta \leq 5$
y_3	1	0	0	$-1/2$	1	$-1/2$	0	$-4+3\theta/2$	$y^* = (6+\theta/2, 0)$
y_1	2	0	1	$1/2$	0	$-1/2$	0	$6+\theta/2$	and $w^* = 180+15\theta$
y_5	3	0	0	0	0	-1^*	1	$5-\theta$	
w	0	−1	0	5	0	0	15	$-105-30\theta$	For $5 \leq \theta$
y_3	1	0	0	$-1/2$	1	0	$-1/2$	$-13/2+2\theta$	$y^* = (7/2+\theta, 0)$
y_1	2	0	1	$1/2$	0	0	$-1/2$	$7/2+\theta$	and $w^* = 105+30\theta$
y_4	3	0	0	0	0	1	−1	$-5+\theta$	

The basic solutions are the same as those obtained in part (a).

$0 \leq \theta \leq 8/3$: y^* from $(2, 8)$ to $(22/3, 0)$

$8/3 \leq \theta \leq 5$: y^* from $(22/3, 0)$ to $(17/2, 0)$

$5 \leq \theta$: $y^* = (7/2 + \theta, 0)$

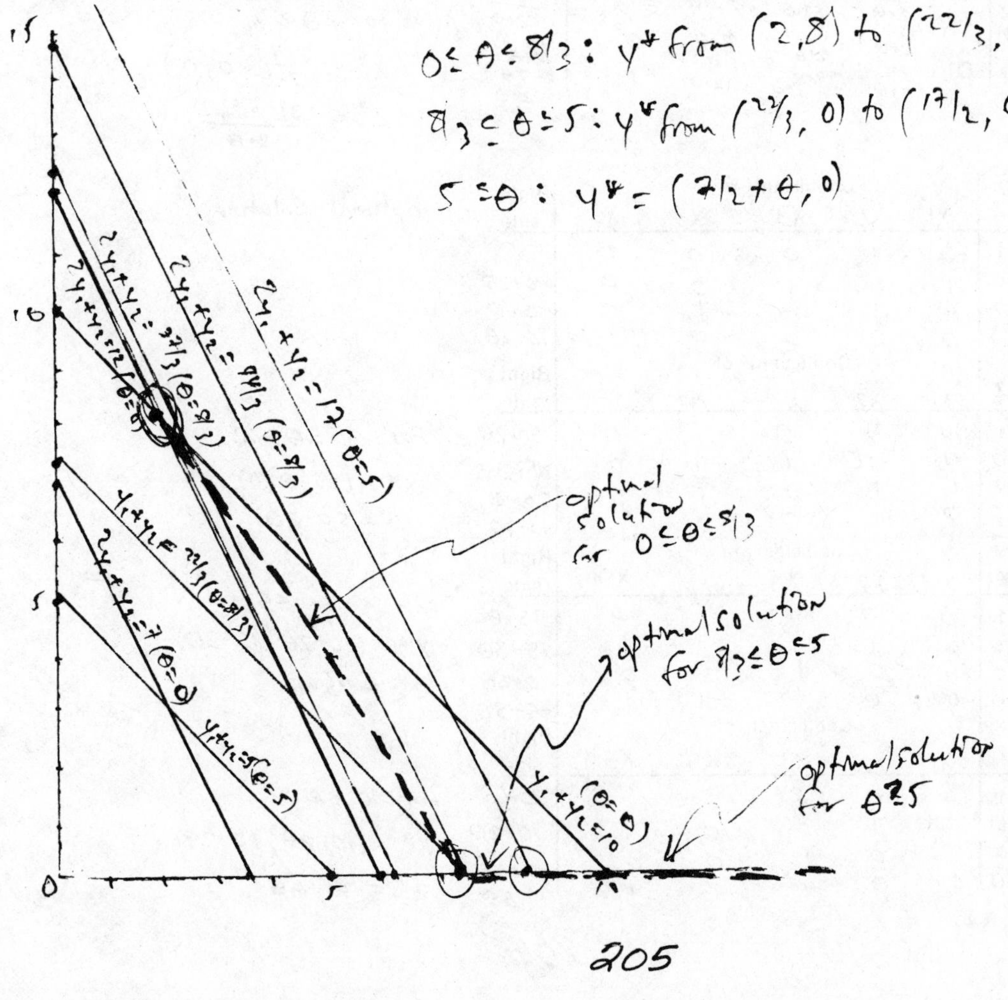

7.2-4 Starting with the optimal tableau for $\theta = 0$ obtained after 2 iterations,

Bas Var	Eq No	Z	X1	X2	X3	X4	X5	X6	Right side
			Coefficient of						
Z	0	1	0	0	$2-\theta$	1	$1-\theta$	0	$18-3\theta$
X2	1	0	0	1	5	1	3	0	24
X6	2	0	0	0	2	0	1*	1	7
X1	3	0	1	0	4	1	2	0	21

OPTIMAL SOLUTION

For $0 \le \theta \le 1$

$X^* = (21, 24, 0)$

$Z^* = 18 - 3\theta$

Bas Var	Eq No	Z	X1	X2	X3	X4	X5	X6	Right side
			Coefficient of						
Z	0	1	0	0	θ	1	0	$-1+\theta$	$11+4\theta$
X2	1	0	0	1	-1	1	0	-3	3
X5	2	0	0	0	2	0	1	1	7
X1	3	0	1	0	0	1	0	-2	7

For $\theta \ge 1$

$X^* = (7, 3, 0)$

$Z^* = 11 + 4\theta$

7.2-5 Starting with the optimal solution for $\theta = 0$ obtained after 2 iterations,

Bas Var	Eq No	Z	X1	X2	X3	X4	X5	Right side
			Coefficient of					
Z	0	1	0	$\frac{2+34\theta}{1+2\theta}$	0	$\frac{2+22\theta}{1+2\theta}$	$\frac{1-4\theta}{1+2\theta}$	$\frac{19+44\theta}{1+2\theta}$
X1	1	0	1	$5/1+2\theta$	0	$3/1+2\theta$	$-1/1+2\theta$	$\frac{1}{1+2\theta}$
X3	2	0	0	$-7+\theta/1+2\theta$	1	$-5-\theta/1+2\theta$	$2+\theta/1+2\theta$ *	$\frac{2+7\theta}{1+2\theta}$

Optimal Solution

For $0 \le \theta \le 1/4$

$X^* = \left(\frac{1}{1+2\theta}, 0, \frac{2+7\theta}{1+2\theta}\right)$

$Z^* = \frac{19+44\theta}{1+2\theta}$

Bas Var	Eq No	Z	X1	X2				Right side
			Coefficient of					
Z	0	1	0	$\frac{11+19\theta}{2+\theta}$	$\frac{-1+4\theta}{2+\theta}$	$\frac{9+9\theta}{2+\theta}$	0	$\frac{36+36\theta}{2+\theta}$
X1	1	0	1	$3/2+\theta$	$1/2+\theta$	$1/2+\theta$	0	$4/2+\theta$
X5	2	0	0	$-\frac{7+\theta}{2+\theta}$	$1+2\theta/2+\theta$	$\frac{-5-\theta}{2+\theta}$	1	$\frac{2+7\theta}{2+\theta}$

For $\theta \ge 1/4$

$X^* = \left(\frac{4}{2+\theta}, 0, 0\right)$

$Z^* = \frac{36+36\theta}{2+\theta}$

7.2-6

Bas Var	Eq No	Z	X1	X2	X3	X4	X5	Right side
			Coefficient of					
Z	0	1	-2	-1	0	0	0	0
X3	1	0	1	0	1	0	0	$10+2\theta$
X4	2	0	1*	1	0	1	0	$25-\theta$
X5	3	0	0	1	0	0	1	$10+2\theta$

optimal Solution

Bas Var	Eq No	Z	X1	X2	X3	X4	X5	Right side
			Coefficient of					
Z	0	1	0	1	0	2	0	$50-2\theta$
X3	1	0	0	-1*	1	-1	0	$-15+3\theta$
X1	2	0	1	1	0	1	0	$25-\theta$
X5	3	0	0	1	0	0	1	$10+2\theta$

For $5 \le \theta \le 25$

$X^* = (25-\theta, 0)$

$Z^* = 50 - 2\theta$

Bas Var	Eq No	Z	X1	X2	X3	X4	X5	Right side
			Coefficient of					
Z	0	1	0	0	1	1	0	$35+\theta$
X2	1	0	0	1	-1	1	0	$15-3\theta$
X1	2	0	1	0	1	0	0	$10+2\theta$
X5	3	0	0	0	1	-1	1	$-5+5\theta$

For $1 \le \theta \le 5$

$X^* = (10+2\theta, 15-3\theta)$

$Z^* = 35 + \theta$

Bas Var	Eq No	Z	X1	X2	X3	X4	X5	Right side
			Coefficient of					
Z	0	1	0	0	2	0	1	$30+6\theta$
X2	1	0	0	1	0	0	1	$10+2\theta$
X1	2	0	1	0	1	0	0	$10+2\theta$
X4	3	0	0	0	-1	1	-1	$5-5\theta$

For $0 \le \theta \le 1$

$X^* = (10+2\theta, 10+2\theta)$

$Z^* = 30 + 6\theta$

7.2-6 cont.:

Graphically we get:

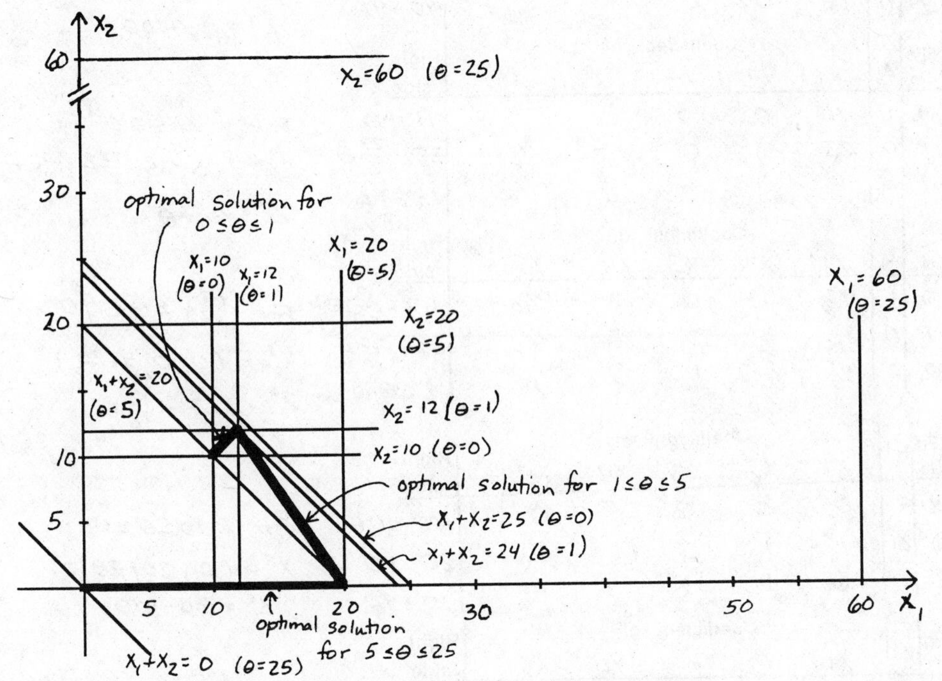

7.2-7 Starting with the optimal tableau for $\theta = 0$ obtained after 2 iterations,

Bas Var	Eq No	Z	X1	X2	X3	X4	X5	X6	X7	Right side
Z	0	1	0	4	1	3	0	0	5	$150+5\theta$
X5	1	0	0	-8	-2	-3	1	0	-3	$45-5\theta$
X6	2	0	0	0	-3*	-2	0	1	-2	$18-3\theta$
X1	3	0	1	2	1	2	0	0	1	$30+\theta$

optimal solution

For $0 \le \theta \le 6$

$x^* = (30+\theta, 0, 0, 0)$

$Z^* = 150 + 5\theta$

Bas Var	Eq No	Z	X1	X2	X3	X4	X5	X6	X7	Right side
Z	0	1	0	4	0	7/3	0	1/3	13/3	$144+4\theta$
X5	1	0	0	-8	0	-5/3	1	-2/3*	-5/3	$33-3\theta$
X3	2	0	0	0	1	2/3	0	-1/3	2/3	$-6+\theta$
X1	3	0	1	2	0	4/3	0	1/3	1/3	36

For $6 \le \theta \le 11$

$x^* = (36, 0, -6+\theta, 0)$

$Z^* = 144 + 4\theta$

Bas Var	Eq No	Z	X1	X2	X3	X4	X5	X6	X7	Right side
Z	0	1	0	0	0	3/2	1/2	0	7/2	$160\frac{1}{2}+\frac{5}{2}\theta$
X6	1	0	0	12	0	5/2	-3/2	1	5/2	$-49\frac{1}{2}+\frac{9}{2}\theta$
X3	2	0	0	4	1	3/2	-1/2	0	3/2	$-22\frac{1}{2}+\frac{5}{2}\theta$
X1	3	0	1	-2	0	1/2	1/2	0	-1/2	$52\frac{1}{2}-\frac{3}{2}\theta$

For $11 \le \theta \le 35$

$x^* = (52\frac{1}{2} - \frac{3}{2}\theta, 0, -22\frac{1}{2} + \frac{5}{2}\theta, 0)$

$Z^* = 160\frac{1}{2} + \frac{5}{2}\theta$

$\theta = 30$ provides the largest value of the objective

$x^*(30) = (7\frac{1}{2}, 0, 52\frac{1}{2}, 0)$, $Z^*(30) = 235\frac{1}{2}$

7.2-8

(a)

Bas Var	Eq No	Z	x_1	x_2	x_3	x_4	x_5	Right side
Z	0	1	0	0	2	5	0	$100+10\theta$
x_2	1	0	-1	1	3	1	0	$20+2\theta$
x_5	2	0	16	0	-2^*	-4	1	$10-9\theta$

OPTIMAL Solution
For $0 \le \theta \le 10/9$
$x^* = (0, 20+2\theta, 0)$
$Z^* = 100+10\theta$

Bas Var	Eq No	Z	x_1	x_2	x_3	x_4	x_5	Right side
Z	0	1	16	0	0	1	1	$110+\theta$
x_2	1	0	23	1	0	-5^*	$3/2$	$35-\frac{23}{2}\theta$
x_3	2	0	-8	0	1	2	$-1/2$	$-5+\frac{9}{2}\theta$

For $10/9 \le \theta \le \frac{70}{23}$
$x^* = (0, 35-\frac{23}{2}\theta, -5+\frac{9}{2}\theta)$
$Z^* = 110+\theta$

Bas Var	Eq No	Z	x_1	x_2	x_3	x_4	x_5	Right side
Z	0	1	$103/5$	$1/5$	0	0	$13/10$	$117-\frac{13}{10}\theta$
x_4	1	0	$-23/5$	$-1/5$	0	1	$-3/10$	$-7+\frac{23}{10}\theta$
x_3	2	0	$6/5$	$2/5$	1	0	$1/10$	$9-\frac{\theta}{10}$

For $70/23 \le \theta \le 90$
$x^* = (0, 0, 9-\frac{\theta}{10})$
$Z^* = 117-\frac{13}{10}\theta$

(b)

Bas Var	Eq No	Z	x_1	x_2	x_3	x_4	x_5	Right side
Z	0	1	0	0	2	5	0	$100-10\theta'$
x_2	1	0	-1^*	1	3	1	0	$20-2\theta'$
x_5	2	0	16	0	-2	-4	1	$10+9\theta'$

For $-10 \le \theta \le 0$
$x^* = (0, 20+2\theta, 0)$
$Z^* = 100-10\theta$

Bas Var	Eq No	Z	x_1	x_2	x_3	x_4	x_5	Right side
Z	0	1	0	0	2	5	0	$100-10\theta'$
x_2	1	0	1	-1	-3	-1	0	$-20+2\theta'$
x_3	2	0	0	16	46	12	1	$330-23\theta'$

For $-\frac{330}{23} \le \theta \le -10$
$x^* = (0, -20-2\theta, 330+23\theta)$
$Z^* = 100-10\theta$

For $\theta < -\frac{330}{23}$ the problem is infeasible.

7.2-9 (a)

Bas Var	Eq No	Z	x_1	x_2	x_3	x_4	x_5	Right side
Z	0	1	0	1	1	0	2	$20-2\theta$
x_4	1	0	0	-1	5	1	-1	$20+4\theta$
x_1	2	0	1	4	-1^*	0	1	$10-\theta$

Optimal Solution
For $0 \le \theta \le 10$
$x^* = (10-\theta, 0, 0)$
$Z^* = 20-2\theta$

Bas Var	Eq No	Z	x_1	x_2	x_3	x_4	x_5	Right side
Z	0	1	1	5	0	0	3	$30-3\theta$
x_4	1	0	5	19	0	1	4	$70-\theta$
x_3	2	0	-1	-4	1	0	-1	$-10+\theta$

For $10 \le \theta \le 70$
$x^* = (0, 0, -10+\theta)$
$Z^* = 30-3\theta$

(b)

Bas Var	Eq No	Z	x_1	x_2	x_3	x_4	x_5	Right side
Z	0	1	0	1	1	0	2	$20+2\theta'$
x_4	1	0	0	-1^*	5	1	-1	$20-4\theta'$
x_1	2	0	1	4	-1	0	1	$10+\theta'$

For $-5 \le \theta \le 0$
$x^* = (10-\theta, 0, 0)$
$Z^* = 20-2\theta$

(cont.)

7.2-9 (b) cont.

Bas Var	Eq No	Z	X1	X2	X3	X4	X5	Right side
Z	0	1	0	0	6	0	1	$40-2\theta'$
X2	1	0	0	1	-5	-1	1	$-20+4\theta'$
X1	2	0	1	0	19	4	-3*	$90-15\theta'$

For $-6 \le \theta \le -5$

$x^* = (90+15\theta, -20+4\theta, 0)$

$z^* = 40+2\theta$

Bas Var	Eq No	Z	X1	X2	X3	X4	X5	Right side
Z	0	1	1/3	0	37/3	4/3	0	$70-7\theta'$
X2	1	0	1/3	1	4/3	1/3	0	$10-\theta'$
X5	2	0	-1/3	0	-19/3	-4/3	1	$-30+5\theta'$

For $-10 \le \theta \le -6$

$x^* = (0, 10+\theta, 0)$

$z^* = 70+7\theta$

For $\theta < -10$ the problem is infeasible.

7.2-10 (a) Let $x^{(k)}$ be the kth optimal solution obtained as θ is increased from 0. Each $x^{(k)}$ is optimal for some θ-interval, say $\theta_k \le \theta \le \theta_{k+1}$, and the objective function $z(\theta) = \alpha_k + \beta_k\theta$ for some α_k and β_k. So $z(\theta)$ is linear in this interval. As the interval changes, so do α_k and β_k so that a different linear function is obtained for each interval.

(b) The problem is maximize $z(\theta) = \sum_{j=1}^{n} (c_j + \alpha_j\theta) x_j$

subject to $\sum_{j=1}^{n} a_{ij} x_j \le b_i \quad i = 1, 2, \ldots, m$

$x_j \ge 0 \quad j = 1, 2, \ldots, n$

Note that the feasible region does not change with θ. Consider $\theta_1 < \theta_2$ and let $\theta_3 = \lambda\theta_1 + (1-\lambda)\theta_2$ for $0 \le \lambda \le 1$. Let $x_j^{(1)}$, $x_j^{(2)}$ and $x_j^{(3)}$ be the optimal values of x_j $(j = 1, 2, \ldots, n)$ for θ_1, θ_2 and θ_3 respectively.

Let $z(\theta, x) = \sum_{j=1}^{n} (c_j + \alpha_j\theta) x_j$.

Now, $z^*(\theta_1) = z(\theta_1, x^{(1)}) \ge z(\theta_1, x^{(3)}) \Rightarrow \lambda z^*(\theta_1) \ge \lambda z(\theta_1, x^{(3)})$

and $z^*(\theta_2) = z(\theta_2, x^{(2)}) \ge z(\theta_2, x^{(3)}) \Rightarrow (1-\lambda) z^*(\theta_2) \ge (1-\lambda) z(\theta_2, x^{(3)})$

Adding gives $\lambda z^*(\theta_1) + (1-\lambda) z^*(\theta_2) \ge \lambda z(\theta_1, x^{(3)}) + (1-\lambda) z(\theta_2, x^{(3)})$

But, $\lambda z(\theta_1, x^{(3)}) + (1-\lambda) z(\theta_2, x^{(3)}) = \lambda \sum_{j=1}^{n} (c_j + \alpha_j\theta_1) x_j^{(3)} + (1-\lambda) \sum_{j=1}^{n} (c_j + \alpha_j\theta_2) x_j^{(3)}$

$$= \sum_{j=1}^{n} (c_j + (\lambda\theta_1 + (1-\lambda)\theta_2)\alpha_j) x_j^{(3)}$$

$$= \sum_{j=1}^{n} (c_j + \alpha_j\theta_3) x_j^{(3)}$$

$$= z(\theta_3, x^{(3)})$$

$$= z^*(\theta_3)$$

Hence, $\lambda z^*(\theta_1) + (1-\lambda) z^*(\theta_2) \ge z^*(\lambda\theta_1 + (1-\lambda)\theta_2)$

Hence, $z^*(\theta)$ is convex.

7.2-11 (a) Same argument as in problem 7.2-10 (a) above.

(b) The problem is maximize $z(\theta) = \sum_{j=1}^{n} c_j x_j$

subject to $\sum_{j=1}^{n} a_{ij} x_j \le b_i + \alpha_i \theta \quad i=1,2,\ldots,m$

$x_j \ge 0 \quad j=1,2,\ldots,n$

Consider $\theta_1 < \theta_2$ and let $\theta_3 = \lambda\theta_1 + (1-\lambda)\theta_2$, $0 \le \lambda \le 1$. Let $x_j^{(1)}$, $x_j^{(2)}$, and $x_j^{(3)}$ be the optimal values of x_j for θ_1, θ_2 and θ_3 respectively.

Thus, $\lambda z^*(\theta_1) + (1-\lambda) z^*(\theta_2) = \lambda \sum_{j=1}^{n} c_j x_j^{(1)} + (1-\lambda)\sum_{j=1}^{n} c_j x_j^{(2)}$

$= \sum_{j=1}^{n} c_j (\lambda x_j^{(1)} + (1-\lambda) x_j^{(2)}) \quad (*)$

Note that if $x_j' = \lambda x_j^{(1)} + (1-\lambda) x_j^{(2)}$ for $j=1,2,\ldots,n$, then x' is feasible for $\theta = \theta_3$ since

$$\sum_{j=1}^{n} a_{ij} x_j' = \lambda \sum_{j=1}^{n} a_{ij} x_j^{(1)} + (1-\lambda)\sum_{j=1}^{n} a_{ij} x_j^{(2)}$$
$$\le \lambda(b_i + \alpha_i\theta_1) + (1-\lambda)(b_i + \alpha_i\theta_2)$$
$$= b_i + \alpha_i\theta_3 \quad i=1,2,\ldots,m$$

Since $x^{(3)}$ is optimal for θ_3

$$\sum_{j=1}^{n} c_j(\lambda x_j^{(1)} + (1-\lambda) x_j^{(2)}) \le \sum_{j=1}^{n} c_j x_j^{(3)} = z^*(\theta_3)$$

So from $(*)$ above, $\lambda z^*(\theta_1) + (1-\lambda) z^*(\theta_2) \le z^*(\theta_3)$

Hence, $z^*(\theta)$ is concave.

7.2-12 From Duality Theory, $z^{**} =$ minimum $\sum_{i=1}^{m} (b_i + k_i) y_i$

subject to: $\sum_{i=1}^{m} a_{ij} y_i \ge c_j$

$y_i \ge 0.$

$(y_1^*, y_2^*, \ldots, y_m^*)$ is feasible for this problem, therefore,

$$z^{**} \le \sum_{i=1}^{m} (b_i + k_i) y_i^* = z^* + \sum_{i=1}^{m} k_i y_i^*.$$

7.3-1

	BV	Eq#	Z	x_1	x_2	x_3	RHS
(0)	Z	0	1	-3	-5	0	0
	x_3	1	0	3	2*	1	18

$x_2 \le 6$ [from $2x_2 \le 12$]
$x_2 \le 9$ from pivot
So x_2 moves to upper bound.

	BV	Eq#	Z	x_1	y_2	x_3	RHS
(1)	Z	0	1	-3	5	0	30
	x_3	1	0	3*	-2	1	6
(2)	Z	0	1	0	3	1	36
	x_1	1	0	1	-2/3	1/3	2

$x_1 \le 4$ from constraint
$x_1 \le 2$ from pivot

So $(x_1, x_2) = (2, 6)$ with $z = 36$ is optimal.

7.3-2 (a) and (c)

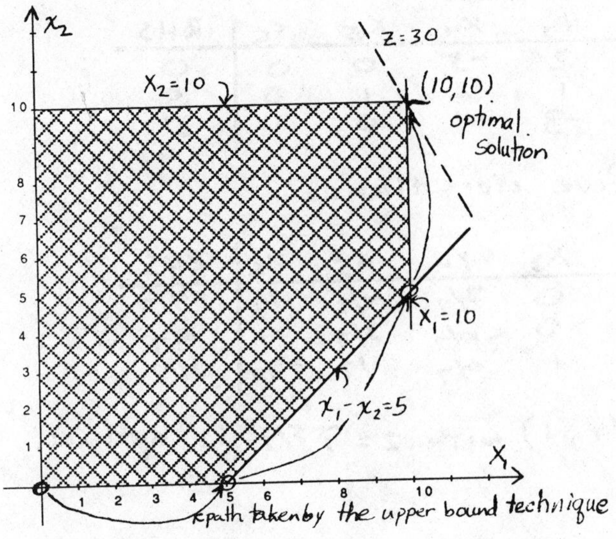

The optimal solution is $(x_1,x_2)=(10,10)$ with $z=30$

(b)

Bas Var	Eq No	Z	X1	X2	X3	Right side	
Z	0	1	-2	-1	0	0	X1 ≤ 10
X3	1	0	1*	-1	1	5	X1 ≤ 5

Bas Var	Eq No	Z	X1	X2	X3	Right side	
Z	0	1	0	-3	2	10	X2 ≤ 10
X1	1	0	1	-1	1	5	X2 ≤ 5

Bas Var	Eq No	Z	Y1	X2	X3	Right side	
Z	0	1	0	-3	2	10	X2 ≤ 10
Y1	1	0	1	1*	-1	5	X2 ≤ 5

Bas Var	Eq No	Z	Y1	X2	X3	Right side	
Z	0	1	3	0	-1	25	X3 ≤ 5
X2	1	0	1	1	-1	5	

BV	EQ	Z	Y1	Y2	X3	RS	
Z	0	1	3	0	-1	25	$X_3 \le 5$
Y2	1	0	-1	1	1*	5	

BV	EQ	Z	Y1	Y2	X3	RS
Z	0	1	2	1	0	30
X3	1	0	-1	1	1	5

(x_1,x_2) is optimal with $z=30$ ←

7.3-3

	BV	Eq. #	Z	x_1	x_2	x_3	x_4	x_5	RHS	
	Z	0	1	-1	-3	2	0	0	0	$x_2 \le 3$
(0)	x_4	1	0	0	1*	-2	1	0	1	$x_2 \le 1$
	x_5	2	0	2	1	2	0	1	8	$x_2 \le 8$
	Z	0	1	-1	0	-4	3	0	3	$x_3 \le 2$
(1)	x_2	1	0	0	1	-2	1	0	1	$x_3 \le 1$
	x_5	2	0	2	0	4	-1	1	7	$x_3 \le 1\frac{3}{4}$

	BV	Eq. #	Z	x_1	y_2	x_3	x_4	x_5	RHS	
	Z	0	1	-1	0	-4	3	0	3	$x_3 \le 2$
(2)	y_2	1	0	0	1	2*	-1	0	2	$x_3 \le 1$
	x_5	2	0	2	0	4	-1	1	7	$x_3 \le 1\frac{3}{4}$
	Z	0	1	-1	2	0	1	0	7	$x_1 \le 1$
(3)	x_3	1	0	0	$\frac{1}{2}$	1	$-\frac{1}{2}$	0	1	$x_1 \le 1\frac{1}{2}$
	x_5	2	0	2	-2	0	1	1	3	

	BV	Eq. #	Z	y_1	y_2	x_3	x_4	x_5	RHS
	Z	0	1	-1	2	0	1	0	8
(4)	x_3	1	0	0	$\frac{1}{2}$	1	$-\frac{1}{2}$	0	1
	x_5	2	0	2	-2	0	1	1	1

So $(x_1,x_2,x_3)=(1,3,1)$ with $z=8$ is optimal.

7.3-4 Initial Tableau:

BV	Eq.#	z	x_1	x_2	x_3	x_4	x_5	x_6	RHS
z	0	1	-2	-3	2	-5	0	0	0
x_5	1	0	2	2	1	2	1	0	5
x_6	2	0	1	2	-3	4	0	1	5

Final Tableau (After five iterations):

BV	Eq.#	z	x_1	y_2	x_3	y_4	x_5	x_6	RHS
z	0	1	0	1/7	0	3/7	4/7	4/7	54/7
x_1	1	0	1	-8/7	0	-10/7	3/7	1/7	2/7
x_3	2	0	0	4/7	1	4/7	1/7	-2/7	3/7

So $(x_1, x_2, x_3, x_4) = (2/7, 1, 3/7, 1)$ with $z = 7\,5/7$ is optimal.

7.3-5. Initial Tableau:

BV	Eq.#	z	x_1	x_2	x_3	x_4	x_5	x_6	x_7	RHS
z	0	1	-2	-5	-3	-4	-1	0	0	0
x_6	1	0	1	3	2	3	1	1	0	6
x_7	2	0	4	6	5	7	1	0	1	15

Final Tableau (after seven iterations):

BV	Eq.#	z	y_1	y_2	y_3	y_4	x_5	x_6	x_7	RHS
z	0	1	2/3	1	1/3	0	1/3	4/3	0	10
y_4	1	0	1/3	1	2/3	1	-1/3	-1/3	0	1
x_7	2	0	-5/3	1	-1/3	0	-4/3	-7/3	1	0

So $(x_1, x_2, x_3, x_4, x_5) = (1, 1, 1, 0, 0)$ with $z = 10$ is optimal.

7.3-6

Bas Var	Eq No	Z	X1	X2	X3	X4	X5	Right side	
-Z	0	1	3	4	2	0	0	0	$x_1 \le 25$
X4	1	0	-1*	-1	0	1	0	-15	$x_1 \le 15$
X5	2	0	0	-1	-1	0	1	-10	

Bas Var	Eq No	Z	X1	X2	X3	X4	X5	Right side	
-Z	0	1	0	1	2	3	0	-45	$X2 \le 5$
X1	1	0	1	1	0	1	0	15	$X2 \le 15$
X5	2	0	0	-1	1	0	1	-10	$X2 \le 10$

Bas Var	Eq No	Z	X1	Y2	X3	X4	X5	Right side	
-Z	0	1	0	-1	2	3	0	-50	$X3 \le 15$
X1	1	0	1	-1	0	1	0	10	
X5	2	0	0	1	-1*	0	1	-5	$X3 \le 5$

(cont.)

7.3-6 (cont.)

Bas Var	Eq No	Z	Coefficient of X1	Y2	X3	X4	X5	Right side
-Z	0	1	0	1	0	3	2	-60
X1	1	0	1	-1	0	1	0	10
X3	2	0	0	-1	1	0	-1	5

$(X1, X2, X3) = (10, 5, 5)$ is optimal with $z = 60$

7.3-7 Intial Tableau :

BV	Eq#	Z	x_1	x_2	x_3	x_4	x_5	x_6	x_7	x_8	x_9	RHS
z	0	-1	8	10	7	6	11	9	0	0	0	0
x_7	1	0	-12	-9	-25	-20	-17	-13	1	0	0	-60
x_8	2	0	-35	-42	-18	-31	-56	-49	0	1	0	-150
x_9	3	0	-37	-53	-28	-24	-29	-20	0	0	1	-125

Final Tableau (After six non-trivial iterations):

BV	Eq. #	Z	Y_1	x_2	x_3	Y_4	x_5	Y_6	x_7	x_8	x_9	RHS
Z	0	-1	.337	0	0	1.816	0	.044	.111	.127	.070	-32.154
x_3	1	0	-.167	0	1	-.530	0	.116	-.096	.016	-.006	.343
x_5	2	0	-.193	0	0	-.430	1	-.989	-.006	-.028	.023	.047
x_2	3	0	-.504	1	0	-.064	0	.103	.028	.006	-.028	.622

7.4-1

It.	X1	X2	Z
0	1	3	7
1	1.04605	4.95395	10.9539
2	0.93406	6.06594	13.0659

7.4-2 (a)

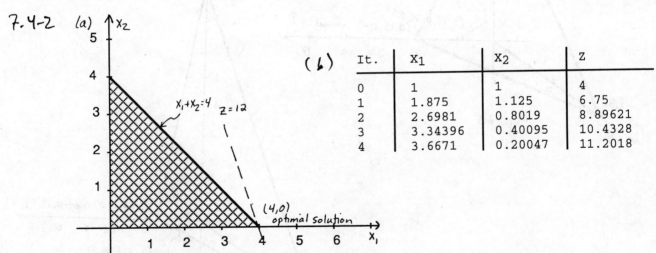

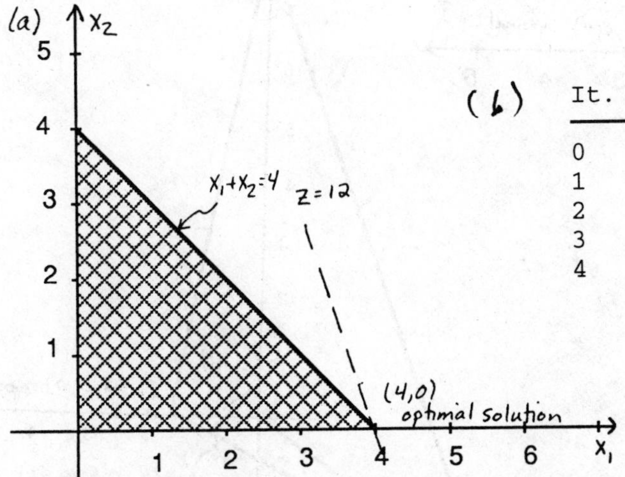

The corner point feasible solutions are (0,0), (0,4) and (4,0). The last one is optimal with $z = 12$.

(b)

It.	X1	X2	Z
0	1	1	4
1	1.875	1.125	6.75
2	2.6981	0.8019	8.89621
3	3.34396	0.40095	10.4328
4	3.6671	0.20047	11.2018

(cont.)

(c)

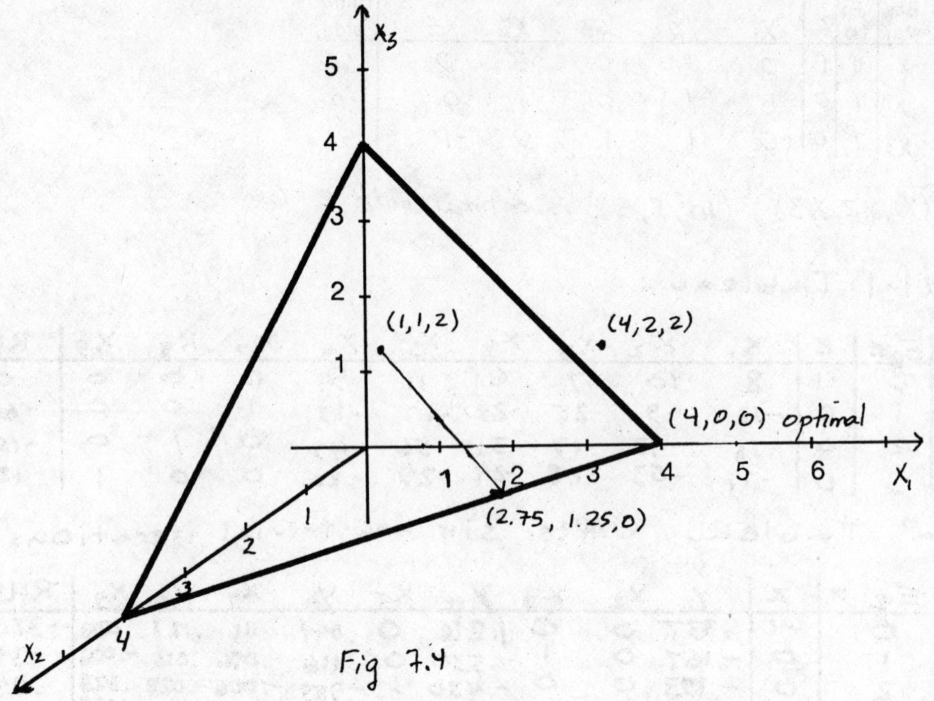

Fig 7.4

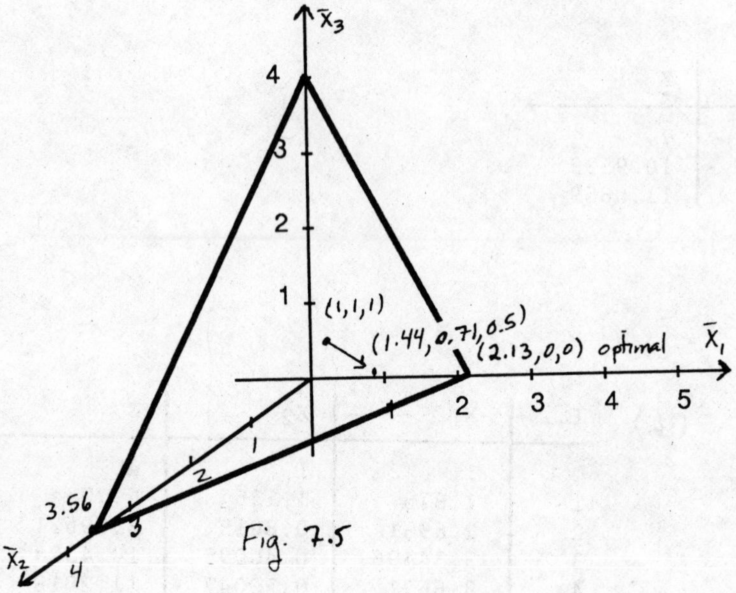

Fig. 7.5

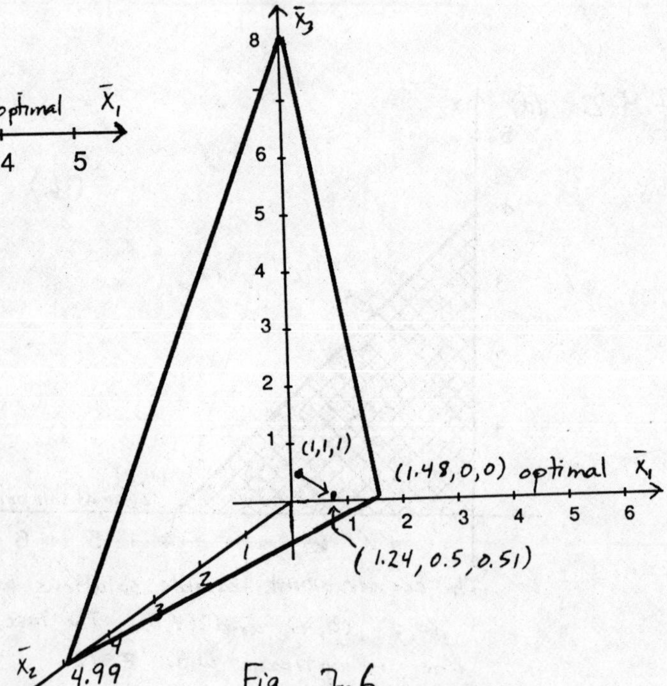

Fig. 7.6

7.4-2 (c) cont.

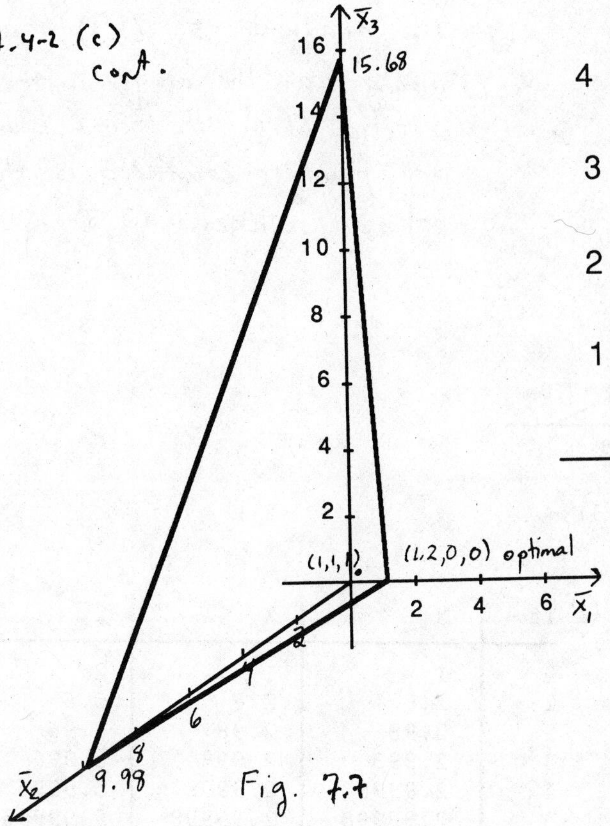

Fig. 7.7

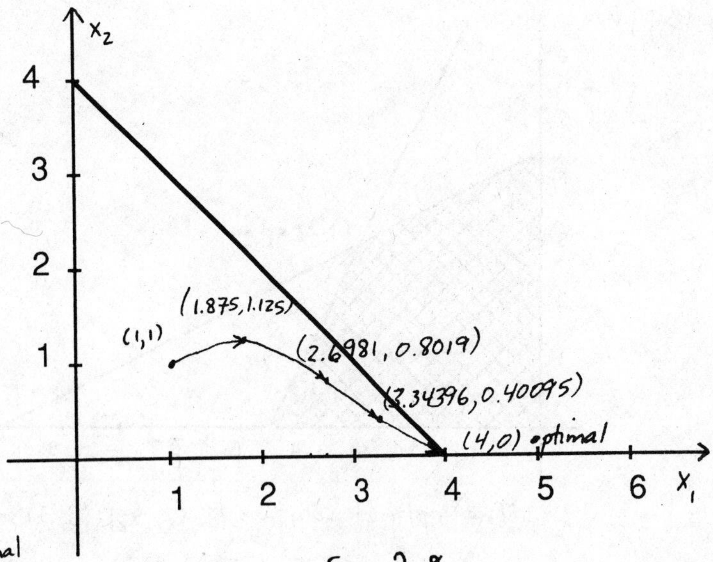

Fig. 7-8

7.4-3 (a) and (c)

It.	x_1	x_2	Z
0	4	4	12
1	2	6	14
2	1	7	15
3	0.5	7.5	15.5
4	0.25	7.75	15.75
5	0.125	7.875	15.875
6	0.0625	7.9375	15.9375
7	0.03125	7.96875	15.9688
8	0.01562	7.98438	15.9844
9	0.00781	7.99219	15.9922

(b) The value of x_1 is halved at each step so subsequent trial solutions should be of the form $(x_1, x_2) = (2^{-i}, 8-2^{-i})$ for $i = 1, 2, \ldots$

(c) We need to determine when $2^{-i} - 2^{-(i+1)} \leq 0.01$. This is true for $i = 6$ with $(x_1, x_2) = (2^{-7}, 8-2^{-7}) = (0.0078, 7.9922)$ on iteration 9.

7.4-4 (a)

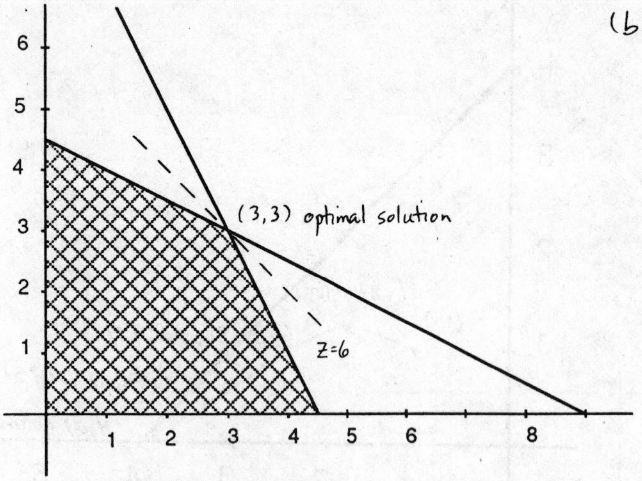

The optimal solution is $(x_1, x_2) = (3, 3)$ with $z = 6$

(b) The gradient is (1,1). Moving from the origin in the direction (1,1), the first boundary point encountered is the optimal solution (3,3).

(c)

It.	x_1	x_2	Z
0	1	1	2
1	2	2	4
2	2.5	2.5	5
3	2.75	2.75	5.5
4	2.875	2.875	5.75
5	2.9375	2.9375	5.875
6	2.96875	2.96875	5.9375
7	2.98437	2.98438	5.96875
8	2.99219	2.99219	5.98438
9	2.99609	2.99609	5.99219
10	2.99805	2.99805	5.99609

alpha = 0.5

(d)

It.	x_1	x_2	Z
0	1	1	2
1	2.8	2.8	5.6
2	2.98	2.98	5.96
3	2.998	2.998	5.996
4	2.9998	2.9998	5.9996
5	2.99998	2.99998	5.99996
6	3	3	6
7	3	3	6
8	3	3	6
9	3	3	6
10	3	3	6

alpha = 0.9

7.4-5 (a)

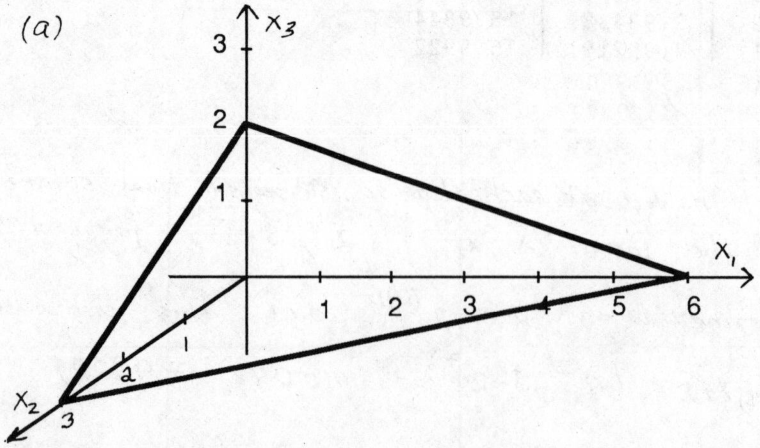

7.4-5 (b) gradient = (2,5,7)

$$\text{projected gradient} = P\begin{pmatrix}2\\5\\7\end{pmatrix} = \left[I - \begin{pmatrix}1\\2\\3\end{pmatrix}\left[(1,2,3)\begin{pmatrix}1\\2\\3\end{pmatrix}\right]^{-1}(1,2,3)\right]\begin{pmatrix}2\\5\\7\end{pmatrix}$$

$$= \begin{pmatrix}2\\5\\7\end{pmatrix} - \frac{1}{14}\begin{pmatrix}33\\66\\99\end{pmatrix} = \frac{1}{14}\begin{pmatrix}-5\\4\\-1\end{pmatrix}$$

(c) and (d)

It.	x_1	x_2	x_3	Z
0	1	1	1	14
1	0.5	1.4	0.9	14.3
2	0.25969	2.19516	0.45	14.6452
3	0.17947	2.57276	0.225	14.7978
4	0.1069	2.7778	0.1125	14.8903
5	0.05595	2.88765	0.05625	14.9439
6	0.0281	2.94376	0.02812	14.9719
7	0.01406	2.97188	0.01406	14.9859
8	0.00703	2.98594	0.00703	14.993
9	0.00352	2.99297	0.00352	14.9965
10	0.00176	2.99648	0.00176	14.9982

7.4-6

It.	x_1	x_2	Z
0	2	2	16
1	2.336	3.496	24.488
2	2.23067	4.65399	29.962
3	2.03597	5.32699	32.7429
4	1.95211	5.6635	34.1738
5	1.95054	5.83175	35.0104
6	1.97169	5.91587	35.4944
7	1.98588	5.95788	35.7471
8	1.99296	5.97891	35.8734
9	1.99648	5.98945	35.9367
10	1.99824	5.99473	35.9684
11	1.99912	5.99736	35.9842
12	1.99956	5.99868	35.9921
13	1.99978	5.99934	35.996
14	1.99989	5.99967	35.998
15	1.99995	5.99984	35.999

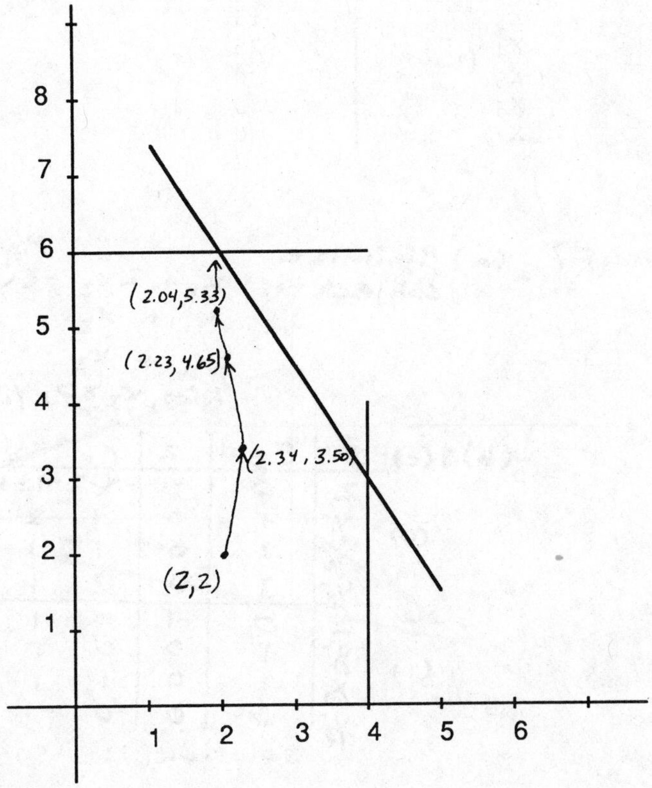

7.5-1 Let x_i = production rate of product i for $i=1,2,3$.

(a) Introduce $y_2^+, y_2^-, y_3^+, y_3^-$ as additional variables. The linear program is:

Max Z = 20 X1 + 15 X2 + 25 X3 - 5 X4 - 5 X5 + 0 X6 - 3 X7

subject to

1) 6 X1 + 4 X2 + 5 X3 - 1 X4 + 1 X5 + 0 X6 + 0 X7 = 50

2) 8 X1 + 7 X2 + 5 X3 + 0 X4 + 0 X5 - 1 X6 + 1 X7 = 75

and

X1 ≥ 0, X2 ≥ 0, X3 ≥ 0, X4 (Y_2^+) ≥ 0, X5 (Y_2^-) ≥ 0, X6 (Y_3^+) ≥ 0, X7 (Y_3^-) ≥ 0.

(b) Solve Automatically by the Simplex Method:

Optimal Solution

Value of the Objective Function: Z = 250

Variable	Value
X1	0
X2	0
X3	15
X4 Y_2^+	25
X5	0
X6	0
X7	0

7.5-2 (a) Minimize $M_1 y_1^+ + M_2 y_2^+ + M_2 y_2^- + y_3^-$

subject to

$$x_1 + 2x_2 - (y_1^+ - y_1^-) = 20$$
$$x_1 + x_2 - (y_2^+ - y_2^-) = 15$$
$$2x_1 + x_2 - (y_3^+ - y_3^-) = 40$$
$$x_1 \ge 0,\ x_2 \ge 0,\ y_1^+ \ge 0,\ y_1^- \ge 0,\ y_2^+ \ge 0,\ y_2^- \ge 0,\ y_3^+ \ge 0,\ y_3^- \ge 0$$

(b) & (c)

	BV	Eq.#	Z	x_1	x_2	y_1^+	y_1^-	y_2^+	y_2^-	y_3^+	y_3^-	RHS
(0)	Z	0	-1	$-M_2-2$	$-M_2-1$	M_1	0	$2M_2$	0	1	0	$-15M_2-40$
	y_1^-	1	0	1	2	-1	1	0	0	0	0	20
	y_2^-	2	0	1*	1	0	0	-1	1	0	0	15
	y_3^-	3	0	2	1	0	0	0	0	-1	1	40
(1)	Z	0	-1	0	1	M_1	0	M_2-2	M_2+2	1	0	-10
	y_1^-	1	0	0	1	-1	1	1	-1	0	0	5
	x_1	2	0	1	1	0	0	-1	1	0	0	15
	y_3^-	3	0	0	-1	0	0	2	-2	-1	1	10

solution is $(x_1, x_2) = (15, 0)$ with $Z = 10$.

7.5-2 (d)

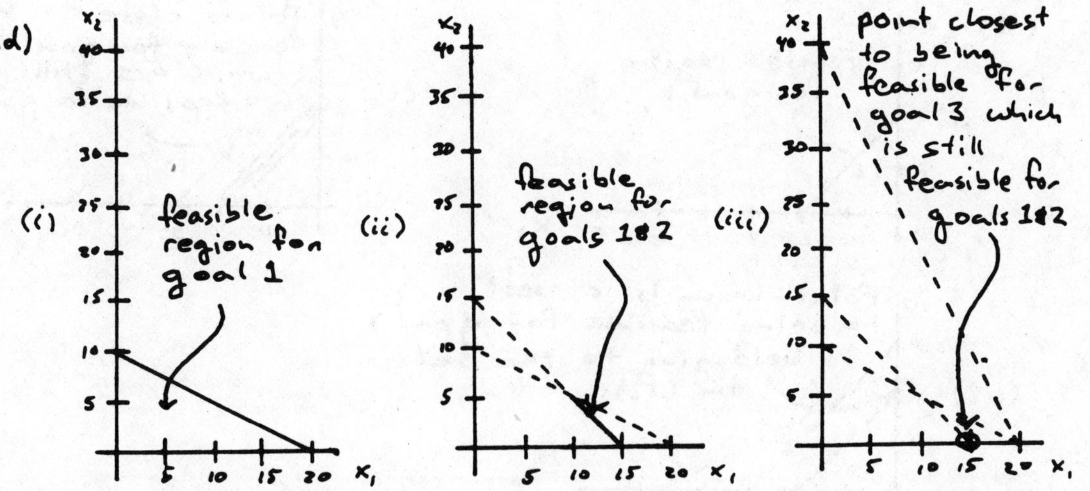

(e) The first program: minimize $z_1 = M_1 y_1^+$

subject to

$$x_1 + 2x_1 - (y_1^+ - y_1^-) = 20$$

$$\left[\begin{array}{l} x_1 + x_2 - (y_2^+ - y_2^-) = 15 \\ 2x_1 + x_1 - (y_3^+ - y_3^-) = 40 \end{array}\right]$$

$$x_1 \geq 0,\ x_2 \geq 0$$

from (iii) the solution is the feasible region in (i) above

Similarly, we let $y_1^+ = 0$ and take $z_2 = M_2 y_2^+ + M_2 y_2^-$ and the resulting program yields the feasible region in (ii).

Finally, letting $y_1^+ = y_2^+ = y_2^- = 0$ and $z_3 = y_3^-$ we get the solution (15,0), $z_3 = 10$.

7.5-3 (a) Minimize $M_1 y_1^+ \qquad + M_2 y_2^- \qquad + y_3^-$

subject to

$$x_1 + x_2 - (y_1^+ - y_1^-) = 20$$

$$x_1 + x_2 - (y_2^+ - y_2^-) = 30$$

$$x_1 + 2x_2 - (y_3^+ - y_3^-) = 50$$

$$x_1 \geq 0,\ x_2 \geq 0,\ y_i^+ \geq 0,\ y_i^- \geq 0 \quad i = 1, 2, 3$$

(b) & (c)

BV	Eq.#	Z	x_1	x_2	y_1^+	y_1^-	y_2^+	y_2^-	y_3^+	y_3^-	RHS
Z	0	−1	$-M_2-1$	$-M_2-2$	M_1	0	M_2	0	1	0	$-30M_2-50$
y_1^-	1	0	1	1*	−1	1	0	0	0	0	20
y_2^-	2	0	1	1	0	0	−1	1	0	0	30
y_3^-	3	0	1	2	0	0	0	0	−1	1	50
Z	0	−1	1	0	M_1-M_2-2	M_2+2	M_2	0	1	0	$-10M_2-10$
x_2	1	0	1	1	−1	1	0	0	0	0	20
y_2^-	2	0	0	0	1	−1	−1	1	0	0	10
y_3^-	3	0	−1	0	2	−2	0	0	−1	1	10

So solution is $(x_1, x_2) = (0, 20)$ with $z = 10M_2 + 10$

7.5-3 (d)

(i)

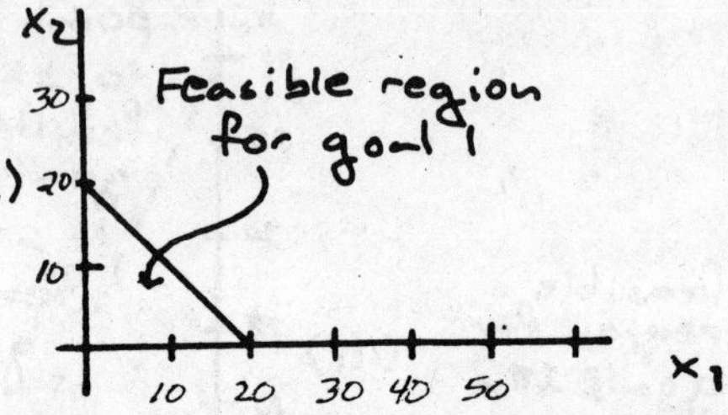

(ii)

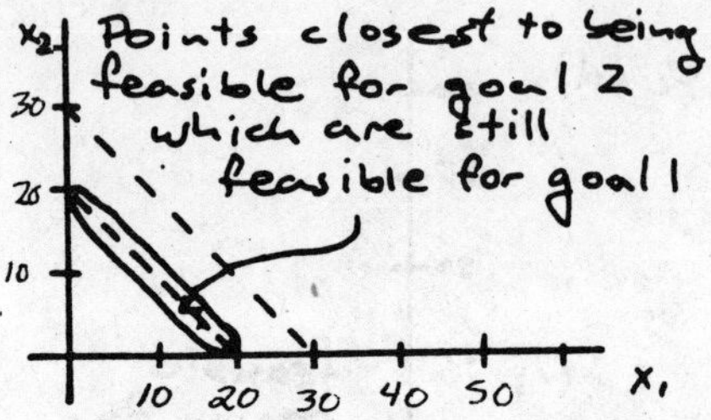

(iii)

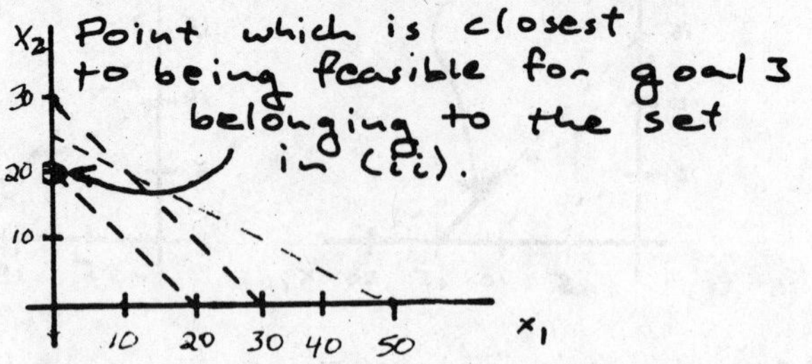

(e) Again, the sequential programing method yields the above regions as well.

7.5-4 (a) Minimize $Z = \frac{1}{100}y_1^- + y_2^- + y_3^+ + y_3^-$

subject to

$$1000x_1 + 1000x_2 + 1000x_3 + x_4 = 15M$$
$$3000x_1 + 5000x_2 + 4000x_3 - (y_1^+ - y_1^-) = 70M$$
$$150x_1 + 75x_2 + 100x_3 - (y_2^+ - y_2^-) = 1.75M$$
$$10x_1 + 15x_2 + 12x_3 - (y_3^+ - y_3^-) = .2M$$
$$x_j \geq 0 \quad j = 1,2,3,4 \qquad y_i^+ \geq 0,\ y_i^- \geq 0 \quad i = 1,2,3$$

(b) Minimize $Z = M_2 y_1^- + M_1 y_2^- + y_3^+ + y_3^-$

subject to

$$1000x_1 + 1000x_2 + 1000x_3 + x_4 = 15M$$
$$3000x_1 + 5000x_2 + 4000x_3 - (y_1^+ - y_1^-) = 70M$$
$$150x_1 + 75x_2 + 100x_3 - (y_2^+ - y_2^-) = 1.75M$$
$$10x_1 + 15x_2 + 12x_3 - (y_3^+ - y_3^-) = .2M$$
$$x_j \geq 0 \quad j = 1,2,3,4 \qquad y_i^+ \geq 0,\ y_i^- \geq 0 \quad i = 1,2,3$$

(cont.)

7.5-4 (c)

BV	Eq#	Z	x_1	x_2	x_3	x_4	y_1^+	y_1^-	y_2^+	y_2^-	y_3^+	y_3^-	RHS
Z	0	-1	$-150M_1$ $-3000M_2$ -10	$-75M_1$ $-5000M_2$ -15	$-100M_1$ $-4000M_2$ -12	0	M_2	0	M_1	0	2	0	$-175M_1$ $-7000M_2$ -20
x_4	1	0	1000	1000	1000	1	0	0	0	0	0	0	1500
y_1^-	2	0	2000	5000	4000	0	-1	1		0	0	0	7000
y_2^-	3	0	150*	75	100	0	0	0	-1	1	0	0	175
y_3^-	4	0	10	15	12	0	0	0	0	0	-1	1	20
Z	0	-1	0	$-3500M_2$ -10	$-2000M_2$ -12	0	M_2	0	$-20M_2$ $-1/15$	M_1+20M_2 $1/15$	2	0	$3500M_2$ $-25/3$
x_4	1	0	0	500*	1000/3	1	0	0	20/3	-20/3	0	0	1000/3
y_1^-	2	0	0	3500	2000	0	-1	1	20	-20	0	0	3500
x_1	3	0	1	1/2	2/3	0	0	0	-1/150	1/150	0	0	7/6
y_3^-	4	0	0	10	12	0	0	0	1/15	-1/15	-1	1	25/3
Z	0	-1	0	0	$1000/3\,M_2+4/3$	$7M_2+1/150$	M_2	0	$80/3\,M_2+1/15$	$M_1-80/3\,M_2-1/15$	2	0	$-\frac{3500}{3}M_2$ $-8/3$
x_2	1	0	0	1	2/3	1/500	0	0	1/75	-1/75	0	0	2/3
y_1^-	2	0	0	0	-1000/3	-7	-1	1	-80/3	80/3	0	0	3500/3
x_1	3	0	1	0	1/3	-1/1000	0	0	0	0	0	0	5/6
y_3^-	4	0	0	0	-4/3	-1/50	0	0	-1/15	1/15	-1	1	5/3

Solution is $(x_1, x_2, x_3) = \left(\frac{50000}{6}, \frac{20000}{3}, 0\right)$, in units of 1000 acres, with $Z = \frac{35{,}000{,}000}{3}M_2 + \frac{50{,}000}{3}$.

(d) With only $M_1 y_2^-$ in the objective function, we get $y_2^- = 0$, $Z = 0$. So fix $y_2^- = 0$ and bring $M_2 y_1^-$ into the objective function; now $y_1^- = 11{,}666{,}666\frac{2}{3}$. Fix y_1^- at this value (remembering to subtract from RHS) and optimize for third priority: now the solution in (c) is reached.

$$x_1 = 8333\tfrac{1}{3},\quad x_2 = 6666\tfrac{2}{3},\quad y_1^- = 11{,}666{,}666\tfrac{2}{3},\quad y_3^- = 16{,}666\tfrac{2}{3}$$

7.5-5 Note that if $z_i = z_i^+ - z_i^-$ where $z_i^+ \ge 0$, $z_i^- \ge 0$ then $|z_i| = z_i^+ + z_i^-$

(a) Minimize $\sum_{i=1}^{n}(z_i^+ + z_i^-)$

subject to $z_i^+ - z_i^- = y_i - (a + bx_i)$ for $i = 1, 2, \ldots, n$

$z_i^+ \ge 0$, $z_i^- \ge 0$ for $i = 1, 2, \ldots, n$

(b) Minimize z

subject to $z_i^+ - z_i^- = y_i - (a + bx_i)$ for $i = 1, 2, \ldots, n$

$0 \le z_i^+ \le z$ for $i = 1, 2, \ldots, n$

$0 \le z_i^- \le z$ for $i = 1, 2, \ldots, n$

Chapter 8
The Transportation and Assignment Problems

8.1-1
a) Transportation Problem Model:

Number of Sources: 3
Number of Destinations: 4

distribution center
Cost Per Unit Distributed

		Destination				
		1	2	3	4	Supply
plant Source	1	500	750	300	450	12
	2	650	800	400	600	17
	3	400	700	500	550	11
Demand		10	10	10	10	

Optimal Solution: The main body of the table shows the optimal number of units (if not zero) to be sent from each source to each destination.

b)

		Destination				
		1	2	3	4	Supply
Source	1			2	10	12
	2		9	8		17
	3	10	1			11
Demand		10	10	10	10	Cost is 20200

8.1-2.(a) Let X1 be the number of pints purchased from Dick today,
X2 be the number of pints purchased from Dick tomorrow,
X3 be the number of pints purchased from Harry today and
X4 be the numbes of pints purchased from Harry tomorrow.

The linear program is:

Min Z = 3 X1 + 2.7 X2 + 2.9 X3 + 2.8 X4

subject to

1 X1 + 1 X2 + 0 X3 + 0 X4 <= 5
0 X1 + 0 X2 + 1 X3 + 1 X4 <= 4
1 X1 + 0 X2 + 1 X3 + 0 X4 = 3
0 X1 + 1 X2 + 0 X3 + 1 X4 >= 4

and

X1 >= 0, X2 >= 0, X3 >= 0, X4 >= 0.

INITIAL TABLEAU

Bas Var	Eq No	Z	X1	X2	X3	X4	X5	X6	X7	X8	X9	Right side
			-1M	-1M	-1M	-1M	1M					-7M
Z	0	-1	3	2.7	2.9	2.8	0	0	0	0	0	0
X6	1	0	1	1	0	0	0	1	0	0	0	5
X7	2	0	0	0	1	1	0	0	1	0	0	4
X8	3	0	1	0	1	0	0	0	0	1	0	3
X9	4	0	0	1	0	1	-1	0	0	0	1	4

8.1-2 (b)

		Destination			Supply
		1 Today	2 Tomorrow	3 Dummy	
Dick	1	3	2.7	0	5
Harry	2	2.9	2.8	0	4
Demand		3	4	2	

c)

		Destination			Supply
		1	2	3	
	1		4	1	5
Source	2	3		1	4
Demand		3	4	2	Cost is 19.5

8.1-3

a)

Cost Per Unit Distributed

		Destination		product		Supply
		1	2	3	dummy 4	
	1	31	45	38	0	400
	2	29	41	35	0	600
Source	3	32	46	40	0	400
plant	4	28	42	1M	0	600
	5	29	43	1M	0	1000
Demand		600	1000	800	600	

b)

		Destination				Supply
		1	2	3	4	
	1			200	200	400
	2			600		600
Source	3				400	400
	4	600				600
	5		1000			1000
Demand		600	1000	800	600	Cost is 88400

8.1-4

a)

		1 Wheat	2 Barley	3 Oats	Supply
England	1	54	40.5	27.6	70
France	2	31.2	36	25	110
Spain	3	52.8	33.6	33.6	80
Demand		125	60	75	

Supplies and demands are in millions of acres.

b)

		Destination			Supply
		1	2	3	
	1			70	70
Source	2	110			110
	3	15	60	5	80
Demand		125	60	75	Cost is 8340

or $8,340,000,000

8.1-5 (a) Customer 5 represents the amount sent to customer 3 in excess of 2 units.
Plant 4 is a "dummy" plant which "sells" units to customers 5 and 4 that they don't really receive.

Cost Per Unit Distributed

		customer Destination 1	2	3	4	5	Supply
plant Source	1	-8	-7	-5	-2	-5	6
	2	-5	-2	-1	-3	-1	8
	3	-6	-4	-3	-5	-3	4
	4	1M	1M	1M	0	0	6
Demand		4	6	2	6	6	

b)

		Destination 1	2	3	4	5	Supply
Source	1		6				6
	2	4			4		8
	3			2	2		4
	4					6	6
Demand		4	6	2	6	6	Cost is -90

8.1-6

(a)

		Distribution Center 1	2	3	4 Dummy	Supply
Plant	1	8	7	4	0	50
	2	6	8	5	0	50
Demand		20	20	20	40	

b)

		Destination 1	2	3	4	Supply
Source	1		20	20	10	50
	2	20			30	50
Demand		20	20	20	40	Cost is 340

$34,000

(c) Let destination $2i-1$ represent the demand of 10 at center i and destination $2i$ the extra demand up to 20 shipped to center i.

Cost Per Unit Distributed

		Destination 1	2	3	4	5	6	7 dummy	Supply
Source	plant 1	8	8	7	7	4	4	0	50
	plant 2	6	6	8	8	5	5	0	50
	dummy 3	1M	0	1M	0	1M	0	1M	30
Demand		10	20	10	20	10	20	40	

d)

		Destination 1	2	3	4	5	6	7	Supply
Source	1			10		10	20	10	50
	2	10	10					30	50
	3		10		20				30
Demand		10	20	10	20	10	20	40	Cost is 310

$31,000

8.1-7 (a) Let Source 1 be initial inventory
2 week 1 regular hours
3 week 1 overtime
4 week 2 regular hours
5 week 2 overtime
6 week 3 regular hours
7 week 3 overtime

	Week 1	2	3	4 Dummy	Supply
Source 1	0	50	100	0	2
2	300	350	400	0	2
3	400	450	500	0	2
4	M	500	550	0	2
5	M	600	650	0	1
6	M	M	400	0	1
7	M	M	500	0	2
Demand	3	3	3	3	

b)

	Destination 1	2	3	4	Supply
Source 1	2				2
2	1	1			2
3		2			2
4				2	2
5				1	1
6			1		1
7			2		2
Demand	3	3	3	3	Cost is $2950

8.1-8 sources: 1 week 1 RT
2 week 1 OT
3 week 2 RT
4 week 2 OT
5 week 3 RT
6 week 3 OT

destinations: 1 product 1, week 1
2 product 2, week 1
3 product 1, week 2
4 product 2, week 2
5 product 1, week 3
6 product 2, week 3
7 dummy

Cost Per Unit Distributed

	Destination 1	2	3	4	5	6	7	Supply
Source 1	15	16	16	18	18	19	0	10
2	18	20	19	22	21	23	0	3
3	1M	1M	17	15	19	16	0	8
4	1M	1M	20	18	22	19	0	2
5	1M	1M	1M	1M	19	17	0	10
6	1M	1M	1M	1M	22	22	0	3
Demand	5	3	3	5	4	4	12	

b)

	Destination 1	2	3	4	5	6	7	Supply
Source 1	5	3	2					10
2							3	3
3			1	5		2		8
4							2	2
5					4	2	4	10
6							3	3
Demand	5	3	3	5	4	4	12	Cost is 389

No overtime is necessary.

8.2-1 a)

	Destination 1	2	3	Supply	Row Difference
Source 1	6	3	5	4	2
Source 2	4	M	7	3	3 ←
Source 3	3	4	3	2	0
Demand	4	2	3		
Column Difference	1	1	2		

Vogel's method would choose x_{21} as the first basic variable.

b)

	Destination 1	2	3	Supply	Row Maximum
1	6 / -6	3 / -M-3	5 / -8	4	6
2	4 / -M-2	M / -M	7 / -M	3	M
3	3 / -7	4 / -M	3 / -8	2	4
Demand	4	2	3		
Column Maximum	6	M	7		

Russell's Method would choose x_{12} as the first basic variable.

c) NW corner rule initial BF solution:

	4			4
	0	2	1	3
			2	2
	4	2	3	

(after the first step, we eliminate the row, as step 3 says)

8.2-2 (a) NW corner rule

	Destination 1	2	3	4	5	Supply
1	2 / B / 4	4 / B / 0	6 / 0	5 / 0	7 / 0	4
2	7 / 0	6 / B / 4	3 / B / 2	M / B / 0	4 / 0	6
3	8 / 0	7 / 0	5 / 0	2 / B / 5	5 / B / 1	6
4	0 / 0	0 / 0	0 / 0	0 / 0	0 / B / 4	4
Demand	4	4	2	5	5	

Cost = 53

(b) Vogel's

	Destination 1	2	3	4	5	Supply
1	2 / B / 4	4 / 0	6 / 0	5 / 0	7 / 0	4
2	7 / 0	6 / 0	3 / B / 2	M / B / 0	4 / B / 4	6
3	8 / B / 0	7 / B / 0	5 / 0	2 / B / 5	5 / B / 1	6
4	0 / 0	0 / B / 4	0 / 0	0 / 0	0 / 0	4
Demand	4	4	2	5	5	

Cost = 45

8.2.2 (c)

	Destination 1	2	3	4	5	Supply	u[i]
1	2 / B / 4	4 / 2	6 / 7	5 / 8	7 / 7	4	-5
2	7 / 1	6 / 0	3 / B / 2	M / 1M- 1	4 / B / 4	6	-1
3	8 / 1	7 / B / 0	5 / 1	2 / B / 5	5 / B / 1	6	0
4	0 / B / 0	0 / B / 4	0 / 3	0 / 5	0 / 2	4	-7
Demand	4	4	2	5	5		
v[j]	7	7	4	2	5		

Cost = 45

Note that the initial BF solutions found by Vogel's and by Russell's methods are optimal.

8.2-3

a) Method used to construct initial basic feasible solution: Northwest Corner Rule

Initial Basic Feasible Solution:

Source	Destination 1	2	3	4	5	6	Supply
1	13 / 3	10 / 2	22	29	18	0	5
2	14	13 / 3	16 / 3	21	1M	0	6
3	3	0	1M / 1	11 / 5	6 / 1	0	7
4	18	9	19	23	11 / 4	0	4
5	30	24	34	36	28 / 1	0 / 2	3
Demand	3	5	4	5	6	2	

Cost = M+279

b) Method used to construct initial basic feasible solution: Vogel's Method

Initial Basic Feasible Solution:

Source	Destination 1	2	3	4	5	6	Supply
1	13	10 / 3	22	29	18 / 2	0	5
2	14 / 1	13 / 1	16 / 4	21	1M	0	6
3	3 / 2	0	1M	11 / 5	6	0	7
4	18	9	19	23	11 / 4	0	4
5	30	24 / 1	34	36	28	0 / 2	3
Demand	3	5	4	5	6	2	

Cost = 286

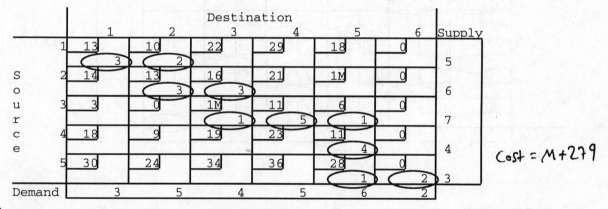

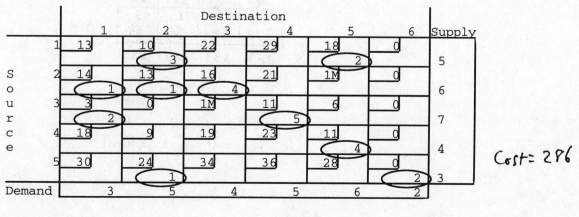

8.2-3 b) Method used to construct initial basic feasible solution: Vogel's Method

Initial Basic Feasible Solution: (arbitrarily breaking tie differently) ↘ !

Destination (cell entries: cost; allocation in parentheses)

Source	1	2	3	4	5	6	Supply
1	13	10 (5)	22	29	18	0	5
2	14	13 (0)	16 (4)	21 (1)	1M (1)	0	6
3	3 (3)	0	1M	11 (4)	6	0	7
4	18	9	19	23	11 (4)	0	4
5	30	24	34	36	28 (1)	0 (2)	3
Demand	3	5	4	5	6	2	

Cost = M+260

c) Method used to construct initial basic feasible solution: Russell's Method

Initial Basic Feasible Solution:

Destination (cell entries: cost; allocation in parentheses)

Source	1	2	3	4	5	6	Supply
1	13 (2)	10 (3)	22	29	18	0	5
2	14	13	16 (4)	21 (2)	1M	0	6
3	3 (1)	0	1M	11	6 (6)	0	7
4	18	9 (2)	19	23 (2)	11	0	4
5	30	24	34	36 (1)	28	0 (2)	3
Demand	3	5	4	5	6	2	

Cost = 301

(8.2-4 is on next page)

8.2-5

(cell entries: cost / value; circled basic variables in parentheses)

				u_i
464 / 15	513 / (20)	654 / 84	867 / (55)	182
352 / (80)	416 / (45)	690 / 217	791 / 21	85
995 / 728	682 / 351	388 / (70)	685 / (30)	0
v_j: 267	331	388	685	

Cost = 152,535.

$c_{ij} - u_i - v_j \geq 0$ for all i and j so the solution is optimal.

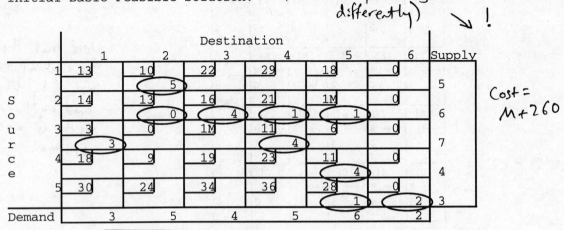

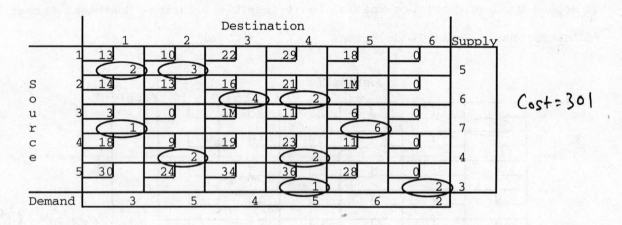

8.2-4

(a) The Integer Solutions Property guarantees that, since supplies and demands are integers, the resulting basic feasible solutions will be integral. Supplies and demands are 1, so the only possible values of variables in a basic feasible solution are 0 or 1. The 1's indicate the assignment of a source to a destination.

(b) There are 7 basic variables in every basic feasible solution and 3 of them are degenerate.

(d)

	Destination 1	2	3	4	Supply $u[i]$	
1	7| ---- 0|	4| ---- 0|	1| ---- B 1|	4| ---- 0|	1|	0
2	4| ---- 0|	6| ---- 0|	7| ---- 0|	2| ---- B 1|	1|	0
3	8| ---- 0|	5| ---- B 1|	4| ---- 0|	6| ---- 0|	1|	0
4	6| ---- B 1|	7| ---- B 0|	6| ---- B 0|	3| ---- B 0|	1|	0
Demand	1	1	1	1		
$v[j]$	0	0	0	0		

The variables are chosen in the order,
x_{13}, x_{24}, x_{44}, x_{32}, x_{41}, x_{43}, x_{42}

(c) and (e)

(0)

	Destination 1	2	3	4	Supply $u[i]$	
1	7| ---- L 1|	4| ---- -5|	1| ---- E -7|	4| ---- -1|	1|	2
2	4| ---- P 0|	6| ---- P 1|	7| ---- 2|	2| ---- 0|	1|	-1
3	8| ---- 5|	5| ---- P 0|	4| ---- P 1|	6| ---- 5|	1|	-2
4	6| ---- 1|	7| ---- 0|	6| ---- B 0|	3| ---- B 1|	1|	0
Demand	1	1	1	1		
$v[j]$	5	7	6	3		

(1)

	Destination 1	2	3	4	Supply $u[i]$	
1	7| ---- 7|	4| ---- 2|	1| ---- B 1|	4| ---- 6|	1|	1
2	4| ---- B 1|	6| ---- B 0|	7| ---- 2|	2| ---- 0|	1|	5
3	8| ---- 5|	5| ---- B 1|	4| ---- B 0|	6| ---- 5|	1|	4
4	6| ---- 1|	7| ---- 0|	6| ---- B 0|	3| ---- B 1|	1|	6
Demand	1	1	1	1		
$v[j]$	-1	1	0	-3		

The optimal assignment is (source, destination):
$(1,3)$, $(2,1)$, $(3,2)$, $(4,4)$

Cost = 13

8.2-6

Destination (each cell: cost / basis marker / value)

	1	2	3	4	5	Supply	u[i]
1	41 / 2	27 / B / 30	28 / B / 30	24 / 1	0 / B / 15	75	0
2	40 / 1	29 / 2	M / 1M-28	23 / B / 15	0 / B / 60	75	0
3	37 / B / 20	30 / 5	27 / 1	21 / B / 25	0 / 2	45	-2
Demand	20	30	30	40	75		
v[j]	39	27	28	23	0		

In the tableau representing the solution from Sect. 8.3 shown above $c_{ij}-u_i-v_j \geq 0$ for all i and j so the solution is optimal.

8.2-7

(0)

Destination

	1	2	3	4	5	Supply	u[i]
1	8 / 1	6 / 3	3 / B / 20	7 / 1	5 / 2	20	2
2	5 / P / 25	M / 1M- 1	8 / 7	4 / P / 5	7 / 6	30	0
3	6 / -1	3 / P / 25	9 / 6	6 / P / 5	8 / 5	30	2
4	0 / E / -4	0 / L / 0	0 / B / 0	0 / -3	0 / B / 20	20	-1
Demand	25	25	20	10	20		
v[j]	5	1	1	4	1		

(1)

Destination

	1	2	3	4	5	Supply	u[i]
1	8 / 5	. 6 / 7	3 / B / 20	7 / 5	5 / 2	20	3
2	5 / P / 25	M / 1M- 1	8 / 3	4 / P / 5	7 / 2	30	5
3	6 / E / -1	3 / B / 25	9 / 2	6 / L / 5	8 / 1	30	7
4	0 / B / 0	0 / 4	0 / B / 0	0 / 1	0 / B / 20	20	0
Demand	25	25	20	10	20		
v[j]	0	-4	0	-1	0		

(2)

Destination

	1	2	3	4	5	Supply	u[i]
1	8 / 5	6 / 6	3 / B / 20	7 / 5	5 / 2	20	3
2	5 / B / 20	M / 1M- 2	8 / 3	4 / B / 10	7 / 2	30	5
3	6 / B / 5	3 / B / 25	9 / 3	6 / 1	8 / 2	30	6
4	0 / B / 0	0 / 3	0 / B / 0	0 / 1	0 / B / 20	20	0
Demand	25	25	20	10	20		
v[j]	0	-3	0	-1	0		

The current solution is optimal:

$x_{13}=20$, $x_{21}=20$, $x_{24}=10$,

$x_{31}=5$, $x_{32}=25$ and $x_{45}=20$

Cost = 305.

The optimality condition is $c_{ij}-u_i-v_j \geq 0$ which has been met.

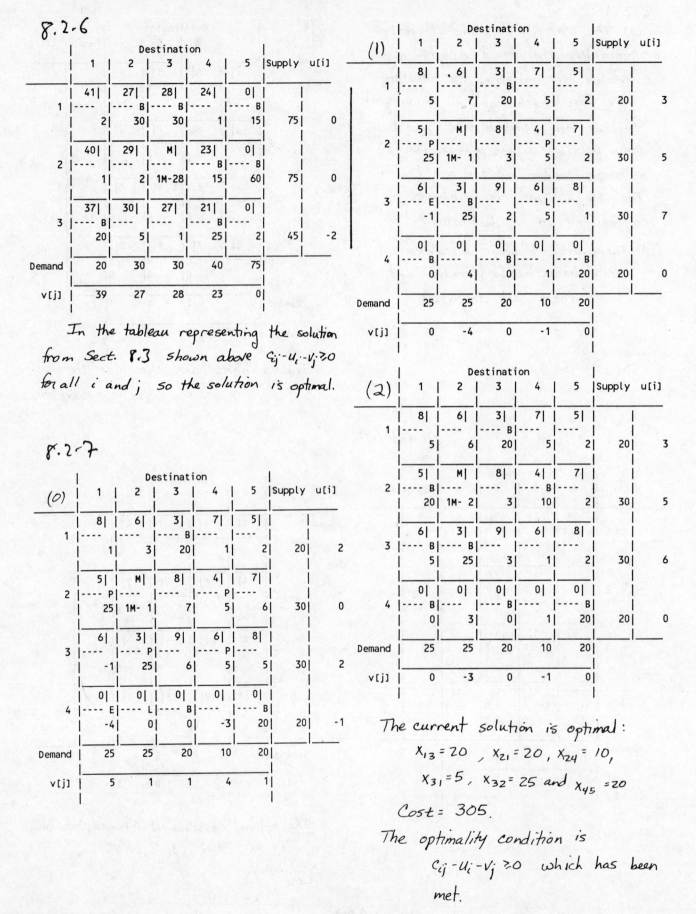

8.2-8

a) Method used to construct initial basic feasible solution: Northwest Corner Rule

Interactive Transportation Simplex Method:

(0)

Source \ Destination	1	2	3	4	Supply	u_i
1	3 / 3	7 / 2	6 / 0	4 / 1	5	0
2	2 / 2	4 / − 1	3 / + 1	2 / 2	2	-3
3	4 / -1	3 / + +	8 / − 1	5 / 2	3	2
Demand	3	3	2	2		
v_j	3	7	6	3	Z = 48	

(1)

Source \ Destination	1	2	3	4	Supply	u_i
1	3 / 3	7 / − 2	6 / 0	4 / + +	5	7
2	2 / 2	4 / 0	3 / 2	2 / -4	2	4
3	4 / 5	3 / + 1	8 / 6	5 / − 2	3	3
Demand	3	3	2	2		
v_j	-4	0	-1	2	Z = 42	

(2)

Source \ Destination	1	2	3	4	Supply	u_i
1	3 / 3	7 / 5	6 / 5	4 / 2	5	0
2	2 / -3	4 / − 0	3 / 2	2 / + +	2	2
3	4 / 0	3 / + 3	8 / 6	5 / − 0	3	1
Demand	3	3	2	2		
v_j	3	2	1	4	Z = 32	

(3)

Source \ Destination	1	2	3	4	Supply	u_i
1	3 / 3	7 / 1	6 / 1	4 / 2	5	2
2	2 / 1	4 / 0	3 / 2	2 / 0	2	0
3	4 / 4	3 / 3	8 / 6	5 / 4	3	-1
Demand	3	3	2	2		
v_j	1	4	3	2	Z = 32	

3 iterations are required to reach optimality.

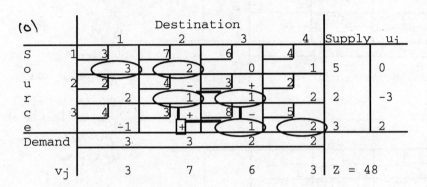

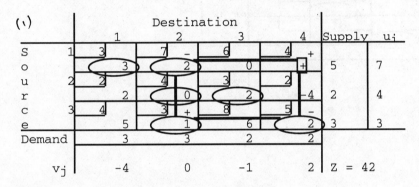

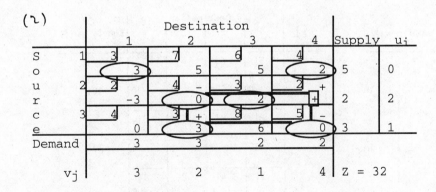

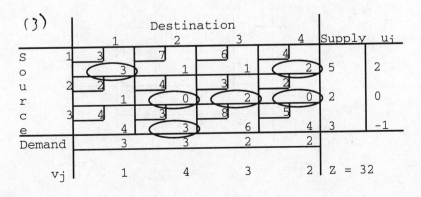

8.2-8 cont.

b) Vogel's

Source	Destination 1	2	3	4	Supply	u_i
1	cost 3, (3)	cost 7, (0)	cost 6, (0)	cost 4, (2)	5	0
2	cost 2, 2	cost 4, 0	cost 3, (2)	cost 2, 1	2	-3
3	cost 4, 5	cost 3, (3)	cost 8, 6	cost 5, 5	3	-4
Demand	3	3	2	2		
v_j	3	7	6	4	Z = 32	

c) Russell's

Source	Destination 1	2	3	4	Supply	u_i
1	cost 3, (3)	cost 7, (0)	cost 6, (0)	cost 4, (2)	5	0
2	cost 2, 2	cost 4, 0	cost 3, (2)	cost 2, 1	2	-3
3	cost 4, 5	cost 3, (3)	cost 8, 6	cost 5, 5	3	-4
Demand	3	3	2	2		
v_j	3	7	6	4	Z = 32	

Both of these initial BF solutions are optimal, so zero iterations of network simplex are required.

8.2-9

(a) and (b)

(0)

	Destination 1	2	3	4	Supply	u[i]
1	5 P 10	6 -1M+ 3	4 -1M+ 3	2 E -1M+ 2	10	1M + 3
2	2 P 10	M L 10	1 -1M+ 3	3 -1M+ 6	20	1M
3	3 1M- 3	4 P 0	2 B 10	1 P 10	20	4
4	2 1M- 5	1 -4	3 0	2 B 10	10	5
Demand	20	10	10	20		
v[j]	-1M + 2	0	-2	-3		

(1)

	Destination 1	2	3	4	Supply	u[i]
1	5 B 0	6 1	4 1	2 B 10	10	1
2	2 B 20	M 1M- 2	1 1	3 4	20	-2
3	3 -1	4 L 10	2 B 10	1 P 0	20	0
4	2 -3	1 E -4	3 0	2 P 10	10	1
Demand	20	10	10	20		
v[j]	4	4	2	1		

cont.

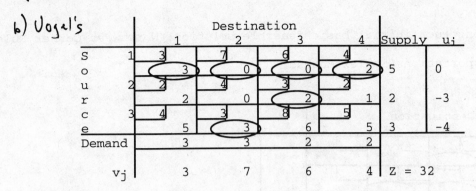

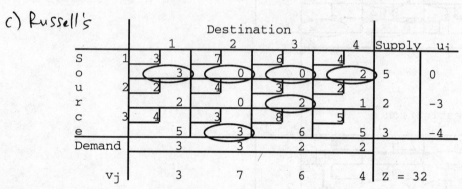

8.2-9 (a) and (b) (cont.)

(2)

```
       |          Destination          |
       |   1   |   2   |   3   |   4   |Supply   u[i]
_______|_______|_______|_______|_______|______________
       |    5| |    6| |    4| |    2| |      |
   1   |---- P|----   |----   |---- P|       |
       |     0|     5|      1|     10|    10|     2
       |______|______|_______|_______|       |
       |    2| |    M| |    1| |    3| |      |
   2   |---- B|----   |----   |----   |       |
       |    20| 1M+ 2|      1|      4|    20|    -1
       |______|______|_______|_______|       |
       |    3| |    4| |    2| |    1| |      |
   3   |----   |----   |---- B|---- B|       |
       |    -1|     4|     10|     10|    20|     1
       |______|______|_______|_______|       |
       |    2| |    1| |    3| |    2| |      |
   4   |---- E|---- B|----   |---- L|       |
       |    -3|    10|      0|      0|    10|     2
       |______|______|_______|_______|_______|______
Demand |    20     10      10      20|
       |_____________________________|
  v[j] |     3     -1       1       0|
       |                             |
```

(3)

```
       |          Destination          |
       |   1   |   2   |   3   |   4   |Supply   u[i]
_______|_______|_______|_______|_______|______________
       |    5| |    6| |    4| |    2| |      |
   1   |---- L|----   |----   |---- P|       |
       |     0|     2|      1|     10|    10|     5
       |______|______|_______|_______|       |
       |    2| |    M| |    1| |    3| |      |
   2   |---- B|----   |----   |----   |       |
       |    20| 1M- 1|      1|      4|    20|     2
       |______|______|_______|_______|       |
       |    3| |    4| |    2| |    1| |      |
   3   |---- E|----   |---- B|---- P|       |
       |    -1|     1|     10|     10|    20|     4
       |______|______|_______|_______|       |
       |    2| |    1| |    3| |    2| |      |
   4   |---- B|---- B|----   |----   |       |
       |     0|    10|      3|      3|    10|     2
       |______|______|_______|_______|_______|______
Demand |    20     10      10      20|
       |_____________________________|
  v[j] |     0     -1      -2      -3|
       |                             |
```

(4)

```
       |          Destination          |
       |   1   |   2   |   3   |   4   |Supply   u[i]
_______|_______|_______|_______|_______|______________
       |    5| |    6| |    4| |    2| |      |
   1   |----   |----   |----   |---- B|       |
       |     1|     3|      1|     10|    10|     1
       |______|______|_______|_______|       |
       |    2| |    M| |    1| |    3| |      |
   2   |---- B|----   |----   |----   |       |
       |    20| 1M- 1|      0|      3|    20|    -1
       |______|______|_______|_______|       |
       |    3| |    4| |    2| |    1| |      |
   3   |---- B|----   |---- B|---- B|       |
       |     0|     2|     10|     10|    20|     0
       |______|______|_______|_______|       |
       |    2| |    1| |    3| |    2| |      |
   4   |---- B|---- B|----   |----   |       |
       |     0|    10|      2|      2|    10|    -1
       |______|______|_______|_______|_______|______
Demand |    20     10      10      20|
       |_____________________________|
  v[j] |     3      2       2       1|
       |                             |
```

The optimal solution is:

$x_{14} = 10$, $x_{21} = 20$, $x_{33} = 10$,

$x_{34} = 10$, $x_{42} = 10$

Cost = 100.

8.2-10

(a)

	1 Electricity	2 Water	3 Space	4 Dummy	Supply
Electricity 1	50	90	80	0	60
Nat. Gas 2	M	60	50	0	40
Solar 3	M	30	40	0	30
Demand	20	10	30	70	

(b) and (c) 8.2-10

(0)

Source	Destination 1	2	3	4	Supply	u[i]
1	50, B, 20	90, P, 10	80, P, 30	0, -30	60	0
2	M, 1M-20	60, 0	50, L, 0	0, P, 40	40	-30
3	M, 1M-20	30, E, -30	40, -10	0, P, 30	30	-30
Demand	20	10	30	70		
v[j]	50	90	80	30		

(1)

Source	Destination 1	2	3	4	Supply	u[i]
1	50, B, 20	90, L, 10	80, B, 30	0, E, -60	60	0
2	M, 1M+10	60, 30	50, 30	0, B, 40	40	-60
3	M, 1M+10	30, P, 0	40, 20	0, P, 30	30	-60
Demand	20	10	30	70		
v[j]	50	90	80	60		

(2)

Source	Destination 1	2	3	4	Supply	u[i]
1	50, B, 20	90, 60	80, P, 30	0, P, 10	60	0
2	M, 1M-50	60, 30	50, -30	0, B, 40	40	0
3	M, 1M-50	30, B, 10	40, E, -40	0, L, 20	30	0
Demand	20	10	30	70		
v[j]	50	30	80	0		

(3)

Source	Destination 1	2	3	4	Supply	u[i]
1	50, B, 20	90, 20	80, L, 10	0, P, 30	60	0
2	M, 1M-50	60, -10	50, E, -30	0, P, 40	40	0
3	M, 1M-10	30, B, 10	40, B, 20	0, 40	30	-40
Demand	20	10	30	70		
v[j]	50	70	80	0		

(4)

Source	Destination 1	2	3	4	Supply	u[i]
1	50, B, 20	90, 50	80, 30	0, B, 40	60	0
2	M, 1M-50	60, 20	50, B, 10	0, B, 30	40	0
3	M, 1M-40	30, B, 10	40, B, 20	0, 10	30	-10
Demand	20	10	30	70		
v[j]	50	40	50	0		

The optimal solution is to meet
- 20 units of electricity demand with electricity
- 10 units of space heating demand with Natural Gas
- 10 units of water heating demand with Solar heating
- 20 units of space heating with solar heating.

Cost = $2600.

8.2-10

The initial BF solution from both Vogel's and Russell's method provides the same optimal solution given in (c).

(f) and (g) Russell's

Source	Destination 1	2	3	4	Supply	u_i
1	50 / (20)	90 / 50	80 / 30	0 / (40)	60	0
2	1M / 1M-50	60 / 20	50 / (10)	0 / (30)	40	0
3	1M / 1M-40	30 / (10)	40 / (20)	0 / 10	30	-10
Demand	20	10	30	70		
v_j	50	40	50	0	Z = 2600	

(d) and (e) Vogel's

(0)

	Destination 1	2	3	4	Supply	u[i]
1	50 B 20	90 50	80 30	0 B 40	60	0
2	M 1M-50	60 20	50 B 10	0 B 30	40	0
3	M 1M-40	30 B 10	40 B 20	0 10	30	-10
Demand	20	10	30	70		
v[j]	50	40	50	0		

8.2-11 Using Vogel's Method.

(0)

	Destination 1	2	3	4	5	Supply	u[i]
1	1.08 B 10	1.09 B 15	1.11 B 0	1.13 0.01	0 0.02	25	-0.02
2	M 1M- 1	1.11 0	1.13 0	1.14 P 15	0 P 20	35	0
3	M 1M- 1	M 1M- 1	1.1 B 25	1.11 B 5	0 0.03	30	-0.03
4	M 1M- 1	M 1M- 1	M 1M- 1	1.13 E -0.01	0 L 10	10	0
Demand	10	15	25	20	30		
v[j]	1.1	1.11	1.13	1.14	0		

(1)

	Destination 1	2	3	4	5	Supply	u[i]
1	1.08 B 10	1.09 B 15	1.11 B 0	1.13 0.01	0 0.02	25	0
2	M 1M- 1	1.11 0	1.13 0	1.14 B 5	0 B 30	35	0.02
3	M 1M- 1	M 1M- 1	1.1 B 25	1.11 B 5	0 0.03	30	-0.01
4	M 1M- 1	M 1M- 1	M 1M- 1	1.13 B 10	0 0.01	10	0.01
Demand	10	15	25	20	30		
v[j]	1.08	1.09	1.11	1.12	-0.02		

The optimal solution is to produce

10 engines in month 1 for installation in month 1

15 engines in month 1 for installation in month 2

5 engines in month 2 for installation in month 4

25 engines in month 3 for installation in month 3

5 engines in month 3 for installation in month 4

10 engines in month 4 for installation in month 4

Cost = 77.3

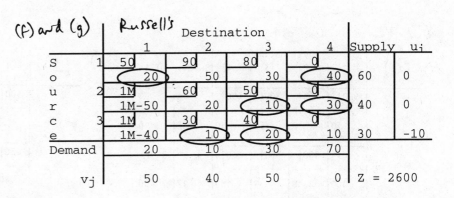

8.2-12

a) (0)

Source	Destination 1	2	3	4	Supply	u[i]
1	500 / P / 10	750 / P / 2	300 / -50	450 / 50	12	0
2	650 / 100	800 / P / 8	400 / P / 9	600 / 150	17	50
3	400 / E / -250	700 / -200	500 / L / 1	550 / B / 10	11	150
Demand	10	10	10	10		
v[j]	500	750	350	400		

b) (1)

Source	Destination 1	2	3	4	Supply	u[i]
1	500 / L / 9	750 / B / 3	300 / -50	450 / E / -200	12	0
2	650 / 100	800 / B / 7	400 / B / 10	600 / -100	17	50
3	400 / P / 1	700 / 50	500 / 250	550 / P / 10	11	-100
Demand	10	10	10	10		
v[j]	500	750	350	650		

(2)

Source	Destination 1	2	3	4	Supply	u[i]
1	500 / 200	750 / L / 3	300 / E / -50	450 / B / 9	12	0
2	650 / 300	800 / P / 7	400 / P / 10	600 / 100	17	50
3	400 / B / 10	700 / -150	500 / 50	550 / B / 1	11	100
Demand	10	10	10	10		
v[j]	300	750	350	450		

(3)

Source	Destination 1	2	3	4	Supply	u[i]
1	500 / 200	750 / 50	300 / P / 3	450 / P / 9	12	0
2	650 / 250	800 / P / 10	400 / P / 7	600 / 50	17	100
3	400 / B / 10	700 / E / -100	500 / 100	550 / L / 1	11	100
Demand	10	10	10	10		
v[j]	300	700	300	450		

(4)

Source	Destination 1	2	3	4	Supply	u[i]
1	500 / 100	750 / 50	300 / B / 2	450 / B / 10	12	0
2	650 / 150	800 / B / 9	400 / B / 8	600 / 50	17	100
3	400 / B / 10	700 / B / 1	500 / 200	550 / 100	11	0
Demand	10	10	10	10		
v[j]	400	700	300	450		

The optimal solution is to send

2 shipments from plant 1 to center 3
10 shipments from plant 1 to center 4
9 shipments from plant 2 to center 2
8 shipments from plant 2 to center 3
10 shipments from plant 3 to center 1
1 shipment from plant 3 to center 2

Total cost: \$ 20,200.

8.2-13

(0)

Source	Destination 1	Destination 2	Destination 3	Supply	u[i]
1	3 / P 3	2.7 / P 2	0 / 0.1	5	0
2	2.9 / E -0.2	2.8 / L 2	0 / B 2	4	0.1
Demand	3	4	2		
v[j]	3	2.7	-0.1		

(1)

Source	Destination 1	Destination 2	Destination 3	Supply	u[i]
1	3 / L 1	2.7 / B 4	0 / E -0.1	5	0
2	2.9 / P 2	2.8 / 0.2	0 / P 2	4	-0.1
Demand	3	4	2		
v[j]	3	2.7	0.1		

Source	Destination 1	Destination 2	Destination 3	Supply	u[i]
1	3 / 0.1	2.7 / B 4	0 / B 1	5	0
2	2.9 / B 3	2.8 / 0.1	0 / B 1	4	0
Demand	3	4	2		
v[j]	2.9	2.7	0		

The optimal solution is:
purchase 4 pints from Dick tomorrow
and 3 pints from Harry today.

Cost: \$19.50

8.2-14

Source	Destination 1	Destination 2	Destination 3	Destination 4	Supply	u_i
1	31 / 1	45 / 1	38 / 200	0 / 200	400	0
2	29 / 2	41 / 0	35 / 600	0 / 3	600	-3
3	32 / 2	46 / 2	40 / 2	0 / 400	400	0
4	28 / 600	42 / 0	1M / 1M-36	0 / 2	600	-2
5	29 / 0	43 / 1000	1M / 1M-37	0 / 1	1000	-1
Demand	600	1000	800	600		
v_j	30	44	38	0	Z = 88400	

The initial solution is optimal.
The corporation should produce
600 units of product 1 at plant 4
1000 units of product 2 at plant 5
200 units of product 3 at plant 1
600 units of product 3 at plant 2

Cost = \$ 88,400

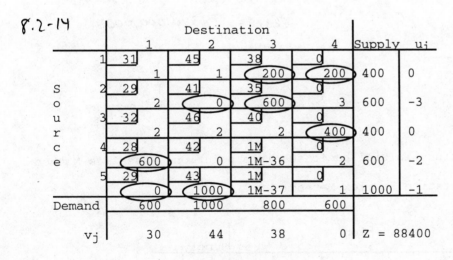

8.2-15

(0)

	Destination 1	2	3	Supply	u[i]
1	54 / P / 70	40.5 / / -18.3	27.6 / E / -31.2	70	22.8
2	31.2 / P / 55	36 / L / 55	25 / / -11	110	0
3	52.8 / / 24	33.6 / P / 5	33.6 / P / 75	80	-2.4
Demand	125	60	75		
v[j]	31.2	36	36		

(1)

	Destination 1	2	3	Supply	u[i]
1	54 / L / 15	40.5 / / 12.9	27.6 / P / 55	70	0
2	31.2 / B / 110	36 / / 31.2	25 / / 20.2	110	-22.8
3	52.8 / E / -7.2	33.6 / B / 60	33.6 / P / 20	80	6
Demand	125	60	75		
v[j]	54	27.6	27.6		

(2)

	Destination 1	2	3	Supply	u[i]
1	54 / / 7.2	40.5 / / 12.9	27.6 / B / 70	70	-6
2	31.2 / B / 110	36 / / 24	25 / / 13	110	-21.6
3	52.8 / B / 15	33.6 / B / 60	33.6 / B / 5	80	0
Demand	125	60	75		
v[j]	52.8	33.6	33.6		

The optimal allocation of land is
70 million acres in England for Oats
110 million acres in France for Wheat
15 million acres in Spain for Wheat
60 million acres in Spain for Barley
5 million acres in Spain for Oats.

Cost = $8,340,000,000.

8.2-16 Method used to construct initial basic feasible solution: Russell's Method

Interactive Transportation Simplex Method:

(0)

Source	Destination 1	2	3	4	5	Supply	u_i
1	-8 / (4) −	-7 / (2) +	-5 / 1	-2 / 6	-5 / 3	6	-5
2	-5 / [+]	-2 / (0) −	-1 / (2)	-3 / (6)	-1 / 2	8	0
3	-6 / -1	-4 / (4)	-3 / 0	-5 / 0	-3 / 2	4	-2
4	1M / 1M	1M / 1M- 1	1M / 1M- 2	0 / (0)	0 / (6)	6	3
Demand	4	6	2	6	6		
v_j	-3	-2	-1	-3	-3	Z = -82	

(cont.)

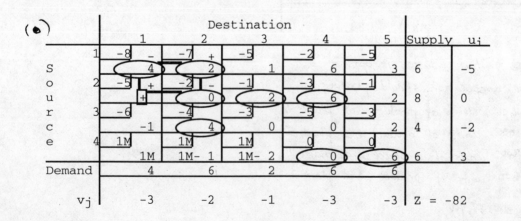

8.2-16 cont.

(1)

Source	1	2	3	4	5	Supply	u_i
1	-8 / (4) −	-7 / (2) +	-5 / -1	-2 / 4	-5 / 1	6	-3
2	-5 / (0) +	-2 / 2	-1 / (2)	-3 / (6) −	-1 / 2	8	0
3	-6 / -1	-4 / (4) −	-3 / -2	-5 / [+]	-3 / 0	4	0
4	1M / 1M+ 2	1M / 1M+ 1	1M / 1M- 2	0 / (0)	0 / (6)	6	3
Demand	4	6	2	6	6		
v_j	-5	-4	-1	-3	-3	Z = -82	

(2)

Source	1	2	3	4	5	Supply	u_i
1	-8 / (0) −	-7 / (6)	-5 / [+] +	-2 / 4	-5 / 1	6	-3
2	-5 / (4) +	-2 / 2	-1 / (2) −	-3 / (2)	-1 / 2	8	0
3	-6 / 1	-4 / 2	-3 / 0	-5 / (4)	-3 / 2	4	-2
4	1M / 1M+ 2	1M / 1M+ 1	1M / 1M- 2	0 / (0)	0 / (6)	6	3
Demand	4	6	2	6	6		
v_j	-5	-4	-1	-3	-3	Z = -90	

(3)

Source	1	2	3	4	5	Supply	u_i
1	-8 / 1	-7 / (6)	-5 / (0)	-2 / 5	-5 / 2	6	-4
2	-5 / (4)	-2 / 1	-1 / (2)	-3 / (2)	-1 / 2	8	0
3	-6 / 1	-4 / 1	-3 / 0	-5 / (4)	-3 / 2	4	-2
4	1M / 1M+ 2	1M / 1M	1M / 1M- 2	0 / (0)	0 / (6)	6	3
Demand	4	6	2	6	6		
v_j	-5	-3	-1	-3	-3	Z = -90	

optimal solution: sell 6 units from plant 1 to cust. 2; 4 from 2 to 1; 2 from 2 to 3; 2 from 2 to 4; 4 from 3 to 4.

→ profit = 90

8.2-17 (a) and (c) [for (b) see 8.1-6(b)]

Northwest Corner Rule

(0)

Source	1	2	3	4	Supply	u_i
1	8 / (20) −	7 / (20)	4 / (10) +	0 / 1	50	0
2	6 / [+] +	8 / 0	5 / (10) −	0 / (40)	50	1
Demand	20	20	20	40		
v_j	8	7	4	-1	Z = 390	

initial BF solution, 22 seconds

→ 15% above optimal (cont.)

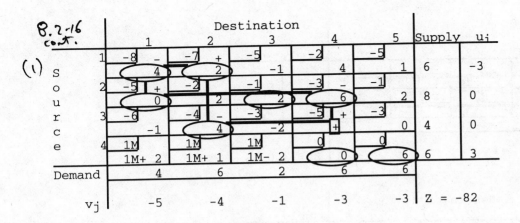

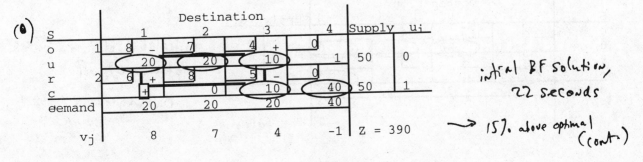

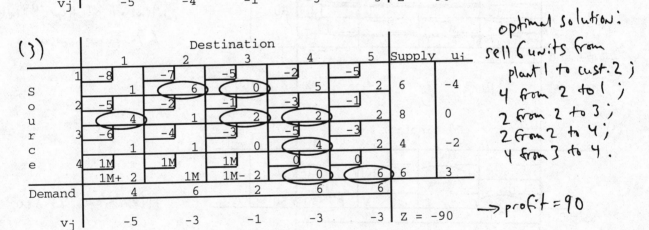

(NW corner) 8.2-17

(1)

Destination

Source	1	2	3	4	Supply	u_i
1 (cost)	8 −	7	4	0 +		
1	(10)	(20)	(20)	[+]	50	0
2 (cost)	6 +	8	5	0 −		
2	(10)	3	3	(40)	50	−2
Demand	20	20	20	40		
v_j	8	7	4	2	Z = 360	

(2)

Destination

Source	1	2	3	4	Supply	u_i
1 (cost)	8	7	4	0		
1	2	(20)	(20)	(10)	50	0
2 (cost)	6	8	5	0		
2	(20)	1	1	(30)	50	0
Demand	20	20	20	40		
v_j	6	7	4	0	Z = 340	

2 iterations, 48 sec.

Vogel's Method

(0)

Destination

Source	1	2	3	4	Supply	u_i
1 (cost)	8 −	7	4	0 +		
1	(10)	(20)	(20)	[+]	50	0
2 (cost)	6 +	8	5	0 −		
2	(10)	3	3	(40)	50	−2
Demand	20	20	20	40		
v_j	8	7	4	2	Z = 360	

initial BF solution 44 sec.
6% above optimal

(1)

Destination

Source	1	2	3	4	Supply	u_i
1 (cost)	8	7	4	0		
1	2	(20)	(20)	(10)	50	0
2 (cost)	6	8	5	0		
2	(20)	1	1	(30)	50	0
Demand	20	20	20	40		
v_j	6	7	4	0	Z = 340	

1 iteration, 28 sec.

Russell's Method

(0)

Destination

Source	1	2	3	4	Supply	u_i
1 (cost)	8	7	4	0		
1	2	(20)	(20)	(10)	50	0
2 (cost)	6	8	5	0		
2	(20)	1	1	(30)	50	0
Demand	20	20	20	40		
v_j	6	7	4	0	Z = 340	

initial BF solution, 25 sec.
optimal, 0% off
0 iterations

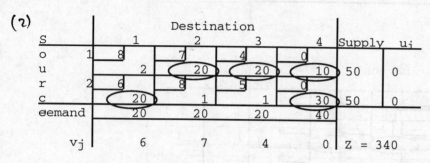

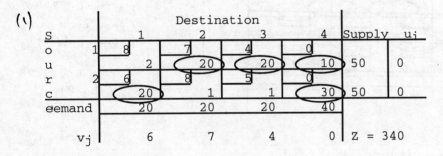

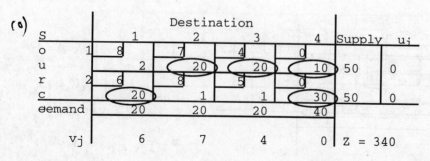

8.2-18

a) NW corner

Source		Dest. 1	2	3	4	5	6	7	Supply	u_i
1	cost	8	8 −	7	7 +	4	4	0		
		10	20	10	10	0	0	1	50	0
2	cost	6	6	8	8 −	5	5	0 +		
		-3	-3	0	10	10	20	10	50	1
3	cost	1M	0 +	1M	0	1M	0	1M −		
		-9	+	-8	-1M- 8	-5	-1M- 5	30	30	1M +1
Demand		10	20	10	20	10	20	40		
v_j		8	8	7	7	4	4	-1	Z = 30M +610	

a) 40 sec., b) M% (lots), c) 7 iterations, 4 minutes

Vogel's

Source		Dest. 1	2	3	4	5	6	7	Supply	u_i
1	cost	8 −	8	7	7	4	4	0 +		
		0	10	10	-1	10	20	+	50	0
2	cost	6 +	6	8	8	5	5	0 −		
		10	0	3	2	3	3	40	50	-2
3	cost	1M	0	1M	0	1M	0	1M		
		1M	10	1M+ 1	20	1M+ 4	4	1M+ 6	30	-8
Demand		10	20	10	20	10	20	40		
v_j		8	8	7	8	4	4	2	Z = 330	

a) 55 sec., b) 6%, c) 2 iterations, 1 minute

Russell's

Source		Dest. 1	2	3	4	5	6	7	Supply	u_i
1	cost	8	8	7	7	4	4	0		
		3	4	0	0	10	0	40	50	-1
2	cost	6	6	8	8 −	5	5 +	0		
		10	1	10	20	0	10	-1	50	0
3	cost	1M	0	1M	0 +	1M	0 −	1M		
		1M- 1	20	1M- 3	+	1M	10	1M+ 4	30	-5
Demand		10	20	10	20	10	20	40		
v_j		6	5	8	8	5	5	1	Z = 390	

a) 1:03, b) 26%, c) 5 iterations, 2 minutes

optimal solution:

Source		Dest. 1	2	3	4	5	6	7	Supply	u_i
1	cost	8	8	7	7	4	4	0		
		2	2	10	1	10	20	10	50	0
2	cost	6	6	8	8	5	5	0		
		10	10	1	2	1	1	30	50	0
3	cost	1M	0	1M	0	1M	0	1M		
		1M	10	1M- 1	20	1M+ 2	2	1M+ 6	30	-6
Demand		10	20	10	20	10	20	40		
v_j		6	6	7	6	4	4	0	Z = 310 ($31,000)	

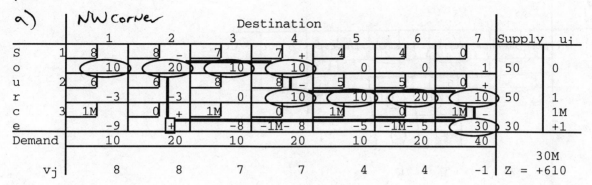

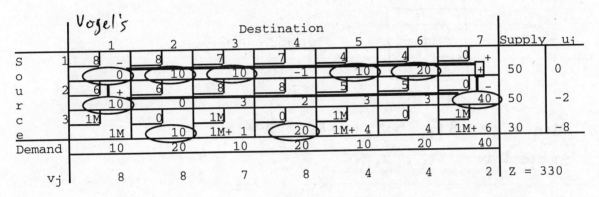

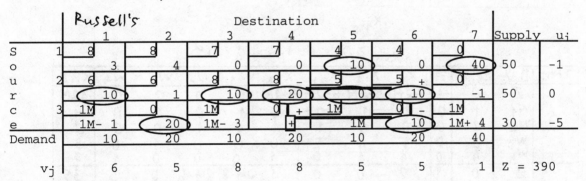

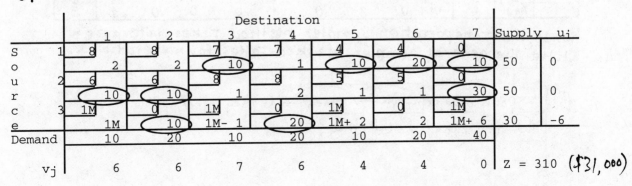

8.2-19

(a) Initial Solution using the Northwest Corner Rule is:

			u_i
	8: (3)	5: (1)	0
	6: -1	4: (2)	-1
v_j	8	5	

Final Tableau:

			u_i
	8: (1)	5: (3)	0
	6: (2)	4: 1	-2
v_j	8	5	

Cost = 35

(b) Minimize $8x_{11} + 5x_{12} + 6x_{21} + 4x_{22}$

subject to

$$x_{11} + x_{12} = 4$$
$$x_{21} + x_{22} = 2$$
$$x_{11} + x_{21} = 3$$
$$x_{12} + x_{22} = 3$$
$$x_{ij} \geq 0 \quad i = 1,2, \; j = 1,2$$

Iter.	B.V.	Eq. #	Z	x_{11}	x_{12}	x_{21}	x_{22}	w_1	w_2	w_3	w_4	RHS
0	Z	0	-1	8-2M	5-2M	6-2M	4-2M	0	0	0	0	-12M
	w_1	1	0	1	1	0	0	1	0	0	0	4
	w_2	2	0	0	0	1	1	0	1	0	0	2
	w_3	3	0	1	0	1	0	0	0	1	0	3
	w_4	4	0	0	1	0	1	0	0	0	1	3
4	Z	0	-1	0	0	0	1	2M-8	2M-6	0	3	-35
	x_{11}	1	0	1	0	0	-1	1	0	0	-1	1
	x_{21}	2	0	0	0	1	1	0	1	0	0	2
	w_3	3	0	0	0	0	0	-1	-1	1	1	0
	x_{12}	4	0	0	1	0	1	0	0	0	1	3

Hence, the transportation simplex method takes 1 iteration while the general simplex method takes four iterations.

Fill in your own computation times — do they agree with the 4:1 ratio? Should they?

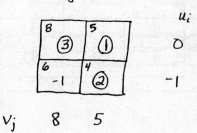

8.2-20 Let $z_1 = x_1 - 10$, $z_2 = x_1 + x_2 - 25$, $z_3 = x_1 + x_2 + x_3 - 50$ and $z_4 = x_1 + x_2 + x_3 + x_4 - 70$

Then Minimize $1.080x_1 + 1.110x_2 + 1.100x_3 + 1.130x_4 + .015(z_1 + z_2 + z_3 + z_4)$

subject to

$$\begin{aligned} x_1 \qquad\qquad\qquad\qquad - z_1 &= 10 \\ x_1 + x_2 \qquad\qquad\qquad - z_2 &= 25 \\ x_1 + x_2 + x_3 \qquad\qquad - z_3 &= 50 \\ x_1 + x_2 + x_3 + x_4 \qquad - z_4 &= 70 \end{aligned}$$

$$0 \le x_1 \le 25$$
$$0 \le x_2 \le 35$$
$$0 \le x_3 \le 30$$
$$0 \le x_4 \le 10$$
$$z_i \ge 0 \quad i = 1,2,3,4.$$

Initial Simplex Tableau

B.V.	Eq.#	Z	x_1	x_2	x_3	x_4	z_1	z_2	z_3	z_4	w_1	w_2	w_3	w_4	Y_1	Y_2	Y_3	Y_4	RHS
Z	0	-1	-4M+1.08	-3M+1.11	-2M+1.1	-M+1.13	M+.015	M+.015	M+.015	M+.015	0	0	0	0	0	0	0	0	-155M
w_1	1		1				-1				1								10
w_2	2		1	1				-1				1							25
w_3	3		1	1	1				-1				1						50
w_4	4		1	1	1	1				-1				1					70
Y_1	5		1												1				25
Y_2	6			1												1			35
Y_3	7				1												1		30
Y_4	8					1												1	10

Simplex tableau: 16 variables and 8 constraints.
Transportation tableau: 20 variables and 9 constraints
But even though the transportation tableau is "larger," it is less work to use than the simplex tableau.

8.2-21 If we multiply the demand constraints by -1, each constraint column will have a +1 entry and a -1 entry with remaining entries 0. If we then sum all constraints, we get

$$0x = \Sigma\text{supplies} - \Sigma\text{demands} = 0 \quad \text{since } \Sigma\text{supplies} = \Sigma\text{demands}$$

Therefore, we have a redundant constraint.

8.2-22 In the initialization step, after selecting the next basic variable, the allocation made is equal to either the (remaining) supply or demand for that row or column. Since these quantities are known to be integer, the allocation will be integer.

Given a current BF solution that is integer, step 3 of an iteration adds and subtracts, around the chain-reaction cycle, the current value of the leaving basic variable. Since we know this is an integer, and all the other basic variables in the cycle began with integer values, the new BF solution must be all integer.

During the initialization step, we can select the next basic variable for allocation arbitrarily from among the rows and columns not already eliminated. Thus by altering our selections we can construct any BF solution as our initial one. And because we've shown that the initialization step gives integer solutions, this means all BF solutions must be integer.

8.2-23(a) Let x_{ij} be the number of tons hauled from pit i (North, South) to site j (1,2,3).

The linear program is:

Minimize $13x_{11} + 16x_{12} + 15x_{13} + 18x_{21} + 15x_{22} + 16x_{23}$

subject to:

$$\begin{aligned} x_{11} + x_{12} + x_{13} &\le 18 \\ x_{21} + x_{22} + x_{23} &\le 14 \\ x_{11} + x_{21} &= 10 \\ x_{12} + x_{22} &= 5 \\ x_{13} + x_{23} &= 10 \end{aligned}$$

$x_{ij} \ge 0$ for $i = 1, 2$ $j = 1, 2, 3$.

Initial Tableau:

Bas Var	Eq No	Z	X1,1	X1,2	X1,3	X2,1	X2,2	X2,3	X7	X8	X9	X10	X11	Right side
Z	0	1	-M+13	-M+16	-M+15	-M+18	-M+15	-M+16	0	0	0	0	0	-25M
X7	1	0	1	1	1	0	0	0	1	0	0	0	0	18
X8	2	0	0	0	0	1	1	1	0	1	0	0	0	14
X9	3	0	1	0	0	1	0	0	0	0	1	0	0	10
X10	4	0	0	1	0	0	1	0	0	0	0	1	0	5
X11	5	0	0	0	1	0	0	1	0	0	0	0	1	10

(b)

	Destination 1	2	3	4 Dummy	Supply
North 1	13	16	15	0	18
South 2	18	15	16	0	14
Demand	10	5	10	7	

This table is much smaller than the simplex tableau necessary to store the same information

(c)

	Destination 1	2	3	4	Supply	u[i]
1	13 ---- B 10	16 ---- B 5	15 ---- -1	0 ---- B 3	18	0
2	18 ---- 5	15 ---- -1	16 ---- B 10	0 ---- B 4	14	0
Demand	10	5	10	7		
v[j]	13	16	16	0		

The solution is not optimal since

$c_{22} - u_2 - v_2 = -1$

and $c_{13} - u_1 - v_3 = -1$.

(d)

(0)	Destination 1	2	3	4	Supply	u[i]
1	13 ---- B 10	16 ---- L 5	15 ---- P 3	0 ---- 1	18	0
2	18 ---- 4	15 ---- E -2	16 ---- P 7	0 ---- B 7	14	1
Demand	10	5	10	7		
v[j]	13	16	15	-1		

(cont.)

d) (1)

	Destination 1	2	3	4	Supply	u[i]
1	13 B 10	16 2	15 B 8	0 1	18	-1
2	18 4	15 B 5	16 B 2	0 B 7	14	0
Demand	10	5	10	7		
v[j]	14	15	16	0		

The optimal solution is to haul

10 tons from the north pit to site 1

5 tons from the south pit to site 2

8 tons from the north pit to site 3

2 tons from the south pit to site 3

Cost = \$357.

(e) From the reduced costs $(c_{ij} - u_i - v_j)$ in the final tableau we see

$$\Delta c_{12} \geq -2 \Rightarrow c_{12} \geq 14$$

$$\Delta c_{21} \geq -4 \Rightarrow c_{21} \geq 14$$

If the contractor can negotiate a hauling cost per ton of 4 or less from the North pit to site 2, or of 2 or less from the South pit to site 1, a new solution, using these options, would give a cost at least as small as \$357, currently optimal.

8.2-24

a) x_{11} is currently nonbasic, so its new reduced cost becomes $5 - u_1 - v_1 = 5 - 0 - 6 = -1 < 0$, so the BF solution in the tableau is no longer optimal. The next network simplex iteration will have x_{11} as the entering variable.

b) x_{13} is basic, so we must recalculate u_i and v_j; leaving $u_1 = 0$ this is easy, $v_3 = 3$ now is the only change. This affects reduced costs:

$$c_{23} - u_2 - v_3 = 6 > 0$$

$$c_{33} - u_3 - v_3 = 0 \leftarrow \text{Now there is an alternate optimal solution involving } x_{33}.$$

$$c_{43} - u_4 - v_3 = 4 > 0$$

The current BF solution is still optimal but not uniquely so.

8-2-25 (a) $\Delta c_{34} = -3 \Rightarrow \Delta(c_{34}-u_3-v_4)^* = -3$

$(c_{34}-u_3-v_4)^* = -2$

New Tableau

Iteration 3	Destination 1	2	3	4	5	Supply	u_i
Source 1	16; +4	16; +4	13; (50)	22; +7	17; +2	50	−7
2	14; +2	14; +2	13; (20)	19; +4	15; (40)	60	−7
3	19; (30)	19; (20)	20; (0)	20; −2	M; M − 22	50	0
4(D)	M; M + 3	0; +3	M; M + 2	0; (30)	0; (20)	50	−22
Demand	30	20	70	30	60	Z = 2460	
v_j	19	19	20	22	22		

The current basic solution is feasible, but not optimal.

(b) $\Delta c_{23} = 3 \Rightarrow \Delta(c_{23}-u_2-v_3) = 3$

we can revise the tableau by changing u_2 from -7 to $-7+3=-4$

This causes v_5 to change to $22-3=19$

u_4 to change to $-22+3=-19$

v_4 to change to $22-3=19$

$\Delta(\text{Reduced cost } x_{41}) = -\Delta u_4 = -3$

$\Delta(\text{Reduced cost } x_{42}) = -\Delta u_4 = -3$

$\Delta(\text{Reduced cost } x_{43}) = -\Delta u_4 = -3$

$\Delta(\text{Reduced cost } x_{34}) = -\Delta v_4 = 3$

$\Delta(\text{Reduced cost } x_{35}) = -\Delta v_5 = 3$

$\Delta(\text{Reduced cost } x_{14}) = -\Delta v_4 = 3$

$\Delta(\text{Reduced cost } x_{15}) = -\Delta v_5 = 3$

The New Tableau is:

Iteration 3	Destination 1	2	3	4	5	Supply	u_i
Source 1	16; +4	16; +4	13; (50)	22; 10	17; 5	50	−7
2	14; +2	14; +2	16; (20)	19; +4	15; (40)	60	−4
3	19; (30)	19; (20)	20; (0)	23; 4	M; M−19	50	0
4(D)	M; M	0; 0	M; M−1	0; (30)	0; (20)	50	−19
Demand	30	20	70	30	60	Z = 2460	
v_j	19	19	20	19	19		

The basic solution remains feasible and optimal.

(c) $\Delta S_2 = -10$, $\Delta d_5 = 10$ $\Rightarrow \Delta x_{25} = 10$

New Tableau:

Iteration 3	Destination 1	2	3	4	5	Supply	u_i
Source 1	16; +4	16; +4	13; (50)	22; +7	17; +2	50	−7
2	14; +2	14; +2	13; (20)	19; +4	15; (30)	50	−7
3	19; (30)	19; (20)	20; (0)	23; +1	M; M − 22	50	0
4(D)	M; M + 3	0; +3	M; M + 2	0; (30)	0; (20)	50	−22
Demand	30	20	70	30	50	Z = 2460	
v_j	19	19	20	22	22		

The basic solution remains feasible and optimal

(d) $\Delta S_2 = 20$, $\Delta d_2 = 20$ $\Rightarrow$ $\Delta x_{23} = 20$, $\Delta x_{33} = -20$, $\Delta x_{32} = 20$

New Tableau:

Iteration 3	Destination 1	2	3	4	5	Supply	u_i
Source 1	16; +4	16; +4	13; (50)	22; +7	17; +2	50	−7
2	14; +2	14; +2	13; (40)	19; +4	15; (40)	80	−7
3	19; (30)	19; (40)	20; (−20)	23; +1	M; M − 22	50	0
4(D)	M; M + 3	0; +3	M; M + 2	0; (30)	0; (20)	50	−22
Demand	30	40	70	30	60	Z = 2460	
v_j	19	19	20	22	22		

This solution satisfies the optimality criterion, but is infeasible.

8.3-1 (a) Ships are assignees and Ports are assignments.

b)

Cost Table

		Task			
		1	2	3	4
	1	5	4	6	7
	2	6	6	7	5
Assignee	3	7	5	7	6
	4	5	4	6	6

Optimal Solution: The X's in the table indicate an optimal assignment of assignees to tasks.

		Task			
		1	2	3	4
	1	X			
	2				X
Assignee	3		X		
	4			X	

Cost is 21

c)

	Destination 1	2	3	4	Supply
1	5	4	6	7	1
2	6	6	7	5	1
3	7	5	7	6	1
4	5	4	6	6	1
Demand	1	1	1	1	

(d) and (e)

(0)

	Destination 1	2	3	4	Supply	u[i]
1	5 / P / 1	4 / P / 0	6 / 1	7 / 3	1	0
2	6 / -1	6 / P / 1	7 / P / 0	5 / -1	1	2
3	7 / 0	5 / -1	7 / L / 1	6 / P / 0	1	2
4	5 / E / -2	4 / -2	6 / -1	6 / P / 1	1	2
Demand	1	1	1	1		
v[j]	5	4	5	4		

(1)

	Destination 1	2	3	4	Supply	u[i]
1	5 / P / 0	4 / P / 1	6 / 1	7 / 1	1	0
2	6 / -1	6 / L / 0	7 / B / 1	5 / E / -3	1	2
3	7 / 2	5 / 1	7 / 2	6 / B / 1	1	0
4	5 / P / 1	4 / 0	6 / 1	6 / P / 0	1	0
Demand	1	1	1	1		
v[j]	5	4	5	6		

(cont.)

8.3-1(e) cont.

(2)

	Dest. 1	Dest. 2	Dest. 3	Dest. 4	Supply	u[i]
1	5 B / 0	4 B / 1	6 / -2	7 / 1	1	6
2	6 / 2	6 / 3	7 P / 1	5 P / 0	1	5
3	7 / 2	5 / 1	7 / -1	6 B / 1	1	6
4	5 B / 1	4 / 0	6 E / -2	6 L / 0	1	6
Demand	1	1	1	1		
v[j]	-1	-2	2	0		

(3)

	Dest. 1	Dest. 2	Dest. 3	Dest. 4	Supply	u[i]
1	5 P / 0	4 P / 1	6 / 0	7 / 3	1	0
2	6 / 0	6 / 1	7 L / 1	5 P / 0	1	1
3	7 / 0	5 E / -1	7 / -1	6 P / 1	1	2
4	5 P / 1	4 / 0	6 P / 0	6 / 2	1	0
Demand	1	1	1	1		
v[j]	5	4	6	4		

(4)

	Dest. 1	Dest. 2	Dest. 3	Dest. 4	Supply	u[i]
1	5 B / 1	4 B / 0	6 / 0	7 / 2	1	0
2	6 / 1	6 / 2	7 / 1	5 B / 1	1	0
3	7 / 1	5 B / 1	7 / 0	6 / 0	1	1
4	5 B / 0	4 / 0	6 B / 1	6 / 1	1	0
Demand	1	1	1	1		
v[j]	5	4	6	5		

One optimal assignment is (ship, port) = (1,1), (2,4), (3,2), (4,3)

Cost = 21

f) Continuing to pivot where reduced cost are 0, we get

(5)

	Dest. 1	Dest. 2	Dest. 3	Dest. 4	Supply	u[i]
1	5 B / 1	4 B / 0	6 / 0	7 / 2	1	4
2	6 / 1	6 / 2	7 / 1	5 B / 1	1	4
3	7 / 1	5 P / 1	7 E / 0	6 B / 0	1	5
4	5 / 0	4 P / 0	6 L / 1	6 / 1	1	4
Demand	1	1	1	1		
v[j]	1	0	2	1		

Alternative optimal matching (ship, port) (1,1) (2,4) (3,3) (4,2)

(cont.)

8.3-1(f) (6)
cont.

	Destination 1	2	3	4	Supply	u[i]
1	5 / ---- L / 1	4 / ---- P / 0	6 / ---- / 0	7 / ---- / 2	1	-1
2	6 / ---- / 1	6 / ---- / 2	7 / ---- / 1	5 / ---- B / 1	1	-1
3	7 / ---- / 1	5 / ---- B / 0	7 / ---- B / 1	6 / ---- B / 0	1	0
4	5 / ---- E / 0	4 / ---- P / 1	6 / ---- / 0	6 / ---- / 1	1	-1
Demand	1	1	1	1		
v[j]	6	5	7	6		

Alternative optimal matching (ship, port)
(1,2), (2,4), (3,3), (4,1)

(7)

	Destination 1	2	3	4	Supply	u[i]
1	5 / ---- / 0	4 / ---- P / 1	6 / ---- E / 0	7 / ---- / 2	1	-1
2	6 / ---- / 1	6 / ---- / 2	7 / ---- / 1	5 / ---- B / 1	1	-1
3	7 / ---- / 1	5 / ---- P / 0	7 / ---- L / 1	6 / ---- B / 0	1	0
4	5 / ---- B / 1	4 / ---- B / 0	6 / ---- / 0	6 / ---- / 1	1	-1
Demand	1	1	1	1		
v[j]	6	5	7	6		

Alternative optimal matching (ship, port)
(1,3), (2,4), (3,2), (4,1)

8.3-2 a)

Cost Table

Assignee \ Task	1	2	3	4	5
1	7440	18000	12160	0	0
2	6960	16400	11200	0	0
3	7680	18400	12800	0	0
4	6720	16800	1M	0	0
5	6960	17200	1M	0	0

b)

Assignee \ Task	1	2	3	4	5
1				X	
2			X		
3					X
4		X			
5	X				

Cost is 34960

c)

Plant \ Product	1	2	3	4	5	Supply
1	74.4	180	121.6	0	0	1
2	69.6	164	112	0	0	1
3	76.8	184	128	0	0	1
4	67.2	168	M	0	0	1
5	69.6	172	M	0	0	1
Demand	1	1	1	1	1	

8.3-2 (d)

(0)

	1	2	3	4	5	Supply	u[i]
1	74.4 / 4.8	180 / 9.6	122 / 3.2	0 / 0	0 B / 1	1	6.4
2	69.6 / 6.4	164 B / 0	112 B / 1	0 / 6.4	0 / 6.4	1	0
3	76.8 / 7.2	184 / 13.6	128 / 9.6	0 B / 1	0 B / 0	1	6.4
4	67.2 B / 0	168 B / 1	M / 1M-e3	0 / 2.4	0 / 2.4	1	4
5	69.6 B / 1	172 / 1.6	M / 1M-e3	0 / 0	0 B / 0	1	6.4
Demand	1	1	1	1	1		
v[j]	63.2	164	112	-6.4	-6.4		

The initial solution from Vogel's Method is optimal.

Plant 2 produces Product 3
Plant 4 produces Product 2
Plant 5 produces Product 1
Cost = 349.6

8.3-3

(a) After adding a "dummy" stroke which everyone can swim in 0 seconds, the problem becomes that of assigning 5 swimmers to 5 strokes

see cost table below

The optimal solution is
David swims the backstroke
Tony swims the breaststroke
Chris swims the butterfly
Carl swims Freestyle.

Time = 126.2 sec.

8.3-3 a)

Cost Table

		Task				
		Carl 1	Chris 2	David 3	Tony 4	Ken 5
	back 1	37.7	32.9	33.8	37	35.4
	breast 2	43.4	33.1	42.2	34.7	41.8
Assignee	fly 3	33.3	28.5	38.9	30.4	33.6
	free 4	29.2	26.4	29.6	28.5	31.1
	dummy 5	0	0	0	0	0

Optimal Solution: The X's in the table indicate an optimal assignment of assignees to tasks.

b)

		Task				
		1	2	3	4	5
	1			X		
	2				X	
Assignee	3		X			
	4	X				
	5					X

Cost is
126.2

8.3-4

(a) The assignments are the loads needed at sites 1, 2 and 3 and the assignees are the three trucks from North and 2 from South

		Sites				
		1	1′	2	3	3′
North	1	65	65	80	75	75
North	2	65	65	80	75	75
North	3	65	65	80	75	75
South	4	90	90	75	80	80
South	5	90	90	75	80	80

b)

		Task				
		1	2	3	4	5
Assignee	1	X				
	2		X			
	3				X	
	4			X		
	5					X

Cost 360

c)

		Site			
		1	2	3	Supply
North	1	65	80	75	3
South	2	90	75	80	2
Demand		2	1	2	

d)

		Destination			
		1	2	3	Supply
Source	1	2		1	3
	2		1	1	2
Demand		2	1	2	

Cost is 360

8.3-5 (a)

		Product					
		1	2	3	4	5	Supply
Plant	1	820	810	840	960	0	2
	2	800	870	M	920	0	2
	3	740	900	810	840	0	1
Demand		1	1	1	1	1	

(b) and (c)

```
        |              Destination               |
        |  1  |  2  |  3  |  4  |  5  |Supply  u[i]
________|_____|_____|_____|_____|_____|______________
        | 820| | 810| | 840| | 960| |   0| |      |
      1 |----  |---- B|---- B|----  |---- B|      |
        |   20|    1|    1|   40|    0|     2|    0
        |_____|_____|_____|_____|_____|      |
        | 800| | 870| |   M| | 920| |   0| |      |
      2 |---- B|----  |----  |---- B|---- B|      |
        |    1|   60|1M-e3|    0|    1|     2|    0
        |_____|_____|_____|_____|_____|      |
        | 740| | 900| | 810| | 840| |   0| |      |
      3 |----  |----  |----  |---- B|----  |      |
        |   20|  170|   50|    1|   80|     1|  -80
        |_____|_____|_____|_____|_____|______|_____
Demand  |    1     1     1     1     1|
        |____________________________|
  v[j]  |  800   810   840   920     0|
        |                            |
```

Since all reduced costs are nonnegative, this solution is optimal.

d)

		Product					
		1	2	3	4	5	Supply
Plant	1	820	810	840	960	0	1
	2	820	810	840	960	0	1
	3	800	870	M	920	0	1
	4	800	870	M	920	0	1
	5	740	900	810	840	M	1
Demand		1	1	1	1	1	

This is identical to the table in part (a) except Plants 1 and 2 have been split into 2 plants each.

8.3-5(e)

Source		Destination 1	2	3	4	5	Supply	u[i]
1	cost	820	810	840	960	0		
		----	---- B	----	----	----		
		20	1	0	40	0	1	0
2	cost	820	810	840	960	0		
		----	---- B	---- B	----	---- B		
		20	0	1	40	0	1	0
3	cost	800	870	M	920	0		
		---- B	----	----	----	----		
		1	60	1M-e3	0	0	1	0
4	cost	800	870	M	920	0		
		---- B	----	----	---- B	---- B		
		0	60	1M-e3	0	1	1	0
5	cost	740	900	810	840	M		
		----	----	----	---- B	----		
		20	170	50	1	1M+80	1	-80
Demand		1	1	1	1	1		
v[j]		800	810	840	920	0		

The basic feasible solution for the transformed problem above corresponds to that given in part (c).

8.3-6

0

Source		Destination 1	2	3	4	Supply	u[i]
1	cost	13	16	12	11		
		----	----	----	---- B		
		7	8	8	1	1	-9
2	cost	15	M	13	20		
		---- B	----	---- P	---- L		
		1	1M-17	0	0	1	0
3	cost	5	7	10	6		
		---- B	---- B	----	----		
		0	1	7	-4	1	-10
4	cost	0	0	0	0		
		----	----	---- P	---- E		
		-2	-4	1	-7	1	-13
Demand		1	1	1	1		
v[j]		15	17	13	20		

(1)

Source		Destination 1	2	3	4	Supply	u[i]
1	cost	13	16	12	11		
		----	----	----	---- B		
		0	1	1	1	1	-2
2	cost	15	M	13	20		
		---- L	----	---- P	----		
		1	1M-17	0	7	1	0
3	cost	5	7	10	6		
		---- P	---- P	----	----		
		0	1	7	3	1	-10
4	cost	0	0	0	0		
		----	---- E	---- P	---- B		
		-2	-4	1	0	1	-13
Demand		1	1	1	1		
v[j]		15	17	13	13		

(2)

Source		Destination 1	2	3	4	Supply	u[i]
1	cost	13	16	12	11		
		----	----	----	---- B		
		4	5	1	1	1	11
2	cost	15	M	13	20		
		----	----	---- B	----		
		4	1M-13	1	7	1	13
3	cost	5	7	10	6		
		---- B	---- L	----	---- E		
		1	0	3	-1	1	7
4	cost	0	0	0	0		
		----	---- P	---- B	---- P		
		2	1	0	0	1	0
Demand		1	1	1	1		
v[j]		-2	0	0	0		

(cont.)

8.3-6 (cont.)

(3)

	Destination 1	2	3	4	Supply	u[i]
1	13 / 3	16 / 5	12 / 1	11 B / 1	1	11
2	15 / 3	M / 1M-13	13 B / 1	20 / 7	1	13
3	5 B / 1	7 / 1	10 / 4	6 B / 0	1	6
4	0 / 1	0 B / 1	0 B / 0	0 B / 0	1	0
Demand	1	1	1	1		
v[j]	-1	0	0	0		

This solution corresponds to that given in Sec. 8.3, though the set of basic variables is different, variable values are the same.

8.3-7 a) let assignees 1 and 2 represent Plant A; assignees 3 and 4 represent Plant B; and tasks be distribution centers.

Cost Table

		Task 1	2	3	dummy 4
Assignee	1	80	140	120	0
	2	80	140	120	0
	3	60	160	150	0
	4	60	160	150	0

b)

		Task 1	2	3	4
Assignee	1		X		
	2			X	
	3	X			
	4				X

Cost is 320

8.3-7 c)

Cost Per Unit Distributed

		Destination 1	2	3	4	Supply
Source	1	80	140	120	0	1
	2	80	140	120	0	1
	3	60	160	150	0	1
	4	60	160	150	0	1
Demand		1	1	1	1	

d)

		Destination 1	2	3	4	Supply
Source	1		1			1
	2			1		1
	3	1				1
	4				1	1
Demand		1	1	1	1	Cost is 320

e)

Cost Per Unit Distributed

		Destination 1	2	3	4	Supply
Source	1	80	140	120	0	2
	2	60	160	150	0	2
Demand		1	1	1	1	

f)

		Destination 1	2	3	4	Supply
Source	1		1	1		2
	2	1			1	2
Demand		1	1	1	1	Cost is 320

8.3-8

a)

		Task 1	2	3
Assignee	1			X
	2	X		
	3		X	

Cost 10

b)

Cost Per Unit Distributed

		Destination 1	2	3	Supply
Source	1	5	7	4	1
	2	3	6	5	1
	3	2	3	4	1
Demand		1	1	1	

c)

		Destination 1	2	3	Supply
Source	1			1	1
	2	1			1
	3		1		1
Demand		1	1	1	Cost is 10

8.3-9 Minimize $\sum_{i=1}^{n}\sum_{j=1}^{n} c_{ij} x_{ij}$

subject to $\sum_{j=1}^{n} x_{ij} = 1$ for $i = 1, 2, \ldots, n$

$\sum_{i=1}^{n} x_{ij} = 1$ for $j = 1, 2, \ldots, n$

$x_{ij} \geq 0$ for $i = 1, 2, \ldots, n$; $j = 1, 2, \ldots, n$.

The table of constraint coefficients is identical to that for the transportation problem (Table 7.6). The assignment problem has a more special structure because $m = n$ and $s_i = d_i = 1$ for all i.

d) A transportation problem of size $m \times n$ has $m+n-1$ basic variables; since $m=n$ for the assignment problem, there are $2(3)-1=5$ basic variables, but only 3 assignments. Thus, 2 basic variables are degenerate (equal to zero). Assignment problems will always be highly degenerate. If you use the interactive routine in the OR Courseware you'll see this.

e) x_{A1}, x_{A2}, x_{B2} are nonbasic; and one of (x_{B3}, x_{C3}) is.

x_{C1} and one of (x_{B3}, x_{C3}) are basic and $= 0$.

(from network simplex – try working it out yourself).

dual variables:

				u_i
	[5] +3	[7] +4	1	0
	1	[6] +2	[5] 0	1
	0	1	0	0
v_j	2	3	4	

looking at $c_{ij} - u_i - v_j$, we see that allowable ranges to stay optimal for c_{ij} are: $c_{A1} \geq 2$, $c_{A2} \geq 3$, $c_{B2} \geq 4$, $c_{B3} \geq 5$

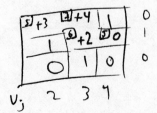

Chapter 9
Network Analysis, Including PERT-CPM

9.2-1

a) AD - DC - CE - EF (A → D → C → E → F) is a directed path from A to F

AD - FD (A → D → F)
CA - CE - EF (A → C → E → F)
AD - ED - EF (A → D – E → F)
} are undirected paths from A to F

b) AD - DC - CA
DC - CE - ED
DC - CE - EF - FD
} are directed cycles

CA - CE - EF - FD - DB - AB is an undirected cycle which includes every node.

c) {CA, CE, DC, FD, DB} is a spanning tree.

d)

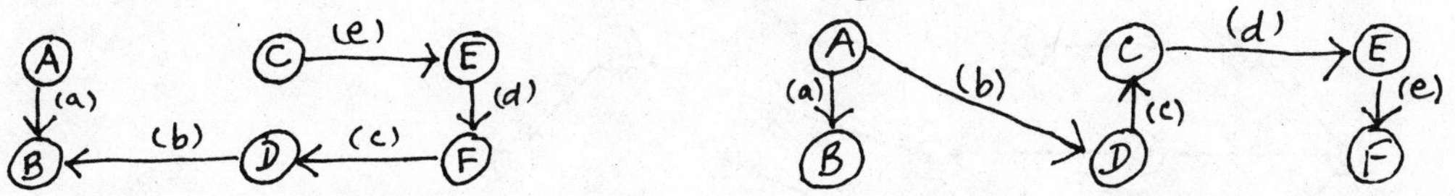

9.3-1

(a) Nodes are the years

d_{ij} = cost of using same tractor from end of year i to end of year j.

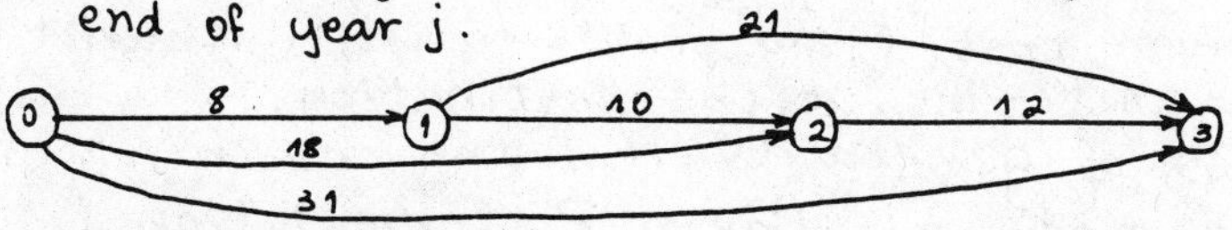

(b)

n	Solved nodes connected to unsolved nodes	its closest connected unsolved node	total distance involved	n^{th} nearest node	its minimum distance	its last connection
1	0	1	8	1	8	01
2	0	2	18	2	18	02
	1	2	8+10 = 18	2		12
3	0	3	31			
	1	3	8+21 = 29	3	29	13
	2	3	18+12 = 30			

After buying new tractor, replace it at end of year 1 and then keep the new till the end of year 3, for total cost of 29.

9.3-2

(a)

0	4	5	5	10	9	16
O	A	B	C	D	E	T
OA-4 OC-5 ~~OB-6~~	AB-1 ~~AD-7~~	~~BA-1~~ ~~BC-2~~ BE-4 BD-5	~~CB-2~~ ~~CE-5~~	~~DE-1~~ ~~DB-5~~ DT-6 DA-7	ED-1 ~~EB-4~~ ~~EC-5~~ ~~ET-8~~	

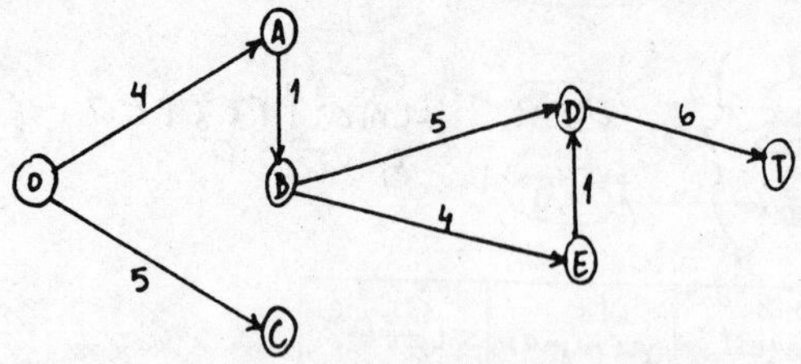

Lenght of Shortest Path = 16

(b)

0	4	3	6	7	9	8	10	11	14	17
O	A	B	C	D	E	F	G	H	I	T
OB-3 OA-4 OC-6	AD-3 ~~AC-5~~	~~BC-4~~ BE-6	~~CD-2~~ CF-2 ~~CB-4~~ ~~CE-5~~ ~~CA-5~~	~~DC-2~~ ~~DF-2~~ ~~DA-3~~ ~~DG-4~~	~~EF-1~~ EH-2 EI-5 ~~EC-5~~ ~~EB-6~~	FE-1 ~~FC-2~~ ~~FD-2~~ FG-2 ~~FH-5~~	~~GF-2~~ ~~GH-2~~ ~~GD-4~~ GT-7	~~HE-2~~ ~~HG-2~~ ~~HI-3~~ ~~HF-5~~ ~~HT-8~~	~~IH-3~~ ~~IT-4~~ ~~IE-5~~	

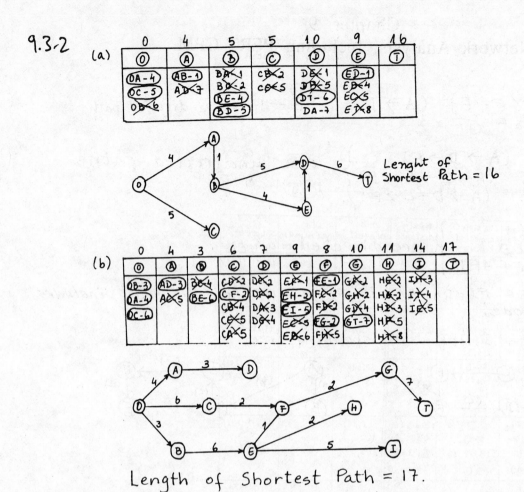

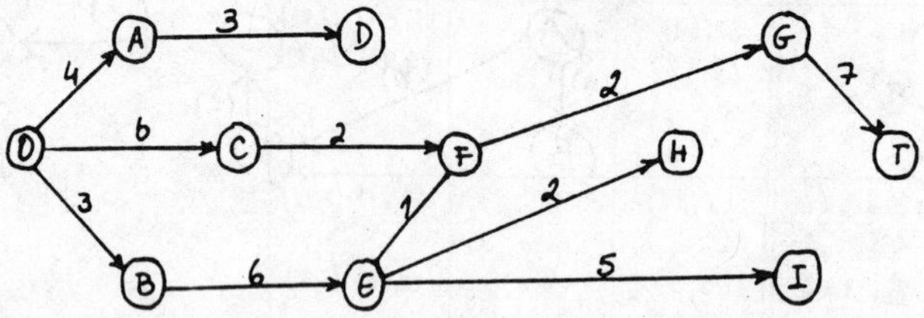

Length of Shortest Path = 17.

9.3-3

This is just the minimum cost flow problem with a unit source at the origin and a unit sink at the destination.

Assume without loss of generality that the origin is node 1 and the destination is node n. The LP formulation is

$$\text{min.} \quad Z = \sum_{i=1}^{n} \sum_{j=1}^{n} c_{ij} x_{ij}$$

subject to

$$\sum_{j=1}^{n} x_{1j} - \sum_{j=1}^{n} x_{j1} = 1$$

$$\sum_{j=1}^{n} x_{ij} - \sum_{j=1}^{n} x_{ji} = 0 \qquad 2 \le i \le n-1$$

$$\sum_{j=1}^{n} x_{nj} - \sum_{j=1}^{n} x_{jn} = -1$$

$$0 \le x_{ij} \le 1, \quad 1 \le i, j \le n$$

9.3-4 (a) Let node (i,j) denote phase i being completed with j left to spend. $t_{(i,j),(i+1,k)}$ = the time taken to complete phase $i+1$ if $(j-k)$ million is spent.

The network is:

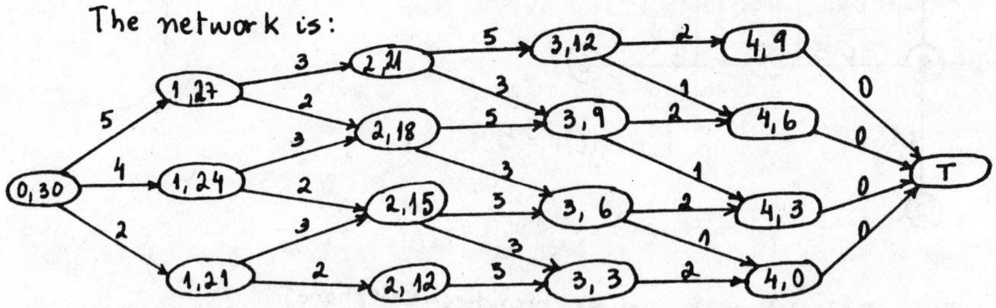

(b)

n	solved nodes connected to unsolved nodes	its closest connected unsolved node	total distance involved	nth nearest node	its minimum distance	its last connection
1	(0,30)	(1,21)	2	(1,21)	2	(0,30)-(1,21)
2	(0,30)	(1,24)	4	(1,24)	4	(0,30)-(1,24)
	(1,21)	(2,12)	2+2=4	(2,12)	4	(1,21)-(2,12)
4	(0,30)	(1,27)	5	(1,27)	5	(0,30)-(1,27)
	(1,21)	(2,15)	2+3=5	(2,15)	5	(1,21)-(2,15)
	(1,24)	(2,15)	4+2=6			
	(2,12)	(3,3)	4+5=9			
6	(1,24)	(2,18)	4+3=7	(2,18)	7	(1,24)-(2,18)
	(1,27)	(2,18)	5+2=7	(2,18)	7	(1,27)-(2,18)
	(2,12)	(3,3)	4+5=9			
	(2,15)	(3,3)	5+3=8			
7	(1,27)	(2,21)	5+3=8	(2,21)	8	(1,27)-(2,21)
	(2,12)	(3,3)	4+5=9			
	(2,15)	(3,3)	5+3=8	(3,3)	8	(2,15)-(3,3)
	(2,18)	(3,6)	7+3=10			
9	(2,15)	(3,6)	5+5=10	(3,6)	10	(2,15)-(3,6)
	(2,18)	(3,6)	7+3=10	(3,6)	10	(2,18)-(3,6)
	(2,21)	(3,9)	8+3=11			
	(3,3)	(4,0)	8+2=10	(4,0)	10	(3,3)-(4,0)
11	(2,18)	(3,9)	7+5=12			
	(2,21)	(3,9)	8+3=11			
	(3,6)	(4,3)	10+2=12			
	(4,0)	T	10+0=10	T	10	(4,0)-T

Shortest Route: (0,30) —2→ (1,21) —3→ (2,15) —3→ (3,3) —2→ (4,0) —0→ (T)

Phase	Level	Cost	Time
Research	crash	9	2
Development	priority	6	3
Design	crash	12	3
Production	priority	3	2

Total time = 10

9.4-1

(a)

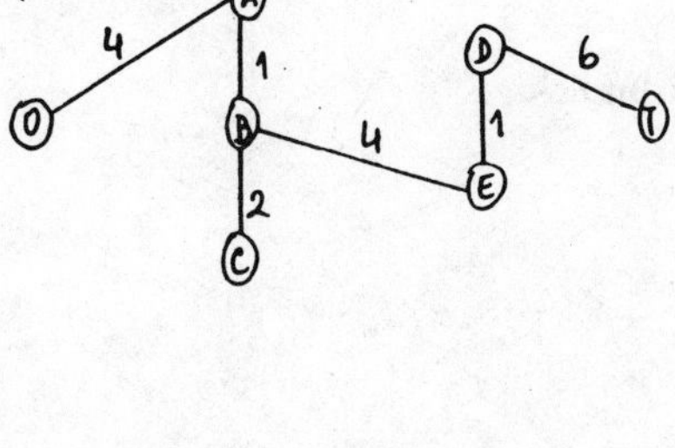

Length = 18

(b)

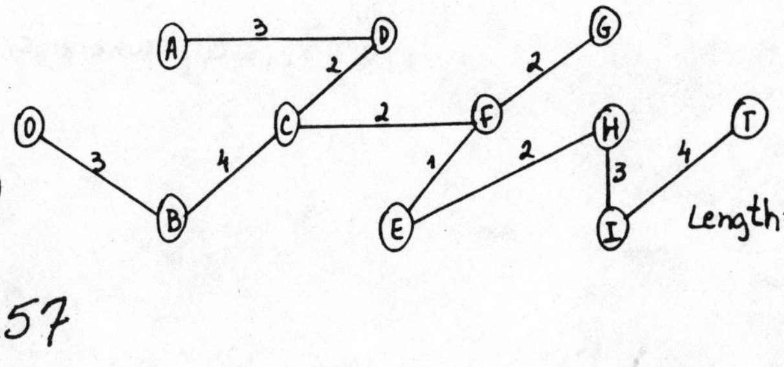

Length = 26

9.4-2 (a) nodes ~ groves, branches ~ roads

(b)

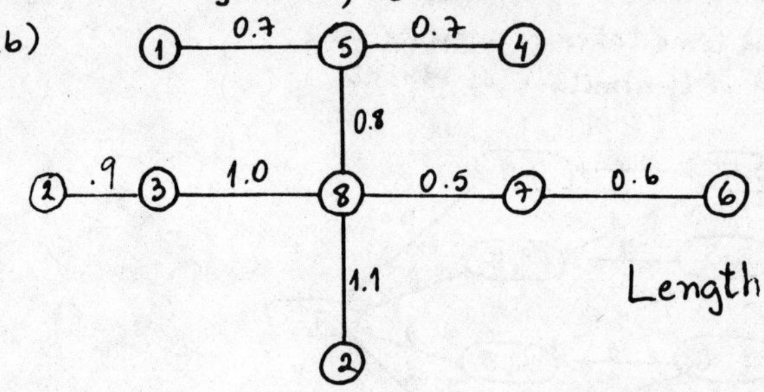

Length = 5.4

9.4-3 (a) nodes ~ {Main office, Branch 1, ..., Branch 5}, branches ~ telephone lines

(b)

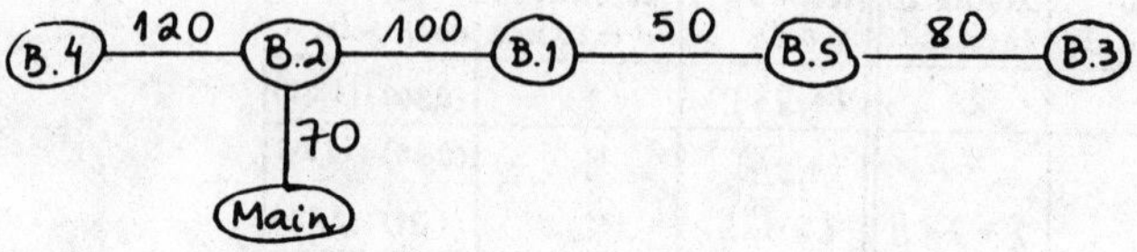

9.5-1 (a)

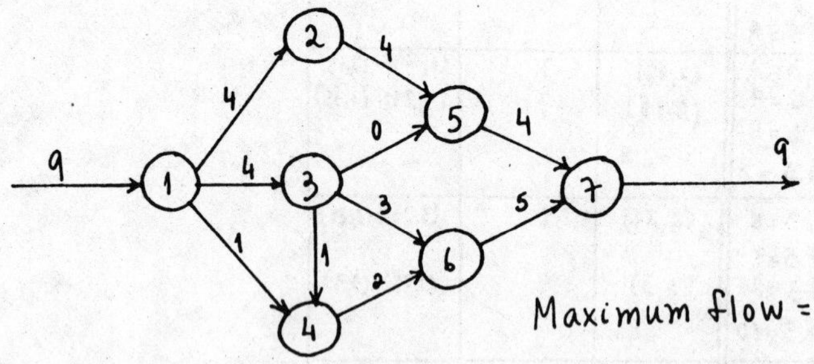

Maximum flow = 9

(b)

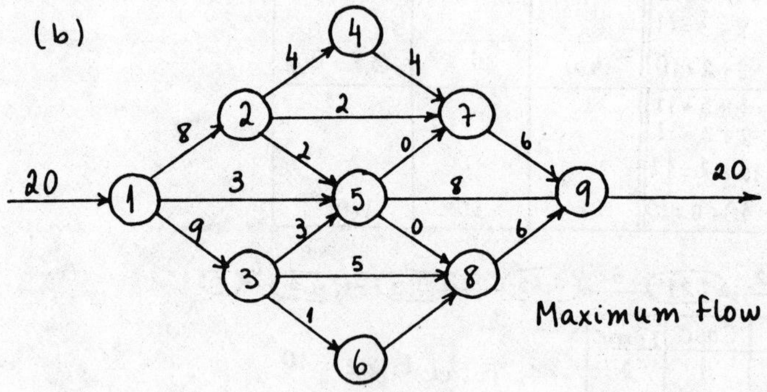

Maximum flow = 20

9.5-2 Let node 1 be the source and node N be the sink. Then:

Maximize $\sum_{j=2}^{N} x_{1j}$

subject to $\sum_{\substack{j=1 \\ j \neq i}}^{N} x_{ij} - \sum_{\substack{j=1 \\ j \neq i}}^{N} x_{ji} = 0$ for $i = 2, 3, \ldots, N-1$

$0 \leq x_{ij} \leq c_{ij}$ where $c_{ij} = 0$ if (i,j) is not a branch

9.5-3 For convenience, call Faireparc station siding 0 and the Portstown station siding $s+1$. Let node (i,j) represent siding i at time j for $i=0,1,\ldots,s,s+1$ and $j=0,.1,.2,\ldots,23.9$. Node $(0,0)$ is the source and node $(s+1,23.9)$ the sink.
Arcs with capacity 1 will exist between nodes (i,j) and $(i+1, j+t_i)$ if and only if a freight train leaving siding i at time j could not be overtaken by a scheduled passenger train before it reached siding $i+1$. Arcs with capacity n_i will exist between nodes (i,j) and $(i,j+1)$ for $j=0,.1,.2,\ldots,23.8$
No other arcs exist.
For example, if $t_i=1.3$ and a scheduled passenger train could overtake a freight train leaving siding i at time 5.7 before it reached siding $i+1$, the following would be a portion of the network.

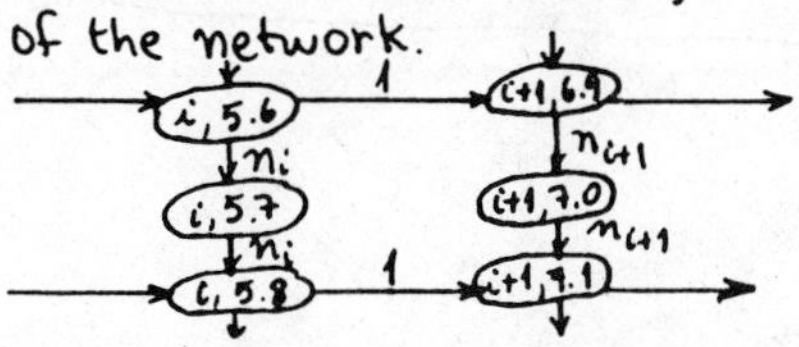

Solving the maximal flow problem will maximize the number of freight trains that are sent.

9.5-4

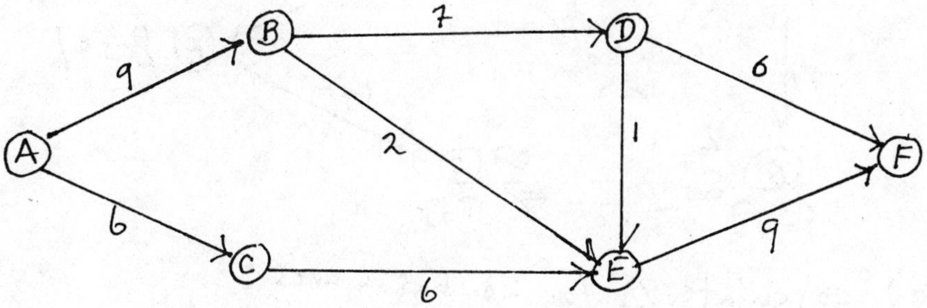

9.6-1

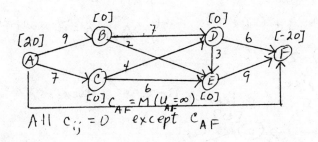

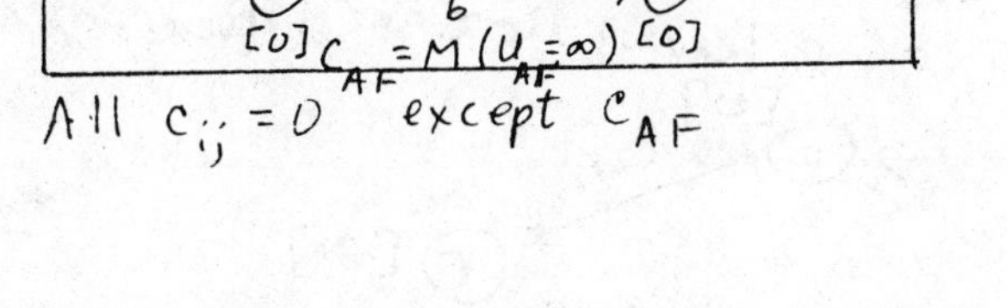

All $c_{ij} = 0$ except c_{AF}

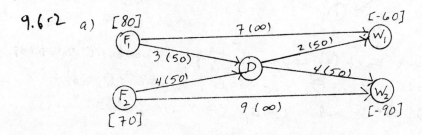

9.6-2 a)

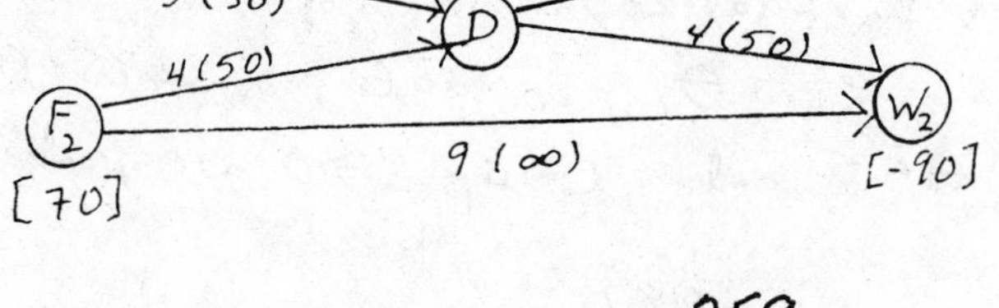

9.6-2 b) Min $7x_{F_1W_1} + 3x_{F_1D} + 2x_{DW_1} + 4x_{F_2D} + 4x_{DW_2} + 9x_{F_2W_2}$

Subject to

$$x_{F_1W_1} + x_{F_1D} = 80$$
$$x_{F_2D} + x_{F_2W_2} = 70$$
$$x_{F_1W_1} + x_{DW_1} = 60$$
$$x_{DW_2} + x_{F_2W_2} = 90$$
$$x_{F_1D} - x_{DW_1} + x_{F_2D} - x_{DW_2} = 0$$
$$0 \le x_{F_1D},\ x_{F_2D},\ x_{DW_1},\ x_{DW_2} \le 50$$

9.6-3

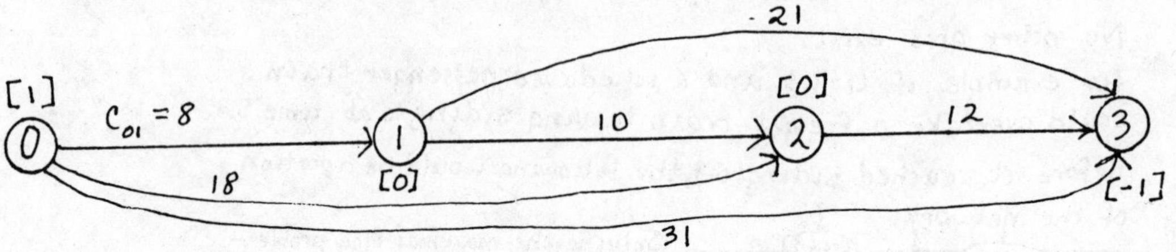

9.7-1 a)

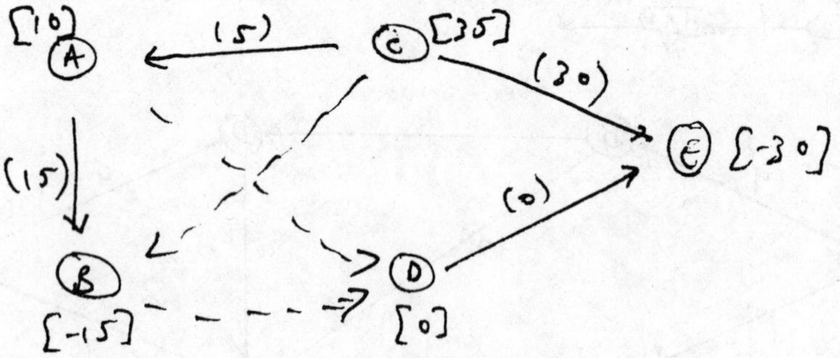

b) calculate Δ for nonbasic arcs:

$\Delta_{BD} = 5 + 4 - 3 + (-6) + 2 = 2$

$\Delta_{AD} = 5 + 4 - 3 + (-6) = 0$

$\Delta_{CB} = (-3) - 2 - (-6) = 1$

all ≥ 0 ⇒ optimal

$\Delta_{AD} = 0$ ⇒ multiple optima exist

Network simplex:

$\theta = 5$, CA is leaving basic arc (reverses)

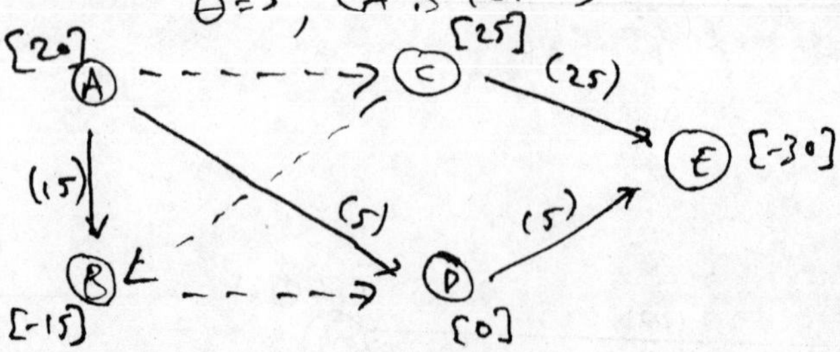

From this and part (a) we see that optimal nonbasic solutions have $x_{AB} = 15$, $x_{AC} = \theta$, $x_{AD} = 5 - \theta$, $x_{CE} = 25 + \theta$, $x_{DE} = 5 - \theta$, where $0 \le \theta \le 5$ and $C \to B$, $B \to D$ are nonbasic arcs.

9.7-1c) starting from

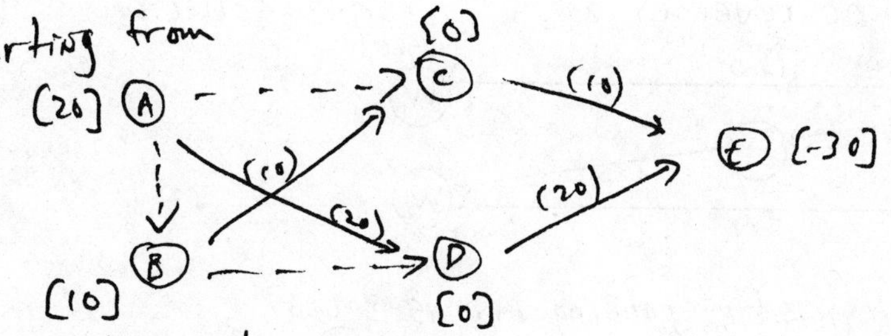

network simplex gives

$\Delta_{AC} = 6+3-4-5=0$

$\Delta_{AB} = 2+3+3-4-5=-1<0$ ← entering arc

$\Delta_{BD} = 5+4-3-3=3$

$\theta=15$, BC is leaving arc (reverses)

next BF solution is

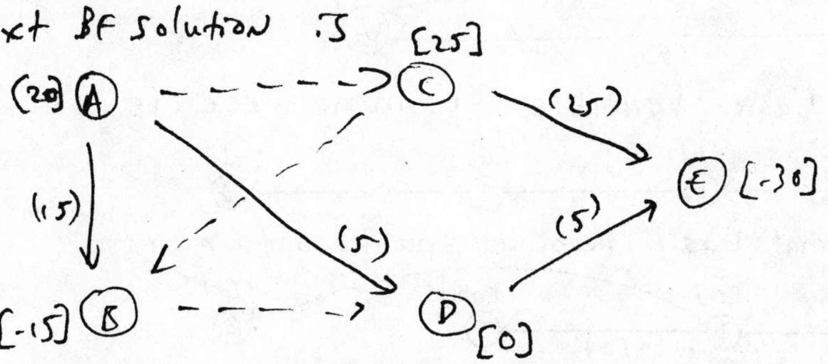

From (6) we recognize this as optimal.

9.7-2

a)

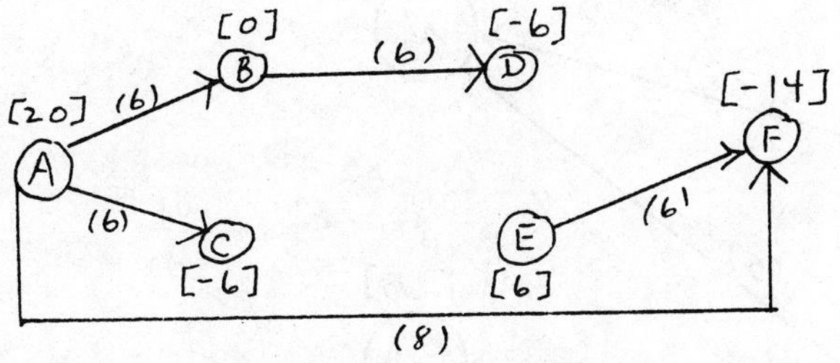

b) The final feasible spanning tree is

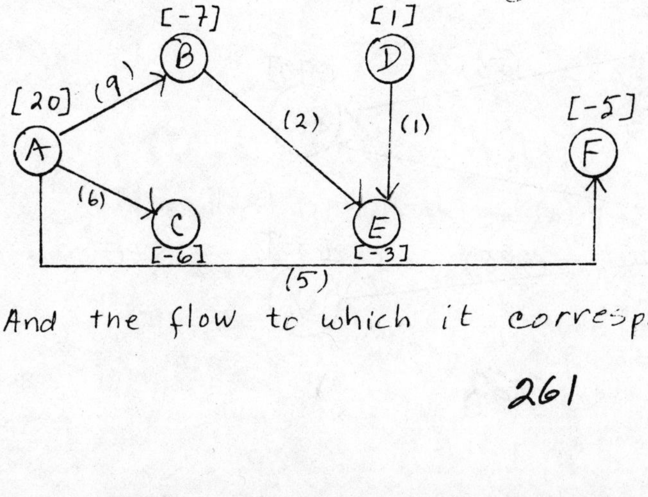

And the flow to which it corresponds is the same as in 9.5-4.

9.7-3 There are no reverse arcs in this solution

a)

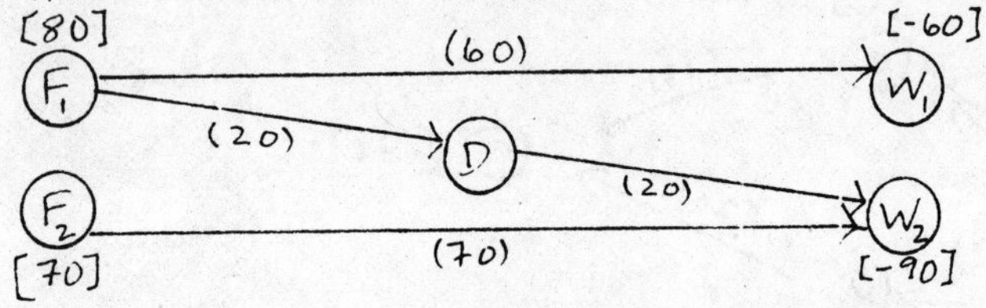

b) The optimal basic feasible spanning tree is

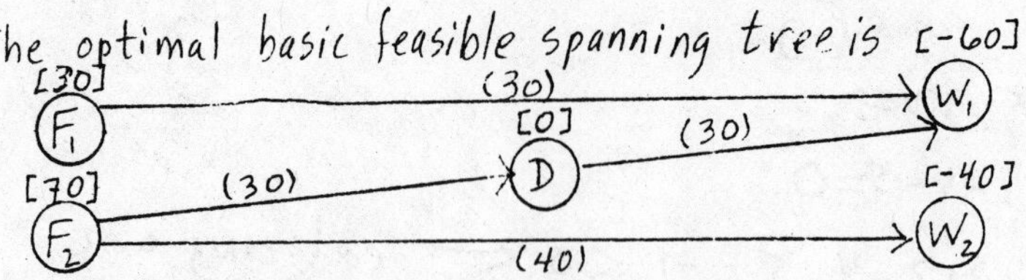

Which corresponds to a real flow of

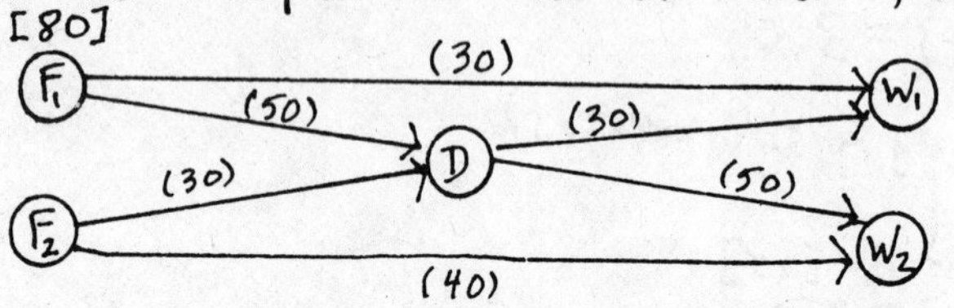

and a cost of 110.

9.7-4 Initial basic feasible spanning tree is

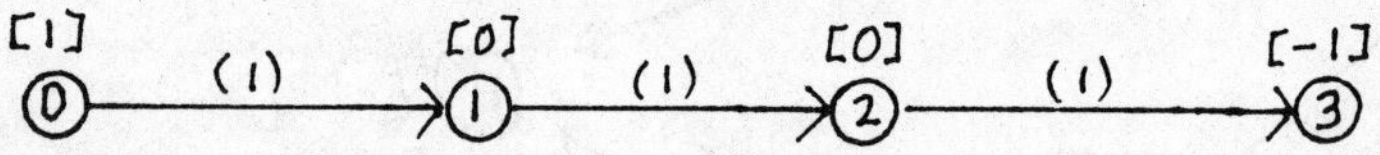

The optimal basic feasible spanning tree is

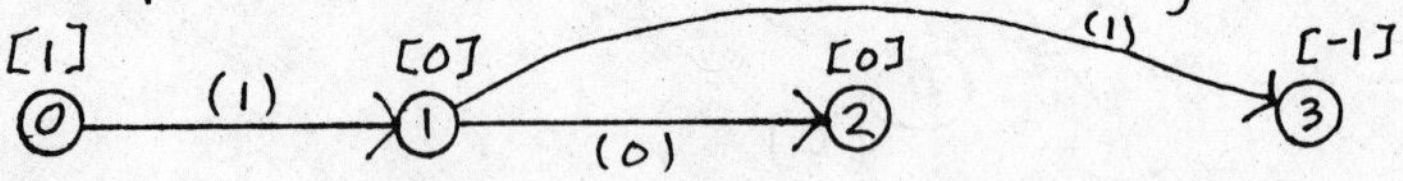

which has a real flow of

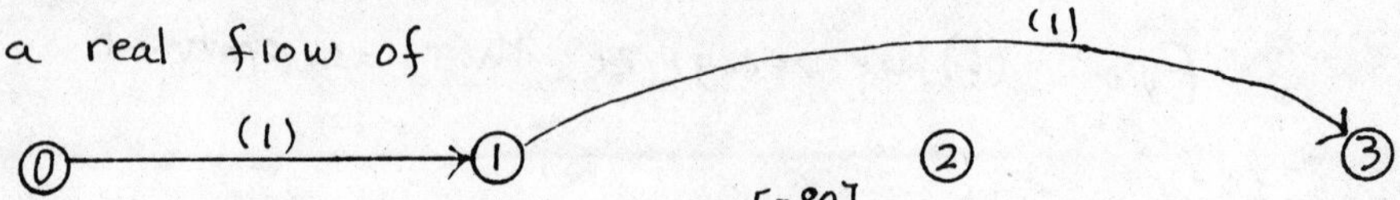

and a cost of 29.

9.7-5

Initial basic spanning tree:

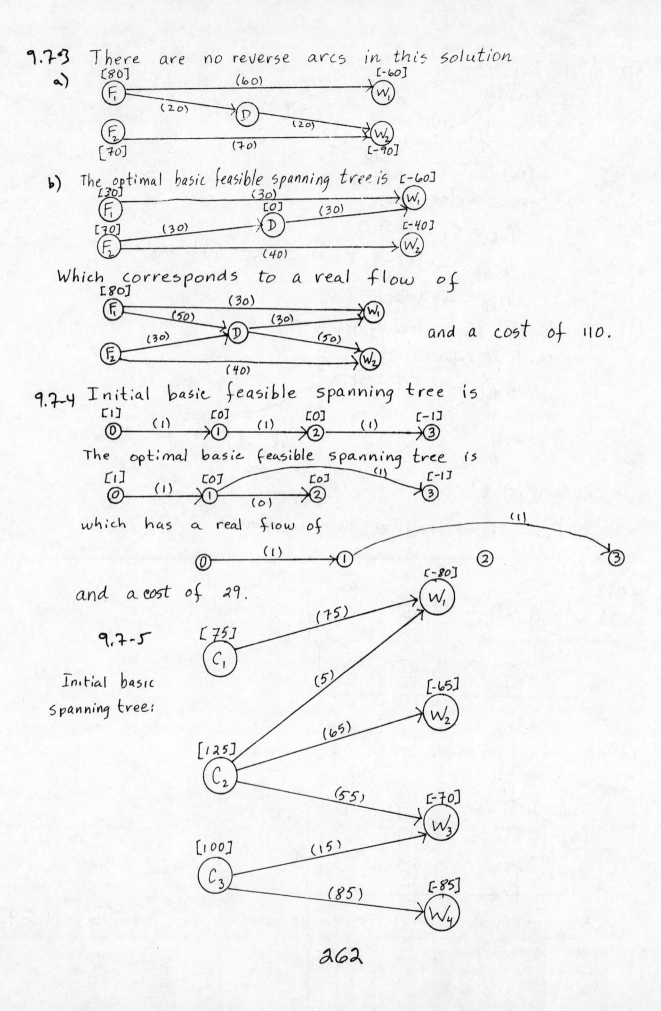

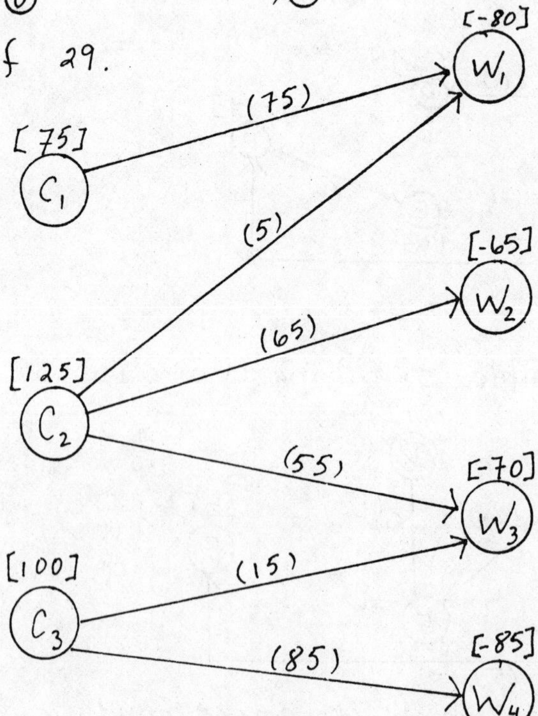

9.7-5 (continued)
The optimal basic feasible spanning tree is:

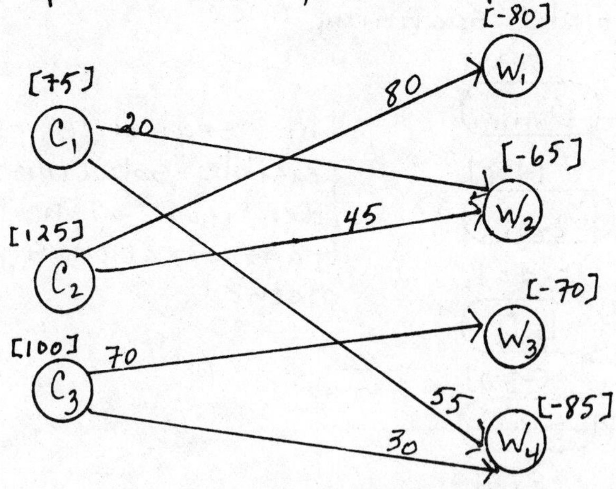

which corresponds to the optimal solution given in Sec. 8.1.

9.7-6 a)

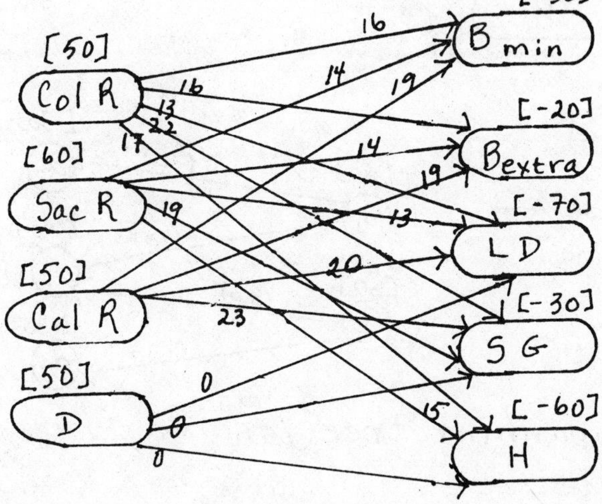

b) Initial basic feasible spanning tree

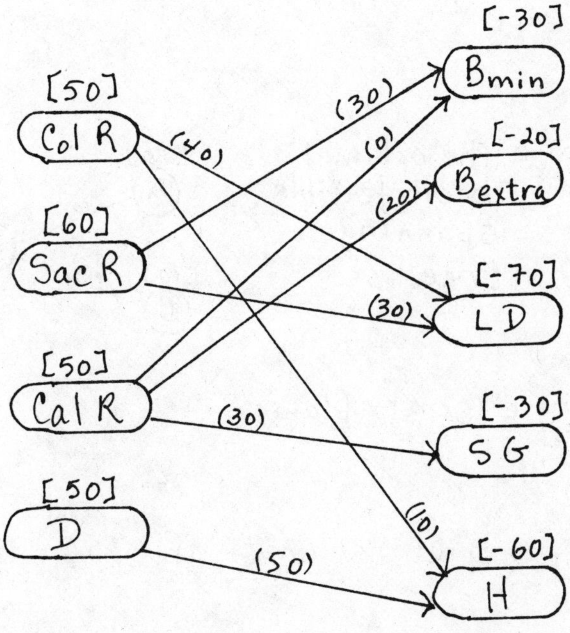

9.7-6 b) (continued)

The optimal basic feasible spanning tree is:

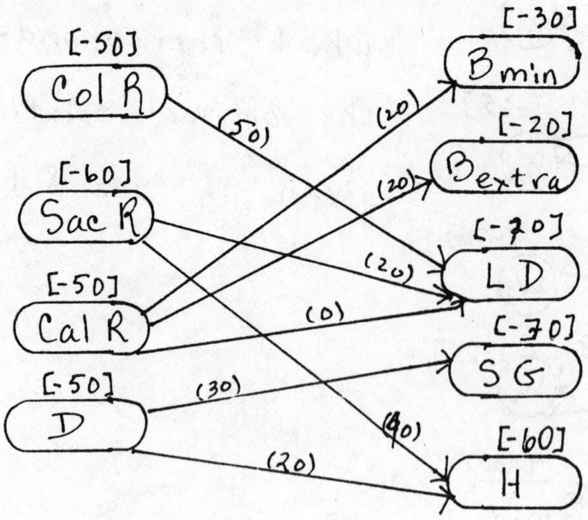

The sequence of basic feasible solutions is identical with the transportation simplex method.

9.7-7

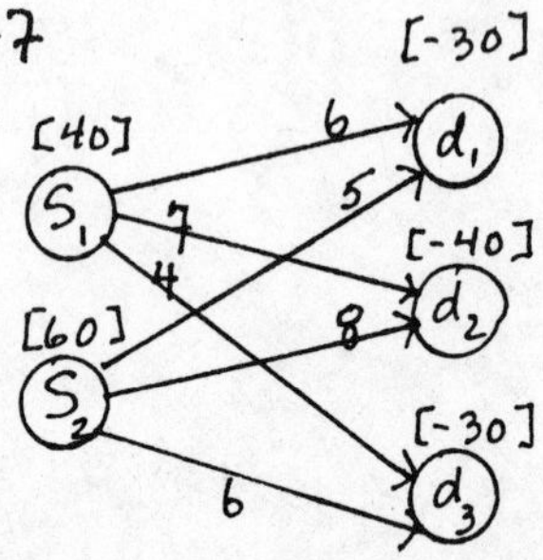

Initial Basic Feasible Spanning Tree →

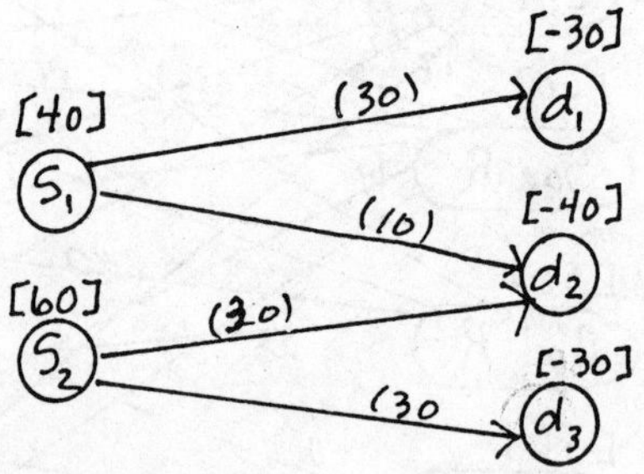

The optimal feasible spanning tree is:

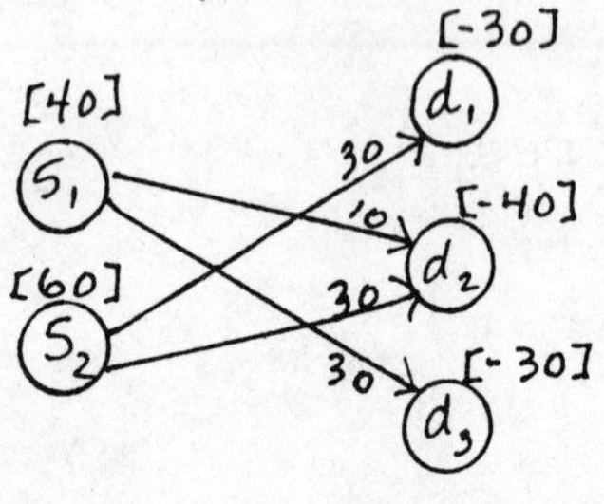

With a cost of 580

9.7-8

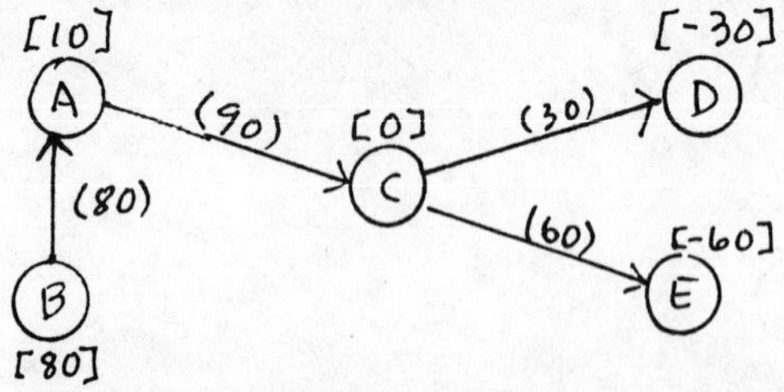

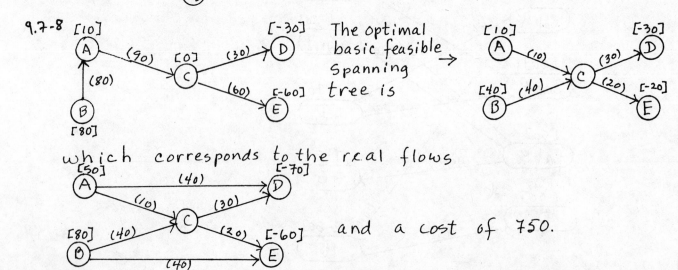

The optimal basic feasible spanning tree is →

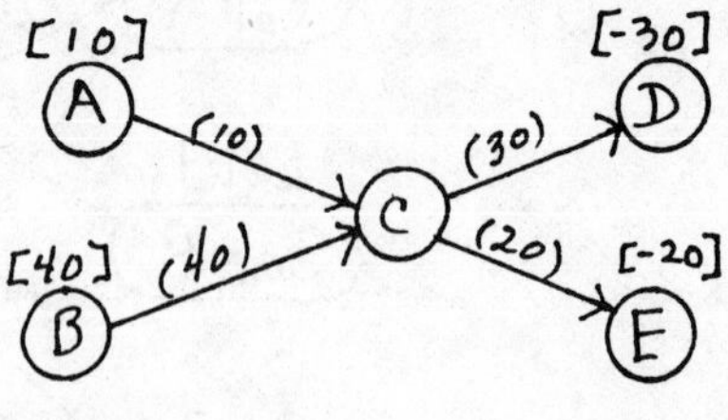

which corresponds to the real flows

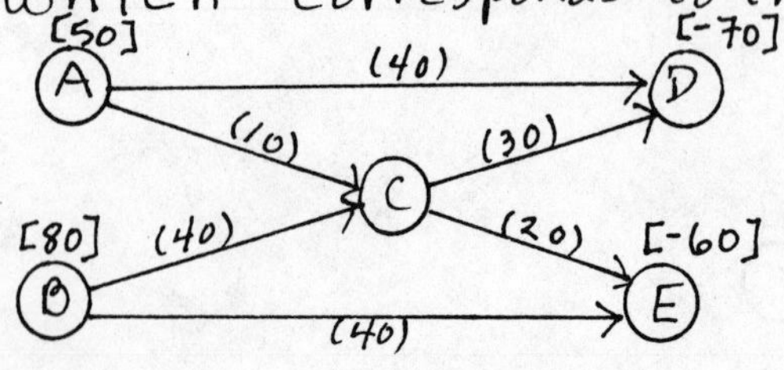

and a cost of 750.

9.8-1

Event	Earliest Time	Latest Time	Slack	Activity	Slack
1	0	0	0	(1,2)	1
2	6	7	1	(1,3)	0
3	3	3	0	(1,4)	1
4	5	6	1	(2,5)	1
5	10	11	1	(2,8)	3
6	10	10	0	(3,6)	0
7	11	13	2	(4,6)	1
8	14	14	0	(4,7)	2
9	13	15	2	(5,8)	1
10	20	20	0	(6,8)	0
				(6,9)	2
				(7,9)	2
				(8,10)	0
				(9,10)	2

Critical path is:

$1 \rightarrow 3 \rightarrow 6 \rightarrow 8 \rightarrow 10$

9.8-2

Event	Earliest Time	Latest Time	Slack	Activity	Slack
1	0	0	0	(1,2)	0
2	5	5	0	(1,3)	1
3	2	3	1	(2,4)	6
4	9	15	6	(2,5)	0
5	12	12	0	(3,5)	1
6	10	19	9	(3,6)	9
7	22	26	4	(4,7)	6
8	24	24	0	(5,7)	4
9	28	28	0	(5,8)	0
				(6,8)	9
				(7,9)	4
				(8,9)	0

Critical path is:

$1 \rightarrow 2 \rightarrow 5 \rightarrow 8 \rightarrow 9$

9.8-3

a)

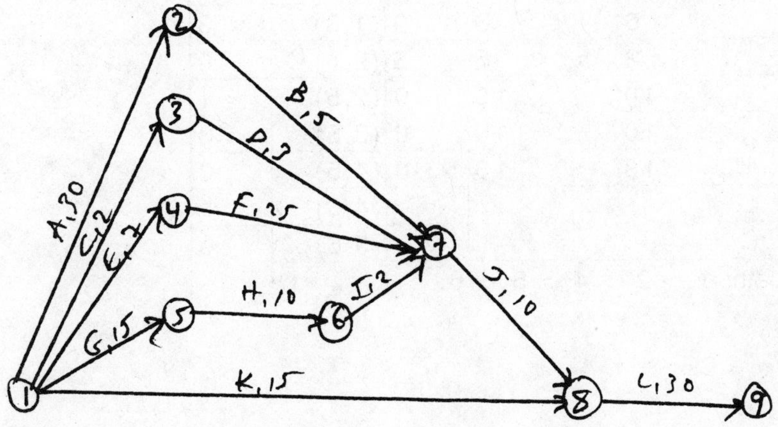

9.8-3 b)

Event	Earliest Time	Latest Time	Slack	Activity	Slack
1	0	0	0	(1,2)	0
2	30	30	0	(1,3)	30
3	2	32	30	(1,4)	3
4	7	10	3	(1,5)	8
5	15	23	8	(1,8)	30
6	25	33	8	(2,7)	0
7	35	35	0	(3,7)	30
8	45	45	0	(4,7)	3
9	75	75	0	(5,6)	8
				(6,7)	8
				(7,8)	0
				(8,9)	0

Critical path is:

1 → 2 → 7 → 8 → 9

c) 6 minutes delay - 3 min slack = 3 min

Thus the dinner will be delayed by at least 3 minutes.

If food processor is used, then slack for activity (1,4) (Task 5) is increased to 8, thus the dinner need not necessarily be delayed (but will be if it took 3 minutes to start Task 5)

9.8-4 The critical path(s) and longest path(s) are the same. Their length is the earliest time of the final event.

9.8-5

event	earliest time	latest time	slack	activity	slack
1	0	0	0	(1,2)	0
2	6	6	0	(1,3)	3
3	2	5	3	(2,4)	0
4	10	10	0	(2,5)	1
5	10	10	0	(3,5)	3
6	13	13	0	(4,5)	0
				(4,6)	1
				(5,6)	0

critical path: 1 -> 2 -> 4 -> 5 -> 6

9.8-6

a)

event	earliest time	latest time	slack	activity	slack
1	0	0	0	(1,2)	4
2	6	10	4	(1,3)	0
3	4	4	0	(2,4)	4
4	13	13	0	(3,4)	0
5	16	17	1	(3,5)	1
6	14	21	7	(3,6)	7
7	22	22	0	(4,7)	0
8	19	25	6	(5,7)	1
9	34	34	0	(5,8)	6
				(6,8)	7
				(7,9)	0
				(8,9)	6
critical path: 1 -> 3 -> 4 -> 7 -> 9					

b) 6 days

9.8-7

a)

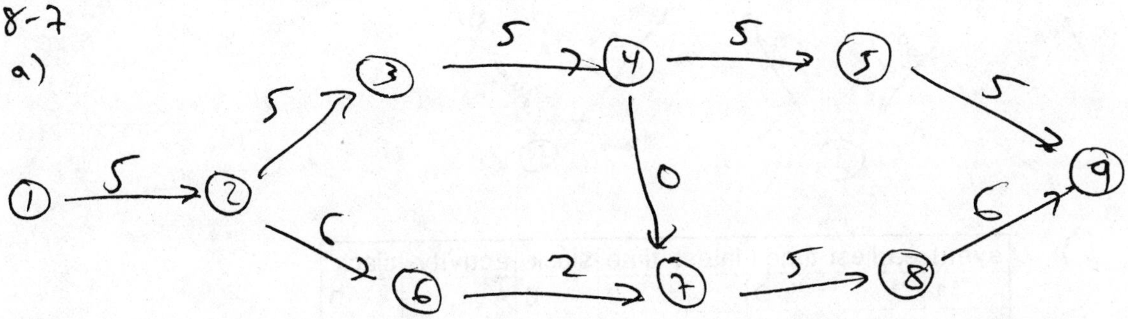

((4,7) is a dummy arc)

b)

event	earliest time	latest time	slack	activity	slack
1	0	0	0	(1,2)	4
2	5	5	0	(2,3)	0
3	10	10	0	(3,4)	4
4	15	15	0	(4,5)	0
5	20	21	1	(5,9)	1
6	11	13	2	(2,6)	7
7	15	15	0	(6,7)	0
8	20	20	0	(7,8)	1
9	26	26	0	(8,9)	6
				(4,7)	7
critical path: 1 -> 2 -> 3 -> 4 -> 7 -> 8 -> 9					

c) 1 unit (new critical path would be 1→2→3→4→5→9, 25 time units)

9.8-8
a)

event	earliest time	latest time	slack	activity	slack
1	0	0	0	(1,2)	0
2	2	2	0	(2,3)	1
3	5	6	1	(2,4)	0
4	4	4	0	(3,6)	1
5	11	11	0	(4,5)	0
6	11	11	0	(5,6)	0
7	17	17	0	(5,7)	2
				(6,7)	0
critical path: 1 -> 2 -> 4 -> 5 -> 6 -> 7					

b) 1 time unit (lose slack in top path, gain it in bottom path)

9.8-9
a)

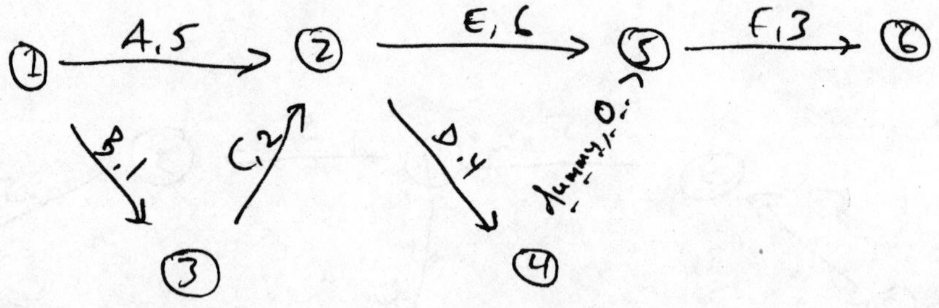

b)

event	earliest time	latest time	slack	activity	slack
1	0	0	0	A	0
2	5	5	0	B	2
3	1	3	2	C	2
4	9	11	2	D	2
5	11	11	0	E	0
6	14	14	0	F	0
				dummy	2
critical path: 1 -> 2 -> 5 -> 6 or A - E - F					

c) 6 time units (4 + slack of 2)

9.8-10 a) 9 time units (see problem 9.8-4)

b) $LT(3) = ET(6) -$ longest time from (3 to 6) $= 9-6 = \boxed{3}$

c) critical path has length 9, so event 4 is not on the critical path; since all paths from 1 to 6 through 4 require time 8, slack $= 9-8 = \boxed{1}$

9.8-11

Since $x \geq 0$, $ET(3) = 2 + x$. $ET(5) = \begin{cases} 6, & x \leq 4 \\ 2+x, & x > 4 \end{cases}$. Now $ET(6)$ is the length of the critical path. $ET(6) = \begin{cases} 2+x+y, & x+y \geq 8 \text{ and } y \geq 4 \\ 2+x+0+4, & y \leq 4 \\ 2+1+3+4, & x+y \leq 8 \end{cases}$

In order for $1 \to 2 \to 3 \to 6$ to be a critical path, we need $\boxed{x+y \geq 8 \text{ and } y \geq 4}$. Note $(x,y) = (0,8)$ is OK: in this case $1 \to 3 \to 6$ is also a critical path, but $1 \to 2 \to 3 \to 6$ still is too.

9.8-12

a) False. Events are a modelling tool; we need only activity times.

b) False. There are many counterexamples to this statement in the preceding problems. Suppose events 1 and 2 are on the critical path: ...

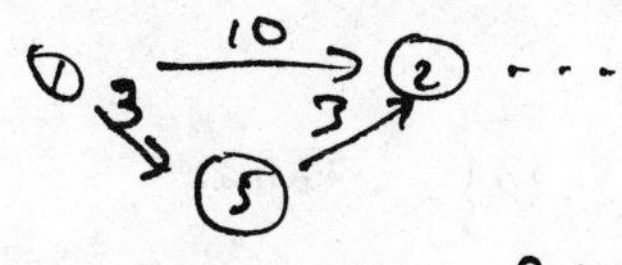

... activity (5,2) has nonzero slack.

c) True. See the description of dummy activities at the beginning of section 9.8.

9.8-13

Expected value:

$$t_e = \frac{1}{3}\left[2 \times 36 + \frac{1}{2}(30+48)\right] = 37$$

Variance:

$$\sigma^2 = \left[\frac{1}{6}(48-30)\right]^2 = 9$$

9.8-14

(a) Critical path: $1 \to 3 \to 4 \to 5 \to 7$

(b) Project Time $\sim N(19, 36)$

$P\{\text{project time} \leq 22\} = 1 - P\{\text{project time} \geq 22\} =$

$= 1 - P\{N(19,36) \geq 22\} =$

$= 1 - P\{N(0,1) \geq .5\} =$

$= 1 - .3085 = .6915$

9.8-14 Contd. c)

- Path $1 \to 2 \to 5 \to 7$

$P\{N(17,25) \le 22\} = 1 - P\{N(17,25) \ge 22\} =$

$= 1 - P\{N(0,1) \ge 1\} =$

$= 1 - .1587 = .8413$

- Path $1 \to 2 \to 4 \to 5 \to 7$

$P\{N(18,33) \le 22\} = 1 - P\{N(18,33) \ge 22\} =$

$= 1 - P\{N(0,1) \ge .70\} =$

$= 1 - .2420 = .7580$

- Path $1 \to 2 \to 4 \to 6 \to 7$

$P\{N(16,25) \le 22\} = 1 - P\{N(0,1) \ge 1.2\} = .8849$

- Path $1 \to 3 \to 4 \to 6 \to 7$

$P\{N(17,28) \le 22\} = 1 - P\{N(0,1) \ge .94\} = .8264$

- Path $1 \to 3 \to 6 \to 7$

$P\{N(18,31) \le 22\} = 1 - P\{N(0,1) \ge .72\} = .7642$

9.8-15 (a)

Activity	$t_e = \frac{1}{3}[2m + (a+b)/2]$	$\sigma = (b-a)/6$
(1,2)	32	1.333
(1,3)	27.667	1.667
(2,6)	36	3.333
(3,4)	16	0.667
(3,5)	32	0
(3,6)	53.667	5.667
(4,5)	16.667	2
(5,6)	20.333	1.667
(5,7)	34	2.667
(6,7)	17.667	3

(b) Critical path: $1 \to 3 \to 6 \to 7$

c) $P\{\text{project time} \le 100\} = P\{N(99, \frac{395}{9}) \le 100\}$

$= 1 - P\{N(0,1) \ge \frac{1}{6.62}\}$

$= 1 - P\{N(0,1) \ge 0.15\}$

$= 1 - .4404 = .5596$

9.8-16

a)

activity	$t_e = \frac{1}{3}\left[2m + \frac{(a+b)}{2}\right]$	$\sigma = \frac{b-a}{6}$	σ^2
$1 \to 2$	12	0	0
$1 \to 3$	23	4	16
$2 \to 4$	15	1	1
$3 \to 6$	27	3	9
$4 \to 5$	18	2	4
$5 \to 6$	6	2	4

b) $1 \to 2 \to 4 \to 5 \to 6$

c) $P\{\text{time} \leq 57 \text{ days}\} = P\{N(51, 9) \leq 57\}$

$= 1 - P\{N(0,1) \geq 2\}$

$= 1 - .0228 = \underline{.9772}$

d) $1 \to 3 \to 6$

e) $P\{N(50, 25) \leq 57\} = P\{N(0,1) \leq 1.4\}$

$= 1 - P\{N(0,1) \leq 1.4\}$

$= 1 - .0808 = \underline{.9192}$

f) This depends on what penalty you assign to missing the deadline. If the penalty would be very high then you'd want to proceed with the 91.92% number. If you just want to be "on the safe side" you could split the difference and use 94.82%.

9.8-17 a) True. See definitions under "The PERT Three-Estimate Approach."

b) False. Assumption 2: <u>beta</u> distribution.

c) False. <u>Maximum</u> not minimum from Assumption 4.

9.8-18 a) $S_{12} = -5000$, $S_{24} = -4000$

LP: max. $5000\,x_{12} + 4000\,x_{24}$

s.t. $5 \le x_{12} \le 8 \qquad 4 \le x_{24} \le 6$

$x_{12} \le y_2 \le y_N - x_{24} \le 12 - x_{24}$

$\Rightarrow \; x_{12} + x_{24} \le 12$

b) $S_{13} = -5000$, $S_{34} = -6000$

LP: max $5000\,x_{13} + 6000\,x_{34}$

s.t. $7 \le x_{13} \le 9 \qquad 4 \le x_{34} \le 7$

$x_{13} + x_{34} \le 12$

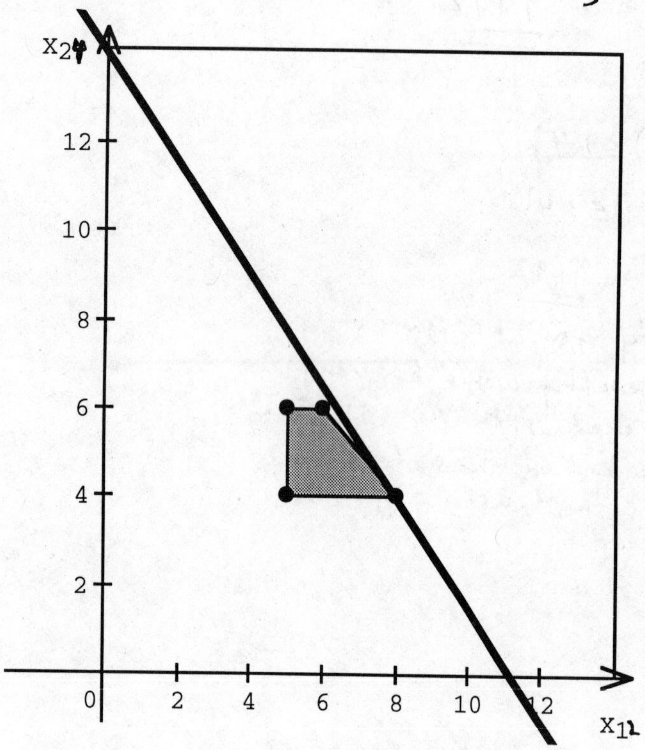

Optimal value of Z: 56,000

Optimal solution: (8,4)

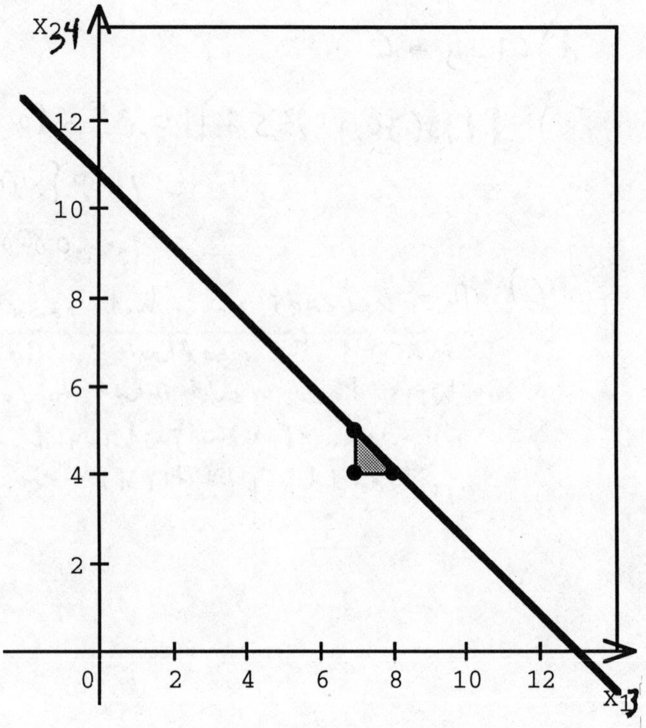

Optimal value of Z: 65,000

Optimal solution: (7, 5)

c) just combine (a) and (b): all the constraints, objective is

max. $5\,x_{12} + 4\,x_{24} + 5\,x_{13} + 6\,x_{34}$

9.8-18

d)

Activity	Activity Time	Cost
1 → 2	8	25000
2 → 4	4	24000
1 → 3	7	30000
3 → 4	5	39000

Event	Earliest Time
1	0
2	8
3	7
4	12

Total Cost = 118000

Project Completion Time = 12

e)

Activity	Activity Time	Cost
1 → 2	7	30000
2 → 4	4	24000
1 → 3	7	30000
3 → 4	4	45000

Event	Earliest Time
1	0
2	7
3	7
4	11

Total Cost = 129000

Project Completion Time = 11

Activity	Activity Time	Cost
1 → 2	8	25000
2 → 4	5	20000
1 → 3	7	30000
3 → 4	6	33000

Event	Earliest Time
1	0
2	8
3	7
4	13

Total Cost = 108000

Project Completion Time = 13

9.8-19 a) LP formulation:

objective uses slopes:

max. $5x_{12} + 10x_{13} + 4x_{24} + 6x_{25} + 8x_{34} + 6x_{35} + 5x_{46} + 7x_{56}$

s.t. (precedences) $x_{12} \le y_2$ $\quad x_{13} \le y_3$ $\quad y_2 + x_{24} \le y_4$

$y_2 + x_{25} \le y_5$ $\quad y_3 + x_{34} \le y_4$ $\quad y_3 + x_{35} \le y_5$ $\quad y_4 + x_{46} \le y_6$

$y_5 + x_{56} \le y_6$ $\quad y_6 \le T = 15$

(bounds)

$3 \le x_{12} \le 5$ $\quad 2 \le x_{13} \le 3$ $\quad 4 \le x_{34} \le 5$ $\quad 5 \le x_{46} \le 9$

$2 \le x_{24} \le 4$ $\quad 3 \le x_{25} \le 6$ $\quad 4 \le x_{35} \le 7$ $\quad 6 \le x_{56} \le 8$

$y_1, y_2, y_3, y_4, y_5, y_6 \ge 0$

9.8-19

b)

Activity	Activity Time	Cost
1 → 2	3	30
1 → 3	2	20
2 → 4	4	16
2 → 5	6	25
3 → 4	5	22
3 → 5	7	30
4 → 6	8	30
5 → 6	6	44

Event	Earliest Time
1	0
2	3
3	2
4	7
5	9
6	15

Total Cost = 217

Project Completion Time = 15

9.8-20

Activity	d_{ij}	D_{ij}	C_{ij}
1→2	28	36	1.25
1→3	22	32	1
2→6	26	46	0.5
3→4	14	18	2.5
3→5	28	36	1.25
3→6	40	74	0.294
4→5	12	24	0.833
5→6	16	26	1
5→7	26	42	0.625
6→7	12	30	0.556

$$\text{Maximize} \quad z = \sum_{(i,j)} C_{ij} x_{ij}$$

subject to

$$\left.\begin{array}{r} x_{ij} \geq d_{ij} \\ x_{ij} \leq D_{ij} \\ y_{ij} + x_{ij} - y_j \geq 0 \end{array}\right\} \text{for all activities } (i,j)$$

$$y_i \geq 0 \quad \text{for } i = 1, \ldots, 7$$

Activity	Activity Time	Cost
1 → 2	36	0
1 → 3	22	10
2 → 6	46	0
3 → 4	18	0
3 → 5	36	0
3 → 6	62	3.52941
4 → 5	18	5
5 → 6	26	0
5 → 7	42	0
6 → 7	16	7.77778

Event	Earliest Time
1	0
2	38
3	22
4	40
5	58
6	84
7	100

Total Cost = 26.30719

Project Completion Time = 100

9.8-21

a) This is just as in 9.8-19 and 9.8-20. We can do it with 10 variables ($x_{12}, x_{13}, x_{24}, x_{35}, x_{46}, x_{56}$) + ($y_2, y_3, y_4, y_5$)

$y_1 \equiv 0$, $y_6 \equiv 13$ (from theorem)

and 19 constraints

(12 for upper and lower bounds on x_{ij} variables)

(7 for precedences, including $y_2 \le y_5$)

b) Solve Automatically by the Simplex Method:

Optimal Solution

Value of the
Objective Function: Z = 285

Variable		Value
X1	x_{12}	4
X2	x_{13}	2
X3	x_{24}	4
X4	x_{35}	5
X5	x_{46}	5
X6	x_{56}	6
X7	y_2	4
X8	y_3	2
X9	y_4	8
X10	y_5	7

c)

Optimal Solution

Value of the
Objective Function: Z = 75

Variable		Value
X1	x_{12}'	0
X2	x_{13}'	1
X3	x_{24}'	2
X4	x_{35}'	2
X5	x_{46}'	1
X6	x_{56}'	0
X7		4
X8		2
X9		8
X10		7

c) let $x'_{ij} = x_{ij} - d_{ij}$

Now we need only 13 constraints (no lower bounds, just use nonnegativity)

example $x_{12}' = x_{12} - 4$

$x_{12}' \le 2$ is new constraint

Also must adjust precedence constraints:

$x_{12} \le y_2$ becomes $x_{12}' \le y_2 - 4$

or $x_{12}' - y_2 \le -4$

thus the courseware gives us

$x_{12}' = 0 \Rightarrow x_{12} = 4$

etc.

for same solution as in (b)

9.8-21

d)

Activity	Activity Time	Cost
1 → 2	4	6200
1 → 3	2	1800
2 → 4	4	5400
3 → 5	5	3600
4 → 6	5	8300
5 → 6	6	8700

Event	Earliest Time
1	0
2	4
3	2
4	8
5	7
6	13

Total Cost = 34000

Project Completion Time = 13

9.8-22

a)

Activity	d_{ij}	D_{ij}	C_{ij}
(1,2)	1	2	500
(2,3)	2	4	200
(3,4)	7	10	366.667
(4,5)	3	4	800
(4,6)	4	6	200
(4,7)	5	7	150
(5,7)	3	5	200
(6,8)	4	7	200
(7,9)	6	8	150
(8,10)	6	9	166.667
(9,11)	3	4	200
(9,12)	3	5	250
(10,13)	1	2	500
(12,13)	3	6	233.333

Maximize $Z = \sum_{(i,j)} C_{ij} x_{ij}$

subject to

$$\left.\begin{aligned} x_{ij} &\geq d_{ij} \\ x_{ij} &\leq D_{ij} \\ y_i + x_{ij} - y_j &\geq 0 \end{aligned}\right\} \text{for all activities } (i,j)$$

$$y_{13} \leq 40$$

$$y_i \geq 0 \quad \text{for } i = 1,2,\ldots,13$$

b)

Activity	Activity Time	Cost
1 → 2	2	1800
2 → 3	4	3200
3 → 4	10	6200
4 → 5	4	4100
4 → 6	6	2600
4 → 7	7	2100
5 → 7	3	2200
6 → 8	7	9000
7 → 9	6	4600
8 → 10	9	2000
9 → 11	4	1600
9 → 12	5	2500
10 → 13	2	1000
12 → 13	6	3300

Event	Earliest Time
1	0
2	2
3	6
4	16
5	20
6	22
7	23
8	29
9	29
10	38
11	33
12	34
13	40

Total Cost = 46200

Project Completion Time = 40

Chapter 10
Dynamic Programming

10.2-1 (a) Notice that the nodes of the network may be divided in "layers": the nodes in the nth layer are accessible from the origin only through nodes in the $(n-1)^{st}$ layer (i.e., the columns of nodes in the figure constitute the layers).

Stage n — n^{th} column, $n = 1, 2, 3, 4$
States — nodes of the network
x_n (decision on stage n) — immediate destination on stage n
c_{ij} — distance between nodes i and j

$f_n^*(s) = \min_{x_n} (c_{s x_n} + f_{n+1}^*(x_n))$

$f_4^*(T) = 0$

(b)

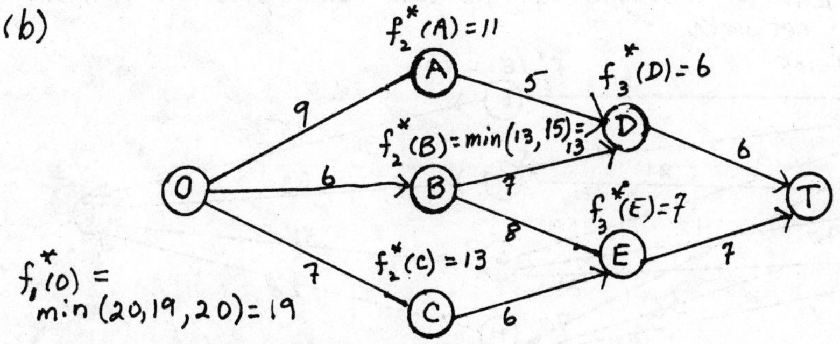

Optimal route is O-B-D-T.

(c) Number of Stages = 3

Calculations:

	S3	f3*(S3)	X3*
Node D	1	6	0
Node E	2	7	0

	S2 \ X2	f2(S2, X2): 1	2	f2*(S2)	X2*
Node A	3	11	---	11	1
Node B	4	13	15	13	1
Node C	5	---	13	13	2

	S1 \ X1	f1(S1, X1): 3	4	5	f1*(S1)	X1*
Node O	6	20	19	20	19	4

Optimal solution(s):

Optimal solution	X1*	X2*	X3*
1	4	1	0

10.2-1 (d) Applying the shortest route algorithm

n	Solved nodes directly connected to unsolved nodes	Closest connected unsolved node	total distance	nth nearest node	Distance to nth nearest node	Last connection
1	O	B	6	B	6	OB
2	O	C	7	C	7	OC
	B	D	6+7=13			
3	O	A	9	A	9	OA
	B	D	6+7=13			
	C	E	7+6=13			
4	A	D	9+5=14	D	13	BD
	B	D	6+7=13	E		CE
	C	E	7+6=13			
5	D	T	13+6=19	T	20	DT
	E	T	13+7=20			

Using the shortest route algorithm we had to do 8 sums and 6 comparisons, while using dynamic programming we did only 7 sums and 3 comparisons. The latter approach seems to be more efficient for this type of shortest route problems, i.e., shortest route problems in "layered" networks.

10.2-2.(a)

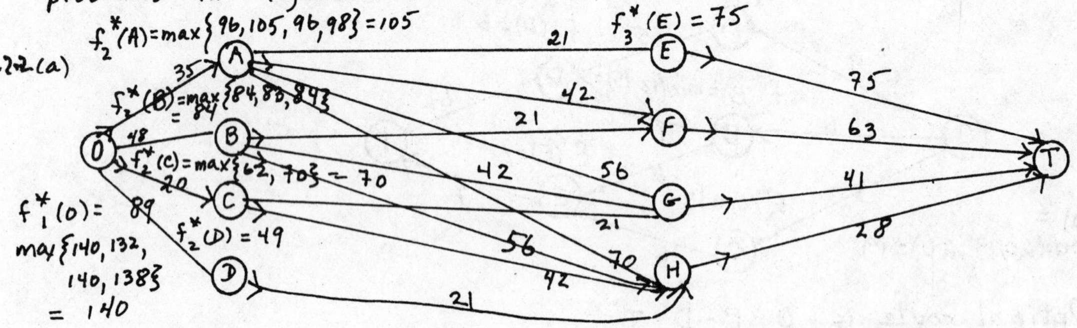

Optimal routes: O - A - F - T and 140 is the corresponding sales income.
O - C - H - T

Optimal Solution:

	Region 1	2	3
number of salespeople	1	2	3
	3	2	1

(b) Stage n — region n
state s_n — number of salespeople remaining to be allocated at stage n
x_n — number of salespeople allocated to region n
$c_n(x_n)$ — increase in sales in region n if x_n salespeople are allocated to it

INTERACTIVE DETERMINISTIC DYNAMIC PROGRAMMING ALGORITHM SOLUTION

Number of Stages = 3

Calculations:

S3	f3*(S3)	X3*
1	28	1
2	41	2
3	63	3
4	75	4

S2 \ X2	f2(S2, X2) 1	2	3	4	f2*(S2)	X2*
2	49	---	---	---	49	1
3	62	70	---	---	70	2
4	84	83	84	---	84	1,3
5	96	105	97	98	105	2

10.2-2 (b) (Continued)

S1\	1	2	3	4	f1*(S1)	X1*
\X1		f1(S1, X1)				
6	140	132	140	138	140	1,3

Optimal solution(s):

Optimal solution	X1*	X2*	X3*
1	1	2	3
2	3	2	1

10.2-3

a) stages: 5 "columns" in network

states: nodes of the network

let t_{ij} be times for activities, given:

$$f_m^*(s) = \min_{x_m} (t_{s,x_m} + f_{m+1}^*(x_m))$$

$$f_m^*(9) = 0$$

b)

$f_4^*(6) = 5$

$f_3^*(4) = \max(6,8) = 8$

$f_2^*(2) = \max(12,12) = 12$

$f_4^*(7) = 4$

$f_1^*(1) = \max(17,16) = 17$

$f_2^*(3) = 13$

$f_3^*(5) = \max(10,9) = 10$

$f_4^*(8) = 7$

Optimal path: $1 \to 2 \to 4 \to 7 \to 9$

or $1 \to 2 \to 5 \to 7 \to 9$

c) Interactive Deterministic Dynamic Programming Algorithm:

S4	f4*(S4)	X4*
1	5	1
2	4	1
3	7	1

S2\	1	2	f2*(S2)	X2*
\X2 — f2(S2, X2)				
1	12	12	12	1,2
2	13	---	13	1

S1\	1	2	f1*(S1)	X1*
\X1 — f1(S1, X1)				
1	17	16	17	1

S3\	1	2	f3*(S3)	X3*
\X3 — f3(S3, X3)				
1	6	8	8	2
2	10	9	10	1

Optimal Sol.	X1*	X2*	X3*	X4*
1	1	1	2	1
2	1	2	1	1

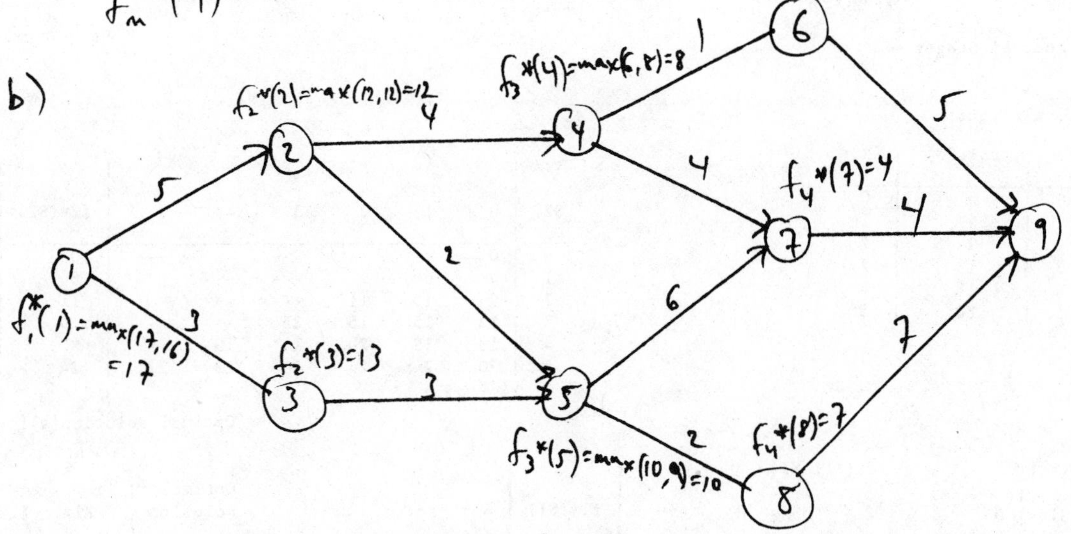

10.2-4

a) False. "preceding" should read "following": feature No. 7, section 10.2.

b) False. The optimal decision for that stage onward was found by the solution procedure. How you got there is no longer important. (feature No. 5, section 10.2, principle of optimality)

c) False. This is the principle of optimality again; need only know current state, not history.

10.3-1 Let x_n be the number of crates allocated to store n.
Let $p_n(x_n)$ be the expected profit from allocating x_n crates to store n.
Let s_n be the number of crates remaining.
Then, $f_n^*(s_n) = \max_{0 \le x_n \le s_n} [p_n(x_n) + f_{n+1}^*(s_n - x_n)]$

Number of Stages = 3

Calculations:

S3	f3*(S3)	X3*
0	0	0
1	4	1
2	9	2
3	13	3
4	18	4
5	20	5

S2 \ X2	f2(S2, X2): 0	1	2	3	4	5	f2*(S2)	X2*
0	0	---	---	---	---	---	0	0
1	4	6	---	---	---	---	6	1
2	9	10	11	---	---	---	11	2
3	13	15	15	15	---	---	15	1,2,3
4	18	19	20	19	19	---	20	2
5	20	24	24	24	23	22	24	1,2,3

S1 \ X1	f1(S1, X1): 0	1	2	3	4	5	f1*(S1)	X1*
5	24	25	24	25	23	21	25	1,3

Optimal solution(s):

Optimal solution	X1*	X2*	X3*
1	1	2	2
2	3	2	0

10.3-2 Let x_n be the number of study days allocated to course n.
Let $p_n(x_n)$ be the number of grade points expected when x_n days are spent on course n.
Let s_n be the number of study days not yet allocated.
Then, $f_n^*(s_n) = \max_{1 \le x_n \le \min(s_n, 4)} [p_n(x_n) + f_{n+1}^*(s_n - x_n)]$

Number of Stages = 4

Calculations:

S4	f4*(S4)	X4*
1	6	1
2	7	2
3	9	3
4	9	4

S3 \ X3	f3(S3, X3): 1	2	3	4	f3*(S3)	X3*
2	8	---	---	---	8	1
3	9	10	---	---	10	2
4	11	11	13	---	13	3
5	11	13	14	14	14	3,4

10.32 (continued)

S2 \ X2	f2(S2, X2) 1	2	3	4	f2*(S2)	X2*
3	13	---	---	---	13	1
4	15	13	---	---	15	1
5	18	15	14	---	18	1
6	19	18	16	17	19	1

S1 \ X1	f1(S1, X1) 1	2	3	4	f1*(S1)	X1*
7	22	23	21	20	23	2

Optimal solution(s):

Optimal solution	X1*	X2*	X3*	X4*
1	2	1	3	1

10.33 Let x_n = advertising dollars (in millions) spent on product n
Let s_n = amount of advertising budget remaining
Let $p_n(x_n)$ be the increase in sales of product n when x_n million dollars are spent on product n.
Then $f_n^*(s_n) = \max_{1 \le x_n \le s_n} \{p_n(x_n) + f_{n+1}^*(s_n - x_n)\}$

INTERACTIVE DETERMINISTIC DYNAMIC PROGRAMMING ALGORITHM SOLUTION

Number of Stages = 3

Calculations:

S3	f3*(S3)	X3*
1	6	1
2	9	2
3	13	3
4	15	4

S2 \ X2	f2(S2, X2) 1	2	3	4	f2*(S2)	X2*
2	10	---	---	---	10	1
3	13	14	---	---	14	2
4	17	17	17	---	17	1,2,3
5	19	21	20	20	21	2

S1 \ X1	f1(S1, X1) 1	2	3	4	f1*(S1)	X1*
6	28	27	28	27	28	1,3

Optimal solution(s):

Optimal solution	X1*	X2*	X3*
1	1	2	3
2	3	2	1

10.34 Let x_n = number of commercials run in area n.
Let $p_n(x_n)$ = number of votes garnered when x_n commercials are run in area n
Let s_n = number of commercials remaining
Then $f_n^*(s_n) = \max_{0 \le x_n \le s_n} \{p_n(x_n) + f_{n+1}^*(s_n - x_n)\}$

INTERACTIVE DETERMINISTIC DYNAMIC PROGRAMMING ALGORITHM SOLUTION

Number of Stages = 4

Calculations:

S4	f4*(S4)	X4*
0	0	0
1	3	1
2	7	2
3	12	3
4	14	4
5	16	5

10.34 (continued)

S3 \ X3	0	1	2	3	4	5	f3*(S3)	X3*
0	0	---	---	---	---	---	0	0
1	3	5	---	---	---	---	5	1
2	7	8	9	---	---	---	9	2
3	12	12	12	11	---	---	12	0,1,2
4	14	17	16	14	10	---	17	1
5	16	19	21	18	13	9	21	2

(f3(S3, X3))

S2 \ X2	0	1	2	3	4	5	f2*(S2)	X2*
0	0	---	---	---	---	---	0	0
1	5	6	---	---	---	---	6	1
2	9	11	8	---	---	---	11	1
3	12	15	13	10	---	---	15	1
4	17	18	17	15	11	---	18	1
5	21	23	20	19	16	12	23	1

(f2(S2, X2))

S1 \ X1	0	1	2	3	4	5	f1*(S1)	X1*
5	23	22	22	20	18	15	23	0

(f1(S1, X1))

Optimal solution(s):

Optimal solution	X1*	X2*	X3*	X4*
1	0	1	1	3

10.35 Let x_n be the number of workers allocated to precinct n.
Let $p_n(x_n)$ be the increase in the number of votes if x_n workers are assigned to precinct n.
Let s_n be the number of workers remaining.
Then $f_n^*(s_n) = \max_{1 \le x_n \le s_n} [p_n(x_n) + f_{n+1}^*(s_n - x_n)]$.

INTERACTIVE DETERMINISTIC DYNAMIC PROGRAMMING ALGORITHM SOLUTION

Number of Stages = 4

Calculations:

S4	f4*(S4)	X4*
0	0	0
1	6	1
2	11	2
3	14	3
4	15	4
5	17	5
6	18	6

S3 \ X3	0	1	2	3	4	5	6	f3*(S3)	X3*
0	0	---	---	---	---	---	---	0	0
1	6	5	---	---	---	---	---	6	0
2	11	11	10	---	---	---	---	11	0,1
3	14	16	16	15	---	---	---	16	1,2
4	16	19	21	21	18	---	---	21	2,3
5	17	21	24	26	24	21	---	26	3
6	18	22	26	29	29	27	22	29	3,4

(f3(S3, X3))

S2 \ X2	0	1	2	3	4	5	6	f2*(S2)	X2*
0	0	---	---	---	---	---	---	0	0
1	6	7	---	---	---	---	---	7	1
2	11	13	11	---	---	---	---	13	1
3	16	18	17	16	---	---	---	18	1
4	21	23	22	22	18	---	---	23	1
5	26	28	27	27	24	20	---	28	1
6	29	33	32	32	29	26	21	33	1

(f2(S2, X2))

(continued)

10.3-5

S1 \ X1	f1(S1, X1): 0	1	2	3	4	5	6	f1*(S1)	X1*
6	33	32	32	33	31	29	24	33	0,3

Optimal solution(s):

Optimal solution	Precinct 1: X1*	2: X2*	3: X3*	4: X4*
1	0	1	3	2
2	3	1	0	2
3	3	1	1	1

number of workers

10.3-6 Let x_n be the number produced in month n.
Let s_n be the inventory.
Then $f_n^*(s_n) = \min_{\max[r_n - s_n, 0] \le x_n \le m_n} [c_n x_n + d_n \max[s_n + x_n - r_n, 0] + f_{n+1}^*(\max[s_n + x_n - r_n, 0])]$

where

Month	r_n	m_n	c_n	d_n
1	2	5	5.40	.075
2	3	7	5.55	.075
3	5	6	5.50	.075
4	4	2	5.65	.075

$n = 4$:

s_4	$f_4^*(s_4)$	x_4^*
2	11.30	2
3	5.65	1
4	0.00	0

$n = 3$:

s_3 \ x_3	$f_3(s_3, x_3)$: 0	1	2	3	4	5	6	$f_3^*(s_3)$	x_3^*
1	—	—	—	—	—	—	44.45	44.45	6
2	—	—	—	—	—	38.95	38.875	38.876	6
3	—	—	—	—	33.45	38.375	33.30	33.30	6
4	—	—	—	27.95	27.875	27.80	—	27.80	5
5	—	—	22.45	22.375	22.30	—	—	22.30	4
6	—	16.95	16.875	16.80	—	—	—	16.80	3
7	11.45	11.375	11.30	—	—	—	—	11.30	2

$n = 2$:

s_2 \ x_2	$f_2(s_2, x_2)$: 0	1	2	3	4	5	6	7	$f_2^*(s_2)$	x_2^*
0	—	—	—	—	66.725	66.775	66.825	66.95	66.725	4
1	—	—	—	61.175	61.225	61.275	61.40	61.175	61.175	3
2	—	—	55.625	55.675	55.725	55.85	55.975	55.625	55.625	2
3	—	50.075	50.125	50.175	50.30	50.425	50.55	50.675	50.075	1

$n = 1$:

s_1 \ x_1	$f_1(s_1, x_1)$: 0	1	2	3	4	5	$f_1^*(s_1)$	x_1^*
0	—	—	77.525	77.45	77.375	77.30	77.30	5

Hence, produce five in period 1, one in period 2
six in period 3 and two in period 4.

10.3-7 Let x_n be the number of widgets made in week n.
Let s_n be the number of widgets on hand at the start of the week.
For week n, let c_n be the unit production cost in regular time, r_n be the maximum regular time production and m_n be the maximum total production.

10.3-7
(continued)

Let $p_n(s_n, x_n) = c_n x_n + 2000 \max(0, x_n - r_n) + 1000 \max(0, s_n + x_n - 3)$.

Then $f_n^*(s_n) = \min_{3 - s_n \le x_n \le m_n} [p_n(s_n, x_n) + f_{n+1}^*(s_n + x_n - 3)]$

n=3:

s_3	$f_3^*(s_3)$	x_3^*
0	28 000	3
1	18 000	2
2	8 000	1
$3 \le s_3$	$1000(s_3 - 3)$	0

n=2:

s_2 \ x_2	$f_2(s_2, x_2)$: 0	1	2	3	$f_2^*(s_2)$	x_2^*
0	—	—	—	60000	60 000	3
1	—	—	48000	51 000	48 000	2
2	—	38000	39000	42000	38000	1
3	28000	29000	30000	35000	28000	0
4	19100	13000	23000	37000	19000	0
5	10000	10000	25000	39000	10000	0,1
6	3000	15000	27000	41000	3000	0

n=1:

s_1 \ x_1	$f_1(s_1, x_1)$: 0	1	2	3	4	$f_1^*(s_1)$	x_1^*
2	-	66 000	61000	60000	59000	59000	4

So the optimal plan is to produce four widgets in period 1, store three of them until period 2, and produce three in period 3, with total cost $59000.

10.3-8 (a) Let x_n (in $1,000,000) be amount spent in phase n.
Let s_n (in $1,000,000) be amount yet to be spent.
Let $p_n(x_n)$ be: ① the initial share of the market attained in phase 1 when x_1 is spent in phase 1 or ② the fraction of this market share retained in phase n when x_n is spent in phase n ($n = 2$ or 3).

INTERACTIVE DETERMINISTIC DYNAMIC PROGRAMMING ALGORITHM SOLUTION

Number of Stages = 3

Calculations:

S3	f3*(S3)	X3*
0	0.3	0
1	0.5	1
2	0.6	2
3	0.7	3

S2 \ X2	f2(S2, X2): 0	1	2	3	f2*(S2)	X2*
0	0.06	---	---	---	0.06	0
1	0.1	0.12	---	---	0.12	1
2	0.12	0.2	0.15	---	0.2	1
3	0.14	0.24	0.25	0.18	0.25	2

S1 \ X1	f1(S1, X1): 1	2	3	4	f1*(S1)	X1*
4	5	6	4.8	3	6	2

Optimal solution(s):

Optimal solution	X1*	X2*	X3*
1	2	1	1

Hence, the optimal plan is to spend $2,000,000 in Phase 1 and $1,000,000 in each of Phases 2 and 3, which will result in a final market share of [ ]%.

10.3-8

b) **Phase 3:**

s	$f_3^*(s)$	x_3^*
$0 \le s \le 4$	$.6 + .07s$	s

Phase 2: $f_2(s, x_2) = (.4 + .1x_2)(.6 + .07(s - x_2))$

$$= -.007x_2^2 + (.007s + .032)x_2 + (.24 + .028s)$$

for $0 \le x_2 \le s$

$$\frac{\partial f(s, x_2)}{\partial x_2} = -.014x_2 + .007s + .032 = 0$$

$$\Rightarrow x_2 = \frac{.007s + .032}{.014} = \frac{s}{2} + \frac{16}{7}$$

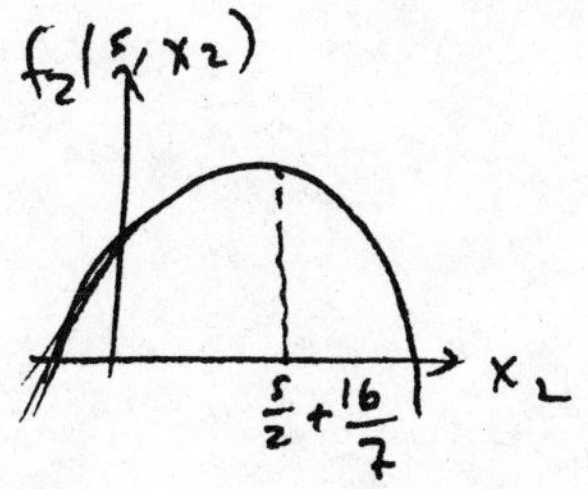

$\therefore$ If $s \le \frac{s}{2} + \frac{16}{7}$ then $x_2^* = s$ because $f_2(s, x_2)$ is strictly increasing on $[0, \frac{s}{2} + \frac{16}{7}]$ and hence is strictly increasing on $[0, s]$. If $s > \frac{s}{2} + \frac{16}{7}$ then $x_2^* = \frac{s}{2} + \frac{16}{7}$ because the unconstrained maximum is then feasible.

$\Rightarrow x_2^* = \min\{\frac{s}{2} + \frac{16}{7}, s\}$

But $0 \le s \le \frac{32}{7} \Rightarrow s \le \frac{s}{2} + \frac{16}{7}$, and $s \le 4 \le \frac{32}{7}$

$\Rightarrow x_2^* = s$ and $f_2^*(s) = .06s + .24$

Phase 1: $f_1(4, x_1) = (10x_1 - x_1^2)(.06(4 - x_1) + .24)$

$$= .06x_1^3 - 1.08x_1^2 + 4.8x_1$$

$$\frac{\partial f_1(4, x_1)}{\partial x_1} = .18x_1^2 - 2.16x_1 + 4.8 = 0$$

$$\Rightarrow x_1 = \frac{2.16 \pm \sqrt{2.16^2 - 4(.18)(4.8)}}{2(.18)} = 2.945 \text{ or } 9.055$$

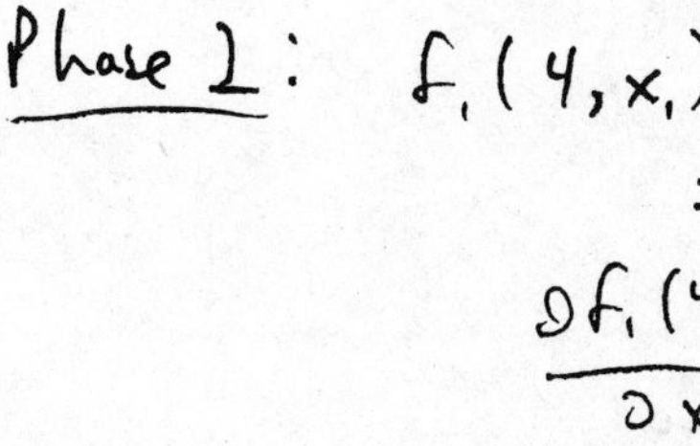

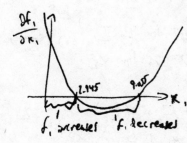

Thus, $f_1(4, x_1)$ achieves its maximum in the interval $[0, 4]$ at $x_1^* = 2.945$ with $f_1^*(4) = 6.302$. Thus, optimally \$2,945,000 is spent in Phase 1, \$1,055,000 in Phase 2 and none in Phase 3, which gives a market share of 6.302%.

10.3-9 a) stages are products

states are % capacity left, in 20% blocks,

so $s \in \{0,1,2,3,4,5\}$

Interactive Deterministic Dynamic Programming Algorithm:

S_3	$f_3^*(S_3)$	X_3^*
0	0	0
1	1	1
2	2	2
3	3	3
4	4	4
5	5	5

S_2 \ X_2	$f_2(S_2,X_2)$ 0	1	2	$f_2^*(S_2)$	X_2^*
0	0	---	---	0	0
1	1	---	---	1	0
2	2	1	---	2	0
3	3	2	---	3	0
4	4	3	4	4	0, 2
5	5	4	5	5	0, 2

S_1 \ X_1	$f_1(S_1,X_1)$ 0	1	2	3	$f_1^*(S_1)$	X_1^*
5	5	3	4	5	5	0, 3

Optimal Sol.	X_1^*	X_2^*	X_3^*
1	0	0	5
2	0	2	1
3	3	0	2

b) Product 3: $f_3^*(s_3) = s_3/20$, $x_3^* = s_3/20$

Product 2: $f_2^*(s_2) = \max\limits_{0 \le x_2 \le s_2/40} \{3x_2 - 2I_{\{x_2>0\}} + \frac{s_2 - 40x_2}{20}\}$

$I_{\{x_2>0\}} = \begin{cases} 1, & x_2>0 \\ 0, & x_2 \le 0 \end{cases}$

this is linear in x_2 except for the $I_{\{x_2>0\}}$ term; need examine only endpoints of range for x_2:

If $x_2 = 0$, we get $\frac{s_2}{20}$

If $x_2 = s_2/40$, we get $3(\frac{s_2}{40}) - 2 + \frac{s_2}{20} - 2(\frac{s_2}{40}) = \frac{3s_2}{40} - 2$

So the 'pivot' is $s_2 = 80$; $x_2^* = \begin{cases} 0, & s_2 \le 80 \\ \frac{s_2}{40}, & s_2 \ge 80 \end{cases}$

(10.3-9 cont.)(b)

$$f_2^*(s_2) = \begin{cases} s_2/20, & s_2 \le 80 \\ \frac{3s_2}{40} - 2, & s_2 \ge 80 \end{cases}$$

Product 1: $f_1^*(100) = \max_{0 \le x_1 \le 3} \{2x_1 - 3I_{\{x_1 > 0\}} + f_2^*(100 - 20x_1)\}$

Again, linear except for $I_{\{x_1>0\}}$, so look at endpoints:

$x_1 = 0$: $f_2^*(100) = 5.5$

$x_1 = 3$: $6 - 3 + f_2^*(40) = 3 + 2 = 5$

So $x_1^* = 0$, $f_1^*(100) = 5.5$

Optimal solution is to produce $2\frac{1}{2}$ units of product 2, profit: 5.5

(better than with integer restriction in (a), as we'd expect)

10.3-? Let x_n be the number of parallel units of component n that are installed.

Let $p_n(x_n)$ be the probability that the component will function if it contains x_n parallel units.

Let $c_n(x_n)$ be the cost of installing x_n units of component n.

Let s_n be the number of dollars (in hundreds of \$) remaining to be spent.

Then $f_n^*(s_n) = \max_{x_n = 0, \ldots, \min\{3, \alpha_{s_n}\}} [p_n(x_n) f_{n+1}^*(s_n - c_n(x_n))]$

where $\alpha_{s_n} = \max\{\alpha : c_n(\alpha) \le s_n, \alpha \in \mathbb{Z}\}$

$n = 4$:

s_4	$f_4^*(s_4)$	x_4^*
0, 1	0	0
2	.5	1
3	.7	2
$4 \le s_4 \le 10$	.9	3

$n = 3$:

s_3 \ x_3	$f_3(s_3,x_3) = p_3(x_3) f_4^*(s_3 - c_3(x_3))$: 0	1	2	3	$f_3^*(s_3)$	x_3^*
0	0	—	—	—	0	0
1, 2	0	0	—	—	0	0, 1
3	0	.35	0	—	.35	1
4	0	.49	0	0	.49	1
5	0	.63	.4	0	.63	1
6	0	.63	.56	.45	.63	1
7	0	.63	.72	.63	.72	2
$8 \le s_3 \le 10$	0	.63	.72	.81	.81	3

$n = 2$:

s_2 \ x_2	$f_2(s_2,x_2) = p_2(x_2) f_3^*(s_2 - c_2(x_2))$: 0	1	2	3	$f_2^*(s_2)$	x_2^*
0, 1	0	—	—	—	0	0
2, 3	0	0	—	—	0	0, 1
4	0	0	0	—	0	0, 1, 2
5	0	.21	0	0	.21	1
6	0	.294	0	0	.294	1
7	0	.378	.245	0	.378	1
8	0	.378	.343	.28	.378	1
9	0	.432	.441	.392	.441	2
10	0	.486	.441	.504	.504	3

(cont.)

10.3-10 cont.

$n=1$:

$s_1 \backslash x_1$	0	1	2	3	$f_1^*(s_1)$	x_1^*
	$f_1(s_1,x_1) = p_1(x_1)f_2^*(s_1 - c_1(x_1))$					
10	0	.22	.227	.302	.302	3

Thus, the optimal solution is $x_1^* = 3$, $x_2^* = 1$, $x_3^* = 1$, $x_4^* = 3$ yielding a system reliability of .3024.

10.3-11 Interactive Deterministic Dynamic Programming Algorithm:

S_2	$f_2^*(S_2)$	X_2^*
0	0	0
1	0	0
2	4	1
3	4	1
4	12	2

stages are x_1, x_2
state is amount of slack remaining in constraint
find $f_1^*(4)$:

$S_1 \backslash X_1$	0	1	2	3	4	$f_1^*(S_1)$	X_1^*
	$f_1(S_1, X_1)$						
4	12	6	8	0	-16	12	0

Optimal Sol.	X_1^*	X_2^*
1	0	2

10.3-12 stages x_1, x_2, x_3
state as in 10.3-11; find $f_1^*(11)$

s_3	$f_3^*(s_3)$	x_3^*
0	0	0
1	0	0
2	0	0
3	10	1
4	10	1
5	10	1
6	20	2
7	20	2
8	20	2
9	30	3
10	30	3
11	30	3

$s_2 \backslash x_2$	0	1	2	$f_2^*(s_2)$	x_2^*
	$f_2(s_2, x_2)$				
0	0	—	—	0	0
1	0	—	—	0	0
2	0	—	—	0	0
3	10	—	—	10	0
4	10	20	—	20	1
5	10	20	—	20	1
6	20	20	—	20	0,1
7	20	30	—	30	1
8	20	30	40	40	2
9	30	30	40	40	2
10	30	40	40	40	1,2
11	30	40	50	50	2

$s_1 \backslash x_1$	0	1	2	3	4	5	$f_1^*(s_1)$	x_1^*
	$f_1(s_1, x_1)$							
11	50	57	62	65	66	65	66	4

optimal solution: $x_1^* = 4$, $x_2^* = 0$, $x_3^* = 1$
$z = 66$

10.3-13 Let s_n denote the remaining slack in the constraint

$$x_1 + 2x_2 + 3x_3 \le 10$$

Let $p_n = x_n^n$

Then $f_3^*(s_3) = \max\limits_{1 \le x_3 \le s_3/3} [p_3]$ and

$$f_n^*(s_n) = \max_{1 \le x_n \le \frac{s_n}{n}} [p_n f_{n+1}^*(s_n - n x_n)] \text{ for } n = 1, 2$$

n=3:

s_3	$f_3^*(s_3)$	x_3^*
$0 \le s_3 \le 2$	—	—
$3 \le s_3 \le 5$	1	1
$6 \le s_3 \le 8$	8	2
9, 10	27	3

n=2:

s_2 \ x_2	$f_2(s_2, x_2)$: 1	2	3	4	$f_2^*(s_2)$	x_2^*
$0 \le s_2 \le 4$	—	—	—	—	—	—
5, 6	1	—	—	—	1	1
7	1	4	—	—	4	2
8	8	4	—	—	8	1
9	8	4	9	—	9	3
10	8	32	9	—	32	2

n=1:

s_1 \ x_1	$f_1(s_1, x_1)$: 1	2	3	4	5	6	$f_1^*(s_1)$	x_1^*
10	9	16	12	4	5	—	16	2

so $(x_1, x_2, x_3) = (2, 1, 2)$ is optimal with $Z = 16$.

10.3-14 Let s_n denote the slack remaining in the constraint $x_1 + x_2 \le 3$.

$$f_2^*(s_2) = \max_{0 \le x_2 \le s_2} [36x_2 - 3x_2^3]$$

$$\frac{\partial f_2(s_2, x_2)}{\partial x_2} = 36 - 9x_2^2 \begin{cases} > 0 & \text{for } 0 \le x_2 < 2 \\ = 0 & \text{for } x_2 = 2 \\ < 0 & \text{for } x_2 > 2 \end{cases} \Rightarrow x_3^* \begin{cases} s_2 & \text{for } 0 \le s_2 \le 2 \\ 2 & \text{for } 2 \le s_2 \le 3. \end{cases}$$

$$f_1^*(3) = \max_{0 \le x_1 \le 3} [36x_1 + 9x_1^2 - 6x_1^3 + f_2^*(3 - x_1)]$$

$$= \max\Big[\max_{0 \le x_1 \le 1} [36x_1 + 3x_1^2 - 6x_1^3 + 48] + \max_{1 \le x_1 \le 3} [36x_1 + 9x_1^2 - 6x_1^3 + 36(3 - x_1) - 3(3 - x_1)^3]\Big)$$

for $0 \le x_1 \le 1$ $\quad \frac{\partial f_1(3, x_1)}{\partial x_1} = -18(x_1^2 - x_1 - 2) > 0 \Rightarrow x_{1\,max} = 1$

for $1 \le x_1 \le 3$ $\quad \frac{\partial f_1(3, x_1)}{\partial x_1} = -9(x_1^2 + 4x_1 - 9) \begin{cases} > 0 & \text{for } 1 \le x_1 < -2 + \sqrt{13} \\ = 0 & \text{for } x_1 = -2 + \sqrt{13} \\ < 0 & \text{for } x_1 > -2 + \sqrt{13} \end{cases}$

$\therefore x_{1\,max} = -2 + \sqrt{13}$

Hence, $f_1(3, x_1)$ attains its maximum at $x_1 = -2 + \sqrt{13}$

summarizing:

s_1	$f_1^*(3)$	x_1^*
3	98.233	$-2 + \sqrt{13} = 1.606$

; $(x_1^*, x_2^*) = (-2 + \sqrt{13}, 5 - \sqrt{13}) = (1.606, 1.394)$; $Z^* = 98.233$

10.3-15 $f_n^*(s_n) = \min\limits_{r_n \le x_n \le 255} [100(x_n - s_n)^2 + 2000(x_n - r_n) + f_{n+1}^*(x_n)]$

n=4:

s_4	$f_4^*(s_4)$	x_4^*
$200 \le s_4 \le 255$	$100(255 - s_4)^2$	255

(Cont.)

10.3-15 (cont.)

$n=3$: $f_3(s_3,x_3) = 100(x_3-s_3)^2 + 2000(x_3-200) + 100(255-x_3)^2$

$$\frac{\partial f_3(s_3,x_3)}{\partial x_3} = 200(x_3-s_3)+2000-200(255-x_3) = 200(2x_3-(s_3+245))=0$$

$$\Rightarrow x_3 = \frac{s_3+245}{2}$$

$$200 \le \frac{s_3+245}{2} \Rightarrow s_3 \ge 155 \text{ and } \frac{s_3+245}{2} \le 255 \Rightarrow s_3 \le 265$$

Hence, $x_3 = \frac{s_3+245}{2}$ is feasible for $240 \le s_3 \le 255$ so

$$f_3^*(s_3) = 100((s_3+245)/2 - s_3)^2 + 2000((s_3+245)/2 - 200) + 100(255-(s_3+245)/2)$$

$$= 25(245-s_3)^2 + 25(265-3)^2 + 1000(s_3-155) \quad \text{or}$$

s_3	$f_3^*(s_3)$	x_3^*
$240 \le s_3 \le 255$	$25(245-s_3)^2 + 25(265-s_3)^2 + 1000(s_3-155)$	$\frac{s_3+245}{2}$

$n=2$: $f_2(s_2,x_2) = 100(x_2-s_2)^2 + 2000(x_2-240) + f_3^*(x_2)$

$$\frac{\partial f_2(s_2,x_2)}{\partial x_2} = 200(x_2-s_2)+2000-50(245-x_2)-50(265-x_2)+1000$$

$$= 100(3x_2-(2s_2+225)) = 0 \Rightarrow x_2 = \frac{2s_2+255}{3}$$

$240 \le \frac{2s_2+255}{3} \le 255 \Rightarrow 247.5 \le s_2 \le 270$. So, for

$247.5 \le s_2 \le 255$, $x_2^* = \frac{2s_2+225}{3}$ and

$$f_2^*(s_2) = 100\left(\frac{2s_2+225}{3} - s_2\right)^2 + 2000\left(\frac{2s_2+225}{3} - 240\right) + f_3^*\left(\frac{2s_2+225}{3}\right)$$

$$= \frac{100}{9}\left[(225-s_2)^2 + (255-s_2)^2 + (285-s_2)^2 + 60(3s_2-615)\right].$$

Now for $220 \le s_2 \le 247.5$, $\frac{2s_2+225}{3} \le 240 \le x_2 \Rightarrow \frac{\partial f_2(s_2,x_2)}{\partial x_2} \ge 0 \Rightarrow x_2^* = 240.$

and $f_2^*(s_2) = 100(240-s_2)^2 + 2000(240-240) + f_3^*(240) = 100(240-s_2)^2 + 101,250$ or

s	$f_2^*(s_2)$	x_2^*
$220 \le s_2 \le 247.5$	$100(240-s_2)^2 + 101,250$	240
$247.5 \le s_2 \le 255$	$\frac{100}{9}[(225-s_2)^2 + (255-s_2)^2 + (285-s_2)^2 + 60(3s_2-165)]$	$\frac{2s_2+225}{3}$

$n=1$: $f_1(255,x_1) = 100(x_1-255)^2 + 2000(x_1-220) + f_2^*(x_1)$

for $220 \le x_1 \le 247.5$ $\quad \frac{\partial f_1(255,x_1)}{\partial x_1} = 200(2x_1-485) = 0 \Rightarrow x_1^* = 242.5$

for $247.5 \le x_1 \le 255$ $\quad \frac{\partial f_1(255,x_1)}{\partial x_1} = \frac{800}{3}(x_1-240) > 0 \Rightarrow x_1^* = 247.5$

Hence, $x_1^* = 242.5$ and $f_1^*(255) = 100(242.5-255)^2 + 2000(242.5-220) + 100(240-242.5)^2 + 101,250 = 162,500$

or

s_1	$f_1^*(s_1)$	x_1^*
255	162,500	242.5

And so the optimal solution is:

Summer	242.5
Autumn	240
Winter	242.5
Spring	255

with cost = 162,500

10.3-16 let s_n be the amount of the RHS resource remaining (4 in stage 1)

$\underline{x_3}$ $\max_{0 \le x_3 \le s_3} \{4x_3 - x_3^2\}$ $\frac{\partial}{\partial x_3} = 4 - 2x_3 = 0 \Rightarrow x_3^* = 2$

$\frac{\partial^2}{\partial x_3^2} = -2 < 0$ so this is a maximum

$0 \le s_3 \le 2$: $x_3^* = s_3$, $f_3^* = 4s_3 - s_3^2$

$2 \le s_3 \le 4$: $x_3^* = 2$, $f_3^* = 4$

$\underline{x_2}$ $\max_{0 \le x_2 \le s_2} \{2x_2 + f_3^*(s_2 - x_2)\}$

$0 \le s_2 - x_2 \le 2$: $\max \{2x_2 + 4(s_2 - x_2) - (s_2 - x_2)^2\}$

$\frac{\partial}{\partial x_2} = -2 + 2s_2 - 2x_2 = 0 \Rightarrow x_2^* = s_2 - 1$

$\frac{\partial^2}{\partial x_2^2} = -2 < 0$, so maximum

Thus if we choose x_2 between $s_2 - 2$ and s_2, we should choose $x_2^* = s_2 - 1$, leaving 1 for stage 3

$f_2^* = 2(s_2 - 1) + 4(1) - (1)^2 = 2s_2 + 1$

$2 \le s_2 - x_2 \le 4$: $\max \{2x_2 + 4\}$ so let x_2 be as large as possible, i.e. $x_2^* = s_2 - 2$

$f_2^* = 2(s_2 - 2) + 4 = 2s_2 < 2s_2 + 1$,

so this is inferior to $x_2^* = s_2 - 1$, $f_2^* = 2s_2 + 1$ $\quad 1 \le s_2 \le 4$

(If $0 \le s_2 \le 1$, $x_2^* = 0$, $f_2^* = 4s_2 - s_2^2$)

$\underline{x_1}$ $\max_{0 \le x_1 \le 2} \left(2x_1^2 + f_2^*(4 - 2x_1)\right)$

$0 \le 4 - 2x_1 \le 1$: $\max.\ 2x_1^2 + 4(4 - 2x_1) - (4 - 2x_1)^2$

$= -2x_1^2 + 8x_1$

$\frac{\partial}{\partial x_1} = -4x_1 + 8 = 0 \Rightarrow x_1 = -2$

but this is infeasible

Smallest feasible x_1 is $x_1^* = 3/2$ for $f_1^* = 7\frac{1}{2}$

(since we want to be near $x_1 = -2$)

(cont.)

$1 \le 4-2x_1 \le 4$: max. $2x_1^2 + 1 + 2(4-2x_1) = 2x_1^2 - 4x_1 + 9$

$\frac{\partial}{\partial x_1} = 4x_1 - 4 = 0 \Rightarrow x_1 = 1$

$\frac{\partial^2}{\partial x_1^2} = 4 > 0$ → this is a minimum

So we look at the endpoints of the range $1 \le 4-2x_1 \le 4$

$0 \le x_1 \le 3/2$

$x_1 = 3/2 \rightarrow f_1^* = 7\frac{1}{2}$ we saw above

$x_1 = 0 \rightarrow f_1^* = 0 + 1 + 8 = 9$, best

So optimal solution: $x_1^* = 0$, $x_2^* = 3$, $x_3^* = 1$, $z = 9$

10.3-17 $\underline{\underline{x_2}}$ $\max\limits_{0 \le x_2 \le \sqrt{s_2}} x_2^2$

$\Rightarrow x_2^* = s_2$, $f_2^*(s_2) = s_2^2$

$\underline{\underline{x_1}}$ $\max\limits_{0 \le x_1 \le 2} (2x_1 + f_2^*(4-x_1^2))$

$= 2x_1 + (4-x_1^2)^2$

$= 2x_1 + 16 - 8x_1^2 + x_1^4$

$\frac{\partial}{\partial x_1} = 2 - 16x_1 + 4x_1^3 = 0$

evaluated at	$\frac{\partial}{\partial x_1} =$
0	2
1	-10
2	2
3	62

So the function has a zero between 0 and 1, and another between 1 and 2.

$\frac{\partial^2}{\partial x_1^2} = -16 + 12x_1^2$ which has zeros at $\pm \frac{2}{\sqrt{3}} \approx 1.15$ and is negative at 0, so the zero of $\frac{\partial}{\partial x_1}$ between 0,1 is a local max.

With a few quick calculations we can "zero in" on this zero as 0.1254

$\Rightarrow x_1^* = .1254$, $x_2^* = \sqrt{4 - .1254^2} = 1.996$

$f_1^* \approx 4.235$

10.3-18 $\underline{x_2}$ $\min. \ 2x_2^2$
$x_2^2 \geq s_2$

where s_2 represents the amount of the original 2 that still must be used up by x_2^2

$\Rightarrow x_2^* = \sqrt{s_2}, \ f_2^* = 2s_2$

$\underline{x_1}$ $\min_{x_1} \{x_1^4 + f_2^*(2-x_1^2)^+\}$ where $(2-x_1^2)^+$ denotes the positive part of $(2-x_1^2)$ i.e. $\max\{0, 2-x_1^2\}$

$x_1^4 + 2(2-x_1^2)$

$x_1^4 + 4 - 2x_1^2$

$\frac{\partial}{\partial x_1} = 4x_1^3 - 4x_1 = 0$

$4x_1(x_1^2 - 1) = 0$

$x_1^* = 0, 1, -1$

$\frac{\partial^2}{\partial x_1^2} = 12x_1^2 - 4$

$0 \rightarrow -$ not ok, max.
$1 \rightarrow +$ } ok, min.
$-1 \rightarrow +$

So $(x_1, x_2)^* = $ (1,1), (1,-1), (-1,1), (-1,-1) all with $\underline{Z=3}$

10.3-19 Let S_n be the slack in the constraint $f_2(S_2, X_2) = X_2$ $X_2 \leq S_2$

$\therefore f_2^*(S_2) = S_2$ and $X_2^* = S_2$

$f_1(2, X_1) = X_1^2(f_2^*(2 - X_1^2) = X_1^2(2 - X_1^*)$

$\frac{\partial f_1(2,X_1)}{\partial X_1} = 2X_1(2 - X_1^2) - X_1^2 2X_1 = 4(X_1 - X_1^3) = 0 \Rightarrow X_1 = -1, 0$ or $+1$

$\frac{\partial^2 f_1(2,X_1)}{\partial x_1^2} = 4(1 - 3x_1^2) \Rightarrow f_1$ is locally concave around $x_1 = \pm 1$

$\Rightarrow X_1 = 1$ and $X_1 = -1$ are local maxima.

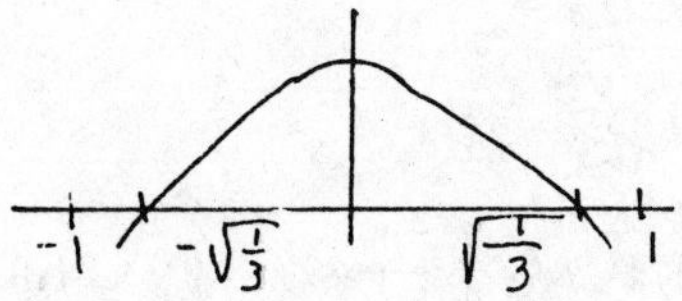

Furthermore, $f_1(2,-1) = f_1(2,1) = 1 \Rightarrow X_1 = 1$ and $X_1 = -1$ are global maxima

$\therefore X_1^* = \pm 1$ and $f_1^*(2) = 1$

$\therefore$ the optimal solutions are $(x_1^*, x_2^*) = (1,1)$ or $(-1,1)$ and the optimal objective function value is $Z=1$.

10.3-20(a) Since the only integer factors of 4 are 1, 2 and 4, let S_n be the remaining factor of 4 entering stage n.

$n=3$:

S_3	$f_3^*(S_3)$	X_3^*
1	16	1
2	32	2
4	64	3

(cont.)

10.3-20 (a) (continued)

n = 2:

s_2 \ x_2	1	2	4	$f_2^*(s_2)$	x_2^*
1	20	—	—	20	1
2	36	32	—	36	1
4	68	48	80	80	4

n = 1:

s_1 \ x_1	1	2	4	$f_1^*(s_1)$	x_1^*
4	81	44	84	84	4

And so the optimal solution is $x_1^* = 4$, $x_2^* = 1$ and $x_3^* = 1$ with a value of 84.

(b) As above let s_n = the (not necessarily integer) factor remaining at stage n.

$f_3^*(s_3) = 16 s_3$ and $x_3^* = s_3$

$$f_2^*(s_2) = \max_{1 \le x_2 \le s_2} \{4x_2^2 + f_3^*(s_2/x_2)\} = \max_{1 \le x_2 \le s_2} \{4x_2^2 + 16 s_2/x_2\}$$

$$\frac{\partial f_2(x_2, s_2)}{\partial x_2} = 4x_2 - \frac{16 s_2}{x_2^2} \quad \text{and}$$

$$\frac{\partial^2 f_2(x_2, s_2)}{\partial x_2^2} = 4 + \frac{32 s_2}{x_2^3} > 0 \quad \text{when } x_2, s_2 \ge 0$$

Thus, $f_2(x_2, s_2)$ is a convex function of x_2 when $s_2, x_2 \ge 0$

And so the maximum of f_2 must occur when $x_2 = 1$ or $x_2 = s_2$ (the endpoints of the interval over which we are maximizing) but $f_2(1, s_2) = 4 + 16 s_2$ and $f_2(s_2, s_2) = 4s_2^2 + 16$

so $f_2(1, s_2) \ge f_2(s_2, s_2) \Leftrightarrow 4 + 16 s_2 \ge 4s_2^2 + 16$

$\Leftrightarrow 4s_2^2 - 16 s_2 + 12 \le 0 \Leftrightarrow 4(s_2 - 1)(s_2 - 3) \le 0 \Leftrightarrow 1 \le s_2 \le 3$

Thus, $$x_2^* = \begin{cases} 1 & 1 \le s_2 \le 3 \\ s_2 & 3 \le s_2 \le 4 \end{cases}$$

$$f_2^*(s_2) = \begin{cases} 4 + 16 s_2 & 1 \le s_2 \le 3 \\ 4s_2^2 + 16 & 3 \le s_2 \le 4 \end{cases}$$

$$f_1^*(s_1) = \max_{1 \le x_1 \le 4} \{x_1^3 + f^*(\tfrac{4}{x_1})\}$$

$$= \max\left\{ \max_{1 \le x_1 \le \frac{4}{3}} \{x_1^3 + 4(\tfrac{16}{x_1^2}) + 16\}, \max_{\frac{4}{3} \le x_1 \le 4} \{x_1^3 + 4 + 16(\tfrac{4}{x_1})\}\right\}$$

$$\frac{\partial^2 [x_1^3 + \frac{64}{x_1^2} + 16]}{\partial x_1^2} = 6x_1 + \frac{204}{x_1^4} > 0 \quad \text{when } x_1 \ge 0 \quad \text{and}$$

$$\frac{\partial^2 [x_1^3 + 4 + \frac{64}{x_1}]}{\partial x_1^2} = 6x_1 + \frac{128}{x_1^2} > 0 \quad \text{when } x_1 \ge 0$$

and so we need only check the end points of each interval for the maximum:

10.3.20 (b) (continued)

$f_1^*(s_1) = \max\{80, 54\frac{10}{27}, 54\frac{10}{27}, 84\} = 84$ which occurs when $x_1^* = 4$, $x_2^* = 1$ and $x_3^* = 1$ as in the integer case.

10.3.21 Let s_n be the slack remaining in the constraint $x_1 - x_2 + x_3 \le 1$ entering the nth stage.

$$f_3^*(s_3) = \max_{0 \le x_3 \le s_3} \{x_3\} = s_3 \quad \text{and} \quad x_3^* = s_3$$

$$f_2^*(s_2) = \max_{x_2 \ge \max\{-s_2, 0\}} \{(1-x_2) f_3^*(s_2 + x_2)\}$$

$$= \max_{x_2 \ge \max\{-s_2, 0\}} \{(1-x_2)(s_2 + x_2)\} = \max_{x_2 \ge \max\{-s_2, 0\}} \{-x_2^2 + (1-s_2)x_2 + s_2\}$$

$\frac{\partial^2 f_2(x_2, s_2)}{\partial s^2} = -2$ and so f_2 is concave with respect to x_2 for fixed s_2, and thus, the maximum of f_2 will occur at the endpoint or when $\frac{\partial f_2}{\partial x_1} = 0$.

$$\frac{\partial f_2(x_2, s_2)}{\partial x_2} = -2x_2 + (s_2 - 1) = 0 \Rightarrow x_2 = \frac{1 - s_2}{2}$$

but x_2 must be greater than $-s_2$ for this to be the maximum

$\Rightarrow \frac{1-s_2}{2} \ge -s_2 \Rightarrow s_2 \ge -1$ and so

$$f_2^*(s_2) = \begin{cases} \frac{(1-s_2)^2}{4} + s_2 & \text{if } s_2 \ge -1 \\ 0 & \text{if } s_2 \le -1 \end{cases}$$

and

$$x_2^* = \begin{cases} \frac{1-s_2}{2} & \text{if } s_2 \ge -1 \\ -s_2 & \text{if } s_2 \le -1 \end{cases}$$

$$f_1^*(s_1) = \max_{x_1 > 0} \{x_1 f_1^*(1 - x_1)\} = \max\left\{\max_{0 \le x_1 \le 2} \left\{x_1\left(\frac{x_1^2}{4} + (1 - x_1)\right)\right\}, 0\right\}$$

$$= \max_{0 \le x_1 \le 2} \left\{\frac{x_1^3}{4} - x_1^2 + x_1\right\}$$

$$\frac{\partial\left[\frac{x^3}{4} - x_1^2 + x_1\right]}{\partial x_1} = \frac{3x_1^2}{4} - 2x_1 + 1 = 0$$

$$\Rightarrow x_1 = \frac{2 \pm \sqrt{4-3}}{\frac{3}{2}} = \frac{4}{3} \pm \frac{2}{3} \quad \text{and so}$$

this function has a relative maximum and minimum at $x_1 = \frac{2}{3}$ and $x_1 = 2$. Plotting the function we find

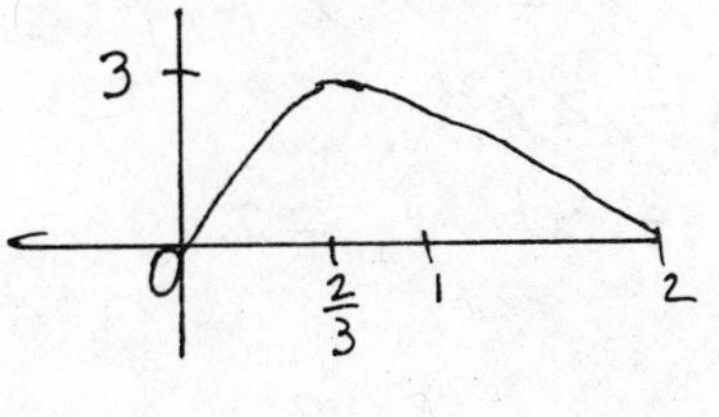

$\Rightarrow x_1^* = \frac{2}{3}$, $x_2^* = \frac{1}{3}$, $x_3^* = \frac{2}{3}$ and

$$z^* = \frac{8}{27}.$$

10.3-22 Let $s = (R_1, R_2)$ where R_i is the slack in the ith constraint.
$f_2(R_1, R_2, x_2) = 2x_2 \quad 0 \le x_2 \le \min\{\frac{R_1}{2}, R_2\}$

$n=2$:

s	$f_2^*(s)$	x_2^*
$\begin{bmatrix} R_1 \\ R_2 \end{bmatrix}$	$10\min\{\frac{R_1}{2}, R_2\}$	$\min\{\frac{R_1}{2}, R_2\}$

$n=1$: $f_1(6,8,x_1) = 15x_1 + f_2^*(6-x_1, 8-3x_1)$

$= 15x_1 + 10\min\{\frac{6-x_1}{2}, 8-3x_1\} \quad 0 \le x_1 \le \frac{8}{3}$

$0 \le x_1 \le 2 \Rightarrow \min\{\frac{6-x_1}{2}, 8-3x_1\} = \frac{6-x_1}{2}$

$\Rightarrow f_1(6,8,x_1) = 15x_1 + 30 - 5x_1 = 10x_1 + 30$

$\Rightarrow \max_{0 \le x_1 \le 2} [f_1(6,8,x_1)] = 50$ at $x_1 = 2$

$2 \le x_1 \le \frac{8}{3} \Rightarrow \min\{\frac{6-x_1}{2}, 8-3x_1\} = 8-3x_1$

$\Rightarrow f_1(6,8,x_1) = 15x_1 + 80 - 30x_2 = 80 - 15x_1$

$\Rightarrow \max_{2 \le x_1 \le \frac{8}{3}} [f_1(6,8,x_1)] = 50$ at $x_1 = 2$

$\Rightarrow f_1^*(6,8) = \max_{0 \le x_1 \le \frac{8}{3}} [f_1(6,8,x_1)] = 50$ at $x_1^* = 2$

$\Rightarrow x_1^* = 2$ and $x_2^* = 2$ is the optimal solution with objective function value $Z^* = 50$.

10.3-23 Let $s = (R_1, R_2)$ where R_i is the slack in the ith constraint
$f_2(R_1, R_2, x_2) = x_2 \quad 0 \le x_2 \le \min\{R_1, R_2\}$

s	$f_1^*(s)$	x_2^*
$\begin{pmatrix} R_1 \\ R_2 \end{pmatrix}$	$\min\{R_1, R_2\}$	$\min\{R_1, R_2\}$

$f_1(13,9,x_1) = 5x_1 + f_2^*(13-2x_1^2, 9-x_1^2, x_1)$

$= 5x_1 + \min\{13-2x_1^2, 9-x_1^2\}$

$0 \le x_1 \le 2 \Rightarrow \min\{13-2x_1^2, 9-x_1^2\} = 9-x_1^2$

$\Rightarrow f_1(13,9,x_1) = 5x_1 + 9 - x_1^2$

$\Rightarrow \max_{0 \le x_1 \le 2} \{f_1(13,9,x_1)\} = 15$ at $x_1 = 2$

$x_1 \ge 2 \Rightarrow \min\{13-2x_1^2, 9-x_1^2\} = 13-2x_1^2$

$\Rightarrow f_1(13,9,x_1) = 5x_1 + 13 - 2x_1^2$

$\Rightarrow \max_{x_1 \ge 2} \{f_1(13,9,x_1)\} = 15$ at $x_1 = 2$

10.3-23 (continued)

and so $f_1^*(13,9) = \max_{x_1 \geq 0} \{f_1(13,9,x_1)\} = 15$ at $x_1^* = 2$

$\Rightarrow x_1^* = 2,\ x_2^* = 5$ is the optimal solution with an objective function value of $Z^* = 15$.

10.3-24 Let $s = (R_1, R_2)$ where R_i is the slack in the ith constraint

$$f_3(R_1,R_2,x_3) = \begin{cases} 0 & \text{if } x_3 = 0 \\ -1 + x_3 & \text{if } x_3 > 0 \end{cases}$$

$$\Rightarrow f_3^*(R_1,R_2) = \max\{0, \max_{0 \leq x_3 \leq \frac{R_i}{2}} [-1 + x_3]\}$$

$$= \max\{0, (R_1/2) - 1\}$$

$$= \begin{cases} 0 & \text{if } R_1 \geq 2 \\ \frac{R_1}{2} - 1 & \text{if } 0 \leq R_1 \leq 2 \end{cases}$$

$$x_3^* = \begin{cases} 0 & \text{if } R_1 \geq 2 \\ \frac{R_1}{2} & \text{if } 0 \leq R_1 \leq 2 \end{cases}$$

$$f_2^*(R_1,R_2) = \max_{0 \leq x_2 \leq \min\{\frac{R_1}{3}, R_2\}} [7x_2 + f_3^*(R_1 - 3x_2, R_2)]$$

$$\Rightarrow f_2(R_1,R_2,x_2) = \begin{cases} 7x_2 & \text{if } R_1 - 3x_2 \geq 2 \\ 7x_2 + \frac{R_1 - 3x_2}{2} - 1 & \text{if } 0 \leq R_1 - 3x_2 \leq 2 \end{cases}$$

$$\Rightarrow f_2^*(R_1,R_2) = \begin{cases} \frac{17R_2}{2} + \frac{R_1}{2} - 1 & \text{if } R_2 \leq \frac{R_1 - 2}{3} \\ 7R_2 & \text{if } \frac{R_1-2}{3} \leq R_2 \leq \frac{R_1}{3} \\ \frac{7R_1}{3} & \text{if } \frac{R_1}{3} \leq R_2 \end{cases}$$

$$x_2^* = \begin{cases} R_2 & \text{if } R_2 \leq \frac{R_1 - 2}{3} \\ R_2 & \text{if } \frac{R_1-2}{3} \leq R_2 \leq \frac{R_1}{3} \\ \frac{R_1}{3} & \text{if } \frac{R_1}{3} \leq R_2 \end{cases}$$

$$f_3^*(R_1,R_2) = \max_{0 \leq x_1 \leq 5} [3x_1 + f_2^*(6 - x_1, 5 - x_1)]$$

$$= \max\left\{\max_{0 \leq x_1 \leq \frac{9}{2}} \left[3x_1 + \frac{7(6-x_1)}{3}\right], \max_{\frac{9}{2} \leq x_1 \leq 5} [3x_1 + 7(5-x_1)]\right\}$$

$$= \max\left\{\max_{0 \leq x_1 \leq \frac{9}{2}} \left[\frac{2x_1}{3} + 14\right], \max_{\frac{9}{2} \leq x_1 \leq 5} [35 - 2x_1]\right\} = 17$$

at $x_1^* = \frac{9}{2}$

$\Rightarrow x_1^* = \frac{9}{2},\ x_2^* = \frac{1}{2}$ and $x_1^* = 0$ with $Z^* = 17$

is optimal.

Let S_n be the current fortune of the player

10.4-1 Let A be the event "have \$100 at the end."

Let X_n be the amount bet at the nth match

$$f_3^*(S_3) = \max_{0 \le X_3 \le S_3} \{ P\{A \mid S_3\} \}$$

if $0 \le S_3 < 50$ $\quad f_3(S_3) = 0$

if $50 \le S_3 < 100$ $\quad f_3(S_3) = \begin{cases} 0 & \text{if } X_3 \ne 100 - S_3 \\ 1/2 & \text{if } X_3 = 100 - S_3 \end{cases}$

if $S_3 = 100$ $\quad f_3(S_3) = \begin{cases} 0 & \text{if } X_3 > 0 \\ 1 & \text{if } X_3 = 0 \end{cases}$

if $S_3 > 100$ $\quad f_3(S_3) = \begin{cases} 0 & \text{if } X_3 \ne S_3 - 100 \\ 1/2 & \text{if } X_3 = S_3 - 100 \end{cases}$

S_3	$f_3^*(S_3)$	X_3^*
$0 \le S_3 \le 50$	0	$0 \le X_3^* \le 50$
$50 \le S_3 < 100$	1/2	$100 - S_3$
100	1	0
$100 < S_3$	1/2	$S_3 - 100$

$$f_2^*(S_2) = \max_{0 \le X_2 \le S_2} \left[f^*(S_2 - X_2)\tfrac{1}{2} + f^*(S_2 + X_2)\tfrac{1}{2} \right]$$

S_2	$f_2(S_2, X_2)$	X_2
$0 \le S_2 < 25$	0	$0 \le X_2 \le S_2$
$25 \le S_2 < 50$	0	$0 \le X_2 < 50 - S_2$
	$\frac{1}{4}$	$50 - S_2 \le X_2 \le S_2$
$S_2 = 50$	$\frac{1}{4}$	$0 \le X_2 < 50$
	1/2	$X_2 = 50$
$50 \le S_2 < 75$	1/2	$0 \le X_2 \le S_2 - 50$
	1/4	$S_2 - 50 < X_2 < 100 - S_2$
	1/2	$X_2 = 100 - S_2$
	1/4	$100 - S_2 < X_2 \le S_2$
$S_2 = 75$	1/2	$0 \le X_2 < 25$
	3/4	$X_2 = 25$
	1/4	$25 \le X_2 \le 75$
$75 < S_2 < 100$	1/2	$0 \le X_2 < 100 - S_2$
	3/4	$X_2 = 100 - S_2$
	1/2	$100 - S_2 < X_2 \le S_2 - 50$
	1/4	$S_2 - 50 < X_2 \le S_2$
$S_2 = 100$	1	$X_2 = 0$
	1/2	$0 < X_2 \le 50$
	1/4	$50 \le X_2 \le 100$
$S_2 > 100$	1/2	$0 \le X_2 < S_2 - 100$
	3/4	$X_2 = S_2 - 100$
	1/2	$S_2 - 100 < X_2 \le S_2 - 50$
	1/4	$S_2 - 50 < X_2 \le S_2$

10.4-1 cont. ⇒

s_2	$f_2^*(s_2)$	x_2^*
$0 \le s_2 < 25$	0	$0 \le x_2 < s_2$
$25 \le s_2 < 50$	1/4	$20 - s_2 \le x_2^* \le s_2$
50	1/2	50
$50 < s_2 < 75$	1/2	$0 \le x_2^* \le s_2 - 50$ or $100 - s_2$
75	3/4	25
$75 < s_2 < 100$	3/4	$100 - s_2$
100	1	0
$40 < s_2$	3/4	$s_2 - 100$

$$f_1^*(75) = \max_{0 \le x_1 \le 75} \left[f_2^*(s - x_1)\tfrac{1}{2} + f_2^*(s_1 + x_1)\tfrac{1}{2} \right]$$

$$f_1(75, x_1) = \begin{cases} 3/4 & \text{if } x_1 = 0 \\ 5/8 & \text{if } 0 < x_1 < 25 \\ 3/4 & \text{if } x_1 = 25 \\ 1/2 & \text{if } 25 < x_1 \le 50 \\ 3/8 & \text{if } 50 < x_1 \le 75 \end{cases}$$

s_1	$f_1^*(s_1)$	x_1^*
75	3/4	0 or 25

policy #	x_1	won 1st bet	lost 1st bet	won 2nd bet	lost 2nd bet
1	0	25	25	0	50
2	25	0	50	0	0

10.4-2 (a) Let x_n be the investment made in year n; that is, $x_n = 0, A, B$.
Let s_n be the amount of money on hand at the begining of the year.
Let $f_n(s_n, x_n)$ be the maximum expected amount of money at the end of the third year given s_n and x_n in year n.

For $s_n \ge 5000$
$$f_n(s_n, x_n) = \begin{cases} f_{n+1}^*(s_n) & x_n = 0 \\ .3 f_{n+1}^*(s_n - 5000) + .7 f_{n+1}^*(s_n + 5000) & x_n = A \\ .9 f_{n+1}^*(s_n) + .1 f_{n+1}^*(s_n + 5000) & x_n = B \end{cases}$$

For $0 \le s_n < 5000$ $\quad f_n(s_n, x_n) = f_{n+1}^*(s_n)$ and $x_n = 0$
(one cannot invest less than 5000)

$n = 3$:

s_3	$f_3^*(s_3)$	x_3^*
$0 \le s_3 < 5000$	s_3	0
$s_3 \ge 5000$	$s_3 + 2000$	A

$n = 2$:

s_2 \ x_2	$f_2(s_2, x_2)$: 0	A	B	$f_2^*(s_2)$	x_2^*
$0 \le s_2 < 5000$	s_2	—	—	s_2	0
$5000 \le s_2 < 10000$	$s_2 + 2000$	$s_2 + 3400$	$s_2 + 2500$	$s_2 + 3400$	A
$10000 \le s_2$	$s_2 + 2000$	$s_2 + 4000$	$s_2 + 2500$	$s_2 + 4000$	A

10.4-2 cont.

$n=1$:

s_1 \ x_1	$f_1(s_1,x_1)$: 0	A	B	$f_1^*(s_1)$	x_1^*
5000	8400	9800	8150	9800	A

The optimal policy is to always invest in A with an expected fortune after three years of \$9800.

(b) Let x_n and s_n be as in part (a).
Let $f_n(s_n,x_n)$ be the maximum probability of having at least \$10,000 after 3 years given s_n and x_n.

$n=3$:

s_3 \ x_3	$f_3(s_3,x_3)$: 0	A	B	$f_3^*(s_3)$	x_3^*
$0 \le s_3 < 5000$	0	—	—	0	0
$5000 \le s_3 < 10000$	0	.7	.1	.7	A
$10000 \le s_3 < 15000$	1	.7	1	1	0 or B
$15000 \le s_3$	1	1	1	1	0, A or B

$n=2$:

s_2 \ x_2	$f_2(s_2,x_2)$: 0	A	B	$f_2^*(s_2)$	x_2^*
$0 \le s_2 < 5000$	0	—	—	0	0
$5000 \le s_2 < 10000$	.7	.7	.73	.73	B
$10000 \le s_2$	1	.73	1	1	0 or B

$n=1$:

s_1 \ x_1	$f_1(s_1,x_1)$: 0	A	B	$f_1^*(s_1)$	x_1^*
5000	.73	.7	.757	.757	B

Hence, the optimal policies are (using the numbers on the arcs to represent the return on the investment indicated at the nodes).

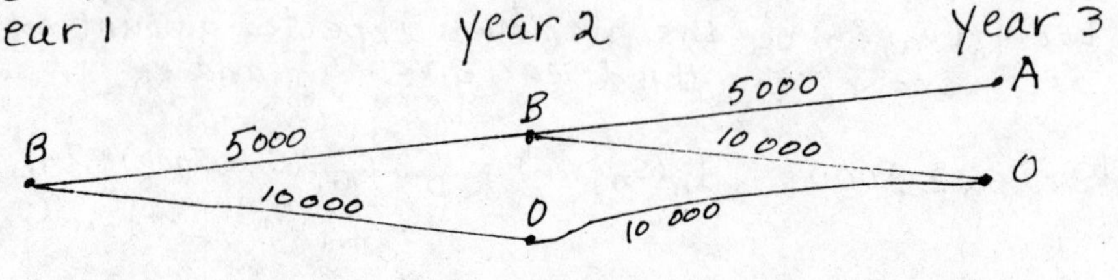

or

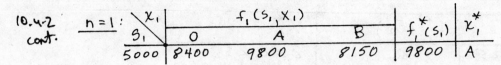

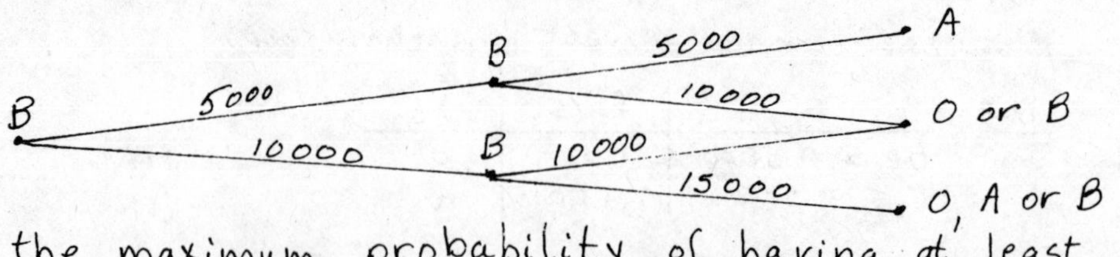

and the maximum probability of having at least \$10,00 at the end of three years is .757.

10.4-3 $f_n(1,x_n) = K + x_n + (\frac{1}{3})^{x_n} f_{n+1}^*(1) + [1-(\frac{1}{3})^{x_n}] f_{n+1}^*(0)$
$= K + x_n + (\frac{1}{3})^{x_n} f_{n+1}^*(1)$ since $f_{n+1}^*(0) = 0$
where $f_3^*(1) = 16$, $f_3^*(0) = 0$ and $K = \begin{cases} 0 & \text{if } x_n = 0 \\ 3 & \text{if } x_n > 0 \end{cases}$

10.4-3 cont.

$\underline{n=2}$:

$s_2 \backslash x_2$	0	1	2	3	4	$f_2^*(s_2)$	x_2^*
						0	0

$\underline{n=1}$:

$s_1 \backslash x_1$	$f_1(s_1,x_1)$: 0	1	2	3	4	$f_1^*(s_1)$	x_1^*
1	6.77	6.26	5.75	6.25	7.08	5.75	2

The optimal policy is to produce two on the first run and if none are acceptable, produce two on the second run. The minimum expected cost = \$5.75.

10.4-4 $f_n^*(s_n) = \max_{0 \le x_n} \{ \frac{1}{3} f_{n+1}^*(s_n - x_n) + \frac{2}{3} f_{n+1}^*(s_n + x_n) \}$

where $f_6^*(s_6) = 0$ for $s_6 < 5$ and $f_6^*(s_6) = 1$ for $s_6 \ge 5$

$\underline{n=5}$:

s_5	$f_5^*(s_5)$	x_5^*
0	0	0
1	0	0
2	0	0
3	$\frac{2}{3}$	$x_5^* \ge 2$
4	$\frac{2}{3}$	$x_5^* \ge 1$
$s_5 \ge 5$	1	$x_5^* \le s_5 - 5$

$\underline{n=4}$:

$s_4 \backslash x_4$	$f_4(s_4,x_4)$: 0	1	2	3	4	$f_4^*(s_4)$	x_4^*
0	0	—	—	—	—	0	0
1	0	0	—	—	—	0	0
2	0	4/9	4/9	—	—	4/9	1,2
3	2/3	4/9	2/3	2/3	—	2/3	0,2,3
4	2/3	8/9	2/3	2/3	2/3	8/9	1
$s_4 \ge 5$	1	—	—	—	—	1	$\le s_4 - 5$

$\underline{n=3}$:

$s_3 \backslash x_3$	$f_3(s_3,x_3)$: 0	1	2	3	4	$f_3^*(s_3)$	x_3^*
0	0	—	—	—	—	0	0
1	0	8/27	—	—	—	8/27	1
2	4/9	4/9	16/27	—	—	16/27	2
3	2/3	20/27	2/3	2/3	—	20/27	1
4	8/9	8/9	22/27	2/3	2/3	22/27	0,1
$s_3 \ge 5$	1	—	—	—	—	1	$\le s_3 - 5$

$\underline{n=2}$:

$s_2 \backslash x_2$	$f_2(s_2,x_2)$: 0	1	2	3	4	$f_2^*(s_2)$	x_2^*
0	0	—	—	—	—	0	0
1	8/27	32/81	—	—	—	32/81	1
2	16/27	48/81	48/81	—	—	48/81	0,1,2
3	20/27	64/81	62/81	2/3	—	64/81	1
4	24/27	74/81	70/81	62/81	2/3	74/81	1
$s_2 \ge 5$	1	—	—	—	—	1	$\le s_2 - 5$

$\underline{n=1}$:

$s_1 \backslash x_1$	$f_1(s_1,x_1)$: 0	1	2	$f_1^*(s_1)$	x_1^*
2	48/81	160/243	124/243	160/243	1

So Probability{winning bet using above policy} $= \frac{160}{243} = .658$

10.4-5 Let $x_n = a$ and $x_n = d$ denote the decision to advertise or discontinue the product, respectively, for quarter n ($n = 1, 2, 3$).

Let s_n denote the level of sales above ($s_n \ge 0$) or below ($s_n \le 0$) the breakeven point (in millions) for quarter ($n-1$).

Let $f_n(s_n, x_n)$ denote the maximum expected discounted profit (in millions) from the beginning of period n onward given state s_n and decision x_n.

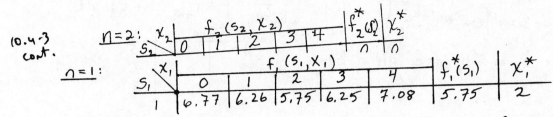

10.4-5 cont. Then $f_n(s_n, x_n) =$

$$-30 + 5\left[s_n + \frac{1}{b_n - a_n}\int_{a_n}^{b_n} t\,dt\right] + \frac{1}{b_n - a_n}\int_{a_n}^{b_n} f^*_{n+1}(s+t)\,dt$$

where a_n and b_n are given by

n	a_n	b_n
1	1	5
2	0	4
3	-1	3

Hence, for $1 \le n \le 3$, $f_n(s_n, a) = -30 + 5\left[s_n + \frac{a_n + b_n}{2}\right] + \frac{1}{b_n - a_n}\int_{a_n}^{b_n} f^*_{n+1}(s_n + t)\,dt$

$f_n(s_n, d) = -20$ and the process stops.

Then $f^*_n(s_n) = \max\{f_n(s_n, a), f_n(s_n, d)\}$ and $f^*_4(s_4) = \begin{cases} -20 & \text{if } 0 > s_4 \\ 40 s_4 & \text{if } s_4 \ge 0 \end{cases}$

n=3:

$f_3(s_3, d) = -20$

$f_3(s_3, a) = -30 + 5(s_3 + 1) + \frac{1}{4}\int_{-1}^{3} f^*_4(s_3 + t)\,dt$

For $-3 \le s_3 \le 1$, $f_3(s_3, a) = -30 + 5(s_3 + 1) + \frac{1}{4}\left[\int_{-1}^{-s_3} -20\,dt + \frac{1}{4}\int_{-s_3}^{3} 40(s_3 + t)\,dt\right]$

$$= 5(s_3 + 4)^2 - 65$$

For $1 \le s_3 \le 5$, $f_3(s_3, a) = -30 + 5(s_3 + 1) + \frac{1}{4}\int_{-1}^{3} 40(s_3 + t)\,dt = 15 + 45 s_3$.

Hence, for $-3 \le s_3 \le 1$, $f^*_3(s_3) = \max\{-20, 5(s_3 + 4)^2 - 65\}$

$$= \begin{cases} -20 & \text{if } -3 \le s_3 \le -1, \quad x^*_3 = d \\ 5(s_3 + 4)^2 - 65 & \text{if } -1 \le s_3 \le 1, \quad x^*_3 = a \end{cases}$$

summarizing:

s_3	$f^*_3(s_3)$	x^*_3
$-3 \le s_3 \le -1$	-20	d
$-1 < s_3 \le 1$	$5(s_3 + 4)^2 - 65$	a
$1 < s_3 \le 5$	$15 + 45 s_3$	a

n=2: for $-3 \le s_2 \le -1$,

$$f_2(s_2, a) = -30 + 5(s_2 + 2) + \frac{1}{4}\left[\int_{0}^{-s_2 - 1} -20\,dt + \int_{-s_2 - 1}^{1 - s_2} (5(s_2 + t + 4)^2 - 65)\,dt + \int_{1 - s_2}^{4} (45(s_2 + t) + 15)\,dt\right]$$

$$= \frac{5}{4}\left(\frac{9}{2}s_2^2 + 47 s_2 + \frac{427}{6}\right)$$

Since $f_2(-3, a) < f_2(s_2, d) = -20 < f_2(-1, a)$, we must find where

$f_2(s_2, a) = f_2(s_2, d)$, that is, $\frac{5}{4}\left(\frac{9}{2}s_2^2 + 47 s_2 + \frac{427}{6}\right) = -20$.

$$s^*_2 = \frac{-47 + 8\sqrt{10}}{9} \doteq -2.411$$

10.4-5 cont.

For $-1 \le S_2 \le 1$, $f_2(S_2, a) = -30 + 5(S_2+2) + \frac{1}{4}\left[\int_0^{1-S_2} (5(S_2+t+4)^2 - 65)\,dt + \int_{1-S_2}^{4} (45(S_2+t)+15)\,dt\right]$

$= \frac{5}{4}\left(-(S_2+4)^3/3 + 9(S_2+4)^2/2 + 20S_2 + 103/6\right)$

Since $f_2(-1, a) = 35\ 5/6$ and $f_2(S_2, a)$ is an increasing function of S_2 over $-1 \le S_2 \le 1$, $x_2^* = a$ is the optimal decision in this interval.

S_2	$f_2^*(S_2)$	x_2^*
$-3 \le S_2 \le S_2^*$	-20	d
$S_2^* < S_2 \le -1$	$5/4\left(\frac{9}{2}S_2^2 + 47S_2 + \frac{427}{6}\right)$	a
$-1 < S_2 \le 1$	$5/4\left[-(S_2+4)^3/3 + \frac{9}{2}(S_2+4)^2 + 20S_2 + \frac{103}{6}\right]$	a

n=1:

$f_1(-20, d) = -20$

$f_1(-20, a) = -30 + 5(-4+3) + \frac{1}{4}\int_1^5 f_2^*(-4+t)\,dt$

$= -35 + \frac{1}{4}\left[\int_1^{S_2^*+4} -20\,dt + \frac{5}{4}\int_{S_2^*+4}^{3} \left(\frac{9}{2}(-4+t)^2 + 47(-4+t) + \frac{427}{6}\right)dt\right]$

$+ \frac{1}{4}\left[\frac{5}{4}\int_3^5 \left(\frac{t^3}{3} + \frac{9t^2}{2} + 20(-4+t) + \frac{103}{6}\right)dt\right] = 4.77$

Summarizing:

S_1	$f_1^*(S_1)$	x_1^*
-4	4.77	a

So the optimal policy is:

First quarter – advertise

Second quarter – if $S_2 \le S_2^*$, discontinue. If $S_2 > S_2^*$, advertise

Third quarter – if $S_3 \le -1$, discontinue. If $S > -1$, advertise.

where $S_2^* \doteq -2.411$.

Chapter 11
Game Theory

11.1-1 Let player I be the labor union with strategy i being to decrease its wage demand by 10(i-1)¢.
Let player II be the management with strategy i being to increase its offer by 10(i-1)¢.

The payoff matrix is:

I \ II	1	2	3	4	5	6
1	1.35	1.2	1.3	1.4	1.5	1.6
2	1.5	1.35	1.3	1.4	1.5	1.6
3	1.4	1.4	1.35	1.4	1.5	1.6
4	1.3	1.3	1.3	1.35	1.5	1.6
5	1.2	1.2	1.2	1.2	1.35	1.6
6	1.1	1.1	1.1	1.1	1.1	1.35

11.1-2 Label the products respectively A and B. Then the strategies for each manufacturer are:

1- Normal development of both products
2- Crash development of product A
3- Crash development of product B

Let $p_{ij} = \dfrac{(\%\text{increase to I from A}) + (\%\text{increase to I from B})}{2}$

The payoff matrix then becomes

I \ II	1	2	3	Row min
1	8	10	10	8 ← max
2	4	-4	13	-4
3	4	13	-4	-4
Column Maximum:	8 ↑ min	13	13	

Hence, both manufacturers should use normal development and I will increase his share of the market by 8%.

11.1-3 Each player has the same strategy set. A strategy must specify the first chip chosen and, for each possible first choice by the opponent, choices of second and third chips. For example, a typical strategy is "Pick i first. If opponent chooses W, pick j_1 and k_1. If opponent chooses R, pick j_2 and k_2. If opponent chooses B, pick j_3 and k_3" where, for $\ell = 1,2,3$ $\{i, j_\ell, k_\ell\} = \{W, R, B\}$. There are 3 choices for i and, for each i, 8 choices of "conditional" strategies, forming 24 distinct strategies. Payoffs are determined from the table (all net payoffs are either \$120, 0 or -120, depending on whether player I wins 3 times, wins 1 time and ties 1 time or loses 3 times).

11.2-1 a) Strategies 4, 5 and 6 of player II are dominated by strategy 3.
Strategies 4, 5 and 6 of player I are dominated by strategy 3.
Strategy 1 of player II is dominated by strategy 3.
Strategy 1 of player I is dominated by strategy 3.
Strategy 2 of player II is dominated by strategy 3.
Strategy 2 of player I is dominated by strategy 3.
Therefore, the optimal strategy is for the labor union to decrease its demand by 20¢ and for management to increase its offer by 20¢.
A wage of \$1.35 will be decided.

b)

		II: 1	2	3	4	5	6	Row Minimum
I	1	1.35	1.2	1.3	1.4	1.5	1.6	1.2
	2	1.5	1.35	1.3	1.4	1.5	1.6	1.3
	3	1.4	1.4	1.35	1.4	1.5	1.6	1.35 ← max
	4	1.3	1.3	1.3	1.35	1.5	1.6	1.3
	5	1.2	1.2	1.2	1.2	1.35	1.6	1.2
	6	1.1	1.1	1.1	1.1	1.1	1.35	1.1
Column Maximum		1.5	1.4	1.35 (↑ min)	1.4	1.5	1.6	

11.2-2 (a) Strategy 3 of player I is dominated by strategy 2.
Strategy 3 of player II is dominated by strategy 1.
Strategy 1 of player I is dominated by strategy 2.
Strategy 2 of player II is dominated by strategy 1.
Therefore, the optimal strategy is for player I to choose strategy 2 and player II to choose strategy 1 resulting in a payoff of 1 to player I.

11.2-2 (b) Strategy 1 of player II is dominated by strategy 3.
Strategy 2 of player I is dominated by both strategies 1 and 3.
Strategy 2 of player II is dominated by strategy 3.
Strategy 1 of player I is dominated by strategy 3.
Therefore, the optimal strategy is for player I to choose strategy 3 and player II to choose strategy 3 resulting in a payoff of 1 to player II.

11.2-3 Strategy 1 of player II is dominated by strategy 3.
Strategy 4 of player II is dominated by strategy 2.
Strategies 1 and 2 of player I are dominated by strategy 3.
Strategy 2 of player II is dominated by strategy 3.
Therefore, the optimal strategy is for player I to choose strategy 3 and player II to choose strategy 3 resulting in a payoff of 1 to player II.

11.2-4

	II: 1	2	3	Row Minimum
I 1	1	-1	1	-1
I 2	-2	0	3	-2
I 3	3	1	2	1 ← max
Column Maximum	3	1 (↑ min)	3	

v = 1, player I uses strategy 3 and player II uses strategy 2.

11.2-5

	II: 1	2	3	4	Row Minimum
I 1	3	-3	-2	-4	-4
I 2	-4	-2	-1	1	-4
I 3	1	-1	2	0	-1 ← max
Column Maximum	3	-1 (↑ min)	2	1	

v = -1, player I uses strategy 3 and player II uses strategy 2.

11.2-6 (a)

	II: 1	2	3	Row Minimum
I 1	2	3	1	1 ← max
I 2	1	4	0	0
I 3	3	-2	-1	-2
Column maximum	3	4	1 (↑ min)	

v = 1, player I uses strategy 1 and player II uses strategy 3.

11.2-6 (b) Strategy 1 of player II is dominated by strategy 3.
Strategy 3 of player I is dominated by strategies 1 and 2.
Strategy 2 of player II is dominated by strategy 3.
Strategy 2 of player I is dominated by strategy 1.
Therefore, the optimal strategy is for player I to choose strategy 1 and player II to choose strategy 3 resulting in a payoff of 1 to player I.

11.2-7 (a)

I \ II	1	2	3	Row Minimum
1	7	-1	3	-1
2	1	0	2	0 ← max
3	-5	-3	1	-5
Column Maximum:	7	0	3	
		↑ min		

Hence, $v=0$ with Politician I using Issue 2 and Politician II using Issue 2.

(b) Let $p_{ij} = P\{$winning or tying election for Politician I$\}$
Then the payoff matrix becomes

I \ II	1	2	3
1	1	0	3/5
2	1/5	0	2/5
3	0	0	1/5

Strategy 3 of Politician I dominated by strategy 2.
Strategy 2 of Politician I dominated by strategy 1.
Strategies 1 and 3 of Politician II dominated by strategy 2.
Hence, eliminating dominated strategies gives $v=0$ with Politician I using Issue 1 and Politician II using Issue 2. Therefore, Politician II can prevent Politician I from winning or tying.

(c) Let $p_{ij} = \begin{cases} 1 & \text{if Politician I will win or tie} \\ 0 & \text{if Politician II will win} \end{cases}$

Then the payoff matrix becomes

I \ II	1	2	3
1	1	0	0
2	0	0	0
3	0	0	0

(cont'd)

11.2-7 (c) cont. Min [Column maxima] = 0 = Max [Row minima].
Hence the minimax criterion yields $v=0$ (Politician I cannot win). Politician I can use any issue and Politician II can use Issue 2 or 3. However, since Issue 1 offers Politician I his only chance of winning, he should use that and hope Politician II makes an error and also uses Issue 1.

11.2-8 Advantages: It provides the best possible guarantee on what the worst outcome can be, regardless of how skillfully the opponent plays the game. Therefore it reduces the risk of very undescrable outcomes to a minimum.

Disadvantages: It is a very conservative approach, and, therefore, it may yield far from the best attainable results if the opponent is not skillful.

11.3-1 (a)

Strategies for player I	Strategies for player II
1- Pass on heads or tails	1- If player I bets, call.
2- Bet on heads or tails	2- If player I bets, pass
3. Pass on heads, bet on tails	
4- Pass on tails, bet on heads	

b)

I \ II	1	2
1	-5	-5
2	0	5
3	-15/2	0
4	5/2	0

Strategies 1 and 3 of player I are dominated by strategy 2. Eliminating the dominated strategies we obtain the payoff table:

I \ II	1	2
2	0	5
4	5/2	0

11.3-1 (c) The payoff matrix is:

I \ II	1	2	Row minimum
1	-5	-5	-5
2	0	5	0 ← max
3	-15/2	0	-15/2
4	5/2	0	0 ← max
Column maximum	5/2 ↑ min	5	

Min[Column maxima] ≠ Max[Row minima], therefore there is no saddle point.

If either player chose a pure strategy, the other player could adjust his strategy in such a way as to cause the first player to want to change his strategy, too. Mixed strategies are needed.

d) expected payoff $= p_{21} x_2 y_1 + p_{22} x_2 y_2 + p_{41} x_4 y_1 + p_{42} x_4 y_2$,

where $x_2 + x_4 = 1$, $y_1 + y_2 = 1$ are the probabilities of each player using each non-dominated strategy (from (b)).

case (i): $y_1 = 1, y_2 = 0$ $\qquad \frac{5}{2} x_4 = \frac{5}{2}(1 - x_2)$

(ii): $y_1 = 0, y_2 = 1$ $\qquad 5 x_2 = 5(1 - x_4)$

(iii): $y_1 = \frac{1}{2} = y_2$ $\qquad 5 x_2 (\frac{1}{2}) + 5/2\, x_4 (\frac{1}{2})$

$= \frac{5}{2} x_2 + \frac{5}{4}(1 - x_2)$

$= \frac{5}{4} x_2 + \frac{5}{4}$

11.4-1

(y_1, y_2)	Expected Payoff
(1, 0)	$5/2(1 - x_2)$
(0, 1)	$5 x_2$

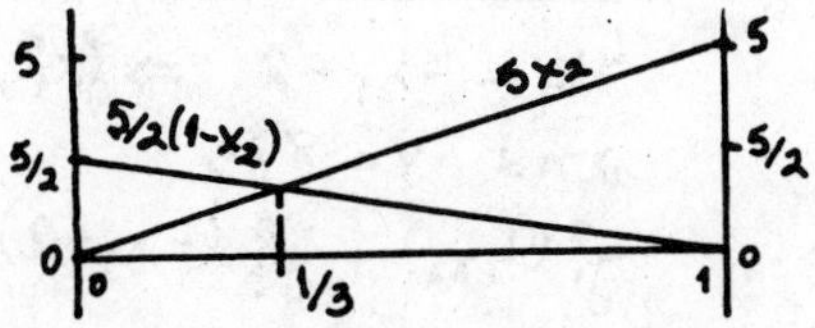

$5/2(1 - x_2) = 5 x_2 \Rightarrow (x_1^*, x_2^*, x_3^*, x_4^*) = (0, 1/3, 0, 2/3)$ and $v = 5/3$

$y_1^*(5/2)(1 - x_2) + y_2^*(5 x_2) = 5/3$ for $0 \le x_2 \le 1 \Rightarrow \frac{5}{2} \cdot y_1^* = 5/3$

$5\, y_2^* = 5/3$

$\Rightarrow (y_1^*, y_2^*) = (2/3, 1/3)$

11.4-2

(y_1, y_2)	Expected Payoff
$(1,0)$	$3x_1 - 1(1-x_1) = 4x_1 - 1$
$(0,1)$	$-2x_1 + 2(1-x_1) = -4x_1 + 2$

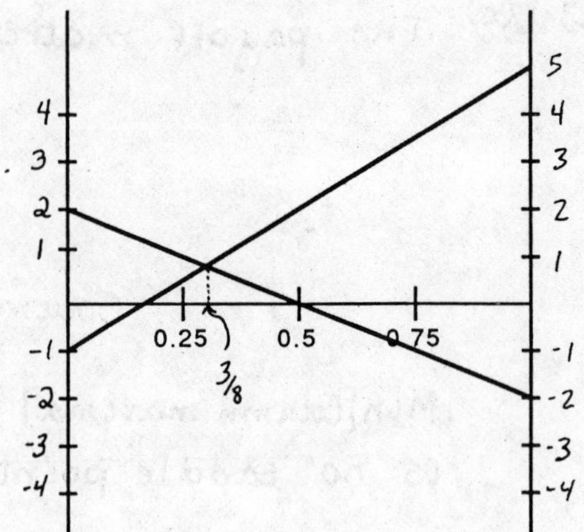

$4x_1 - 1 = -4x_1 + 2 \Rightarrow x_1^* = 3/8,\ x_2^* = 5/8$

$v = 4(3/8) - 1 = 1/2$

$$\left.\begin{array}{l} 3y_1^* - 2y_2^* = 1/2 \\ -y_1^* + 2y_2^* = 1/2 \end{array}\right\} \Rightarrow y_1^* = y_2^* = 1/2$$

The payoff matrix for player II is:

		II: 1	II: 2
I	1	-3	2
	2	1	-2

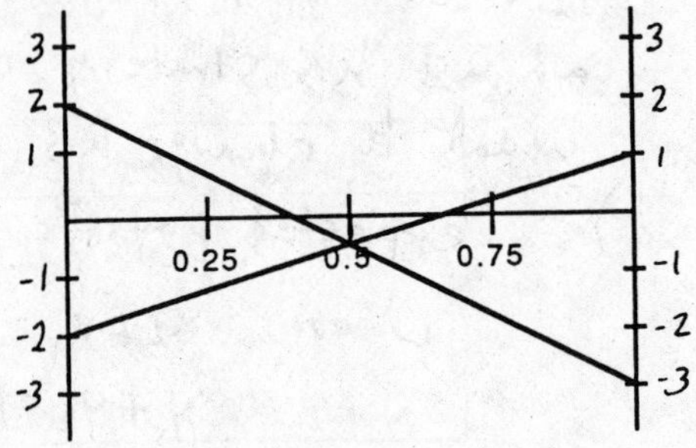

(x_1, x_2)	Expected Payoff
$(1,0)$	$-3y_1 + 2(1-y_1) = -5y_1 + 2$
$(0,1)$	$y_1 - 2(1-y_1) = 3y_1 - 2$

$-5y_1 + 2 = 3y_1 - 2 \Rightarrow y_1^* = \frac{1}{2},\ y_2^* = 1/2$

11.4-3 (a)

(y_1, y_2, y_3)	Expected payoff
$(1, 0, 0)$	$4x_1$
$(0, 1, 0)$	$3x_1 + (1-x_1) = 2x_1 + 1$
$(0, 0, 1)$	$x_1 + 2(1-x_1) = -x_1 + 2$

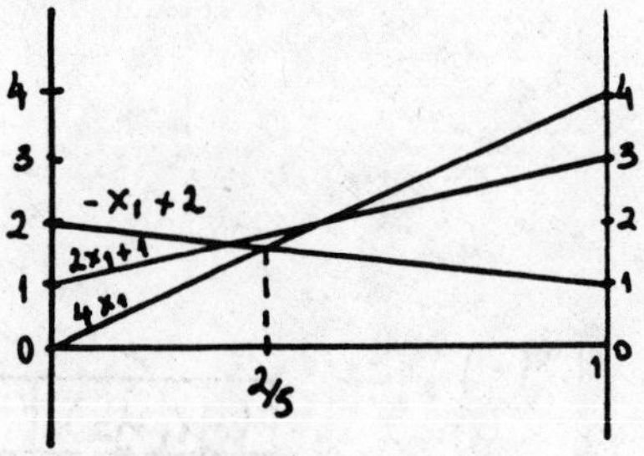

$4x_1 = -x_1 + 2 \Rightarrow (x_1^*, x_2^*) = (2/5, 3/5)$

and $v = 8/5$

$y_1^*(4x_1) + y_3^*(-x_1+2) = 8/5$ for $0 \le x_1 \le 1 \Rightarrow$ $2y_3^* = 8/5$

$4y_1^* + y_3^* = 8/5$

$\Rightarrow (y_1^*, y_2^*, y_3^*) = (1/5, 0, 4/5)$

11.4-3 (b) Strategy 3 of player II is dominated by strategy 1 reducing the table to:

		II 1	2
	1	1	-1
I	2	0	4
	3	3	-2
	4	-3	6

(x_1, x_2, x_3, x_4)	Expected Payoff
(1, 0, 0, 0)	$y_1 - (1-y_1) = 2y_1 - 1$
(0, 1, 0, 0)	$4(1-y_1) = -4y_1 + 4$
(0, 0, 1, 0)	$3y_1 - 2(1-y_1) = 5y_1 - 2$
(0, 0, 0, 1)	$-3y_1 + 6(1-y_1) = -9y_1 + 6$

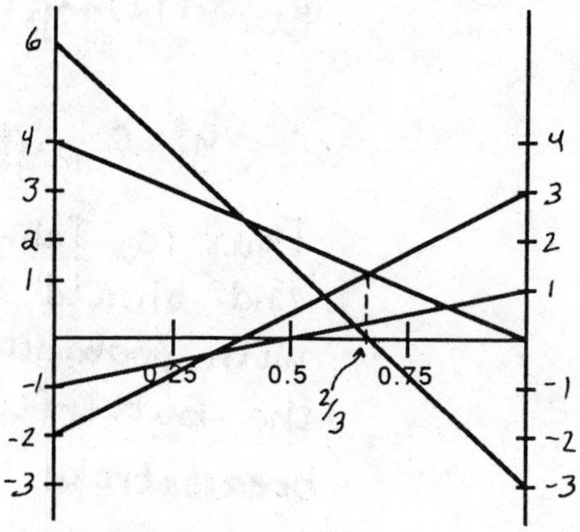

$y_1^* = 2/3 \quad y_2^* = 1/3$

$v = 4/3$

11.4-4 (a)

Strategies for A.J. Team	Strategies for G.N. Team
1. John does not swim butterfly	1. Mark does not swim butterfly
2. John does not swim backstroke	2. Mark does not swim backstroke
3. John does not swim breaststroke	3. Mark does not swim breaststroke

Let the payoff entries be the total points won in all three events when a given pair of strategies are used by the teams. Then the payoff matrix becomes:

A.J. \ G.N.	1	2	3
1	14	13	12
2	13	12	12
3	12	12	13

Strategy 2 of A.J. Team dominated by strategy 1.
Strategy 1 of G.N. Team dominated by strategy 2

Final payoff table

A.J. \ G.N.	2	3
1	13	12
3	12	13

(y_2, y_3)	Expected Pay off
(1, 0)	$13x_1 + 12(1-x_1) = x_1 + 12$
(0, 1)	$12x_1 + 13(1-x_1) = -x_1 + 13$

$\Rightarrow x_1 + 12 = -x_1 + 13$

$\therefore x_1^* = 1/2, \; x_2^* = 0, \; x_3^* = 1/2$

and $v = 12\ 1/2$

11.4-4 (a) (cont.)

$y_2^*(x_1+12)+y_3^*(-x_1+13) = 12\frac{1}{2}$ for $0 \le x_1 \le 1 \Rightarrow 12y_2^* + 13y_3^* = 12\frac{1}{2}$

$13y_2^* + 12y_3^* = 12\frac{1}{2}$

$\therefore\ y_1^* = 0,\ y_2^* = 1/2,\ y_3^* = 1/2$

That is, John should always swim the backstroke and should swim the butterfly or breaststroke each with probability 1/2. Also, Mark should always swim the butterfly and should swim the backstroke or breaststroke each with probability 1/2. And the A.J. Team can expect to get $12\frac{1}{2}$ points in the three events.

(b) The strategies for the two teams are as in part (a).

Let $p_{ij} = \begin{cases} 1/2 & \text{if } p_{ij} \ge 13 \text{ for part (a); that is, A.J. Team wins} \\ -1/2 & \text{if } p_{ij} < 13 \text{ for part (a); that is, A.J. Team loses} \end{cases}$

The payoff matrix becomes

A.J. \ G.N.	1	2	3
1	1/2	1/2	-1/2
2	1/2	-1/2	-1/2
3	-1/2	-1/2	1/2

Strategy 2 of A.J. Team dominated by strategy 1.

Strategy 1 of GN Team dominated by strategy 2.

After eliminating the dominated strategies the matrix is

AJ \ GN	2	3
1	1/2	-1/2
3	-1/2	1/2

If $12\frac{1}{2}$ is added to each entry, the optimal strategies are unchanged. Furthermore, the payoff matrix of part (a) is obtained. Hence the strategies given in part (a) are still optimal and $v = 12\frac{1}{2} - 12\frac{1}{2} = 0$

11.7-4 (c) Since John and Mark are the best swimmers on their respective teams, they will always swim in two events since the team can do no better if they swim in only one or no events. Hence, if either does not swim in the first event, the butterfly, he will surely swim the last two events.

Thus the strategies for the A.J. team are:

1. John enters the butterfly and then enters the backstroke regardless of whether Mark enters the butterfly.
2. John enters the butterfly and then swims the backstroke if Mark enters the butterfly, but swims breaststroke if Mark does not.
3. John enters the butterfly and then swims breaststroke if Mark enters the butterfly, but swims the backstroke if Mark does not.
4. John enters the butterfly and then swims the breaststroke regardless of whether Mark enters the butterfly.
5. John does not swim the butterfly and then enters both the breaststroke and the backstroke.

The strategies for the G.N. Team are as above but with the roles of John and Mark reversed.

The payoff matrix is

A.J. \ G.N.	1	2	3	4	5
1	1/2	1/2	-1/2	-1/2	-1/2
2	1/2	1/2	-1/2	-1/2	1/2
3	-1/2	-1/2	-1/2	-1/2	-1/2
4	-1/2	-1/2	-1/2	-1/2	1/2
5	-1/2	1/2	-1/2	1/2	1/2

Strategy 3 of G.N. Team dominates all others.
Since the resulting payoff matrix is:

A.J. \ G.N.	3
1	-1/2
2	-1/2
3	-1/2
4	-1/2
5	-1/2

if G.N. Team uses strategy 3, it will win, regardless of the strategy chosen by the A.J. Team.

(d) Strategy 2 of AJ Team dominates strategies 1, 3, 4.
Thus, if the coach for the GN Team may choose any of his strategies at random, the coach for the A.J. Team should choose either strategy 2 or 5.
The payoff matrix becomes (after eliminating the dominated strategies of A.J. Team):

A.J. \ G.N.	1	2	3	4	5
2	1/2	1/2	-1/2	-1/2	1/2
5	-1/2	1/2	-1/2	1/2	1/2

The two rows are identical except for columns 1 and 4.
Thus, if the coach for the A.J. Team knows that the other coach has a tendency to enter Mark in butterfly and backstroke more often than breast-stroke, that means column 1 is more likely to be chosen than column 4. Therefore, the coach for the A.J. Team should choose strategy 2.

11.5-1 Adding 3 to the entries of table 12.6 we obtain the payoff table

I \ II	1	2	3
1	3	1	5
2	8	7	0

The new linear programming model for player I is:

Maximize x_3

subject to
$$3x_1 + 8x_2 - x_3 \geq 0$$
$$x_1 + 7x_2 - x_3 \geq 0$$
$$5x_1 \quad - x_3 \geq 0$$
$$x_1 + x_2 = 1$$
$$x_1, x_2, x_3 \geq 0$$

The new linear programming model for player II is:

Minimize y_4

subject to
$$3y_1 + y_2 + 5y_3 - y_4 \leq 0$$
$$8y_1 + 7y_2 \quad - y_4 \leq 0$$
$$y_1 + y_2 + y_3 = 1$$
$$y_1, y_2, y_3, y_4 \geq 0$$

Based on the information given in Section 12.5, the optimal solutions for these new models are:

$(x_1^*, x_2^*, x_3^*) = (7/11, 4/11, 35/11)$ and $(y_1^*, y_2^*, y_3^*, y_4^*) = (0, 5/11, 6/11, 35/11)$

Note that $x_3^* = y_4^*$ and also $x_3^* = y_4^* = v + 3$ where v is the original game value.

11.5-2

a) Maximize x_4

subject to
$$5x_1 + 2x_2 + 3x_3 - x_4 \geq 0$$
$$4x_2 + 2x_3 - x_4 \geq 0$$
$$3x_1 + 3x_2 \quad - x_4 \geq 0$$
$$x_1 + 2x_2 + 4x_3 - x_4 \geq 0$$
$$x_1 + x_2 + x_3 = 1$$
$$x_1, x_2, x_3, x_4 \geq 0$$

b)

Solve Automatically by the Simplex Method:

Optimal Solution

Value of the
Objective Function: Z = 2.36842105

Variable	Value
X_1	0.05263
X_2	0.73684
X_3	0.21053
X_4	2.36842

11.5-3 To insure $x_4 \geq 0$ add 3 to each entry of the payoff table.

a)

$$\begin{aligned} \text{Maximize} \quad & x_4 \\ \text{subject to:} \quad & 7x_1 + 2x_2 + 5x_3 - x_4 \geq 0 \\ & 5x_1 + 3x_2 + 6x_3 - x_4 \geq 0 \\ & 6x_2 + x_3 - x_4 \geq 0 \\ & x_1 + x_2 + x_3 = 1 \\ & x_i \geq 0 \text{ for } i = 1,2,3,4. \end{aligned}$$

Solve Automatically by the Simplex Method:

b) **Optimal Solution**

Value of the
Objective Function: Z = 3.79166667

Variable	Value
X_1	0.33333
X_2	0.625
X_3	0.04167
X_4	3.79167

11.5-4

a) To insure $x_5 \geq 0$ add 4 to each entry of the payoff table.

$$\begin{aligned} \text{maximize} \quad & \\ \text{subject to:} \quad & 5x_1 + 6x_2 + 4x_3 - x_5 \geq 0 \\ & x_1 + 7x_2 + 8x_3 + 4x_4 - x_5 \geq 0 \\ & 6x_1 + 4x_2 + 3x_3 + 2x_4 - x_5 \geq 0 \\ & 2x_1 + 7x_2 + x_3 + 6x_4 - x_5 \geq 0 \\ & 5x_1 + 2x_2 + 6x_3 + 3x_4 - x_5 \geq 0 \\ & x_1 + x_2 + x_3 + x_4 = 1 \end{aligned}$$

$x_i \geq 0$ for $i=1,2,3,4,5$

Solve Automatically by the Simplex Method:

b) **Optimal Solution**

Value of the
Objective Function: Z = 3.98101266

Variable	Value
X_1	0.31013
X_2	0.26582
X_3	0.20886
X_4	0.21519
X_5	3.98101

11.5-5 Following Table 6.14, the dual of player I's problem is:

$$\begin{aligned} \min. \quad & y_{m+1} \\ \text{s.t.} \quad & p_{11} y_1' + p_{12} y_2' + \cdots + p_{1m} y_m' + y_{m+1} \geq 0 \\ & p_{21} y_1' + p_{22} y_2' + \cdots + p_{2m} y_m' + y_{m+1} \geq 0 \\ & \vdots \\ & p_{m1} y_1' + p_{m2} y_2' + \cdots + p_{mm} y_m' + y_{m+1} \geq 0 \\ & -y_1' - y_2' - \cdots - y_m' = 1 \\ & y_i' \leq 0, \quad i = 1,2,\dots,m \quad (y_{m+1} \text{ free}) \end{aligned}$$

Now let $y_i = -y_i'$, $i = 1,2,\dots,m$

and we get the linear program given for player II.

11.5-6 Taking the dual of the player I problem gives:

$$\min \quad y_4$$

s.t.

$$-2y_2' + 2y_3' + y_4 \geq 0$$
$$5y_1' + 4y_2' - 3y_3' + y_4 \geq 0$$
$$-y_1' - y_2' - y_3' = 1$$
$$y_1', y_2', y_3' \leq 0 \qquad y_4 \text{ free}$$

let $y_i = -y_i'$, $i = 1,2,3$

→ substitution produces the given player II problem.

11.5-7

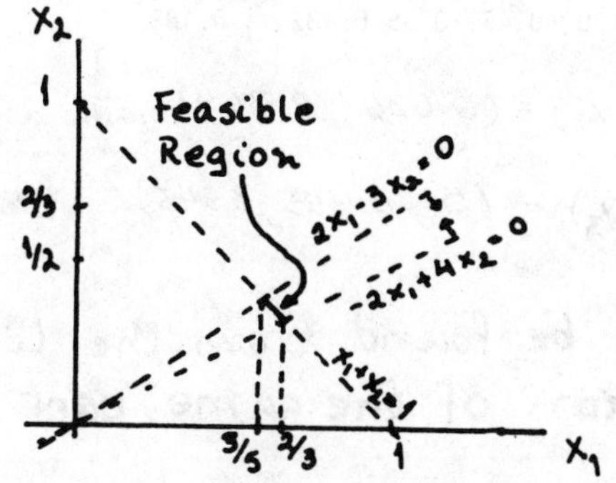

There fore the feasible region may be algebraically described by: $x_2 = 1 - x_1 \quad 3/5 \leq x_1 \leq 2/3$

The restrictions may be rewritten as:

$x_3 \leq -5x_1 + 5 \qquad 3/5 \leq x_1 \leq 2/3$

$x_3 \leq -6x_1 + 4 \qquad 3/5 \leq x_1 \leq 2/3$

$x_3 \leq 5x_1 - 3 \qquad 3/5 \leq x_1 \leq 2/3$

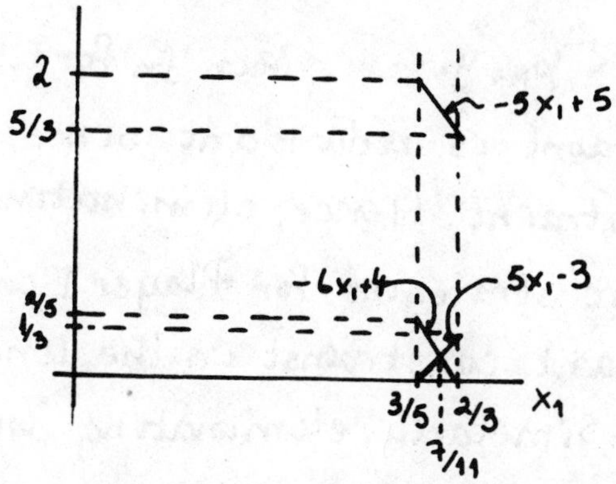

$-6x_1 + 4 = 5x_1 - 3$

$\Rightarrow x_1 = 7/11$

There fore the algebraic expression for the maximizing value of x_3 for any point in the feasible region is:

$$x_3 = \begin{cases} 5x_1 - 3 & \text{for } 3/5 \leq x_1 \leq 7/11 \\ -6x_1 + 4 & \text{for } 7/11 \leq x_1 \leq 2/3 \end{cases}$$

Hence, the optimal solution is:

$$x_1^* = 7/11$$
$$x_2^* = 1 - 7/11 = 4/11$$
$$x_3^* = 5(7/11) - 3 = 2/11$$

11.5-8 AUTOMATIC SIMPLEX METHOD: FINAL TABLEAU

Bas Var	Eq No	Z	X1	X2	X3	X4	X5	X6	X7	X8	X9	X10	Right side
									1M	1M	1M	1M	
Z	0	1	0	0	0	0	0.455	0.545	0	-0.45	-0.55	0.182	0.182
X2	1	0	0	1	0	0	-0.09	0.091	0	0.091	-0.09	0.364	0.364
X4	2	0	0	0	0	1	-0.91	-0.09	-1	0.909	0.091	1.636	1.636
X1	3	0	1	0	0	0	0.091	-0.09	0	-0.09	0.091	0.636	0.636
X3	4	0	0	0	1	0	0.455	0.545	0	-0.45	-0.55	0.182	0.182

The optimal primal solution is $(x_1, x_2) = (0.636, 0.364)$ with a payoff = 0.182

The optimal dual solution is $(y_1, y_2, y_3) = (0, 0.455, 0.545)$

11.5-9 (a) Since saddlepoints can be found from the linear programming formulation of the game, part (a) follows from part (b).

(b) Consider the linear programming formulation of the problem for Player II. The ith and k^{th} constraints are

$$p_{i1}y_1 + p_{i2}y_2 + \cdots + p_{in}y_n \leq y_{n+1}$$

$$p_{k1}y_1 + p_{k2}y_2 + \cdots + p_{kn}y_n \leq y_{n+1}$$

If row k weakly dominates row i, then

$$p_{i1}y_1 + \cdots + p_{in}y_n \leq p_{k1}y_1 + \cdots + p_{kn}y_n \text{ for all } y_1, \ldots, y_n$$

That is, the ith constraint is redundant since it is implied by the kth constraint. Hence, eliminating weakly dominated pure strategies for Player I corresponds to eliminating redundant constrainst in the linear program for Player II. Similarly, eliminating weakly dominated pure strategies for Player II corresponds to eliminating redundant constraints in the linear program for Player I.

Since this process cannot eliminate feasible solutions or create new ones, all optimal strategies cannot be eliminated and new ones cannot be created.

Chapter 12
Integer Programming

12.1-1 (a) $x_{ej} = \begin{cases} 0 & \text{if Eve does not do task } j \\ 1 & \text{if Eve does task } j \end{cases}$

$x_{sj} = \begin{cases} 0 & \text{if Steven does not do task } j \\ 1 & \text{if Steven does task } j \end{cases}$

Let task m = marketing, task c = cooking, task d = dishwashing, task l = laundering.

(a) Then the problem is

$$\text{Minimize } 4.5\,x_{em} + 7.8\,x_{ec} + 3.6\,x_{ed} + 2.9\,x_{el} + 4.9\,x_{sm} + 7.2\,x_{sc} + 4.3\,x_{sd} + 3.1\,x_{sl}$$

Subject to

$$x_{em} + x_{ec} + x_{ed} + x_{el} = 2$$
$$x_{sm} + x_{sc} + x_{sd} + x_{sl} = 2$$
$$x_{em} + x_{sm} = 1$$
$$x_{ec} + x_{sc} = 1$$
$$x_{ed} + x_{sd} = 1$$
$$x_{el} + x_{sl} = 1$$
$$x_{ij} = 0 \text{ or } 1 \quad i = e, s; \; j = m, c, d, l.$$

b)

Automatic Binary Integer Programming Branch and Bound Algorithm:

Solution:

$X_1 = 1$
$X_2 = 0$
$X_3 = 1$
$X_4 = 0$
$X_5 = 0$
$X_6 = 1$
$X_7 = 0$
$X_8 = 1$

$Z = 18.4$

Eve performs the marketing and dishwashing chores.
Steven performs the cooking and laundering chores.

12.1-2. (a) $x_i = \begin{cases} 0 & \text{if investment } i \text{ is not made} \\ 1 & \text{if investment } i \text{ is made} \end{cases}$

Hence, the problem is

Maximize $17x_1 + 10x_2 + 15x_3 + 19x_4 + 7x_5 + 13x_6 + 9x_7$

subject to $43x_1 + 28x_2 + 34x_3 + 48x_4 + 17x_5 + 32x_6 + 23x_7 \le 100$

$x_1 + x_2 \le 1$ (1 and 2 are mutually exclusive)

$x_3 + x_4 \le 1$ (3 and 4 are mutually exclusive)

$x_3 + x_4 \le x_1 + x_2$ (Neither 3 or 4 can be undertaken unless 1 or 2 is)

x_i is binary, for $i = 1, \dots, 7$.

b)

```
Solution:
X1 = 1
X2 = 0
X3 = 1
X4 = 0
X5 = 4.3368e-19   (≈0)
X6 = 0
X7 = 1

Z  = $41 million
```

12.1-3 a) Let x_{ij} = # of trucks hauling from pit i = North, South to site $j = 1, 2, 3$

y_{ij} = tons of gravel hauled from pit i to site j.

The MIP model is:

Minimize $z = 13y_{11} + 16y_{12} + 15y_{13} + 18y_{21} + 15y_{22} + 16y_{23} + 5\sum_{i=1}^{2}\sum_{j=1}^{3} x_{ij}$

$y_{11} + y_{12} + y_{13} \le 18$

$y_{21} + y_{22} + y_{23} \le 14$

$y_{ij} \le 5x_{ij} \quad i = 1, 2, \; j = 1, 2, 3$

$y_{1j} + y_{2j} \ge \begin{cases} 10 & j = 1 \\ 5 & j = 2 \\ 10 & j = 3 \end{cases}$

$y_{ij} \ge 0$ for $i = 1, 2$ $j = 1, 2, 3$ $\quad x_{ij} \ge 0$ and integral for $i = 1, 2$ $j = 1, 2, 3$.

b)

```
Solution:
X1  = 2    x11
X2  = 0
X3  = 1    x13
X4  = 0
X5  = 1    x22
X6  = 1    x23
X7  = 10   y11
X8  = 0
X9  = 5    y13
X10 = 0
X11 = 5    y22
X12 = 5    y23

Z   = 385
```

12.1-4. Let swimmer 1 = Carl, 2 = Chris, 3 = David, 4 = Tony, 5 = Ken

stroke 1 = backstroke, 2 = breaststroke, 3 = butterfly, 4 = freestyle.

t_{ij} = "best time" of swimmer i in stroke j (given data of Problem 8.3-3)

$x_{ij} = \begin{cases} 1 & \text{if swimmer } i \text{ is assigned to swim stroke } j \\ 0 & \text{otherwise} \end{cases}$

Hence, the problem is:

Minimize $\sum_{j=1}^{4} \sum_{i=1}^{5} t_{ij} \cdot x_{ij}$

subject to $\sum_{i=1}^{5} x_{ij} = 1$ for $j = 1, \ldots, 4$

$\sum_{j=1}^{4} x_{ij} \leq 1$ for $i = 1, \ldots, 5$

x_{ij} is binary, for $i = 1, \ldots, 5$; $j = 1, \ldots, 4$

12.2-1 a) let x_i = # units to produce of product i, $i = 1, 2, 3$

$y_i = \begin{cases} 1 & \text{if product } i \text{ is produced} \\ 0 & \text{if product } i \text{ is not produced} \end{cases}$, $i = 1, 2$

max. $2x_1 + 3x_2 + x_3 - 3y_1 - 2y_2$

s.t. $20x_1 + 40x_2 + 20x_3 \leq 100$

$x_1 \leq M y_1$

$x_2 \leq M y_2$

$x_1 \leq 3$

$x_1, x_2, x_3 \geq 0$, integer y_1, y_2 binary

b) (there are other optimal solutions, as seen in ch.10)

Solution:

y_1 ~~X1~~	=	0
y_2 ~~X2~~	=	0
x_1 ~~X3~~	=	0
x_2 ~~X4~~	=	0
x_3 ~~X5~~	=	5
Z	=	5

c) formulation is the same except $x_1, x_2, x_3 \geq 0$ not necessarily integer

d)

Solution:

y_1 ~~X1~~	=	0
y_2 ~~X2~~	=	1
x_1 ~~X3~~	=	0
x_2 ~~X4~~	=	2.5
x_3 ~~X5~~	=	0
Z	=	5.5

12.2-2 Let $y_i = \begin{cases} 1 & \text{if product } i \text{ is produced} \\ 0 & \text{otherwise} \end{cases}$ $i = 1, 2, 3, 4$

Let M be a very large number.

The problem can be formulated as follows:

Maximize $70x_1 + 60x_2 + 90x_3 + 80x_4 - 50000y_1 - 40000y_2$
$-70000y_3 - 60000y_4$

subject to $\sum_{i=1}^{4} y_i \leq 2$ (no more than two of the products can be produced)

$x_i \leq M y_i$ $i = 1, \ldots, 4.$ (production level x_i can be positive only if decision to produce product i has been made)

$y_3 + y_4 \leq y_1 + y_2$ (either product 3 or 4 can be produced only if either product 1 or 2 is produced)

$5x_1 + 3x_2 + 6x_3 + 4x_4 \leq 6000 + zM$
$4x_1 + 6x_2 + 3x_3 + 5x_4 \leq 6000 + (1-z)M$
} only one of the constraints in (3) needs to hold.

$x_i \geq 0$ $i = 1, \ldots, 4.$

y_i binary $i = 1, \ldots, 4$

z binary

12.2-3 Minimize $7y_1 + 5x_1 + 5y_2 + 6x_2$

subject to

(0) $x_1 \leq My_1$

$x_2 \leq My_2$

(1) $x_1 \geq 3 - My_3$

$x_2 \geq 3 - M(1-y_3)$

(2) $2x_1 + x_2 \geq 7 - My_4$

$x_1 + x_2 \geq 5 - My_5$

$x_1 + 2x_2 \geq 7 - My_6$

$y_4 + y_5 + y_6 = 2$

(3) $x_1 - x_2 = 0 \cdot y_7 - 3y_8 + 3y_9 - 6y_{10} + 6y_{11}$

$y_7 + y_8 + y_9 + y_{10} + y_{11} = 1$

(4) $x_i \geq 0$ $i=1,2$ and y_i binary $i=1,\ldots,11$.

12.2-4 Maximize $3x_1 - 10y_1 + 6x_2 + 2x_3 - 9y_2 + 15x_4$

subject to

(0) $x_1 \leq My_1$

$x_4 \leq My_2$

(1) $2x_1 - x_2 + x_3 + 3x_4 \leq 15$

(2) $x_1 + x_2 + x_3 + x_4 \leq 4 + My_3$

$3x_1 - x_2 - x_3 + x_4 \leq 3 + M(1-y_3)$

(3) $5x_1 + 3x_2 + 3x_3 - x_4 \leq 10 + My_4$

$2x_1 + 5x_2 - x_3 + 3x_4 \leq 10 + My_5$

$-x_1 + 3x_2 + 5x_3 + 3x_4 \leq 10 + My_6$

$3x_1 - x_2 + 3x_3 + 5x_4 \leq 10 + My_7$

$y_4 + y_5 + y_6 + y_7 = 2$

(4) $x_3 = y_8 + 2y_9 + 3y_{10}$

$y_8 + y_9 + y_{10} = 1$

(5) $x_i \geq 0$ $i=1,\ldots,4$ and y_j binary $j=1,\ldots,10$

12.2-5

a) Let y_1, y_2 be binary variables indicating whether or not toys 1 and 2 are produced. Let x_1, x_2 be the number of toys 1 and 2 produced. Let $z = \begin{cases} 0 & \text{if factory 1 is used} \\ 1 & \text{if factory 2 is used} \end{cases}$.

IP: max. $10x_1 + 15x_2 - 50000y_1 - 80000y_2$

s.t.

$$x_1 \leq My_1$$
$$x_2 \leq My_2$$
$$x_1/50 + x_2/40 \leq 500 + Mz$$
$$x_1/40 + x_2/25 \leq 700 + M(1-z)$$

$x_1, x_2 \geq 0$, integer $\quad y_1, y_2, z$ binary

Solution:

y_1 = 1
y_2 = 0
z = 1
x_1 = 28000
x_2 = 0

Z = \$230,000

Use factory 2 and produce only toy 1, at a level of 28,000 toys.

12.2-6 (a) Let x_j denote the number of long, medium and short range planes for $j = 1, 2, 3$, respectively.

So Maximize $2.1x_1 + 1.5x_2 + 1.15x_3$

subject to

$$33.5x_1 + 25x_2 + 17.5x_3 \leq 750$$
$$x_1 + x_2 + x_3 \leq 30$$
$$5/3\,x_1 + 4/3\,x_2 + x_3 \leq 40$$

$x_j \geq 0$ and integer for $j = 1, 2, 3$

b) Solution:

X1 = 14
X2 = 0
X3 = 16

Z = \$47.8 million

(cont.)

12.2-6 cont. (c) $x_1 \le \min\left\{\left[\frac{750}{33.5}\right], 30, \left[\frac{40}{5/3}\right]\right\} = \min\{22, 30, 24\} = 22$

$x_2 \le \min\left\{\left[\frac{750}{25}\right], 30, \left[\frac{40}{4/3}\right]\right\} = \min\{30, 30, 30\} = 30$

$x_3 \le \min\left\{\left[\frac{750}{17.5}\right], 30, 40\right\} = \min\{42, 30, 40\} = 30$

(where $[x]$ = integer part of x)

$$x_1 = \sum_{i=0}^{4} 2^i y_{1i}, \quad x_2 = \sum_{i=0}^{4} 2^i y_{2i}, \quad x_3 = \sum_{i=0}^{4} 2^i y_{3i}$$

and the problem may be rewritten as follows:

Maximize $2.1 \sum_{i=0}^{4} 2^i y_{1i} + 1.5 \sum_{i=0}^{4} 2^i y_{2i} + 1.15 \sum_{i=0}^{4} 2^i y_{3i}$

subject to $33.5 \sum_{i=0}^{4} 2^i y_{1i} + 25 \sum_{i=0}^{4} 2^i y_{2i} + 17.5 \sum_{i=0}^{4} 2^i y_{3i} \le 750$

$$\sum_{i=0}^{4} 2^i y_{1i} + \sum_{i=0}^{4} 2^i y_{2i} + \sum_{i=0}^{4} 2^i y_{3i} \le 30$$

$$\frac{5}{3} \sum_{i=0}^{4} 2^i y_{1i} + \frac{4}{3} \sum_{i=0}^{4} 2^i y_{2i} + \sum_{i=0}^{4} 2^i y_{3i} \le 40$$

y_{ij} is binary

d) Solution:

X_1	= 0	
X_2	= 1	0+2+4+8+0 = 14
X_3	= 1	
X_4	= 1	
X_5	= 0	
X_6	= 0	
X_7	= 0	
X_8	= 0	0
X_9	= 0	
X_{10}	= 0	
X_{11}	= 0	
X_{12}	= 0	0+0+0+0+16 = 16
X_{13}	= 0	
X_{14}	= 0	
X_{15}	= 1	[same as in (b)]

Z = \$47.8 million

12.2-7 (a) Let $x_1 = y_{11} + 2y_{12}$; $x_2 = y_{21} + 2y_{22}$

The BIP formulation is:

$$\text{Maximize } Z = y_{11} + 2y_{12} + 5y_{21} + 10y_{22}$$

subject to:

$$y_{11} + 2y_{12} + 10y_{21} + 20y_{22} \le 20$$

$$y_{11} + 2y_{12} \le 2$$

y_{ij} binary for $i = 1,2$ $j = 1,2$.

b) Solution:

X1 = 0   0 = x_1
X2 = 0
X3 = 0   0+2 = 2 = x_2
X4 = 1

Z = 10

12.3-1 Wyndor Glass Co.

introduce y_1, y_2 binary variables

add constraints: $x_1 \le My_1$

$x_2 \le My_2$

(all the old constraints remain) $y_1 + y_2 = 1$

y_1, y_2 binary

12.3-2 introduce binary variables y_1, y_2, y_3 to represent positive (nonzero) production levels

New MIP:

$$\max. \ Z = 50x_1 + 20x_2 + 25x_3$$

s.t.

$$9x_1 + 3x_2 + 5x_3 \le 500$$

$$5x_1 + 4x_2 \le 350$$

$$3x_1 + 2x_3 \le 150$$

$$x_3 \le 20$$

$$x_1 \le My_1, \ x_2 \le My_2, \ x_3 \le My_3$$

$$y_1 + y_2 + y_3 \le 2$$

$x_1, x_2, x_3 \ge 0$ y_1, y_2, y_3 binary

12.3-3 a) let $y_{ij} = \begin{cases} 1 & \text{if } x_i = j \\ 0 & \text{if not} \end{cases}$ (i.e. produce j units of i)

$i = 1, 2, 3$, $j = 1, 2, (3, 4, 5)$

$$\max. \; -1y_{11} + 2y_{12} + 4y_{13} + 1y_{21} + 5y_{22} + 1y_{31} + 3y_{32} + 5y_{33} + 6y_{34} + 7y_{35}$$

s.t.
$$y_{11} + y_{12} + y_{13} \le 1$$
$$y_{21} + y_{22} \le 1$$
$$y_{31} + y_{32} + y_{33} + y_{34} + y_{35} \le 1$$
$$1y_{11} + 2y_{12} + 3y_{13} + 2y_{21} + 4y_{22} + 1y_{31} + 2y_{32} + 3y_{33} + 4y_{34} + 5y_{35} \le 5$$
y_{ij} binary

c) let $y_{ij} = \begin{cases} 1, & x_i \ge j \\ 0, & \text{if not} \end{cases}$

$$\max. \; -1y_{11} + 3y_{12} + 2y_{13} + 1y_{21} + 4y_{22} + 1y_{31} + 2y_{32} + 2y_{33} + 1y_{34} + 1y_{35}$$

s.t.
$$y_{12} \le y_{11}, \quad y_{13} \le y_{12}, \quad y_{22} \le y_{21}$$
$$y_{32} \le y_{31}, \quad y_{33} \le y_{32}, \quad y_{34} \le y_{33}, \quad y_{35} \le y_{34}$$
$$y_{11} + y_{12} + y_{13} + 2y_{21} + 2y_{22} + y_{31} + y_{32} + y_{33} + y_{34} + y_{35} \le 5$$
y_{ij} binary

b)

```
Solution:
      X1  = 0
      X2  = 0
      X3  = 0
      X4  = 0
      X5  = 0
      X6  = 0
      X7  = 0
      X8  = 0
      X9  = 0
y35   X10 = 1   => x3 = 5

      Z   = 7
```

d)

```
Solution:
      X1  = 0
      X2  = 0
      X3  = 0
      X4  = 0
      X5  = 0
y31   X6  = 1
y32   X7  = 1   => x3 = 5
y33   X8  = 1
y34   X9  = 1
y35   X10 = 1

      Z   = 7
```

12.3-4 a) let $y_{ij} = \begin{cases} 1, & x_i = j \\ 0, & \text{if not} \end{cases}$ $i = 1, 2$, $j = 1, 2, 3$

It's simple to work out by hand the objective function contribution for $x_1, x_2 = 0, 1, 2, 3$. This gives:

max. $3y_{11} + 8y_{12} + 9y_{13} + 9y_{21} + 24y_{22} + 9y_{23}$

s.t. $y_{11} + y_{12} + y_{13} \le 1$, $y_{21} + y_{22} + y_{23} \le 1$

$y_{11} + y_{23} \le 1$ $\quad$ $y_{13} + y_{23} \le 1$

$y_{12} + y_{23} \le 1$ $\quad$ $y_{13} + y_{22} \le 1$

$y_{12} + y_{22} \le 1$ $\quad$ $y_{13} + y_{21} \le 1$

y_{ij} binary

b) Solution:

$X_1 = 1$ y_{11}
$X_2 = 0$
$X_3 = 0$
$X_4 = 0$
$X_5 = 1$ y_{22}
$X_6 = 0$
$\Rightarrow x_1 = 1, x_2 = 2$
$Z = 27$

c) let $y_{ij} = \begin{cases} 1, & x_i \ge j \\ 0, & \text{if not} \end{cases}$ $i = 1, 2$, $j = 1, 2, 3$

max. $3y_{11} + 5y_{12} + 1y_{13} + 9y_{21} + 15y_{22} - 15y_{23}$

s.t. $y_{12} \le y_{11}$, $y_{13} \le y_{12}$

$y_{22} \le y_{21}$, $y_{23} \le y_{22}$

$y_{11} + y_{23} \le 1$
$y_{12} + y_{22} \le 1$ $\quad$ ← this is sufficient due to the first four constraints
$y_{13} + y_{21} \le 1$

y_{ij} binary

d) Solution:

$X_1 = 1$ y_{11}
$X_2 = 0$
$X_3 = 0$
$X_4 = 1$ y_{21}
$X_5 = 1$ y_{22}
$X_6 = 0$
$\Rightarrow x_1 = 1, x_2 = 2$
$Z = 27$

12.3-5 a) let $y_{ij} = \begin{cases} 1, & x_i = \frac{1}{j+1} \\ 0, & \text{if not} \end{cases}$ $i = 1, 2$, $j = 1, 2, 3, 4$

max. $3/4\, y_{11} + 5/9\, y_{12} + 7/16\, y_{13} + 9/25\, y_{14}$
$+ 3/4\, y_{21} + 2/3\, y_{22} + 9/16\, y_{23} + 12/25\, y_{24}$

s.t. $\sum_{j=1}^{4} y_{ij} \le 1$, $i = 1, 2$

$y_{11} + y_{21} \le 1$

$y_{11} + y_{22} \le 1$ $\quad$ y_{ij} binary

$y_{12} + y_{21} \le 1$

i) Solution:

$X_1 = 1$ y_{11}
$X_2 = 0$
$X_3 = 0$
$X_4 = 0$
$X_5 = 0$
$X_6 = 0$
$X_7 = 1$ y_{23}
$X_8 = 0$

$Z = 1.3125$

$\Rightarrow x_1 = \frac{1}{2}$, $x_2 = \frac{1}{4}$

12.3-6 a) Let $x_{ij} = \begin{cases} 1 & \text{if arc from node } i \text{ to node } j \text{ is used in shortest route} \\ 0 & \text{otherwise} \end{cases}$

Then the problem is:

Minimize $3x_{12}+6x_{13}+6x_{24}+5x_{25}+4x_{34}+3x_{35}+3x_{46}+2x_{56}$

$x_{12}+x_{13}=1$
$x_{24}+x_{25}+x_{34}+x_{35}=1$
$x_{46}+x_{56}=1$

} at each stage (between col.) exactly one arc is used

$x_{24}+x_{25} \le x_{12}$
$x_{34}+x_{35} \le x_{13}$
$x_{46} \le x_{24}+x_{34}$
$x_{56} \le x_{25}+x_{35}$

} route leaves node i only if route enters node i

x_{ij} is binary

b) Solution:

```
X1  = 1  x12
X2  = 0
X3  = 0
X4  = 1  x25
X5  = 0
X6  = 0
X7  = 0
X8  = 1  x56
path: 1→2→5→6
Z   = 10
```

The first three equations represent mutually exclusive alternatives and the last four equations represent contingent decisions.

12.3-7 Let $x_{ij} = \begin{cases} 1 & \text{if } (i,j) \text{ is in the critical path} \\ 0 & \text{otherwise} \end{cases}$

Maximize $z = 5x_{12}+3x_{13}+4x_{24}+2x_{25}+3x_{35}+1x_{46}+3x_{47}$
$+6x_{57}+2x_{58}+5x_{69}+4x_{79}+7x_{89}$

subject to: $\sum_i x_{ij} - \sum_k x_{jk} = \begin{cases} -1 & \text{for } j=1 \\ 1 & \text{for } j=9 \\ 0 & \text{otherwise} \end{cases}$

x_{ij} binary.

12.3-8 Let $x_{ij} = \begin{cases} 1 & \text{if tract } j \text{ is assigned to station located in tract } i \\ 0 & \text{otherwise} \end{cases}$

a_{ij} = response time to a fire in tract j, if that tract is served by a station Located in tract i (entries in the table are the a_{ij}'s)

Then the problem is:

$$\text{Minimize } 2\sum_{i=1}^{5} a_{i1}x_{i1} + \sum_{i=1}^{5} a_{i2}x_{i2} + 3\sum_{i=1}^{5} a_{i3}x_{i3} + \sum_{i=1}^{5} a_{i4}x_{i4} + 3\sum_{i=1}^{5} a_{i5}x_{i5}$$

subject to

$\sum_{i=1}^{5} x_{ii} = 2$ (have to locate 2 stations)

mutually exclusive alternatives → $\sum_{i=1}^{5} x_{ij} = 1$ for $j=1,\ldots,5$ (each tract is assigned to a station)

contingent decisions → $x_{ij} \leq x_{ii}$ for $i=1,\ldots,5$; $j=1,\ldots,5$ (assign tract j to station in tract i only if there is a station located in tract i)

x_{ij} is binary

12.3-9 a) let $x_i = \begin{cases} 1, & \text{if a station is located in tract } i \\ 0, & \text{if not} \end{cases}$ $i=1,2,3,4,5$

min. $200x_1 + 250x_2 + 400x_3 + 300x_4 + 500x_5$

s.t.

$x_1 + x_3 + x_5 \geq 1$

$x_1 + x_2 + x_4 \geq 1$

$x_2 + x_3 + x_5 \geq 1$

$x_2 + x_3 + x_4 + x_5 \geq 1$

$x_1 + x_3 + x_4 + x_5 \geq 1$

x_i binary, $i=1,2,3,4,5$

c) Solution:

$X_1 = 1$
$X_2 = 1$
$X_3 = 0$
$X_4 = 0$
$X_5 = 0$

$Z = \$450K$

b) Yes, this is a set covering problem. The activities are locating stations, and the characteristics are the fires. S_i is the set of all locations that could cover a fire in tract i, so $S_1 = \{1,3,5\}$ for example. We have $\sum_{j \in S_i} x_j \geq 1 \quad \forall i$.

12.3-10 Let $x_j = \begin{cases} 1 & \text{if district } j \text{ is chosen} \\ 0 & \text{if not} \end{cases}$

y_j = auxiliary variable, will be zero for every j, except for the index of the district with largest c_j that is chosen, will be one for this index.

The problem is:

Minimize $\sum_{j=1}^{N} c_j y_j$

subject to

$$y_j \le x_j \quad j=1,\dots,N$$

$$\sum_{j=1}^{N} y_j = 1$$

$$\sum_{j=1}^{N} c_j y_j \ge c_i x_i \quad i=1,\dots,N$$

$$\sum_{j=1}^{N} x_j = R$$

$$\sum_{j=1}^{N} a_{ij} x_j = 1 \quad i=1,\dots,D$$

x_j and y_j are binary

This is a set partitioning problem with additional constraints.

12.3-11 Let $s_i = \begin{cases} 1 & \text{if skirt } i \text{ is taken} \quad i=1,2,3 \\ 0 & \text{otherwise} \end{cases}$

$p_i = \begin{cases} 1 & \text{if slacks } i \text{ is taken} \quad i=1,2,3 \\ 0 & \text{otherwise} \end{cases}$

$t_i = \begin{cases} 1 & \text{if top } i \text{ is taken} \quad i=1,2,3,4 \\ 0 & \text{otherwise} \end{cases}$

$t_5 = 1$ to indicate the use of the Icelandic sweater "top #5"

$d_i = \begin{cases} 1 & \text{if dress } i \text{ is taken} \quad i=1,2,3 \\ 0 & \text{otherwise} \end{cases}$

$x_{ij} = \begin{cases} 1 & \text{if both skirt } i \text{ and top } j \text{ are taken} \\ 0 & \text{otherwise} \end{cases}$

$y_{ij} = \begin{cases} 1 & \text{if both slacks } i \text{ and top } j \text{ are taken} \\ 0 & \text{otherwise} \end{cases}$

The BIP model is:

$$\text{Maximize } z = x_{11} + x_{12} + x_{15} + x_{21} + x_{24} + x_{32} + x_{33} + x_{34} + x_{35} + y_{11} + y_{13} + y_{21} + y_{22} + y_{24} + y_{25} + y_{33} + y_{34} + y_{35} + d_1 + d_2 + d_3$$

(cont.)

12.3-11 cont. subject to: $600 s_1 + 450 s_2 + 700 s_3 + 600 p_1 + 550 p_2 + 500 p_3 + 350 t_1 + 300 t_2 + 300 t_3 + 450 t_4 + 600 d_1 + 700 d_2 + 800 d_3 \le 4000$

$$5000 s_1 + 3500 s_2 + 3000 s_3 + 3500 p_1 + 6000 p_2 + 4000 p_3 + 4000 t_1 + 3500 t_2 + 3000 t_3 + 5000 t_4 + 6000 d_1 + 5000 d_2 + 4000 d_3 \le 32000$$

$$x_{ij} \le \frac{1}{2}(s_i + t_j)$$

$$y_{ij} \le \frac{1}{2}(p_i + t_j)$$

s_i, p_i, d_i binary for $i = 1,2,3$

t_i binary for $i = 1,2,3,4$

x_{ij}, y_{ij} binary for $i = 1,2,3$ $j = 1,2,3,4,5$

12.4-1 (a)

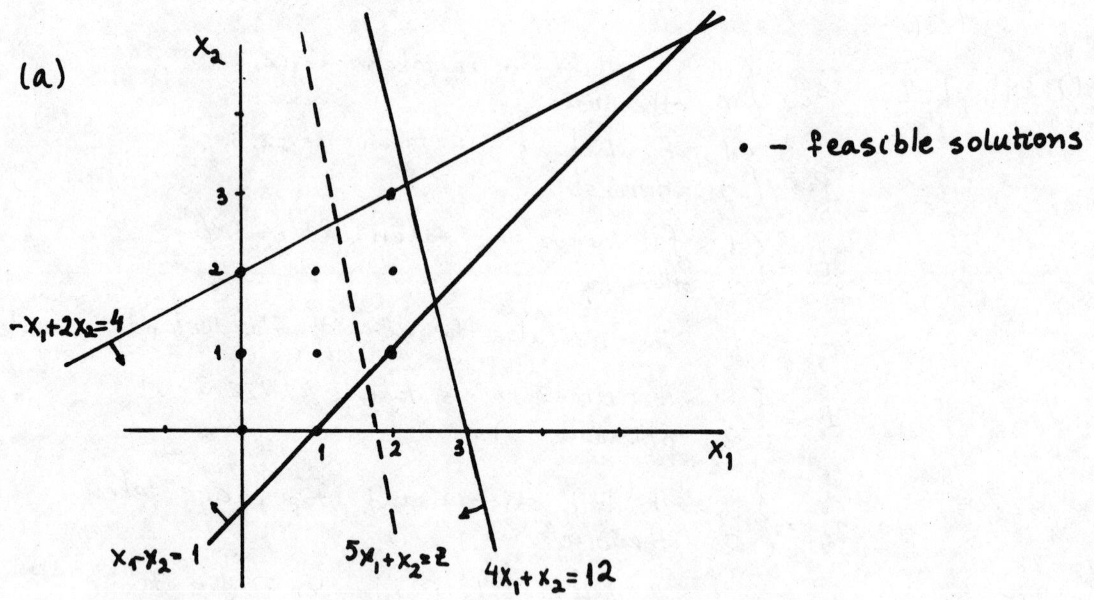

Optimal solution: $(x_1, x_2) = (2, 3)$

$$Z = 5x_1 + x_2 = 13$$

(b) Solving LP-relaxation graphically we obtain the optimal solution $(x_1, x_2) = \left(\frac{13}{5}, \frac{8}{5}\right) = (2.6, 1.6)$

$$Z = 13 + \frac{8}{5} = 14.6$$

(cont.)

12.4-1 b) cont. Rounding the optimal solution to the LP-relaxation:

$(\bar{x}_1, \bar{x}_2) = (3, 2)$ is not feasible $4 \cdot 3 + 2 \nleq 12$

Rounded Solutions	Constraints violated	Z
(3,2)	3rd	-
(3,1)	2nd and 3rd	-
(2,2)	none	12
(2,1)	none	11

So, none of the feasible rounded solutions is optimal for the IP problem.

12.4-2 (a)

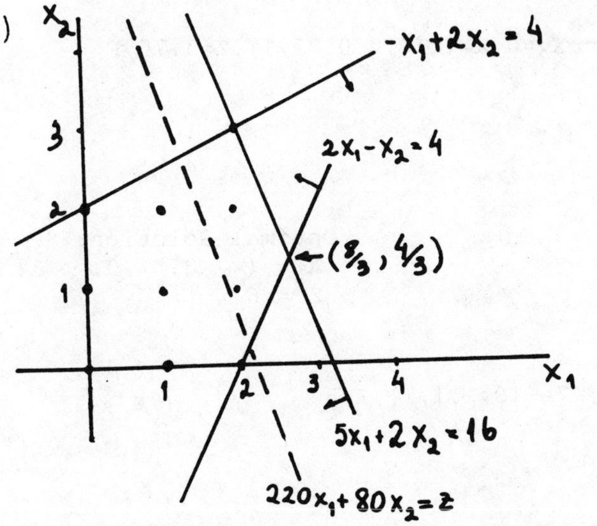

Optimal solution: $(x_1, x_2) = (2,3)$

$z = 220x_1 + 80x_2 = 680$

(b) Optimal solution to LP-relaxation:

$(x_1, x_2) = (8/3, 4/3)$

$z = 2080/3 = 693\ 1/3$

Nearest integer point is (3,1), which is not feasible

Rounded Solution	Constraints violated	z
(3,2)	2nd	-
(3,1)	2nd and 3rd	-
(2,2)	none	600
(2,1)	none	520

12.4-3 a) True. Section 12.4, 3rd paragraph, last line.

b) True. Section 12.4, last paragraph before rounding examples.

c) False. The result will not necessarily be feasible. See problems 12.4-1, 12.4-2 for examples of this. Also see the first "pitfall" mentioned in section 12.4, rounding.

12.5-1 Solution Tree:

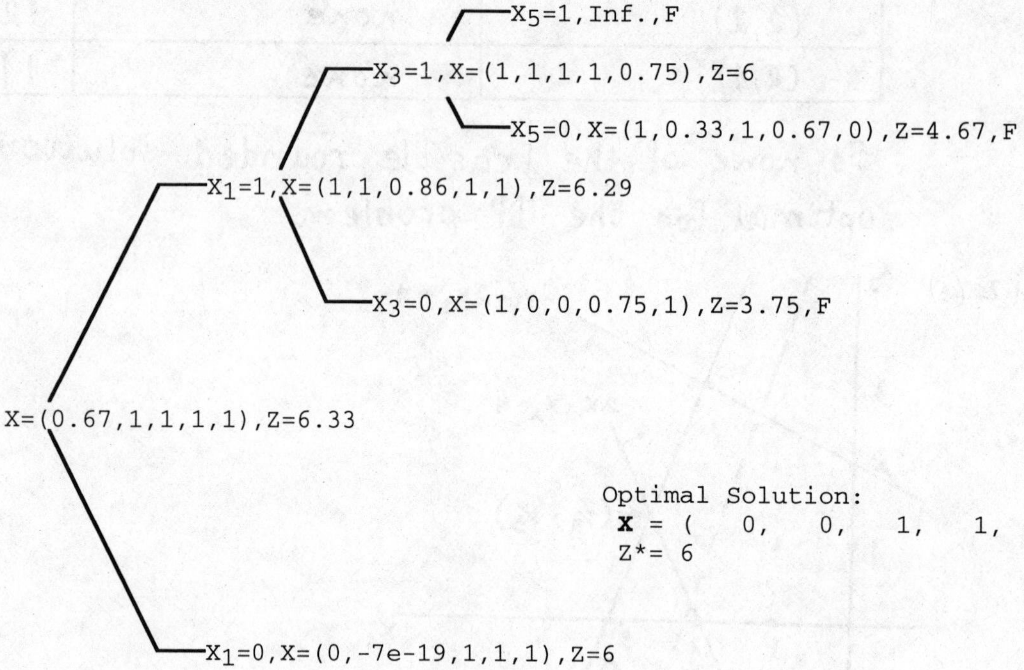

Optimal Solution:
X = (0, 0, 1, 1, 1)
Z*= 6

12.5-2 Solution Tree:

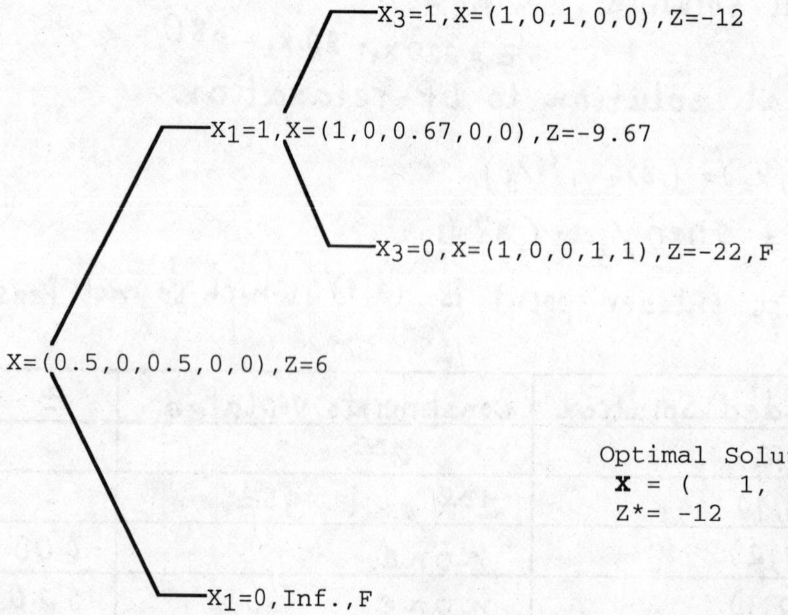

Optimal Solution:
X = (1, 0, 1, 0, 0)
Z*= -12

12.5-3 Solution Tree:

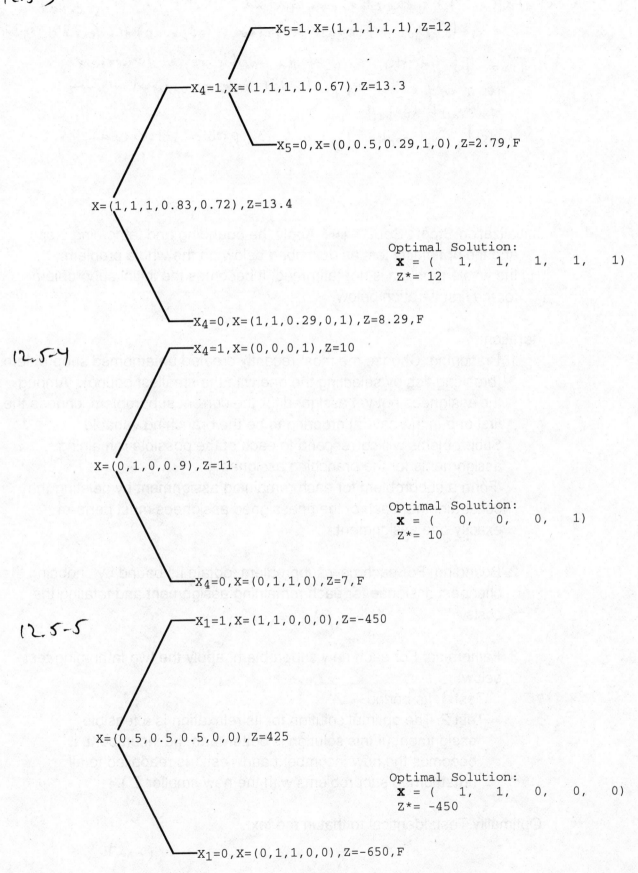

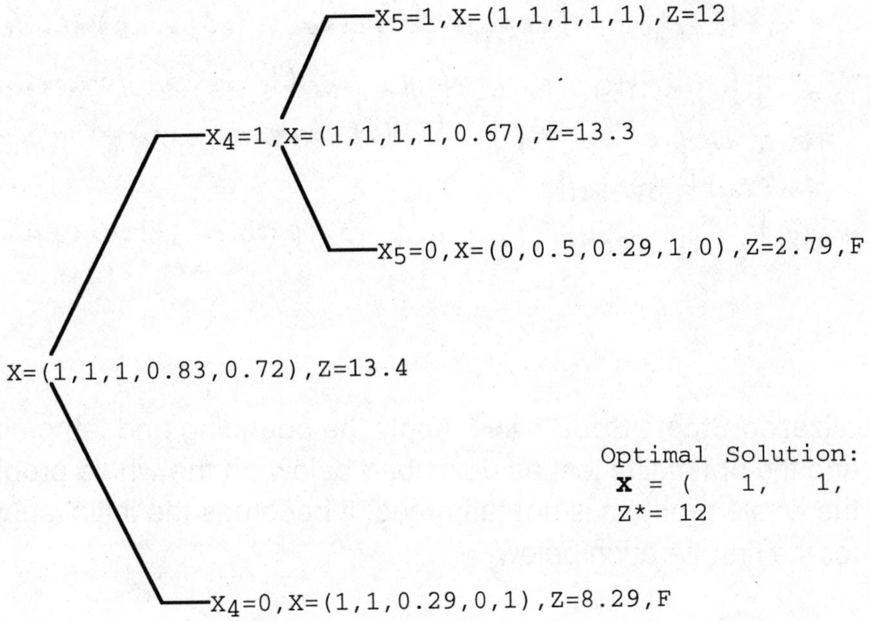

Optimal Solution:
x = (1, 1, 1, 1, 1)
Z*= 12

12.5-4

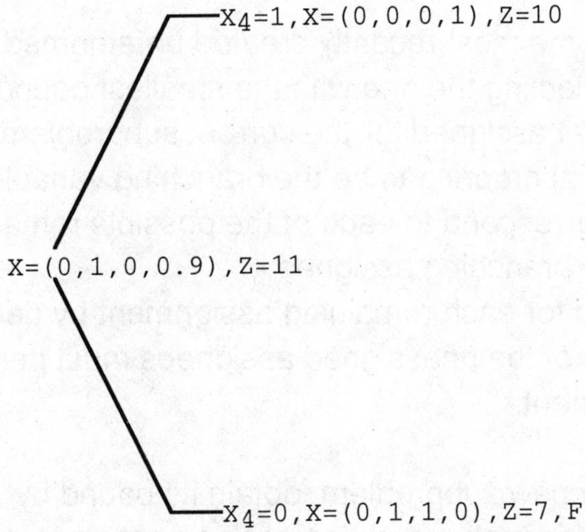

Optimal Solution:
x = (0, 0, 0, 1)
Z*= 10

12.5-5

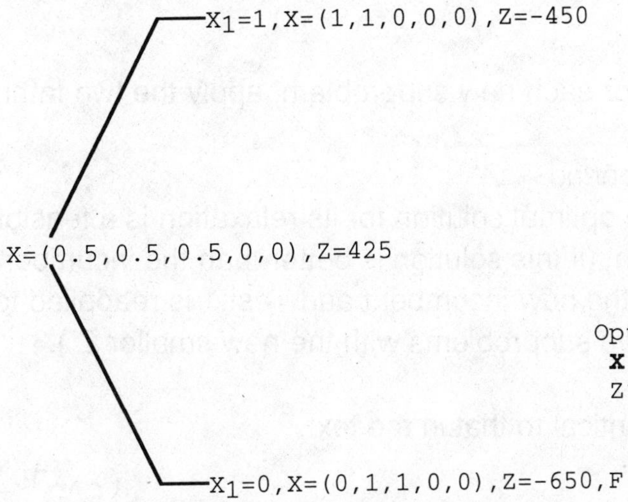

Optimal Solution:
x = (1, 1, 0, 0, 0)
Z*= -450

12.5-6 a) False. It's the other way around. That's why it's called a "relaxation," because it relaxes (expands) the feasible region.

b) True. If you then restrict the feasible region to integers you've only eliminated points that weren't optimal anyway. You can't do better.

c) False! See section 12.4 and its problems for examples.

12.5-7 (a) Initialization Step: Set $Z^*=+\infty$. Apply the bounding and fathoming steps and the optimality test as dexcribed below on the whole problem. If the whole problem is not fathomed, it becomes the initial subproblem for the first iteration below.

Iteration:

1. Branching: Choose the most recently created unfathomed subproblem (breaking ties by selecting the one with the smallest bound). Among the assignees not yet assigned for the current subproblem, choose the first one in the natural ordering to be the branching variable. Subproblems will correspond to each of the possible remaining assignments for the branching assignee.
   Form a subproblem for each remaining assignment by deleting the constraint that each of the unassigned assignees must perform exactly one assignment.

2. Bounding: For each new subproblem, obtain its bound by choosing the cheapest assignee for each remaining assignment and totaling the costs.

3. Fathoming: For each new subproblem, apply the two fathoming test below:
   Test 1. Its bound>= Z^*
   Test 2. The optimal solution for its relaxation is a feasible assignment (if this solution is better than the incumbent, it becomes the new incumbent and Test 1 is reapplied to all unfathomed subproblems with the new smaller Z^*).

Optimality Test: Identical to that in the text.

(cont.)

12.5-7

(b)

Matchings are indicated with the notation (assignee, assignment)

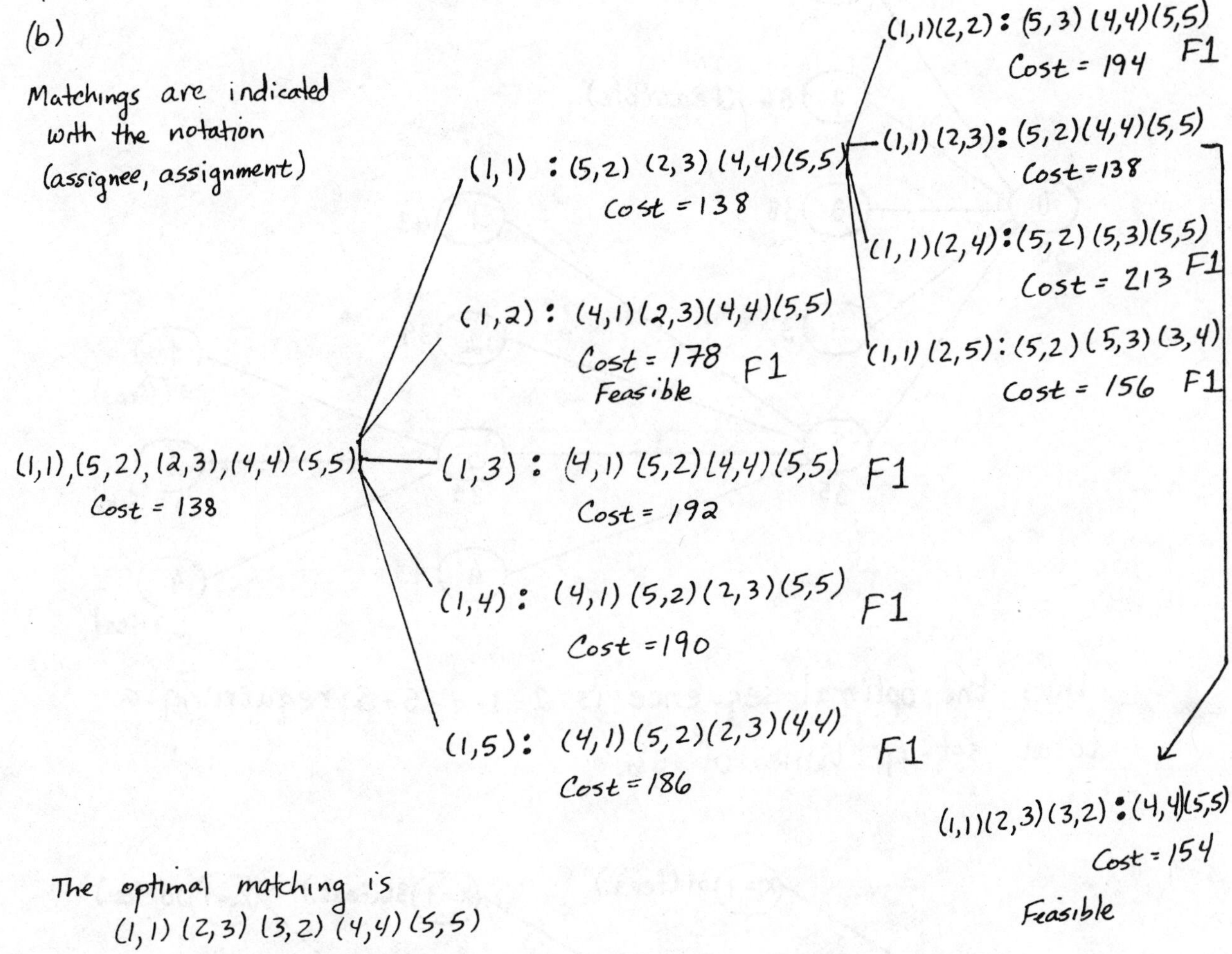

The optimal matching is (1,1) (2,3) (3,2) (4,4) (5,5) with Cost = 154.

12.5-8

(a) <u>Branch step</u> : Best bound rule

<u>Bound step</u> : Given a partial sequencing $J_1, \ldots, J_k$ of the first k jobs, a lower bound on the time for the set-up of the remaining (5-k) jobs is found by adding the minimum elements of the columns corresponding to the remaining jobs, excluding those elements in rows "None", $J_1, J_2, \ldots, J_{k-1}$.

<u>Fathoming step</u>: As specified in the summary of the Branch-and-Bound technique given in Section 13.4.

(cont.)

12.5-8 (b)

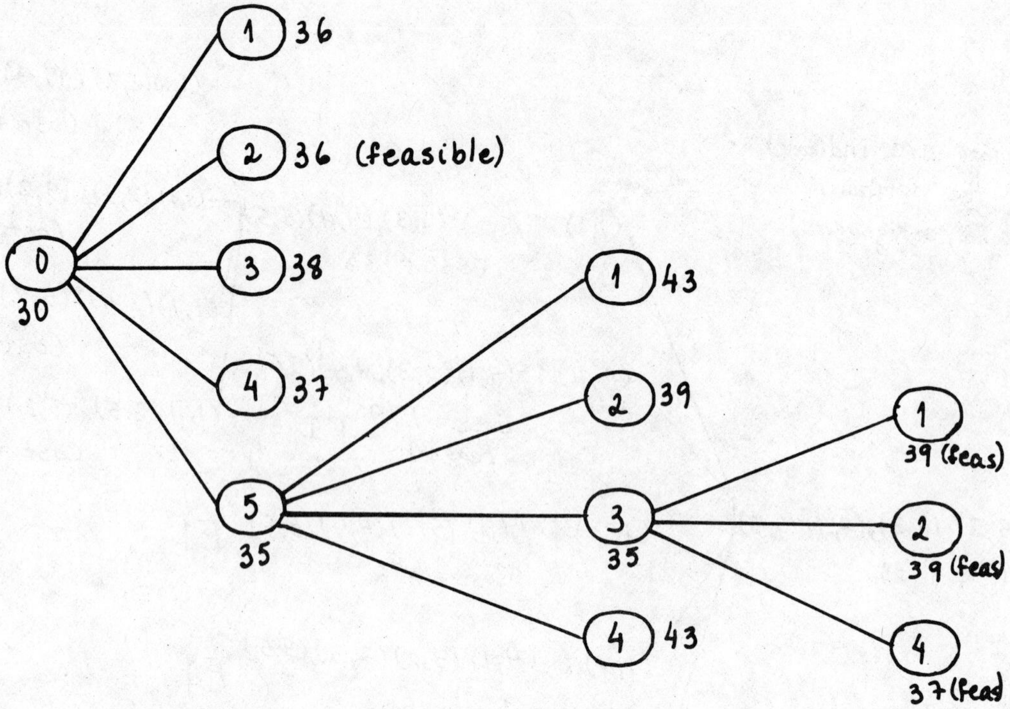

Thus the optimal sequence is 2-1-4-5-3 requiring a total set-up time of 36.

12.5-9

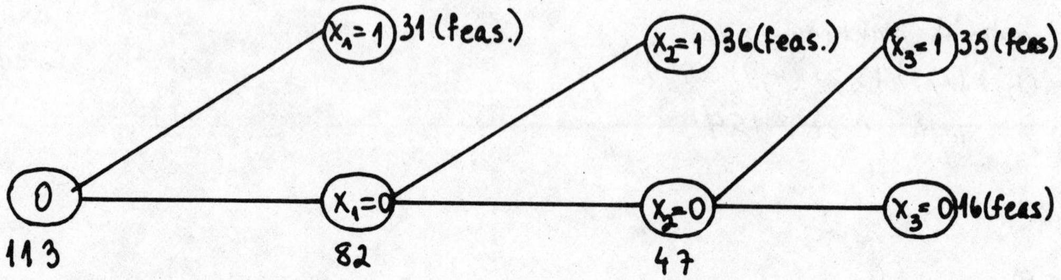

So $(x_1, x_2, x_3, x_4) = (0,1,1,0)$ is optimal, with $z^* = 36$.

12.5-10 a) x is feasible for an MIP. Since the Lagrangian relaxation has no constraints, other than nonnegativity or integer constraints, x is trivially feasible for this problem too.

b) x^* is optimal for MIP $\Rightarrow$ x^* feasible, i.e. $Ax^* \le b$ or $Ax^* - b \le 0$. Since $\lambda \ge 0$, $cx^* - \lambda(Ax^* - b) \ge cx^* = Z$.

From (a), x^* is feasible for the Lagrangian relaxation, so its objective value is a lower bound on Z_R^* [we are maximizing].

So we have $Z \le cx^* - \lambda(Ax^* - b) \le Z_R^*$

$Z \le Z_R^*$

Solve Interactively by the Graphical Method:

12.6-1 a)

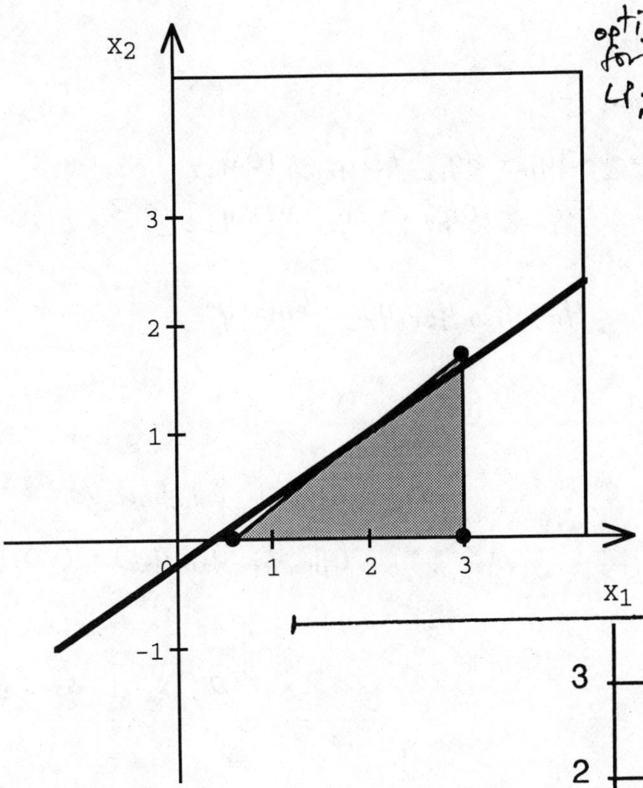

	Corner Points	Z
optimal for LP-relaxation →	(3, 1.7143)	-0.429
	(0.6, 0)	-1.8
	(3, 0)	-9

Optimal value of Z: -1

Optimal integer solution: (2,1)

$x_2 \geq 2$ Branch

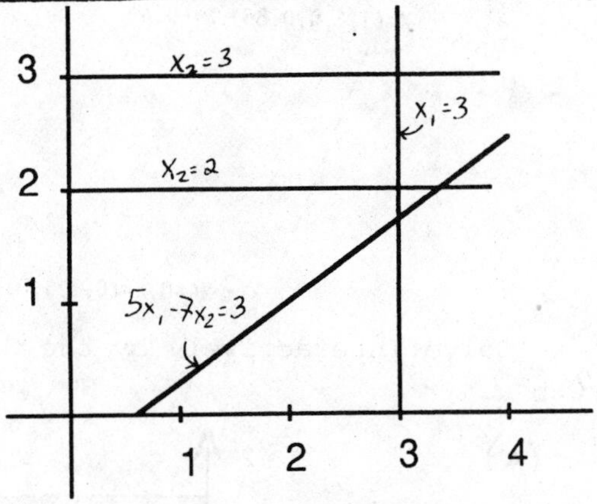

Infeasible Subproblem
Branch is Fathomed.

b)

Linear Relaxation of Entire Problem

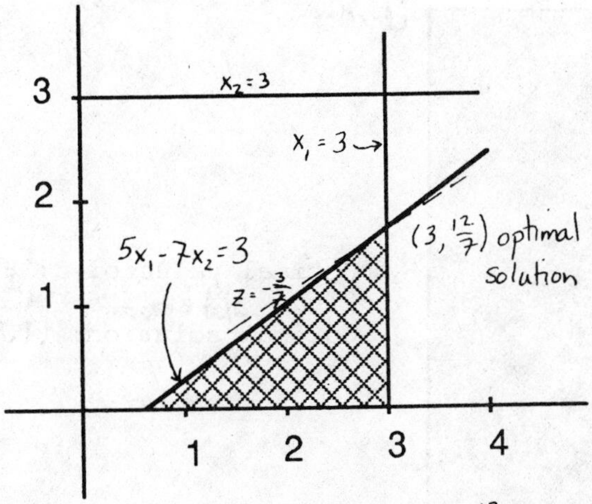

optimal solution $(x_1, x_2) = (3, \frac{12}{7})$

$z = -\frac{3}{7}$

$x_2 \leq 1$ Branch

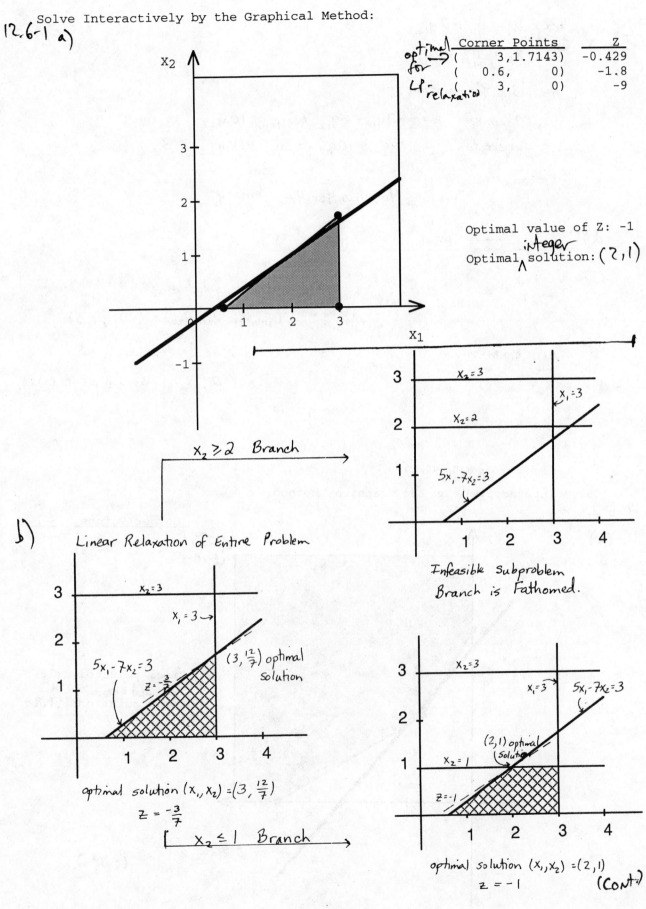

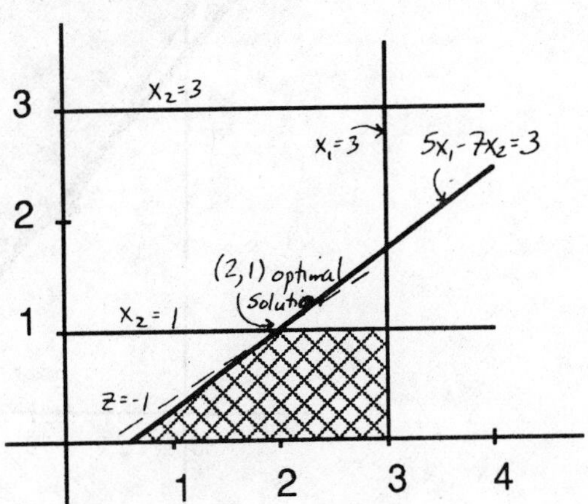

optimal solution $(x_1, x_2) = (2,1)$

$z = -1$

(Cont.)

12.6-1 c) Let $x_1 = y_{11} + 2y_{12}$

$x_2 = y_{21} + 2y_{22}$

The BIP formulation is:

$$\text{Maximize} \quad Z = -3y_{11} - 6y_{12} + 5y_{21} + 10y_{22}$$

$$\text{subject to:} \quad 5y_{11} + 10y_{12} - 7y_{21} - 14y_{22} \geq 3$$

$$y_{11}, y_{12}, y_{21}, y_{22} \text{ binary.}$$

d)

```
                   --- X4=1,Inf.,F
                  /
                 /
                /
               /
              /
             /
            /
X=(1,1,0,0.86),Z=-0.4
            \
             \
              \
               \
                \
                 \
                   --- X4=0,X=(0,1,1,0),Z=-1
```

The optimal solution is:

$(y_{11}, y_{12}, y_{21}, y_{22}) = (0,1,1,0)$

$Z = -1$

so $x_1 = 2$, $x_2 = 1$ as in part (a).

Solve Interactively by the Graphical Method:

12.6-2

(a)

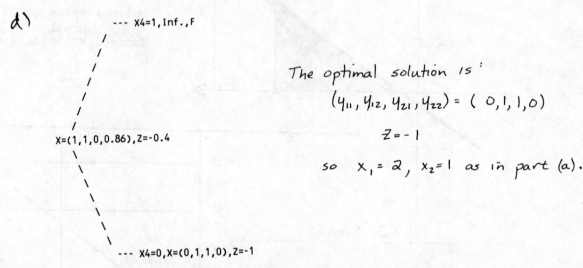

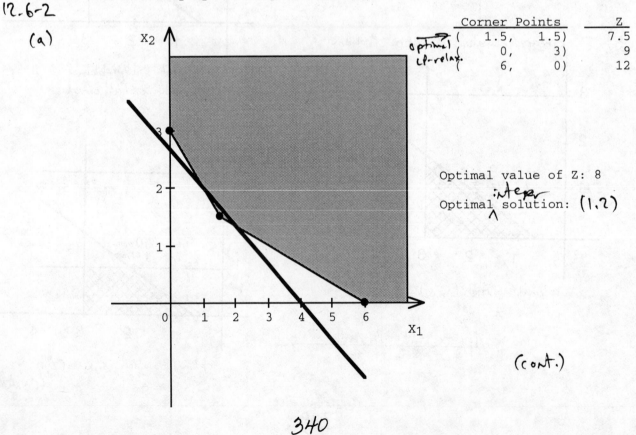

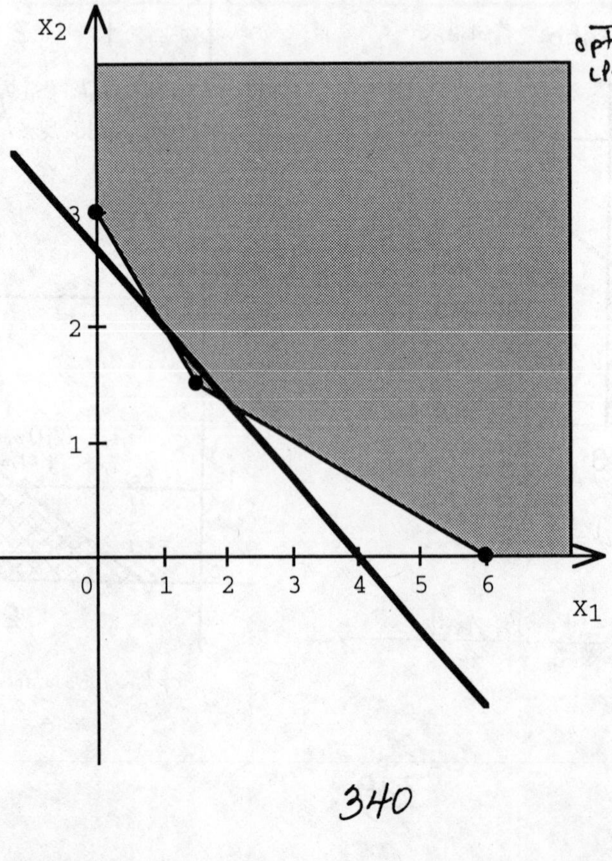

Corner Points		Z
(1.5,	1.5)	7.5
(0,	3)	9
(6,	0)	12

(optimal LP-relax. → (1.5, 1.5))

Optimal value of Z: 8

Optimal integer solution: (1,2)

(cont.)

12.6-2 b)

Linear Programming Relaxation of Entire Problem

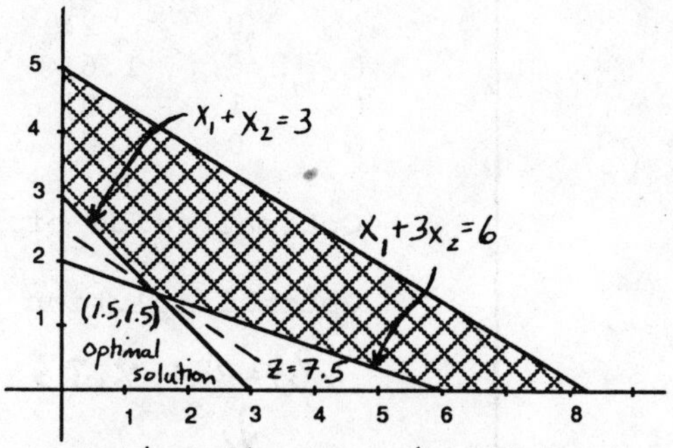

optimal solution $(x_1, x_2) = (1.5, 1.5)$

Z = 7.5

$x_1 \le 1$ Branch

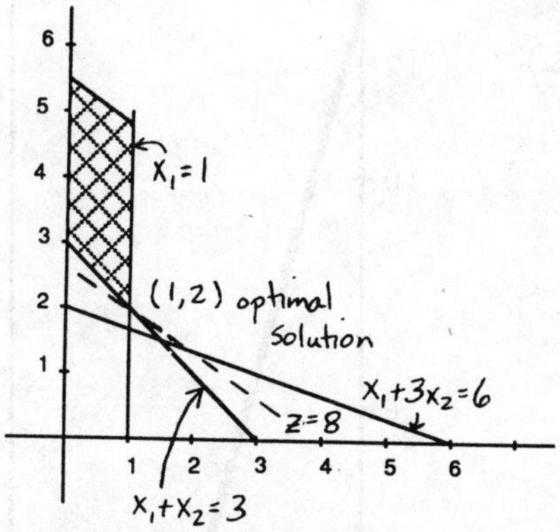

optimal solution $(x_1, x_2) = (1, 2)$

Z = 8

Feasible for original problem

$x_1 \ge 2$ Branch

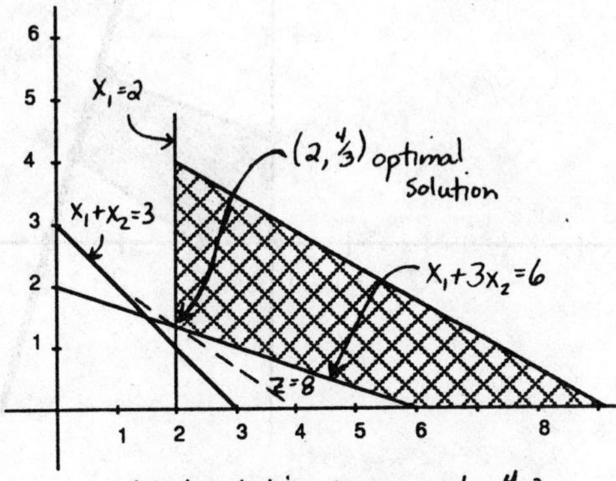

optimal solution $(x_1, x_2) = (2, \frac{4}{3})$

Z = 8

$x_2 \le 1$ Branch

$x_2 \ge 2$ Branch

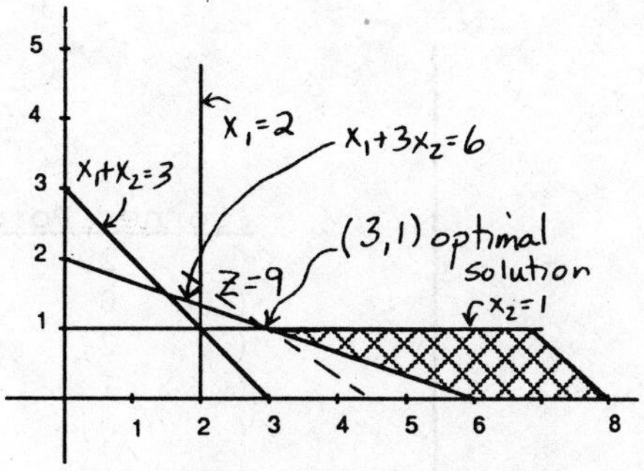

optimal solution $(x_1, x_2) = (3, 1)$

Z = 9

F1

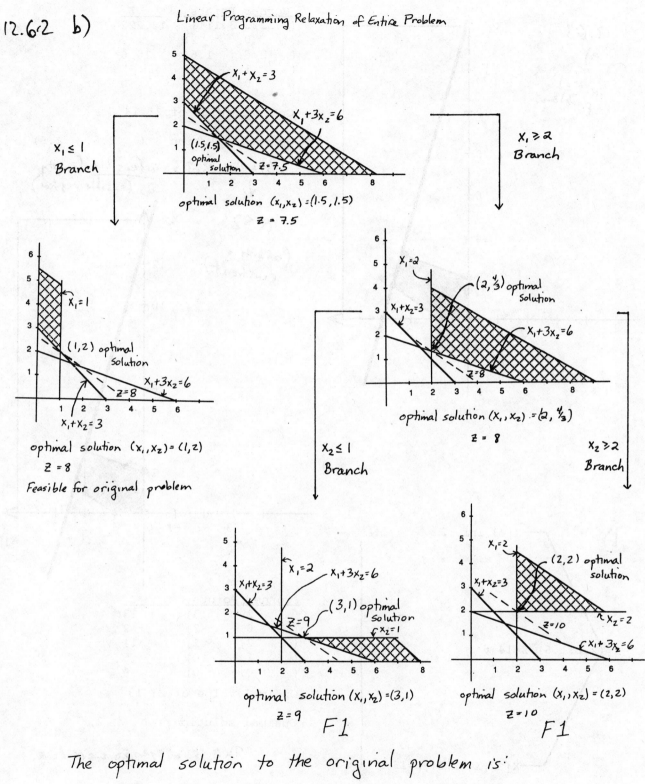

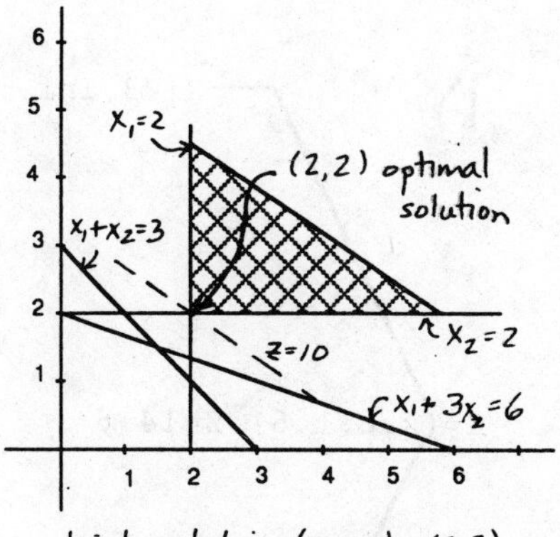

optimal solution $(x_1, x_2) = (2, 2)$

Z = 10

F1

The optimal solution to the original problem is:

$(x_1, x_2) = (1, 2)$ with $Z = 8$

12.6-3

a)

initial problem:

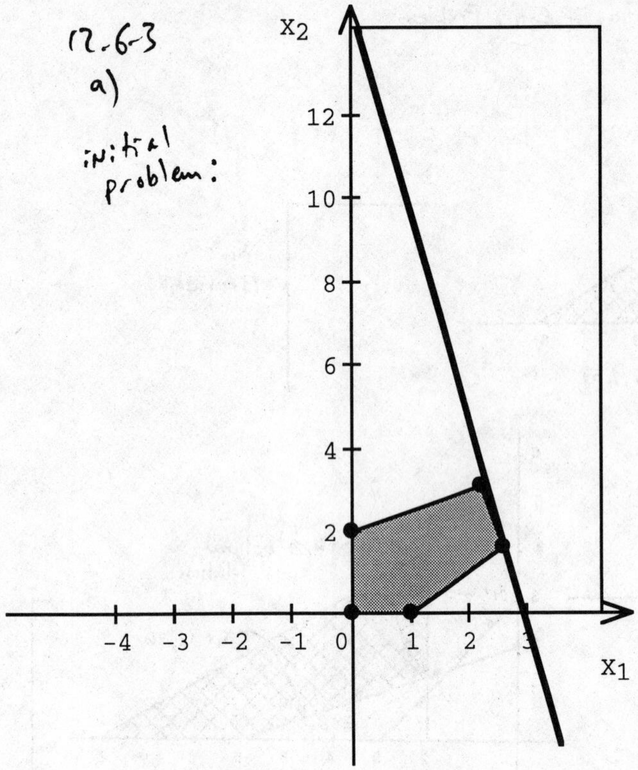

Corner Points	Z
(2.2222,3.1111)	14.222
(0, 2)	2
(2.6, 1.6)	14.6*
(1, 0)	5
(0, 0)	0

Optimal value of Z: 14.6

Optimal solution: (2.6, 1.6)

Branch: $x_1 \geq 3$ infeasible (empty feasible region)

↓

$x_1 \leq 2$:

(add this constraint)

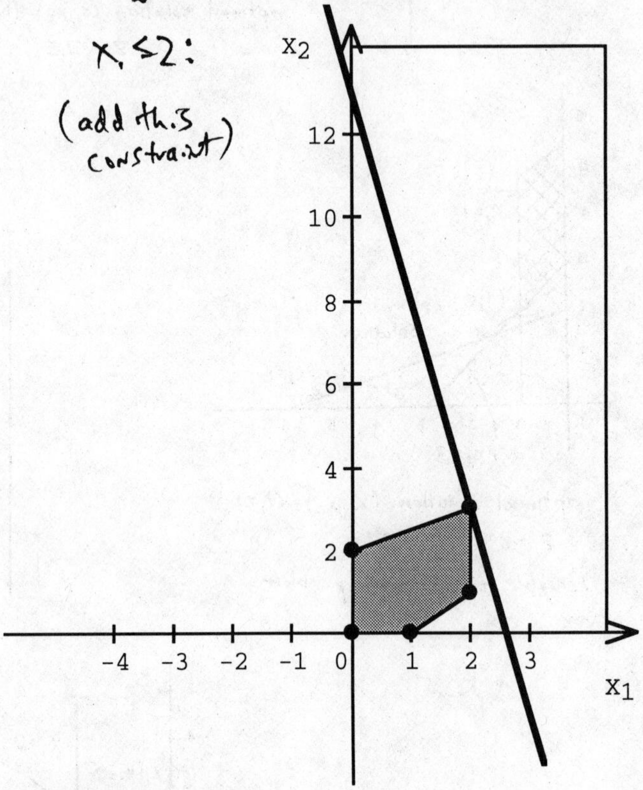

Corner Points	Z
(2, 3)	13*
(0, 2)	2
(2, 1)	11
(1, 0)	5
(0, 0)	0

Optimal value of Z: 13

Optimal solution: (2, 3)

This is integer, so we're done.

b)

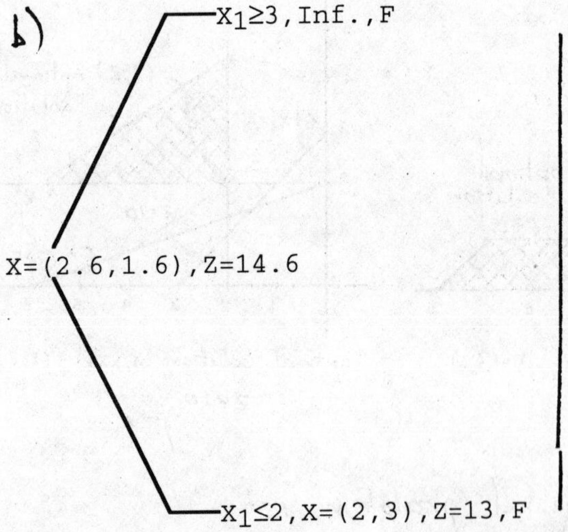

Optimal Solution:
x = (2, 3)
Z*= 13

c) Solution:
X_1 = 2
X_2 = 3

Z = 13

12.6-4

a)

initial problem:

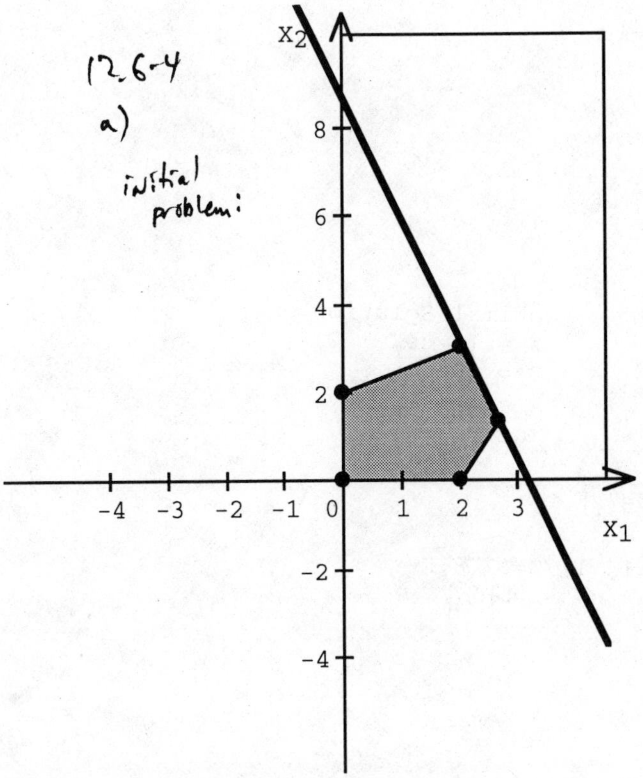

Corner Points		Z
(2.6667,	1.3333)	693.33*
(2,	3)	680
(2,	0)	440
(0,	2)	160
(0,	0)	0

Optimal value of Z: 693.33

Optimal solution: (2.6667,1.3333)

Branch: $x_1 \geq 3$ infeasible

↓

$x_1 \leq 2$ (adding constraint):

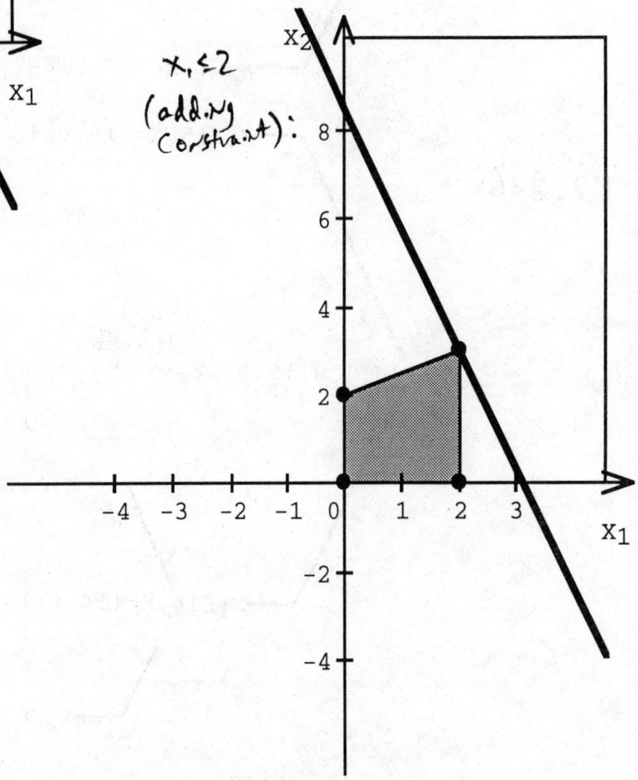

Corner Points		Z
(2,	3)	680*
(2,	0)	440
(0,	2)	160
(0,	0)	0

Optimal value of Z: 680

Optimal solutions: (2, 3)
(2, 3)
(2, 3)

integer → finished

b)

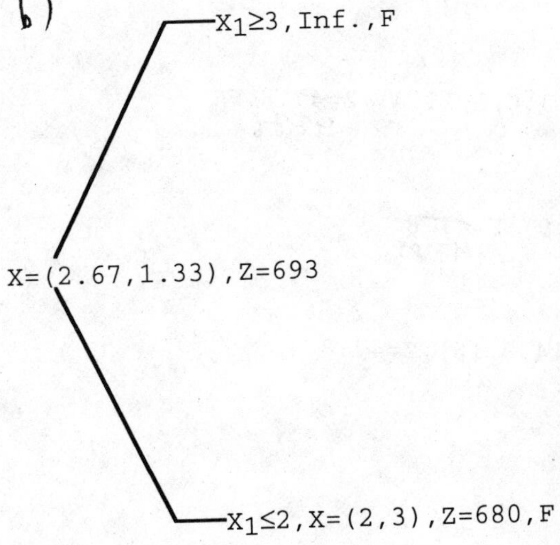

Optimal Solution:
X = (2, 3)
Z*= 680

c) Solution:

X_1 = 2
X_2 = 3

Z = 680

12.6-5

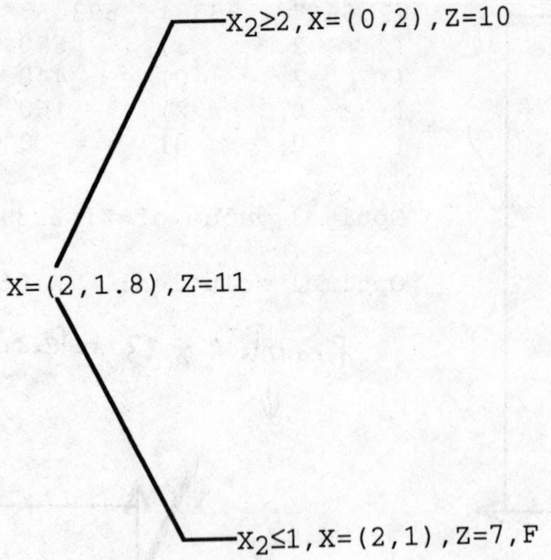

Optimal Solution:
x = (0, 2)
Z*= 10

12.6-6

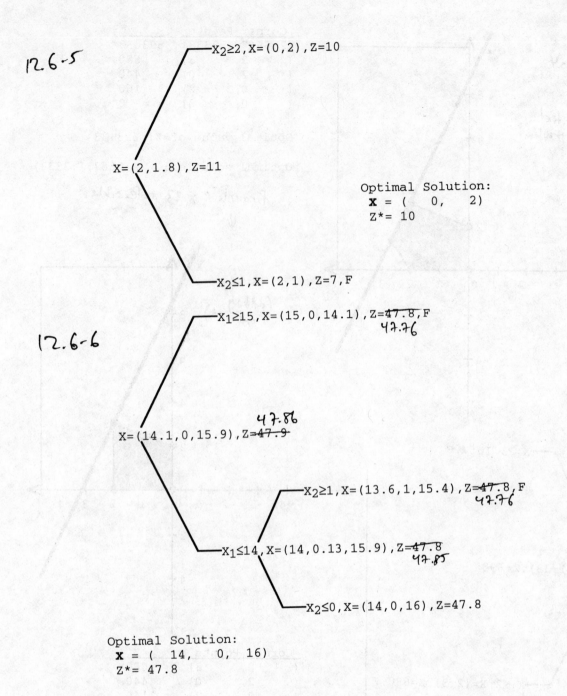

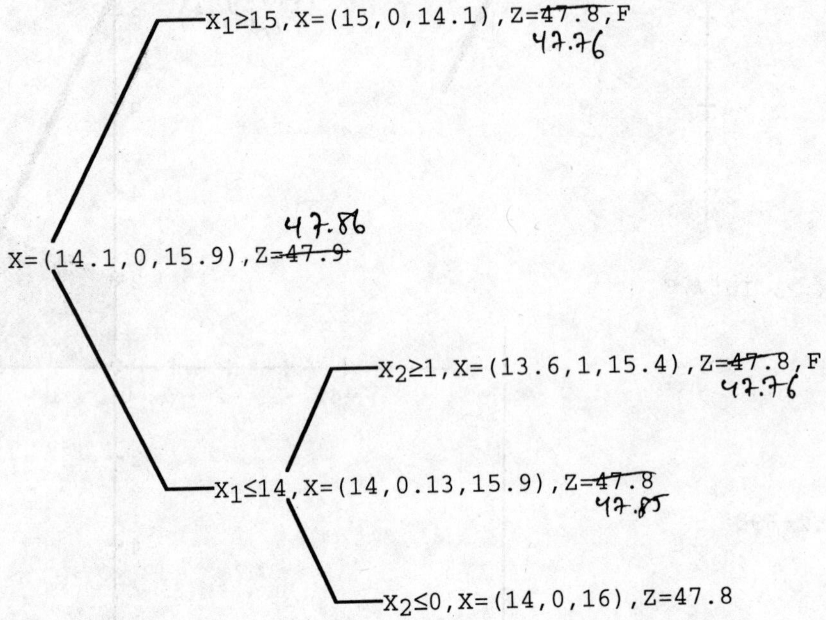

Optimal Solution:
x = (14, 0, 16)
Z*= 47.8

12.6-7 a) let x_i = # of 1/4 units of product i to produce, i=1,2

max. $4x_1 + 2.5x_2$

s.t. $3/4\,x_1 + 1/2\,x_2 \leq 8$

$1/2\,x_1 + 3/4\,x_2 \leq 7$

$x_1, x_2 \geq 0$, integer

(cont.)

b)

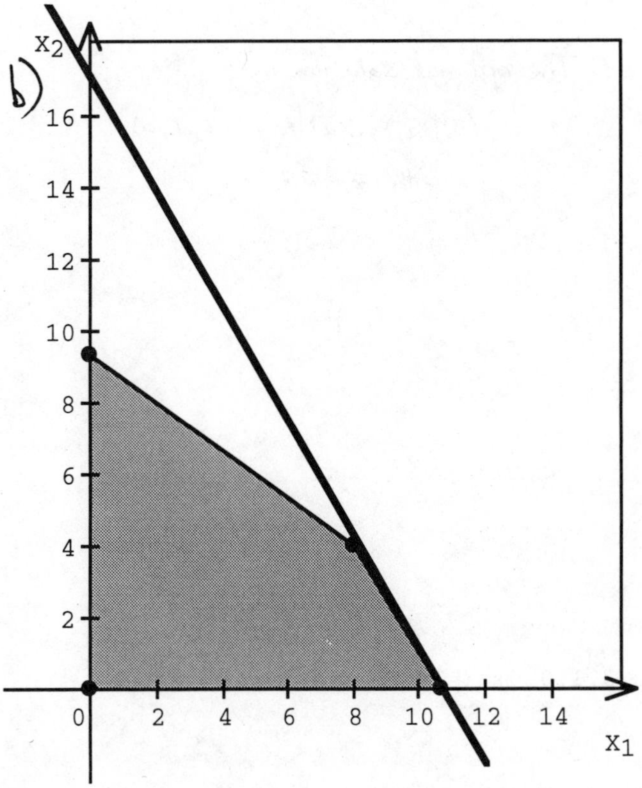

Corner Points		Z
(8,	4)	42
(10.667,	0)	42.667*
(0,	9.3333)	23.333
(0,	0)	0

Optimal value of Z: 42.667

Optimal solution: (10.667, 0)

c) $x_1 \geq 11 \rightarrow$ infeasible

$x_1 \leq 10$ ↓

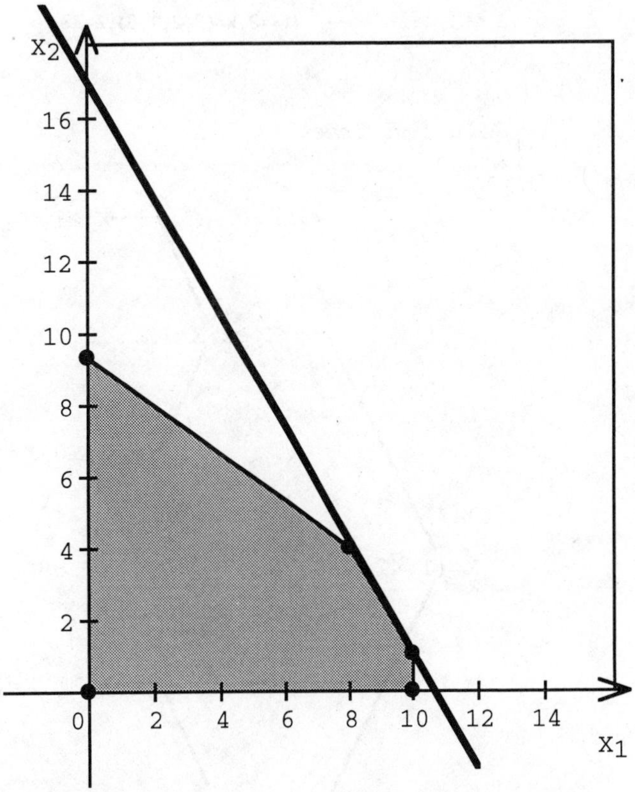

Corner Points		Z
(8,	4)	42
(10,	1)	42.5*
(0,	9.3333)	23.333
(10,	0)	40
(0,	0)	0

Optimal value of Z: 42.5

Optimal solution: (10, 1)

integer ⇒ optimal for IP

d)

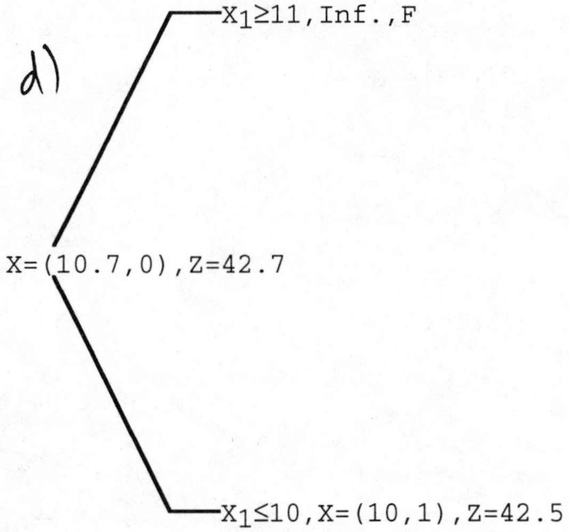

Optimal Solution:
x = (10, 1)
Z*= 42.5

e) Solution:

X_1 = 10
X_2 = 1

Z = 42.5

12.6-8

```
                     --- X1>=3,X=(3,0,0,0),Z=15,F
                    /
                   /
                  /
                 /
                /
               /
X=(2.5,2.5,0,0),Z=22.5
               \
                \
                 \
                  \
                   \
                    \
                     --- X1<=2,X=(2,2,1,0),Z=22
```

The optimal solution is

$(x_1, x_2, x_3, x_4) = (2, 2, 1, 0)$

with $Z = 22$.

Solution Tree:

```
                          —X3≥1,X=(2,3,1,0,0),Z=14,F
                         /
          —X1≥2,X=(2,0,0.33,0,0),Z=10.3
         /               \
        /                 —X3≤0,X=(2,2,0,0,0),Z=12
       /
X=(1.42,0.08,0.42,0,0),Z=7.58
       \
        \                 —X3≥1,X=(1,0,1,0,2),Z=12
         \               /
          —X1≤1,X=(1,0,0.5,0,2),Z=11.5
                         \
                          —X3≤0,X=(1,0,0,3,2),Z=17,F
```

Optimal Solution:
X = (1, 0, 1, 0, 2) , (2,2,0,0,0)
Z*= 12

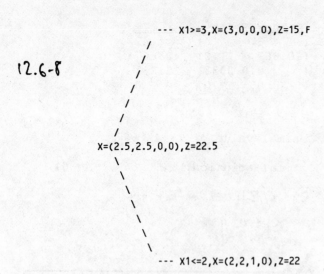

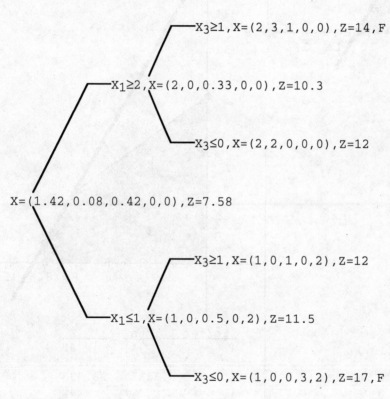

12.6-9.

Solution Tree:

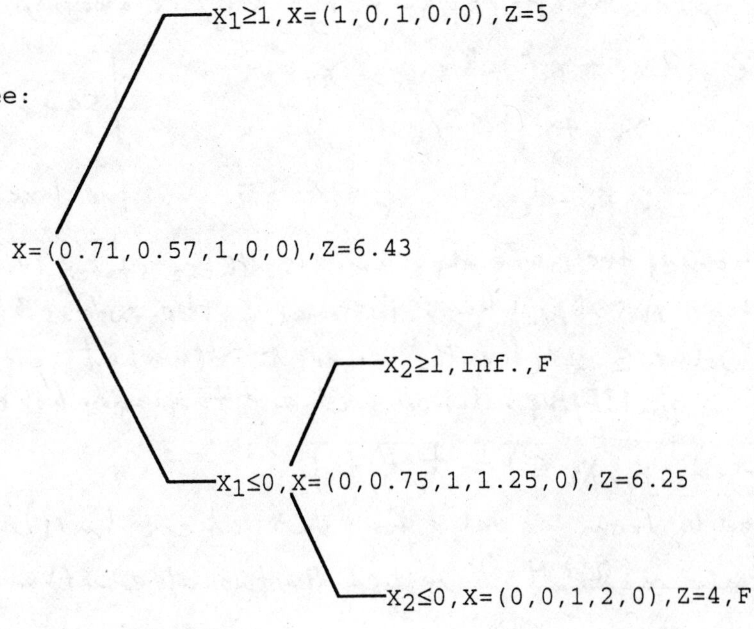

Optimal Solution:
X = (1, 0, 1, 0, 0)
Z*= 5

12.6-10 Solution Tree:

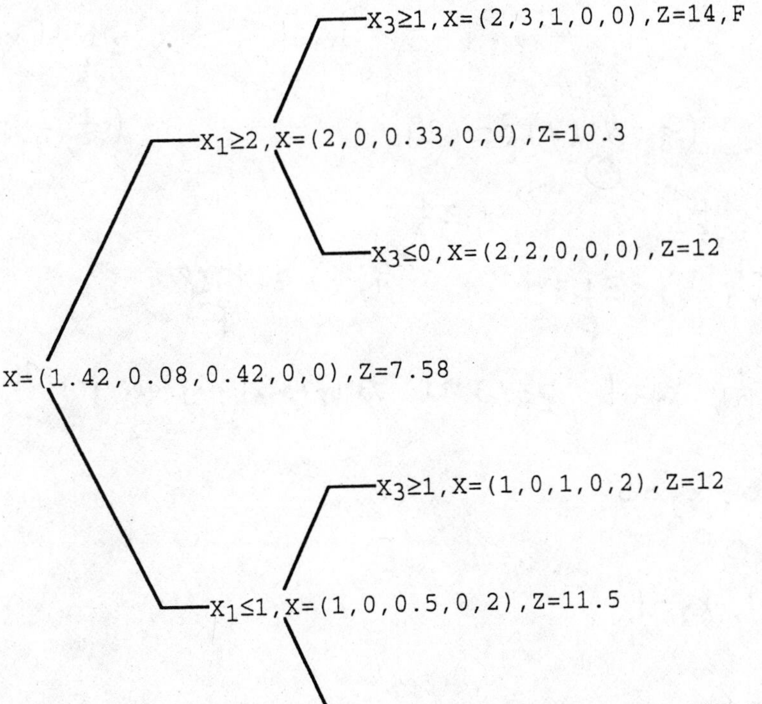

Optimal Solution:
X = (1, 0, 1, 0, 2)
Z*= 12 <u>or</u> x=(2,2,0,0,0)

12.6-11

a) (1) Use the quadratic programming (QP) relaxation:

$$\max. \; z = 2x_1 - x_1^2 + 3x_2 - 3x_2^2$$

s.t.
$$x_1 + x_2 \leq 3/4 \qquad \text{| same}$$

$$\tfrac{1}{5} \leq x_1 \leq \tfrac{1}{2} \;,\; \tfrac{1}{5} \leq x_2 \leq \tfrac{1}{2} \qquad \text{| relaxed}$$

(2) The fathoming tests are the same as those stated in the chapter. A subproblem is fathomed if its infeasible, has value $\leq z^*$ for the current incumbent, or has a <u>qualifying</u> solution, where to qualify here we need $x_1, x_2 \in \{\tfrac{1}{5}, \tfrac{1}{4}, \tfrac{1}{3}, \tfrac{1}{2}\}$.

(3) To branch from a value for x_j^* where $(m+1)^{-1} < x_j^* < m^{-1}$ for some $m = 2, 3, 4$, we use the two alternative constraints

$$x_j \leq (m+1)^{-1} \qquad \underline{or} \qquad x_j \geq m^{-1}$$

b) The branch & bound tree will look like this:

relaxed soln.
(.4375, .3125) z = 1.328

①Branch → $x_1 \geq \tfrac{1}{2}$ [$x_1 = \tfrac{1}{2}$ in th.3 problem]

$x_1 \leq \tfrac{1}{3}$

$(\tfrac{1}{3}, .4167)$ z = 1.29

$(\tfrac{1}{2}, \tfrac{1}{4})$ z = 1.3125
Incumbent

②
$x_2 \leq \tfrac{1}{3}$ → $x_2 \geq \tfrac{1}{2}$

$(\tfrac{1}{3}, \tfrac{1}{3})$ z = 1.22
F

$(\tfrac{1}{4}, \tfrac{1}{2})$ z = 1.188
F

✓ optimal!

So $x_1 = \tfrac{1}{2}$, $x_2 = \tfrac{1}{4}$, z = 1.3125 is optimal, agreeing with 12.3-5.

12.7-1

a) $x_1 = 0$, $x_3 = 0$

b) $x_1 = 0$

c) $x_1 = 1$, $x_3 = 1$

12.7-2

a) $x_1 = 0$

b) $x_1 = 1$, $x_2 = 0$

c) $x_1 = 0$, $x_2 = 1$

12.7-3 From eqn. 1, $x_3 = 0$; this makes eqn. 1 redundant.
From eqn. 3, $x_5 = 0$, $x_6 = 1$; now eqn. 3 is redundant
Since $x_6 = 1$, from eqn. 2 $x_2 = x_4 = 0$, and this is redundant.
Finally eqn. 4 reduces to $x_1 = 0$, which leaves all equations redundant. We have $x_1 = x_2 = x_3 = x_4 = x_5 = 0$, $x_6 = 1$, x_7 ?

12.7-4

a) redundant, because even if all variables are 1, $2+1+2 \leq 5$

b) not redundant, as (1,0,1) violates this ($8 \nleq 5$)

c) not redundant, as (0,0,0) (for example) violates

d) redundant, because $(0,1,1) \rightarrow 0-1-2 \geq -4$ still; this is the worst case, because we let variables with positive coefficients $=0$ and variables with negative coefficients $=1$ to try to violate the ≥ -4 condition, and we can't do it.

12.7-5

$$3x_1 - 2x_2 + x_3 \leq 3$$

$$S = 4 < 3 + |a_1| = 6$$

$$\bar{a}_1 = S - b = 1 \qquad \bar{b} = S - a_1 = 1$$

$$\rightarrow x_1 - 2x_2 + x_3 \leq 1$$

$$S = 2 < 1 + |a_2|$$

$$a_2 := b - S = -1$$

$$\rightarrow \boxed{x_1 - x_2 + x_3 \leq 1}, \text{ done.}$$

Check for yourself that the same binary (x_1, x_2, x_3) vectors satisfy both the original and the tightened constraint.

12.7-6

$$x_1 - x_2 + 3x_3 + 4x_4 \geq 1$$

$$-x_1 + x_2 - 3x_3 - 4x_4 \leq -1$$

$$S = 1 < -1 + |a_3| = 2$$

$$\rightarrow -x_1 + x_2 - 2x_3 - 4x_4 \leq -1$$

$$S = 1 < -1 + |a_4| = 3$$

$$\rightarrow \boxed{-x_1 + x_2 - 2x_3 - 2x_4 \leq -1}, \text{ done.}$$

(these steps could have been done at the same time, since they involve $a_j < 0$)

12.7-7

a) $x_1 + 3x_2 - 4x_3 \leq 2$

$S = 4 < 2 + |a_2|$

$\rightarrow x_1 + 2x_2 - 4x_3 \leq 1$

$S = 3 < 1 + |a_3|$

$\rightarrow \boxed{x_1 + 2x_2 - 2x_3 \leq 1}$

b) $3x_1 - x_2 + 4x_3 \geq 1$

$-3x_1 + x_2 - 4x_3 \leq -1$

$S = 1 < -1 + |a_1|, -1 + |a_3|$

$\rightarrow \boxed{-2x_1 + x_2 - 2x_3 \leq -1}$

12.7-8 $2x_1 + 3x_2 \leq 4$

minimum cover is $\{x_1, x_2\}$

$\longrightarrow \boxed{x_1 + x_2 \leq 1}$ ✓ same as with tightening

12.7-9 $x_1 + 3x_2 + 2x_3 + 4x_4 \leq 5$

minimum covers: $\{x_2, x_4\} \rightarrow x_2 + x_4 \leq 1$

$\{x_3, x_4\} \rightarrow x_3 + x_4 \leq 1$

$\{x_1, x_2, x_3\} \rightarrow x_1 + x_2 + x_3 \leq 2$

12.7-10

$3x_1 + 4x_2 + 2x_3 + 5x_4 \leq 7$

minimum covers: $\{x_1, x_4\} \rightarrow x_1 + x_4 \leq 1$

$\{x_2, x_4\} \rightarrow x_2 + x_4 \leq 1$

$\{x_1, x_2, x_3\} \rightarrow x_1 + x_2 + x_3 \leq 2$

12.7-11 $3x_1 + 5x_2 + 4x_3 + 8x_4 \leq 10$

cutting planes:

$x_1 + x_4 \leq 1$

$x_2 + x_4 \leq 1$

$x_3 + x_4 \leq 1$

$x_1 + x_2 + x_3 \leq 2$

12.7-12

$5x_1 + 3x_2 + 7x_3 + 4x_4 + 6x_5 \le 9$

cutting planes:

$x_1 + x_3 \le 1$

$x_1 + x_5 \le 1$

$x_2 + x_3 \le 1$

$x_3 + x_4 \le 1$

$x_3 + x_5 \le 1$

$x_4 + x_5 \le 1$

$x_1 + x_2 + x_4 \le 2$

12.7-13

1) $3x_2 + x_4 + x_5 \ge 3 \Rightarrow x_2 = 1$, leaving a redundant constraint

2) $x_1 + x_2 \le 1$, with $x_2 = 1$ we set $x_1 = 0$, redundant now

3) $x_2 + x_4 - x_5 - x_6 \le -1$, $x_2 = 1 \Rightarrow x_4 = 0,\ x_5 = x_6 = 1$, eliminate

4) $x_2 + 2x_6 + 3x_7 + x_8 + 2x_9 \ge 4$

$x_2 = x_6 = 1 \rightarrow 3x_7 + x_8 + 2x_9 \ge 1$

tighten: $\rightarrow x_7 + x_8 + x_9 \ge 1$

5) $-x_3 + 2x_5 + x_6 + 2x_7 - 2x_8 + x_9 \le 5$

$x_5 = x_6 = 1 \rightarrow -x_3 + 2x_7 - 2x_8 + x_9 \le 2$

tighten: $\rightarrow -x_3 + x_7 - x_8 + x_9 \le 1$

Now we have

max. $x_3 + 2x_7 + x_8 + 3x_9$

s.t. $x_7 + x_8 + x_9 \ge 1$

$-x_3 + x_7 - x_8 + x_9 \le 1$

Since we're maximizing & all variables have positive coefficients in objective, try $(1,1,1,1) \rightarrow$ $3 \ge 1$ ✓

$0 \le 1$ ✓ feasible, so optimal!

$x_2 = x_5 = x_6 = x_3 = x_7 = x_8 = x_9 = 1 \Rightarrow Z = 15$

CP12-1 a) decision variables:

$$x_{ij} = \begin{cases} 1 & \text{if students from area } i \text{ are assigned to school } j \\ 0 & \text{if not} \end{cases}$$

$i = 1,2,3,4,5,6 \quad j = 1,2,3$

let c_{ij} = bussing cost (data from Chapter 3)
s_i = student population of area i
k_j = capacity of school j

model: minimize $\sum_{i=1}^{6} \sum_{j=1}^{3} c_{ij} s_i x_{ij}$

s.t. $\sum_i s_i x_{ij} \le k_j \quad j = 1,2,3$

$\sum_j x_{ij} = 1 \quad i = 1,2,3,4,5,6$

$\sum_i (35 - p_{ik}) s_i x_{ij} \ge 0 \quad j = 1,2,3, \; k = 6,7,8$

x_{ij} binary $\forall i,j$

Note $x_{21} = x_{43} = x_{52} = 0$ due to infeasibility

b) The models really aren't too different; x_{ij} are binary here, which amounts to forcing their value in the LP of CP3-1 to be either 0 or S_i. We can leave out the 3 variables known to be 0, and also 9 redundant constraints. The LP-relaxation of this model, with $0 \le x_{ij} \le 1$, would allow us to interpret x_{ij} as the fraction of students from area i to be assigned to school j. This obviously would be a more general model, equivalent to that in CP3-1.

c) When using the Courseware be careful to keep up with the meaning of each variable, since we can't give them names like X_{61} for area 6, school 1 —
The solution is to assign areas 1 and 6 to school 1, areas 2 and 4 to school 2, and areas 3 and 5 to school 3.

d) The cost is now \$1,085,000, compared to \$644,700 from CP3-1(c), so this restriction costs \$440,300.

[printout for (c) next page]

CP 12-1 (c)

Automatic Binary Integer Programming Branch and Bound Algorithm:

Model:

Number of binary (0-1) variables: 15
Number of general integer variables: 0
Number of continuous variables: 0
Number of functional constraints: 18

$$\text{Min } Z = 135 X_1 + 315 X_3 + 240 X_4 + 300 X_5 + 330 X_6 + 165 X_7 + 110 X_8 + 70 X_9 + 175 X_{10} + 200 X_{12} + 225 X_{13} + 135 X_{14}$$

subject to

1) $45 X_1 + 55 X_6 + 35 X_9 + 50 X_{11} + 45 X_{13} \leq 95$

2) $45 X_2 + 60 X_4 + 55 X_7 + 35 X_{10} + 45 X_{14} \leq 115$

3) $45 X_3 + 60 X_5 + 55 X_8 + 50 X_{12} + 45 X_{15} \leq 105$

4) $1 X_1 + 1 X_2 + 1 X_3 = 1$

5) $1 X_4 + 1 X_5 = 1$

6) $1 X_6 + 1 X_7 + 1 X_8 = 1$

7) $1 X_9 + 1 X_{10} = 1$

8) $1 X_{11} + 1 X_{12} = 1$

9) $1 X_{13} + 1 X_{14} + 1 X_{15} = 1$

10) $135 X_1 + 275 X_6 + 245 X_9 - 200 X_{11} + 45 X_{13} \geq 0$

11) $-135 X_1 + 165 X_6 - 175 X_9 + 50 X_{11} + 315 X_{13} \geq 0$

12) $225 X_1 - 165 X_6 + 105 X_9 + 400 X_{11} - 135 X_{13} \geq 0$

13) $135 X_2 - 120 X_4 + 275 X_7 + 245 X_{10} + 45 X_{14} \geq 0$

14) $-135 X_2 + 420 X_4 + 165 X_7 - 175 X_{10} + 315 X_{14} \geq 0$

15) $225 X_2 - 165 X_7 + 105 X_{10} - 135 X_{14} \geq 0$

16) $135 X_3 - 120 X_5 + 275 X_8 - 200 X_{12} + 45 X_{15} \geq 0$

17) $-135 X_3 + 420 X_5 + 165 X_8 + 50 X_{12} + 315 X_{15} \geq 0$

18) $225 X_3 - 165 X_8 + 400 X_{12} - 135 X_{15} \geq 0$

and

$X_1 = \{0,1\}$, $X_2 = \{0,1\}$, $X_3 = \{0,1\}$, $X_4 = \{0,1\}$, $X_5 = \{0,1\}$, $X_6 = \{0,1\}$, $X_7 = \{0,1\}$, $X_8 = \{0,1\}$, $X_9 = \{0,1\}$, $X_{10} = \{0,1\}$, $X_{11} = \{0,1\}$, $X_{12} = \{0,1\}$, $X_{13} = \{0,1\}$, $X_{14} = \{0,1\}$, $X_{15} = \{0,1\}$.

(solution next page)

CP 12-1 cont.

(c) Solution:

X_1	= 1	X_{11}
X_2	= 0	
X_3	= 0	
X_4	= 1	X_{22}
X_5	= 0	
X_6	= 0	
X_7	= 0	
X_8	= 1	X_{33}
X_9	= 0	
X_{10}	= 1	X_{42}
X_{11}	= 0	
X_{12}	= 1	X_{53}
X_{13}	= 1	X_{61}
X_{14}	= 0	
X_{15}	= 0	
Z	= 1085	

e) Solution:

X_1	= 1
X_2	= 0
X_3	= 0
X_4	= 1
X_5	= 0
X_6	= 0
X_7	= 0
X_8	= 1
X_9	= 0
X_{10}	= 1
X_{11}	= 0
X_{12}	= 1
X_{13}	= 1
X_{14}	= 0
X_{15}	= 0
Z	= 975

f) Solution:

X_1	= 1
X_2	= 0
X_3	= 0
X_4	= 1
X_5	= 0
X_6	= 0
X_7	= 0
X_8	= 1
X_9	= 0
X_{10}	= 1
X_{11}	= 0
X_{12}	= 1
X_{13}	= 1
X_{14}	= 0
X_{15}	= 0
Z	= 840

Solution is the same in (e) and (f), just cheaper, saving $110,000 for Option 1 and another $135,000 for Option 2.

g)

option	cost	# students walking > 1 mile	# students walking > 1.5 miles
0 (current)	1085	0	0
1	975	550	0
2	840	1000	450

h) Option 2 has a greater marginal benefit than Option 1; going from the current plan to Option 1 saves $110K and produces 550 additional walkers, while going from Option 1 to Option 2 saves more and adds fewer walkers. So it seems somewhat unlikely Option 1 is best, although it would depend on the magnitude of the safety concerns. If the concerns were very great, however, one would expect Option 0, the status quo, to be chosen.

Chapter 13: Nonlinear Programming

13.1-1. Maximize $f(x) = 100x_1^{2/3} + 10x_1 + 40x_2^{3/4} + 5x_2 + 50x_3^{1/2} + 5x_3$

subject to:

$$
\begin{aligned}
9x_1 + 3x_2 + 5x_3 &\le 500 \\
5x_1 + 4x_2 &\le 350 \\
3x_1 + 2x_3 &\le 150 \\
x_3 &\le 20
\end{aligned}
$$

$x_1 \ge 0,\ x_2 \ge 0,\ x_3 \ge 0$

13.1-2. Marginal Cost:

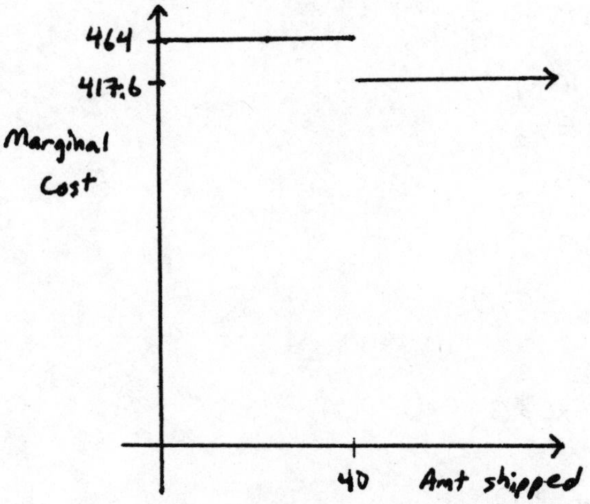

Total Cost:

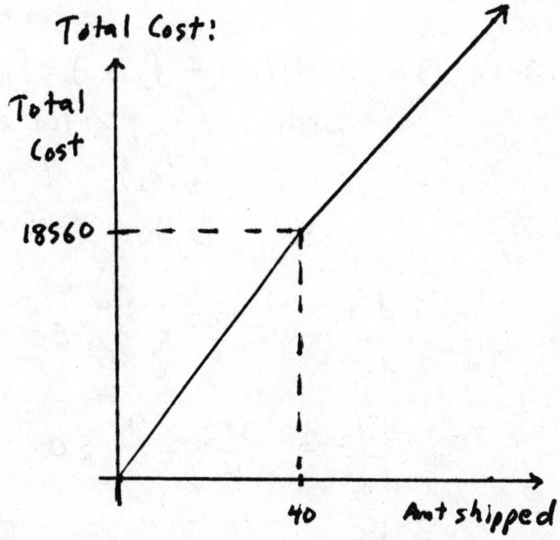

Each term in the objective function changes (as above) from $a_{ij}x_{ij}$ to

$$a_{ij}x_{ij} - 0.1\,a_{ij}(x_{ij}-40)\,S(x_{ij}-40)$$

where a_{ij} is the shipping cost from cannery i to warehouse j

and $S(x) = \begin{cases} 0 & x < 0 \\ 1 & x \ge 0 \end{cases}$

otherwise, the formulation is the same.

13.1-3. a) Maximize $5x_1 + 10x_2 - \beta(4x_1^2 + 5x_1x_2 + 100x_2^2)$
subject to $20x_1 + 30x_2 \le 50$
$x_1 \ge 0,\ x_2 \ge 0$

b) Results:

β	x_1	x_2	Z
0.02	1.447	0.702	13.000
0.1	2.186	0.209	10.445
0.5	1.206	0.070	3.365

$\beta = 0 \Rightarrow x_1^* = 0,\ x_2^* = 5/3$
$\beta = \infty \Rightarrow$ minimize $4x_1^2 + 5x_1x_2 + 100x_2^2$
subject to $20x_1 + 30x_2 \le 50$
$x_1 \ge 0,\ x_2 \ge 0$

$\Rightarrow x_1^* = 0,\ x_2^* = 0$

Relative concentrations:

β	% stock 1	% stock 2
0	0	100
0.02	67.3	32.7
0.1	91.3	8.7
0.5	94.5	5.5
∞	—	—

13.2-1. $f(x) = f_1(x_1) + f_2(x_2) + f_3(x_3)$
with $f_1(x_1) = 100x_1^{2/3} + 10x_1$
$f_2(x_2) = 40x_2^{3/4} + 5x_2$
$f_3(x_3) = 50x_3^{1/2} + 5x_3$

$$\frac{d^2f_1}{dx_1^2} = -\frac{200}{9}x_1^{-4/3} \le 0 \text{ for } x_1 \ge 0$$

$$\frac{d^2f_2}{dx_2^2} = -\frac{120}{16}x_2^{-5/4} \le 0 \text{ for } x_2 \ge 0$$

$$\frac{d^2f_3}{dx_3^2} = -\frac{50}{4}x_3^{-3/2} \le 0 \text{ for } x_3 \ge 0$$

f_1, f_2 and f_3 are concave over the non-negative orthant so f must be concave in the same region. The constraints are linear and, therefore, convex so the problem is a convex programming problem.

13.2-2. $\frac{\partial^2 f}{\partial x_1^2} = -8\beta \le 0 \quad \forall \beta \ge 0$

$\frac{\partial^2 f}{\partial x_2^2} = -200\beta \le 0 \quad \forall \beta \ge 0$

$\frac{\partial^2 f}{\partial x_1 \partial x_2} = -5\beta$

$\Rightarrow \frac{\partial^2 f}{\partial x_1^2}\frac{\partial^2 f}{\partial x_2^2} - \left[\frac{\partial^2 f}{\partial x_1 \partial x_2}\right]^2 = 1600\beta^2 - 25\beta^2 = 1575\beta^2 \ge 0$

$\Rightarrow$ f is concave everywhere $\forall \beta \ge 0$

13.2-3. Objective function: $Z = 3x_1 + 5x_2$

$\Rightarrow x_2 = -3/5\, x_1 + 1/5\, Z$

$\Rightarrow$ slope is $-3/5$

Constraint boundary: $9x_1^2 + 5x_2^2 = 216$

$\Rightarrow x_2 = \sqrt{1/5(216 - 9x_1^2)}$

$\Rightarrow \frac{\partial x}{\partial x_1} = -\frac{1}{5}\frac{9x_1}{\sqrt{1/5(216-9x_1^2)}}$

$= -3/5$ for $x_1 = 2$

So the objective function is tangent to this constraint at $(x_1, x_2) = (2, 6)$

13.2-4. Constraint boundary: $3x_1 + 2x_2 = 18$

$\Rightarrow g(x_1) = x_2 = -3/2\, x_1 + 9$

$\Rightarrow \frac{dg(x_1)}{dx_1} = -3/2$

Objective function at $(8/3, 5)$:

$(9x_1^2 - 126x_1 + 857) - 182x_2 + 13x^2 = 0$

$\Rightarrow f(x_1) = x_2 = \frac{182 - 2\sqrt{-2860 + 1638x_1 - 117x^2}}{26}$

$\Rightarrow \frac{df(x_1)}{dx_1} = -\frac{1}{26}\frac{1638 - 234x_1}{\sqrt{-2860 + 1638x_1 - 117x_1^2}}$

$\Rightarrow \frac{df(8/3)}{dx_1} = -3/2$

and $f(8/3) = 5$, $g(8/3) = 5$

so the objective function is tangent to this constraint at $(x_1, x_2) = (8/3, 5)$

13.2-5. (a) $\frac{df}{dx} = 48 - 120x + 3x^2 = 0$

$\Rightarrow x^* = \frac{120 \pm \sqrt{120^2 - 4 \cdot 3 \cdot 48}}{6}$

$= .4041$ or 39.596

$\frac{d^2 f(.4041)}{dx^2} = -117.6 \Rightarrow f(.4041) = 2.475$ is a local maximum

$\frac{d^2 f(39.596)}{dx^2} = 117.6 \Rightarrow f(39.596) = .0253$ is a local minimum

13.2-5. (b) for $x > 39.596$ $\frac{df}{dx} > 0$ and $\frac{d^2f}{dx^2} = 6x - 120 > 0$

$\Rightarrow$ f is unbounded above.

for $x < .4041$ $\frac{df}{dx} < 0$ and $\frac{d^2f}{dx^2} < 0$

$\Rightarrow$ f is unbounded below.

13.2-6. (a) $\frac{d^2f}{dx^2} = -2 \quad \forall x \Rightarrow$ f is concave

(b) $\frac{d^2f}{dx^2} = 12x^2 + 12 > 0 \quad \forall x \Rightarrow$ f is convex

(c) $\frac{d^2f}{dx^2} = 12x - 6 \begin{cases} > 0 & \text{for } x > \frac{1}{2} \\ < 0 & \text{for } x < \frac{1}{2} \end{cases} \Rightarrow$ f is neither convex nor concave

(d) $\frac{d^2f}{dx^2} = 12x^2 + 2 > 0 \quad \forall x \Rightarrow$ f is convex

(e) $\frac{d^2f}{dx^2} = 6x + 12x^2 \begin{cases} > 0 & \text{for } x < -\frac{1}{2} \text{ or } x > 0 \\ < 0 & \text{for } -\frac{1}{2} < x < 0 \end{cases}$

$\Rightarrow$ f is neither convex nor concave.

13.2-7. (a) $\frac{\partial^2 f}{\partial x_1^2} = -2 < 0 \quad \forall (x_1, x_2)$

$\frac{\partial^2 f}{\partial x_2^2} = -2 < 0 \quad \forall (x_1, x_2)$

$\frac{\partial^2 f}{\partial x_1^2}\frac{\partial^2 f}{\partial x_2^2} - \left[\frac{\partial^2 f}{\partial x_1 \partial x_2}\right]^2 = 4 - 1^2 = 3 > 0 \quad \forall (x_1, x_2)$

$\Rightarrow$ f is concave

(b) $\frac{\partial^2 f}{\partial x_1^2} = 4 > 0 \quad \forall (x_1, x_2)$

$\frac{\partial^2 f}{\partial x_2^2} = 2 > 0 \quad \forall (x_1, x_2)$

$\frac{\partial^2 f}{\partial x_1^2}\frac{\partial^2 f}{\partial x_2^2} - \left[\frac{\partial^2 f}{\partial x_1 \partial x_2}\right]^2 = 8 - (2)^2 = 4 > 0 \quad \forall (x_1, x_2)$

$\Rightarrow$ f is convex

(c) $\frac{\partial^2 f}{\partial x_1^2} = 2 > 0 \quad \forall (x_1, x_2)$ $\quad \frac{\partial^2 f}{\partial x_2^2} = 4 > 0 \quad \forall (x_1, x_2)$

$\frac{\partial^2 f}{\partial x_1^2}\frac{\partial^2 f}{\partial x_2^2} - \left[\frac{\partial^2 f}{\partial x_1 \partial x_2}\right]^2 = -1 < 0$

$\Rightarrow$ f is neither convex nor concave

(d) $\frac{\partial^2 f}{\partial x_1^2} = \frac{\partial^2 f}{\partial x_2^2} = \frac{\partial^2 f}{\partial x_1 \partial x_2} = 0$

$\Rightarrow \frac{\partial^2 f}{\partial x_1^2}\frac{\partial^2 f}{\partial x_2^2} - \left[\frac{\partial^2 f}{\partial x_1 \partial x_2}\right]^2 = 0$

$\Rightarrow$ f is both convex and concave

13.2-7. (e) $\frac{\partial^2 f}{\partial x_1^2} = \frac{\partial^2 f}{\partial x_2^2} = 0 \quad \forall (x_1, x_2)$

$$\frac{\partial^2 f}{\partial x_1^2}\frac{\partial^2 f}{\partial x_2^2} - \left[\frac{\partial^2 f}{\partial x_1 \partial x_2}\right]^2 = -1 < 0$$

$\Rightarrow f$ is neither convex nor concave

13.2-8. Let $f = f_1 + f_2 + f_{34} + f_{56} + f_{67}$

where
$f_1 = 5x_1$
$f_2 = 2x_2^2$
$f_{34} = x_3^2 - 3x_3x_4 + 4x_4^2$
$f_{56} = x_5^2 + 3x_5x_6 + 3x_6^2$
$f_{67} = 3x_6^2 + 3x_6x_7 + x_7^2$

$\frac{d^2 f_1}{dx_1^2} = 0 \quad \forall x_1 \Rightarrow f_1$ is convex (and concave).

$\frac{d^2 f_2}{dx_2^2} = 4 \quad \forall x_2 \Rightarrow f_2$ is convex

$\frac{\partial^2 f_{34}}{\partial x_3^2} = 2 > 0 \quad \forall (x_3, x_4) \quad \frac{\partial^2 f_{34}}{\partial x_4^2} = 8 > 0 \quad \forall (x_3, x_4)$

$$\frac{\partial^2 f_{34}}{\partial x_3^2}\frac{\partial^2 f_{34}}{\partial x_4^2} - \left[\frac{\partial^2 f_{34}}{\partial x_3 \partial x_4}\right]^2 = 16 - 3^2 = 7 > 0 \quad \forall (x_3, x_4)$$

$\Rightarrow f_{34}$ is convex

$\frac{\partial^2 f_{56}}{\partial x_5^2} = 2 > 0 \quad \forall (x_5, x_6) \quad \frac{\partial^2 f_{56}}{\partial x_6^2} = 6 > 0 \quad \forall (x_5, x_6)$

$$\frac{\partial^2 f_{56}}{\partial x_5^2}\frac{\partial^2 f_{56}}{\partial x_6^2} - \left[\frac{\partial^2 f_{56}}{\partial x_5 \partial x_6}\right]^2 = 12 - 3^2 = 3 > 0 \quad \forall (x_5, x_6)$$

$\Rightarrow f_{56}$ is convex

$f_{67}(x_6, x_7) = f_{56}(x_7, x_6) \Rightarrow f_{67}$ is convex.

$\Rightarrow f$ is convex

13.2-9. (a) maximize $f(\underline{x}) = x_1 + x_2$
subject to $g(\underline{x}) = x_1^2 + x_2^2 \leq 1$
$\underline{x} \geq 0$

$\frac{\partial^2 f}{\partial x_1^2} = \frac{\partial^2 f}{\partial x_2^2} = \frac{\partial^2 f}{\partial x_1 \partial x_2} = 0$

$$\Rightarrow \frac{\partial^2 f}{\partial x_1^2}\frac{\partial^2 f}{\partial x_2^2} - \left[\frac{\partial^2 f}{\partial x_1 \partial x_2}\right]^2 = 0$$

$\Rightarrow f$ is concave (and convex)

$\frac{\partial^2 g}{\partial x_1^2} = 2 > 0 \quad \forall (x_1, x_2) \quad \frac{\partial^2 g}{\partial x_2^2} = 2 > 0 \quad \forall (x_1, x_2)$

$$\frac{\partial^2 g}{\partial x_1^2}\frac{\partial^2 g}{\partial x_2^2} - \left[\frac{\partial^2 g}{\partial x_1 \partial x_2}\right]^2 = 4 - 0^2 = 4 > 0 \quad \forall (x_1, x_2)$$

$\Rightarrow g_1$ is convex

$\Rightarrow$ the problem is a convex programming problem.

13.2-9. (b)

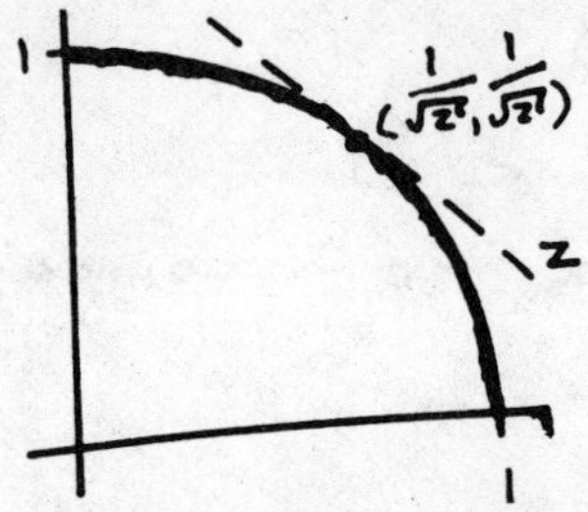

13.2-10. a)

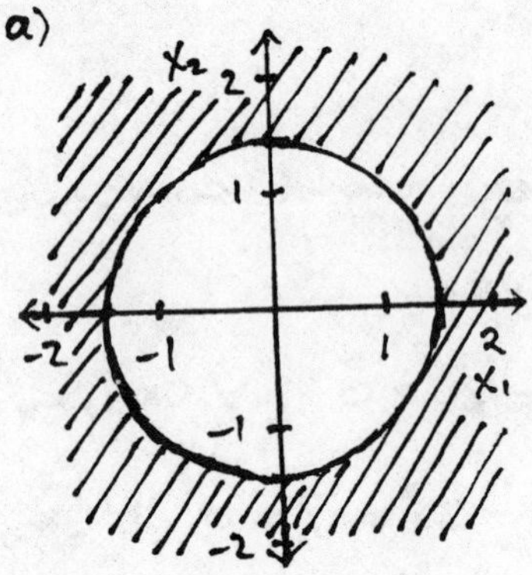

$x_1^2 + x_2^2 \geq 2$

Clearly, this is <u>not</u> a convex feasible region

(Take $(0, \sqrt{2})$ and $(0, -\sqrt{2})$, $(0,0) = \frac{1}{2}(0, \sqrt{2}) + \frac{1}{2}(0, -\sqrt{2})$ is not feasible)

b) Feasible region: $-x_1^2 - x_2^2 \leq -2$

$g_1(x_1) = -x_1^2$ and $g_2(x_2) = -x_2^2$ are both <u>concave</u> functions, not convex, so the feasible region does not need to be convex.

$\left(\frac{\partial^2}{\partial x_i^2} g_i(x_i) = -1 < 0\right)$

To <u>prove</u> that the feasible region is not convex, we need to show there are y and z both feasible, but $\alpha y + (1-\alpha) z$ not feasible $(0<\alpha<1)$, as shown in (a).

13.3-1. Since we are <u>minimizing</u> a <u>concave</u> function (see 13.1-2.) this is a nonconvex programming problem.

13.3-2. $\frac{df}{dx} = -6 + 6x - 6x^2 = 0$

$\Rightarrow x = \frac{-6 \pm \sqrt{36 - 4 \cdot 36}}{12}$ has no real solution

$\frac{d^2 f}{dx^2} = 6 - 12x \begin{cases} > 0, & x < \frac{1}{2} \\ < 0, & x > \frac{1}{2} \end{cases}$

So the slope of f increases from -6 at $x = 0$ to $-9/2$ at $x = \frac{1}{2}$ and decreases for all x thereafter.

Thus, $x^* = 0$ is optimal.

13.3-3. a) Linearly constrained convex program:

$\frac{\partial^2 f}{\partial x_1^2} = -12x_1^2 - 4 < 0 \quad \forall(x_1, x_2) \quad \frac{\partial^2 f}{\partial x_2^2} = -8 < 0 \quad \forall(x_1, x_2)$

$\frac{\partial^2 f}{\partial x_1^2}\frac{\partial^2 f}{\partial x_2^2} - \left[\frac{\partial^2 f}{\partial x_1 \partial x_2}\right] = 96x_1^2 + 32 - (-2)^2 > 0 \quad \forall(x_1, x_2)$

$\Rightarrow f$ is concave

g_1 and g_2 are linear and, hence, convex.

Geometric Program:

$f(\underline{x}) = c_1 x_1^{a_{11}} x_2^{a_{12}} + c_2 x_1^{a_{21}} x_2^{a_{22}} + c_3 x_1^{a_{31}} x_2^{a_{32}} + c_4 x_1^{a_{41}} x_2^{a_{42}}$

with $c_1 = 1 \quad a_{11} = 4 \quad a_{12} = 0$
$c_2 = 2 \quad a_{21} = 2 \quad a_{22} = 0$
$c_3 = 2 \quad a_{31} = 1 \quad a_{32} = 1$
$c_4 = 4 \quad a_{41} = 0 \quad a_{42} = 2$

$g_1(\underline{x}) = c_1 x_1^{a_{11}} x_2^{a_{12}} + c_2 x_1^{a_{21}} x_2^{a_{22}}$

with $c_1 = -2 \quad a_{11} = 1 \quad a_{12} = 0$
$c_2 = -1 \quad a_{21} = 0 \quad a_{22} = 1$

$g_2(\underline{x}) = c_1 x_1^{a_{11}} x_2^{a_{12}} + c_2 x_1^{a_{21}} x_2^{a_{22}}$

with $c_1 = -1 \quad a_{11} = 1 \quad a_{12} = 0$
$c_2 = -2 \quad a_{21} = 0 \quad a_{22} = 1$

Fractional Program:

$f' = f_1 / f_2$ where $f_1 = f$ & $f_2 = 1$

b) Let $y_1 = x_1 - 1$ and $y_2 = x_2 - 1$

$\Rightarrow$ Minimize $y_1^4 + 4y_1^3 + 8y_1^2 + 10y_1 + 2y_1y_2 + 4y_2^2 + 10y_2$
subject to $2y_1 + y_2 \geq 7$
$y_1 + 2y_2 \geq 7$
$y_1 \geq 0, \; y_2 \geq 0$

13.3-4. a) Let $x_1 = e^{y_1}$ and $x_2 = e^{y_2}$

$\Rightarrow$ Minimize $2e^{-2y_1 - y_2} + e^{-y_1 - 2y_2}$
subject to $4e^{y_1 + y_2} + e^{2y_1 + 2y_2} \leq 12$
$e^{y_1} \geq 0, \; e^{y_2} \geq 0$

b) $\frac{\partial^2 f}{\partial y_1^2} = -8e^{-2y_1 - y_2} - e^{-y_1 - 2y_2} \leq 0 \quad \forall(y_1, y_2)$

$\frac{\partial^2 f}{\partial y_2^2} = -2e^{-2y_1 - y_2} - 4e^{-y_1 - 2y_2} \leq 0 \quad \forall(y_1, y_2)$

$\frac{\partial^2 f}{\partial y_1^2}\frac{\partial^2 f}{\partial y_2^2} - \left[\frac{\partial^2 f}{\partial y_1 \partial y_2}\right]^2 = 18e^{-3y_1 - 3y_2} \geq 0 \quad \forall(y_1, y_2)$

so f is concave

13.3-4. b) (cont') for $g(y_1,y_2) = 4e^{y_1+y_2} + e^{2y_1+2y_2} - 12$

$$\frac{\partial^2 g}{\partial y_1^2} = 4e^{y_1+y_2} + 4e^{2y_1+2y_2} \geq 0 \quad \forall (y_1,y_2)$$

$$\frac{\partial^2 g}{\partial y_2^2} = 4e^{y_1+y_2} + 4e^{2y_1+2y_2} \geq 0 \quad \forall (y_1,y_2)$$

$$\frac{\partial^2 g}{\partial y_1^2}\frac{\partial^2 g}{\partial y_2^2} - \left[\frac{\partial^2 g}{\partial y_1 \partial y_2}\right]^2 = 0 \quad \forall (y_1,y_2)$$

so g is convex

$e^{y_1} \geq 0$, $e^{y_2} \geq 0$ $\forall (y_1,y_2)$

Now there is, in fact, no non-negativity constraints on the y's, and so, strictly speaking, according to the definition in the book this isn't quite a convex program. However, in general, the entire theory of convex programming applies as long as the feasible region is convex which is the case here.

13.3-5. (a) Maximize $10y_1 + 20y_2 + 10t$

subject to

$$y_1 + 3y_2 - 50t \leq 0$$
$$3y_1 + 2y_2 - 80t \leq 0$$
$$3y_1 + 4y_2 + 20t = 1$$
$$y_1 \geq 0, \; y_2 \geq 0, \; t \geq 0$$

(b)

Bas Var	Eq No	Z	X1	X2	X3	X4	X5	X6	Right side
								1M	
Z	0	1	3.269	0	0	1.385	0	3.962	3.962
X2	1	0	0.654	1	0	0.077	0	0.192	0.192
X5	2	0	3.231	0	0	-1.38	1	0.538	0.538
X3	3	0	0.019	0	1	-0.02	0	0.012	0.012

Variables (x_1, x_2, x_3) from the courseware solution correspond to (y_1, y_2, t) for part (a) variables, respectively. Therefore, the optimal solution has $(y_1, y_2, t) = (0, 0.192, 0.012)$ with $Z = 3.962$. The optimal solution to the original problem is $(x_1, x_2) = (0, 16.67)$ with $f(x) = 3.962$.

13.3-6. The KKT conditions may be rewritten:

$$Qx + A^T u - c = y$$
$$-Ax + b = v$$

$$x \geq 0, \; u \geq 0, \; y \geq 0, \; v \geq 0$$

$$x^T(Qx + A^T u - c) + u^T(-Ax + b) = 0$$

and this is the Linear Complementarity Problem with $z = \begin{pmatrix} x \\ u \end{pmatrix}$ $M = \begin{bmatrix} Q & A^T \\ -A & 0 \end{bmatrix}$ $q = \begin{pmatrix} -c \\ b \end{pmatrix}$

and $w = \begin{bmatrix} Qx + A^T u - c \\ -Ax + b \end{bmatrix}$

13.4-1.

Iteration	df(X)/dX	X(L)	X(U)	New X'	f(X')
0		0	2.4	1.2	0.7296
1	-0.208	0	1.2	0.6	0.6636
2	+0.464	0.6	1.2	0.9	0.745
3	+0.101	0.9	1.2	1.05	0.7487
4	- 0.05	0.9	1.05	0.975	0.7497
5	+0.025	0.975	1.05	1.0125	0.7499
Stop					

13.4-2. a)

Iteration	df(X)/dX	X(L)	X(U)	New X'	f(X')
0		0	4.8	2.4	8.64
1	+ 1.2	2.4	4.8	3.6	8.64
2	- 1.2	2.4	3.6	3	9
3	+ 0	3	3.6	3.3	8.91
4	- 0.6	3	3.3	3.15	8.9775
5	- 0.3	3	3.15	3.075	8.9944
6	- 0.15	3	3.075	3.0375	8.9986
Stop					

b)

Iteration	df(X)/dX	X(L)	X(U)	New X'	f(X')
0		-4	1	-1.5	-1.688
1	- 1.5	-1.5	1	-0.25	-1.121
2	+3.188	-1.5	-0.25	-0.875	-1.984
3	+0.258	-1.5	-0.875	-1.188	-1.964
4	-0.401	-1.188	-0.875	-1.031	-1.999
5	-0.063	-1.031	-0.875	-0.953	-1.998
6	+0.094	-1.031	-0.953	-0.992	-2
Stop					

13.4-3.

Iteration	df(X)/dX	X(L)	X(U)	New X'	f(X')
0		-1	4	1.5	-16.69
1	- 100	-1	1.5	0.25	0.3047
2	+0.156	0.25	1.5	0.875	0.2482
3	-0.923	0.25	0.875	0.5625	0.3125
4	-0.001	0.25	0.5625	0.4063	0.3124
5	+0.004	0.4063	0.5625	0.4844	0.3125
Stop					

13.4-4.

Iteration	df(X)/dX	X(L)	X(U)	New X'	f(X')
0		0	2	1	25
1	+ 13	1	2	1.5	20.109
2	-44.81	1	1.5	1.25	26.068
3	-6.748	1	1.25	1.125	26.146
4	+4.844	1.125	1.25	1.1875	26.288
Stop					

13.4-5. (a) $f'(x) = 4x^3 + 2x - 4$
$f'(0) = -4$
$f'(1) = 2$
$f'(2) = 32$

since $f'(x)$ is continuous there must be a point in $0 \le x \le 1$ such that $f'(x) = 0$, and so since f is a concave function (this is a convex program) the optimal solution must be in the interval $0 \le x \le 1$.

(b)

Iteration	df(X)/dX	X(L)	X(U)	New X'	f(X')
0		0	2	1	-2
1	+ 2	0	1	0.5	-1.688
2	- 2.5	0.5	1	0.75	-2.121
3	-0.813	0.75	1	0.875	-2.148
4	+ 0.43	0.75	0.875	0.8125	-2.154
5	-0.229	0.8125	0.875	0.8438	-2.156
6	+ 0.09	0.8125	0.8438	0.8281	-2.156
Stop					

13.4-6. a) Claim: $(\bar{x}_{n+1} - \underline{x}_{n+1}) = \frac{1}{2}(\bar{x}_n - \underline{x}_n)$. To see this consider the two cases:

Case 1: $\bar{x}_{n+1} = \bar{x}_n$, $\underline{x}_{n+1} = x_n'$, then $\bar{x}_{n+1} - \underline{x}_{n+1} = \bar{x}_n - x_n' = \bar{x}_n - \frac{1}{2}(\bar{x}_n + \underline{x}_n)$
$= \frac{1}{2}(\bar{x}_n - \underline{x}_n)$

Case 2: $\bar{x}_{n+1} = x_n'$, $\underline{x}_{n+1} = \underline{x}_n$, then $\bar{x}_{n+1} - \underline{x}_{n+1} = x_n' - \underline{x}_n = \frac{1}{2}(\bar{x}_n + \underline{x}_n) - \underline{x}_n$
$= \frac{1}{2}(\bar{x}_n - \underline{x}_n)$

Therefore, we have $(\bar{x}_{n+1} - \underline{x}_{n+1}) = \frac{1}{2}(\bar{x}_n - \underline{x}_n) = \ldots = \frac{1}{2^{n+1}}(\bar{x}_0 - \underline{x}_0)$

so $\lim_{n\to\infty}(\bar{x}_{n+1} - \underline{x}_{n+1}) = \lim_{n\to\infty} 2^{-n}(\bar{x}_0 - \underline{x}_0) = 0$

Suppose the points generated by this procedure do not converge, then we know there is $\varepsilon > 0$ such that, no matter what N we choose, there will be $n \ge N$ and $m \ge N$ so that $|x_n' - x_m'| > \varepsilon$. But if we choose N so that $2^{-N}(\bar{x}_0 - \underline{x}_0) < \varepsilon$ then for all $n \ge N$ $x_n' \in [\bar{x}_N, \underline{x}_N]$ and so for $n \ge N$ and $m \ge N$ and $|x_n' - x_m'| > \varepsilon$ we have $\varepsilon < |x_n' - x_m'| \le |\bar{x}_N - \underline{x}_N| = 2^{-N}(\bar{x}_0 - \underline{x}_0) < \varepsilon$, a contradiction. Thus, the sequence of trial solutions must converge.

(b) Let $\bar{x}$ be the limitting solution. Then we know $f'(x) \ge 0$ for $x < \bar{x}$ and $f'(x) \le 0$ for $x > \bar{x}$. Suppose $\bar{x}$ is not the global maximum, but that $\hat{x}$ is. Then $f(\hat{x}) > f(\bar{x})$.

Case 1: $\hat{x} > \bar{x}$. By the Mean Value Theorm there is a z with $\hat{x} > z > x$ such that $f(\hat{x}) - f(\bar{x}) = (\hat{x} - \bar{x})f'(z)$. The right hand side is non-positive, since $z > \bar{x}$, $f'(z) \le 0$ and $\hat{x} > \bar{x} \Rightarrow (\hat{x} - \bar{x}) > 0$, so $f(\hat{x}) - f(\bar{x}) \le 0$, a contradiction.

Case 2: $\hat{x} < \bar{x}$. Using the Mean Value Theorm, we have z with $\hat{x} < z < \bar{x}$, $f(\hat{x}) - f(\bar{x}) = (\hat{x} - \bar{x})f'(z) \ge 0$ which implies $f(\hat{x}) \ge f(\bar{x})$, a contradiction.

So $\bar{x}$ must be the global maximum.

13.4-6. (c) The argument follows as in part (b) by observing that the z of the Mean Value Theorem (which is between $\bar{x}$ and $\hat{x}$) is in the part of the domain where f is concave.

(d)

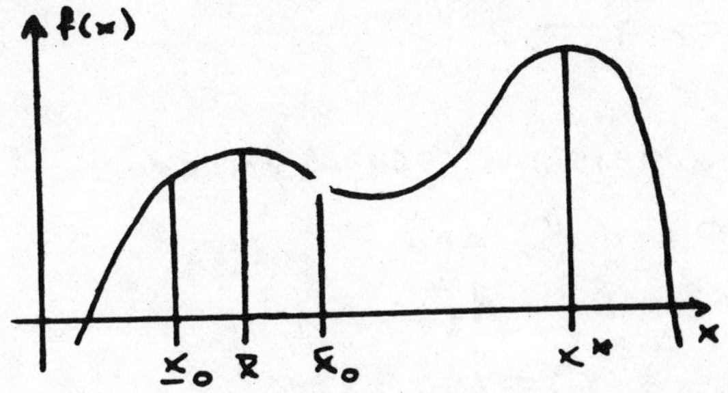

The procedure would converge to $\bar{x}$, not to x^* which is the global maximum.

(e) Suppose $f'(x)<0$, but that a global maximum occurs at $\hat{x}$. Let $x<\hat{x}$. By the Mean Value Theorem, there exists a z with $\hat{x}>z>x$ and $f(\hat{x})-f(x)=(\hat{x}-x)f'(z)$, or $f(x)=f(\hat{x})+(x-\hat{x})f'(z)>f(x')$, a contradiction. So a global maximumum cannot occur.

Suppose $f'(x)>0$, but that a global maximum occurs at $\hat{x}$. Let $x>\hat{x}$. By the Mean Value Theorem, there exists a z with $x>z>\hat{x}$ and $f(\hat{x})-f(x)=(\hat{x}-x)f'(z)$, or $f(x)=f(\hat{x})+(x-\hat{x})f'(z)>f(x')$, a contradiction. So a global maximum cannot occur.

(f) Suppose $f(x)$ is concave and $\lim_{x\to-\infty} f'(x)<0$, but that an $\underline{x}_0$ exists. So $f'(\underline{x}_0)\geq 0$. But $f'(x)$ is monotone decreasing, so for $x<\underline{x}_0$, $f'(x)\geq 0$ and $\lim_{x\to-\infty} f'(x)\geq 0$, a contradiction. So no $\underline{x}_0$ exists.

Suppose $f(x)$ is concave and $\lim_{x\to\infty} f'(x)>0$, but that an $\bar{x}_0$ exists. So $f'(\underline{x}_0)\leq 0$. But $f'(x)$ is monotone decreasing, so for $x>\bar{x}_0$, $f'(x)\leq 0$, and $\lim_{x\to\infty} f'(x)\leq 0$, a contradiction. So no $\underline{x}_0$ exists.

In either case, we know there is no global maximum from part (e).

13.4-7. $f(x) = f_1(x_1) + f_2(x_2)$

$f_1(x_1) = 32x_1 - x_1^4$

$f_2(x_2) = 50x_2 - 10x_2^2 + x_2^3 - x_2^4$

$\frac{df_1}{dx_1} = 32 - 4x_1^3 \equiv 0 \Rightarrow x_1 = 2$

Using the automatic one-dimensional search procedure ($\varepsilon = 0.001$) with initial bounds 0 and 4, and

$f(x) = 48 + 50x_2 - 10x_2^2 + x_2^3 - x_2^4$

we get: $x_2 = 1.8076$, $f(x) = 100.936$

$3x_1 + x_2 = 7.8076 < 11$

$2x_1 + 5x_2 = 13.038 < 16$

Since the optimum for the unconstrained problem is in the interior of the feasible region for the constrained problem, it is also optimal for the original constrained problem.

13.5-1. (a)

It.	X'	grad f(X')	X' + t[grad f(X')]	t*	X'+t[grad f]
1	(1, 1)	(0, -1)	(1+ 0t, 1- 1t)	0.25	(1, 0.75)
2	(1, 0.75)	(-0.5, 0)	(1- 0.5t, 0.75+ 0t)	0.5	(0.75, 0.75)
3	(0.75, 0.75)	(0, -0.5)	(0.75+ 0t, 0.75- 0.5t)	0.25	(0.75,0.625)
4	(0.75,0.625)	(-0.25, 0)			

(b) $-2x_1 + 2x_2 = 0$, $-2x_1 + 4x_2 = 1$ $\Longrightarrow$ $x_2 = 1/2$, $x_1 = 1/2$ so $(1/2, 1/2)$ is optimal.

(c)

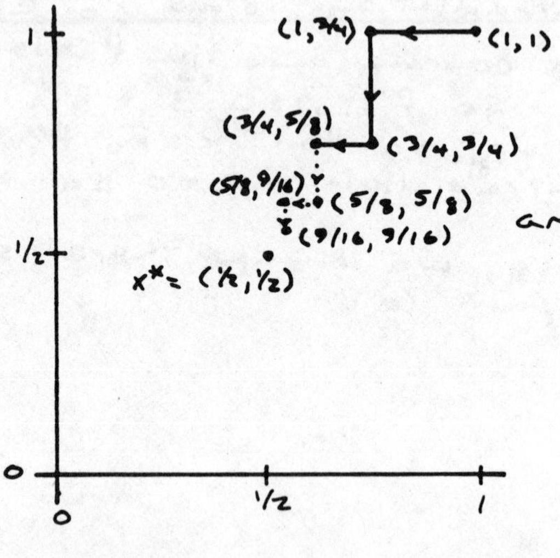

are the next iterations

(d) The software gives: Solution:

$(X_1, X_2) = (0.508, 0.504)$

grad $f(X_1, X_2) = (-8e-3, 6e-8)$

13.5-2. (a)

It.	X'	grad f(X')	X' + t[grad f(X')]	t*	X'+t[grad f]
1	(1, 1)	(-2, 0)	(1- 2t, 1+ 0t)	0.25	(0.5, 1)
2	(0.5, 1)	(0, -1)	(0.5+ 0t, 1- 1t)	0.5	(0.5, 0.5)
3	(0.5, 0.5)	(-1, 0)	(0.5- 1t, 0.5+ 0t)	0.25	(0.25, 0.5)
4	(0.25, 0.5)	(0, -0.5)			

(b) $-4x_1 - 2x_2 = 0$
$2x_1 - 2x_2 = 0$ $\Rightarrow$ $(0,0)$ is optimal.

(c)

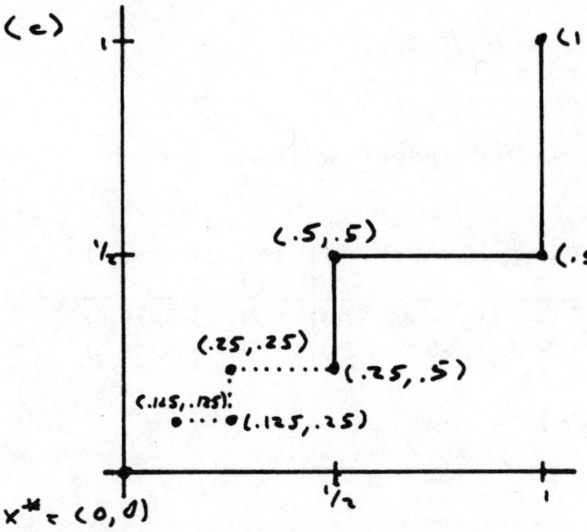

(d) with the automatic routine:

Solution:

$(X_1,X_2) = (0.004,0.008)$

grad $f(X_1,X_2) = ($ 1e-8,-8e-3$)$

13.5-3.

It.	X'	grad f(X')	X' + t[grad f(X')]	t*	X'+t[grad f]
1	(1, 1)	(0, -2)	(1+ 0t, 1- 2t)	0.167	(1,0.667)
2	(1,0.667)	(-1.33, 0)	(1-1.33t,0.667+ 0t)	0.25	(0.667,0.667)
3	(0.667,0.667)	(0,-1.33)			

The automatic routine ($\varepsilon = 0.01$) gives:

Solution:

$(X_1,X_2) = (0.005,0.003)$

grad $f(X_1,X_2) =$ (-7e-3, 3e-8)

$\nabla f = (4x_2 - 4x_1 \;,\; 4x_1 - 6x_2)$

$\nabla f = 0 \Rightarrow (x_1, x_2) = (0,0)$ is the optimal solution.

13.5-4.

It.	X'	grad f(X')	X' + t[grad f(X')]	t*	X'+t[grad f]
1	(0, 0)	(8, -12)	(0+ 8t, 0- 12t)	0.191	(1.529,-2.29)
2	(1.529,-2.29)	(0.361,0.219)	(1.529+0.36t,-2.29+0.22t)	1.31	(2.002, -2)
3	(2.002, -2)	(-0,0.003)			

Automatic routine ($\varepsilon = 0.01$):

Solution:

$(X_1, X_2) = (1.997, -2)$

$\text{grad } f(X_1, X_2) = (0.002, 0.001)$

$\nabla f = (-2x_1 + 2x_2 + 8, \ 2x_1 - 4x_2 - 12)$

$\nabla f = 0 \Rightarrow (x_1, x_2) = (2, -2)$ is the optimal solution

13.5-5.

It.	X'	grad f(X')	X' + t[grad f(X')]	t*	X'+t[grad f]
1	(0, 0)	(6, -2)	(0+ 6t, 0- 2t)	0.2	(1.2, -0.4)
2	(1.2, -0.4)	(0.4, 1.2)	(1.2+ 0.4t, -0.4+ 1.2t)	1	(1.6, 0.8)
3	(1.6, 0.8)	(1.2, -0.4)			

Automatic routine ($\varepsilon = 0.01$)

Solution:

$(X_1, X_2) = (1.994, 0.989)$

$\text{grad } f(X_1, X_2) = (0.003, 0.01)$

$\nabla f = (-4x_1 + 2x_2 + 6, \ 2x_1 - 2x_2 - 2)$

$\nabla f = 0 \Rightarrow (x_1, x_2) = (2, 1)$

13.5-6. $\nabla f(x_1, x_2) = (4 - 2x_1 - 4x_1^3 - 2x_2, \ 2 - 2x_1 - 2x_2)$

Iter.	x_n	$\nabla f(x_n)$	$f(x_n + t\nabla f(x_n))$	Iter.	t'	$\frac{d}{dt} f(t)$
1	(0,0)	(4,2)	$20t - 36t^2 - 256t^4$	1	.5	-144
				2	.25	-14
					$t^* = .125$	
(2)	(1/2, 1/4)					

$\Rightarrow x + t^* \nabla f(x) = (0.500, 0.250)$ is our estimate.

13.5-7. a) We can rewrite f as $f = f_1(x_1, x_2) + f_2(x_2, x_3)$

with $f_1 = 3x_1x_2 - x_1^2 - 3x_2^2$

$f_2 = 3x_2x_3 - x_3^2 - 3x_2^2$

For any given x_2 (including the optimal one) we realize that by symmetry $x_1 = x_3$ at the maximizing point for f with x_2 at the given value. Therefore, to maximize f we can maximize f_1 (or f_2) and obtain (x_1, x_2). From the solution to maximize f_1 we can set $x_3 = x_1$ and $f = 2f_1$ to find the solution to our original problem. We can solve maximize f_1 with the courseware.

b) Using $f(x) = 3x_1x_2 - x_1^2 - 3x_2^2$:

It.	**X'**	grad f(**X'**)	**X'** + t[grad f(**X'**)]	t*	**X'**+t*[grad f]
1	(1, 1)	(1, -3)	(1+ 1t, 1- 3t)	0.135	(1.135,0.595)
2	(1.135,0.595)	(-0.49,-0.16)	(1.14-0.49t,0.59-0.16t)	1.616	(0.343,0.336)
3	(0.343,0.336)	(0.323,-0.99)	(0.34+0.32t,0.34-0.99t)	0.135	(0.387,0.202)
4	(0.387,0.202)	(-0.17,-0.05)	(0.39-0.17t, 0.2-0.05t)	1.427	(0.144,0.131)
5	(0.144,0.131)	(0.103,-0.35)	(0.14+ 0.1t,0.13-0.35t)	0.139	(0.158,0.083)
6	(0.158,0.083)	(-0.07,-0.02)	(0.16-0.07t,0.08-0.02t)	1.361	(0.063,0.056)
7	(0.063,0.056)	(0.042,-0.15)	(0.06+0.04t,0.06-0.15t)	0.135	(0.069,0.036)

Final solution: (X1, X2) = (0.069,0.036)

The estimated solution to the original problem will be

$(x_1, x_2, x_3) = (0.069, 0.036, 0.069)$

c) Automatic routine ($\varepsilon = 0.005$) gives:

Solution:

(X1,X2) = (0.004,0.002)

grad f(X1,X2) = (-2e-3,-6e-4)

13.5-8. (a)

It.	X'	grad f(X')	X' + t[grad f(X')]	t*	X'+t[grad f]
1	(0, 0)	(0, 3)	(0+ 0t, 0+ 3t)	0.5	(0, 1.5)
2	(0, 1.5)	(1.5, 0)	(0+ 1.5t, 1.5+ 0t)	0.5	(0.75, 1.5)
3	(0.75, 1.5)	(0, 0.75)			

Automatic routine ($\varepsilon = 0.01$):

Solution:

(X1,X2) = (0.996,1.998)

grad f(X1,X2) = (0.006,-2e-8)

(b)

It.	X'	grad f(X')	X' + t[grad f(X')]	t*	X'+t[grad f]
1	(0, 0)	(4, -4)	(0+ 4t, 0- 4t)	0.193	(0.771,-0.77)
2	(0.771,-0.77)	(0.002, -0)			

Automatic routine ($\varepsilon = 0.01$):

(Note: min f(x) ⟺ max -f(x))

Solution:

(X1,X2) = (0.771,-0.77)

grad f(X1,X2) = (8e-6,-8e-6)

13.6-1. Converting min to max, the KKT conditions are:

1) $-4x^3-2x+4-u \le 0$

2) $x(-4x^3-2x+4-u)=0$

3) $x-2 \le 0$

4) $u(x-2)=0$

5) $x \ge 0$

6) $u \ge 0$ → (Also can get this from (1) and (6))

From 13.4-5. (a), $0 \le x \le 1$, so $x \ne 2$ and (4) $\Rightarrow u=0$.

From (1), we see that $x \ne 0$ ($4 \not\le 0$), so from (2), we have $-4x^3-2x+4=0$ (or $2x^3+x-2=0$)

Solving for the root (real) of this cubic, we get

$$x = \sqrt[3]{\frac{1}{2}+\sqrt{\frac{55}{216}}} + \sqrt[3]{\frac{1}{2}-\sqrt{\frac{55}{216}}} = .83512$$

13.6-2. The KKT conditions are.

1 (j=1). $1-2ux_1 \le 0$

2 (j=1). $x_1(1-2ux_1)=0$

1 (j=2). $1-2ux_2 \le 0$

2 (j=2). $x_2(1-2ux_2)=0$

3. $x_1^2+x_2^2-1 \le 0$

4. $u(x_1^2+x_2^2-1)=0$

5. $x_1 \ge 0,\ x_2 \ge 0$

6. $u \ge 0$

For $x=\left(\frac{1}{\sqrt{2}}, \frac{1}{\sqrt{2}}\right)$, 2 (j=1) $\Rightarrow 1-2u\frac{1}{\sqrt{2}}=0 \Rightarrow u=\frac{1}{\sqrt{2}}$

This satisfies all the KKT conditions, so $x=\left(\frac{1}{\sqrt{2}}, \frac{1}{\sqrt{2}}\right)$, $u=\frac{1}{\sqrt{2}}$ is optimal.

13.6-3. KKT conditions:

1 a) $-4x_1^3-4x_1-2x_2+2u_1+u_2 \le 0$

2 a) $x_1(-4x_1^3-4x_1-2x_2+2u_1+u_2)=0$

1 b) $-2x_1-8x_2+u_1+2u_2 \le 0$

2 b) $x_2(-2x_1-8x_2+u_1+2u_2)=0$

3 a) $2x_1+x_2 \ge 10$

3 b) $x_1+2x_2 \ge 10$

4 a) $u_1(-2x_1-x_2+10)=0$

4 b) $u_2(-x_1-2x_2+10)=0$

5) $x_1 \ge 0,\ x_2 \ge 0$

6) $u_1 \ge 0,\ u_2 \ge 0$

for $(x_1,x_2)=(0,10)$ 2 b) $\Rightarrow u_1+2u_2=80$

and 4b) $\Rightarrow u_2=0$ so $u_1=80$

but then 1a) does not hold

so $(x_1,x_2)=(0,10)$ is not optimal

13.6-4. (a) the KKT conditions:

1a) $24 - 2x_1 - u_1 \le 0$

2a) $x_1(24 - 2x_1 - u_1) = 0$

1b) $10 - 2x_2 - u_2 \le 0$

2b) $x_2(10 - 2x_2 - u_2) = 0$

3) $x_1 \le 8,\ x_2 \le 7$

4a) $u_1(x_1 - 8) = 0$

4b) $u_2(x_2 - 7) = 0$

5) $x_1 \ge 0,\ x_2 \ge 0$

6) $u_1 \ge 0,\ u_2 \ge 0$

Take $x_1 = 8$ 2a) $\Rightarrow u_1 = 8$
then 1a), 3), 4a), 5) and 6) are satisfied

Take $u_2 = 0$ 2b) $\Rightarrow x_2 = 5$
then 1b), 3), 4b), 5) and 6) are satisfied

So $(x_1, x_2) = (8, 5)$ is optimal since this is a convex program.

(b)

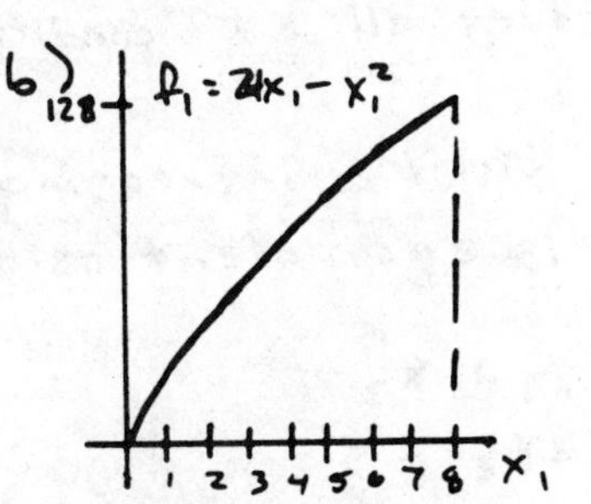

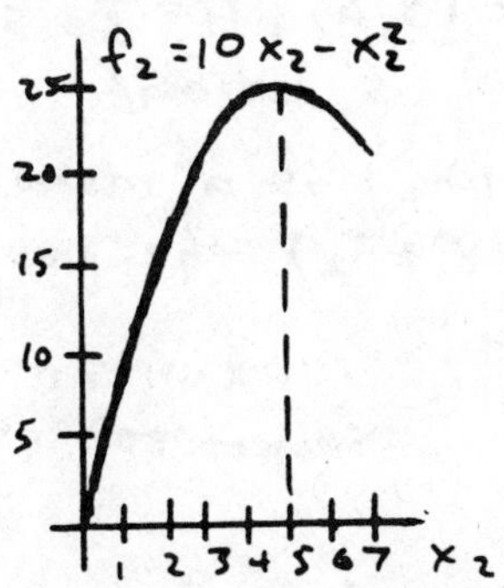

$\frac{\partial f}{\partial x_1} = 24 - 2x_1 > 0 \quad \forall\, 0 \le x_1 \le 8 \Rightarrow x_1 = 8$ is the maximum over the feasible region.

$\frac{\partial f}{\partial x_2} = 10 - 2x_2 = 0$ at $x_2 = 5$ and $\frac{\partial^2 f}{\partial x_2} = -2 \le 0$
so $x_2 = 5$ is a global maximum.

13.6-5. a) $\frac{\partial^2 f}{\partial x_1^2} = -\frac{1}{(1+x_1+x_2)^2} \le 0 \quad \forall\, x_1, x_2 \ge 0$

$\frac{\partial^2 f}{\partial x_2^2} = -\frac{1}{(1+x_1+x_2)^2} \le 0 \quad \forall\, x_1, x_2 \ge 0$

$\frac{\partial^2 f}{\partial x_1^2}\frac{\partial^2 f}{\partial x_2^2} - \left[\frac{\partial f}{\partial x_1 \partial x_2}\right]^2 = 0 \quad \forall\, x_1, x_2 \ge 0$

So f is concave for $x_1, x_2 \ge 0$

$g = x_1 + 2x_1 - 5$ is linear and, hence, convex

Thus, this is a convex program.

13.6-5, b) The KKT conditions are:

1a) $\frac{1}{1+x_1+x_2} - u \leq 0$

2a) $x_1\left(\frac{1}{1+x_1+x_2} - u\right) = 0$

1b) $\frac{1}{1+x_1+x_2} - 2u \leq 0$

2b) $x_2\left(\frac{1}{1+x_1+x_2} - 2u\right) = 0$

3) $x_1 + 2x_2 - 5 \leq 0$

4) $u(x_1 + 2x_2 - 5) = 0$

5) $x_1 \geq 0, x_2 \geq 0$

6) $u \geq 0$

Trying $u \neq 0$, (4) $\Rightarrow x_1 + 2x_2 = 5$

Trying $x_2 = 0 \Rightarrow x_1 = 5$, then 2a) $\Rightarrow u = \frac{1}{1+x_1+x_2} = \frac{1}{5}$

Since $(x_1, x_2) = (5, 0)$, $u = \frac{1}{5}$ satisfies all KKT conditions, $(x_1, x_2) = (5, 0)$ is optimal.

c) Since $\ln(1+x_1+x_2)$ is a monotone strictly increasing function of $(1+x_1+x_2)$, the problem is equivalent to the linear program:

$$\begin{aligned} \text{maximize } & 1 + x_1 + x_2 \\ \text{subject to } & x_1 + 2x_2 \leq 5 \\ & x_1 \geq 0, x_2 \geq 0 \end{aligned}$$

and so we expect an extreme point solution. The extreme points of the feasible region are $(5,0)$, $(0, \frac{5}{2})$ and $(0,0)$, and it is clear that, of the three, $(5,0)$ is optimal.

13.6-6. (a) $\frac{\partial^2 f}{\partial x_1^2} = -\frac{1}{(x_1+1)^2} \leq 0 \quad \forall (x_1, x_2): x_1 \neq -1$

$\frac{\partial^2 f}{\partial x_2^2} = -2 \leq 0 \quad \forall (x_1, x_2)$

$\frac{\partial^2 f}{\partial x_1^2}\frac{\partial^2 f}{\partial x_2^2} - \left[\frac{\partial f}{\partial x_1 \partial x_2}\right]^2 = \frac{2}{(x_1+1)^2} \geq 0 \quad \forall (x_1, x_2): x_1 \neq -1$

$\Rightarrow f$ is concave

$g = x_1 + 2x_2 - 3$ is linear, and, hence, convex.

so this is a convex program.

13.6-6. (b) The KKT conditions:

1a) $\frac{1}{x_1+1} - u \le 0$

2a) $x_1\left[\frac{1}{x_1+1} - u\right] = 0$

1b) $-2x_2 - 2u \le 0$

2b) $x_2[-2x_2 - 2u] \le 0$

3) $x_1 + 2x_2 \le 3$

4) $u(x_1 + 2x_2 - 3) = 0$

5) $x_1 \ge 0$, $x_2 \ge 0$

6) $u \ge 0$

Trying $u \ne 0$ 4) $\Rightarrow$ $x_1 + 2x_2 = 3$

Trying $x_2 = 0$ $\Rightarrow$ $x_1 = 3$ 2a) $\Rightarrow$ $u = \frac{1}{4}$

and $(3, 0, \frac{1}{4})$ satisfies 1a), 1b), 2b), 3), 5) & 6)

so $(x_1, x_2) = (3, 0)$ is optimal.

(c) Since $-x_2^2$ is monotonically strictly decreasing for $x_2 \ge 0$ and $\ln(x_1+1)$ is monotonically strictly increasing, it is intuitively clear that one would like to increase x_1 as much as possible and decrease x_2 toward 0 as much as possible in an optimal solution. The feasible region is "nice" in this respect since if we take F to be the feasible region:

$$\max_{x_1}[\min_{x_2} F] = \min_{x_2}[\max_{x_1} F] = \{(3,0)\}.$$

13.6-7. (a) The KKT conditions:

1a) $10 - 4x_1 - 3x_1^2 - u \le 0$

2a) $x_1(10 - 4x_1 - 3x_1^2 - u) = 0$

1b) $8 - 2x_2 - u \le 0$

2b) $x_2(8 - 2x_2 - u) = 0$

3) $x_1 + x_2 \le 2$

4) $u(x_1 + x_2 - 2) = 0$

5) $x_1 \ge 0$, $x_2 \ge 0$

6) $u \ge 0$

so if $(x_1, x_2) = (1, 1)$

2a) $\Rightarrow$ $u = 3$

2b) $\Rightarrow$ $u = 6$

thus, the KKT conditions cannot be met at $(x_1, x_2) = (1, 1)$ so $(1, 1)$ is not optimal.

(b) $(x_1, x_2) = (\sqrt{3} - 1, 3 - \sqrt{3})$, and $u = 2(1 + \sqrt{3})$ satisfies all the KKT conditions, and so since we have a convex program $(\sqrt{3} - 1, 3 - \sqrt{3})$ is optimal

13.6-8. The KKT conditions:

1a) $36 + 18x_1 - 18x_1^2 - u \le 0$

2a) $x_1(36 + 18x_1 - 18x_1^2 - u) = 0$

1b) $36 - 9x_2^2 - u \le 0$

2b) $x_2(36 - 9x_2^2 - u) = 0$

3) $x_1 + x_2 \le 3$

4) $u(x_1 + x_2 - 3) = 0$

5) $x_1 \ge 0,\ x_2 \ge 0$

6) $u \ge 0$

So for $(x_1, x_2) = (1, 2)$

2a) $\Rightarrow$ $u = 36$

2b) $\Rightarrow$ $u = 0$

Thus, the KKT conditions cannot be met at $(x_1, x_2) = (1, 2)$, and so $(1, 2)$ is not optimal.

13.6-9. (a) The KKT conditions:

1a) $\frac{1}{x_2+1} - u \le 0$

2a) $x_1\left[\frac{1}{x_2+1} - u\right] = 0$

1b) $-\frac{x_1}{(x_2+1)^2} + u \le 0$

2b) $x_2\left[-\frac{x_1}{(x_2+1)^2} + u\right] = 0$

3) $x_1 - x_2 \le 2$

4) $u[x_1 - x_2 - 2] = 0$

5) $x_1 \ge 0,\ x_2 \ge 0$

6) $u \ge 0$

for $(x_1, x_2) = (4, 2)$

2a) $\Rightarrow u = 1/3$

2b) $\Rightarrow u = 4/9$

So $(x_1, x_2) = (4, 2)$ does not satisfy the KKT condition, and, hence, is not optimal.

(b) Try $x_2 = 0,\ u \ne 0$ 2a) $\Rightarrow u = 1$

4) $\Rightarrow x_1 = 2$

and $(2, 0, 1)$ satisfies 1a), 1b), 2a), 3), 5) & 6)

So $(x_1, x_2) = (2, 0)$ satisfies the KKT conditions

(c) $\frac{\partial^2 f}{\partial x_1^2} = 0 \quad \forall (x_1, x_2)$

$\frac{\partial^2 f}{\partial x_2^2} = \frac{2x_1}{(x_2+1)^3} \ge 0 \quad \forall x_1 \ge 0, x_2 \ge 0$

Thus, f cannot be concave, and so this is not a convex program.

13.6-9. (d) $f(x)$ is a monotone strictly increasing function of x_2 and is monotone strictly decreasing in x_2 for $x_2 > -1$, and, thus, any optimal solution in a bounded feasible region with $x_2 > -1$ will have x_1 increased as high as possible and x_2 decreased toward -1 as much as possible. The feasible region here allows x_1 to be increased without bound. However, then x_2 can only be decreased to the line $x_1 - x_2 = 2$ or $x_1 = 2 + x_2$:

$$f(x_2+2, x_2) = \frac{x_2+2}{x_2+1} \longrightarrow 1 \text{ as } x_2 \to \infty$$
$$= 2 \text{ at } x_2 = 0$$

Conversely, if we then decrease x_2 to 0 we can increase x_1 to $x_1 = 2$. Thus, the feasible region is "nice" and the optimal solution is at $(x_1, x_2) = (2, 0)$.

(e) Maximize x_1
subject to
$$x_1 - x_2 - 2t \le 0$$
$$x_2 + t = 1$$
$$x_1 \ge 0,\ x_2 \ge 0,\ t \ge 0$$

$\Leftrightarrow$ Maximize x_1
subject to
$$x_1 + x_2 \le 2$$
$$x_2 \le 1$$
$$x_1 \ge 0,\ x_2 \ge 0$$

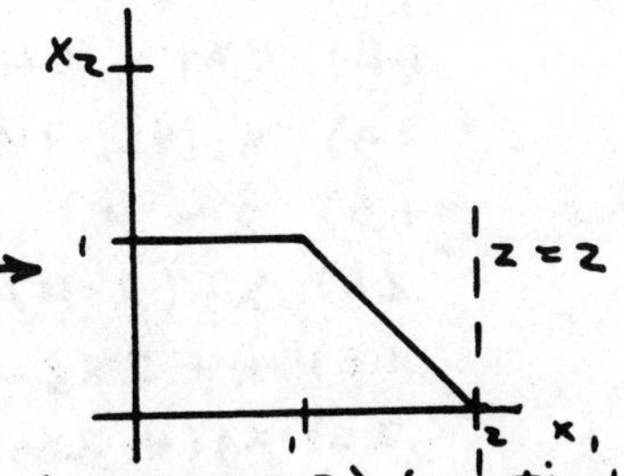

$(x_1, x_2) = (2, 0)$ is optimal

13.6-10. (a) The KKT conditions:

1a) $1 - u \le 0$
2a) $x_1(1 - u) = 0$
1b) $2 - 3x_2^2 - u \le 0$
2b) $x_2(2 - 3x_2^2 - u) = 0$
3) $x_1 + x_2 \le 1$
4) $u(x_1 + x_2 - 1) = 0$
5) $x_1 \ge 0,\ x_2 \ge 0$
6) $u \ge 0$

It is easy to check that $(x_1, x_2, u) = \left(1 - \frac{\sqrt{3}}{3}, \frac{\sqrt{3}}{3}, 1\right)$ satisfies the KKT conditions. Thus, $(x_1, x_2) = \left(1 - \frac{\sqrt{3}}{3}, \frac{\sqrt{3}}{3}\right)$ is optimal since this is a convex program.

13.6-10. (b) The KKT conditions:

1a) $20 - u_1 2x_1 - u_2 \le 0$

2a) $x_1(20 - u_1 2x_1 - u_2) = 0$

1b) $10 - u_1 2x_2 - 2u_2 \le 0$

2b) $x_2(10 - u_1 2x_2 - 2u_2) = 0$

3a) $x_1^2 + x_2^2 \le 1$

b) $x_1 + 2x_2 \le 2$

4a) $u_1(x_1^2 + x_2^2 - 1) = 0$

b) $u_2(x_1 + 2x_2 - 2) = 0$

5) $x_1 \ge 0,\ x_2 \ge 0$

6) $u_1 \ge 0,\ u_2 \ge 0$

It is easy to check that $(x_1, x_2, u_1, u_2) = \left(\frac{2\sqrt{5}}{5}, \frac{\sqrt{5}}{5}, 5\sqrt{5}, 0\right)$ satisfies the KKT conditions, and so since we have a convex program again $(x_1, x_2) = \left(\frac{2\sqrt{5}}{5}, \frac{\sqrt{5}}{5}\right)$ is optimal.

13.6-11. a) The KKT conditions:

1a) $4x_1 - 2u \le 0$

2a) $x_1(4x_1 - 2u) = 0$

1b) $2 - u \le 0$

2b) $x_2(2-u) = 0$

1c) $4 - 2x_3 - u \le 0$

2c) $x_3(4 - 2x_3 - u) = 0$

3) $2x_1 + x_2 + x_3 - 4 \le 0$

4) $u(2x_1 + x_2 + x_3 - 4) = 0$

5) $x_1 \ge 0, x_2 \ge 0, x_3 \ge 0$

6) $u \ge 0$

$x_1 = 1$ so (2a) $\Rightarrow u = 2$

Since $(x_1, x_2, x_3) = (1,1,1)$ and $u = 2$ satisfies all the KKT conditions, this can be optimal.

b) No, the objective function is not convex.

13.6-12.

Minimize $f(\underline{x})$ subject to $g_i(\underline{x}) \ge b_i$, $\underline{x} \ge 0$ $\Longleftrightarrow$ Maximize $-f(\underline{x})$ subject to $-g_i(\underline{x}) \le -b_i$, $\underline{x} \ge 0$

has KKT conditions:

1) $\sum_{i=1}^{m} u_i \frac{\partial g_i}{\partial x_j} - \frac{\partial f}{\partial x_j} \le 0$

2) $x_j^*\left(\sum_{i=1}^{m} u_i \frac{\partial g_i}{\partial x_j} - \frac{\partial f}{\partial x_j}\right) = 0$

} at $x_j = x_j^*$ for $j = 1, \ldots, n$

3) $g_i(x^*) \ge b_i$

4) $u_i(b_i - g_i(x^*)) = 0$

} for $i = 1, \ldots, m$

5) $x_j^* \ge 0 \quad j = 1, \ldots, n$

6) $u_i \ge 0 \quad i = 1, \ldots, m$

13.6-13. (a) An equivalent nonlinear programming problem is:

$$\text{MAXIMIZE} \quad Z = -2x_1^2 - x_2^2$$

subject to: $x_1 + x_2 \le 10$

$-x_1 - x_2 \le -10 \quad x_1 \ge 0 \quad x_2 \ge 0.$

This nonlinear program fits the following types:

- Linearly Constrained Optimization Problem, because all constraints are linear.
- Quadratic Programming Problem, because all constraints are linear and the objective only involves the squares of variables.
- Convex Programming Problem, because the objective is concave as shown below and the constraints are linear and, therefore, convex

Using the test in the appendix $\frac{\partial^2 f}{\partial x_1^2}\frac{\partial^2 f}{\partial x_2^2} - \left[\frac{\partial^2 f}{\partial x_1 \partial x_2}\right]^2 = (-4)(-2) - 0$

$= 8 \ge 0$

so f is concave

- Geometric Programming Problem, because the first constraint can be written as $g_1(x_1, x_2) = c_1 P_1(x_1, x_2) + c_2 P_2(x_1, x_2)$ with $c_1 = 1 = c_2$ $P_1 = x_1$ and $P_2 = x_2$. Similarly for the second constraint and the objective function.
- Fractional Programming Problem, because $f(x_1, x_2) = -2x_1^2 - x_2^2 = \frac{f_1(x)}{f_2(x)}$ with $f_1(x) = -2x_1^2 - x_2^2$ and $f_2(x) = 1$.

(b) The KKT conditions are:

1(a) $-4x_1 - u_1 + u_2 \le 0$

(b) $-2x_2 - u_1 + u_2 \le 0$

2(a) $x_1(-4x_1 - u_1 + u_2) = 0$

(b) $x_2(-2x_2 - u_1 + u_2) = 0$

3(a) $x_1 + x_2 - 10 \le 0$

(b) $-x_1 - x_2 + 10 \le 0$

4(a) $u_1(x_1 + x_2 - 10) = 0$

(b) $u_2(-x_1 - x_2 + 10) = 0$

5 $x_1 \ge 0, \; x_2 \ge 0$

6 $u_1 \ge 0, \; u_2 \ge 0$

c) From 3(a) + (b), $x_1 + x_2 = 10$, so 4(a) + (b) are automatically satisfied. Let us try $x_1, x_2 \ne 0$. Then 2(a) + (b) give

$$-4x_1 - u_1 + u_2 = 0 = -2x_2 - u_1 + u_2$$

$$\Rightarrow x_2 = 2x_1$$

$$\Rightarrow x_1 + 2x_1 = 10 \Rightarrow x_1 = \tfrac{10}{3}, \; x_2 = \tfrac{20}{3}$$

Now 2(a) gives $-u_1 + u_2 = \frac{40}{3}$

$u_1 = 0, \; u_2 = \frac{40}{3}$ satisfies this

(actually $u_1 = c \ge 0, \; u_2 = \frac{40}{3} + c$ works)

$(x_1, x_2) = (\frac{10}{3}, \frac{20}{3}), \; (u_1, u_2) = (0, \frac{40}{3})$ satisfies all KKT conditions, so $(x_1, x_2) = (\frac{10}{3}, \frac{20}{3})$ is optimal.

13.6-14. (a) An equivalent nonlinear programming problem is:

Maximize $f(y) = -(y_1+1)^3 - 4(y_2+1)^2 - 16(y_3+1)$

subject to: $y_1 + y_2 + y_3 \le 2$

$-y_1 - y_2 - y_3 \le -2$

$y_1 \ge 0 \quad y_2 \ge 0 \quad y_3 \ge 0$

(b) The KKT Conditions are:

1 (a) $-3(y_1+1)^2 - u_1 + u_2 \le 0$

(b) $-8(y_2+1) - u_1 + u_2 \le 0$

(c) $-16 \quad - u_1 + u_2 \le 0$

2 (a) $y_1(-3(y_1+1)^2 - u_1 + u_2) = 0$

(b) $y_2(-8(y_2+1)^2 - u_1 + u_2) = 0$

(c) $y_3(-16 - u_1 + u_2) = 0$

3 (a) $y_1 + y_2 + y_3 - 2 \le 0$

(b) $-y_1 - y_2 - y_3 + 2 \le 0$

4 (a) $u_1(y_1 + y_2 + y_3 - 2) = 0$

(b) $u_2(-y_1 - y_2 - y_3 + 2) = 0$

5 $y_1 \ge 0 \quad y_2 \ge 0 \quad y_3 \ge 0$

6 $u_1 \ge 0 \quad u_2 \ge 0.$

(c) For $x = (2,1,2)$ we have $y = (1,0,1)$

2 (a) implies $-3(2^2) - u_1 + u_2 = 0$ or $-u_1 + u_2 = 12$

2 (c) implies $-16 - u_1 + u_2 = 0$ or $-u_1 + u_2 = 16$

The KKT Conditions are not satisfied by $x = (2,1,2)$

13.6-15. (a) The KKT conditions:

1 a) $6 - 2x_1 - u \le 0$

2 a) $x_1(6 - 2x_1 - u) = 0$

1 b) $3 - 3x_2^2 - u \le 0$

2 b) $x_2(3 - 3x_2^2 - u) = 0$

3) $x_1 + x_2 \le 1$

4) $u(x_1 + x_2 - 1) = 0$

5) $x_1 \ge 0, x_2 \ge 0$

6) $u \ge 0$.

(b) for $(x_1, x_2) = (1/2, 1/2)$

2a) $\Rightarrow u = 5$

2b) $\Rightarrow u = 9/4$

so $(x_1, x_2) = (1/2, 1/2)$ is not optimal.

(c) It is easy to check that $(x_1, x_2, u) = (1, 0, 4)$ satisfies the KKT condition, and once again we have a convex program so $(x_1, x_2) = (1, 0)$ is optimal.

13.6-16. (a) The KKT conditions:

1a) $8 - 2x_1 - u \le 0$
2a) $x_1(8 - 2x_1 - u) = 0$
1b) $2 - 3u \le 0$
2b) $x_2(2 - 3u) = 0$
1c) $1 - 2u \le 0$
2c) $x_3(1 - 2u) = 0$
3) $x_1 + 3x_2 + 2x_3 \le 12$
4) $u(x_1 + 3x_2 + 2x_3 - 12) = 0$
5) $x_1 \ge 0,\ x_2 \ge 0,\ x_3 \ge 0$
6) $u \ge 0$

for $(x_1, x_2, x_3) = (2, 2, 2)$
2a) $\Rightarrow$ $u = 4$
2b) $\Rightarrow$ $u = 2/3$
2c) $\Rightarrow$ $u = 1/2$

so $(2, 2, 2)$ cannot be an optimal solution.

(b) It is easy to check that $(x_1, x_2, x_3, u) = (11/3, 25/9, 0, 2/3)$ satisfies the KKT conditions, and so $(x_1, x_2, x_3) = (11/3, 25/9, 0)$ is optimal since the program is convex.

13.6-17. The KKT conditions:

1a) $-2 - u(-2x_1) \le 0$
2a) $x_1(-2 + u2x_1) = 0$
1b) $-3x_2^2 - u(-4x_2) \le 0$
2b) $x_2(-3x_2^2 + u4x_2 = 0$
1c) $-2x_3 - u(-2x_3) \le 0$
2c) $x_3(-2x_3 + u2x_3) = 0$
3) $x_1^2 + 2x_2^2 + x_3^2 \ge 4$
4) $u(4 - x_1^2 - 2x_2^2 - x_3^2) = 0$
5) $x_1 \ge 0,\ x_2 \ge 0,\ x_3 \ge 0$
6) $u \ge 0$

For $(x_1, x_2, x_3) = (1, 1, 1)$
2a) $\Rightarrow$ $u = 1$
2b) $\Rightarrow$ $u = 3/4$
2c) $\Rightarrow$ $u = 1$

so $(x_1, x_2, x_3) = (1, 1, 1)$ cannot be optimal

13.6-18. KKT conditions:

1a) $-4x_1^3 + 2x_1 u \le 0$
2a) $x_1(-4x_1^3 + 2x_1 u) = 0$
1b) $-4x_2 + 2x_2 u \le 0$
2b) $x_2(-4x_2 + 2x_2 u) = 0$
3) $-x_1^2 - x_2^2 + 2 \le 0$
4) $u(-x_1^2 - x_2^2 + 2) = 0$
5) $x_1 \ge 0,\ x_2 \ge 0$
6) $u \ge 0$

If $x_1 = x_2 = 1$, 2a) $\Rightarrow$ $-4 + 2u = 0$ or $u = 2$

$(x_1, x_2) = (1, 1)$, $u = 2$ satisfies all KKT conditions, so $(1, 1)$ is optimal.

13.6-19. The KKT conditions:

1a) $32 - 4x_1^3 - 3u_1 - 2u_2 \leq 0$

2a) $x_1(32 - 4x_1^3 - 3u_1 - 2u_2) = 0$

1b) $50 - 20x_2 + 3x_2^2 - 4x_2^3 - u_1 - 5u_2 \leq 0$

2b) $x_2(50 - 20x_2 + 3x_2^2 - 4x_2^3 - u_1 - 5u_2) = 0$

3a) $3x_1 + x_2 \leq 11$

4a) $u_1(3x_1 + x_2 - 11) = 0$

3b) $2x_1 + 5x_2 \leq 16$

4b) $u_2(2x_1 + 5x_2 - 16) = 0$

5) $x_1 \geq 0,\ x_2 \geq 0$

6) $u_1 \geq 0,\ u_2 \geq 0$

for $(x_1, x_2) = (2,2)$ 2a) & 6) $\Rightarrow u_1 = u_2 = 0$

2b) $\Rightarrow u_1 + 5u_2 = -10$

$\Rightarrow (x_1, x_2) = (2,2)$ is not optimal.

13.7-1. (a) $\frac{\partial^2 f}{\partial x_1^2} = -4 < 0 \quad \forall (x_1, x_2)$

$\frac{\partial^2 f}{\partial x_2^2} = -8 < 0 \quad \forall (x_1, x_2)$

$\frac{\partial^2 f}{\partial x_1^2}\frac{\partial^2 f}{\partial x_2^2} - \left[\frac{\partial^2 f}{\partial x_1 \partial x_2}\right]^2 = 16 > 0 \quad \forall (x_1, x_2)$

$\Rightarrow f$ is strictly concave.

(b) $x^T Q x = 4x_1^2 - 8x_1x_2 + 8x_2^2 = 4(x_1 - x_2)^2 + 4x_2^2 > 0$

$\forall (x_1, x_2) \neq (0,0)$

$\Rightarrow Q$ is positive definite.

(c) The KKT conditions:

1a) $15 + 4x_2 - 4x_1 - u \leq 0$

2a) $x_1(15 + 4x_2 - 4x_1 - u) = 0$

1b) $30 + 4x_1 - 8x_2 - 2u \leq 0$

2b) $x_2(30 + 4x_1 - 8x_2 - 2u) = 0$

3) $x_1 + 2x_2 \leq 30$

4) $u(x_1 + 2x_2 - 30) = 0$

5) $x_1 \geq 0,\ x_2 \geq 0$

6) $u \geq 0$

It is easy to verify that $(x_1, x_2, u) = (12, 9, 3)$ satisfies these conditions.

13.7-2. (a) The KKT conditions:

1 a) $8 - 2x_1 - u \le 0$
2 a) $x_1(8 - 2x_1 - u) = 0$
1 b) $4 - 2x_2 - u \le 0$
2 b) $x_2(4 - 2x_2 - u) = 0$
3) $x_1 + x_2 \le 2$
4) $u(x_1 + x_2 - 2) = 0$
5) $x_1 \ge 0,\ x_2 \ge 0$
6) $u \ge 0$

It is easy to verify that $(x_1, x_2, u) = (2, 0, 4)$ satisfies the above conditions; hence, since this is a convex program $(x_1, x_2) = (2, 0)$ is optimal.

(b) The objective function in vector notation is:

Maximize $(8, 4)\begin{pmatrix} x_1 \\ x_2 \end{pmatrix} - \frac{1}{2}(x_1, x_2)\begin{pmatrix} 2 & 0 \\ 0 & 2 \end{pmatrix}\begin{pmatrix} x_1 \\ x_2 \end{pmatrix}$

Hence, the equivalent problem is:

Minimize $z_1 + z_2$

subject to

$$2x_1 - y_1 + y_3 + z_1 = 8$$
$$2x_2 - y_2 + y_3 + z_2 = 4$$
$$x_1 + x_2 + x_3 = 2$$
$$x_1 \ge 0,\ x_2 \ge 0,\ x_3 \ge 0$$
$$y_1 \ge 0,\ y_2 \ge 0,\ y_3 \ge 0$$
$$z_1 \ge 0,\ z_2 \ge 0$$

The complementarity constraint is: $x_1 y_1 + x_2 y_2 + x_3 y_3 = 0$

(c)

(0)

Bas Var	Eq No	Z	X1	X2	X3	X4	X5	X6	X7	X8	Right side
Z	0	1	-2	-2	-2	1	1	0	0	0	-12
X6	1	0	2	0	1	-1	0	1	0	0	8
X7	2	0	0	2	1	0	-1	0	1	0	4
X8	3	0	1*	1	0	0	0	0	0	1	2

(1)

Bas Var	Eq No	Z	X1	X2	X3	X4	X5	X6	X7	X8	Right side
Z	0	1	0	0	-2	1	1	0	0	2	-8
X6	1	0	0	-2	1*	-1	0	1	0	-2	4
X7	2	0	0	2	1	0	-1	0	1	0	4
X1	3	0	1	1	0	0	0	0	0	1	2

13.7-2. (c) (cont.)

(2)

Bas Var	Eq No	Z	X1	X2	X3	X4	X5	X6	X7	X8	Right side
Z	0	1	0	-4	0	-1	1	2	0	-2	0
X3	1	0	0	-2	1	-1	0	1	0	-2	4
X7	2	0	0	4*	0	1	-1	-1	1	2	0
X1	3	0	1	1	0	0	0	0	0	1	2

(3)

Bas Var	Eq No	Z	X1	X2	X3	X4	X5	X6	X7	X8	Right side
Z	0	1	0	0	0	0	0	1	1	0	0
X3	1	0	0	0	1	-0.5	-0.5	0.5	0.5	-1	4
X2	2	0	0	1	0	0.25	-0.25	-0.25	0.25	0.5	0
X1	3	0	1	0	0	-0.25	0.25	0.25	-0.25	0.5	2

This provides the optimal solution $x_1 = 2, x_2 = 0, u = 4$.

13.7-3. (a) The objective function in vector notation is:

Maximize $(20, 50)\begin{pmatrix} x_1 \\ x_2 \end{pmatrix} - \frac{1}{2}(x_1, x_2)\begin{pmatrix} 40 & -20 \\ -20 & 10 \end{pmatrix}\begin{pmatrix} x_1 \\ x_2 \end{pmatrix}$

Hence, the equivalent problem is:

Minimize $z_1 + z_2$

subject to

$$40x_1 - 20x_2 - y_1 + y_3 + y_4 + z_1 = 20$$
$$-20x_1 + 10x_2 - y_2 + y_3 + 4y_4 + z_2 = 50$$
$$x_1 + x_2 + x_3 = 6$$
$$x_1 + 4x_2 + x_4 = 18$$
$$x_1 \geq 0, x_2 \geq 0, x_3 \geq 0, x_4 \geq 0, y_1 \geq 0, y_2 \geq 0, y_3 \geq 0, y_4 \geq 0, z_1 \geq 0, z_2 \geq 0$$

The enforced complementarity constraint is:

$$x_1 y_1 + x_2 y_2 + x_3 y_3 + x_4 y_4 = 0$$

(b)

(0)

Bas Var	Eq No	Z	X1	X2	X3	X4	X5	X6	X7	X8	X9	X10	Right side
Z	0	1	-20	10	-2	-5	1	1	0	0	0	0	-70
X7	1	0	40*	-20	1	1	-1	0	1	0	0	0	20
X8	2	0	-20	10	1	4	0	-1	0	1	0	0	50
X9	3	0	1	1	0	0	0	0	0	0	1	0	6
Xe	4	0	1	4	0	0	0	0	0	0	0	1	18

(1)

Bas Var	Eq No	Z	X1	X2	X3	X4	X5	X6	X7	X8	X9	X10	Right side
Z	0	1	0	0	-1.5	-4.5	0.5	1	0.5	0	0	0	-60
X1	1	0	1	-0.5	0.025	0.025	-0.03	0	0.025	0	0	0	0.5
X8	2	0	0	0	1.5	4.5	-0.5	-1	0.5	1	0	0	60
X9	3	0	0	1.5*	-0.03	-0.03	0.025	0	-0.03	0	1	0	5.5
Xe	4	0	0	4.5	-0.03	-0.03	0.025	0	-0.03	0	0	1	17.5

13.7-3. (b) (cont.)

(2)

Bas Var	Eq No	Z	X1	X2	X3	X4	X5	X6	X7	X8	X9	X10	Right side
Z	0	1	0	0	-1.5	-4.5	0.5	1	0.5	0	0	0	-60
X1	1	0	1	0	0.017	0.017	-0.02	0	0.017	0	0.333	0	2.333
X8	2	0	0	0	1.5	4.5	-0.5	-1	0.5	1	0	0	60
X2	3	0	0	1	-0.02	-0.02	0.017	0	-0.02	0	0.667	0	3.667
Xe	4	0	0	0	0.05*	0.05	-0.05	0	0.05	0	-3	1	1

(3)

Bas Var	Eq No	Z	X1	X2	X3	X4	X5	X6	X7	X8	X9	X10	Right side
Z	0	1	0	0	0	-3	-1	1	2	0	-90	30	-30
X1	1	0	1	0	0	0	0	0	0	0	1.353	-0.34	1.993
X8	2	0	0	0	0	3*	1	-1	-1	1	90	-30	30
X2	3	0	0	1	0.003	0.003	-0	0	0.003	0	-0.53	0.4	4.067
X3	4	0	0	0	1	1	-1	0	1	0	-60	20	20

(4)

Bas Var	Eq No	Z	X1	X2	X3	X4	X5	X6	X7	X8	X9	X10	Right side
Z	0	1	0	0	0	0	0	0	1	1	0	0	0
X1	1	0	1	0	0	0	0	0	0	0	1.353	-0.34	1.993
X4	2	0	0	0	0	1	0.333	-0.33	-0.33	0.333	30	-10	10
X2	3	0	0	1	0.003	0	-0	0.001	0.004	-0	-0.63	0.433	4.033
X3	4	0	0	0	1	0	-1.33	0.333	1.333	-0.33	-90	30	10

This provides the optimal solution $(x_1, x_2) = (1.993, 4.033)$
$(u_1, u_2) = (10, 10)$

13.7-4. a) The KKT conditions:

1a) $2 - 2x_1 - u \leq 0$

2a) $x_1(2 - 2x_1 - u) = 0$

1b) $4 - 3x_2 - u \leq 0$

2b) $x_2(4 - 3x_2 - u) = 0$

3) $x_1 + x_2 \leq 2$

4) $u(x_1 + x_2 - 2) = 0$

5) $x_1 \geq 0, x_2 \geq 0$

6) $u \geq 0$

If you plot the points obtained in (a) it is pretty clear that you are converging to a boundary point solution. So $x_1, x_2, u \neq 0$ $\Rightarrow (x_1, x_2, u) = (.8, 1.2, .4)$ satisfies the above conditions. So $(x_1, x_2) = (.8, 1.2)$ is optimal.

13.7-4. b) Minimize $z_1 + z_2$

subject to

$$2x_1 - y_1 + y_3 + z_1 = 2$$
$$3x_2 - y_2 + y_3 + z_2 = 4$$
$$x_1 + x_2 + x_3 = 2$$
$$x_1 \geq 0,\ x_2 \geq 0,\ x_3 \geq 0,\ y_1 \geq 0,\ y_2 \geq 0,\ y_3 \geq 0,\ z_1 \geq 0,\ z_2 \geq 0$$

The enforced complementarity constraint is:

$$x_1 y_1 + x_2 y_2 + x_3 y_3 = 0$$

c) for $x_1 = .8$, $x_2 = 1.2$, $u = y_3 = .4$

the first constraint becomes $-y_1 + z_1 = 0$

the second constraint becomes $-y_2 + z_2 = 0$

the third constraint becomes $x_3 = 0$

and, hence, the complementarity constraint becomes $.8y_1 + 1.2y_2 = 0$, but $y_1 \geq 0$ & $y_2 \geq 0$

$\Rightarrow y_1 = 0,\ y_2 = 0$

so $z_1 = z_2 = 0 \Rightarrow Z = 0$

Thus, $(.8, 1.2) = (x_1, x_2)$ is optimal

d)

(0)

Bas Var	Eq No	Z	X1	X2	X3	X4	X5	X6	X7	X8	Right side
Z	0	1	-2	-3	-2	1	1	0	0	0	-6
X6	1	0	2	0	1	-1	0	1	0	0	2
X7	2	0	0	3*	1	0	-1	0	1	0	4
X8	3	0	1	1	0	0	0	0	0	1	2

(1)

Bas Var	Eq No	Z	X1	X2	X3	X4	X5	X6	X7	X8	Right side
Z	0	1	-2	0	-1	1	0	0	1	0	-2
X6	1	0	2	0	1	-1	0	1	0	0	2
X2	2	0	0	1	0.333	0	-0.33	0	0.333	0	1.333
X8	3	0	1*	0	-0.33	0	0.333	0	-0.33	1	0.667

(2)

Bas Var	Eq No	Z	X1	X2	X3	X4	X5	X6	X7	X8	Right side
Z	0	1	0	0	-1.67	1	0.667	0	0.333	2	-0.67
X6	1	0	0	0	1.667*	-1	-0.67	1	0.667	-2	0.667
X2	2	0	0	1	0.333	0	-0.33	0	0.333	0	1.333
X1	3	0	1	0	-0.33	0	0.333	0	-0.33	1	0.667

13.7-4. d) (cont')

Bas Var	Eq No	Z	X1	X2	X3	X4	X5	X6	X7	X8	Right side
Z	0	1	0	0	0	0	0	1	1	0	0
X3	1	0	0	0	1	-0.6	-0.4	0.6	0.4	-1.2	0.4
X2	2	0	0	1	0	0.2	-0.2	-0.2	0.2	0.4	1.2
X1	3	0	1	0	0	-0.2	0.2	0.2	-0.2	0.6	0.8

(3)

This provides the optimal solution $(x_1, x_2) - (0.8, 1.2)$
$u = 0.4$

13.7-5. a) The KKT conditions:

1a) $126 - 18x_1 - u_1 - 3u_3 \le 0$
2a) $x_1(126 - 18x_1 - u_1 - 3u_3) = 0$
1b) $182 - 26x_2 - 2u_2 - 2u_3 \le 0$
2b) $x_2(182 - 26x_2 - 2u_2 - 2u_3) = 0$
3a) $x_1 \le 4$
4a) $u_1(x_1 - 4) = 0$
3b) $2x_2 \le 12$
4b) $u_2(2x_2 - 12) = 0$
3c) $3x_1 + 2x_2 \le 18$
4c) $u_3(3x_1 + 2x_2 - 18) = 0$

It is easy to verify that $(x_1, x_2, u_1, u_2, u_3) = (8/5, 5, 0, 0, 26)$ satisfies the above conditions, and, hence, $(x_1, x_2) = (8/3, 5)$ is optimal.

b) Minimize $z_1 + z_2$

subject to

$$
\begin{aligned}
18x_1 \quad - y_1 \quad + y_3 + 3y_5 + z_1 &= 126 \\
26x_2 \quad - y_2 \quad + 2y_4 + 2y_5 + z_2 &= 182 \\
x_1 + x_3 &= 4 \\
2x_2 + x_4 &= 12 \\
3x_1 + 2x_2 + x_5 &= 18
\end{aligned}
$$

$x_i \ge 0 \quad i = 1, \ldots, 5 \qquad y_i \ge 0 \quad i = 1, \ldots, 5 \qquad z_1 \ge 0, z_2 \ge 0$

c) for $(8/3, 5, 26) = (x_1, x_2, u_3) = (x_1, x_2, y_5)$
the third constraint $\Rightarrow x_3 = 1/3$
the fourth constraint $\Rightarrow x_4 = 2$
the fifth constraint $\Rightarrow x_5 = 0$
the first constraint $\Rightarrow y_3 - y_1 + z_1 = 0$
the second constraint $\Rightarrow 2y_4 - y_2 + z_2 = 0$
the complementary constraint $\Rightarrow 8/3 y_1 + 5y_2 + 1/3 y_3 + 2y_4 = 0$
so non-negativity $\Rightarrow y_1 = y_2 = y_3 = y_4 = 0$
$\Rightarrow z_1 = z_2 = 0$
$\Rightarrow (8/3, 5) = (x_1, x_2)$ is optimal

13.7-6. (a) The KKT Conditions are:

1(a) $-2(x_1-1)+3-4u_1-u_2 \le 0$

(b) $-2(x_2-2)+3-u_1-4u_2 \le 0$

2(a) $x_1(-2(x_1-1)+3-4u_1-u_2)=0$

(b) $x_2(-2(x_2-2)+3-u_1-4u_2)=0$

3(a) $4x_1+x_2-20 \le 0$

(b) $x_1+4x_2-20 \le 0$

4(a) $u_1(4x_1+x_2-20)=0$

(b) $u_2(x_1+4x_2-20)=0$

5 $x_1 \ge 0 \quad x_2 \ge 0$

6 $u_1 \ge 0 \quad u_2 \ge 0$

(b) Since the optimal solution is not on a boundary from 2(a), 2(b), 4(a) and 4(b), respectively, we have:

$$-2(x_1-1)+3-4u_1-u_2=0$$
$$-2(x_2-2)+3-u_1-4u_2=0$$
$$u_1=0$$
$$u_2=0$$

Substituting the last 2 into the first 2 we get

$$-2x_1+5=0$$
$$-2x_2+7=0$$

So, the optimal solution is $x_1=5/2 \quad x_2=7/2$.

(c) Minimize z_1+z_2

subject to:

$$2x_1 + 4u_1 + u_2 - y_1 + z_1 = 5$$
$$2x_2 + u_1 + 4u_2 - y_2 + z_2 = 7$$
$$4x_1 + x_2 + v_1 = 20$$
$$x_1 + 4x_2 + v_2 = 20$$

$$x_i \ge 0,\ u_i \ge 0,\ y_i \ge 0,\ v_i \ge 0,\ z_i \ge 0 \text{ for } i=1,2.$$

Complementarity Constraint is: $x_1y_1+x_2y_2+u_1v_1+u_2v_2=0$

(d)

	Bas Var	Eq No	Z	X1	X2	X3	X4	X5	X6	X7	X8	X9	X10	Right side
	Z	0	1	-2	-2	-5	-5	1	1	0	0	0	0	-12
	X7	1	0	2*	0	4	1	-1	0	1	0	0	0	5
(0)	X8	2	0	0	2	1	4	0	-1	0	1	0	0	7
	X9	3	0	4	1	0	0	0	0	0	0	1	0	20
	Xe	4	0	1	4	0	0	0	0	0	0	0	1	20

13.7-6. d) (cont')

(1)

Bas Var	Eq No	Z	X1	X2	X3	X4	X5	X6	X7	X8	X9	X10	Right side
Z	0	1	0	-2	-1	-4	0	1	1	0	0	0	-7
X1	1	0	1	0	2	0.5	-0.5	0	0.5	0	0	0	2.5
X8	2	0	0	2*	1	4	0	-1	0	1	0	0	7
X9	3	0	0	1	-8	-2	2	0	-2	0	1	0	10
Xe	4	0	0	4	-2	-0.5	0.5	0	-0.5	0	0	1	17.5

(2)

Bas Var	Eq No	Z	X1	X2	X3	X4	X5	X6	X7	X8	X9	X10	Right side
Z	0	1	0	0	0	0	0	0	1	1	0	0	0
X1	1	0	1	0	2	0.5	-0.5	0	0.5	0	0	0	2.5
X2	2	0	0	1	0.5	2	0	-0.5	0	0.5	0	0	3.5
X9	3	0	0	0	-8.5	-4	2	0.5	-2	-0.5	1	0	6.5
Xe	4	0	0	0	-4	-8.5	0.5	2	-0.5	-2	0	1	3.5

This shows $x_1 = \frac{5}{2}$ $x_2 = \frac{7}{2}$ is optimal with $u_1 = u_2 = 0$

13.8-1. a) Let $x_1 = x_{11} + x_{12}$ and $x_2 = x_{21} + x_{22}$, $f_1(x_1) = (x_1 - 1)^2 - 3x_1$ and $f_2(x_2) = (x_2 - 2)^2 - 3x_2$.

$f_1(0) = 1$, $f_1(2.5) = -5.25$, $f_1(5) = 1$, $f_2(0) = 4$, $f_2(2.5) = -7.25$ and $f_2(5) = -6$

so $s_{11} = \dfrac{1 + 5.25}{0 - 2.5} = -2.5$ $\qquad s_{12} = \dfrac{-5.25 - 1}{2.5 - 5} = 2.5$

$s_{21} = \dfrac{4 + 7.25}{0 - 2.5} = -4.5$ $\qquad s_{22} = \dfrac{-7.25 + 6}{2.5 - 5} = \frac{1}{2}$

The approximate linear programming model is:

Minimize $\quad -2.5x_{11} + 2.5x_{12} - 4.5x_{21} + \frac{1}{2}x_{22}$

subject to:

$4x_{11} + 4x_{12} + x_{21} + x_{22} \le 20$

$x_{11} + x_{12} + 4x_{21} + 4x_{22} \le 20$

$0 \le x_{ij} \le 2.5$ for $i = 1, 2$ and $j = 1, 2$.

b)

Bas Var	Eq No	Z	X1	X2	X3	X4	X5	X6	X7	X8	X9	X10	Right side
Z	0	-1	0	2.5	0	0.5	0	0	2.5	0	4.5	0	17.5
X5	1	0	0	4	0	1	1	0	-4	0	-1	0	7.5
X6	2	0	0	1	0	4	0	1	-1	0	-4	0	7.5
X1	3	0	1	0	0	0	0	0	1	0	0	0	2.5
X8	4	0	0	1	0	0	0	0	0	1	0	0	2.5
X3	5	0	0	0	1	0	0	0	0	0	1	0	2.5
Xe	6	0	0	0	0	1	0	0	0	0	0	1	2.5

The optimal solution is $x_{11} = 2.5$, $x_{12} = 0$, $x_{21} = 2.5$, $x_{22} = 0$

In terms of the original variables we have $x_1 = x_{11} + x_{12} = 2.5$, $x_2 = x_{21} + x_{22} = 2.5$

13.8-1. c) i) Let $x_1 = x_{11} + x_{12} + x_{13} + x_{14} + x_{15}$, $x_2 = x_{21} + x_{22} + x_{23} + x_{24} + x_{25}$

$f_1(x_1) = (x_2 - 1)^2 - 3x_1$, $f_2(x_2) = (x_2 - 2)^2 - 3x_2$

$f_1(0) = 1,\ f_1(1) = -3,\ f_1(2) = -5,\ f_1(3) = -5,\ f_1(4) = -3,\ f_1(5) = 1$

$f_2(0) = 4,\ f_2(1) = -2,\ f_2(2) = -6,\ f_2(3) = -8,\ f_2(4) = -8,\ f_2(5) = -6$

So, $s_{11} = \dfrac{1-(-3)}{0-1} = -4$, $s_{12} = \dfrac{-3-(-5)}{1-2} = -2$, $s_{13} = 0$, $s_{14} = 2$, $s_{15} = 4$

$s_{21} = -6$, $s_{22} = -4$, $s_{23} = -2$, $s_{24} = 0$, $s_{25} = 2$

The approximate linear programming model is:

Minimize $-4x_{11} - 2x_{12} + 2x_{14} + 4x_{15} - 6x_{21} - 4x_{22} - 2x_{23} + 2x_{25}$

subject to $4x_{11} + 4x_{12} + 4x_{13} + 4x_{14} + 4x_{15} + x_{21} + x_{22} + x_{23} + x_{24} + x_{25} \le 20$

$x_{11} + x_{12} + x_{13} + x_{14} + x_{15} + 4x_{21} + 4x_{22} + 4x_{23} + 4x_{24} + 4x_{25} \le 20$

$0 \le x_{ij} \le 1$ for $i = 1, 2$ and $j = 1, 2, 3, 4, 5$.

ii) Solving this using the Simplex Method, we get:

Optimal Solution

Value of the
Objective Function: Z = -18

Variable	Value
X1 (x_{11})	1
X2 (x_{12})	1
X3 (x_{13})	0
X4 (x_{14})	0
X5 (x_{15})	0
X6 (x_{21})	1
X7 (x_{22})	1
X8 (x_{23})	1
X9 (x_{24})	0
X10 (x_{25})	0

In terms of the original variable, we have

$x_1 = x_{11} + x_{12} + x_{13} + x_{14} + x_{15} = 2$

$x_2 = x_{21} + x_{22} + x_{23} + x_{24} + x_{25} = 3$

(Note that we improved by $\frac{1}{2}$; Z went from -17.5 to -18)

13.8-2. a) Maximize $36x_{11} + 3x_{12} + 24x_{21} + 12x_{22} + 9x_{23} + 45x_{31} + 30x_{32} + 18x_{33}$

subject to

$$x_{11} + x_{12} + x_{21} + x_{22} + x_{23} + x_{31} + x_{32} + x_{33} \le 60$$
$$3x_{11} + 3x_{12} + 2x_{21} + 2x_{22} + 2x_{23} \le 200$$
$$x_{11} + x_{12} + x_{31} + x_{32} + x_{33} \le 70$$
$$0 \le x_{11} \le 15,\ 0 \le x_{12}$$
$$0 \le x_{21} \le 20,\ 0 \le x_{22} \le 20,\ 0 \le x_{23}$$
$$0 \le x_{31} \le 10,\ 0 \le x_{32} \le 5,\ 0 \le x_{33}$$

where $x_1 = x_{11} + x_{12}$, $x_2 = x_{21} + x_{22} + x_{23}$ & $x_3 = x_{31} + x_{32} + x_{33}$

b) Solving automatically by the Simplex Method:

Optimal Solution

Value of the
Objective Function: Z = 1800

Variable		Value
X1	(x_{11})	15
X2	(x_{12})	0
X3	(x_{21})	20
X4	(x_{22})	0
X5	(x_{23})	0
X6	(x_{31})	10
X7	(x_{32})	5
X8	(x_{33})	10

In terms of the original variables, we have

$x_1 = x_{11} + x_{12} = 15$, $x_2 = x_{21} + x_{22} + x_{23} = 20$, $x_3 = x_{31} + x_{32} + x_{33} = 25$.

c) The restriction on profit from products 1 and 2 can be modeled by adding the following constraint to the linear program in part (a):

$$36x_{11} + 3x_{12} + 24x_{21} + 12x_{22} + 9x_{23} \ge 900$$

d) The Simplex Method gives the optimal solution:

Value of the
Objective Function: Z = 1800

Variable	Value
X1	15
X2	0
X3	20
X4	0
X5	0
X6	10
X7	5
X8	10

Note that the optimal hasn't changed. This is because $\underset{\sim}{x}$ still is feasible with the new constraint. (i.e. $36x_{11} + 3x_{12} + 24x_{21} + 12x_{22} + 9x_{23} = 1020 > 900$)

In terms of the original variables, we (still) have

$x_1 = 15$, $x_2 = 20$, $x_3 = 25$.

13.8-3. a) The KKT conditions:

1a) $4 - 3x_1^2 - u_1 - 5u_2 \le 0$

2a) $x_1(4 - 3x_1^2 - u_1 - 5u_2) = 0$

1b) $6 - 4x_2 - 3u_1 - 2u_2 \le 0$

2b) $x_2(6 - 4x_2 - 3u_1 - 2u_2) = 0$

3a) $x_1 + 3x_2 \le 8$

4a) $u_1(x_1 + 3x_2 - 8) = 0$

3b) $5x_1 + 2x_2 \le 14$

4b) $u_2(5x_1 + 2x_2 - 14) = 0$

5) $x_1 \ge 0, \; x_2 \ge 0$

6) $u_1 \ge 0, \; u_2 \ge 0$

It is easy to verify that $(x_1, x_2, u_1, u_2) = (\frac{2}{\sqrt{3}}, \frac{3}{2}, 0, 0)$ satisfies the above conditions, and so $(x_1, x_2) = (\frac{2}{\sqrt{3}}, \frac{3}{2})$ is optimal with $z = 7.58$

b) Let $x_1 = x_{11} + x_{12} + x_{13}$, $x_2 = x_{21} + x_{22} + x_{23}$, $f_1(x_1) = 4x_1 - x_1^3$, $f_2(x_2) = 6x_2 - 2x_2^2$

$f_1(0) = 0$, $f_1(1) = 3$, $f_1(2) = 0$, $f_1(3) = -15$

$f_2(0) = 0$, $f_2(1) = 4$, $f_2(2) = 4$, $f_2(3) = 0$

$s_{11} = \frac{3-0}{1-0} = 3$, $s_{12} = \frac{0-3}{2-1} = -3$, $s_{13} = -15$

$s_{21} = 4$, $s_{22} = 0$, $s_{23} = -4$

The approximate linear programming model is:

Maximize $3x_{11} - 3x_{12} - 15x_{13} + 4x_{21} \qquad - 4x_{23}$

subject to: $x_{11} + x_{12} + x_{13} + 3x_{21} + 3x_{22} + 3x_{23} \le 8$

$5x_{11} + 5x_{12} + 5x_{13} + 2x_{21} + 2x_{22} + 2x_{23} \le 14$

$0 \le x_{ij} \le 1$ for $i = 1, 2$ and $j = 1, 2, 3$.

c) The Simplex method gives the solution:

Value of the
Objective Function: Z = 7

Variable		Value
X1	(x_{11})	1
X2	(x_{12})	0
X3	(x_{13})	0
X4	(x_{21})	1
X5	(x_{22})	0
X6	(x_{23})	0

or $x_1 = x_{11} + x_{12} + x_{13} = 1$

$x_2 = x_{21} + x_{22} + x_{23} = 1$

(also $x_2 = 2$ gives optimal objective value $z = 7$)

$x_{12} = 0 \Rightarrow x_{13} = 0$ (also $x_{11} = 0 \Rightarrow x_{12} = 0$ since $x_{11} \ne 0$

$x_{22} = 0 \Rightarrow x_{23} = 0$ $\qquad x_{21} = 0 \Rightarrow x_{22} = 0$ since $x_{21} \ne 0$)

So special restriction for the model is satisfied.

The approximate solution is fairly close: $(1,1)$ or $(1,2)$ $\approx (1.155, 1.5)$ ← optimal

+ z is close.

13.8-4. Since regular time production is cheaper than overtime, the objective of minimizing cost will force regular time to be used first. (If not increasing regular time by a small amount and decreasing overtime by the same amount will yield a feasible solution with a better objective value.)

13.8-5. (a) Let $x_1 = x_{11} + x_{12} + x_{13}$, $x_2 = x_{21} + x_{22} + x_{23}$, $f_1(x_1) = 32x_1 - x_1^4$ and $f_2(x_2) = 50x_2 - 10x_2^2 + x_2^3 - x_2^4$.

We will have $s_{11} = 31$, $s_{12} = 17$, $s_{13} = -33$, $s_{21} = 40$, $s_{22} = 12$ and $s_{23} = -46$.

The approximate linear programming model is:

Maximize $31x_{11} + 17x_{12} - 33x_{13} + 40x_{21} + 12x_{22} - 46x_{23}$

subject to: $3x_{11} + 3x_{12} + 3x_{13} + x_{21} + x_{22} + x_{23} \leq 11$

$2x_{11} + 2x_{12} + 2x_{13} + 5x_{21} + 5x_{22} + 5x_{23} \leq 16$

$0 \leq x_{ij} \leq 1$ for $i = 1,2$ and $j = 1,2,3$.

b) The automatic routine (Simplex method) gives the solution:

Value of the
Objective Function: Z = 100

Variable		Value
X1	(x_{11})	1
X2	(x_{12})	1
X3	(x_{13})	0
X4	(x_{21})	1
X5	(x_{22})	1
X6	(x_{23})	0

In terms of the original variables, we have:

$x_1 = x_{11} + x_{12} + x_{13} = 2$, $x_2 = x_{21} + x_{22} + x_{23} = 2$.

13.8-6. Let $f_1(x_1) = \begin{cases} 5x_1 & 0 \leq x_1 \leq 2 \\ 2 + 4x_1 & 2 \leq x_1 \leq 5 \\ 12 + 2x_1 & 5 \leq x_1 \end{cases}$

$f_2(x_2) = \begin{cases} 4x_2 & 0 \leq x_2 \leq 3 \\ 9 + x_2 & 3 \leq x_2 \leq 4 \end{cases}$

So Maximize $f_1(x_1) + f_2(x_2)$

subject to $3x_1 + 2x_2 \leq 25$

$2x_1 - x_2 \leq 10$

$x_2 \leq 4$

$x_1 \geq 0$, $x_2 \geq 0$

Possibly, the $f_i(x_i)$ are piecewise-linear approximations of the true objective function.

13.8-7. (a) Assume that in the optimal solution of the linear program there exists an x_{ij} such that $x_{ij} < u_{ij}$ and $x_{i(j+1)} > 0$. Create a new solution with $x'_{ij} = \min\{u_{ij}, x_{ij} + x_{i(j+1)}\}$, $x'_{i(j+1)} = \max\{0, x_{ij} + x_{i(j+1)} - u_{ij}\}$. This solution is feasible since the g_i's are all linear and $x_{ij} + x_{i(j+1)} = x'_{ij} + x'_{i(j+1)}$.

But $s_{ij}x'_{ij} + s_{i(j+1)}x'_{i(j+1)} = \begin{cases} s_{ij}(x_{ij} + x_{i(j+1)}) & x_{ij} + x_{i(j+1)} \le u_{ij} \\ s_{ij}u_{ij} + s_{i(j+1)}(x_{ij} + x_{i(j+1)} - u_{ij}) & \text{otherwise.} \end{cases}$

Clearly, $s_{ij}(x_{ij} + x_{i(j+1)}) > s_{ij}x_{ij} + s_{i(j+1)}x_{i(j+1)}$ since $s_{ij} \ge s_{i(j+1)}$

Furthermore, $(s_{ij} - s_{i(j+1)})u_{ij} > (s_{ij} - s_{i(j+1)})x_{ij}$ from $x_{ij} < u_{ij}$

$$\Rightarrow s_{ij}u_{ij} + s_{i(j+1)}(x_{ij} - u_{ij}) > s_{ij}x_{ij}$$
$$\Rightarrow s_{ij}u_{ij} + s_{i(j+1)}(x_{ij} + x_{i(j+1)} - u_{ij}) > s_{ij}x_{ij} + s_{i(j+1)}x_{i(j+1)}$$

So $s_{ij}x'_{ij} + s_{i(j+1)}x'_{i(j+1)} > s_{ij}x_{ij} + s_{i(j+1)}x_{i(j+1)}$

Thus, the original solution was not optimal.

(b) Make the same assumptions as above and construct x' from x as above. For the linear approximate of g_i we will have $\ldots a_{ij}x_{ij} + a_{i(j+1)}x_{i(j+1)} \ldots \le b_i$ with $a_{ij} \le a_{i(j+1)}$ since g_i was convex. Thus, it can be shown by the analysis above if we reverse the inequalities in the appropriate places:

$$a_{ij}x'_{ij} + a_{i(j+1)}x'_{i(j+1)} < a_{ij}x_{ij} + a_{i(j+1)}x_{i(j+1)}$$

So x' is feasible. Further, by above

$s_{ij}x'_{ij} + s_{i(j+1)}x'_{i(j+1)} > s_{ij}x_{ij} + s_{i(j+1)}x_{i(j+1)}$

So x was not optimal.

13.8-8. Let $f_1(x_1) = \begin{cases} 15x_1 & 0 \le x_1 \le 2000 \\ 25x_1 - 20{,}000 & 2000 \le x_1 \end{cases}$

$f_2(x) = \begin{cases} 16x_2 & 0 \le x_2 \le 1000 \\ 24x_2 - 8000 & 1000 \le x_1 \end{cases}$

The (non-linear) programming problem is:

Maximize $z = x_1 + x_2$

subject to $f_1(x_1) + f_2(x_2) \le 60{,}000$

$x_1 \le 3000$

$x_2 \le 1500$

$x_1 \ge 0,\ x_2 \ge 0$

(a) Let x_i^R, x_i^O denote regular and overtime production at plant i. The LP is:

Maximize $z = x_1^R + x_1^O + x_2^R + x_2^O$

subject to $15x_1^R + 25x_1^O + 16x_2^R + 24x_2^O \le 60{,}000$

$x_1^R \le 2000$

$x_1^O \le 1000$

$x_2^R \le 1000$

$x_2^O \le 500$

$x_1^R \ge 0,\ x_1^O \ge 0,\ x_2^R \ge 0,\ x_2^O \ge 0$

13.8-8. (b) Since overtime production is more costly than regular time, the objective of maximizing total production time will force the regular time to be used first.

13.8-9. (a) The objective function is linear and, therefore, concave.

$$\frac{\partial^2 g_1}{\partial x_1^2} \cdot \frac{\partial^2 g_1}{\partial x_2^2} - \left(\frac{\partial^2 g_1}{\partial x_1 \partial x_2}\right)^2 = 4 \cdot 0 - 0^2 = 0 \geq 0$$ so from the test in the appendix $g_1(x_1, x_2)$ is convex. Similarly

$$\frac{\partial^2 g_2}{\partial x_1^2} \cdot \frac{\partial^2 g_2}{\partial x_2^2} - \left(\frac{\partial^2 g_2}{\partial x_1 \partial x_2}\right)^2 = 2 \cdot 0 - 0^2 = 0 \geq 0$$ so $g_2(x_1, x_2)$ is also convex.

(b) Let $x_1 = x_{11} + x_{12} + x_{13}$. From constraint 1 we know $2x_1^2 \leq 13$ or $x_1 \leq \sqrt{\frac{13}{2}} \approx 2.55$, therefore, using integer breakpoints will require 3 linear pieces. Let $g_{11}(x_1) = 2x_1^2$, $g_{12}(x_2) = x_2$, $g_{21}(x_1) = x_1^2$ and $g_{22}(x_2) = x_2$

Constraint 1 = $g_{11}(x_1) + g_{12}(x_2)$ and Constraint 2 = $g_{21}(x_1) + g_{22}(x_2)$

$g_{11}(0) = 0$, $g_{11}(1) = 2$, $g_{11}(2) = 8$, $g_{11}(3) = 18$, $g_{21}(0) = 0$, $g_{21}(1) = 1$, $g_{21}(2) = 4$ and $g_{21}(3) = 9$.

Let $s_{11} = \frac{2-0}{1-0} = 2$ $\quad s_{12} = \frac{8-2}{2-1} = 6$ $\quad s_{13} = \frac{18-8}{3-2} = 10$

$s_{21} = \frac{1-0}{1-0} = 1$ $\quad s_{22} = \frac{4-1}{2-1} = 3$ $\quad s_{23} = \frac{9-4}{3-2} = 5$

The approximate linear program is:

Maximize $5x_{11} + 5x_{12} + 5x_{13} + x_2$

subject to: $2x_{11} + 6x_{12} + 10x_{13} + x_2 \leq 13$

$x_{11} + 3x_{12} + 5x_{13} + x_2 \leq 9$

$0 \leq x_{11} \leq 1 \quad 0 \leq x_{12} \leq 1 \quad x_{13} \geq 0 \quad x_2 \geq 0.$

We could have $0 \leq x_{13} \leq 1$ but the constraints will enforce the upper bound.

(c)

Bas Var	Eq No	Z	X1	X2	X3	X4	X5	X6	X7	X8	Right side
Z	0	1	0	0	0	0	0	1	4	2	15
X3	1	0	0	0	1	0	0.2	-0.2	-0.2	-0.6	0
X4	2	0	0	0	0	1	-1	2	0	0	5
X1	3	0	1	0	0	0	0	0	1	0	1
X2	4	0	0	1	0	0	0	0	0	1	1

In terms of the original variables, the optimal solution to the approximate problem is: $X_1 = X_{11} + X_{12} + X_{13} = 1 + 1 + 0 = 2$

$X_2 = 5$

13.8-10. a) Let $X_1 = X_{11} + X_{12} + X_{13}$, $X_2 = X_{21} + X_{22} + X_{23}$

Obj: $f_1(x_1) = 32x_1 - x_1^4$ $\quad \left(\frac{\partial^2 f_1}{\partial x_1^2} = -12x_1^2 \le 0\right)$ } concave

$f_2(x_2) = 4x_2 - x_2^2$ $\quad \left(\frac{\partial^2 f_2}{\partial x_2^2} = -2 < 0\right)$

$f_1(0) = 0,\ f_1(1) = 31,\ f_1(2) = 48,\ f_1(3) = 15$

$f_2(0) = 0,\ f_2(1) = 3,\ f_2(2) = 4,\ f_2(3) = 3$

So, $s_{11} = \frac{31-0}{1-0} = 31,\ s_{12} = 17,\ s_{13} = -33$

$s_{21} = 3,\ s_{22} = 1,\ s_{23} = -1$

Constraints: $g_{11}(x_1) = x_1^2,\ g_{12}(x_2) = x_2^2$ $\quad \left(\frac{\partial^2 g_{11}}{\partial x_1^2} = \frac{\partial^2 g_{12}}{\partial x_2^2} = 2 > 0, \text{convex}\right)$

$g_{11}(0) = 0,\ g_{11}(1) = 1,\ g_{11}(2) = 4,\ g_{11}(3) = 9$

$g_{12}(0) = 0,\ g_{12}(1) = 1,\ g_{12}(2) = 4,\ g_{12}(3) = 9$

$t_{11} = \frac{1-0}{1-0} = 1,\ t_{12} = \frac{4-1}{2-1} = 3,\ t_{13} = 5$

$t_{21} = 1,\ t_{22} = 3,\ t_{23} = 5$

The approximate linear program is:

Maximize $\quad 31X_{11} + 17X_{12} - 33X_{13} + 3X_{21} + X_{22} - X_{23}$

subject to $\quad X_{11} + 3X_{12} + 5X_{13} + X_{21} + 3X_{22} + 5X_{23} \le 9$

$X_{11} \ge 0,\ X_{12} \ge 0,\ X_{13} \ge 0,\ X_{21} \ge 0,\ X_{22} \ge 0,\ X_{23} \ge 0$

$X_{11} \le 1,\ X_{12} \le 1,\ (X_{13} \le 1),\ X_{21} \le 1,\ X_{22} \le 1,\ (X_{23} \le 1)$

b) The Simplex Method gives the solution:

Value of the
Objective Function: Z = 52

Variable		Value
X1	(X_{11})	1
X2	(X_{12})	1
X3	(X_{13})	0
X4	(X_{21})	1
X5	(X_{22})	1
X6	(X_{23})	0

In terms of the original variables, we have

$x_1 = x_{11} + x_{12} + x_{13} = 2,\ x_2 = x_{21} + x_{22} + x_{23} = 2.$

c) The KKT conditions:

1 a) $32 - 4x_1^3 - 2x_1 u \le 0$

2 a) $x_1(32 - 4x_1^3 - 2x_1 u) = 0$

1 b) $4 - 2x_2 - 2x_2 u \le 0$

2 b) $x_2(4 - 2x_2 - 2x_2 u) = 0$

3) $x_1^2 + x_2^2 - 9 \le 0$

4) $u(x_1^2 + x_2^2 - 9) = 0$

5) $x_1 \ge 0,\ x_2 \ge 0$

6) $u \ge 0$

From (4), $x_1 = 2 = x_2 \Rightarrow u = 0$

These values satisfy all of the KKT conditions

So the solution to the linear approximation is, in fact, the optimal to the original problem.

13.8-11. a) $f(x) = f_1(x_1) + f_2(x_2)$

$f_1(x_1) = 3x_1^2 - x_1^3$

$f_2(x_2) = 5x_2^2 - x_2^3$

$\frac{\partial^2 f_1}{\partial x_1^2} = 6 - 6x_1 \quad \leftarrow \quad > 0 \text{ if } 0 \le x_1 < 1$

$\frac{\partial^2 f_2}{\partial x_2^2} = 10 - 6x_2 \quad \leftarrow \quad > 0 \text{ if } 0 \le x_2 < \frac{5}{3}$

Neither f_1 nor f_2 are concave (we only need to show one of these are not concave), so $f(x)$ is not concave.

b) Let $x_1 = x_{11} + x_{12} + x_{13} + x_{14}$

$x_2 = x_{21} + x_{22}$

$f_1(0) = 0$, $f_1(1) = 2$, $f_1(2) = 4$, $f_1(3) = 0$, $f_1(4) = -16$

$f_2(0) = 0$, $f_2(1) = 4$, $f_2(2) = 12$

So, $s_{11} = \frac{2-0}{1-0} = 2$, $s_{12} = \frac{4-2}{2-1} = 2$, $s_{13} = -4$, $s_{14} = -16$

$s_{21} = 4$, $s_{22} = 8$

We need special restrictions

i) $x_{12} = 0$ if $x_{11} < 1$

ii) $x_{13} = 0$ if $x_{12} < 1$

iii) $x_{14} = 0$ if $x_{13} < 1$

iv) $x_{22} = 0$ if $x_{21} < 1$

Since $s_{12} > s_{13} > s_{14}$, (ii) and (iii) are automatically satisfied upon optimizing.

The approximate BIP formulation is:

Maximize $2x_{11} + 2x_{12} - 4x_{13} - 16x_{14} + 4x_{21} + 8x_{22}$

subject to: $x_{11} + x_{12} + x_{13} + x_{14} + 2x_{21} + 2x_{22} \le 4$

$-x_{11} + x_{12} \le 0$

$-x_{21} + x_{22} \le 0$

x_{ij} binary $(i,j) = (1,1), \ldots, (2,2)$

c) The solution (by BIP automatic routine) is:

$x_{11} = 0$, $x_{12} = 0$, $x_{13} = 0$, $x_{14} = 0$, $x_{21} = 1$, $x_{22} = 1$ and $Z = 12$

In terms of the original variables, we have

$x_1 = x_{11} + x_{12} + x_{13} + x_{14} = 0$, $x_2 = x_{21} + x_{22} = 2$

(An alternate solution is $x_1 = 2$, $x_2 = 1$ which also gives the optimal objective value $Z = 12$)

13.9-1. $\nabla f(x_1,x_2) = \left(\frac{1}{1+x_1+x_2}, \frac{1}{1+x_1+x_2}\right)$

$\nabla f(1,1) = (\frac{1}{3},\frac{1}{3})$

Solving: max $\frac{1}{3}x_1 + \frac{1}{3}x_2$
s.t. $x_1 + 2x_2 \le 5$
$x_1 \ge 0,\ x_2 \ge 0$ $\Rightarrow$ $x_1 = 5,\ x_2 = 0$

$x^{(1)} = (1,1) + t(4,-1)$

$t^* = 1$ f(x) increases as t increases

New $x = (5,0)$ (which is the solution found in 13.6-5(b))

2nd iter: $\nabla f(5,0) = (\frac{1}{6},\frac{1}{6})$

Solving LP: max $\frac{1}{6}x_1 + \frac{1}{6}x_2$
s.t. $x_1 + 2x_2 \le 5$
$x_1 \ge 0,\ x_2 \ge 0$ $\Rightarrow$ $x_1 = 5,\ x_2 = 0$

$x^{(2)} = (5,0) + t(0,0)$

So $x = (5,0)$ is optimal

Since $\nabla f(x_1,x_2) = (c_1,c_2)$ $c_1 = c_2 \ge 0$, the LP to be solved is max $c_1x_1 + c_1x_2$
s.t. $x_1 + 2x_2 \le 5$
$x_1 \ge 0,\ x_2 \ge 0$ $\Rightarrow$ $x_1 = 5,\ x_2 = 0$ is always the solution.

Thus, $x^{(1)} = (x_1^{(0)}, x_2^{(0)}) + t(5 - x_1^{(0)}, 0 - x_2^{(0)}) = (5,0)$ (at $t=1$) after 1st iteration.

($t^* = 1$ since f(x) increases with t)

(There are no complications for $(x_1,x_2) = (0,0)$)

13-9-2. $\nabla f(x_1,x_2) = \left(\frac{1}{x_1+1}, -2x_2\right)$

$\nabla f(0,0) = (1,0)$

Solving: max x_1
s.t. $x_1 + 2x_2 \le 3$
$x_1 \ge 0,\ x_2 \ge 0$ $\Rightarrow$ $x_1 = 3,\ x_2 = 0$

$x^{(1)} = (0,0) + t(3,0)$

$t^* = 1$ (f(x) increases with t)

$x^{(1)} = (3,0)$ (the solution found in 13.6-6(b))

2nd iter: $\nabla f(3,0) = (\frac{1}{4}, 0)$

Solving LP: max $\frac{1}{4}x_1$
s.t. $x_1 + 2x_2 \le 3$
$x_1 \ge 0,\ x_2 \ge 0$ $\Rightarrow$ $x_1 = 3,\ x_2 = 0$

$x^{(2)} = (3,0) + t(0,0)$

So $x = (3,0)$ is optimal.

13.9-3.

k	$\mathbf{x}^{(k-1)}$	c1	c2	$\mathbf{x}_{LP}^{(k)}$	t*	$\mathbf{x}^{(k)}$
1	(0, 0)	-6	-3	(1, 0)	1	(1, 0)
2	(1, 0)	-4	-3	(1, 0)	1e-8	(1, 0)

Final solution: (1, 0).

$\nabla f(x_1, x_2) = (2x_1 - 6,\ 3x_2^2 - 3)$

but since $x_1 \le 1, x_2 \le 1$ (since $x_1 + x_2 \le 1, x_1 \ge 0, x_2 \ge 0$)

$2x_1 - 6 < 3x_2^2 - 3 \qquad (2x_1 - 6 \le -4 < -3 \le 3x_2^2 - 3)$

So the resulting LP will be of the form

$\min\ c_1 x_1 + c_2 x_2 \qquad c_1 < c_2$

s.t. $x_1 + x_2 \le 1$

$x_1 \ge 0, x_2 \ge 0$ $\Rightarrow$ $(1,0)$ will always be the optimal solution.

$x^{(1)} = (x_1^{(0)}, x_2^{(0)}) + t(1 - x_1^{(0)}, -x_2^{(0)})$

So at $t^* = 1$, $x^{(1)} = (1,0)$, the optimal

13.9-4.

k	$\mathbf{x}^{(k-1)}$	c1	c2	c3	$\mathbf{x}_{LP}^{(k)}$	t*	$\mathbf{x}^{(k)}$
1	(0, 0, 0)	8	2	1	(12, 0, 0)	0.33	(4, 0, 0)
2	(4, 0, 0)	0	2	1	(0, 4, 0)	0.25	(3, 1, 0)

Final solution: (3, 1, 0).

13.9-5.

k	$\mathbf{x}^{(k-1)}$	c1	c2	$\mathbf{x}_{LP}^{(k)}$	t*	$\mathbf{x}^{(k)}$
1	(5, 5)	15	10	(30, 0)	0.088	(7.196,4.561)
2	(7.196,4.561)	4.459	22.3	(0, 15)	0.119	(6.337,5.807)
3	(6.337,5.807)	12.88	8.89	(30, 0)	0.07	(7.996, 5.4)
4	(7.996, 5.4)	4.615	18.79	(0, 15)	0.089	(7.283,6.256)
5	(7.283,6.256)	10.89	9.082	(30, 0)	0.054	(8.514,5.917)
6	(8.514,5.917)	4.611	16.72	(0, 15)	0.072	(7.903,6.569)
7	(7.903,6.569)	9.666	9.056	(30, 0)	0.045	(8.887,6.277)

Final solution: (8.8866, 6.277).

13.9-6.

a)

k	$\mathbf{x}^{(k-1)}$	c_1	c_2	$\mathbf{x}_{LP}^{(k)}$	t^*	$\mathbf{x}^{(k)}$
1	(0, 0)	2	3	(0, 2)	0.75	(0, 1.5)
2	(0, 1.5)	2	0	(2, 0)	0.32	(0.64, 1.02)
3	(0.64, 1.02)	0.72	0.96	(0, 2)	0.175	(0.528,1.192)
4	(0.528,1.192)	0.944	0.617	(2, 0)	0.092	(0.663,1.082)
5	(0.663,1.082)	0.674	0.835	(0, 2)	0.126	(0.579,1.198)
6	(0.579,1.198)	0.842	0.603	(2, 0)	0.068	(0.676,1.117)

Final solution: (0.676,1.1166).

b)

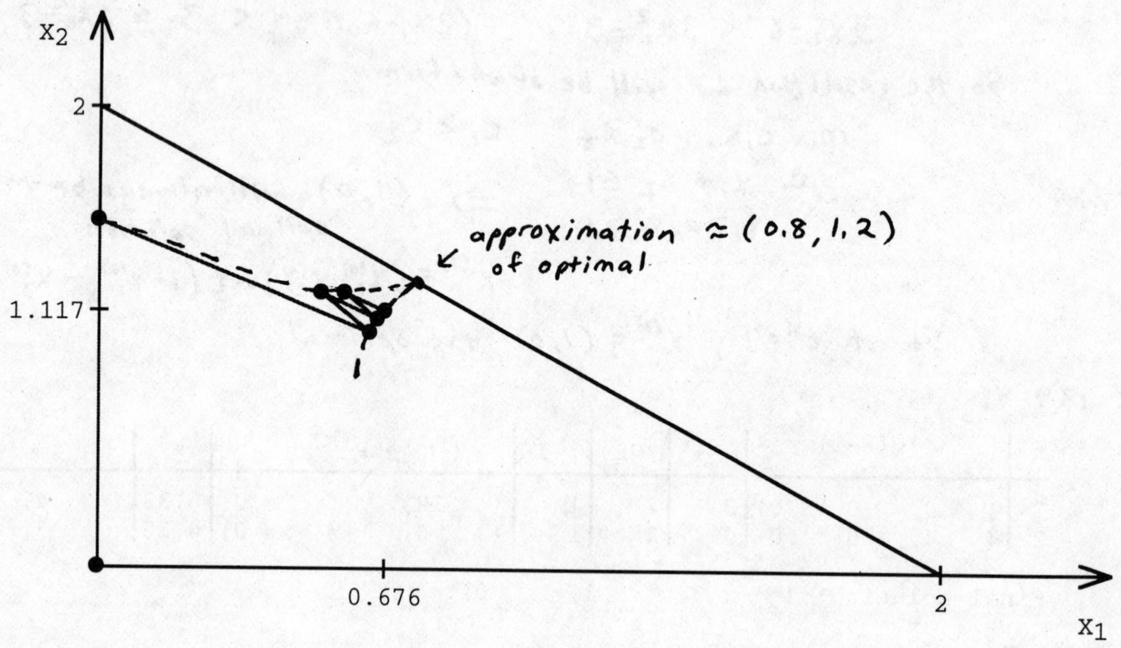

13.9-7.

k	$\mathbf{x}^{(k-1)}$	c_1	c_2	$\mathbf{x}_{LP}^{(k)}$	t^*	$\mathbf{x}^{(k)}$
1	(0, 0)	126	182	(2, 6)	1	(2, 6)
2	(2, 6)	90	26	(4, 3)	0.333	(2.667, 5)
3	(2.667, 5)	78	52	(4, 3)	1e-8	(2.667, 5)

Final solution: (2.6667, 5).

This is optimal since iter. 3 gave same point as iter. 2

13.9-8.

k	$\mathbf{x}^{(k-1)}$	c1	c2	$\mathbf{x}_{LP}^{(k)}$	t*	$\mathbf{x}^{(k)}$
1	(0, 0)	32	50	(3, 2)	0.729	(2.188,1.458)
2	(2.188,1.458)	-9.87	14.81	(0, 3.2)	0.131	(1.902,1.686)
3	(1.902,1.686)	4.499	5.634	(3, 2)	0.111	(2.024,1.721)
4	(2.024,1.721)	-1.15	4.078	(0, 3.2)	0.028	(1.966,1.763)

Final solution: (1.9662,1.7629).

13.9-9.

k	X^(k-1)	c1	c2	X[LP]^k	t*	X^k
1	(0, 0)	40	30	(3, 0)	0.616	(1.847, 0)
2	(1.847, 0)	0.001	35.54	(0, 2)	0.406	(1.097,0.812)

13.9-10. (a)

k	X^(k-1)	c1	c2	X[LP]^k	t*	X^k
1	(0.25, 0.25)	2.813	3.5	(0, 1)	1	(0, 1)
2	(0, 1)	3	2	(1, 0)	0.333	(0.333,0.667)
3	(0.333,0.667)	2.667	2.667	(1, 0)	0.001	(0.334,0.666)

(b) The KKT conditions:

1a) $3-3x_1^2-u\le 0$

2a) $x_1(3-3x_1^2-u)=0$

1b) $4-2x_2-u\le 0$

2b) $x_2(4-2x_2-u)=0$

3) $x_1+x_2\le 1$

4) $u(x_1+x_2-1)=0$

5) $x_1\ge 0,\ x_2\ge 0$

6) $u\ge 0$

It is easy to verify that $(x_1,x_2,u)=(1/3,2/3,8/3)$ satisfies these conditions, so $(x_1,x_2)=(1/3,2/3)$, the estimated solution from part (a), is optimal.

13.9-11. a)

k	$\mathbf{x}^{(k-1)}$	c_1	c_2	$\mathbf{x}_{LP}^{(k)}$	t^*	$\mathbf{x}^{(k)}$
1	(0.5, 0.5)	3.5	1	(1.25, 0)	0.541	(0.906,0.229)
2	(0.906,0.229)	1.027	1.541	(0, 2.5)	0.148	(0.771,0.566)
3	(0.771,0.566)	2.164	0.867	(1.25, 0)	0.216	(0.875,0.444)
4	(0.875,0.444)	1.323	1.112	(0, 2.5)	0.076	(0.808,0.601)

Final solution: (0.8079,0.6011).

b)

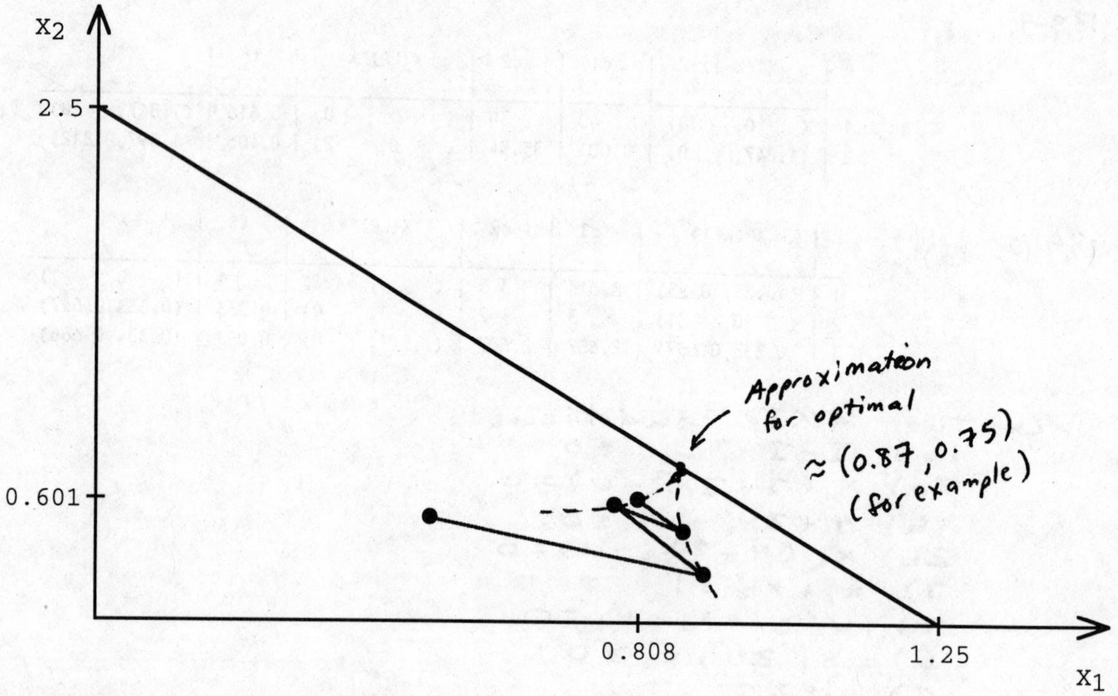

(c) The KKT conditions:

1a) $4 - 4x_1^3 - 4u \le 0$

2a) $x_1(4 - 4x_1^3 - 4u) = 0$

1b) $2 - 2x_2 - 2u \le 0$

2b) $x_2(2 - 2x_2 - 2u) = 0$

3) $4x_1 + 2x_2 \le 5$

4) $u(4x_1 + 2x_2 - 5) = 0$

5) $x_1 \ge 0, x_2 \ge 0$

6) $u \ge 0$

Are satisfied by $(x_1, x_2, u) = (.8934, .7131, .5737)$ so $(x_1, x_2) = (.8934, .7131)$ is optimal.

13.10-1. a) $P(\underline{x};r) = 3x_1 + 4x_2 - x_1^3 - x_2^2 - r\left[\frac{1}{1-x_1-x_2} + \frac{1}{x_1} + \frac{1}{x_2}\right]$

b) $\nabla P(\underline{x};r) = \begin{bmatrix} 3 - 3x_1^2 + r\left[\frac{-1}{(1-x_1-x_2)^2} + \frac{1}{x_1^2}\right] \\ 4 - 2x_2 + r\left[\frac{-1}{(1-x_1-x_2)^2} + \frac{1}{x_2^2}\right] \end{bmatrix}$

$\Rightarrow \nabla P((\frac{1}{4},\frac{1}{4});1) = \begin{bmatrix} 14\frac{13}{16} \\ 15\frac{1}{2} \end{bmatrix}$

$x' + t\nabla P(x';1) = (\frac{1}{4} + 14\frac{13}{16}t, \frac{1}{4} + 15\frac{1}{2}t)$

$t^* = 0.006606$

New $x' = (0.3479, 0.3524)$

c)

k	r	x_1	x_2	f(**x**)
0		0.25	0.25	1.672
1	1	0.343	0.357	2.29
2	0.01	0.322	0.619	3.023
3	0.0001	0.331	0.663	3.169

d) The true solution is $(\frac{1}{3}, \frac{2}{3})$. The percentage error in:

x_1 is $\frac{|1/3 - .331|}{1/3} = 0.70\%$

x_2 is $\frac{|2/3 - .663|}{2/3} = 0.55\%$

$f(x)$ is $\frac{|3\frac{5}{27} - 3.169|}{3\frac{5}{27}} = 0.51\%$

13.10-2. a) $P(\underline{x};r) = 4x_1 - x_1^4 + 2x_2 - x_2^2 - r\left[\frac{1}{5-4x_1-2x_2} + \frac{1}{x_1} + \frac{1}{x_2}\right]$

b) $\nabla P(\underline{x};r) = \begin{bmatrix} 4 - 4x_1^3 + r\left[\frac{-4}{(5-4x_1-2x_2)^2} + \frac{1}{x_1^2}\right] \\ 2 - 2x_2 + r\left[\frac{-2}{(5-4x_1-2x_2)^2} + \frac{1}{x_2^2}\right] \end{bmatrix}$

$\Rightarrow \nabla P((\frac{1}{2},\frac{1}{2});1) = \begin{bmatrix} 6\frac{1}{2} \\ 4\frac{1}{2} \end{bmatrix}$

$x' + t\nabla P(x';1) = (\frac{1}{2} + 6\frac{1}{2}t, \frac{1}{2} + 4\frac{1}{2}t)$

$t^* = 0.03167$

New $x' = (0.7058, 0.6425)$

13.10-2. c)

k	r	x_1	x_2	f(**x**)
0		0.5	0.5	2.688
1	1	0.669	0.716	3.395
2	0.01	0.871	0.671	3.801
3	0.0001	0.891	0.708	3.849
4	0.000001	0.894	0.712	3.854

13.10-3. a) $P(\underset{\sim}{x};r) = -x_1^4 - 2x_1^2 - 2x_1x_2 - 4x_2^2 - r\left[\frac{1}{2x_1+x_2-10} + \frac{1}{x_1+2x_2-10} + \frac{1}{x_1} + \frac{1}{x_2}\right]$

b) $\nabla P(\underset{\sim}{x};100) = \begin{bmatrix} -4x_1^3 - 4x_1 - 2x_2 + 100\left[\frac{2}{(2x_1+x_2-10)^2} + \frac{1}{(x_1+2x_2-10)^2} + \frac{1}{x_1^2}\right] \\ -2x_1 - 8x_2 + 100\left[\frac{1}{(2x_1+x_2-10)^2} + \frac{2}{(x_1+2x_2-10)^2} + \frac{1}{x_2^2}\right] \end{bmatrix}$

$\Rightarrow \nabla P((5,5);100) = \begin{bmatrix} -514 \\ -34 \end{bmatrix}$

$x' + t\nabla P(x';100) = (5-514t,\ 5-34t)$

$t^* = 0.003529$

New $x' = (3.1862,\ 4.8802)$

c)

k	r	x_1	x_2	f(**x**)
0		5	5	-825
1	100	2.725	6.072	-251
2	1	2.587	4.976	-183
3	0.01	2.562	4.891	-177
4	0.0001	2.557	4.888	-176

Note that because of minimization, we converted

Min $f(x)$ to Max $-f(x)$

Also, $g(x) \geq b$

becomes $-g(x) \leq -b$.

13.10-4. (a) The KKT conditions:

1a) $x_2 - 2u_1x_1 \le 0$

2a) $x_1(x_2 - 2u_1x_1) = 0$

1b) $x_1 - u_1 \le 0$

2b) $x_2(x_1 - u_1) = 0$

3) $x_1^2 + x_2 \le 3$

4) $u_1(x_1^2 + x_2 - 3) = 0$

5) $x_1 \ge 0,\ x_2 \ge 0$

6) $u_1 \ge 0$

$(x_1, x_2) = (1,2)$ satisfies these with $u_1 = 1$.

(b)

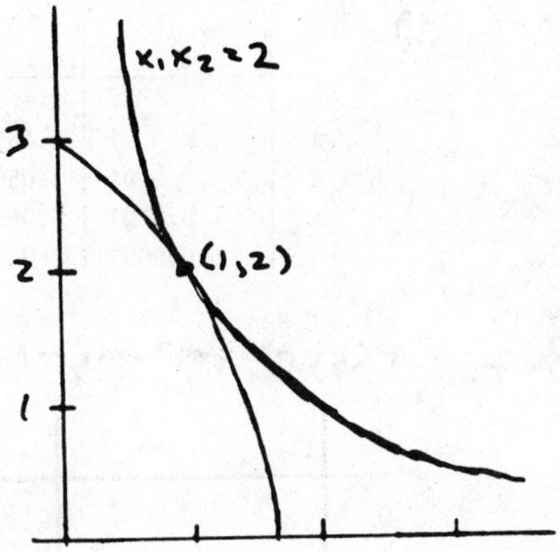

13.10-5. a) $P(\underline{x};r) = -2x_1 - (x_2-3)^2 - r\left(\frac{1}{x_1-3} + \frac{1}{x_2-3}\right)$

b) $\frac{\partial P(x;r)}{\partial x_1} = -2 + \frac{r}{(x_1-3)^2} = 0 \Rightarrow x_1 = \sqrt{\frac{r}{2}} + 3$

$\frac{\partial P(x;r)}{\partial x_2} = -2x_2 + 6 + \frac{r}{(x_2-3)^2} = 0 \Rightarrow x_2 = \sqrt[3]{\frac{r}{2}} + 3$

r	x_1	x_2
1	3.7071	3.7937
10^{-2}	3.0707	3.1710
10^{-4}	3.0071	3.0368
10^{-6}	3.0007	3.0079

Note $(x_1, x_2) \to (3,3)$ as $r \to 0$, so $(x_1, x_2) = (3,3)$ is optimal

c)

k	r	X1	X2	f(X)
0		4	4	-9
1	1	3.707	3.794	-8.044
2	0.01	3.07	3.179	-6.172
3	0.0001	3.007	3.056	-6.017
4	0.000001	3.001	3.011	-6.002

13.10-6. a) $P(x;r) = -\frac{(x_1+1)^3}{3} - x_2 - r\left(\frac{1}{x_1-1} + \frac{1}{x_2}\right)$

b) $\frac{\partial P(x;r)}{\partial x_1} = -(x_1+1)^2 + \frac{r}{(x_1-1)^2} = 0 \Rightarrow x_1 = \sqrt{1+\sqrt{r}}$

$\frac{\partial P(x;r)}{\partial x_2} = -1 + \frac{r}{x_2^2} = 0 \Rightarrow x_2 = \sqrt{r}$

r	x_1	x_2
1	1.4142	1
10^{-2}	1.0488	0.1
10^{-4}	1.0050	0.01
10^{-6}	1.0005	0.001

Note that $(x_1, x_2) \to (1,0)$ as $r \to 0$, so $(x_1, x_2) = (1,0)$ is optimal.

13.10-6. c)

k	r	X1	X2	f(X)
0		2	1	-8
1	1	1.459	1	-4.762
2	0.01	1.056	0.1	-2.273
3	0.0001	1.006	0.01	-2.027
4	0.000001	1.001	0.001	-2.003

13.10-7. $P(x;r) = -x_1^2 - x_2^2 - x_1 - x_2 + x_1 x_2 - r/x_2$

k	r	X_1	X_2	f(**X**)
0		1	1	-3
1	1	-0.18	0.638	-1.01
2	0.01	-0.46	0.079	0.127
3	0.0001	-0.5	0.008	0.238

13.10-8. $P(x;r) = 2x_1 + 3x_2 - x_1^2 - x_2^2 - r\left(\frac{1}{2-x_1-x_2} + \frac{1}{x_1} + \frac{1}{x_2}\right)$

k	r	X_1	X_2	f(**X**)
0		0.5	0.5	2
1	1	0.649	0.781	2.61
2	0.01	0.691	1.184	3.055
3	0.0001	0.743	1.243	3.118
4	0.000001	0.749	1.249	3.124

13.10-9. $P(x;r) = 126x_1 - 9x_1^2 + 182x_2 - 13x_2^2 - r\left(\frac{1}{4-x_1} + \frac{1}{12-2x_2} + \frac{1}{18-3x_1-2x_2} + \frac{1}{x_1} + \frac{1}{x_2}\right)$

k	r	X_1	X_2	f(**X**)
0		2	3	645
1	100	2.292	4.523	798.8
2	1	2.62	4.972	851.9
3	0.01	2.661	4.999	856.5
4	0.0001	2.665	5.002	856.9

13.10-10. (a) Solving for the roots of $x^2+x-500=0$ we find x is feasible in the range $[0, \frac{-1+\sqrt{2001}}{2}]$ or $[0, 21.866]$

$$f'(x) = 1000 - 800x + 120x^2 - 4x^3$$

$$f''(x) = -800 + 240x - 12x^2$$

$$f'''(x) = 240 - 24x$$

A rough sketch of f(x):

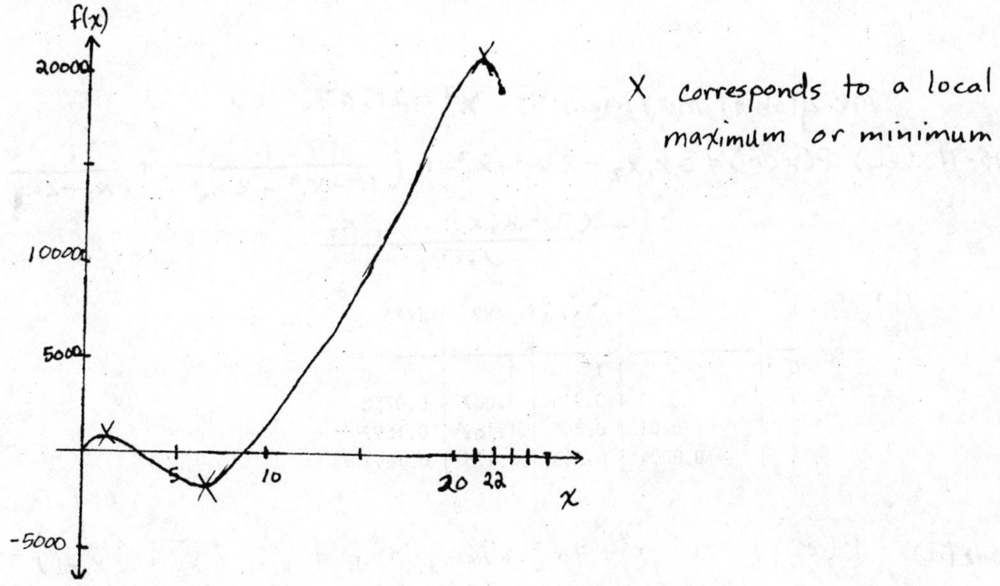

(b)

Iteration	df(X)/dX	X(L)	X(U)	New X'	f(X')
0		0	5	2.5	585.94
1	-312.5	0	2.5	1.25	700.68
2	+179.7	1.25	2.5	1.875	720.06
3	-104.5	1.25	1.875	1.5625	732.56
4	+27.71	1.5625	1.875	1.7188	731.48
5	-40.82	1.5625	1.7188	1.6406	733.36
6	-7.166	1.5625	1.6406	1.6016	733.3
Stop					

Iteration	df(X)/dX	X(L)	X(U)	New X'	f(X')
0		18	21.866	19.933	19931
1	+ 1053	19.933	21.866	20.899	20546
2	+180.4	20.899	21.866	21.383	20509
3	-346.2	20.899	21.383	21.141	20559
4	- 75.1	20.899	21.141	21.02	20560
5	+54.58	21.02	21.141	21.081	20562
6	-9.778	21.02	21.081	21.051	20561
Stop					

There is a local maximum near 1.6016 and a global maximum near 21.051

13.10-10. c)

k	r	X_1	f(**X**)
0		3	399
1	1000	2.171	672.8
2	100	1.704	732
3	10	1.633	733.4
4	1	1.625	733.4
0		15	9375
1	1000	21.04	20561
2	100	21.07	20562
3	10	21.07	20562
4	1	21.07	20562

Initial trial solution $X = 3$ gives $X = 1.625$ $(f(x) = 733.4)$ as max

Initial trial solution $X = 15$ gives $X = 21.07$ $(f(x) = 20562)$ as max

The global maximum is $X^* = 21.07$

13.10-11. (a) $P(x;r) = 3x_1x_2 - 2x_1^2 - x_1^2 - r\left(\frac{1}{4 - x_1^2 - 2x_2^2} + \frac{1}{x_2 - 2x_4} + \frac{1}{x_1} + \frac{1}{x_2}\right) - \frac{(2 - x_1x_2^2 - x_1^2x_2)^2}{\sqrt{r}}$

(b)

k	r	X1	X2	f(X)
0		1	1	0
1	1	0.915	1.007	0.0758
2	0.01	0.848	1.169	0.1692
3	0.0001	0.843	1.175	0.1697

13.10-12. (a) $P(x;r) = x_1^3 + 4x_2^2 + 16x_3 + r\left(\frac{1}{x_1 - 1} + \frac{1}{x_2 - 1} + \frac{1}{x_3 - 1}\right) + \frac{(5 - x_1 - x_2 - x_3)^2}{\sqrt{r}}$

(b)

k	r	X1	X2	X3	f(X)
0		1.5	1.5	2	-44.38
1	0.01	1.95	1.434	1.047	-32.38
2	0.0001	2.179	1.743	1.007	-38.62
3	0.000001	2.208	1.784	1.001	-39.51
4	0.00000001	2.21	1.786	1.002	-39.6

13.10-13. (a) $P(x;r) = \sin 3x_1 + \cos 3x_2 + \sin(x_1 + x_2) + r\left(\frac{1}{1 + x_1^2 - 10x_2} + \frac{1}{100 - 10x_1 - x_2^2} + \frac{1}{x_1} + \frac{1}{x_2}\right)$

(b) SUMT can be used to obtain the global minimum if "enough" different starting points are used and SUMT is run from each. If we choose a lattice of points over the feasible region so that the adjacent points don't change by more than $\frac{2}{3}\pi$ then this set of points will work for f(x). Since sin and cos have period 2π, choosing lattice points with grid size not greater than $\frac{2}{3}\pi$ will ensure that the arguments of the sin and cos terms in f will not change by more than 2π between adjacent lattice points. Since the second constraint ensures $x_1 \le 10$ and $x_2 \le 10$, we can see that at most $\left(\frac{10}{2\pi/3}\right)^2 \approx 23$ starting points are required if chosen well.

13.11-1. a) Yes. $f(\underset{\sim}{x}) = f_1(x_1) + f_2(x_2)$

$f_1(x_1) = 4x_1 - x_1^2 \qquad \frac{\partial^2 f_1}{\partial x_1^2} = -2 < 0$

$f_2(x_2) = 10x_2 - x_2^2 \qquad \frac{\partial^2 f_2}{\partial x_2^2} = -2 < 0$

So $f(\underset{\sim}{x})$ is concave.

$g(x) = x_1^2 + 4x_2^2$ is convex (again $g = g_1(x_1) + g_2(x_2)$, $g_1(x_1) = x_1^2$, $g_2(x_2) = 4x_2^2$ both convex)

So this is a convex programming problem.

b) No. This is not a quadratic programming problem since the constraints are not linear.

c) No. The Frank-Wolfe algorithm in 13.9 requires linear constraints so cannot be used for this problem.

d) KKT conditions are:

1a) $4 - 2x_1 - 2x_1 u \le 0$

1b) $x_1(4 - 2x_1 - 2x_1 u) = 0$

2a) $10 - 2x_2 - 8x_2 u \le 0$

2b) $x_2(10 - 2x_2 - 8x_2 u) = 0$

3) $x_1^2 + 4x_2^2 - 16 \le 0$

4) $u(x_1^2 + 4x_2^2 - 16) = 0$

5) $x_1 \ge 0, x_2 \ge 0$

6) $u \ge 0$

If $x_1 = 1$, (1b) $\Rightarrow u = 1$ but this violates (4) so $(x_1, x_2) = (1,1)$ cannot be optimal.

e) Let $x_1 = x_{11} + x_{12} + x_{13} + x_{14}$, $x_2 = x_{21} + x_{22}$

Obj: $f_1(x_1) = 4x_1 - x_1^2$, $f_2(x_2) = 10x_2 - x_2^2$

$f_1(0) = 0$, $f_1(1) = 3$, $f_1(2) = 4$, $f_1(3) = 3$, $f_1(4) = 0$

$f_2(0) = 0$, $f_2(1) = 9$, $f_2(2) = 16$

$s_{11} = \frac{3-0}{1-0} = 3$, $s_{12} = \frac{4-3}{2-1} = 1$, $s_{13} = -1$, $s_{14} = -3$

$s_{21} = 9$, $s_{22} = 7$

Constraints: $g_1(x_1) = x_1^2$, $g_2(x_2) = 4x_2^2$

$g_1(0) = 0$, $g_1(1) = 1$, $g_1(2) = 4$, $g_1(3) = 9$, $g_1(4) = 16$

$g_2(0) = 0$, $g_2(1) = 4$, $g_2(2) = 16$

$t_{11} = \frac{1-0}{1-0} = 1$, $t_{12} = \frac{4-1}{2-1} = 3$, $t_{13} = 5$, $t_{14} = 7$

$t_{21} = 4$, $t_{22} = 12$

13.11-1. e) (cont')

The approximate LP is:

Maximize $3X_{11} + X_{12} - X_{13} - 3X_{14} + 9X_{21} + 7X_{22}$

subject to: $X_{11} + 3X_{12} + 5X_{13} + 7X_{14} + 4X_{21} + 12X_{22} \le 16$

$$0 \le X_{ij} \le 1 \quad (\text{all } i,j)$$

f) The Simplex Method gives the solution:

Value of the
Objective Function: Z = 18.4166667

Variable		Value
X1	(X_{11})	1
X2	(X_{12})	0
X3	(X_{13})	0
X4	(X_{14})	0
X5	(X_{21})	1
X6	(X_{22})	0.91667

In terms of the original variables, we have

$X_1 = X_{11}+X_{12}+X_{13}+X_{14} = 1$, $X_2 = X_{21}+X_{22} = 1.91667$

g) $P(\underline{x};r) = 4x_1 - x_1^2 + 10x_2 - x_2^2 - r\left[\frac{1}{16-x_1^2-4x_2^2} + \frac{1}{x_1} + \frac{1}{x_2}\right]$

h)

k	r	X1	X2	f(**X**)
0		2	1	13
1	1	1.504	1.754	18.22
2	0.01	1.409	1.862	18.8
3	0.0001	1.41	1.871	18.86
4	0.000001	1.411	1.871	18.86

Chapter 14
Markov Chains

14.2-1. a) Since the probability of weather tomorrow is only dependent on today, Markovian property holds for evolution of the weather.

b) Let 0 = Rain, 1 = Clear,

Then
$$P = P^{(1)} = \begin{array}{c} \\ 0 \\ 1 \end{array}\begin{array}{c} \begin{array}{cc} 0 & 1 \end{array} \\ \begin{bmatrix} .5 & .5 \\ .1 & .9 \end{bmatrix} \end{array}$$

14.2-2. Let 1 = increased today and yesterday
2 = increased today but decreased yesterday
3 = decreased today but increased yesterday
4 = decreased today and yesterday

Then
$$P = P^{(1)} = \begin{array}{c} \\ 1 \\ 2 \\ 3 \\ 4 \end{array}\begin{array}{c} \begin{array}{cccc} 1 & 2 & 3 & 4 \end{array} \\ \begin{bmatrix} \alpha_1 & 0 & 1-\alpha_1 & 0 \\ \alpha_2 & 0 & 1-\alpha_2 & 0 \\ 0 & \alpha_3 & 0 & 1-\alpha_3 \\ 0 & \alpha_4 & 0 & 1-\alpha_4 \end{bmatrix} \end{array}$$

14.2-3.

Yes, it can be formulated as a Markov Chain with the following 8 $(= 2^3)$ states

state	today	1 day ago	2 days ago
1	inc	inc	inc
2	inc	inc	dec
3	inc	dec	inc
4	inc	dec	dec
5	dec	inc	inc
6	dec	inc	dec
7	dec	dec	inc
8	dec	dec	dec

These states have included all the information needed to predict tomorrow's stockmarket whereas states in Prob. 14.2-2 doesn't consider the day before yesterday, which

14.3-1. a)
$$P^2 = \begin{bmatrix} 0.3 & 0.7 \\ 0.14 & 0.86 \end{bmatrix} \qquad P^5 = \begin{bmatrix} 0.175 & 0.825 \\ 0.165 & 0.835 \end{bmatrix}$$

$$P^{10} = \begin{bmatrix} 0.167 & 0.833 \\ 0.167 & 0.833 \end{bmatrix} \qquad P^{20} = \begin{bmatrix} 0.167 & 0.833 \\ 0.167 & 0.833 \end{bmatrix}$$

14.3-1. (b) P(rain n days from now | rain today) = P_{11}^n

If the probability it will rain today is 0.5,

P(rain ndays from now) = $P_n = 0.5 \cdot P_{11}^n$

Thus, $P_2 = 0.15$, $P_5 = 0.0875$, $P_{10} = 0.0835$, $P_{20} = 0.0835$

(c) We find $\pi_1 = 0.167$

$\pi_2 = 0.833$

Obviously when n grows large, every row of $P^{(n)}$ approaches to the stationary probabilies.

14.3-2. (a) Let states 0 and 1 denote that a 0 and a 1 have been recorded, respectively.

$$P = \begin{bmatrix} 1-q & q \\ q & 1-q \end{bmatrix} \quad \text{where } q = 0.01$$

(b) $$P^{(10)} = \begin{bmatrix} 0.909 & 0.091 \\ 0.091 & 0.909 \end{bmatrix}$$

The probability that a digit would recorded accurately is 0.909

(c) $$P^{(10)} = \begin{bmatrix} 0.99 & 0.01 \\ 0.01 & 0.99 \end{bmatrix}$$

The probability is 0.99.

14.3-3. a) Transition Matrix, P =

$$\begin{bmatrix} 0 & 0.5 & 0 & 0 & 0.5 \\ 0.5 & 0 & 0.5 & 0 & 0 \\ 0 & 0.5 & 0 & 0.5 & 0 \\ 0 & 0 & 0.5 & 0 & 0.5 \\ 0.5 & 0 & 0 & 0.5 & 0 \end{bmatrix}$$

(b)

$$P^5 = \begin{bmatrix} 0.062 & 0.312 & 0.156 & 0.156 & 0.312 \\ 0.312 & 0.062 & 0.312 & 0.156 & 0.156 \\ 0.156 & 0.312 & 0.062 & 0.312 & 0.156 \\ 0.156 & 0.156 & 0.312 & 0.062 & 0.312 \\ 0.312 & 0.156 & 0.156 & 0.312 & 0.062 \end{bmatrix}$$

$$P^{10} = \begin{bmatrix} 0.248 & 0.161 & 0.215 & 0.215 & 0.161 \\ 0.161 & 0.248 & 0.161 & 0.215 & 0.215 \\ 0.215 & 0.161 & 0.248 & 0.161 & 0.215 \\ 0.215 & 0.215 & 0.161 & 0.248 & 0.161 \\ 0.161 & 0.215 & 0.215 & 0.161 & 0.248 \end{bmatrix}$$

14.3-3. (b) (continued)

$$P^{20} = \begin{bmatrix} 0.206 & 0.195 & 0.202 & 0.202 & 0.195 \\ 0.195 & 0.206 & 0.195 & 0.202 & 0.202 \\ 0.202 & 0.195 & 0.206 & 0.195 & 0.202 \\ 0.202 & 0.202 & 0.195 & 0.206 & 0.195 \\ 0.195 & 0.202 & 0.202 & 0.195 & 0.206 \end{bmatrix}$$

$$P^{40} = \begin{bmatrix} 0.2 & 0.2 & 0.2 & 0.2 & 0.2 \\ 0.2 & 0.2 & 0.2 & 0.2 & 0.2 \\ 0.2 & 0.2 & 0.2 & 0.2 & 0.2 \\ 0.2 & 0.2 & 0.2 & 0.2 & 0.2 \\ 0.2 & 0.2 & 0.2 & 0.2 & 0.2 \end{bmatrix}$$

$$P^{80} = \begin{bmatrix} 0.2 & 0.2 & 0.2 & 0.2 & 0.2 \\ 0.2 & 0.2 & 0.2 & 0.2 & 0.2 \\ 0.2 & 0.2 & 0.2 & 0.2 & 0.2 \\ 0.2 & 0.2 & 0.2 & 0.2 & 0.2 \\ 0.2 & 0.2 & 0.2 & 0.2 & 0.2 \end{bmatrix}$$

(c) We can easily find out $\pi_1 = \pi_2 = \pi_3 = \pi_4 = \pi_5 = 0.2$

14.4-1. (a) P has one recurrent communicating class: $\{0, 1, 2, 3\}$

(b) P has three communicating classes:

$\{0\}$ is absorbing and, therefore, recurrent

$\{1, 2\}$ is recurrent

$\{3\}$ is transient

14.4-2. (a) P has one recurrent communicating class: $\{0, 1, 2, 3\}$

(b) P has one recurrent communicating class: $\{0, 1, 2\}$

14.4-3. This matrix has three communicating classes:

$\{0, 1\}$ is recurrent

$\{2\}$ is transient

$\{3, 4\}$ is recurrent

14.5-1. (a) The process satisfies the four points listed in Sec. 15.3, and is thus Makovian.

Let 0 = Working

1 = Failed

$$P = \begin{matrix} & 0 & 1 \\ 0 & .9 & .1 \\ 1 & .65 & .35 \end{matrix}$$

(b) $\pi P = \pi \Rightarrow \pi = (13/15, 2/15)$

14.5-2. (a) Let 0 = operational, 1 = down, 2 = repaired

Then

$$P = \begin{array}{c} \\ 0 \\ 1 \\ 2 \end{array} \begin{array}{c} \begin{array}{ccc} 0 & 1 & 2 \end{array} \\ \begin{bmatrix} 0.9 & 0.1 & 0 \\ 0 & 0 & 1 \\ 0.9 & 0.1 & 0 \end{bmatrix} \end{array}$$

(b) From sec 14.5, we have $\mu_{ij} = 1 + \sum_{k \neq j} p_{ik}\mu_{kj}$

So, $\begin{cases} \mu_{00} = 1 + 0.1\mu_{10} \\ \mu_{10} = 1 + \mu_{20} \\ \mu_{20} = 1 + 0.1\mu_{10} \end{cases}$ such that $\begin{cases} \mu_{00} = \frac{11}{9} \\ \mu_{10} = \frac{20}{9} \\ \mu_{20} = \frac{11}{9} \end{cases}$

$\begin{cases} \mu_{01} = 1 + 0.9\mu_{01} \\ \mu_{11} = 1 + \mu_{21} \\ \mu_{21} = 1 + 0.9\mu_{01} \end{cases}$ such that $\begin{cases} \mu_{01} = 10 \\ \mu_{11} = 11 \\ \mu_{21} = 10 \end{cases}$

$\begin{cases} \mu_{02} = 1 + 0.9\mu_{02} + 0.1\mu_{12} \\ \mu_{12} = 1 + 0 \\ \mu_{22} = 1 + 0.9\mu_{02} + 0.1\mu_{12} \end{cases}$ such that $\begin{cases} \mu_{02} = 11 \\ \mu_{12} = 1 \\ \mu_{22} = 2.09 \end{cases}$

The expected number of days that machine will remain operational is 10.

(C) It would be the same due to the Markovian Property.

14.5-3. (a)

$$P = \begin{array}{c} \\ (1,1) \\ (0,1) \\ (1,0) \end{array} \begin{array}{c} \begin{array}{ccc} (1,1) & (0,1) & (1,0) \end{array} \\ \begin{bmatrix} 0.9 & 0.1 & 0 \\ 0.9 & 0 & 0.1 \\ 0.9 & 0.1 & 0 \end{bmatrix} \end{array}$$

(b) $\begin{cases} \mu_{13} = 1 + 0.9\mu_{13} + 0.1\mu_{23} \\ \mu_{23} = 1 + 0.9\mu_{13} \\ \mu_{33} = 1 + 0.9\mu_{13} + 0.1\mu_{23} \end{cases}$

And we can get $\mu_{33} = 110$ which is the expected recurrence time of state (1, 0)

14.6-1. $P = \begin{bmatrix} \alpha & 1-\alpha \\ 1-\beta & \beta \end{bmatrix}$

From $\pi P = P \Rightarrow \alpha\pi_1 + (1-\beta)\pi_2 = \pi_1$

$\pi_1 + \pi_2 = 1$

$\Rightarrow \pi = \left(\frac{1-\beta}{2-\alpha-\beta}, \frac{1-\alpha}{2-\alpha-\beta}\right)$

14.6-2

Must show that $\pi_j = \frac{1}{M+1}$ for $j = 0, 1, \ldots, M$ satisfies the steady state equations: $\pi_j = \sum_{i=0}^{M} p_{ij}\pi_j$, for $j = 0, \ldots, M$ and $\sum_{j=0}^{M}\pi_j = 1$.

Since $\sum_{i=0}^{M} p_{ij} = 1$ for all j, this is easily verified.

Since the chain is irreducible, aperiodic and positive recurrent this is the unique solution.

14.6-3. Since $M=5$, $\pi_1 = \pi_2 = \pi_3 = \pi_4 = \pi_5 = \frac{1}{5} = 0.2$

The steady-state probabilities don't change if the probability for moving steps changes.

14.6-4. Run the OR courseware and we can find

$\pi_1 = 0.346$

$\pi_2 = 0.385$

$\pi_3 = 0.269$

which means the steady-state market share for A and B are 0.346 and 0.385 respectively.

14.6-5. (a) Assume demand occurs after the delivery:

$$P = \begin{array}{c} \\ 1 \\ 2 \\ 3 \\ 4 \\ 5 \\ 6 \\ 7 \end{array}\begin{array}{c} \begin{array}{ccccccc} 1 & 2 & 3 & 4 & 5 & 6 & 7 \end{array} \\ \begin{bmatrix} .6 & .4 & 0 & 0 & 0 & 0 & 0 \\ .3 & .3 & .4 & 0 & 0 & 0 & 0 \\ .1 & .2 & .3 & .4 & 0 & 0 & 0 \\ 0 & .1 & .2 & .3 & .4 & 0 & 0 \\ 0 & 0 & .1 & .2 & .3 & .4 & 0 \\ 0 & 0 & 0 & .1 & .2 & .3 & .4 \\ 0 & 0 & 0 & 0 & .1 & .2 & .7 \end{bmatrix} \end{array}$$

14.6-5. [continued]

(b) $\pi P = \pi \Rightarrow (.139, .139, .139, .138, .141, .130, .174)$

(C) The steady probability that a pint of blood is to be discarded

$= P\{D=0\} \cdot P\{\text{state is in } 7\} = 0.4 \times 0.174 = 0.0696$

(d) P{emergency deliveries}

$= \sum_{i=1}^{2} P\{\text{state } i\} \cdot P\{D > i\}$

$= 0.139 \times (0.2 + 0.1) + 0.139 \times 0.1 = 0.0556$

14.6-6. (a) Let 0 = Low
1 = High

Never advertize $\Rightarrow P = \begin{matrix} & 0 & 1 \\ 0 & 3/4 & 1/4 \\ 1 & 1/2 & 1/2 \end{matrix}$

Always advertize $\Rightarrow P = \begin{matrix} & 0 & 1 \\ 0 & 1/2 & 1/2 \\ 1 & 1/4 & 3/4 \end{matrix}$

Marketing Manager's Proposal $\Rightarrow P = \begin{matrix} & 0 & 1 \\ 0 & 1/2 & 1/2 \\ 1 & 1/2 & 1/2 \end{matrix}$

(b) Never advertize $\Rightarrow \pi = (2/3, 1/3)$
Always advertize $\Rightarrow \pi = (1/3, 2/3)$
Marketing Manager's Proposal $\Rightarrow \pi = (1/2, 1/2)$

(c) Never advertize $\Rightarrow$ profit $= \frac{2}{3} \times 2 + \frac{1}{3} \times 4 = 2\frac{2}{3}$ million

Always advertize $\Rightarrow$ profit $= \frac{1}{3} \times 2 + \frac{2}{3} \times 4 - 1 = 2\frac{1}{3}$ million

Proposal $\Rightarrow$ profit $= \frac{1}{2} \times (2-1) + \frac{1}{2} \times 4 = 3$ million

So, the Marketing Manager's Proposal is the best.

14.6-7(a). Transition Matrix, $P = \begin{bmatrix} 0.25 & 0.5 & 0.25 \\ 0.75 & 0.25 & 0 \\ 0.25 & 0.5 & 0.25 \end{bmatrix}$

(b)

$$P^2 = \begin{bmatrix} 0.5 & 0.375 & 0.125 \\ 0.375 & 0.438 & 0.188 \\ 0.5 & 0.375 & 0.125 \end{bmatrix}$$

14.6-7.(b)(continued)

$$P^5 = \begin{bmatrix} 0.449 & 0.4 & 0.15 \\ 0.451 & 0.399 & 0.149 \\ 0.449 & 0.4 & 0.15 \end{bmatrix} \quad P^{10} = \begin{bmatrix} 0.45 & 0.4 & 0.15 \\ 0.45 & 0.4 & 0.15 \\ 0.45 & 0.4 & 0.15 \end{bmatrix}$$

(c)
$$\begin{cases} \mu_{00} = 1 + 0.5\mu_{10} + 0.25\mu_{20} \\ \mu_{10} = 1 + 0.25\mu_{10} \\ \mu_{20} = 1 + 0.5\mu_{10} + 0.25\mu_{20} \end{cases} \Rightarrow \begin{cases} \mu_{00} = 20/9 \\ \mu_{10} = 4/3 \\ \mu_{20} = 20/9 \end{cases}$$

$$\begin{cases} \mu_{01} = 1 + 0.25\mu_{01} + 0.25\mu_{21} \\ \mu_{11} = 1 + 0.75\mu_{01} \\ \mu_{21} = 1 + 0.25\mu_{01} + 0.25\mu_{21} \end{cases} \Rightarrow \begin{cases} \mu_{01} = 2 \\ \mu_{11} = 2\frac{1}{2} \\ \mu_{21} = 2 \end{cases}$$

$$\begin{cases} \mu_{02} = 1 + 0.25\mu_{02} + 0.5\mu_{12} \\ \mu_{12} = 1 + 0.75\mu_{02} + 0.25\mu_{12} \\ \mu_{22} = 1 + 0.25\mu_{02} + 0.5\mu_{12} \end{cases} \Rightarrow \begin{cases} \mu_{02} = 20/3 \\ \mu_{12} = 8 \\ \mu_{22} = 20/3 \end{cases}$$

(d) The steady-state probabilities is (0.45, 0.4, 0.15)

(e) $\pi \cdot C = 0(0.45) + 2(0.4) + 8(0.15) = \$2/\text{week}$.

14.6-8.

(a) Transition Matrix, $P = \begin{bmatrix} 0 & 0.875 & 0.062 & 0.062 \\ 0 & 0.75 & 0.125 & 0.125 \\ 0 & 0 & 0.5 & 0.5 \\ 1 & 0 & 0 & 0 \end{bmatrix}$

Solution:

$\pi_1 = 0.154$
$\pi_2 = 0.538$
$\pi_3 = 0.154$
$\pi_4 = 0.154$

(b) $\pi \cdot C = 1(0.538) + 3(0.154) + 6(0.154) = \$1923.08$

(c)
$$\begin{cases} \mu_{00} = 1 + 0.875\mu_{10} + 0.0625\mu_{20} + 0.0625\mu_{30} \\ \mu_{10} = 1 + 0.75\mu_{10} + 0.125\mu_{20} + 0.125\mu_{30} \\ \mu_{20} = 1 + 0.5\mu_{20} + 0.5\mu_{30} \\ \mu_{30} = 0 + 1 \end{cases}$$

$\Rightarrow \mu_{00} = 6.5$, which is expected recurren time for state 0.

14.6-9.

For a (s,S) policy with s=2 and S=3,

$$C(x_{t-1}, D_t) = \begin{cases} 10 + (25)(3-x_{t-1}) + 50\max\{D_t - 3, 0\} & \text{for } x_{t-1} < 2 \\ 50\max\{D_t - x_{t-1}, 0\} & \text{for } x_{t-1} \geq 2 \end{cases}$$

Thus

$$K(0) = E[C(0,D_t)] = 85 + 50\left[\sum_{j=4}^{\infty}(j-3)P\{D_t = j\}\right] \approx 86.2$$

$$K(1) = E[C(1,D_t)] = 60 + 50\left[\sum_{j=4}^{\infty}(j-3)P\{D_t = j\}\right] \approx 61.2$$

$$K(2) = E[C(2,D_t)] = 0 + 50\left[\sum_{j=4}^{\infty}(j-2)P\{D_t = j\}\right] \approx 5.2$$

$$K(3) = E[C(3,D_t)] = 0 + 50\left[\sum_{j=4}^{\infty}(j-3)P\{D_t = j\}\right] \approx 1.2$$

Again for a (2,3) policy,

$$X_{t+1} = \begin{cases} \max\{3 - D_{t+1}, 0\} & \text{for } X_t < 2 \\ \max\{X_t - D_{t+1}, 0\} & \text{for } X_t \geq 2 \end{cases}$$

So

$$P = \begin{bmatrix} .080 & .184 & .368 & .368 \\ .080 & .184 & .368 & .368 \\ .264 & .368 & .368 & 0 \\ .080 & .184 & .368 & .368 \end{bmatrix}$$

Solving the steady state equations gives $\pi_0 = .148$, $\pi_1 = .252$, $\pi_2 = .368$, $\pi_3 = .232$

Hence, the long-run average cost per week is

$$\sum_{j=0}^{3} K(j)\pi_j = 30.37$$

14.6-10.

$$x_{t+1} = \begin{cases} \max\{x_t + 2 - D_{t+1}, 0\} & \text{for } x_t \leq 1 \\ \max\{x_t - D_{t+1}, 0\} & \text{for } x_t \geq 2 \end{cases}$$

$$\text{So } P = \begin{bmatrix} .264 & .368 & .368 & 0 \\ .080 & .184 & .368 & .368 \\ .264 & .368 & .368 & 0 \\ .080 & .184 & .368 & .368 \end{bmatrix}$$

Solving the steady state equations gives $\pi_0 = .182$, $\pi_1 = .285$, $\pi_2 = .368$, $\pi_3 = .165$

(b) $K(0) = E[C(0,D_t)] = 60 + 50\left[\sum_{j=3}^{\infty}(j-2)P\{D_t = j\}\right] = 65.2$

$K(1) = E[C(1,D_t)] = 60 + 50\left[\sum_{j=4}^{\infty}(j-3)P\{D_t = j\}\right] = 61.2$

$K(2) = E[C(2,D_t)] = 50\left[\sum_{j=3}^{\infty}(j-2)P\{D_t = j\}\right] = 5.2$

$K(3) = E[C(3,D_t)] = 50\left[\sum_{j=4}^{\infty}(j-3)P\{D_t = j\}\right] = 1.2$

Hence, the long range cost per week is $\sum_{j=0}^{3} K(j)\pi_j = 31.42$

14.6-11. (a) $P_{11} = P\{D_{n+1} = 0\} + P\{D_{n+1} = 2\} + P\{D_{n+1} = 4\} = 3/5$

$P_{12} = P\{D_{n+1} = 1\} + P\{D_{n+1} = 3\} = 2/5$

$P_{21} = P\{D_{n+1} = 1\} + P\{D_{n+1} = 3\} = 2/5$

$P_{22} = P\{D_{n+1} = 0\} + P\{D_{n+1} = 2\} + P\{D_{n+1} = 4\} = 3/5$

so $P = \begin{bmatrix} 3/5 & 2/5 \\ 2/5 & 3/5 \end{bmatrix}$

(c) (b) Since P is doubly stochastic, $\pi_0 = \pi_1 = 1/2$.

(d) $K(1) = E[c(1, D_n)] = (2/5)[3 + 2(1)] + (2/5)[3 + 2(2)] + (1/5)(1) +$
$+ (4/5)[1 + 2 + 3] = 9.8$

$K(2) = E[c(2, D_n)] = (2/5)[3 + 2(1)] + (1/5)[3 + 2(2)] + 1/5[2 + 1]$
$+ (4/5)[1 + 2] = 6.4$

So long-run average cost per unit time is
$9.8(1/2) + 6.4(1/2) = 8.10$.

14.6-12 (a) P{waiting on line in Period n} $= P_{02}^{(n)}$
and

$P^2 = \begin{bmatrix} 0.64 & 0.16 & 0.04 & 0.16 \\ 0.64 & 0.36 & 0 & 0 \\ 0 & 0 & 0.2 & 0.8 \\ 0.64 & 0.16 & 0.04 & 0.16 \end{bmatrix}$ $P^5 = \begin{bmatrix} 0.62 & 0.195 & 0.037 & 0.148 \\ 0.594 & 0.174 & 0.046 & 0.186 \\ 0.64 & 0.232 & 0.026 & 0.102 \\ 0.62 & 0.195 & 0.037 & 0.148 \end{bmatrix}$

$P^{10} = \begin{bmatrix} 0.615 & 0.192 & 0.039 & 0.154 \\ 0.616 & 0.193 & 0.038 & 0.153 \\ 0.614 & 0.191 & 0.039 & 0.156 \\ 0.615 & 0.192 & 0.039 & 0.154 \end{bmatrix}$ $P^{20} = \begin{bmatrix} 0.615 & 0.192 & 0.038 & 0.154 \\ 0.615 & 0.192 & 0.038 & 0.154 \\ 0.615 & 0.192 & 0.038 & 0.154 \\ 0.615 & 0.192 & 0.038 & 0.154 \end{bmatrix}$

So, $n = 2$, $p = 0.04$; $n = 5$, $p = 0.037$
$n = 10$, $p = 0.039$; $n = 20$, $p = 0.038$

(b) $\pi_1 = 0.615$, $\pi_2 = 0.192$, $\pi_3 = 0.038$, $\pi_4 = 0.154$

(C) Long-run average cost per period $= \$30,000\,\pi_2 = \$5,760$

14.7-1. (a) For the transition matrix,

$P_{00} = P_{TT} = 1$, $P_{i,i-1} = q$, $P_{i,i+1} = p$. $P_{i,k} = 0$ else.

And,

14.7-1. (continued)

$$P = \begin{bmatrix} 1 & 0 & 0 & 0 & & & \\ q & 0 & p & 0 & \cdots & & \\ \vdots & & & \ddots & & & \\ \vdots & & & & q & 0 & p & 0 \\ & & & & 0 & q & 0 & p \\ & & & & 0 & 0 & 0 & 1 \end{bmatrix}$$

(b) Class 1: $\{0\}$ which is absorbing

Class 2: $\{T\}$ which is absorbing

Class 3: $\{1, 2, \ldots, T-1\}$ which is transient

(c) Let $f_{ik} = P\{\text{absorbtion at } k \text{ given start at } i\}$

Then $f_{i0} = 1 - \dfrac{1+\rho+\rho^2+\cdots+\rho^{i-1}}{1+\rho+\rho^2+\cdots+\rho^{T-1}} = \dfrac{\rho^i+\rho^{i+1}+\cdots+\rho^{T-1}}{1+\rho+\rho^2+\cdots+\rho^{T-1}}$

Now $\rho = q/p = 7/3 \Rightarrow f_{10} = (\rho+\rho^2)/(1+\rho+\rho^2) = 70/79 = .89$

$f_{1T} = 1 - f_{10} = 9/79 = .11$

$f_{20} = \rho^2/(1+\rho+\rho^2) = 49/79 = .62$

$f_{2T} = 1 - f_{20} = 30/79 = .38$

(d) Now $\rho = 3/7 \Rightarrow$ $f_{10} = (\rho+\rho^2)/(1+\rho+\rho^2) = 30/79 = .38$

$f_{1T} = 1 - f_{10} = 49/79 = .62$

$f_{20} = \rho^2/(1+\rho+\rho^2) = 9/79 = .11$

$f_{2T} = 1 - f_{20} = 70/79 = .89$

It appears that $p > 1/2 \Rightarrow$ drift to T

$p < 1/2 \Rightarrow$ drift to 0

14.7-2. (a) 0 = Have to honor warranty

1 = Reorder in 1st year

2 = Reorder in 2nd year

3 = Reorder 3 years or older

$$P = \begin{array}{c} \\ 0 \\ 1 \\ 2 \\ 3 \end{array} \begin{array}{c} \begin{array}{cccc} 0 & 1 & 2 & 3 \end{array} \\ \begin{bmatrix} 1 & 0 & 0 & 0 \\ .01 & 0 & .99 & 0 \\ .05 & 0 & 0 & .95 \\ 0 & 0 & 0 & 1 \end{bmatrix} \end{array}$$

(b) Probability manufacturer has to honor warranty $= f_{10}$

$f_{10} = .01 f_{00} + 0 f_{10} + .99 f_{20} + 0 f_{30}$

$f_{20} = .05 f_{00} + 0 f_{10} + 0 f_{20} + .95 f_{30}$

but $f_{00} = 1$ and $f_{30} = 0$

$\Rightarrow f_{10} = .01 + .99 f_{20}$

$f_{20} = .05$

$\Rightarrow f_{10} = .0595 = 5.95\%$

14.8-1. (a)

state :

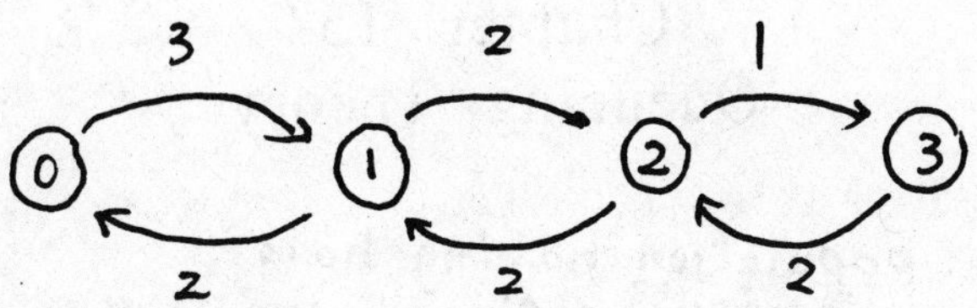

(b) Balance equations :

$$3\pi_0 = 2\pi_1$$
$$4\pi_1 = 3\pi_0 + 2\pi_2$$
$$3\pi_2 = 2\pi_1 + 2\pi_3$$
$$2\pi_3 = \pi_2$$
$$\pi_1 + \pi_2 + \pi_3 + \pi_0 = 1$$

(c) Solve them, we get $\pi_0 = \frac{4}{19}$, $\pi_1 = \frac{6}{19}$, $\pi_2 = \frac{6}{19}$, $\pi_3 = \frac{3}{19}$

14.8-2. (a) state : number of jobs at the work center

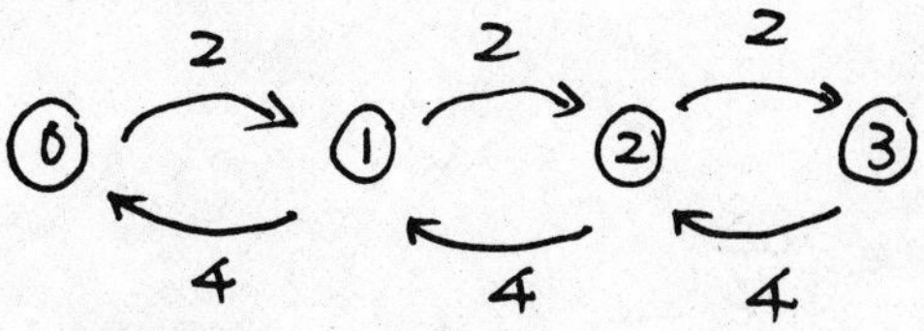

(b) Steady-state equations ;

$$2\pi_0 = 4\pi_1$$
$$6\pi_1 = 2\pi_0 + 4\pi_2$$
$$6\pi_2 = 2\pi_1 + 4\pi_3$$
$$2\pi_2 = 4\pi_3 \quad , \quad \pi_0 + \pi_1 + \pi_2 + \pi_3 = 1$$

(c) We can easily get

$$\pi = \left(\frac{8}{15}, \frac{4}{15}, \frac{2}{15}, \frac{1}{15}\right)$$

Chapter 15
Queueing Theory

15.2-1 input source: population having hair
calling units: customers wanting haircuts
queue: customers waiting for a barber
Service discipline: usually first in, first out.
service mechanism: barbers and equipment.

15.2-2 a) $L = \sum_{n=0}^{4} nP_n = \frac{1}{16}\cdot 0 + \frac{4}{16}\cdot 1 + \frac{6}{16}\cdot 2 + \frac{4}{16}\cdot 3 + \frac{1}{16}\cdot 4$

$= 2$

b) $L_q = \sum_{n=3}^{4} (n-2)P_n = \frac{4}{16}\cdot 1 + \frac{1}{16}\cdot 2 = \frac{3}{8}$

c) $E(\text{\# cutomers being served}) = 1\cdot P_1 + 2(P_2 + P_3 + P_4)$

$= \frac{4}{16} + 2(\frac{6}{16} + \frac{4}{16} + \frac{1}{16}) = \frac{13}{8}$

d) $W = L/\lambda = 1$

$W_q = L_q/\lambda = \frac{3}{8}/2 = \frac{3}{16}$

e) Expected service time $= W - W_q = \frac{13}{16}$

15.2-3 $\lambda_2 = 2\lambda_1$, $\mu_2 = 2\mu_1$, $L_2 = 2L_1$

$\frac{W_2}{W_1} = \frac{L_2/\lambda_2}{L_1/\lambda_1} = 1$

15.2-4 (a) $L = \begin{cases} L_q & \text{when no one is in the system} \\ L_q + 1 & \text{otherwise} \end{cases}$

So $L = P_0 L_q + (1-P_0)(L_q+1) = L_q + (1-P_0)$

(b) $L = \lambda W = \lambda(W_q + 1/\mu) = \lambda W_q + \lambda/\mu = L_q + \rho$

(c) $L = L_q + \rho = L_q + (1-P_0)$ from (a) and (b). So $\rho = 1 - P_0$.

15.2-5 $L = \sum_{n=0}^{\infty} nP_n = \sum_{n=0}^{s-1} nP_n + \sum_{n=s}^{\infty} nP_n = \sum_{n=0}^{s-1} nP_n + \sum_{n=s}^{\infty}(n-s)P_n + \sum_{n=s}^{\infty} sP_n =$

$= \sum_{n=0}^{s-1} nP_n + L_q + s\sum_{n=s}^{\infty} P_n =$

$= \sum_{n=0}^{s-1} nP_n + L_q + s(1 - \sum_{n=0}^{s-1} P_n)$

15.3-1

Part	customers	servers
(a)	customers waiting checkout	checkers
(b)	fires	fire fighting units
(c)	cars	toll collectors
(d)	broken bicycles	bicycle repairpersons
(e)	ships to be loaded or unloaded	Longshoremen + equipment
(f)	machines needing operator	operator
(g)	materials to be handled	handling equipment
(h)	calls for plumbers	plumbers
(i)	custom orders	customized process
(j)	typing requests	typists

15.4-1 $\lambda_n = 1/2$ for $n > 0$ and $\mu_n = \begin{cases} 1/2 & \text{for } n=1 \\ 1 & \text{for } n \geq 2 \end{cases}$

(a) $P\{\text{next arrival before 1:00}\} = 1 - e^{-1/2} = .393$

$P\{\text{next arrival between 1:00 and 2:00}\} = (1-e^{-1/2 \cdot 2}) - (1 - e^{-1/2}) = .239$

$P\{\text{next arrival after 2:00}\} = e^{-2 \cdot 1/2} = .368$

(b) $P\{\text{next arrival between 1:00 and 2:00} \mid \text{no arrivals between 12:00 and 1:00}\} = 1 - e^{-1/2} = .393$

(c) $P\{\text{no arrivals between 1:00 and 2:00}\} = \frac{(\lambda t)^0 e^{-\lambda t}}{0!} = e^{-1/2} = .607$

$P\{\text{one arrival between 1:00 and 2:00}\} = \frac{(\lambda t)^1 e^{-\lambda t}}{1!} = \frac{1}{2} \cdot e^{-1/2} = .303$

$P\{\text{two or more arrivals between 1:00 and 2:00}\} = 1 - e^{-1/2} - \frac{1}{2} e^{-1/2}$

(d) $P\{\text{none served by 2:00}\} = e^{-1} = .368$

$P\{\text{none served by 1:10}\} = e^{-1(1/6)} = .846$

$P\{\text{none served by 1:01}\} = e^{-1(1/60)} = .983$

15.4-2 $\lambda_n = 2$ for $n \geq 0 \Rightarrow P\{n \text{ arrivals in an hour}\} = \frac{2^n e^{-2}}{n!}$

(a) $P\{0 \text{ arrivals in an hour}\} = e^{-2} = .135$

b) $P\{2 \text{ arrivals in an hour}\} = \frac{2^2 e^{-2}}{2!} = 2e^{-2} = .270$

c) $P\{5 \text{ or more arrivals in an hour}\} = 1 - \sum_{n=0}^{4} P\{n \text{ arrivals in an hour}\}$

$= 1 - e^{-2} - 2e^{-2} - 2e^{-2} - (4/3) \cdot e^{-2} - (2/3)e^{-2}$

$= 1 - 7e^{-2} = .0527$

15.4-3 $\text{Pay} = 100 \cdot P\{T<2\} + 80 \cdot P\{T>2\} = 100 - 20 \cdot P\{T>2\}$

$P\{T_{old} > 2\} = e^{-\frac{1}{4} \cdot 2} = e^{-\frac{1}{2}} = 0.607$

15.4-3 (continued)

$P\{T_{special} > 2\} = e^{-\frac{1}{2}\cdot 2} = e^{-1}$

Increase $= Pay_{special} - Pay_{old} = 20(P\{T_{old} > 2\} - P\{T_{special} > 2\})$

$= 20(e^{-\frac{1}{2}} - e^{-1})$

15.4-4 Given the memoryless property, the system turns into a two-server queue after first completion occurs.

T = amount of time after 1 and before next service completion

$P\{T < t\} = P\{\min(T_2, T_3) < t\}$

So, T satisfies exponential distribution with mean $0.5/2 = 0.25$ (property 3)

15.4-5 By memoryless property, $U = \min(T_1, T_2, T_3)$

$T_1 \sim exp(1/20)$, $T_2 \sim exp(1/15)$, $T_3 \sim exp(1/10)$

$U \sim exp(\frac{1}{20} + \frac{1}{15} + \frac{1}{10}) = exp(\frac{13}{60})$

So, expected waiting time $= \frac{60}{13} = 4\frac{8}{13}$ minutes

15.4-6 a) From aggregation property of poisson process, the arrival process is still poisson with mean rate 10 per hour. So, distribution of time between consecutive arrivals is exponential with mean of 6 minutes.

b) The probability distribution is the minimum of two exponential random variables. By property 3, it is exponential with mean of 5 minutes.

15.4-7 a) Exponential with mean of 5 minutes.

b) $W = W_q + T_s$, W_q and T_s are independent

$EW = EW_q + ET_s = 5 + 10 = 15$ minutes $= \frac{1}{4}$ hour

$var W = var W_q + var T_s = (\frac{1}{12})^2 + (\frac{1}{6})^2 = \frac{5}{144} = 0.0347$

d) $\bar{W} = 5 + W_s$

$\bar{W}$ has mean of 20 minutes, but holds the same variance as W_s

15.4-8 a) $P\{T_X < T_Y\} = \frac{\lambda_X}{\lambda_X + \lambda_Y} = \frac{1}{2} = P\{X$ completes before $Y\}$

b) (continued)

$P\{Z \text{ completes before } X\} = P\{Y \text{ completes before } X,\ Z \text{ completes before } X\}$

$= P\{T_Y < T_X\} \cdot P\{T_Z < T_X'\} = \frac{1}{2} \cdot \frac{1}{2} = \frac{1}{4}$

T_X starts from the end of 15-minute interval

T_X' starts from the moment Y leaves the system

c) Same as b), $\frac{1}{4}$

d) $T_X = \frac{1}{4} + \exp(4)$

So, $F_X(t) = \begin{cases} 0 & t < \frac{1}{4} \\ 1 - e^{-4t} & t \geq \frac{1}{4} \end{cases}$

$ET_X = \frac{1}{4} + \frac{1}{4} = \frac{1}{2}$ hour, $\quad \text{var } T_X = \left(\frac{1}{4}\right)^2 = \frac{1}{16} = 0.0625$

e) $T_Y = \frac{1}{6} + \exp(4)$

So, $F_Y(t) = \begin{cases} 0 & t < \frac{1}{6} \\ 1 - e^{-4t} & t \geq \frac{1}{6} \end{cases}$

$ET_Y = \frac{1}{4} + \frac{1}{6} = \frac{5}{12}$, $\quad \text{var } T_Y = \left(\frac{1}{4}\right)^2 = \frac{1}{16} = 0.0625$

f) $W_Z = W_q + T_Z$, $\quad W_q \sim \exp(8)$, $\quad T_Z \sim \exp(4)$

So, $EW_Z = \frac{1}{8} + \frac{1}{4} = \frac{3}{8}$, $\quad \text{var } W_Z = \frac{1}{16} + \frac{1}{64} = \frac{5}{64} = 0.0781$

g) $P\{2 \text{ arrivals}\} = \frac{(\lambda t)^2 e^{-\lambda t}}{2!} = \frac{e^{-1}}{2!} = \frac{1}{2e} \quad (\lambda = 1)$

$= 0.1839$

15.4-9 a) False

b) False

c) False

15.5-1 a)

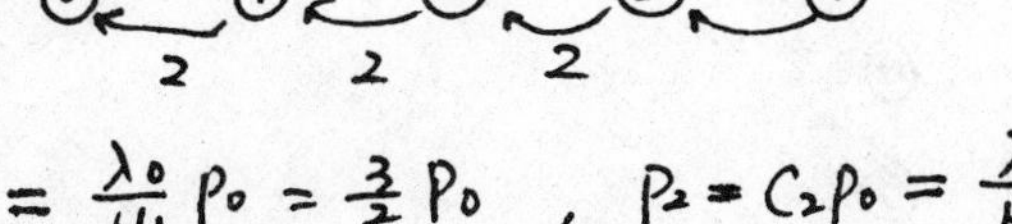

b) $P_1 = \frac{\lambda_0}{\mu_1} P_0 = \frac{3}{2} P_0$, $\quad P_2 = C_2 P_0 = \frac{\lambda_0 \lambda_1}{\mu_1 \mu_2} \cdot P_0 = \frac{3}{2} P_0$

$P_3 = \frac{\lambda_0 \lambda_1 \lambda_2}{\mu_1 \mu_2 \mu_3} P_0 = \frac{3}{4} P_0$, $\quad P_4 = P_5 = \cdots = 0$

$p_0+p_1+p_2+p_3=(1+\frac{3}{2}+\frac{3}{2}+\frac{3}{4})p_0=1$, $p_0=\frac{4}{19}$

$p_1=\frac{12}{38}$, $p_2=\frac{12}{38}$, $p_3=\frac{6}{38}$

c) $L=\sum_{n=0}^{\infty} np_n = p_1+2p_2+3p_3=\frac{12}{38}+\frac{24}{38}+\frac{9}{19}=\frac{27}{19}=1.421$

$L_q = p_2+2p_3=\frac{12}{19}=0.632$

$\bar{\lambda}=\sum_{n=0}^{\infty}\lambda_n p_n = 3p_0+2p_1+p_2=\frac{30}{19}=1.579$

$W=L/\bar{\lambda}=\frac{27}{19}\times\frac{19}{30}=\frac{9}{10}=0.9$

$W_q=L_q/\bar{\lambda}=\frac{12}{19}\cdot\frac{19}{30}=\frac{2}{5}=0.4$

15.5-2 a)

b) $\begin{cases} 2p_1=p_0 & p_0+2p_2=3p_1 \\ p_1=2p_2 & p_0+p_1+p_2=1 \end{cases}$

c) $p_0=\frac{4}{7}$ $p_1=\frac{2}{7}$ $p_2=\frac{1}{7}$

d) $p_1=\frac{\lambda_0}{\mu_1}p_0=\frac{1}{2}p_0$ $p_2=\frac{\lambda_0\lambda_1}{\mu_1\mu_2}p_0=\frac{1}{4}p_0$

$(1+\frac{1}{2}+\frac{1}{4})p_0=p_1+p_2+p_3=1$, we have $p_0=\frac{4}{7}$, $p_1=\frac{2}{7}$, $p_2=\frac{1}{7}$

$L=p_1+2p_2=\frac{4}{7}$ $L_q=p_2=\frac{1}{7}$ $\bar{\lambda}=\lambda_0p_0+\lambda_1p_1=\frac{6}{7}$

$W=L/\bar{\lambda}=\frac{2}{3}$ $W_q=L_q/\lambda=\frac{1}{6}$

15.5-3 a)

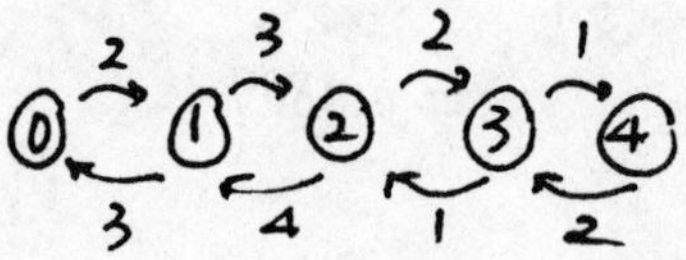

b) $\begin{cases} 2p_0=3p_1 & ① \\ 2p_0+4p_2=6p_1 & ② \\ 3p_1+p_3=6p_2 & ③ \\ 2p_2+2p_4=2p_3 & ④ \\ p_3=2p_4 & ⑤ \\ p_1+p_2+p_3+p_4=1 & ⑥ \end{cases}$

c) ① $\Rightarrow$ $p_1 = \frac{2}{3} p_0$

② $\Rightarrow$ $p_2 = (6 \cdot \frac{2}{3} p_0 - 2p_0)/4 = \frac{1}{2} p_0$

③ $\Rightarrow$ $p_3 = \frac{1}{2} \cdot 6p_0 - 3 \cdot \frac{2}{3} p_0 = p_0$

④ $\Rightarrow$ $p_4 = (2p_0 - 2 \cdot \frac{1}{2} p_0)/2 = \frac{1}{2} p_0$

⑤ $p_0 + \frac{2}{3} p_0 + \frac{1}{2} p_0 + p_0 + \frac{1}{2} p_0 = 1$

$\Rightarrow$ $p_0 = \frac{3}{11}$ $\quad p_1 = \frac{2}{11}$ $\quad p_2 = \frac{3}{22}$ $\quad p_3 = \frac{3}{11}$ $\quad p_4 = \frac{3}{22}$

d) $p_1 = \frac{\lambda_0}{\mu_1} \cdot p_0 = \frac{2}{3} p_0$,

$p_2 = \frac{\lambda_0 \lambda_1}{\mu_1 \mu_2} \cdot p_0 = \frac{1}{2} p_0$

$p_3 = \frac{\lambda_0 \lambda_1 \lambda_2}{\mu_1 \mu_2 \mu_3} \cdot p_0 = p_0$

$p_4 = \frac{\lambda_0 \lambda_1 \lambda_2 \lambda_3}{\mu_1 \mu_2 \mu_3 \mu_4} \cdot p_0 = \frac{1}{2} p_0$

From $p_0 + p_1 + p_2 + p_3 + p_4 = 1 \Rightarrow p_0 = \frac{3}{11}$.

$L = p_1 + 2p_2 + 3p_3 = \frac{20}{11}$

$L_q = p_2 + 2p_3 = \frac{12}{11}$

$\bar{\lambda} = \lambda_0 p_0 + \lambda_1 p_1 + \lambda_2 p_2 + \lambda_3 p_3 = \frac{18}{11}$

$W = L/\bar{\lambda} = \frac{10}{9}$ $\qquad W_q = L_q/\bar{\lambda} = \frac{2}{3}$

15.5-4 a)

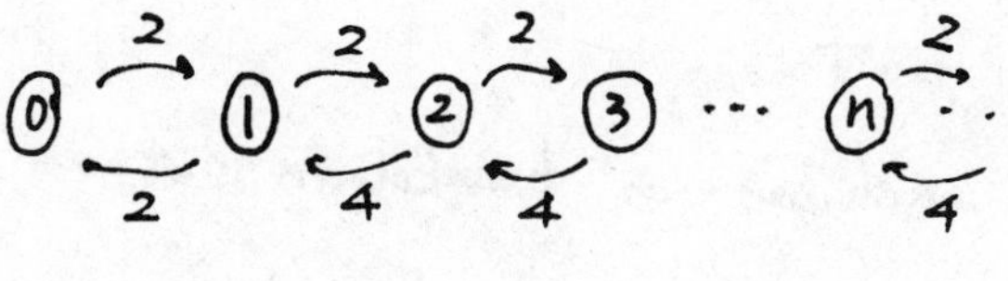

b) $p_1 = \frac{2}{2} p_0$

$p_2 = \frac{1}{2} p_0 \quad \cdots \quad p_n = (\frac{1}{2})^{n-1} p_0$

$\sum_{n=0}^{\infty} p_n = \sum_{n=0}^{\infty} (\frac{1}{2})^n p_0 + p_0 = 3p_0 = 1$, $\quad p_0 = \frac{1}{3}$

$p_n = (\frac{1}{2})^{n-1} \cdot \frac{1}{3}$

c) arrival rate 1,
service rate 2.

15.5-5 a)

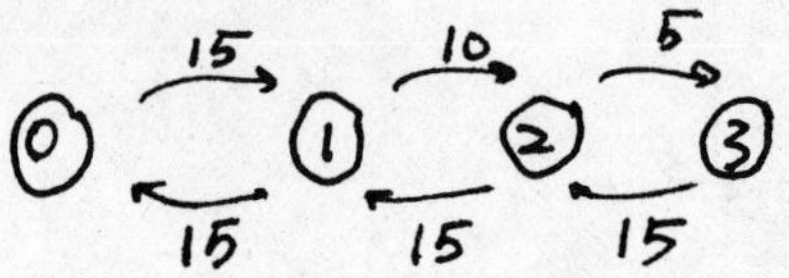

b) $$\begin{cases} 15p_0 = 15p_1 & ① \\ 15p_0 + 15p_2 = 25p_1 & ② \\ 10p_0 + 15p_3 = 20p_2 & ③ \\ 5p_2 = 15p_3 & ④ \end{cases}$$

c) $p_0 = p_1$, $p_2 = \frac{5p_1 - 3p_0}{3} = \frac{2}{3}p_0$, $p_3 = \frac{1}{3}p_2 = \frac{2}{9}p_0$

$p_0 + p_1 + p_2 + p_3 = 1 = \frac{26}{9}p_0 \Rightarrow p_0 = \frac{9}{26}$

$p_1 = \frac{9}{26}$ $\quad p_2 = \frac{3}{13}$ $\quad p_3 = \frac{1}{13}$

Or $p_1 = \frac{\lambda_0}{\mu_1} p_0 = p_0$

$p_2 = \frac{\lambda_0 \lambda_1}{\mu_1 \mu_2} p_0 = \frac{2}{3} p_0$

$p_3 = \frac{\lambda_0 \lambda_1 \lambda_2}{\mu_1 \mu_2 \mu_3} p_0 = \frac{2}{9} p_0$

d) $L = p_1 + 2p_2 + 3p_3 = \frac{27}{26} = 1.04$, $\bar{\lambda} = \lambda_0 p_0 + \lambda_1 p_1 + \lambda_2 p_2 = \frac{255}{26} = 9.81$

$W = L/\bar{\lambda} = \frac{9}{85}$ (hour) $= 0.106$

15.5-6 a)

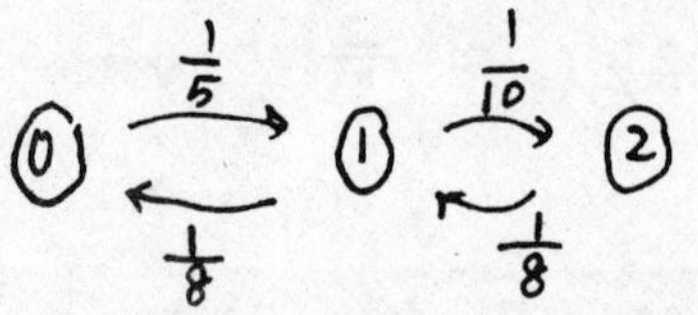

state = # of machines in breakdown state.

b) $p_1 = \frac{8}{5} p_0$, $p_2 = \frac{8}{5} \cdot \frac{8}{10} p_0 = \frac{32}{25} p_0$,

$p_0 + p_1 + p_2 = 1 \Rightarrow p_0 = \frac{25}{97}$, $p_1 = \frac{40}{97}$, $p_2 = \frac{32}{97}$

c) $\bar{\lambda} = p_0 \cdot \lambda_0 + p_1 \lambda_1 = \frac{1}{5} \cdot \frac{25}{97} + \frac{1}{10} \cdot \frac{40}{97} = \frac{9}{97} = 0.093$

$L = p_1 + 2p_2 = \frac{104}{97} = 1.072$, $L_q = \frac{32}{97} = 0.330$

$W = L/\bar{\lambda} = \frac{104}{9}$, $W_q = \frac{32}{9} = 3.556$

d) $p_1 + p_2 = \frac{72}{97} = 0.742$

e) $p_0 + p_1 = \frac{65}{97} = 0.670$

15.5-7 a)

(b) $\mu P_1 = \lambda P_0$

$\lambda P_0 + (\mu + \theta) P_2 = (\mu + \lambda) P_1$

$\vdots$

$\lambda P_{n-1} + (\mu + n\theta) P_{n+1} = (\lambda + \mu + (n-1)\theta) P_n$

$\vdots$

15.5-8 a)

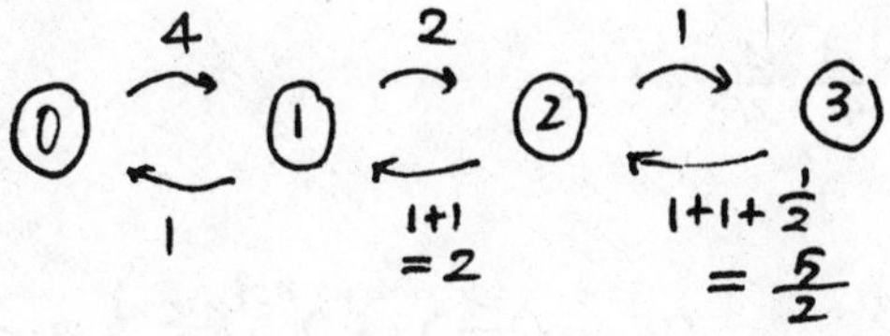

b) $p_1 = 4p_0$, $p_2 = 4p_0$, $p_3 = \frac{2}{5} p_0$

$p_0 + p_1 + p_2 + p_3 = (1 + 4 + 4 + \frac{2}{5}) p_0 = 1 \Rightarrow p_0 = \frac{5}{47}$

$p_1 = \frac{20}{47}$, $p_2 = \frac{20}{47}$, $p_3 = \frac{2}{47}$

c) Fraction of lost customers $= p_1 \cdot \frac{1}{2} + p_2 \cdot \frac{3}{4} + p_3 \cdot 1 = \frac{27}{47}$

d) $L = p_1 + 2p_2 + 3p_3 = \frac{66}{47} = 1.404$

$L_q = p_2 + 2 \cdot p_3 = \frac{24}{47} = 0.511$

15.5-9 a)

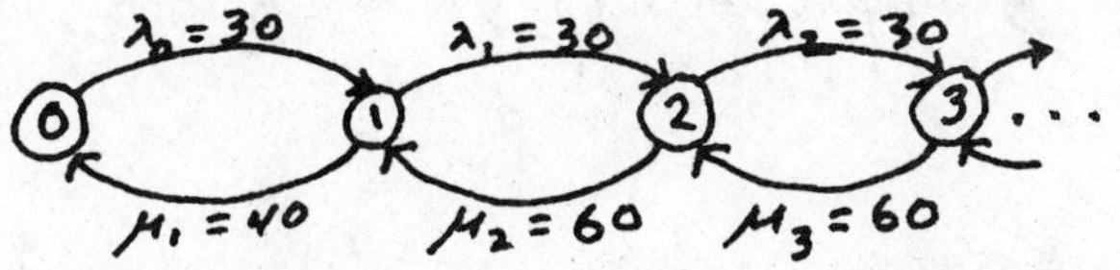

(b) $P_0 = \left[1 + \sum_{n=1}^{\infty} \frac{\lambda^n}{\mu_1 \mu_2^{n-1}}\right]^{-1} = \left[1 + \frac{\lambda}{\mu_1} \sum_{n=1}^{\infty} \left(\frac{\lambda}{\mu_2}\right)^{n-1}\right]^{-1} = \left[1 + \frac{\lambda}{\mu_1}\left(\frac{1}{1 - \frac{\lambda}{\mu_2}}\right)\right]^{-1}$

$= \left[1 + \frac{3}{4}\left(\frac{1}{1 - 1/2}\right)\right]^{-1} = 2/5 = .4$

$P_n = P_0 \frac{\lambda^n}{\mu_1 \mu_2^{n-1}} = \left(\frac{3}{5}\right)\left(\frac{1}{2}\right)^n$ for $n \geq 1$

c) $L = \sum_{n=0}^{\infty} n P_n = \frac{3}{5} \sum_{n=1}^{\infty} n \left(\frac{1}{2}\right)^n = \frac{3}{5} \cdot \frac{1}{2} \sum_{n=1}^{\infty} n \left(\frac{1}{2}\right)^{n-1} = \frac{3}{5} \cdot \frac{1}{2} \cdot \frac{1}{(1 - 1/2)^2} = \frac{6}{5}$

$L_q = L - (1 - P_0) = 6/5 - (1 - 2/5) = 3/5$

(continued)

$W = L/\lambda = 1/25$

$W_q = L_q/\lambda = 1/50$

15.5-10 a)

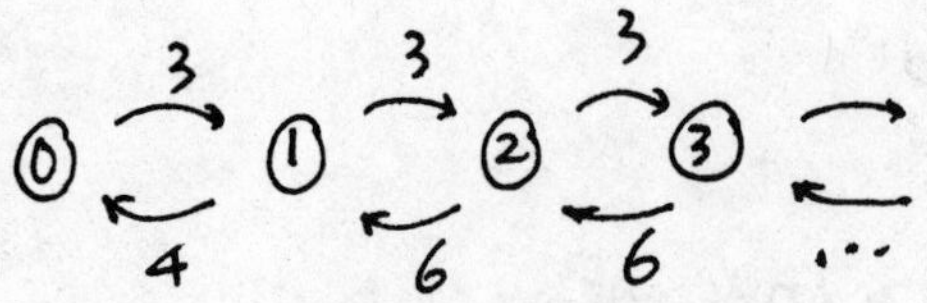

b) $p_1 = \frac{3}{4} p_0$, $p_2 = \frac{3}{4} \cdot \frac{1}{2} p_0$, ... , $p_n = \frac{3}{4} \cdot (\frac{1}{2})^{n-1} p_0$

$$\sum_{n=0}^{\infty} p_n = p_0 + \frac{3}{4} p_0 + \frac{3}{4} \cdot \frac{1}{2} p_0 + \cdots$$

$$= \frac{5}{2} p_0 = 1$$

So, $p_0 = \frac{2}{5}$, $p_1 = \frac{3}{10}$, $p_n = (\frac{3}{4})(\frac{1}{2})^{n-1}(\frac{2}{5}) = \frac{3}{10} \cdot (\frac{1}{2})^{n-1}$

Let $p_i' = P\{$in steady-state i documents have been received but not yet completed$\}$

Then $p_0' = p_0 + p_1 = \frac{7}{10}$

$p_n' = p_{n+1} = \frac{3}{10} \cdot (\frac{1}{2})^n$, $n \geq 1$

c) $L = \sum_{n=1}^{\infty} n p_n = \frac{3}{10} (1 + 2 \cdot \frac{1}{2} + 3 \cdot \frac{1}{2^2} + \cdots)$

$$= \frac{3}{10} \cdot 4 \cdot (\frac{1}{2^2} + \frac{2}{2^3} + \frac{3}{2^4} + \cdots)$$

$$= -\frac{6}{5} \frac{d}{d\rho} \left(\frac{1}{\rho - 1}\right) \bigg|_{\rho = 2} = \frac{6}{5}$$

$W = L/\lambda = \frac{2}{3}$

$L_q = \sum_{n=1}^{\infty} (n-1) p_n = L - (1 - p_0) = \frac{3}{5}$

$W_q = L_q/\lambda = \frac{1}{5}$

15.5-11

(a) $L_q = W_q = 0$

(b)

(continued)

(c) $P_n = \frac{\lambda^n}{n!\mu^n} P_0 = \frac{\rho^n}{n!} P_0$

(d) $P_0 = \frac{1}{\sum_{i=0}^{\infty} \frac{\rho^n}{n!}} = \frac{1}{e^\rho} = e^{-\rho}$ notice that ρ need not be ≤ 1 in this case

(e) $W = 1/\mu$, $L = \lambda W = \lambda/\mu = \rho$

15.5-12

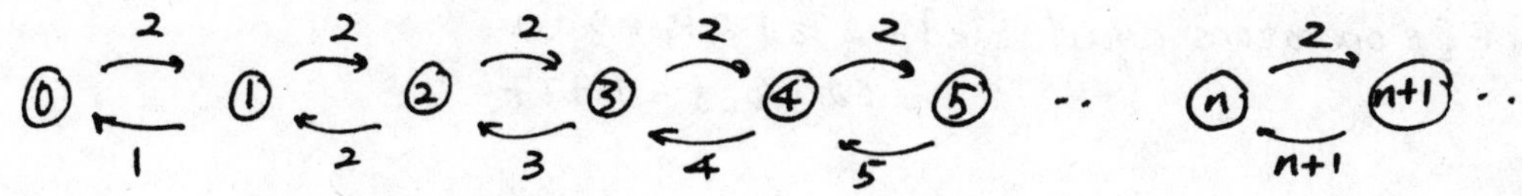

Then, $p_1 = \frac{\lambda_0}{\mu_1} p_0 = 2p_0$,

$p_2 = 2 \cdot 1 \cdot p_0$

$\vdots$

$p_n = \frac{2^n}{n!} \cdot p_0$

$\sum_{n=0}^{\infty} p_n = e^2 \cdot p_0 = 1$, So $p_0 = e^{-2}$, $p_1 = 2e^{-2}$

15.5-13 a)

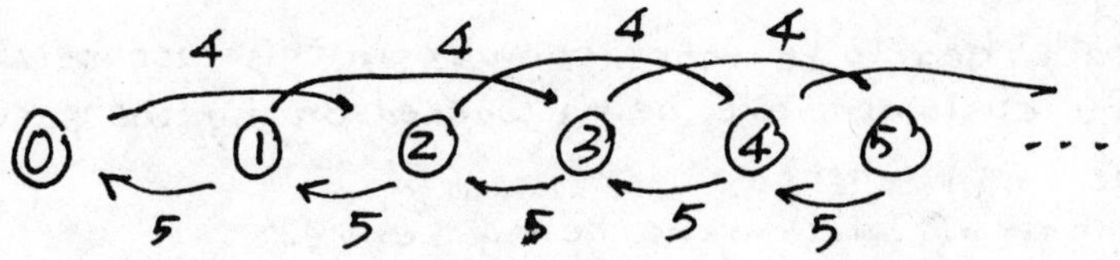

b) $5p_1 = 4p_0$

$5p_2 = 9p_1$

$5p_3 + 4p_0 = 9p_2$

$\vdots$

$5p_{n+1} + 4p_{n-2} = 9p_n$

$\vdots$

c)

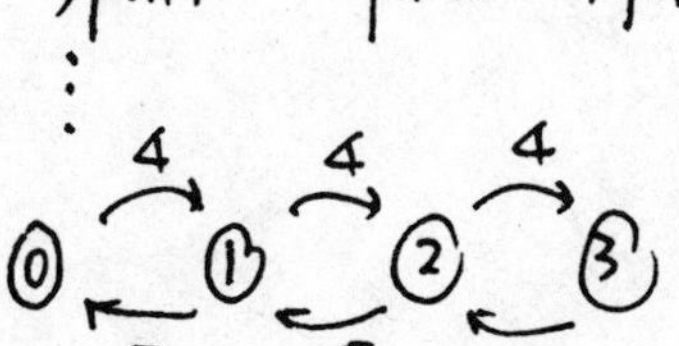

15.5-14 (a) State n = # machines broken down.
Since the 3rd machine is shut off when the 2nd machine breaks, $n = 0, 1$ or 2.

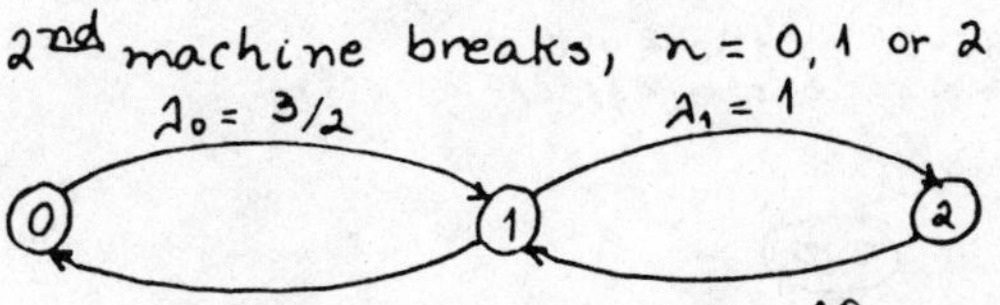

(continued)

(b) The balance equations are:

$$5P_1 = (3/2)P_0$$
$$(3/2)P_0 + 20P_2 = 6P_1$$
$$P_1 = 20P_2$$

Solving the balance equations we obtain

$$(P_0, P_1, P_2) = (200/263, 60/263, 3/263) = (.760, .228, .011)$$

(c) $E[\#\text{ operators available}] = 2P_0 + 2P_1 + 0P_2 =$
$= 520/263 = 1.977$

15.5-15 (a) Let n = number of customers in the system. Then the rate diagram is:

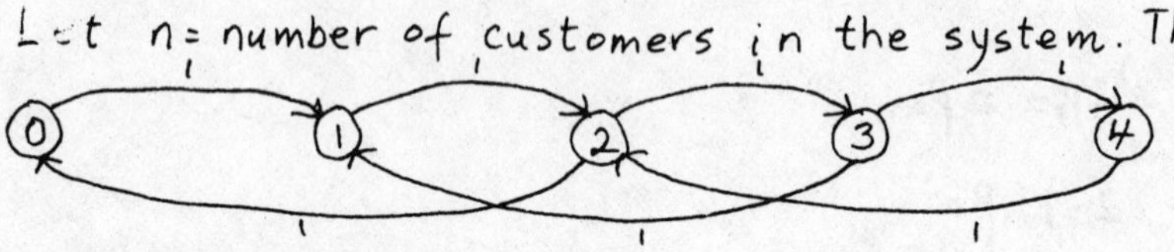

The balance equations are:

$$P_0 = P_2$$
$$P_1 = P_0 + P_3$$
$$2P_2 = P_1 + P_4$$
$$2P_3 = P_2$$
$$P_4 = P_3$$

(b) The state space has to be more complex in this case because you need to know how many customers are being worked on by the server.
Let the state be (s, q) where
s = number of customers being served
q = number of customers in the queue
Then the rate diagram is

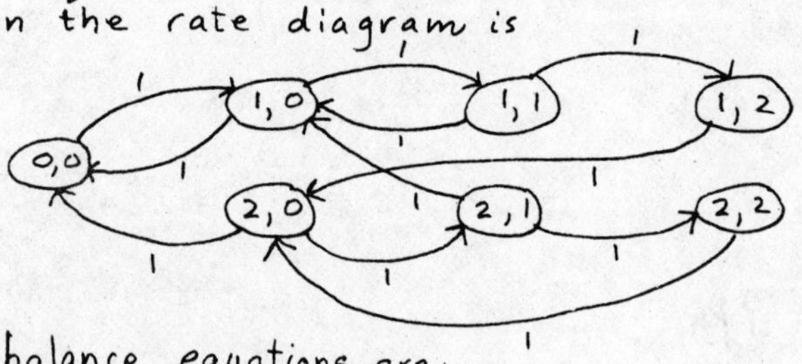

The balance equations are:

$$P_{00} = P_{10} + P_{20}$$
$$2P_{10} = P_{00} + P_{11} + P_{21}$$
$$2P_{11} = P_{10}$$
$$P_{12} = P_{11}$$
$$2P_{20} = P_{12} + P_{22}$$
$$2P_{21} = P_{20}$$
$$P_{22} = P_{21}$$

15.5-16 (a) Let the state be (n_1, n_2) where
n_1 = number of type 1 customers in the system
n_2 = number of type 2 customers in the system
Then the rate diagram is:

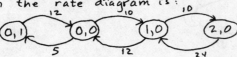

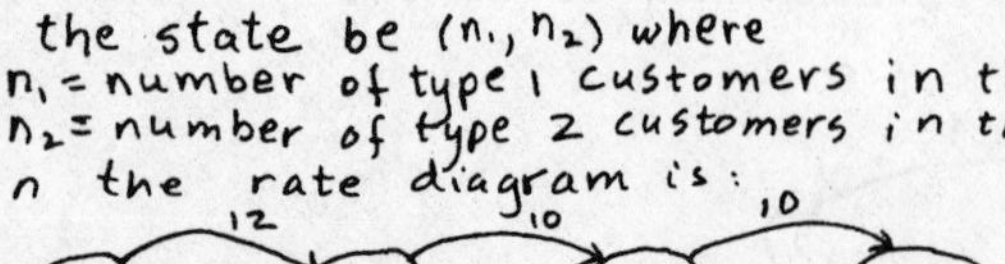

(continued)

(b) The balance equations are:

(c)

$$12 P_{01} = 5 P_{00}$$
$$15 P_{00} = 12 (P_{01} + P_{10})$$
$$22 P_{10} = 10 P_{00} + 24 P_{20}$$
$$24 P_{20} = 10 P_{10}$$
$$(P_{00} + P_{10} + P_{01} + P_{20} = 1)$$
$$\Rightarrow P_{00} = \frac{72}{187},\ P_{10} = \frac{60}{187},\ P_{01} = \frac{30}{187},\ P_{20} = \frac{25}{187}$$

(d) Type 1 customers are blocked when the system is in state (2,0) or (0,1) which means that the fraction unable to enter the system is $P_{20} + P_{01} = 55/187$.
Type 2 customers are blocked when the system is in state (2,0),(1,0) or (0,1) which means that the fraction unable to enter the system is $P_{20} + P_{10} + P_{01} = 115/187$.

15.6-1 $\lambda = 10,\ \mu = 15,\ P_0 = (1 - \frac{\lambda}{\mu}) = \frac{1}{3}$ = propotion of time no one is waiting

15.6-2 (a) $\mathcal{W} \sim \exp(\mu - \lambda),\ W = \frac{1}{\mu - \lambda}$

$$P\{\mathcal{W} > W\} = (\mu-\lambda) e^{-(\mu-\lambda)\frac{1}{\mu-\lambda}} = (\mu-\lambda)/e$$

(b) $W_q = \frac{\lambda}{\mu(\mu-\lambda)},\ \mathcal{W}_q(t) = \begin{cases} 1-\rho & t=0 \\ 1-\rho e^{-\mu(1-\rho)t} & t>0 \end{cases}$

$$\text{So, } P\{\mathcal{W}_q > W_q\} = 1 - \mathcal{W}_q(W_q) = \rho e^{-\mu(1-\rho)\frac{\lambda}{\mu(\mu-\lambda)}}$$
$$= \frac{\lambda}{\mu} \cdot e^{-\frac{\lambda}{\mu}}$$

15.6-3 $P_0 = 1 - \rho,\ W_q = \frac{\lambda}{\mu(\mu-\lambda)}$

$$\frac{(1-P_0)^2}{W_q P_0} = \frac{\rho^2}{\frac{\lambda}{\mu(\mu-\lambda)} \cdot (1 - \frac{\lambda}{\mu})} = \frac{\lambda^2/\mu}{\lambda/\mu^2} = \lambda$$

$$\frac{1-P_0}{W_q P_0} = \frac{\rho}{\frac{\lambda}{\mu(\mu-\lambda)} \cdot \frac{\mu-\lambda}{\mu}} = \frac{\lambda/\mu}{\lambda/\mu^2} = \mu$$

15.6-4 $\lambda = 2,\ \mu = 4,\ s = 1,\ \rho = 1/2$

For M/M/1 queue, $P_0 = 1 - \lambda/\mu = 1/2$ and $P_n = (1-\rho)\rho^n = (1/2)^{n+1}$

desired proportion of time $= \sum_{i=0}^{4} P_i = 31/32$

15.6-5 $\lambda = 3,\ \mu = 4,\ s = 1,\ \rho = 3/4$

The system without the storage restriction is a M/M/1 queue. If n square feet of floor space were available for waiting, the proportion of time this would be sufficient is $\sum_{i=0}^{n+1} P_i$. Thus we want to find n_ℓ such that $\sum_{i=0}^{n_\ell+1} P_i \geq q_\ell$ for $\ell = 1,2,3$, where $q_1 = .5,\ q_2 = .9,\ q_3 = .99$.

(continued)

Now $\sum_{i=0}^{n_e+1} P_i \geq q_e \Leftrightarrow \sum_{i=0}^{n_e+1} (1-\rho)\rho^i \geq q_e \Leftrightarrow (1-\rho)\frac{(1-\rho^{n_e+2})}{(1-\rho)} \geq q_e \Leftrightarrow$

$\Leftrightarrow 1-\rho^{n_e+2} \geq q_e \Leftrightarrow \rho^{n_e+2} \leq 1-q_e \Leftrightarrow (n_e+2)\ln\rho \leq \ln(1-q_e)$

$\Leftrightarrow (n_e+2) \geq \frac{\ln(1-q_e)}{\ln\rho} \Leftrightarrow n_e \geq \frac{\ln(1-q_e)}{\ln\rho} - 2$

part	q_e	$\frac{\ln(1-q_e)}{\ln\rho} - 2$	floor space required
(a)	.50	.409	1
(b)	.90	6.004	7
(c)	.99	14.008	15

15.6-6. a) True

b) False. $L = \lambda W = \frac{\rho}{1-\rho}$

c) False. $L = \rho/(1-\rho)$, $L = 9$ when $\rho = 0.9$, but $L = 99$ when $\rho = 0.99$

15.6-7 a) False

b) True. when $\rho > 1$, $L \to \infty$

c) TRUE

15.6-8 a) True

b) False

c) True

15.6-9.

(a)

λ	L	L_q	W	W_q	$P\{W > 5\}$
.5	1	.50	2	1	.082
.9	9	8.10	10	9	.607
.99	99	98.01	100	99	.951

(b)

λ	λ/μ	ρ	P_0	L	L_q	W	W_q	$P\{W>5\}$
.5	1	.5	.3333	1.333	.333	2.667	.667	.150
.9	1.8	.9	.0526	9.474	7.674	10.526	8.526	.641
.99	1.98	.99	.0050	99.497	97.517	100.503	98.503	.956

15.6-10. Run OR courseware, we have the following Results:

S	L_q	L	W_q	W	$P\{W_q > 0\}$	$P\{W > 10\}$	ΣP_n
1	4.167	5	0.417	0.5	0.833	0.717	0.306
2	0.175	1.008	0.018	0.101	0.245	0.191	0.898
3	0.022	0.856	0.002	0.086	0.058	0.141	0.984
4	0.003	0.836	0	0.084	0.011	0.135	0.998
5	0	0.834	0	0.083	0.002	0.135	0.999

So, a) S=3

b) S=3

c) S=2

d) S=1

e) S=3

f) S=3

g) S=3

15.6-11. (a)

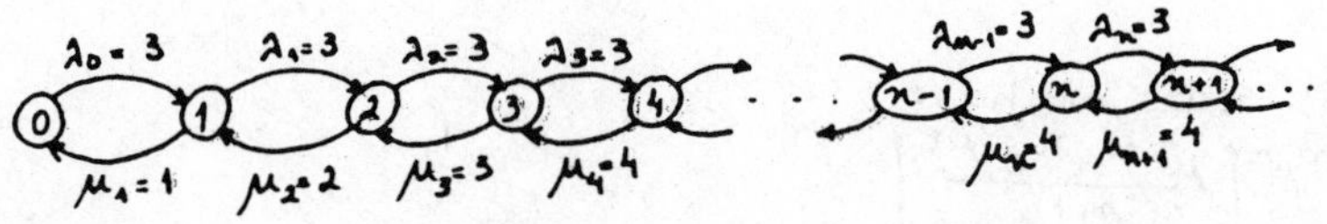

(b)(c)

The M/M/s Model:

λ = 10	P_0 = 0.43457
	P_1 = 0.36214
μ = 12	P_2 = 0.15089
	P_3 = 0.04191
s = 5	P_4 = 0.00873
	P_5 = 0.00146
	P_6 = 0.00024
	P_7 = 0.00004
	P_8 = 0.00001
	P_9 = 0
L = 0.834	P_{10} = 0
	P_{11} = 0
L_q= 0	P_{12} = 0
	P_{13} = 0
W = 0.083	P_{14} = 0
	P_{15} = 0
W_q= 0	P_{16} = 0
	P_{17} = 0
P($\mathcal{W}$ > t) = 0.135, where t = 0.167	P_{18} = 0
	P_{19} = 0
P($\mathcal{W}_q$ > t) = 0.002, where t = 0	P_{20} = 0

15.6-12. $\lambda = 20$, $\mu = 30$, This is M/M/1 Queue.

E(number of airplanes at the end of the thundestorm)

= E(# airplanes before thunderstone) + E(# arrived planes during the thunderstorm)

$$= L_q + \lambda t = \lambda(W_q + t) = 20\left(\frac{20}{30(30-20)} + 0.5\right) = 11.33$$

15.6-13. $\lambda = 15$, $\mu = 20$, this is a M/M/1 Queue

$$P\{\text{customer does not have to wait}\} = P_0 = 1 - \frac{\lambda}{\mu} = \frac{1}{3}$$

$$\text{price/per gallon} = 1.2 \times \frac{1}{3} + 1 \times \frac{2}{3} = 1.067$$

15.6-14. $$\text{Expected cost} = \sum_{n=1}^{\infty} n \cdot P_n = \sum_{n=1}^{\infty} n \cdot \rho^n (1-\rho) = \frac{\rho}{1-\rho} = \frac{\lambda}{\mu - \lambda}$$

15.6-15. Let $P\{\mathcal{W} \leq t\} = G(t)$ and let $\frac{dG(t)}{dt} = g(t)$

Then $P\{\mathcal{W} > t\} = 1 - P(t)$

So $$[1 - G(t)] = \sum_{n=0}^{\infty} P_n \, P\{S_{n+1} > t\} =$$

$$= \sum_{n=0}^{\infty} (1-\rho)\rho^n \left[\int_t^{\infty} \frac{\mu^{n+1} x^n e^{-\mu x}}{n!} dx\right] =$$

$$= \sum_{n=0}^{\infty} (1-\rho)\rho^n \left[1 - \int_0^{t} \frac{\mu^{n+1} x^n e^{-\mu x}}{n!} dx\right]$$

15.6-15 (*continued*)

Differentiating both sides, we have:

$$g(t) = \sum_{n=0}^{\infty} (1-\rho)\rho^n \left[\frac{\mu^{n+1} t^n e^{-\mu t}}{n!}\right]$$

$$= (1-\rho)\mu e^{-\mu t} \sum_{n=0}^{\infty} \frac{(\lambda t)^n}{n!}$$

$$= (1-\rho)\mu e^{-\mu t} e^{\lambda t}$$

$$= \mu(1-\rho) e^{-\mu(1-\rho)t}$$

Hence, by integration, $P\{\mathcal{W} > t\} = 1 - \int_0^t g(x)dx = e^{-\mu(1-\rho)t}$

15.6-16 (a) Let $P\{\mathcal{W}_q \le t\} = G(t)$ and let $\frac{dG(t)}{dt} = g(t)$

Then $P\{\mathcal{W}_q > t\} = 1 - G(t)$

So $[1 - G(t)] = \sum_{n=1}^{\infty} P_n P\{S_n > t\} = \sum_{n=1}^{\infty} (1-\rho)\rho^n \left[1 - \int_0^t \frac{\mu^n x^{n-1} e^{-\mu x}}{(n-1)!} dx\right]$

Differentiating both sides gives:

$$g(t) = \sum_{n=1}^{\infty} (1-\rho)\rho^n \left[\frac{\mu^n t^{n-1} e^{-\mu t}}{(n-1)!}\right]$$

$$= (1-\rho)\lambda e^{-\mu t} \sum_{n=1}^{\infty} \frac{(\lambda t)^{n-1}}{(n-1)!}$$

$$= (1-\rho)\lambda e^{-\mu t} e^{\lambda t}$$

$$= \left(\frac{\lambda}{\mu}\right)(\mu - \lambda) e^{-(\mu-\lambda)t}$$

Then $W_q = \left(\frac{\lambda}{\mu}\right)\int_0^{\infty} t(\mu-\lambda)e^{-(\mu-\lambda)t} dt = \frac{\lambda}{\mu(\mu-\lambda)}$

(b) Let $P\{\mathcal{W}_q \le t\} = G(t)$ and let $\frac{dG(t)}{dt} = g(t)$

Then $P\{\mathcal{W}_q > t\} = 1 - G(t)$

So $[1 - G(t)] = \sum_{n=s}^{\infty} P_n P\{S_{n-s+1} > t\}$

$$= \sum_{n=s}^{\infty} P_n \left[1 - \int_0^t \frac{(s\mu)^{n-s+1} x^{n-s} e^{-(s\mu)x}}{(n-s)!} dx\right]$$

Now $P_n = \frac{(\lambda/\mu)^n}{s!\, s^{n-s}} P_0$ for $n \ge s$

So differentiating both sides gives

$$g(t) = \sum_{n=s}^{\infty} \left[\frac{(\lambda/\mu)^n P_0}{s!\, s^{n-s}}\right]\left[\frac{(s\mu)^{n-s+1} t^{n-s} e^{-(s\mu)t}}{(n-s)!}\right]$$

$$= \frac{P_0 (s\mu)(\lambda/\mu)^s}{s!} e^{-s\mu t} \sum_{n=s}^{\infty} \frac{(\lambda t)^{n-s}}{(n-s)!}$$

$$= \frac{P_0 (s\mu)(\lambda/\mu)^s}{s!} e^{-s\mu t} e^{\lambda t}$$

$$= \frac{P_0 (s\mu)(\lambda/\mu)^s}{s!} e^{-(s\mu)(1-\rho)t}$$

So $W_q = \frac{P_0 (\lambda/\mu)^s}{s!} \int_0^{\infty} t(s\mu) e^{-(s\mu)(1-\rho)t} dt$

$$= \frac{P_0 (\lambda/\mu)^s}{s!(1-\rho)} \int_0^{\infty} t(s\mu)(1-\rho) e^{-(s\mu)(1-\rho)t} dt$$

$$= \frac{P_0 (\lambda/\mu)^s}{s!(1-\rho)^2 (s\mu)}$$

$$= \frac{P_0 (\lambda/\mu)^s \rho}{s!(1-\rho)^2 \lambda}$$

$$= L_q / \lambda$$

15.6-17.

$\lambda = 4$

$\mu = 3$

$s = 2$

$L = 2.4$

$L_q = 1.067$

$W = 0.6$

$W_q = 0.267$

$P(\mathcal{W} > t) = 1$, where $t = 0$

$P(\mathcal{W}_q > t) = 0.533$, where $t = 0$

P_0	= 0.2
P_1	= 0.26667
P_2	= 0.17778
P_3	= 0.11852
P_4	= 0.07901
P_5	= 0.05267
P_6	= 0.03512
P_7	= 0.02341
P_8	= 0.01561
P_9	= 0.0104
P_{10}	= 0.00694
P_{11}	= 0.00462
P_{12}	= 0.00308
P_{13}	= 0.00206
P_{14}	= 0.00137
P_{15}	= 0.00091
P_{16}	= 0.00061
P_{17}	= 0.00041
P_{18}	= 0.00027
P_{19}	= 0.00018
P_{20}	= 0.00012

$$\text{The mean rate} = \frac{P_1 + P_2}{1 - P_0} = \frac{0.26667 + 0.17778}{0.8} = 0.556$$

15.6-18.

$\lambda = 4$

$\mu = 6$

$s = 2$

$L = 0.75$

$L_q = 0.083$

$W = 0.188$

$W_q = 0.021$

$P(\mathcal{W} > t) = 1$, where $t = 0$

$P(\mathcal{W}_q > t) = 0.003$, where $t = 0.5$

P_0	= 0.5
P_1	= 0.33333
P_2	= 0.11111
P_3	= 0.03704
P_4	= 0.01235
P_5	= 0.00412
P_6	= 0.00137
P_7	= 0.00046
P_8	= 0.00015
P_9	= 0.00005
P_{10}	= 0.00002
P_{11}	= 0.00001
P_{12}	= 0
P_{13}	= 0
P_{14}	= 0
P_{15}	= 0
P_{16}	= 0
P_{17}	= 0
P_{18}	= 0
P_{19}	= 0
P_{20}	= 0

$$P\{W_q > 0.5 \mid \#\text{ customers} \geq 2\} = \frac{P\{W_q > 0.5,\ \#\text{ customers} \geq 2\}}{P\{\#\text{ customers} \geq 2\}}$$

$$= \frac{P\{W_q > 0.5\}}{1 - P_0 - P_1} = \frac{0.003}{1 - (0.5 + 0.3333)} = 0.018$$

15.6-19. when $\lambda = 10$, $\mu = 7.5$, $S = 2$, (current system)

$L = 2.4$, $L_q = 1.067$, $W = 0.24$, $W_q = 0.107$

When $\lambda = 5$, $\mu = 7.5$, $s = 1$, (next year)

$L = 2$, $L_q = 1.333$, $W = 0.4$, $W_q = 0.267$

So, next year yields smaller L but larger L_q, W and W_q

15.6-20. (a) $W = \frac{1}{\mu - \lambda}$

$W_{clara} = \frac{1}{20-16} = \frac{1}{4}$ hour $= 15$ minutes

$W_{clarence} = \frac{1}{20-14} = \frac{1}{6}$ hour $= 10$ minutes

$W_{total} = P\{clara\} \cdot W_{clara} + P\{clarence\} \cdot W_{clarence}$

$= \frac{16}{30} \cdot 15 + \frac{14}{30} \cdot 10 = 12.67$ minutes $= 0.211$ hour

(b) It is M/M/2 queue, $\lambda = 16 + 14 = 30$, $\mu = 20$, $S = 2$

Run OR courseware, $W = 0.114$ hour

(c) $\mu = 60/3.5$, $W = 0.249$

$\mu = 60/3.4$, $W = 0.204$

$\mu = 60/3.45$, $W = 0.225$

$\mu = 60/3.425$, $W = 0.214$

$\mu = 60/3.419$, $W = 0.212$

$\mu = 60/3.4185$, $W = 0.211$

$\vdots$

So, if the expected processing time is 3.4185 minutes, it cause the same expected waiting time.

15.6-21. $L = 8$, $W = 2$, $\lambda = L/W = 4$

$W = \frac{1}{\mu - \lambda} = 2 \Rightarrow \mu = \frac{1}{2} + \lambda = 4\frac{1}{2}$

$P\{T_s > \frac{1}{3}\} = e^{-\frac{9}{2} \cdot \frac{1}{3}} = e^{-\frac{3}{4}}$

15.6-22. (a) The future evolution of the queueing system is affected by whether the parameter of the service time distribution for the customer currently in service is μ_1 or μ_2. So the current state of the system needs to include this information from the history of the process.

The states are (n, s) where

n = number of customers in the system ($n = 1, 2, \cdots$)

$s = \begin{cases} 1 & \text{if the current parameter is } \mu_1 \\ 2 & \text{if the current parameter is } \mu_2 \end{cases}$

except that $n = 0$ does not need s. Then we have:

15.6-22. (continued)

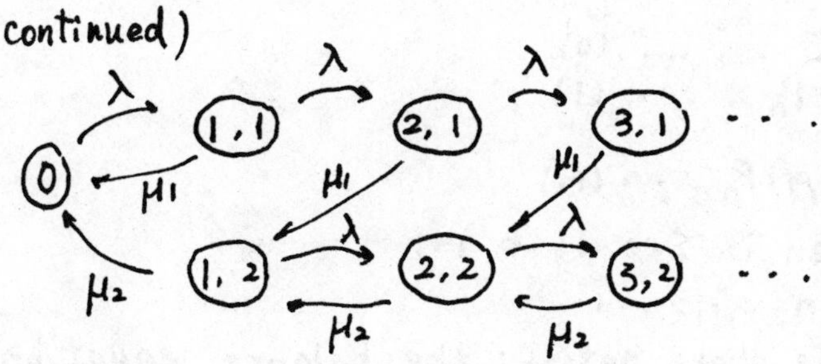

(b) $\lambda P_0 = \mu_1 \cdot P_{1,1} + \mu_2 \cdot P_{1,2}$

$(\lambda+\mu_1)P_{1,1} = \lambda P_0$

$\vdots$

$(\lambda+\mu_1)P_{n,1} = \lambda P_{n-1,1}$

$\vdots$

$(\lambda+\mu_2)P_{1,2} = \mu_1 \cdot P_{2,1} + \mu_2 P_{2,2}$

$\vdots$

$(\lambda+\mu_2)P_{n,2} = \lambda P_{n-1,2} + \mu_1 P_{n+1,1} + \mu_2 P_{n+1,2} \quad (n \geq 2)$

$\vdots$

(c) Truncate (cut off) the balance equations at a very large n and then solve the resulting finite system of equations numerically. The resulting approximation of the stationary distribution should be essentially exact if the probability of exceeding the truncating value of n (in the exact model) is negligible.

(d) $L = \sum_{n=1}^{\infty} n(P_{n,1}+P_{n,2})$, $W = \frac{L}{\lambda}$

$L_q = \sum_{n=1}^{\infty} (n-1)(P_{n,1}+P_{n,2})$, $W_q = \frac{L_q}{\lambda}$

(e) Because the input is Poisson, the distribution of the state of the system is the same just before an arrival and at an arbitrary point in time

$$P\{W \leq t\} = P\{W \leq t \mid \text{arrival finds state } 0\} P_0 + \sum_{n=1}^{\infty} P\{W \leq t \mid \text{arrival finds state } (n,1)\} P_{n,1} + \sum_{n=1}^{\infty} P\{W \leq t \mid \text{arrival finds state } (n,2)\} P_{n,2}$$

These 3 conditional distributions of W are, respectively (1) $\exp(\mu_1)$ (2) a convolution of $\exp(\mu_1)$ and Erlang$(1/\mu_2, n)$ and (3) Erlang$((n+1)\mu_2, n+1)$

Then,
$$P\{W \leq t\} = (1-e^{-\mu_1 t})P_0 + \sum_{n=1}^{\infty}\left[\int_0^t [1-e^{-\mu_1(t-t_1)}] \cdot \frac{\mu_2^n t_1^{n-1} e^{-\mu_2 t_1}}{(n-1)!} dt_1\right] P_{n,1} + \sum_{n=1}^{\infty}\left[\int_0^t \frac{\mu_2^{n+1} x^n e^{-\mu_2 x}}{n!} dx\right] P_{n,2}$$

15.6-23. (a) $\lambda P_0 = \mu P_1 \quad \ldots \quad (0)$

$\lambda P_0 + \mu P_2 = (\lambda+\mu) P_n \quad \ldots \quad (1)$

$\vdots$

$\lambda P_{n-1} + \mu P_{n+1} = (\lambda+\mu) P_n \quad \ldots \quad (n)$

The solution given in Sec. 16.6 is:

$P_n = (1-\rho)\rho^n$ for $n = 0, 1, 2 \ldots$

Verifying that the above satisfy the balance equations:

equation (0): $\lambda\cdot(1-\rho) = \mu(1-\rho)\cdot\rho \Leftrightarrow \lambda = \mu\cdot\rho = \mu\frac{\lambda}{\mu}$ <u>OK</u>

equation (n): $\lambda(1-\rho)\rho^{n-1} + \mu(1-\rho)\rho^{n+1} = (\lambda+\mu)(1-\rho)\rho^n$

$$\Leftrightarrow \lambda + \mu\rho^2 = (\lambda+\mu)\cdot\rho$$

$$\lambda + \frac{\lambda^2}{\mu} \qquad \frac{\lambda^2}{\mu} + \lambda \qquad \underline{\text{OK}}$$

(b) $\lambda P_0 = \mu P_1$

$\lambda P_0 + \mu P_2 = (\lambda+\mu) P_1$

$\lambda P_1 = \mu P_2$

The solution given in Sec. 16.6 is:

$$P_n = \left(\frac{1-\rho}{1-\rho^3}\right)\rho^n \quad \text{for } n = 0, 1, 2$$

Verifying:

- $\lambda\cdot\frac{1-\rho}{1-\rho^3} = \mu\cdot\frac{1-\rho}{1-\rho^3}\cdot\rho \Leftrightarrow \lambda = \mu\cdot\rho = \mu\cdot\frac{\lambda}{\mu} \quad \ldots$ <u>OK</u>
- $\lambda\cdot\frac{1-\rho}{1-\rho^3} + \mu\frac{1-\rho}{1-\rho^3}\cdot\rho^2 = (\lambda+\mu)\frac{1-\rho}{1-\rho^3}\rho \Leftrightarrow \lambda + \mu\cdot\rho^2 = (\lambda+\mu)\cdot\rho$

$$\lambda + \frac{\lambda^2}{\mu} \qquad \frac{\lambda^2}{\mu} + \lambda$$

- $\lambda\cdot\frac{1-\rho}{1-\rho^3}\cdot\rho = \mu\frac{1-\rho}{1-\rho^3}\cdot\rho^2 \Leftrightarrow \lambda\cdot\rho = \mu\rho^2 \quad \ldots$ <u>OK</u>

$$\frac{\lambda^2}{\mu} \qquad \frac{\lambda^2}{\mu}$$

(c) $2\lambda P_0 = \mu P_1$

$2\lambda P_0 + \mu P_2 = (\lambda+\mu) P_1$

$2 P_1 = \mu P_2$

The solution given in Sec. 16.6 is:

$$P_0 = \left[\sum_{n=0}^{2}\frac{2!}{(2-n)!}\left(\frac{\lambda}{\mu}\right)^n\right]^{-1} = \left[1 + 2\left(\frac{\lambda}{\mu}\right) + 2\left(\frac{\lambda}{\mu}\right)^2\right]^{-1}$$

$$P_n = \frac{2!}{(2-n)!}\left(\frac{\lambda}{\mu}\right)^n P_0 \quad \text{for } n = 1, 2$$

Verifying:

- $2\lambda/(1 + 2(\frac{\lambda}{\mu}) + 2(\frac{\lambda}{\mu})^2) = \mu\cdot 2(\frac{\lambda}{\mu})/(1 + 2(\frac{\lambda}{\mu}) + 2(\frac{\lambda}{\mu})^2)$

$\Leftrightarrow 2\lambda = \mu\cdot 2\cdot\frac{\lambda}{\mu} \quad \ldots$ <u>OK</u>

15.6-23. (continued)

- $2\lambda/(1+2(\frac{\lambda}{\mu})+2(\frac{\lambda}{\mu})^2)+\mu\cdot 2(\frac{\lambda}{\mu})^2/(1+2(\frac{\lambda}{\mu})+2(\frac{\lambda}{\mu})^2) =$
$= (\lambda+\mu)2(\lambda/\mu)/(1+2(\lambda/\mu)+2(\lambda/\mu)^2) \Leftrightarrow 2\lambda+2\mu(\frac{\lambda}{\mu})^2 = 2(\lambda+\mu)(\frac{\lambda}{\mu})$
$2(\lambda+\frac{\lambda^2}{\mu}) = 2(\frac{\lambda^2}{\mu}+\lambda) \ldots$
- $\lambda\cdot 2(\frac{\lambda}{\mu})/(1+2(\lambda/\mu)+2(\lambda/\mu)^2) = \mu\cdot 2\cdot(\lambda/\mu)^2/(1+2(\lambda/\mu)+2(\lambda/\mu)^2)$
$\Leftrightarrow 2\frac{\lambda^2}{\mu} = 2\frac{\lambda^2}{\mu}$ ... OK

15.6-24. (a) The M/M/s Model:

λ = 6	P_0 = 0.21053
μ = 4	P_1 = 0.31579
s = 3	P_2 = 0.23684
	P_3 = 0.11842
	P_4 = 0.05921
	P_5 = 0.02961
	P_6 = 0.0148
	P_7 = 0.0074
	P_8 = 0.0037
	P_9 = 0.00185
L = 1.737	P_{10} = 0.00093
	P_{11} = 0.00046
L_q = 0.237	P_{12} = 0.00023
	P_{13} = 0.00012
W = 0.289	P_{14} = 0.00006
	P_{15} = 0.00003
W_q = 0.039	P_{16} = 0.00001
	P_{17} = 0.00001
P(W > t) = 0.026, where t = 1	P_{18} = 0
	P_{19} = 0
P(W_q > t) = 0.237, where t = 0	P_{20} = 0

(b) $P\{\text{a phone is answered immediately}\} = 1 - P\{W_q > 0\} = 0.763$

Or, $= P\{\text{at least one server is free}\} = P_0 + P_1 + P_2$
$= 0.21053 + 0.31579 + 0.23684 = 0.763$

(c) $P\{n \text{ calls on hold}\} = P'_n = P_{n+3} \quad (n \geq 1)$

$P'_0 = P_0 + P_1 + P_2 + P_3 = 0.88158$

(d) The printed measures are in the next page.

$P\{\text{arriving call is lost}\}$
$= P\{\text{all three servers are busy}\}$
$= P_3 = 0.13433$

15.6-24. (continued)

Finite Queue Variation of the M/M/s Model:

$\lambda = 6$	$P_0 = 0.23881$
$\mu = 4$	$P_1 = 0.35821$
$s = 3$	$P_2 = 0.26866$
$K = 3$	$P_3 = 0.13433$
	$P_4 = 0$
$L = 1.299$	$P_5 = 0$
$L_q = 0$	$P_6 = 0$
$W = 0.25$	$P_7 = 0$
$W_q = 0$	$P_8 = 0$
	$P_9 = 0$
	$P_{10} = 0$
	$P_{11} = 0$
	$P_{12} = 0$
	$P_{13} = 0$
	$P_{14} = 0$
	$P_{15} = 0$
	$P_{16} = 0$
	$P_{17} = 0$
	$P_{18} = 0$
	$P_{19} = 0$
	$P_{20} = 0$

15.6-25. (a) This is a finite Calling Population of M/M/s Model.

Here $\lambda = 1$, $\mu = 2$, $S = 1$, $N = 3$

(b) Finite Calling Population of the M/M/s Model:

$\lambda = 1$	$P_0 = 0.21053$
$\mu = 2$	$P_1 = 0.31579$
$s = 1$	$P_2 = 0.31579$
$N = 3$	$P_3 = 0.15789$
	$P_4 = 0$
$L = 1.421$	$P_5 = 0$
$L_q = 0.632$	$P_6 = 0$
$W = 0.9$	$P_7 = 0$
$W_q = 0.4$	$P_8 = 0$
	$P_9 = 0$
	$P_{10} = 0$
	$P_{11} = 0$
	$P_{12} = 0$
	$P_{13} = 0$
	$P_{14} = 0$
	$P_{15} = 0$
	$P_{16} = 0$
	$P_{17} = 0$
	$P_{18} = 0$
	$P_{19} = 0$
	$P_{20} = 0$

15.6-26. This is a M/M/2/K queue with K = 3, $\lambda = 15$, $\mu = 15$.

(a)

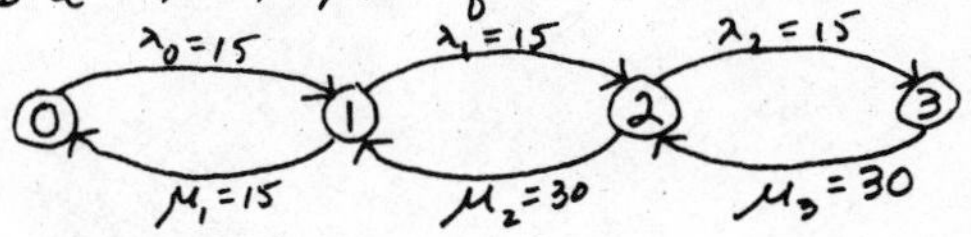

(b)

λ = 15

μ = 15

s = 2

K = 3

L = 1

L_q = 0.091

W = 0.073

W_q = 0.007

P0	=	0.36364
P1	=	0.36364
P2	=	0.18182
P3	=	0.09091
P4	=	0
P5	=	0
P6	=	0
P7	=	0
P8	=	0
P9	=	0
P10	=	0
P11	=	0
P12	=	0
P13	=	0
P14	=	0
P15	=	0
P16	=	0

So, $P\{(i)\} = P_0 + P_1 = 0.727$

$P\{(ii)\} = P_2 = 0.182$

$P\{(iii)\} = P_3 = 0.091$

15.6-27 This is a M/M/1/K queue with K = 1, 3 and 5, respectively. Also, $\lambda = 1/4$ and $\mu = 1/3$ so that $\rho = 3/4$.
The fraction of customers lost $= P_K = \frac{(1-\rho)}{(1-\rho^{K+1})} \cdot \rho^K$

(a) zero spaces : $P_1 = \frac{(1-3/4)}{(1-(3/4)^2)} \cdot (3/4) = \frac{3}{7} = .429$

(b) two spaces : $P_3 = \frac{(1-3/4)}{(1-(3/4)^4)} \cdot (3/4)^3 = \frac{27}{175} = .154$

(c) four spaces : $P_5 = \frac{(1-3/4)}{(1-(3/4)^6)} \cdot (3/4)^5 = \frac{243}{3367} = .072$

15.6-28. M/M/s/K model

$$L_q = \sum_{n=s}^{\infty} (n-s) P_n =$$

$$= \sum_{n=s}^{K} (n-s) \frac{(\lambda/\mu)^n}{s!\, s^{n-s}} P_0$$

$$= \frac{P_0 (\lambda/\mu)^{s+1}}{s!\, s} \sum_{n=s}^{K} (n-s) \left(\frac{\lambda}{s\mu}\right)^{n-s-1} =$$

$$= \frac{P_0 (\lambda/\mu)^s \rho}{s!} \sum_{j=0}^{K-s} j \rho^{j-1} =$$

$$= \frac{P_0 (\lambda/\mu)^s \rho}{s!} \sum_{j=0}^{K-s} \frac{d(\rho^j)}{d\rho} =$$

15.6-28 (continued)

$$= \frac{P_0 (\lambda/\mu)^s \rho}{s!} \frac{d}{d\rho}\left[\sum_{j=0}^{K-s} \rho^j\right] =$$

$$= \frac{P_0 (\lambda/\mu)^s \rho}{s!} \frac{d}{d\rho}\left(\frac{1-\rho^{K-s+1}}{1-\rho}\right) =$$

$$= \frac{P_0 (\lambda/\mu)^s \rho}{s!} \left[\frac{1-\rho^{K-s} - (K-s)\rho^{K-s}(1-\rho)}{(1-\rho)^2}\right]$$

15.6-29.

$\mathcal{W}$ and $\mathcal{W}_q$ represent the waiting times of arriving customers who <u>enter</u> the system. The probability that such a customer finds n customers already there is:

$$P\{n \text{ customers in system} | \text{system not full}\} = \begin{cases} \frac{P_n}{1-P_K} & 0 \le n \le K-1 \\ 0 & n = K \end{cases}$$

And so:

(a) $P\{\mathcal{W} > t\} = \frac{1}{1-P_K} \sum_{n=0}^{K-1} P_n P\{S_{n+1} > t\}$

(b) $P\{\mathcal{W}_q > t\} = \frac{1}{1-P_K} \sum_{n=0}^{K-1} P_n P\{S_n > t\}$

15.6-30. (a) Finite Calling Population of the M/M/s Model:

λ = 0.111		P0	= 0.4929
		P1	= 0.3286
μ = 0.5		P2	= 0.14604
		P3	= 0.03245
s = 1		P4	= 0
		P5	= 0
N = 3		P6	= 0
		P7	= 0
		P8	= 0
		P9	= 0
L = 0.718		P10	= 0
		P11	= 0
Lq= 0.211		P12	= 0
		P13	= 0
W = 2.832		P14	= 0
		P15	= 0
Wq= 0.832		P16	= 0

$E(\#\text{ of machines not running}) = P_1 + 2P_2 + 3P_3 = 0.718$

(b) (i) This is a M/M/1 queue with $\lambda = 1/3$ and $\mu = 1/2$

So $P_0 = 1 - \rho = 1/3 = .333$

$P_1 = (1-\rho)\rho = 2/9 = .222$

$P_2 = (1-\rho)\rho^2 = 4/27 = .148$

$P_3 = (1-\rho)\rho^3 = 8/81 = .099$

$L = \lambda/(\mu-\lambda) = \rho/(1-\rho) = 2$

(ii) This is a M/M/1/K queue with $K=3, \lambda = 1/3, \mu = 1/2$

Thus, $P_0 = \frac{1-\rho}{1-\rho^{K+1}} = \frac{1-2/3}{1-(2/3)^4} = \frac{27}{65} = .415$

$P_1 = \rho P_0 = \frac{2}{3} \cdot \frac{27}{65} = \frac{18}{65} = .277$

$P_2 = \rho^2 P_0 = \frac{4}{9} \cdot \frac{27}{65} = \frac{12}{65} = .185$

$P_3 = \rho^3 P_0 = \frac{8}{27} \cdot \frac{27}{65} = \frac{8}{65} = .123$

$L = \frac{\rho}{1-\rho} - \frac{(K+1)\rho^{K+1}}{1-\rho^{K+1}} = \frac{66}{65} = 1.015$

Summarizing,

Part	P_0	P_1	P_2	P_3	L
(a)	.493	.329	.146	.032	.718
(b)(i)	.333	.222	.148	.099	2.000
(ii)	.415	.277	.185	.123	1.015

(C) Finite Calling Population of the M/M/s Model:

λ = 0.111

μ = 0.5

s = 2

N = 3

L = 0.553

Lq= 0.009

W = 2.033

Wq= 0.033

P0 = 0.54607
P1 = 0.36404
P2 = 0.0809
P3 = 0.00899
P4 = 0
P5 = 0
P6 = 0
P7 = 0
P8 = 0
P9 = 0
P10 = 0
P11 = 0
P12 = 0
P13 = 0
P14 = 0
P15 = 0
P16 = 0

E(# of machines not running) = $P_1 + 2P_2 + 3P_3 = 0.553$

15.6-31. It is a finite calling population of M/M/1 model with $N=3$.

(a) Let N = # of machines assigned to an operator

L = expected number of machines in service

It is desired $L \le 0.11N = (1-0.89)N$, and

N	L	Is $L \le 0.11N$
1	0.91	yes
2	0.197	yes
3	0.321	yes
4	0.461	No

So, the operator can be assigned at most 3 machines

(b) For 3-machine case, we have

Finite Calling Population of the M/M/s Model:

λ = 0.4	P0 = 0.73206
	P1 = 0.21962
μ = 4	P2 = 0.04392
	P3 = 0.00439
s = 1	P4 = 0
	P5 = 0
N = 3	P6 = 0
	P7 = 0
	P8 = 0
	P9 = 0
L = 0.321	P10 = 0
	P11 = 0
Lq= 0.053	P12 = 0
	P13 = 0
W = 0.299	P14 = 0
	P15 = 0
Wq= 0.049	P16 = 0

E[fraction of time operator will be busy] $= 1 - P_0 = 0.268$

15.6-32. (a) state is (n,i) where n is the number of failed machines $(n = 0,1,2,3)$ and i is the stage of service (which operation) for the machine under repair ($i = 0$ if no machines are failed), 1, 2).

(b)

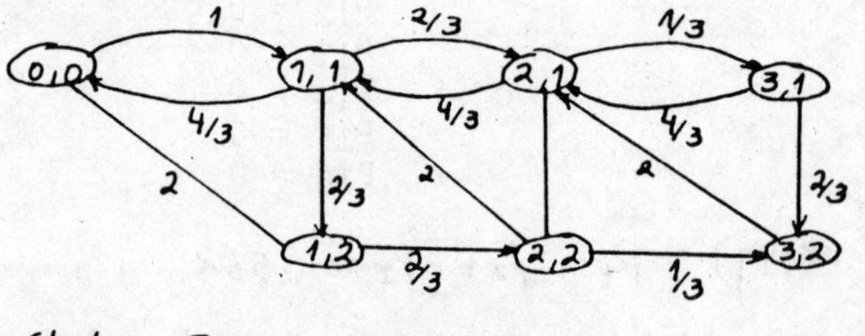

(c)

State	Rate in = Rate out
(0,0)	$4/3\, P_{1,1} + 2\, P_{1,2} = P_{0,0}$
(1,1)	$P_{0,0} + 4/3\, P_{2,1} + 2\, P_{2,2} = (4/3 + 2/3 + 2/3)\, P_{1,1}$
(2,1)	$2/3\, P_{1,1} + 4/3\, P_{3,1} + 2\, P_{3,2} = (4/3 + 2/3 + 1/3)\, P_{2,1}$
(3,1)	$1/3\, P_{2,1} = (4/3 + 2/3)\, P_{3,1}$
(1,2)	$2/3\, P_{1,1} = (2 + 2/3)\, P_{1,2}$
(2,2)	$2/3\,(P_{1,2} + P_{2,1}) = (2 + 1/3)\, P_{2,2}$
(3,2)	$1/3\, P_{2,2} + 2/3\, P_{3,1} = 2\, P_{3,2}$

15.6-33.

$\mu_1 = 1/8$

(a) $\mu_4 = 1/4 = 4^c(1/8) \Rightarrow 2 = 4^c \Rightarrow c = 1/2$

(b) $\mu_4 = 1/5 = 4^c(1/8) \Rightarrow 8/5 = 4^c \Rightarrow c = \dfrac{\ln(8/5)}{\ln 4} = .339$

15.6-34. Using the L's of figure 16.10 and those calculated in problem 9,

$\frac{\lambda_0}{s\mu_1}$ \ c		.20	.40	.60
.50	s = 1	.7800	.6500	.6000
	s = 2	.9000	.8475	.7875
.90	s = 1	.2444	.1667	.1333
	s = 2	.3464	.2624	.2257
.99	s = 1	.0288	.0177	.0139
	s = 2	.0454	.0303	. 252

15.7-1. (a) (i) exponential: $W_q = \frac{\lambda}{\mu(\mu-\lambda)}$

(ii) constant: $W_q = \frac{1}{2} \cdot \frac{\lambda}{\mu(\mu-\lambda)}$

(iii) Erlang: $\sigma = \frac{1}{2}\left(0 + \frac{1}{\mu}\right) = \frac{1}{2\mu} \Rightarrow \sigma^2 = \frac{1}{4\mu^2} \Rightarrow k = 4$

$$W_q = \frac{1+4}{8} \cdot \frac{\lambda}{\mu(\mu-\lambda)} = \frac{5}{8}\,\frac{\lambda}{\mu(\mu-\lambda)}$$

So $W_q^{exp} = 2\,W_q^{c} = (8/5)\,W_q^{Erlang}$

(b) Let B = 1, (1/2) and (5/8) when the distribution is exponential, constant or Erlang, respectively.
Now $\lambda^{(2)} = 2\lambda^{(1)}$ and $\mu^{(2)} = 2\mu^{(1)}$

$$W_q^{(2)} = B\left[\frac{2\lambda^{(1)}}{2\mu^{(1)}(2\mu^{(1)} - 2\lambda^{(1)})}\right] = \frac{W_q^{(1)}}{2}$$

$$L_q^{(2)} = \lambda^{(2)} W_q^{(2)} = 2\lambda^{(1)} W_q^{(1)}/2 = \lambda^{(1)} W_q^{(1)} = L_q^{(1)}$$

So the waiting time is cut in half while the queue lenght is unchanged.

15.7-2. For M/G/1, $L = \rho + \frac{\rho^2 + \lambda^2\sigma_s^2}{2(1-\rho)}$, $L_q = \frac{\rho^2 + \lambda^2\sigma_s^2}{2(1-\rho)}$ $W = L/\lambda$, $W_q = \frac{L_q}{\lambda}$

(a) False. when L increases, W also increases.

(b) False. when μ and σ^2 are small, L_q is not necessarily small.

(c) True. For exponential service time, $L_q = \frac{2\rho^2}{2(1-\rho)}$ since $\sigma_s^2 = 1/\mu^2$
For constant service time, $L_q = \frac{\rho^2}{2(1-\rho)}$ since $\sigma_s^2 = 0$

(d) False. We can easily find distribution with $\sigma_s^2 > \frac{1}{\mu^2}$

15.7-3. (a) Poisson Input
Erlang service with $\mu = 1/12$ and $k = 4$

(b) Poisson Input
General service with mean $3 + 9 = 12$ and
variance $\frac{1}{(k\mu_1^2)} + \frac{1}{(k\mu_2^2)} = 30$

15.7-4. Under the current policy, the queueing system has ..... input with $\lambda = 1$ and exponential service with $\mu = 2$. Under the proposal, the queueing system would have exponential Poisson input with $\lambda = 1/4$ and Erlang service with $\mu = 1/2$ and $K = 4$. On the basis of the information provided, there is no apparent difference in the service cost of the two alternatives. Therefore, any differences in cost must be due to differences in waiting costs of the planes. Let C denote the cost per day of an idle airplane. Then, as explained in Section 17.3 of Chapter 17, CL is the expected waiting costs per day for both alternatives. Thus a comparison of the two alternatives reduces to a Comparison of their respective values for L.

For the current policy, $L = \frac{\lambda}{\mu - \lambda} = \frac{1}{2-1} = 1$

For the proposal, $L = \left(\frac{K+1}{2K}\right)\left(\frac{\lambda^2}{\mu(\mu-\lambda)}\right) + \frac{\lambda}{\mu} = \frac{13}{16}$

Hence the proposal should be adopted.

15.7-5. (a)

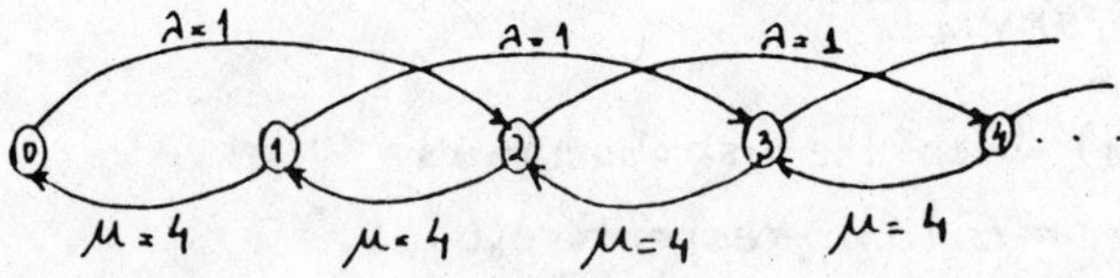

$\mu P_1 = \lambda P_0$

$\mu P_2 = (\lambda + \mu) P_1$

$\lambda P_0 + \mu P_3 = (\lambda + \mu) P_2$

$\vdots$

$\lambda P_{n-2} + \mu P_{n+1} = (\lambda + \mu) P_n$

(b) Poisson input with $\lambda = 1$ and Erlang Service with $\mu = 4/2 = 2$ and $K = 2$.

$W = \left(\frac{1+K}{2K}\right)\frac{\lambda}{\mu(\mu-\lambda)} + \frac{1}{\mu} = \frac{7}{8}$

15.7-6 (a) Let the state be (n,s) where
n = # airplanes at the base
s = stage of service of the airplane being overhauled

(b) The rate diagram is:

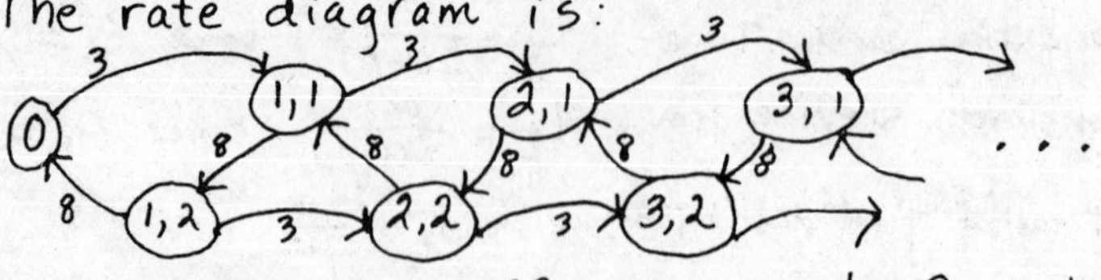

(c) $L_q = \frac{27}{16}$ airplanes, $L = \frac{39}{16}$ airplanes, $W_q = \frac{9}{16}$ weeks, $W = \frac{13}{16}$ weeks

15.7-7. For the current arrangement, $\lambda = 24$ and $\mu = 30 \Rightarrow \rho = .8$

For the proposal, $\lambda = 48$, $\mu = 30$ and $s = 2 \Rightarrow \rho = .8$

Model	Current			Proposal	
	L at each crib	Total L	$W = L/\lambda$	L	$W = L/\lambda$
Figure 16.7	4.0	8.0	0.167	4.444	0.093
Figure 16.11	2.4	4.8	0.098	3.1	0.064
Figure 16.13	3.2	6.4	0.133	3.7	0.078
Figure 16.14	2.2	4.4	0.091	2.8	0.058

15.7-8. (a) Let state (i,j) denote i calling units in the system, with the calling unit being served at the jth stage of his service. Then the state space is: $\{(0,0),(1,2),(1,1),(2,2),(2,1)\}$. The rate diagram is:

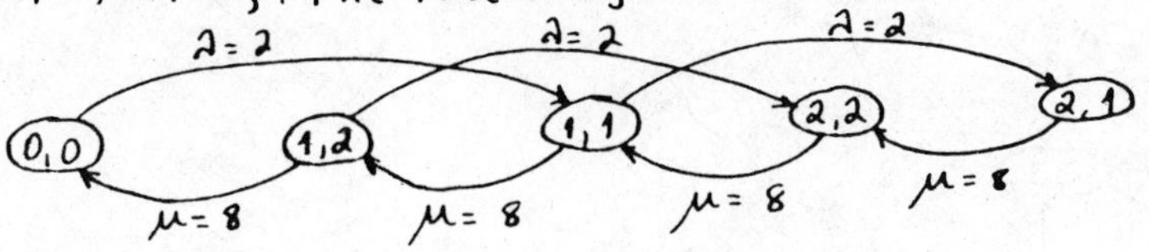

Note this analysis is possible because an Erlang distribution with $1/\mu = 1/4$ and $k=2$ is equivalent to the sum of two independent exponentials with parameter $1/\mu = 1/8$.

Hence, the steady state equations are:

$8\,P_{1,2} = 2\,P_{0,0}$

$8\,P_{1,1} = 10\,P_{1,2}$

$2\,P_{0,0} + 8\,P_{2,2} = 10\,P_{1,1}$

$2\,P_{1,2} + 8\,P_{2,1} = 8\,P_{2,2}$

$2\,P_{1,1} = 8\,P_{2,1}$

(b) The solution to these equations is:

$(P_{0,0};\ P_{1,2};\ P_{1,1};\ P_{2,2};\ P_{2,1}) = (64/114,\ 16/114,\ 20/114,\ 9/114,\ 5/114)$

Hence $P_0 = \frac{64}{114} = .561$

$P_1 = \frac{16+20}{114} = .316$

$P_2 = \frac{9+5}{114} = .123$

$L = \frac{18+14}{52} = .561$

(c) If the service time is exponential, then the system is an M/M/1 queue limited to $K=2$ and with $\lambda = 2$ and $\mu = 4$. So,

$P_0 = \frac{1-\rho}{1-\rho^{K+1}} = \frac{(1/2)}{(1-1/8)} = \frac{4}{7} = .571$

$P_1 = \left(\frac{1}{2}\right) P_0 = \frac{2}{7} = .286$

$P_2 = \left(\frac{1}{2}\right)^2 P_0 = \frac{1}{7} = .143$

$L = \frac{2+2}{7} = \frac{4}{7} = .571$

15.7-9. state is (n, i) where n is the number of customers in the system $(n \geq 1)$ and i is the number of completed arrival stages for currently arriving customer $(i = 0, 1)$.

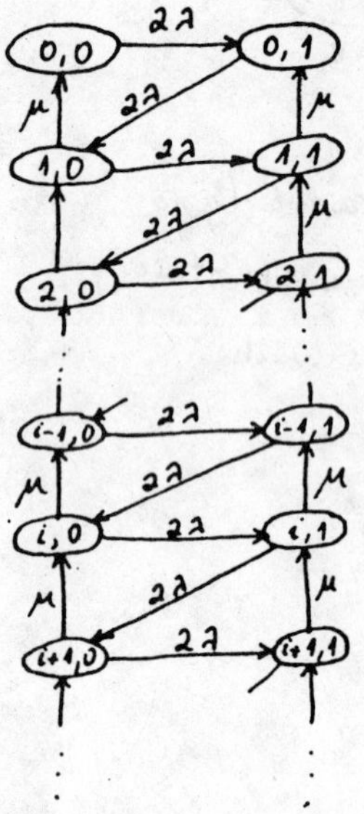

15.7-10. (a) Let T be the repair time.

$$E(T) = E(T \mid \text{minor repair needed}) \cdot (0.9) + E(T \mid \text{major repair needed}) \cdot (0.1) = \tfrac{1}{2}(0.9) + 5(0.1) = .95 \text{ hours}$$

Now let X be a binary random variable with $P(X=1) = p = 0.9$ and $P(X=0) = q = 0.1$, Y_i be an exponential random variable with mean $1/\lambda_i$ $(i = 1, 2)$, with $\frac{1}{\lambda_1} = \frac{1}{2}$ and $\frac{1}{\lambda_2} = 5$. Then we may express T as follows:

$T = Y_1 \cdot X + Y_2(1-X)$ where X, Y_1, Y_2 are independent

To calculate $\sigma^2 = Var(T)$ we use the formula:

$$Var(T) = E(Var(T \mid X)) + Var(E(T \mid X))$$

$$Var(T \mid X) = Var(Y_1) \cdot X + Var(Y_2)(1-X) = (1/\lambda_1^2)X + (1/\lambda_2^2)(1-X)$$

$$\therefore E(Var(T \mid X)) = p/\lambda_1^2 + q/\lambda_2^2$$

$$E(T \mid X) = E(Y_1) \cdot X + E(Y_2) \cdot (1-X) = \frac{1}{\lambda_1} \cdot X + \frac{1}{\lambda_2} \cdot (1-X) = \frac{1}{\lambda_2} + \left(\frac{1}{\lambda_1} - \frac{1}{\lambda_2}\right) X$$

$$\therefore Var(E(T \mid X)) = \left(\frac{1}{\lambda_1} - \frac{1}{\lambda_2}\right)^2 \cdot Var X = \left(\frac{1}{\lambda_1} - \frac{1}{\lambda_2}\right)^2 pq$$

15.7-10. (continued)

Therefore,

$$Var(T) = \frac{p}{\lambda_1^2} + \frac{q}{\lambda_2^2} + \left(\frac{1}{\lambda_1} - \frac{1}{\lambda_2}\right)^2 pq = 4.5475$$

Now we can see that T has a variance much bigger than that of an exponential random variable with same mean, which would be $(.95)^2 = .9025$

(b) $\left.\begin{array}{l}\mu = \frac{1}{.95} \\ \lambda = 1\end{array}\right\} \Rightarrow \rho = .95$

Since this is an M/G/1 queue we can apply the following formulas:

$P_0 = 1 - \rho = 1. - .95 = .05$

$L_q = \frac{\lambda^2 \sigma^2 + \rho^2}{2(1-\rho)} = \frac{(4.5475)^2 + (.95)^2}{2 \times .05} = 215.82$

$L = \rho + L_q = 216.77$

$W_q = \frac{L_q}{\lambda} = 215.82$

$W = W_q + \frac{1}{\mu} = 216.77$

(c) W | major repair needed = $W_q + 5 = 220.82$

W | minor repair needed = $W_q + .5 = 216.32$

$L_{\text{major repair machines}} = (\lambda)(0.1)(220.82) = 22.082$

$L_{\text{minor repair machines}} = (\lambda)(0.9)(216.32) = 194.69$

(d) state is (n, i) where n is the number of failed machines and i is the type of repair being done on machine under repair ($i = 1$ denotes minor repair and $i = 2$ denotes major repair).

(e)

15.7-11. $\{X_n\}$ is an imbedded Markov chain with states.

And $X_{n+1} = \begin{cases} X_n - 1 + A_{n+1} & X_n \geq 1 \\ A_{n+1} & X_n = 0 \end{cases}$ and $X_{n+1} \leq 3$

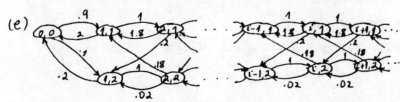

15.7-11. (continued)

A_{n+1} is the number of arrivals in the 10 minutes.

$$Pr(A=n) = \frac{e^{-\lambda t}(\lambda t)^n}{n!} = a_n, \text{ and } \lambda t = \frac{60}{50}\cdot\frac{10}{60} = 0.2$$

So, the transition matrix is

$$P = \begin{bmatrix} a_0 & a_1 & a_2 & 1-a_0-a_1-a_2 \\ a_0 & a_1 & a_2 & 1-a_0-a_1-a_2 \\ 0 & a_0 & a_1 & 1-a_0-a_1 \\ 0 & 0 & a_0 & 1-a_0 \end{bmatrix}$$

$$= \begin{bmatrix} 0.819 & 0.164 & 0.016 & 0.001 \\ 0.819 & 0.164 & 0.016 & 0.001 \\ 0 & 0.819 & 0.164 & 0.017 \\ 0 & 0 & 0.819 & 0.181 \end{bmatrix}$$

b) Run OR courseware, we get

$p_0 = 0.801$, $p_1 = 0.177$, $p_2 = 0.02$, $p_3 = 0.002$

c) $L = p_1 + 2p_2 + 3p_3 = 0.223$

In M/D/1 model, $L^\infty = \rho + \frac{\rho^2}{2(1-\rho)} = 0.2 + \frac{0.04}{2(1-0.2)} = 0.225$

So, $L^\infty > L$

15.8-1.

	W_{q1}	L_{q1}	W_1	L_1	W_{q2}	L_{q2}	W_2	L_2
$s=1$, $\mu=10$	.133	.533	.233	.933	.667	2.667	.767	3.067
$s=2$, $\mu=5$	.119	.474	.319	1.274	.593	2.370	.793	3.170

If W_1 is the primary concern, one should choose the first alternative (one fast server). On the other hand, if W_{q1} is the primary concern, one should choose the second alternative (two slow servers).

15.8-2.

$\lambda = 8$, $\lambda_1 = 2$, $\lambda_2 = 4$, $\lambda_3 = 2$, $\mu = 10$

(a) First come, first served : $W = \frac{1}{\mu-\lambda} = \frac{1}{2}$ days

(b) Nonpreemptive:

$A = \frac{\mu^2}{\lambda} = \frac{25}{2}$

$B_1 = 1 - (\lambda_1/\mu) = 4/5$

$B_2 = 1 - (\lambda_1+\lambda_2)/\mu = 2/5$

$B_3 = 1 - \lambda/\mu = 1/5$

15.8-2. (continued)

so $W_1 = \frac{1}{AB_1} + \frac{1}{\mu} = \frac{1}{5} = .20$ days

$W_2 = \frac{1}{AB_1B_2} + \frac{1}{\mu} = \frac{7}{20} = .35$ days

$W_3 = \frac{1}{AB_2B_3} + \frac{1}{\mu} = \frac{11}{10} = 1.1$ days

(c) Preemptive:

$W_1 = \frac{1/\mu}{B_1} = \frac{1}{8} = .125$ days

$W_2 = \frac{1/\mu}{B_1B_2} = \frac{5}{16} = .3125$ days

$W_3 = \frac{1/\mu}{B_2B_3} = \frac{5}{4} = 1.25$ days

15.8-3. $\lambda_1 = 0.1,\ \lambda_2 = 0.4,\ \lambda_3 = 1.5,\ \lambda = \sum_{i=1}^{3} \lambda_i = 2,\ \mu = 3$

	Preemptive Priorities		Nonpreemptive Priorities	
	s = 1	s = 2	s = 1	s = 2
A	...	...	4.5	36
B_1	.967	...	.967	.983
B_2	.833	...	.833	.917
B_3	.333	...	.333	.667
$W_1 - \frac{1}{\mu}$	.011	.00009	.230	.028
$W_2 - \frac{1}{\mu}$	.080	.00289	.276	.031
$W_3 - \frac{1}{\mu}$	.867	.05493	.800	.045

15.8-4. a) The expected number of customers wouldn't change since customers of both types have exactly same arrival pattern and service times. The change of the prority wouldn't affect the total service rate from the server's view and thus the total queue size stays the same

b) Run OR courseware, for Nonpreemptive Prority-Disciplie Queueing model, we have

$\mu = 6$ $\lambda_1 = 5$, $\lambda_2 = 5$ $L_1 = 1.37446$, $L_2 = 4.08009$

$s = 2$

$N = 2$ $L_p = L_1 + L_2 = 5.45455$

$W_1 = 0.27489$ $(W_q)_1 = 0.10823$

$W_2 = 0.81602$ $(W_q)_2 = 0.64935$

for M/M/2 queueing system,

$\lambda = 10$ $L = 5.455$

$\mu = 6$ $L_q = 3.788$ Thus, $L_p = L$.

$s = 2$ $W = 0.545$

15.8-5.

Let state (i,j) denote i jobs of high priority and j jobs of low priority.

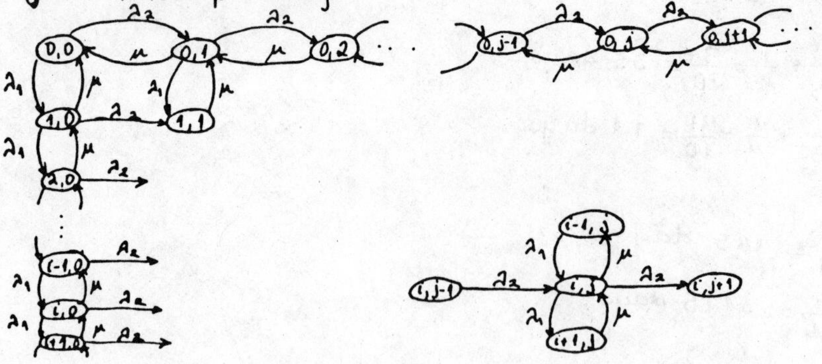

state	Rate in = Rate out
$(0,0)$	$\mu(P_{1,0}+P_{0,1}) = (\lambda_1+\lambda_2)P_{0,0}$
$(i,0)$ for $i\geq 1$	$\mu P_{i+1,0} + \lambda_1 P_{i-1,0} = (\mu+\lambda_1+\lambda_2)P_{i,0}$
$(0,j)$ for $j\geq 1$	$\mu(P_{1,j}+P_{0,j+1}) + \lambda_2 P_{0,j-1} = (\mu+\lambda_1+\lambda_2)P_{0,j}$
(i,j) for $i,j\geq 1$	$\mu P_{i+1,j} + \lambda_1 P_{i-1,j} + \lambda_2 P_{i,j-1} = (\mu+\lambda_1+\lambda_2)P_{i,j}$

15.9-1. (a) Let the state be n_1 = number of type 1 customers in the system
Then the rate diagram for type 1 customers is:

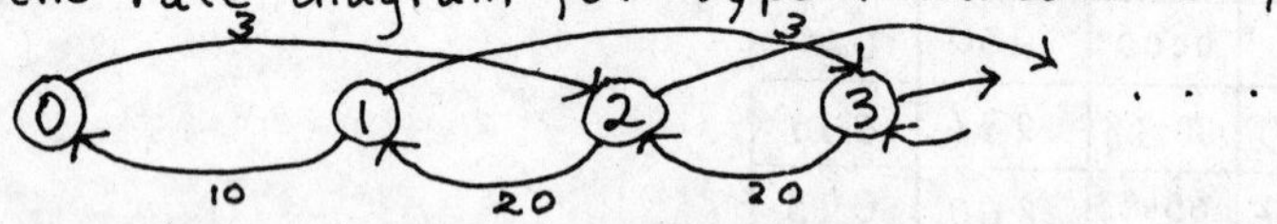

(b) Let the state be n = number of customers in the system
Then the rate diagram for the total number of customers is:

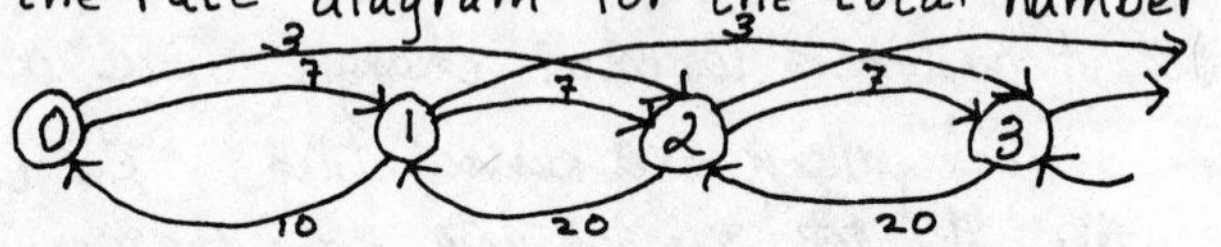

(c) Let the state be (n_1, n_2) where
n_1 = number of type 1 customers in the system
n_2 = number of type 2 customers in the system
Then the rate diagram is:

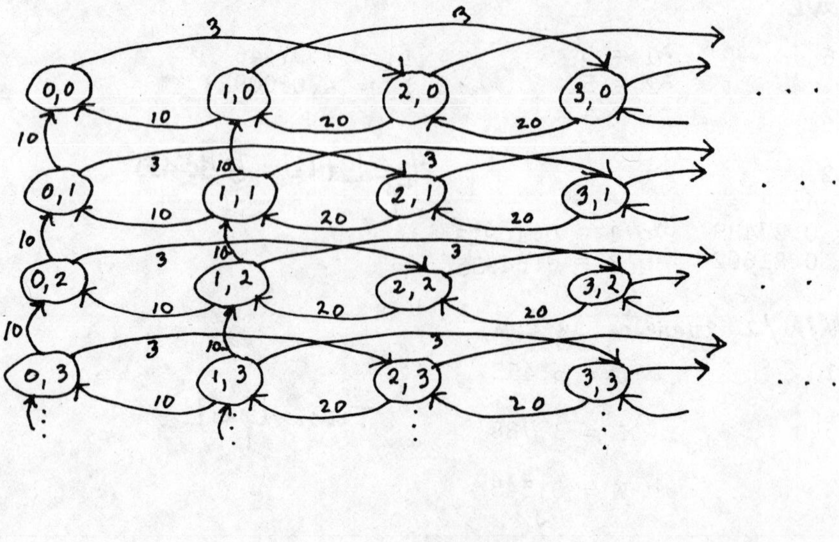

15.9-2. (a) $P_{n_1} = (\frac{1}{2})(\frac{1}{2})^{n_1}$

$P_{n_2} = (\frac{1}{3})(\frac{2}{3})^{n_2}$

$P\{(N_1, N_2) = (n_1, n_2)\} = P_{n_1} P_{n_2} = (\frac{1}{6})(\frac{1}{2})^{n_1}(\frac{2}{3})^{n_2}$

(b) $P\{(N_1, N_2) = (0,0)\} = \frac{1}{6}$

(c) $L = L_1 + L_2 = 1 + 2 = 3$

$W = W_1 + W_2 = \frac{1}{10} + \frac{2}{10} = .3$ hour = 18 minutes

15.9-3.

Facility j	a_j	p_{ij}: j=1	j=2	j=3	...	j=m-1	j=m
j=1	λ	0	1	0	...	0	0
j=2	0	0	0	1	...	0	0
⋮		⋮	⋮	⋮	...	⋮	⋮
j=m-1	0	0	0	0	...	0	1
j=m	0	0	0	0	...	0	0

15.9-4. (a)

Facility j	aj	Pij: i = 1	i = 2	i = 3
j = 1	10	0	0.3	0.4
j = 2	15	0.5	0	0.5
j = 3	3	0.3	0.2	0

Results

$\lambda_1 = 30$
$\lambda_2 = 40$
$\lambda_3 = 20$

(b) $P_{n_1} = (\frac{1}{4})(\frac{3}{4})^{n_1}$

$P_{n_2} = (\frac{1}{5})(\frac{4}{5})^{n_2}$

$P_{n_3} = (\frac{1}{3})(\frac{2}{3})^{n_3}$

$P\{(N_1, N_2, N_3) = (n_1, n_2, n_3)\} = (\frac{1}{60})(\frac{3}{4})^{n_1}(\frac{4}{5})^{n_2}(\frac{2}{3})^{n_3}$

(c) $P = (P_0 + P_1)(P_0 + P_1)(P_0 + P_1)$ (facility 1, facility 2, facility 3)

$= (\frac{7}{16})(\frac{9}{25})(\frac{5}{9}) = \frac{7}{80} = 0.088$

(d) $L = L_1 + L_2 + L_3 = 3 + 4 + 2 = 9$

(e) $W = \frac{L}{a_1 + a_2 + a_3} = \frac{9}{28} = 0.321$

CASE PROBLEM

(a) Status quo: At machine, it is M/M/10 queue with $\lambda = 70$, $\mu = 10$.

Run OR courseware, $L_m = 7.517$

At the inspection station, it is a $M/E_{25}/1$ queue

where $L_{in} = \frac{1+K}{2K} \cdot \frac{\lambda^2}{\mu(\mu-\lambda)} + \frac{\lambda}{\mu} = 4.06$ since in a tandem queueing network like this, the input rate for inspection station is the same as the input rate for the machines. So $\lambda = 70$, $\mu = 80$.

Now, inventory cost $= (7.517 + 4.06) \times 5 = 57.885$ dollars per hour

machine cost $= 7 \times 10 = 70$ \$ per hour

inspector cost $= 14$ \$ per hour

Then, total cost $= 57.885 + 70 + 14 = 141.885$ \$ per hour

(b) Proposal 1: For the machines, $\mu = 60/7$, $\lambda = 70$, then

$L_m = 10.16$

On the other hand, the input rate to inspection hasn't changed at all. So, $L_{in} = 4.06$

Then, inventory cost $= (10.16 + 4.06) \times 5 = 71.1$ \$ / hour

machine cost $= 6.5 \times 10 = 65$ \$ / hour

inspector cost $= 14$ \$ /per hour

So, total cost $= 71.1 + 65 + 14 = 150.1$ \$ > 141.885 \$

Proposal 1 is worse than status quo and shouldn't be adoped. The main reason is that slowing down machines won't change work-in-process for the inspection station

(c) Proposal 2: For the inspector, $\lambda = 70$, $\mu = 83.3$, $K = 2$.

$$L_{in} = \frac{3}{4} \cdot \frac{\lambda^2}{\mu(\mu-\lambda)} + \frac{\lambda}{\mu} = 4.15$$

such that inventory cost $= (4.15 + 7.517) \times 5 = 58.3$ /hour

machine cost $= 70$ \$ / hour

inspector cost $= 16$ \$ / hour

So, total cost $= 70 + 16 + 58.3 = 144.3$ /hour

Obviously, proposal 2 is not better This is due to the variability of inspection time.

d) To reduce the average level of in-process inventory, the most effective approach is to reduce the processing times. Let's reduce the processing times of the machines to the minimum 5 minutes.

Now, $\lambda = 70$, $\mu = 12$, $s = 10$, OR courseware gives us $L = 5.955$
We should still use the slower inspector with less variability such that our total cost is

$$(5.955 + 4.06) \times 5 + 7.5 \times 10 + 14 = 139.1 \$ / \text{hour}$$

which is better that status quo.

Chapter 16
The Application of Queueing Theory

16.2-1.

	Service Costs	Waiting Costs
(a)	Salaries of checkers, cost of cash registers	Lost profit from lost business
(b)	Salaries of firemen, cost of fire trucks	Expected $ destruction due to waiting
(c)	Salaries of toll-takers, cost of constructing toll lane	Social cost of waiting by commuters
(d)	Salaries of repairpersons, cost of tools	Lost profit from lost business
(e)	Salaries of Longshoremen, cost of equipment	Lost profit from ships not loaded or unloaded
(f)	Salary of an operator as a function of their experience	Lost profit from lost productivity of unused machines
(g)	Salaries of operators, cost of equipment	Lost profit due to lost productivity of materials not handled
(h)	Salaries of plumbers, cost of tools	Lost profit from lost business
(i)	Salaries of employees, cost of equipment	Lost profit from lost business
(j)	Salaries of typists, cost of typewriters	Lost profit due to typing jobs being unfinished

16-3-1.

$s = 1, \lambda = 2, \mu = 4 \Rightarrow \rho = 1/2 \Rightarrow P_n = (1/2)^{n+1}$ and $f_n(t) = 2e^{-2t}$

The answers to (a) through (d) are based on the following identities:

(i) $$\sum_{n=0}^{\infty} n\,x^n = \frac{x}{(1-x)^2} \qquad \text{if } |x|<1$$

(ii) $$\sum_{n=0}^{\infty} n^2\,x^n = \frac{2x^2}{(1-x)^3} + \frac{x}{(1-x)^2} \qquad \text{if } |x|<1$$

(iii) $$\sum_{n=0}^{\infty} n^3\,x^n = \frac{6x^3}{(1-x)^4} + \frac{6x^2}{(1-x)^3} + \frac{x}{(1-x)^2} \qquad \text{if } |x|<1$$

(iv) $$\int_0^b x\,e^{-\alpha x}\,dx = \frac{1}{\alpha^2}\left(1 - e^{-\alpha b} - \alpha b\,e^{-\alpha b}\right)$$

(v) $$\int_0^\infty x\,e^{-\alpha x}\,dx = \frac{1}{\alpha^2}$$

(vi) $$\int_0^\infty x^2\,e^{-\alpha x}\,dx = \frac{b^2}{\alpha}e^{-\alpha b} + \frac{2b}{\alpha^2}e^{-\alpha b} + \frac{2}{\alpha^3}e^{-\alpha b}$$

(vii) $$\int_0^\infty x^3\,e^{-\alpha x}\,dx = \frac{6}{\alpha^4}$$

(a) $$E[WC] = \sum_{n=0}^{\infty}(10n + 2n^2)P_n = 10\sum_{n=0}^{\infty} n\left(\frac{1}{2}\right)^{n+1} + 2\sum_{n=0}^{\infty} n^2\left(\frac{1}{2}\right)^{n+1}$$

$$= 5\sum_{n=0}^{\infty} n\left(\frac{1}{2}\right)^{n} + \sum_{n=0}^{\infty} n^2\left(\frac{1}{2}\right)^{n}$$

16.3-1. (continued)

$$= 5\left(\frac{\frac{1}{2}}{(1-\frac{1}{2})^2}\right) + \left(\frac{2\left(\frac{1}{2}\right)^2}{(1-\frac{1}{2})^3} + \frac{\frac{1}{2}}{(1-\frac{1}{2})^2}\right) \quad \text{by (i) and (ii)}$$

$$= 16$$

(b)

$$E[WC] = \lambda E[h(w)] = 2\int_0^{\infty} (25w + w^3)(2e^{-2w})\,dw$$

$$= 100\int_0^{\infty} w e^{-2w}\,dw + 4\int_0^{\infty} w^3 e^{-2w}\,dw \quad = \text{by (v) and (vii)}$$

$$= 100 . \frac{1}{2^2} + 4 . \frac{6}{2^4} = 26.5$$

16.3-2 (a)

$$E[WC] = \sum_{n=0}^{2} 10\,n\left(\frac{1}{2}\right)^{n+1} + \sum_{n=3}^{5} 6\,n^2\left(\frac{1}{2}\right)^{n+1} + \sum_{n=6}^{\infty} n^3\left(\frac{1}{2}\right)^{n+1}$$

$$= 10\left(\frac{1}{4}\right) + 20\left(\frac{1}{8}\right) + 54\left(\frac{1}{16}\right) + 96\left(\frac{1}{32}\right) + 150\left(\frac{1}{64}\right) + \sum_{n=6}^{\infty} n^3\left(\frac{1}{2}\right)^{n+1}$$

$$= 20 + \frac{419}{128} = 23.273$$

(b)

$$E[WC] = 2\int_0^1 w(2e^{-2w}\,dw + 2\int_1^{\infty} w^2(2e^{-2w})\,dw$$

$$= 4\left[\frac{1}{2^2}(1 - e^{-2} - 2e^{-2})\right] + 4\left[\frac{e^{-2}}{2} + \frac{2e^{-2}}{2^2} + \frac{2e^{-2}}{2^3}\right]$$

$$= 1 - 3e^{-2} + 5e^{-2} = 1 + 2e^{-2} = 1.271$$

16.4-1

$$\lambda = 4,\ \mu = 5,\ c_s = 20 \text{ and } g(n) = \begin{cases} 0 & \text{for } N = 0 \\ 120 & \text{for } N = 1 \\ 120 + 180(N-1) & \text{for } N \geq 2 \end{cases}$$

$$E[WC] = \sum_{n=0}^{\infty} g(n)P_n = 120\sum_{n=1}^{\infty} P_n + 180\sum_{n=2}^{\infty} N \cdot P_n - 180\sum_{n=2}^{\infty} P_n$$

$$= 120(1 - P_0) + 180[L - P_1] - 180[1 - P_0 - P_1] = 60P_o + 180L - 60$$

s	$\rho = 4/5s$	P_0	L	E[WC]	E[SC]	E[TC]
1	.8	.2	4.0	672.00	20.0	692.00
2	.4	.43	.95	136.80	40.0	176.80
3	.267	.45	.82	114.60	60.0	174.60
4	.2	.44	.80	110.40	80.0	190.40

Hence, s* = 3 and E[TC] = $ 174.60 per hour.

16.4-2 (a) Model 2, with s fixed (equal to 1), A = { 40, 60 },

$$f(\mu) = \begin{cases} 10 & \text{for } \mu = 40 \\ 15 & \text{for } \mu = 60 \end{cases}, \quad \lambda = 30$$

That is, we must choose between a slow server (cashier) and a fast server (cashier + box boy)

(b) $E[WC] = \lambda E[h(W)] = \lambda E[(.05)W] = \lambda(.05)W = (.05)L = (.05)\cdot\frac{\lambda}{\mu-\lambda}$

Therefore we have

μ	$sf(\mu)$	E[WC]	E[TC]	
40	10	.15	10.15	← minimum
60	15	.05	15.05	

Hence the status quo should be maintained.

16.4-3. $\lambda=30$, $\mu_x=50$, $\mu_y=40$. Thus, $\rho_x=0.6$, $\rho_y=0.75$

$EW=\frac{1}{\mu-\lambda}$, $EW_x=\frac{1}{20}$ hour = 3 minutes, $EW_y=\frac{1}{10}$ hour = 6 minutes

Then, compensation difference $\leq 6000\left(\frac{1}{3}-\frac{1}{6}\right)=1000$

16.4-4 $\lambda=4, \mu_A=5, \mu_B=6\,2/3$, $h(W) = \begin{cases} 20W & \text{for } 0\leq W\leq 1 \\ 20W+(W-1)100 & \text{for } W\geq 1 \end{cases}$

$$E[h(W)] = \int_0^1 (20w)(\alpha e^{-\alpha w})\,dw + \int_1^\infty [20w+100(w-1)]\alpha e^{-\alpha w}\,dw$$

where $\alpha = \mu(1-\rho)$. Simplifying, $E[h(W)] = \frac{20}{\alpha}(1+4e^{-\alpha})$ where $\alpha = \begin{cases} 1 & \text{for A} \\ 8/3 & \text{for B} \end{cases}$

So $E[WC] = \lambda E[h(W)] = \begin{cases} 80(1+4e^{-1}) & \text{for A} \\ 30(1+4e^{-8/3}) & \text{for B} \end{cases}$

Alternative	E(SC)	E[WC]	E[TC]
A	50	197.72	247.72
B	150	38.34	188.34

Hence, purchase equipment B, E [TC] = \$188.34 per hour.

16.4-5 For alternative 1, the system has Poisson input with $\lambda = 1/5$, constant service with $\mu = 1/6$ and s = 2. For Alternative 2, the system has Poisson input with $\lambda = 1/5$, constant service with $\mu = 1/3$ and s = 1.

Alternative	E[SC]	ρ	L (from Fig. 16.11)	E[WC] = 50 L	E[TC]
1	34.25	3/5	1.2	60	94.25
2	45.66	3/5	1.0	50	95.66

Hence, Alternative 1 should be chosen, E [TC] = \$94.25 per hour.

16.4-6 For alternative A, the system has Poisson input with $\lambda = 1/45$, Erlang service with $k = 2$ and $\mu = 1/36$ and $s = 2$. For Alternative B, the system has Poisson input with $\lambda = 1/45$, Erlang service with $k = 2$ and $\mu = 1/18$ and $s = 1$. Planes arrive at the rate of one every 45 hours or, equivalently, $8760 / 45 \approx 195$ arrivals per year. Since each plane goes to the maintenance shop five times a year, there are approximately $195/5 = 39$ planes.
So, for Alternative A, E [SC] = \$100,000 x 39 / 8760 = \$1780.82 per hour
and for Alternative B, E [SC] = \$550,000 x 39 / 8760 = \$2448.63 per hour.

Also for Alternative A, $\rho = \dfrac{(\frac{1}{45})}{(2)\ (\frac{1}{36})} = \dfrac{2}{5} \Rightarrow L = .91$ from Fig. 16.13

and for Alternative B, $L = \left(\dfrac{1+k}{2k}\right)\left(\dfrac{\lambda^2}{\mu(\mu-\lambda)}\right) + \dfrac{\lambda}{\mu} = \dfrac{3}{4}\left[\dfrac{\left(\frac{1}{45}\right)^2}{\left(\frac{1}{18}\right)\left(\frac{1}{18}-\frac{1}{45}\right)}\right] + \dfrac{\left(\frac{1}{45}\right)}{\left(\frac{1}{18}\right)} = \dfrac{3}{5}$

Alternative	E[SC]	E[WC] = 3000L	E[TC]
A	1780.82	2730.00	4510.82
B	2448.63	1800.00	4248.63

So choose Alternative B with E [TC] = \$4248.63 per hour.

16.4-7. For Status Quo, the system has Poisson input with $\lambda = 3$, expenential service with $\mu = 4$ and $s = 1$. So $L = \dfrac{\lambda}{\lambda - \mu} = 3$.
For the Proposal, the system has Poisson input with $\lambda = 3$, and general service with $\mu = \dfrac{1}{\left(\frac{1}{10}+\frac{1}{5}\right)} = \dfrac{10}{3}$

and
$\sigma^2 = \dfrac{1}{200} + \dfrac{1}{50} = \dfrac{1}{40}$ with $s = 1$. So,

$$L = \frac{\lambda^2\ \sigma^2 + \rho^2}{2(1-\rho)} + \rho = \frac{\left(\frac{9}{40}\right) + \left(\frac{9}{10}\right)^2}{2\ (1 - \frac{9}{10})} + \frac{9}{10} = 6.075$$

Alternative	E[SC]	E[WC] = 10 L	E[TC]
Status Quo	20	30.00	50.00
Proposal	15	60.75	75.75

So continue Status Quo with E [TC] = \$50.00 per hour.

16.4-8. For Alternative 1, the system has Poisson input with $\lambda = 0.3$, exponential service with $\mu = 0.2$, and $s = 2$. So

Running MMS model in PROMOD, we can easily find $L = 3.43$

For alternative 2, the system has Poisson input with $\lambda = 0.3$, general service (sum of $E(\mu_1, k_1)$ and $E(\mu_2, k_2)$ where $k_1 = k_2 = 4$, $\mu_1 = 0.5$ and $\mu_2 = 1$ - $E(\mu, k)$ denotes Erlang distribution with parameters μ and k, see Section 16.7) with $\mu = 1/3$ and $\sigma^2 = 5/4$

$$\text{So } L = \rho + \frac{\lambda^2\sigma^2 + \rho^2}{2(1-\rho)} = 0.9 + \frac{0.9 \cdot \frac{5}{4} + 0.81}{0.2} = 5.51$$

Alternative	E[SC]	E[WC] = 100 L	E[TC]
1	2000	343	2343
2	1500	551	2051

So choose Alternative 2, with E [TC] = 2051 per week.

16.4-9. <u>For the status quo</u>, the system has Poisson input with $\lambda = 15$, exponential service with $\mu = 15$, $s = 1$ and limited waiting room with $k = 4$. There is a waiting cost of 6 W_q for each customer due to loss of good will and also a waiting cost of \$45 per hour when the system is full (4 cars in system) due to loss of potential customers. So

$$E[TC] = E[WC] = \lambda 6 W_q + 45 P_4 = 6 L_q + 45 P_4.$$

In this case, $\frac{\lambda}{\mu} = 1$, so

$$P_0 = \frac{1}{k+1}, \quad P_n = \frac{1}{k+1} \quad n = 1, 2, \ldots, k \quad \therefore P_4 = \frac{1}{5}$$

$$L = \sum_{n=1}^{k} n P_n = \frac{1}{k+1} \sum_{n=1}^{k} n = \frac{k(k+1)}{2(k+1)} = \frac{k}{2}$$

$$L_q = L - (1 - P_0) = \frac{k}{2} - 1 + \frac{1}{k+1} = \frac{4}{2} - 1 + \frac{1}{5} = \frac{6}{5}$$

Thus, $E[TC] = 6(6/5) + 45(1/5) = \$16.20$ per hour.

<u>For Proposal 1</u>, the system has Poisson input with $\lambda = 15$, exponential service with $\mu = 20$ and $s = 1$. In addition to the waiting cost of 6 L_q due to los of good will, there is an expected waiting cost of \$2 per customer that waits longer than 1 /2 hour before his car is ready. The expected value of this additional waiting cost is given by

$$2\lambda P\{W > 1/2\} = 2\lambda e^{-\mu(1-\rho)/2} = 30 e^{-2.5} = 2.46.$$

Also, $6 L_q = \frac{6\lambda^2}{\mu(\mu - \lambda)} = \frac{6 \times 225}{20 \times 5} = 13.50$

Hence, $E[TC] = 3 + 13.50 + 2.46 = 18.96$ per hour (where 3 is the capitalized cost of the new equipment.)

<u>For Proposal 2</u>, the system has a Poisson input with $\lambda = 15$, Erlang service with $\mu = 30$ and $k = 2$, and $s = 1$. The only waiting cost is 6 L_q due to loss of good will. In this case,

$$L_q = \left(\frac{k+1}{2k}\right)\left(\frac{\lambda^2}{\mu(\mu - \lambda)}\right) = \left(\frac{3}{4}\right)\left(\frac{225}{30 \times 15}\right) = \frac{3}{8} = 0.375.$$ Hence, $E[TC] = 10 + 2.25 = 12.25$.

Summarizing, Status Quo: $E[TC] = 0 + 6L_q + 45 P_4 = 16.20$

Proposal 1: $E[TC] = 3 + 6 L_q + 30 P\{W \geq 1/2\} = 18.96$

Proposal 2: $E[TC] = 10 + 6 L_q = 10 + 2.25 = 12.25$.

Hence, Proposal 2 should be adopted.

16.4-10 (a)

s	$L = \frac{\lambda}{\mu_s - \lambda}$	$E[WC] = 15L$	$E[SC] = 10s$	$E[TC]$
1	∞	∞	10	∞
2	1	15.00	20	35.00
3	1/2	7.50	30	37.50

Since clearly $E[SC] > 35$ for $s \geq 4$, it follows that $s^* = 2$

(b)

s	$\mu_s = \sqrt{s}$	$L = \frac{\lambda}{\mu_s - \lambda}$	$E[WC] = 15L$	$E[SC] = 10s$	$E[TC]$
1	1.0	∞	∞	10	∞
2	1.414	2.414	36.21	20	56.21
3	1.732	1.366	20.49	30	50.49
4	2.0	1.000	15.00	40	55.00
5	2.236	.809	13.75	50	63.75

Since clearly $E[SC] > 50.49$ for $s \geq 6$, it follows that $s^* = 3$.

16.4-11. $\lambda = 4$, $\mu = 6n$, $EN = \frac{\lambda}{\mu - \lambda} = \frac{4}{6n-4}$

Hourly cost $= C(n) = 18n + 20\,EN = 18n + \frac{80}{6n-4}$

Easy to see $c(n)$ is convex. Enumerate $c(n)$ at $n = 1, 2, 3, \ldots$

We can easily find that $C(n)$ attain its minimum (when n is integer) at $n = 2$. So, two loaders would minimize the expected hourly cost.

16.4-12. $\lambda = 3$, $ET = \frac{1}{\mu - 3}$

Expect cost $= C(\mu) = 5\mu + 60\,ET \cdot \lambda = 5\mu + \frac{60 \cdot 3}{\mu - 3}$

$C'(\mu) = 5 - \frac{180}{(\mu-3)^2}$ So when $\mu = 9$, $C(\mu)$ attains its minimum

Then, the hourly wage of 45\$ per hour would minimize the total cost

16.4-13 This is an $M/E_2/1$ model with $\lambda = 3$ and so:

$$E[TC] = 40{,}000 + 10{,}000\mu + 90{,}000\left[\frac{27}{4\mu(\mu-3)} + \frac{3}{\mu}\right]$$

$$\frac{dE[TC]}{d\mu} = 10{,}000 - 90{,}000\left[\frac{27}{4\mu(\mu-3)^2} + \frac{27}{4\mu^2(\mu-3)} + \frac{3}{\mu^2}\right] = 0.$$ Solving for μ

we get $\mu = 7.774$,

at which point $E[TC] = \$168{,}840/\text{wk}$.

If we check $\frac{d^2E[TC]}{d\mu^2} = 90{,}000\left[\frac{6}{\mu^3} + \frac{27}{2\mu(\mu-3)^3} + \frac{27}{2\mu^2(\mu-3)^2} + \frac{27}{2\mu^3(\mu-3)}\right] \geq 0$

if $\mu \geq 3$.

16.4-14. $E[SC] = .10\mu^2$ and $E[WC] = .20L = \frac{.20(1/2)}{\mu - 1/2} = \frac{.10}{\mu - 1/2}$

So $E[TC] = .10\mu^2 + \frac{.10}{\mu - 1/2}$

μ	E[TC]
.5	∞
.75	.45625
1.00	.30000
1.10	.28767
1.15	.28610
1.20	.28656
1.25	.28958
1.50	.32500
1.75	.38625
2.00	.46667

So $\mu^* = 1.15$

16.4-18 (continued)

(ii) the resulting system is a collection of independent M/M/1 with finite calling populations and the appropriate decision model is a combination of Models 2 and 3 since in this case we have to determine μ (the service rate of a crew depends on how many operators are assigned to the crew) and λ (the mean arrival rate depends on the number of machines assigned to a crew) and s is fixed equal to 1.

(iii) the resulting system doesn't fit any of the models described in Chapter 15.

Each of the proposed alternatives allows, in varied degrees, the sharing of resources (the operators) in contrast to the original proposal. Now, since in the original proposal the operators would be idle most of the time, it is reasonable to expect that if we allow interaction, the production rate obtained with the same number of operators will increase, and thus, the required number of operators that are needed to achieve the desired production rate will decrease.

What might prevent this from happening? In alternatives (i) and (iii), the travel time (not taken into account in the above argument) may pose a problem (instead of turning idle time into service time we may be turning idle time into travel time). Also, in alternative (iii) the service rate of a group of workers may be smaller than the individual service rate, since they won't be working together regularly. And finally, although this is not the case in Alternative (ii) (the components of a crew do work together regularly) even then we may have that $\mu' < n\mu$ (where μ' is the service rate of crew of n operators and μ is the individual service rate).

16.4-15. Given that $s=1$ (by the Optimality of the Single Server result), $E[TC] = C_r\mu + C_w L = C_r\mu + C_w\left(\frac{\lambda}{\mu-\lambda}\right)$

$$\frac{dE[TC]}{d\mu} = C_r - \frac{C_w\lambda}{(\mu-\lambda)^2} = 0 \Rightarrow (\mu-\lambda)^2 = \frac{\lambda C_w}{C_r}$$

$$\Rightarrow \mu = \lambda + \sqrt{\lambda C_w/C_r}$$

$$\frac{d^2E[TC]}{d\mu^2} = \frac{2\lambda C_w}{(\mu-\lambda)^3} > 0 \text{ for all } \mu>\lambda.$$

Hence, $\mu = \lambda + \sqrt{\lambda C_w/C_r}$ is the minimizing value.

16.4-16. $E[TC] = D\mu + \lambda C/(\mu-\lambda)^2$

$$\frac{dE[TC]}{d\mu} = D - \frac{2\lambda C}{(\mu-\lambda)^3} = 0 \Rightarrow (\mu-\lambda)^3 = \frac{2\lambda C}{D} \Rightarrow \mu = \lambda + \left(\frac{2\lambda C}{D}\right)^{1/3}$$

Also, $\frac{d^2E[TC]}{d\mu^2} = \frac{6\lambda C}{(\mu-\lambda)^4} > 0$ when $C>0$

Hence, $\mu = \lambda + \left(\frac{2\lambda C}{D}\right)^{1/3}$ is the minimizing value.

16.4-17 (a) Original design would give a smaller number (expected) of customers in the system. This is due to the pooling effect of multiple servers.

(b) Original design is a M/M/2 queue where $\lambda=5$, $\mu=6$.
Run ProMod, we find $L=$
Alternative design is two M/M/1 queue, under which
$L = \frac{2\lambda}{\mu-\lambda} = 10$. This has varified what we claimed in (a).

16.4-18. (a) Part (a) of Problem 15.6-3 is a special case of Model 3, in which we want to determine λ (since determining the number of machines assigned to one operator is equivalent to determining λ, the mean arrival rate) and s is fixed (equal to 1 in this case).

(b) (i) the resulting system would be a M/M/s with finite calling population (size of population is equal to the total number of machines) and the associated decision problem fits Model 1 (unknown s).

16.4-19. $a = b = c = d = 300$ and $v = 3$ miles/hour $= 264$ feet/min

So $E[T] = \frac{1}{264}\left[\frac{(300)^2+(300)^2}{(300+300)} + \frac{(300)^2+(300)^2}{(300+300)}\right] =$

$= 600/264$ minutes $= 2.27$ minutes.

16.4-20. $\mu = 30$, $s = 1$, $\lambda_p = 24$, $C_f = 20$, $C_s = 15$, $C_t = 25$.

$\underline{n=1}$: $\lambda = \frac{\lambda_p}{n} = 24$

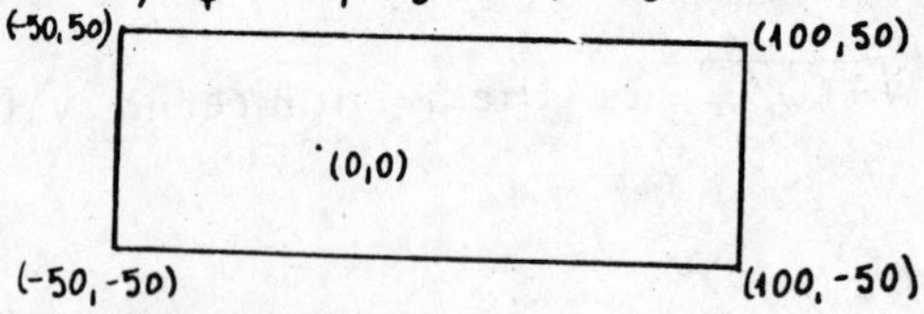

So $a = 50, b = 50, c = 100, d = 50$

$\therefore E(T) = \frac{1}{5,000}\left(\frac{50^2+100^2}{50+100} + \frac{50^2+50^2}{50+50}\right) = .0267$ hrs.

Also, $L = \frac{\lambda}{\mu-\lambda} = \frac{24}{30-24} = 4$

$\underline{n=2}$: $\lambda = \frac{\lambda_p}{n} = 12$

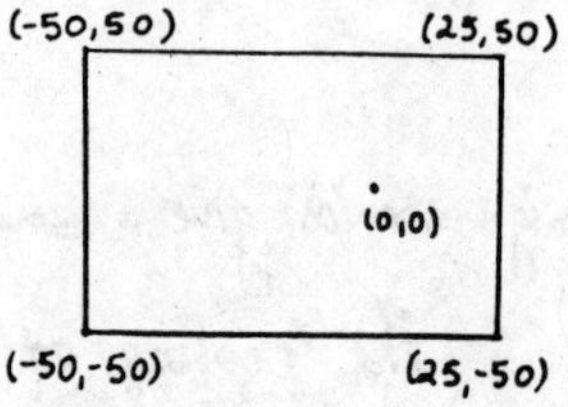

Relabelling symmetric areas,

So $a = 50$, $b = 50$, $c = 25$, $d = 50$

$E(T) = \frac{1}{5000}\left(\frac{50^2+25^2}{50+25} + \frac{50^2+50^2}{50+50}\right) = .0183$ hrs.

Also, $L = \frac{\lambda}{\mu-\lambda} = \frac{12}{30-12} = \frac{2}{3}$

Hence, $E(TC) = n[(C_f + C_s) + C_t L + \frac{24}{n} C_t E(T)]$

n	λ	$E[T]$	L	$C_f + C_s$	$C_t L$	$\lambda C_t E(T)$	$E[TC]$
1	24	.0267	4	35	100	16	151
2	12	.0183	2/3	35	50/3	5.5	114.33

So there should be two facilities.

16.4-21. From Table 16.4 and adjacent text

	$s=1$	$s=2$
$W_1 - 1/\mu$	.024	.00037
$W_2 - 1/\mu$	.154	.00793
$W_3 - 1/\mu$	1.033	.06542

Note that $\lambda_1 = .2$, $\lambda_2 = .6$ and $\lambda_3 = 1.2$

S	E[waiting costs]				E[SC]	E[TC]
	critical	serious	stable	total		
1	480.00	92.40	12.40	584.80	40.00	624.80
2	7.40	4.76	0.79	12.95	80.00	92.95

So there should be two doctors.

16.4-22. The system is a non-preemptive queueing system with $\mu = 4$, $\lambda_1 = 6$, $\lambda_2 = 4$ and $\lambda_3 = 2$, where Class 1 is government jobs, Class 2 is commercial jobs and Class 3 is standard jobs. The problem is to determine whether $s = 4$ or $s = 5$.

For $s = 4$, $A = 31.41$, $B_0 = 1$, $B_1 = 5/8$, $B_2 = 3/8$, $B_3 = 1/4$ $\Rightarrow$ $W_1 = .30094$, $W_2 = .38585$, $W_3 = .58962$

For $s = 5$, $A = 52.35$, $B_0 = 1$, $B_1 = 7/10$, $B_2 = 1/2$, $B_3 = 2/5$ $\Rightarrow$ $W_1 = .27729$, $W_2 = .30458$, $W_3 = .34552$

S	E[WC]				E[SC]	E[TC]
	Government	Commercial	Standard	Total		
4	6771.15	3472.65	884.43	11128.23	5000	16128.23
5	6239.02	2741.22	518.28	9498.52	6250	15748.52

So two additional lathes should be obtained.

Chapter 17
Inventory Theory

17-3.1

(a) $K=15,\ h=30,\ a=30 \Rightarrow Q^*=\sqrt{\dfrac{(2)(30)(15)}{0.30}} = 54.77$

$t^* = Q^*/a = 1.83$ months

(b) $p=3 \Rightarrow Q^*=\sqrt{\dfrac{(2)(30)(15)}{0.30}}\cdot\sqrt{\dfrac{3+0.30}{3}} = 57.45$

$S^*=\sqrt{\dfrac{(2)(30)(15)}{0.30}}\cdot\sqrt{\dfrac{3}{3+0.30}} = 52.22$

$t^* = Q^*/a = 1.91$ months

17.3-2

(a) $K=25,\ h=0.05,\ a=600 \Rightarrow Q^*=\sqrt{\dfrac{(2)(600)(25)}{0.05}} = 774.60$

$t^* = Q^*/a = 1.29$ weeks

(b) $p=2 \Rightarrow Q^*=\sqrt{\dfrac{(2)(600)(25)}{0.05}}\sqrt{\dfrac{2+0.05}{2}} = 784.22$

$S^*=\sqrt{\dfrac{(2)(600)(25)}{0.05}}\sqrt{\dfrac{2}{2+0.05}} = 765.09$

$t^* = Q^*/a = 1.31$ weeks

17.3-3

$\lambda = 1$ week (delivery lag)

Since $\lambda_a = 600 < 816.24 = Q^*$, by remark 5 in the Continuous Review-Uniform Demand section, the same amount (816.24) should be ordered one week earlier.

17.3-4

$K=12{,}000,\ h=0.30,\ a=8{,}000,\ p=5$

$Q^*=\sqrt{\dfrac{(2)(8000)(12000)}{0.30}}\sqrt{\dfrac{5+0.30}{5}} = 26{,}046$

$S^*=\sqrt{\dfrac{(2)(8000)(12000)}{0.30}}\sqrt{\dfrac{5}{5+0.30}} = 24{,}572$

$t^* = Q^*/a = 3.26$ months

17.3-5

(a) $K=1{,}000,\ h=0.01,\ a=8{,}500 \Rightarrow Q^*=\sqrt{\dfrac{(2)(8500)(1000)}{0.01}} = 41{,}231$

$t^* = Q^*/a = 4.85$ months

(b) $p=0.50 \Rightarrow Q^*=\sqrt{\dfrac{(2)(8500)(1000)}{0.01}}\sqrt{\dfrac{0.50+0.01}{0.50}} = 41{,}641$

$S^*=\sqrt{\dfrac{(2)(8500)(1000)}{0.01}}\sqrt{\dfrac{0.50}{0.50+0.01}} = 40{,}825$

$t^* = Q^*/a = 4.90$ months

17.3-6

$c_1 = 1.05$ if $Q < 50{,}000$
$c_2 = 1.00$ if $Q \geq 50{,}000$
Let $T_1 = \frac{aK}{Q} + ac_1 + \frac{hQ}{2}$ and $T_2 = \frac{ak}{Q} + ac_2 + \frac{hQ}{2}$. Both curves attain their minimum at $Q = 41{,}231$, but $T_1 \geq T_2$ and $T_1(41{,}231) = 9337 > 8920 = T_2(50{,}000)$. Therefore, $Q^* = 50{,}000$ and $t^* = Q^*/a = 5.88$ months.

17.3-7

Let $c_1 = 1.20$, $c_2 = 1.10$ and $c_3 = 1.00$
Let T_1 be the cost per unit time for $0 \leq Q < 20{,}000$
Let T_2 be the cost per unit time for $20{,}000 < Q < 40{,}000$
Let T_3 be the cost per unit time for $40{,}000 < Q$.

$$T_1 = \frac{aK}{Q} + ac_1 + \frac{hQ}{2}$$

$$T_2 = \frac{K + c_1(20{,}000) + c_2(Q - 20{,}000) + (hQ^2/2a)}{Q/a} =$$

$$= \frac{aK}{Q} + c_2 a + \frac{hQ}{2} + \frac{(20{,}000)(c_1 - c_2)a}{Q}$$

$$T_3 = \frac{K + c_1(20{,}000) + c_2(20{,}000) + c_3(Q - 40{,}000) + (hQ^2/2a)}{Q/a} =$$

$$= \frac{aK}{Q} + c_3 a + \frac{hQ}{2} + \frac{[(c_1 - c_3)(20{,}000) + (c_2 - c_3)(20{,}000)]a}{Q}$$

$\frac{dT_1(Q)}{dQ} = -\frac{aK}{Q^2} + \frac{h}{2} = 0 \Rightarrow T_1$ attains its minimum at $Q = \sqrt{\frac{2aK}{h}} = 41{,}231$ (since $\frac{d^2T_1}{dQ^2} > 0$)

$\frac{dT_2(Q)}{dQ} = -\frac{aK}{Q^2} + \frac{h}{2} - \frac{(20{,}000)(c_1 - c_2)a}{Q^2} = 0 \Rightarrow T_2$ attains its minimum at $Q = \sqrt{\frac{2aK + 2a(20{,}000)(c_1 - c_2)}{h}} = 71{,}414$

since $d^2T/dQ^2 > 0$

$\frac{dT_3(Q)}{dQ} = -\frac{aK}{Q^2} + \frac{h}{2} + \frac{[2c_3 - c_1 - c_2](20{,}000)a}{Q^2} = 0 \Rightarrow T_3$ attains its minimum at $Q = \sqrt{\frac{2aK + 2a(20{,}000)(c_1 + c_2 - 2c_3)}{h}} =$
$= 109{,}087$ (since $d^2T_3/dQ^2 > 0$)

Since for fixed Q $T_j < T_{j-1}$ for all j, we have that $T_3(109.087) < T_3(71414) < T_2(71414) < T_2(41231) < T_1(41231)$ (2nd and 4th inequalities follow from minimization results). Therefore, the optimal policy is to order $Q^* = 109{,}087$ gallons every $t^* = Q^*/a = 12.83$ months.

17.3-8

$$S = a8Q \Rightarrow T = \frac{ak}{Q} + ac + 0.32hQ + 0.02pQ$$

$$= \frac{ak}{Q} + ac + (0.32h + 0.02p)Q$$

$$\frac{\partial T}{\partial Q} = -\frac{ak}{Q^2} + (0.32h + 0.02p) = 0$$

$$\Rightarrow Q^* = \sqrt{\frac{ak}{0.32h + 0.02p}}$$

17.3-9

(a) Maximum inventory = $\frac{(b-a)Q}{b}$

Length of interval I = $\frac{Q}{b}$ | Length of interval II = $Q/a - Q/b$

Average inventory in interval I = $\frac{(b-a)Q}{2b}$ | Average inventory in interval II = $\frac{(b-a)Q}{2b}$

Thus, the average inventory per cycle is: $\frac{(b-a)Q}{2b}$

Thus, the holding cost per cycle is: $\frac{(b-a)Q}{2ab}$

$\Rightarrow T = \frac{-ak}{Q} + \frac{(b-a)hQ}{2b} + ac$

(b) $\frac{\partial T}{\partial Q} = \frac{-ak}{Q^2} + \frac{(b-a)h}{2b} = 0 \Rightarrow Q^* = \sqrt{\frac{2abk}{(b-a)h}}$

17.3-10

$C_5 = 4 + 3 = 7$

$c_4^{(4)} = 7 + 4 + 2 = 13$; $c_4^{(5)} = 4 + 5 + .3\,(3) = 9.9$; $\mathbf{C_4 = c_4^{(5)} = 9.9}$

$c_3^{(3)} = 9.9 + 4 + 2 = 15.9$; $c_3^{(4)} = 7 + 4 + 4 + .3\,(2) = 15.6$; $c_3^{(5)} = 4 + 7 + .3\,(2 + 6) = 13.4$

$\mathbf{C_3 = c_3^{(5)} = 13.5}$

$c_2^{(2)} = 13.5 + 4 + 4 = 21.5$; $c_2^{(3)} = 9.9 + 4 + 6 + .3\,(2) = 20.5$; $c_2^{(4)} = 7 + 4 + 8 + .3\,(2 + 4) = 20.8$

$c_2^{(5)} = 4 + 11 + .3\,(2 + 4 + 9) = 19.5$; $\mathbf{C_2 = c_2^{(5)} = 19.5}$

$c_1^{(1)} = 19.5 + 4 + 2 = 25.5$; $c_1^{(2)} = 13.5 + 4 + 6 + .3\,(4) = 24.7$; $c_1^{(3)} = 9.9 + 4 + 8 + .3\,(4 + 4) = 24.3$

$c_1^{(4)} = 7 + 4 + 10 + .3\,(4 + 4 + 6) = 25.2$; $c_1^{(5)} = 4 + 13 + .3\,(4 + 4 + 6 + 12) = 24.8$; $\mathbf{C_1 = c_1^{(3)} = 24.3}$

The optimal production schedule is to producee 8 in period 1 and 5 in period 4 at a cost of $24.30.

17.3-11

$k = 2, c = 1, h = 0.20, \quad (r_1, r_2, r_3, r_4) = (4, 3, 4, 3)$

$C_4 = 2 + 3 = 5$

$c_3^{(3)} = 5 + 2 + 4 = 11$; $c_3^{(4)} = 2 + 7 + .2\,(3) = 9.6$; $\mathbf{C_3 = c_3^{(4)} = 9.6}$

$c_2^{(2)} = 9.6 + 2 + 3 = 14.6$; $c_2^{(3)} = 5 + 2 + 7 + .3\,(4) = 15.2$; $c_2^{(4)} = 2 + 10 + .3\,(4 + 6) = 15$;

$\mathbf{C_2 = c_2^{(2)} = 14.6}$

$c_1^{(1)} = 14.6 + 2 + 4 = 20.6$; $c_1^{(2)} = 9.6 + 2 + 7 + .2\,(3) = 19.2$;

$c_1^{(3)} = 5 + 2 + 11 + .2\,(3 + 8) = 20.2$; $c_1^{(4)} = 2 + 14 + .2\,(3 + 8 + 9) = 20.0$; $\mathbf{C_1 = c_1^{(2)} = 19.2.}$

The optimal production schedule is to produce 7 in period 1 and 7 in period 3 at a cost of 19.2.

17.3-12

$k = 2, \quad (c_1, c_2, c_3, c_4) = (1.4, 1, 1.4, 1)\,, h = .2, \quad (r_1, r_2, r_3, r_4) = (3, 2, 3, 2)$

x_4	z_4	$c^*(x_4)$	z_4^*
0	2	4	2
1	1	3	1
2	0	0	0

(continued)

x_3 \ z_3	0	1	2	3	4	5	$c^*(x_3)$	z_3^*
0	—	—	—	10.2	10.8	9.4	9.4	5
1	—	—	8.8	9.4	8.0	—	8.0	4
2	—	7.4	8.0	6.6	—	—	6.6	3
3	4	6.6	5.2	—	—	—	4	0
4	3.2	3.8	—	—	—	—	3.2	0
5	0.4	—	—	—	—	—	0.4	0

x_2 \ z_2	0	1	2	3	4	5	6	7	$c^*(x_2)$	z_2^*
0	—	—	13.4	13.2	14.0	11.6	13.0	10.4	10.4	7
1	—	12.4	12.2	13.0	10.6	12.0	9.4	—	9.4	6
2	9.4	11.2	12.0	9.6	11.0	8.4	—	—	8.4	5
3	8.2	11.0	8.6	10.0	7.4	—	—	—	7.4	4
4	7.0	7.6	9.0	6.4	—	—	—	—	6.4	3
5	4.6	8.0	5.4	—	—	—	—	—	4.6	0
6	4.0	4.4	—	—	—	—	—	—	4.0	0
7	1.4	—	—	—	—	—	—	—	1.4	0

x_1 \ z_1	3	4	5	6	7	8	9	10	$c^*(x_1)$	z_1^*
0	16.8	17.2	17.8	18.4	19.0	18.8	19.8	18.8	16.8	3

The optimal production schedule is to produce 3 units in the first period and 7 units in the second period at a cost of 16.8.

17-3-13

$h = 2.$

$$B(x_n, z_n) = \begin{cases} k_n + c_n z_n + 2 \cdot \max[0, z_n - 3] + h(x_n + z_n - r_n) & \text{for } 0 < z_n \le 4 \\ h \cdot (x_n - r_n) & \text{for } z_n = 0 \end{cases}$$

x_3	z_3	$C^*(x_3)$	z_3^*
0	4	47	4
1	3	36	3
2	2	27	2
3	1	18	1
4	0	4	0

x_2 \ z_2	0	1	2	3	4	$C^*(x_2)$	z_2^*
0	—	—	—	87	90	87	3
1	—	—	77	78	83	77	2
2	—	67	68	71	76	67	1
3	47	58	61	64	64	47	0
4	38	51	54	52	—	38	0

x_1 \ z_1	0	1	2	3	4	$C^*(x_1)$	z_1^*
1	87	92	92	82	85	82	3

The optimal production schedule is to produce 3 units in period 1 and 4 units in period 3, at a cost of 82.

17-3-14

$c_2 = 5 + 36 = \mathbf{41}$

$c_1^{(1)} = 41 + 5 + 27 = 73$; $c_1^{(2)} = 5 + 63 + .3\,(3) = 68.9$; $\mathbf{c_1} = c_1^{(2)} = \mathbf{68.9}$.

The optimal schedule is to produce all 7 in the first period at a cost of 68.9 .

17-4-1

$$\Phi(y^o) = \frac{y^o - 200}{100} = \frac{p-c}{p+n} = \frac{25-18}{25+0.1}\text{ . So } y^o = 100\left(2+\frac{7}{25.1}\right) \approx 228$$

17.4-2

(a) $y^o = -\lambda \ln\left(\frac{c+h}{p+h}\right) = -50 \ln\left(\frac{1000+300}{10000+300}\right) \approx 103$

(b) $C(y) = c\,(y - x_o) + L\,(y)$ and so when we take the derivative with respect to y the term involving the initial inventory disappears, and so the optimal policy is to order up to the same amount as in part (a). So order 103 - 23 = 80 parts.

(c) We want the y such that $P\{D \le y\} = 0.90$

$$\Phi(y) = 1 - e^{-\frac{y}{50}} = 0.9$$

$$\Rightarrow e^{-\frac{y}{50}} = 0.1 \quad \Rightarrow -\frac{y}{50} = \ln(0.1) \quad \Rightarrow y = -50\ln(0.1) \approx 115$$

(d) $\left(\frac{p-c}{p+h}\right) = 0.9 \Rightarrow \frac{p-1000}{p+300} = 0.9 \quad \Rightarrow 0.1\,p = 1,270 \quad \Rightarrow p = \$12,700$

17.4-3

Let $C(D,y)$ be the cost to the manufacturer of meeting demand D, given an inventory y. Then what we seek is y^o such that y^o minimizes $E(C(D,y))$.

Now $C(D,y) = 40y + 40(D-y)^+ - 60\min(y,D) - 30(y-D)^+$

(where $x^+ = \max(0,x)$).

There fore,

$$C(D,y) = \begin{cases} 40D - 60y & \text{if } D > y \\ 10y - 30D & \text{if } D \le y \end{cases}$$

$$E[C(D,y)] = \begin{cases} 60000 - 60y & \text{if } 1000 > y \\ (7y^2/200) - 130y + 95000 & \text{if } 1000 \le y \le 2000 \\ 10y - 45000 & \text{if } 2000 < y \end{cases}$$

Clearly, the minimum must be attained in the region $1000 \le y \le 2000$

Setting the derivative of $E[C(D,y)]$ in this region equal to zero, we obtain: $0 = (7y/100) - 130$

$\Rightarrow y^o \cong 1857$

and since the second derivative is $7/100 > 0$, y^o is indeed a minimum.

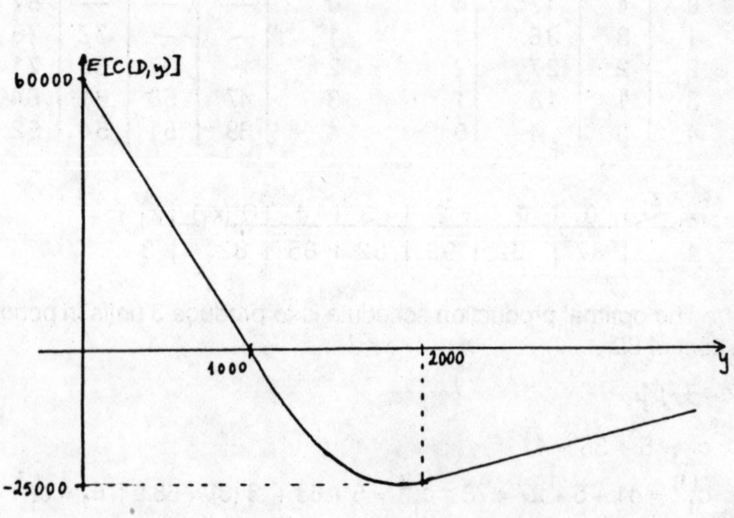

17-4.4

$p = 50,\ c = 1,\ h = 2 \Rightarrow \frac{p-c}{p+h} = \frac{49}{52} = .942$

y^0 = smallest y such that $F(y) \geq .942 \Rightarrow y^0 = 1{,}600$

So the student should buy 4 additional \$100 checks.

17.4-5

Following the development in Sec. 18.4

$$C(y) = cy + h\int_0^y (y-\xi)\,\vartheta_D(\xi)\,d\xi + p\int_y^\infty (\xi - y)\,\vartheta_D(\xi)\,d\xi + kP\{D \geq y\}$$

but if D is uniform on [a, b] then $P\{D \geq y\} = \frac{b-y}{b-a}$, and so

$$C(y) = cy + k\,\frac{b-y}{b-a} + L(y) \Rightarrow \frac{\delta(C_y)}{\delta y} = c - \frac{k}{b-a} + h\Phi(y) - p[1 - \Phi(y)]$$

and so the minimum occurs when

$$\Phi(y) = \frac{p + \frac{k}{b-a} - c}{p+h}.$$ In this case, $p = c+2,\ k = 14,\ h = -(c-1),\ [a, b] = [40, 40]$

and so: $\Phi(y) = \frac{y-40}{20} = \frac{2.7}{3} = 0.9 \Rightarrow y = 58$.

17.4-6

(a) $C(x,y) = c(y-x) + p\cdot P\{D>y\} = c(y-x) + pe^{-y} = (cy + pe^{-y}) - cx$

$\frac{dC(x,y)}{dy} = c - pe^{-y} = 0 \Rightarrow e^{-y} = c/p \Rightarrow y^0 = -\ln(c/p)$

So order up to y^0 if $x < y^0$, and do not order otherwise.

(b) $C(x,y) = \begin{cases} K + c(y-x) + pe^{-y} & \text{if } y > x \\ pe^{-x} & \text{if } y = x \end{cases}$

An (s, S) policy will be optimal with $S = -\ln(c/p)$ and s the smallest value such that $cs + pe^{-s} \leq K - c\ln(c/p) + c$

17.4-7.

$L(y) = 1\int_0^y (y-\xi)\,d\xi/20 + 3\int_y^{20} (\xi - y)\,d\xi/20 = y^2/10 - 3y + 30$

So $cy + L(y) = y^2/10 - y + 30$

$\Phi(S) = S/20 = (p-c)/(p+h) = (3-2)/(3+1) = 1/4 \Rightarrow S = 5$

$cs + L(s) = K + cS + L(S) \Rightarrow s^2/10 - s + 30 = 1.5 + 27.5$

$\Rightarrow s^2/10 - s + 1 = 0$

$\Rightarrow s = 5 - \sqrt{15} = 1.13$

So the $(s,S) = (1.13, 5)$ policy is optimal.

17.4-8.

Single Period Model With A Setup Cost:

Demand density is exponential, with lambda = 25.

Unit production or purchasing cost, c = 1

Unit inventory holding cost, h = 0.4

Unit shortage cost, p = 1.5

17.4-8. (continued)

Setup Cost, K = 10

Results:

s = -11.e3

S = 7.63454

17.4-9

$h = .3, \quad p = 2.5$

$$G(y) = .3\int_0^y \frac{(y-\xi)}{25} e^{-\xi/25} d\xi + 2.5\int_y^{\infty} \frac{(\xi-y)}{25} e^{-\xi/25} d\xi =$$

$$= .3y + 70 e^{-y/25} - 7.5$$

$G'(y) = .3 - 2.8 e^{-y/25} = 0 \Rightarrow G(y)$ attains its minimum at $y = 55.84$, since $G''(y) = 2.8 e^{-y/25} > 0$ for any y.

Now K must be found such that $G(K) = G(K+100)$, or

$.3K + 70 e^{-K/25} - 7.5 = .3(K+100) + 70 e^{-(K+100)/25} - 7.5$ or

$70 e^{-K/25}(1 - e^{-4}) = 30$, so $K = 20.72 \approx 21$

Note that $K = 21 < y^0 = 55.84 < K+100 = 121$, and $G(21) \approx G(121)$

Hence, the optimal policy is a $(k, Q) = (21, 100)$ policy.

17.4-10

(a) Single Period Model With No Setup Cost:

Demand density is exponential, with lambda = 25.

Unit production or purchasing cost, c = 10

Unit inventory holding cost, h = 6

Unit shortage cost, p = 15

Results:

y(0) = 6.79834

(b) Two Period Model With No Setup Cost:

Demand density is exponential, with lambda = 25.

Unit production or purchasing cost, c = 10

Unit inventory holding cost, h = 6

Unit shortage cost, p = 15

Results:

y1(0) = 23.2932

y2(0) = 6.79834

17.4-11. (a) Single Period Model With No Setup Cost:

Demand density is uniform between 0 and 50.

Unit production or purchasing cost, c = 10

Unit inventory holding cost, h = 8

Unit shortage cost, p = 15

Results:

y(0) = 10.8696

(b) Two Period Model With No Setup Cost:

Demand density is uniform between 0 and 50.

Unit production or purchasing cost, c = 10

Unit inventory holding cost, h = 8

Unit shortage cost, p = 15

Results:

y1(0) = 9.26156

y2(0) = 10.8696

17.4-12. Infinite Period Model with no Setup Cost:

Demand density is exponential, with lambda = 25.

Unit production or purchasing cost, C=1

Unit inventory holding cost, h=0.25

Unit shortage cost, p=2

Discount Factor = 0.9

Results: y(0) = 46.5188

17.4-13. Two Period Model With No Setup Cost:

Demand density is exponential, with lambda = 25.

Unit production or purchasing cost, c = 1

Unit inventory holding cost, h = 0.25

Unit shortage cost, p = 2

Results:

y1(0) = 36.521

y2(0) = 14.6947

17.4-14. Infinite Period Model With No Setup Cost:

Demand density is exponential, with lambda = 25.

Unit production or purchasing cost, c = 1

Unit inventory holding cost, h = 0.25

Unit shortage cost, p = 2

Discount Factor = 0.9

Results:

y(0) = 46.5188

17.4-15. Infinite Period Model With No Setup Cost:

Demand density is exponential, with lambda = 1.

Unit production or purchasing cost, c = 2

Unit inventory holding cost, h = 1

Unit shortage cost, p = 5

Discount Factor = 0.95

Results:

y(0) = 1.69645

17.4-16. Same as 17-4-15 above.

17.4-17. Infinite Period Model With No Setup Cost:

Demand density is uniform between 0 and 1000.

Unit production or purchasing cost, c = 150

Unit inventory holding cost, h = 2

Unit shortage cost, p = 30

Discount Factor = 0.9

Results:

$y(0) = 468.75 \Rightarrow y^* = 2468.75$

17.4-18. Infinite Period Model With No Setup Cost:

Demand density is exponential, with lambda = 1000.

Unit production or purchasing cost, c = 8

Unit inventory holding cost, h = 0.07

Unit shortage cost, p = 2

Discount Factor = 0.95 Results: y(0) = 1482.57

17.4-19. Since $c=0$, the answer is identical to that for problem 17.4-7.

17.4-20. $L(y) = \int_y^\infty p(\xi - y)\varphi_D(\xi)\,d\xi + \int_0^y h(y-\xi)\varphi_D(\xi)\,d\xi$

$$\frac{dL(y)}{dy} = \int_y^\infty -p\,\varphi_D(\xi)\,d\xi + \int_0^y h\,\varphi_D(\xi)\,d\xi = -p(1-\Phi(y)) + h\,\Phi(y)$$

So $\frac{dL(y)}{dy} + c(1-\alpha) = 0 \Rightarrow -p + p\Phi(y) + h\,\Phi(y) + c(1-\alpha) = 0$

$\Rightarrow \Phi(y) = \frac{p - c(1-\alpha)}{p+h}$, as descred.

17.4-21. Continuous Review Model With Fixed Delivery Lag - Backlogging:
Demand density is uniform between 0 and 30.

Expected number of items demanded per unit time, a = 30

Unit inventory holding cost, h = 0.3

Unit shortage cost, p = 3

Setup Cost, K = 15

Results:

s = 24.2265

Q = 57.735

17.4-22. Continuous Review Model With Fixed Delivery Lag - Backlogging:
Demand density is exponential, with lambda = 1.

Expected number of items demanded per unit time, a = 600

Unit inventory holding cost, h = 0.05

Unit shortage cost, p = 2

Setup Cost, K = 25

Results:

s = 1632.45

Q = 1579.8

17.4-23. Continuous Review Model With Fixed Delivery Lag - Backlogging:
Demand density is uniform between 0 and 4250.

Expected number of items demanded per unit time, a = 8500

Unit inventory holding cost, h = 0.01

17.4-23 (continued)

Unit shortage cost, p = 0.5

Setup Cost, K = 1000

Results:

s = 3835.61

Q = 41438.8

17.4-24.

Continuous Review Model With Fixed Delivery Lag - Backlogging:
Demand density is exponential, with lambda = 0.25.

Expected number of items demanded per unit time, a = 8500

Unit inventory holding cost, h = 0.01

Unit shortage cost, p = 0.5

Setup Cost, K = 1000

Results:

s = 4847.94

Q = 43410.8

17.4-25

$c(Q,s): aK/Q + h[(Q/2)+s-a\lambda] + (pa/Q)a\lambda e^{-\frac{s}{a\lambda}} + ac$

when D is exponential, and so

$$\frac{\partial c(Q,s)}{\partial s} = h - \frac{pa}{Q} e^{-\frac{s}{a\lambda}} = 0$$

$$\Rightarrow e^{-\frac{s}{a\lambda}} = \frac{hQ}{pa}$$

$$\Rightarrow s = -a\lambda \ln\left(\frac{hQ}{pa}\right)$$

17.4-26.

(a) $P\{D>s\} = \frac{t-s}{t} \le V \Rightarrow s \ge (1-V)t$

(b) $$c(Q) = \frac{aK}{Q} + ac + h\left[\frac{Q}{2} + (1-V)t - a\lambda\right] + \left(\frac{pa}{Q}\right)\left[\frac{t}{2} + \frac{(1-V)^2t^2}{2t} - (1-V)t\right]$$

$$= \frac{aK}{Q} + ac + h\left[\frac{Q}{2} + t - Vt - a\lambda\right] + \left(\frac{pa}{Q}\right)\left[\frac{t}{2} + \frac{t}{2} - Vt + \frac{V^2t}{2} - t + Vt\right]$$

$$= \frac{aK}{Q} + ac + h\left[\frac{Q}{2} + t - vt - a\lambda\right] + \frac{pav^2t}{2Q}$$

(c) $$\frac{\partial c(Q)}{\partial Q} = -\frac{aK}{Q^2} + \frac{h}{2} - \frac{pav^2t}{2Q^2} = 0$$

$$\Rightarrow \frac{1}{Q^2}\left[aK + \frac{pav^2t}{2}\right] = \frac{h}{2} \Rightarrow Q^2 = \frac{2a}{h}\left[K + \frac{pv^2}{2}\right] \Rightarrow Q = \sqrt{\frac{2a}{h}\left[K + \frac{pv^2}{2}\right]}$$

17.4-27. (a) $P\{D>s\} = e^{-\frac{s}{a\lambda}} \leq V \Rightarrow s \geq -a\lambda \ln(V)$

(b) $C(Q) = \frac{aK}{Q} + ac + h\left[\frac{Q}{2} - a\lambda \ln(V) - a\lambda\right] + \left(\frac{pa}{Q}\right)a\lambda e^{\ln(V)}$

$= \frac{aK}{Q} + ac + h\left[\frac{Q}{2} - a\lambda \ln(V) - a\lambda\right] + \frac{pa^2\lambda V}{Q}$

(c) $\frac{\partial C(Q)}{\partial Q} = -\frac{aK}{Q^2} + \frac{h}{2} - \frac{pa^2\lambda V}{Q^2} = 0$

$\Rightarrow \frac{1}{Q^2}\left[aK + a^2\lambda p V\right] = \frac{h}{2}$

$\Rightarrow Q^2 = \frac{2a}{h}\left[K + a\lambda p V\right]$

$\Rightarrow Q = \sqrt{\frac{2a}{h}\left[K + a\lambda p V\right]}$

17.4-28. $\int_{s^*}^{\infty} \varphi_D(\xi)d\xi = 1 - \frac{s^*}{t} = \frac{hQ^*}{hQ^*+pa} \Rightarrow s^* = t\left[1 - \frac{hQ^*}{hQ^*+pa}\right] = t\left(\frac{pa}{hQ^*+pa}\right)$

$$Q^* = \sqrt{\frac{2a\left[K + p\int_{s^*}^{\infty}(\xi - s^*)\varphi_D(\xi)d\xi\right]}{h}}$$

$$= \sqrt{\frac{2a\left[K + p\left(\frac{t}{2} + \frac{s^{*2}}{2t} - s^*\right)\right]}{h}}$$

$$= \sqrt{\frac{2aK + apt + aps^{*2}/t - 2aps^{*2}}{h}}$$

17.4-29. $\int_{s^*}^{\infty} \varphi_D(\xi)d\xi = e^{-\frac{s^*}{a\lambda}} = \frac{hQ^*}{hQ^*+pa}$

$\Rightarrow s^* = -a\lambda \ln\left[\frac{hQ^*}{hQ^*+pa}\right]$

$$Q^* = \sqrt{\frac{2a\left[K + p\int_{s^*}^{\infty}(\xi - s^*)\varphi_D(\xi)d\xi\right]}{h}}$$

$$= \sqrt{\frac{2a\left[K + pa\lambda e^{-\frac{s^*}{a\lambda}}\right]}{h}}$$

$$= \sqrt{\frac{2a}{h}\left[K + a\lambda p e^{-\frac{s^*}{\lambda a}}\right]}$$

17.4-30. Continuous Review Model With Fixed Delivery Log - No Backlogging:

Demand density is uniform between 0 and 30.

Expected number of items demanded per unit time, a = 30

Unit inventory holding cost, h = 0.3

Unit shortage cost, p = 3

Setup Cost, K = 15

17.4-30 (continued)

Results:

$Q^* = 56.8172$

$S^* = 25.223$

17.4-31. Continuous Review Model With Fixed Delivery Log - No Backlogging:

Demand density is exponential with $a\lambda = 600$.

Expected number of items demanded per unit time, a = 600

Unit inventory holding cost, h = 0.05

Unit shortage cost, p = 2

Setup Cost, K = 25

Results:

$Q^* = 1522.5$

$S^* = 1691.52$

17.4-32. Continuous Review Model With Fixed Delivery Log - No Backlogging:

Demand density is uniform between 0 and 4250.

Expected number of items demanded per unit time, a = 8500

Unit inventory holding cost, h = 0.01

Unit shortage cost, p = 0.5

Setup Cost, K = 1000

Results:

$Q^* = 41403.3$

$S^* = 3872.72$

17.4-33. Continuous Review Model With Fixed Delivery Log - No Backlogging:

Demand density is exponential with $a\lambda = 2125$.

Expected number of items demanded per unit time, a = 8500

Unit inventory holding cost, h = 0.01

Unit shortage cost, p = 0.5

Setup Cost, K = 1000

Results:

$Q^* = 43205.1$

$S^* = 5063.77$

Chapter 18
Forecasting

18.3-1. $F_{t+1} = \frac{1}{4}(x_{t-3} + x_{t-2} + x_{t-1} + x_t)$

$\Rightarrow F_{t+2} = F_{t+1} + \frac{1}{4}(x_{t+1} - x_{t-3})$

$\Rightarrow F_{t+2} = 2083 + \frac{1}{4}(1975 - 1945) = 2090.5$

18.3-2. $F_{t+1} = .3(1975) + .7(2083) = 2050.6$

18.3-3. $F_{t+1} = .1 \times 794 + .9 \times 782 = 783.2$

18.3-4. $F_{t+1} = F_t + \frac{1}{3}(x_t - x_{t-3}) = 782 + \frac{1}{3}(794 - 805) = 778.3$

18.3-5. $F_{t+1} = F_t + \frac{1}{10}(x_t - x_{t-10}) = 1551 + \frac{1}{10}(1553 - 1632) = 1543.1$

18.3-6. $\alpha = 0 \Rightarrow F_{t+1} = F_t = \ldots = F_1$

in other words, the forecast remains equal to the best initial guess for the variable and never changes.

$\alpha = 1 \Rightarrow F_{t+1} = x_t$

hence, the forecast always equals the current value of the variable.

18.3-7. $F_{1+1} = .3(2800) + .7(2750) = 2765$

$F_{2+1} = .3(2925) + .7(2765) = 2813$

$F_{3+1} = .3(3040) + .7(2813) = 2881.1$

Since we do not have the value of sales in the fourth period our best estimate of sales in the fifth period is the estimate of sales in the fourth period $F_{3+2} = 2881.1$

18.3-8. (a) $F_{t+1} = \alpha x_t + (1-\alpha)F_t \Rightarrow x_t = \frac{1}{\alpha}(F_{t+1} - (1-\alpha)F_t) = 2F_{t+1} - F_t$ in this case

$\Rightarrow$ Actual demand in April $= 2(390) - 380 = 400$

Actual demand in May $= 2(380) - 390 = 370$

(b) $F_{Feb} = .5\,x_{Jan} + .5\,F_{Jan}$

$F_{mar} = .5\,x_{Feb} + .5\,F_{Feb}$

$= .5\,x_{Feb} + .5[.5\,x_{Jan} + .5\,F_{Jan}] = .5\,x_{Feb} + .25\,x_{Jan} + .25\,F_{Jan}$

We know that $x'_{Jan} = x_{Jan} + 32$

$x'_{Feb} = x_{Feb}$

and $F'_{Jan} = F_{Jan}$

$\Rightarrow F'_{march} = F_{march} + .25(32) = 408$

and so we can complete the table

	Jan	Feb	March	April	May	June
Forecast			408	384	392	381
Actual	400		360	400	370	

18.4-1. Initial Estimate : 2750

Initial Trend : 100

Alpha = 0.3 , Beta = 0.3

$F_{20+m} = 4668 + 96.46m$

$F_5 = 3222$

Data:

t	X_t
1	2800
2	2925
3	3040

Results:

t	F_t	S_t	B_t
1	2850	2835	95.5
2	2931	2929	95.01
3	3024	3029	96.46
4	3125	3125	96.46
5	3222	3222	96.46

18.5-1 Exponential Smoothing With Seasonal Effect Forecasting Procedure:

Number of data points: 4

Initial estimate = 7.15

Number of seasons = 4

Alpha = 0.1 Gamma = 0.1

Init. Seas. Factor: Data:

	t	I(t-4)
1-80	1	0.965
4-80	2	0.937
7-80	3	1.105
10-80	4	0.993

Date	t	X(t)
1-81	1	8.2
4-81	2	7
7-81	3	7.3
10-81	4	7.5

Results:

Date	t	F(t)	S(t)	I(t)
1-81	1	6.9	7.285	0.981
4-81	2	6.826	7.303	0.939
7-81	3	8.069	7.234	1.095
10-81	4	7.183	7.266	0.997
10-84	16	7.243	7.266	0.997

18.5-2 Exponential Smoothing With Seasonal Effect Forecasting Procedure:

Number of data points: 4

Initial estimate = 9.575

Number of seasons = 4

Alpha = 0.1 Gamma = 0.1

Init. Seas. Factor: Data:

	t	I(t-4)
1-82	1	0.982
4-82	2	0.961
7-82	3	1.023
10-82	4	1.034

Date	t	X(t)
1-83	1	11.4
4-83	2	10
7-83	3	9.4
10-83	4	8.4

Results:

Date	t	F(t)	S(t)	I(t)
1-83	1	9.4	9.779	1
4-83	2	9.396	9.842	0.966
7-83	3	10.07	9.776	1.017
10-83	4	10.11	9.611	1.018
10-84	8	9.783	9.611	1.018

18.6-1 (a)

Date	X_t	$F_{(t-1)+1}$
1-80	6.9	
4-80	6.7	
7-80	7.9	
10-80	7.1	7.167
1-81	8.2	7.233
4-81	7.0	7.733
7-81	7.3	7.433
10-81	7.5	7.500
1-82	9.4	7.267
4-82	9.2	8.067
7-82	9.8	8.700
10-82	9.9	9.467
1-83	11.4	9.633
4-83	10.0	10.367
7-83	9.4	10.433
10-83	8.4	10.267
1-84	8.8	9.267
4-84	7.6	8.867
7-84	7.5	8.267
10-84		7.967

18.6-1 (continued)

(b) $\frac{1}{16}\sum_{i=1}^{16} E_i^2 = \frac{1}{16}(.004 + .934 + .538 + .018 + 0 + 4.551 + 1.284 + 1.210 + 0.188 + 3.121 + .134 + 1.068 + 3.484 + .218 + 1.604 + .588) = 1.184$

18.6-2

(a) Exponential Smoothing Forecasting Procedure:

Number of data points: 17

Initial estimate = 7.2

Alpha = 0.1

Data:

date	t	X(t)
7-80	1	7.9
10-80	2	7.1
1-81	3	8.2
4-81	4	7
7-81	5	7.3
10-81	6	7.5
1-82	7	9.4
4-82	8	9.2
7-82	9	9.8
10-82	10	9.9
1-83	11	11.4
4-83	12	10
7-83	13	9.4
10-83	14	8.4
1-84	15	8.8
4-84	16	7.6
7-84	17	7.5

Results:

date	t	F(t)
7-80	1	7.2
10-80	2	7.27
1-81	3	7.253
4-81	4	7.348
7-81	5	7.313
10-81	6	7.312
1-82	7	7.33
4-82	8	7.537
7-82	9	7.704
10-82	10	7.913
1-83	11	8.112
4-83	12	8.441
7-83	13	8.597
10-83	14	8.677
1-84	15	8.649
4-84	16	8.664
7-84	17	8.558
10-84	18	8.452

(b) $\frac{1}{16}\sum_{i=1}^{16} E_i^2 = \frac{1}{16}(0.029 + 0.897 + 0.121 + 0 + 0.035 \cdot 4.283 + 2.764 + 4.395 + 3.947 + 10.811 + 2.431 + 0.645 + 0.077 + 0.023 + 1.133 + 1.119) = 2.044$

18.6-3 (a)

Exponential Smoothing Forecasting Procedure:

Number of data points: 17

Initial estimate = 7.2

Alpha = 0.3

Data:

Date	t	X(t)
7-80	1	7.9
10-80	2	7.1
1-81	3	8.2
4-81	4	7
7-81	5	7.3
10-81	6	7.5
1-82	7	9.4
4-82	8	9.2
7-82	9	9.8
10-82	10	9.9
1-83	11	11.4
4-83	12	10
7-83	13	9.4
10-83	14	8.4
1-84	15	8.8
4-84	16	7.6
7-84	17	7.5

Results:

Date	t	F(t)
7-80	1	7.2
10-80	2	7.41
1-81	3	7.317
4-81	4	7.582
7-81	5	7.407
10-81	6	7.375
1-82	7	7.413
4-82	8	8.009
7-82	9	8.366
10-82	10	8.796
1-83	11	9.127
4-83	12	9.809
7-83	13	9.866
10-83	14	9.727
1-84	15	9.329
4-84	16	9.17
7-84	17	8.699
10-84	18	8.339

18.6-3. (b)

$$\frac{1}{16}\sum_{i=1}^{16} E_i^2 = \frac{1}{16}(0.096 + 0.780 + 0.339 + 0.012 + 0.016 + 3.950 + 1.419 + 2.056 + 1.218 + 5.165 + 0.036 + 0.218 + 1.760 + 0.279 + 2.465 + 1.438) = 1.328$$

18.6-4

The moving average forecasts had the lower mean square error and is the computationally easier method and, hence, is the method of choice over exponential smoothing in this instance.

18.6-5.

(a) Exponential Smoothing With Trend Forecasting Procedure:

Number of data points: 16

Initial estimate = 7.2

Initial trend = 0.2

Alpha = 0.1 Beta = 0.1

Note: The Courseware printout will include more information than this problem asks.

Data:

Date	t	X(t)
10-80	1	7.1
1-81	2	8.2
4-81	3	7
7-81	4	7.3
10-81	5	7.5
1-82	6	9.4
4-82	7	9.2
7-82	8	9.8
10-82	9	9.9
1-83	10	11.4
4-83	11	10
7-83	12	9.4
10-83	13	8.4
1-84	14	8.8
4-84	15	7.6
7-84	16	7.5

Results:

Date	t	F(t)	S(t)	B(t)
10-80	1	7.4	7.37	0.197
1-81	2	7.567	7.63	0.203
4-81	3	7.834	7.75	0.195
7-81	4	7.945	7.881	0.189
10-81	5	8.069	8.012	0.183
1-82	6	8.195	8.316	0.195
4-82	7	8.511	8.58	0.202
7-82	8	8.781	8.883	0.212
10-82	9	9.095	9.176	0.22
1-83	10	9.396	9.596	0.24
4-83	11	9.836	9.853	0.242
7-83	12	10.09	10.02	0.235
10-83	13	10.26	10.07	0.216
1-84	14	10.29	10.14	0.201
4-84	15	10.34	10.07	0.174
7-84	16	10.24	9.968	0.146
10-84	17	10.11	10.11	0.146

(b)

$$\frac{1}{16}\sum_{i=1}^{16} E_i^2 = \frac{1}{16}(0.090 + 0.401 + 0.695 + 0.416 + 0.324 + 1.452 + 0.475 + 1.038 + 0.648 + 4.017 + 0.027 + 0.476 + 3.458 + 2.220 + 7.508 + 7.508) = 1.922$$

18.6-6.

The moving average forecasts had the lowest mean square error and is easier computationally. Thus the moving average procedure is the method of choice.

18.6-7. (a)

Quarter	x_t	$F_{(t-1)+1}$
1	546	
2	528	
3	530	
4	508	
5	647	528
6	594	553.25
7	665	569.75
8	630	603.5
9	736	634
10	724	656.25
11	813	688.75
12		725.75

18.6-7 (b) $\frac{1}{7}\sum_{i=5}^{11} E_i^2 = \frac{1}{7}(14161 + 1660.5625 + 9072.5625 + 702.25 + 10404 + 4590.0625$
$+ 15438.0625) = 8004.071$

18.6-8. (a) Exponential Smoothing Forecasting Procedure:

Number of data points: 10

Initial estimate = 546

Alpha = 0.1

Data:

Quarter	t	X(t)
2	1	528
3	2	530
4	3	508
5	4	647
6	5	594
7	6	665
8	7	630
9	8	736
10	9	724
11	10	813

Results:

Quarter	t	F(t)
2	1	546
3	2	544.2
4	3	542.8
5	4	539.3
6	5	550.1
7	6	554.5
8	7	565.5
9	8	572
10	9	588.4
11	10	601.9
12	11	623

(b) $\frac{1}{9}\sum_{i=3}^{11} E_i^2 = \frac{1}{9}(201.640 + 1211.04 + 11599.29 + 1927.21 + 12210.25$
$+ 4160.25 + 26896 + 18387.36 + 44563.21$

$= \frac{120954.61}{9} = 13439.401$

18.6-9. (a) Exponential Smoothing Forecasting Procedure:

Number of data points: 10

Initial estimate = 546

Alpha = 0.3

Data:

Quarter	t	X(t)
2	1	528
3	2	530
4	3	508
5	4	647
6	5	594
7	6	665
8	7	630
9	8	736
10	9	724
11	10	813

Results:

Quarter	t	F(t)
2	1	546
3	2	540.6
4	3	537.4
5	4	528.6
6	5	564.1
7	6	573.1
8	7	600.7
9	8	609.5
10	9	647.4
11	10	670.4
12	11	713.2

(b) $\frac{1}{9}\sum_{i=3}^{11} E_i^2 = \frac{1}{9}(112.36 + 864.36 + 14018.56 + 894.01 + 8445.61 + 858.49 +$
$16002.25 + 5867.56 + 20334.76) = 7488.66$

18.6-10. The mean square error for the moving average technique is less than the mean square error for the exponential smoothing technique, so the moving average technique is the technique of choice.

18.6-11. a) Exponential Smoothing With Trend Forecasting Procedure:

Number of data points: 9

Initial estimate = 546

Initial trend = 18

Alpha = 0.1 Beta = 0.1

Data:

Quarter	t	X(t)
3	1	530
4	2	508
5	3	647
6	4	594
7	5	665
8	6	630
9	7	736
10	8	724
11	9	813

Results:

Quarter	t	F(t)	S(t)	B(t)
3	1	564	560.6	17.66
4	2	578.3	571.2	16.96
5	3	588.2	594.1	17.55
6	4	611.6	609.9	17.37
7	5	627.2	631	17.75
8	6	648.7	646.9	17.56
9	7	664.4	671.6	18.28
10	8	689.9	693.3	18.62
11	9	711.9	722	19.63
12	10	741.6	741.6	19.63

b) First interpretation:

$$\frac{1}{9}\sum_{i=3}^{11} E_i^2 = \frac{1}{9}(2304 + 6789.76 + 2352.25 + 686.44 + 954.81 + 580.81 + 4583.29 + 998.56 + 9980.01)$$

$$= \frac{1}{9}(29229.93) = 3247.77$$

Second interpretation:

$$\frac{1}{9}\sum_{i=3}^{11} E_i^2 = \frac{1}{9}(1156 + 4942.09 + 3457.44 + 309.76 + 1428.84 + 349.69 + 5126.56 + 1162.81 + 10221.21)$$

$$= \frac{1}{9}(28154.4) = 3128.267$$

18.6-12. 13,439 > 8004 > 3248 and 3128. ∴ Choose Exponential Smoothing adjusted for trend.

18.8-1. (a) $\Sigma ty = 29356$, $\Sigma t = 55$, $\Sigma y = 5073$ and $\Sigma t^2 = 385$

$\Rightarrow \hat{Y}(t) = 410\frac{1}{3} + 17.630t$

(b) $\hat{Y}(11) = 604.267$

(c)

t	Y	$\hat{E}(Y)$
1	430	
2	446	
3	464	431.6
4	480	434.84
5	498	439.356
6	514	445.220
7	532	452.098
8	548	460.089
9	570	468.880
10	591	478.992
11	—	490.193

(d)

t	Y	$\hat{E}(Y)$	$\hat{E}(S_t)$	$Y_{t+1,1}$
1	430	430	18	—
2	446	447.6	17.92	—
3	464	465.216	17.859	465.52
4	480	482.460	17.736	483.075
5	498	499.757	17.648	500.196
6	514	516.724	17.512	517.405
7	532	533.789	17.422	534.236
8	548	550.569	17.294	551.212
9	570	568.291	17.380	567.864
10	591	586.736	17.593	585.671
11	—	—	—	604.329

18.8-2. (a) $\hat{Y}(x) = 121.04 - 1.0346x$

$\hat{Y}(55) = 64.137$

(b) $t_{.025:5} = 2.571$, $s_{Y|x} = 6.34$

$\sqrt{1 + \frac{1}{7} + \frac{(x_+ - \bar{x})^2}{\Sigma(x_i - \bar{x})^2}} = 1.0735$

$\Rightarrow$ the 95% prediction interval is [46.64, 81.64]

(c) by interpolation

$t_{.0125:5} = 3.365 - \frac{.0025}{.015}(3.365 - 2.571)$
$= 3.233$

$\Rightarrow$ the simultaneous 95% prediction interval is [42.13, 86.14]

(d) interpolating: $c^{**} = 10.722 + \frac{1}{2}(11.150 - 10.722)$
$= 10.936$

$\Rightarrow$ the simultaneous tolerance interval is [37.1, 91.2]

18.8-3. (a) $\Sigma x = 20$, $\Sigma y = 40$, $\Sigma xy = 242$ and $\Sigma x^2 = 120$

$\Rightarrow \hat{Y}(x) = -.2 + 2.05x$

$\hat{Y}(10) = 20.3$

(b) $s^2_{Y|x} = .6333$, $t_{.025:3} = 3.182$, and $\sqrt{\frac{1}{5} + \frac{(x_0 - \bar{x})^2}{\Sigma(x_i - \bar{x})^2}} = \sqrt{1.1}$

$\Rightarrow$ [17.64, 22.9] is the 95% confidence interval

(c) $\sqrt{1 + \frac{1}{5} + \frac{(x_+ - \bar{x})^2}{\Sigma(x_i - \bar{x})^2}} = \sqrt{2.1}$

$\Rightarrow$ [16.630, 23.970] is the 95% prediction interval

(d) interpolating: $c^{**} = 11.150 + \frac{1}{2}(14.953 - 11.150)$
$= 13.0515$

$\Rightarrow$ [9.406, 31.194] is the simultaneous tolerance interval

18.8-4. (a) $K = 19.96/10 = 1.996$

$\log g = .016 - (1.996)(0) = .016$

$\Rightarrow \log r = .016 + 1.996 \log t$
and at $\log t = 3$ $\log r = 6.004$

(b)

log t	log r	$\hat{E}(\log r)$
-2.0	-3.95	—
-1.0	-2.12	
0.0	0.08	-3.767
1.0	2.20	-3.382
2.0	3.87	-2.824
3.0	—	-2.155

(c)

log t	log r	$\hat{E}(\log r)$	$\hat{E}(K)$	$\log r_{\text{a-i-l}}$
-2.0	-3.95	-3.95	1.996	—
-1.0	-2.12	-1.971	1.994	
0.0	0.08	0.029	1.995	0.024
1.0	2.20	2.042	1.997	2.024
2.0	3.87	4.022	1.995	4.039
3.0	—	—	—	6.017

18.8-5. $Q = \Sigma(y_i - bx_i)^2$

$\frac{dQ}{db} = \Sigma -2x_i(y_i - bx_i) = 0 \Rightarrow B = \frac{\Sigma x_i y_i}{\Sigma x_i^2}$

Chapter 19
Markov Decision Processes

19.2-1 a) State i = the number of customers at the facility, $i=0,1,2$

decision 1 = use the slow service rate

decision 2 = use the fast service rate

expected net immediate cost $= C_{ij}$, $i=1,2$; $j=1,2$

$C_{11} = 3-\frac{3}{5}\times 50 = -27$, $C_{12} = 9-\frac{4}{5}\times 50 = -31$

$C_{21} = -27$, $C_{22} = -31$

b) The four possible stationary policies R_1, R_2, R_3, R_4 are

i	$d_i(R_1)$	$d_i(R_2)$	$d_i(R_3)$	$d_i(R_4)$
1	1	1	2	2
2	1	2	1	2

Transition matrix:

Under R_1: $\begin{bmatrix} \frac{1}{2} & \frac{1}{2} & 0 \\ \frac{3}{10} & \frac{1}{2} & \frac{1}{5} \\ 0 & \frac{3}{5} & \frac{2}{5} \end{bmatrix}$ Under R_2: $\begin{bmatrix} \frac{1}{2} & \frac{1}{2} & 0 \\ \frac{3}{10} & \frac{1}{2} & \frac{1}{5} \\ 0 & \frac{4}{5} & \frac{1}{5} \end{bmatrix}$

Under R_3: $\begin{bmatrix} \frac{1}{2} & \frac{1}{2} & 0 \\ \frac{2}{5} & \frac{1}{2} & \frac{1}{10} \\ 0 & \frac{3}{5} & \frac{2}{5} \end{bmatrix}$ Under R_4: $\begin{bmatrix} \frac{1}{2} & \frac{1}{2} & 0 \\ \frac{2}{5} & \frac{1}{2} & \frac{1}{10} \\ 0 & \frac{4}{5} & \frac{1}{5} \end{bmatrix}$

Expected long-term Average cost:

R_1: $-27(\pi_{11}+\pi_{21}) = C_1$

R_2: $-27\pi_{12} - 31\pi_{22} = C_2$

R_3: $-31\pi_{13} - 27\pi_{23} = C_3$

R_4: $-31(\pi_{14}+\pi_{24}) = C_4$

c) For R_1, $\pi_1 = 0.517$, $\pi_2 = 0.172$, $C_1 = -18.6$

For R_2, $\pi_1 = 0.541$, $\pi_2 = 0.135$, $C_2 = -18.79$

For R_3, $\pi_1 = 0.508$, $\pi_2 = 0.085$, $C_3 = -18.043$

For R_4, $\pi_1 = 0.519$, $\pi_2 = 0.065$, $C_4 = -18.104$.

Obviously, C_2 is the minimum. So, R_2 is the best policy.

19.2-2. a) States = $\begin{cases} 0 & \text{not dented} \\ 1 & \text{dented} \end{cases}$

Decisions at state 0: street, two spaces, lot
Decisions at state 1: repair, not repaired
So, there are 5 decisions.

$$C(ik): \begin{bmatrix} 0 & 4.5 & 5 & - & - \\ - & - & - & 50 & 9 \end{bmatrix}$$

b) There are 5 stationary deterministic policies

c)

state	$d_i(R_1)$	$d_i(R_2)$	$d_i(R_3)$	$d_i(R_4)$	$d_i(R_5)$
0	1	1	2	2	3
1	4	5	4	5	—

R_1: $P = \begin{bmatrix} 0.9 & 0.1 \\ 1 & 0 \end{bmatrix}$ $\quad \pi = (0.909, 0.091)$

$C_1 = \pi_0 \cdot 0 + \pi_1 \cdot 50 = 4.55$

R_2: $P = \begin{bmatrix} 0.9 & 0.1 \\ 0 & 1 \end{bmatrix}$ $\quad \pi = (0, 1)$

$C_2 = 9$

R_3: $P = \begin{bmatrix} 0.98 & 0.02 \\ 1 & 0 \end{bmatrix}$ $\quad \pi = (0.98, 0.02)$

$C_3 = 0.98 \times 4.5 + 0.02 \times 50 = 5.41$

R_4: $P = \begin{bmatrix} 0.98 & 0.02 \\ 0 & 1 \end{bmatrix}$ $\quad \pi = (0, 1)$

$C_4 = 9$

R_5: $P = \begin{bmatrix} 1 & 0 \\ 0 & 1 \end{bmatrix}$, $C_5 = 5$ if initial state of the car is undented

So, R_1, namely, parking in the street and have it repaired when dented, is the optimal policy.

19.2-3. a) Let state 0 = Low sales
1 = High sales

decision 1 = Do not advertise
2 = Advertise

cost matrix, $C(ik)$:

$$\begin{bmatrix} -2 & -1 \\ -4 & -3 \end{bmatrix}$$

19.2-3 (continued)

b) The four possible stationary deterministic policies are:

i	$d_i(R_1)$	$d_i(R_2)$	$d_i(R_3)$	$d_i(R_4)$
0	1	1	2	2
1	1	2	1	2

R_1: $P = \begin{bmatrix} 0.75 & 0.25 \\ 0.5 & 0.5 \end{bmatrix}$ $\quad C_1 = -2\pi_0 - 4\pi_1$

R_2: $P = \begin{bmatrix} 0.75 & 0.25 \\ 0.25 & 0.75 \end{bmatrix}$ $\quad C_2 = -2\pi_0 - 3\pi_1$

R_3: $P = \begin{bmatrix} 0.5 & 0.5 \\ 0.5 & 0.5 \end{bmatrix}$ $\quad C_3 = -\pi_0 - 4\pi_1$

R_4: $P = \begin{bmatrix} 0.5 & 0.5 \\ 0.25 & 0.75 \end{bmatrix}$ $\quad C_4 = -\pi_0 - 3\pi_1$

c) R_1: $\pi = (0.667, 0.333)$, $C_1 = -2.667$

R_2: $\pi = (0.5, 0.5)$, $C_2 = -2.5$

R_3: $\pi = (0.5\ 0.5)$, $C_3 = -2.5$

R_4: $\pi = (0.333, 0.667)$, $C_4 = -2.333$

So, policy R_1 is optimal.

19.2-4 a) Let state 0 = good mood   decision 1 = take her out for dinner
1 = bad mood   2 = not take her out

cost matrix, $C(i k)$:

$$\begin{bmatrix} 14 & 0 \\ 14 & 75 \end{bmatrix}$$

b) The four possible stationary deterministic policies are

i	$d_i(R_1)$	$d_i(R_2)$	$d_i(R_3)$	$d_i(R_4)$
0	1	1	2	2
1	1	2	1	2

19.2-4 (continued)

R_1 : $\begin{bmatrix} 0.875 & 0.125 \\ 0.875 & 0.125 \end{bmatrix}$ $C_1 = 14\pi_0 + 14\pi_1$

R_2 : $\begin{bmatrix} 0.875 & 0.125 \\ 0.125 & 0.875 \end{bmatrix}$ $C_2 = 14\pi_0 + 75\pi_1$

R_3 : $\begin{bmatrix} 0.125 & 0.875 \\ 0.875 & 0.125 \end{bmatrix}$ $C_3 = 14\pi_1$

R_4 : $\begin{bmatrix} 0.125 & 0.875 \\ 0.125 & 0.875 \end{bmatrix}$ $C_4 = 75\pi_1$

c) R_1: $\pi = (0.875, 0.125)$, $C_1 = 14$

R_2: $\pi = (0.5, 0.5)$, $C_2 = 44.5$

R_3: $\pi = (0.5, 0.5)$, $C_3 = 7$

R_4: $\pi = (0.125, 0.875)$, $C_4 = 65.625$

So, optimal policy is R_3.

19.2-5. a) Let state 0 denote that the point is over and that there are two serves for the next point, and let state 1 denote that only one serve for the current point is remaining. Let decision 1 be to attempt an ace and decision 2 be to attempt a lob. The transition

Cost matrix, $C(ik)$:

$C_{01} = 3/8[2/3(-1) + 1/3(1)] = -1/8$

$C_{02} = 7/8[1/3(-1) + 2/3(1)] = 7/24$

$C_{11} = 3/8[2/3(-1) + 1/3(1)] + 5/8(1) = 1/2$

$C_{12} = 7/8[1/3(-1) + 2/3(1)] + 1/8(1) = 5/12$

b) There are four possible stationary deterministic policies:

i	$d_i(R_1)$	$d_i(R_2)$	$d_i(R_3)$	$d_i(R_4)$
0	1	1	2	2
1	1	2	1	2

R_1: $P = \begin{bmatrix} \frac{3}{8} & \frac{5}{8} \\ 1 & 0 \end{bmatrix}$ $C_1 = -\frac{1}{8}\pi_0 + \frac{1}{2}\pi_1$

R_2: $P = \begin{bmatrix} \frac{3}{8} & \frac{5}{8} \\ 1 & 0 \end{bmatrix}$ $C_2 = -\frac{1}{8}\pi_0 + \frac{5}{12}\pi_1$

R_3: $P = \begin{bmatrix} \frac{7}{8} & \frac{1}{8} \\ 1 & 0 \end{bmatrix}$ $C_3 = \frac{7}{24}\pi_0 + \frac{1}{2}\pi_1$

19.2-5 (b) (continued)

$$R_4: \quad P = \begin{bmatrix} \frac{7}{8} & \frac{1}{8} \\ 1 & 0 \end{bmatrix}, \quad C_4 = \frac{7}{24}\pi_0 + \frac{5}{12}\pi_1$$

c) R_1: $\pi = (0.615, 0.385)$, $C_1 = 0.27$

R_2: $\pi = (0.615, 0.385)$, $C_2 = 0.237$

R_3: $\pi = (0.889, 0.111)$, $C_3 = 0.315$

R_4: $\pi = (0.889, 0.111)$, $C_4 = 0.306$

So, R_2 is the optimal policy. (0: attempt ace, 1: attempt lob)

19.2-6 (a) Let states 0, 1, 2 be that the market is currenty at 4400, 4500, 4600, respectively. Let decisions 1, 2 be to invest in the go-go fund and go-slow fund, respectively.

$C_{01} = \frac{5}{10}(-20) + \frac{2}{10}(-50) = -20$

$C_{02} = \frac{5}{10}(-10) + \frac{2}{10}(-20) = -9$

$C_{11} = \frac{1}{10}(20) + \frac{4}{10}(-20) = -6$

$C_{12} = \frac{1}{10}(10) + \frac{4}{10}(-10) = -3$

$C_{21} = \frac{2}{10}(50) + \frac{4}{10}(20) = 18$

$C_{22} = \frac{2}{10}(20) + \frac{4}{10}(10) = 8$

(b) There are 8 possible policies:

i	$d_i(R_1)$	$d_i(R_2)$	$d_i(R_3)$	$d_i(R_4)$	$d_i(R_5)$	$d_i(R_6)$	$d_i(R_7)$	$d_i(R_8)$
0	1	1	1	1	2	2	2	2
1	1	1	2	2	2	1	1	2
2	1	2	2	1	1	2	1	2

R_i's share the same transition matrix

$$P = \begin{bmatrix} 0.3 & 0.5 & 0.2 \\ 0.1 & 0.5 & 0.4 \\ 0.2 & 0.4 & 0.1 \end{bmatrix}$$

R_1: $C_1 = -20\pi_0 - 6\pi_1 + 18\pi_2$

R_2: $C_2 = -20\pi_0 - 6\pi_1 + 8\pi_2$

R_3: $C_3 = -20\pi_0 - 3\pi_1 + 8\pi_2$

R_4: $C_4 = -20\pi_0 - 3\pi_1 + 18\pi_2$

R_5: $C_5 = -9\pi_0 - 3\pi_1 + 18\pi_2$

R_6: $C_6 = -9\pi_0 - 6\pi_1 + 8\pi_2$

R_7: $C_7 = -9\pi_0 - 6\pi_1 + 18\pi_2$

R_8: $C_8 = -9\pi_0 - 3\pi_1 + 8\pi_2$

19.2-6. (continued)

c) From OR courseware, $\pi = (0.171, 0.463, 0.366)$

Such that $R_1 = 0.39$, $R_2 = -3.27$, $R_3 = -1.881$, $R_4 = 1.779$

$R_5 = 3.66$ $R_6 = -1.389$ $R_7 = 2.271$ $R_8 = 0$

R_2 has the lowest value. so, $\begin{pmatrix} 0 : \text{Go-go} \\ 1 : \text{Go-go} \\ 2 : \text{Go-slow} \end{pmatrix}$ is optimal

19.2-7. a) Let state 0 = machine broken down

1 = machine running

decision 1 = Buck works on machine

2 = Bill works on machine

Cost matrix, $C(ik)$:

$$\begin{bmatrix} 0 & 0 \\ -1200 & -1200 \end{bmatrix}$$

b) There are 4 possible (stationary deterministic) policies

i	$d_i(R_1)$	$d_i(R_2)$	$d_i(R_3)$	$d_i(R_4)$
0	1	1	2	2
1	1	2	1	2

R_1: $\begin{bmatrix} 0.4 & 0.6 \\ 0.6 & 0.4 \end{bmatrix}$ $C_1 = -1200\pi_1$

R_2, $\begin{bmatrix} 0.4 & 0.6 \\ 0.4 & 0.6 \end{bmatrix}$ $C_2 = -1200\pi_1$

R_3: $\begin{bmatrix} 0.5 & 0.5 \\ 0.6 & 0.4 \end{bmatrix}$ $C_3 = -1200\pi_1$

R_4: $\begin{bmatrix} 0.5 & 0.5 \\ 0.4 & 0.6 \end{bmatrix}$ $C_4 = -1200\pi_1$

c) R_1 : $\pi = (0.5, 0.5)$, $C_1 = -600$

R_2 ; $\pi = (0.4, 0.6)$, $C_2 = -720$

R_3 ; $\pi = (0.545, 0.455)$, $C_3 = -546$

R_4 : $\pi = (0.444, 0.556)$, $C_4 = -667.2$

19.2-7. c) (continued)

The smallest value is -720.

So, policy R_2 is optimal.

19.2-8. a) Let state 0 = she is in $(20, \infty)$

state 1 = she is in $(10, 19)$

2 = she is in $(-10, 9)$

3 = she is in $(-20, -11)$

Let decision 1 = do not speed

2 = speed

$C_{01} = 0 = C_{02}$, $C_{11} = 4$, $C_{12} = \frac{1}{8} \times (20+4) = 3$.

$C_{21} = 4 = C_{22}$, $C_{31} = 8$, $C_{32} = \frac{1}{8} \times (20+8) + \frac{7}{8} \times 4 = 7$

b) There are four (stationary deterministic) policies.

i	$d_i(R_1)$	$d_i(R_2)$	$d_i(R_3)$	$d_i(R_4)$
0	1	1	1	1
1	1	1	2	2
2	1	1	1	1
3	1	2	1	2

We do not speed at state 0 and 2 since speeding or not, it doesn't help to avoid penalty of lateness.

R_1: $P = \begin{bmatrix} \frac{3}{8} & \frac{1}{4} & \frac{1}{4} & \frac{1}{8} \\ \frac{1}{2} & \frac{1}{4} & \frac{1}{8} & \frac{1}{8} \\ \frac{5}{8} & \frac{1}{4} & \frac{1}{8} & 0 \\ \frac{3}{4} & \frac{1}{4} & 0 & 0 \end{bmatrix}$ $\qquad C_1 = 4\pi_1 + 4\pi_2 + 8\pi_3$

R_2: $P = \begin{bmatrix} \frac{3}{8} & \frac{1}{4} & \frac{1}{4} & \frac{1}{8} \\ \frac{1}{2} & \frac{1}{4} & \frac{1}{8} & \frac{1}{8} \\ \frac{5}{8} & \frac{1}{4} & \frac{1}{8} & 0 \\ \frac{5}{8} & \frac{1}{4} & \frac{1}{8} & 0 \end{bmatrix}$ $\qquad C_2 = 4\pi_1 + 4\pi_2 + 7\pi_3$

R_3: $P = \begin{bmatrix} \frac{3}{8} & \frac{1}{4} & \frac{1}{4} & \frac{1}{8} \\ \frac{3}{8} & \frac{1}{4} & \frac{1}{4} & \frac{1}{8} \\ \frac{5}{8} & \frac{1}{4} & \frac{1}{8} & 0 \\ \frac{3}{4} & \frac{1}{4} & 0 & 0 \end{bmatrix}$ $\qquad C_3 = 3\pi_1 + 4\pi_2 + 8\pi_3$

19.2-9 (b) (continued)

i \ $d_i(R_j)$	7	8	9	10	11	12	13	14	15	16	17	18	19	20	21	22	23	24	25	26	27
0	1	2	3	1	2	3	1	2	3	1	2	3	1	2	3	1	2	3	1	2	3
1	3	3	3	1	1	1	2	2	2	3	3	3	1	1	1	2	2	2	3	3	3
2	1	1	1	2	2	2	2	2	2	2	2	2	3	3	3	3	3	3	3	3	3

19.3-1. (a) Minimize $3y_{01} + 9y_{02} + 3y_{11} + 9y_{12} + 28y_{21} + 34y_{22}$

subject to

$$y_{01} + y_{02} + y_{11} + y_{12} + y_{21} + y_{22} = 1$$

$$y_{01} + y_{02} - \left(\tfrac{1}{2}y_{01} + \tfrac{3}{10}y_{11} + \tfrac{1}{2}y_{02} + \tfrac{2}{5}y_{12}\right) = 0$$

$$y_{11} + y_{12} - \left(\tfrac{1}{2}y_{01} + \tfrac{1}{2}y_{11} + \tfrac{3}{5}y_{21} + \tfrac{1}{2}y_{02} + \tfrac{1}{2}y_{12} + \tfrac{4}{5}y_{22}\right) = 0$$

$$y_{21} + y_{22} - \left(\tfrac{2}{10}y_{11} + \tfrac{2}{5}y_{21} + \tfrac{1}{10}y_{12} + \tfrac{1}{5}y_{22}\right) = 0$$

$$y_{ik} \geq 0 \text{ for } i = 0,1,2 \text{ and } k = 1,2$$

(b) Use simplex-method, we find $y_{01} = 0.32432$, $y_{11} = 0.54054$, $y_{22} = 0.13514$ and other y_{ik}'s are zero. This tells us that we should adopt decision 1 at state 0, decision 2 at state 2, decision at state 1, which means policy 2 is optimal.

19.3-2. (a) Minimize $4.5y_{02} + 5y_{03} + 50y_{14} + 9y_{15}$

subject to

$$y_{01} + y_{02} + y_{03} + y_{14} + y_{15} = 1$$

$$y_{01} + y_{02} + y_{03} - \left(\tfrac{9}{10}y_{01} + \tfrac{49}{50}y_{02} + y_{03} + y_{14}\right) = 0$$

$$y_{14} + y_{15} - \left(\tfrac{1}{10}y_{01} + \tfrac{1}{50}y_{02} + y_{15}\right) = 0$$

$$y_{ik} \geq 0 \quad i = 0,\ k = 1,2,3;\ i = 1,\ k = 4,5.$$

(b) Use simplex method, we find y_{ik}'s are zero except that $y_{01} = 0.90909$, $y_{14} = 0.09091$. So, $R_1 = \begin{bmatrix} 0: 1 \\ 1: 4 \end{bmatrix}$ is optimal.

19.3-3. (a) Minimize $-4y_{01} - 2y_{02} - 3y_{11} - 4y_{12}$

subject to:

$$y_{01} + y_{02} + y_{11} + y_{12} = 1$$

$$y_{01} + y_{11} - \left(\tfrac{3}{4}y_{01} + \tfrac{1}{4}y_{02} + \tfrac{1}{2}y_{11} + \tfrac{1}{2}y_{12}\right) = 0$$

$$y_{02} + y_{12} - \left(\tfrac{1}{2}y_{01} + \tfrac{1}{2}y_{02} + \tfrac{1}{4}y_{11} + \tfrac{3}{4}y_{12}\right) = 0$$

$$y_{ik} \geq 0 \quad i = 0,1 \quad k = 1,2$$

(b) Use simplex method, we find y_{ik}'s are zero excep that $y_{01} = 0.6667$, $y_{11} = 0.3333$. So $R_1 = \begin{bmatrix} 0, \text{ decision } 1 \\ 1: \text{ decision } 1 \end{bmatrix}$ is optimal.

19.3-4. (a) Minimize $75y_{11} + 14y_{02} + 14y_{12}$

subject to

$$y_{01} + y_{11} + y_{02} + y_{12} = 1$$
$$y_{01} + y_{11} - \left(\tfrac{1}{8}y_{01} + \tfrac{1}{8}y_{11} + \tfrac{7}{8}y_{02} + \tfrac{7}{8}y_{12}\right) = 0$$
$$y_{02} + y_{12} - \left(\tfrac{7}{8}y_{01} + \tfrac{7}{8}y_{11} + \tfrac{1}{8}y_{02} + \tfrac{1}{8}y_{12}\right) = 0$$
$$y_{ik} \geq 0 \quad i = 0,1, \; k = 1,2$$

(b) Solve this by simplex-method, we get $y_{02} = y_{11} = 0.5$, $y_{01} = y_{12} = 0$

So, optimal policy is $R_3 = \begin{bmatrix} 0, \text{ decision } 2 \\ 1, \text{ decision } 1 \end{bmatrix}$

19.3-5. (a) Minimize $-\tfrac{1}{8}y_{01} + \tfrac{7}{24}y_{02} + \tfrac{1}{2}y_{11} + \tfrac{5}{12}y_{12}$

subject to

$$y_{01} + y_{02} + y_{11} + y_{12} = 1$$
$$y_{01} + y_{02} - \left(\tfrac{3}{8}y_{01} + y_{11} + \tfrac{7}{8}y_{02} + y_{12}\right) = 0$$
$$y_{11} + y_{12} - \left(\tfrac{5}{8}y_{01} + \tfrac{1}{8}y_{02}\right) = 0$$
$$y_{ik} \geq 0 \quad i = 0,1, \; k = 1,2$$

(b) The Simplex-method yields $y_{02} = 0.8889$, $y_{11} = 0.1111$, $y_{01} = y_{12} = 0$

So, optimal policy is $R_3 = \begin{bmatrix} 0: \text{ attempt ace} \\ 1: \text{ attempt lob} \end{bmatrix}$.

19.3-6. (a) Minimize $-20y_{01} - 9y_{02} - 6y_{11} - 3y_{12} + 18y_{21} + 8y_{22}$

subject to

$$y_{01} + y_{02} + y_{11} + y_{12} + y_{21} + y_{22} = 1$$
$$y_{01} + y_{02} - \left[\tfrac{3}{10}(y_{01}+y_{02}) + \tfrac{1}{10}(y_{11}+y_{12}) + \tfrac{2}{10}(y_{21}+y_{22})\right] = 0$$
$$y_{11} + y_{12} - \left[\tfrac{5}{10}(y_{01}+y_{02}) + \tfrac{5}{10}(y_{11}+y_{12}) + \tfrac{4}{10}(y_{21}+y_{22})\right] = 0$$
$$y_{21} + y_{22} - \left[\tfrac{2}{10}(y_{01}+y_{02}) + \tfrac{4}{10}(y_{11}+y_{12}) + \tfrac{4}{10}(y_{21}+y_{22})\right] = 0$$
$$y_{ik} \geq 0 \quad i = 0,1,2 \quad k = 1,2$$

(b) The Simplex-method yields $y_{01} = 0.171$, $y_{11} = 0.463$, $y_{22} = 0.366$ and $y_{02} = y_{12} = y_{21} = 0$.

So, optimal policy is $R_2 = \begin{bmatrix} 0: \text{ go-go} \\ 1: \text{ go-go} \\ 2: \text{ go-slow} \end{bmatrix}$

19.3-7 (a) Minimize $-1200y_{11} - 1200y_{12}$

Subject to:

$$y_{01} + y_{02} + y_{11} + y_{12} = 1$$
$$y_{01} + y_{02} - (.4y_{01} + .6y_{11} + .5y_{02} + .4y_{12}) = 0$$
$$y_{11} + y_{12} - (.6y_{01} + .4y_{11} + .5y_{02} + .6y_{12}) = 0$$

$y_{ik} \geq 0$ for $i = 0,1$ and $k = 1,2$.

(b) The simplex-method yields $y_{01} = 0.4$, $y_{12} = 0.6$, $y_{02} = y_{11} = 0$

So, optimal policy is $R_2 = \begin{bmatrix} 0; \text{ Buck} \\ 1: \text{ Bill} \end{bmatrix}$.

19.2-8 (b) (continued)

$$R_4: \; P = \begin{bmatrix} \frac{3}{8} & \frac{1}{4} & \frac{1}{4} & \frac{1}{8} \\ \frac{3}{8} & \frac{1}{4} & \frac{1}{4} & \frac{1}{8} \\ \frac{5}{8} & \frac{1}{4} & \frac{1}{8} & 0 \\ \frac{5}{8} & \frac{1}{4} & \frac{1}{8} & 0 \end{bmatrix}, \quad C_4 = 3\pi_1 + 4\pi_2 + 7\pi_3$$

(c) $R_1: \; \pi = (0.484, 0.25, 0.174, 0.092)$ $\quad C_1 = 2.432$

$R_2: \; \pi = (0.475, 0.25, 0.184, 0.091)$ $\quad C_2 = 2.373$

$R_3: \; \pi = (0.459, 0.25, 0.203, 0.089)$ $\quad C_3 = 2.274$

$R_4: \; \pi = (0.45, 0.25, 0.213, 0.087)$ $\quad C_4 = 2.225$

So, R_4 attains the minimum and thus is the optimal policy.

19.2-9

(a) Let the state be the number of items in inventory at the begining of the period.
Let decision 1 = order 0 items
2 = order 1 item
3 = order 2 items
(The strange labeling of decisions here is to conform to the software package standard).

The cost matrix is:

C_{ik}	1	2	3
0	40/3	56/3	24
1	4	19	—
2	4	—	—

The policy, R_5, is:

i	$d_i(R_5)$
0	3
1	1
2	1

$$P(R_6) = \begin{bmatrix} \frac{1}{3} & \frac{1}{3} & \frac{1}{3} \\ \frac{2}{3} & \frac{1}{3} & 0 \\ \frac{1}{3} & \frac{1}{3} & \frac{1}{3} \end{bmatrix} \Rightarrow \pi = (4/9, 3/9, 2/9)$$

$\Rightarrow$ the expected cost $= \frac{4}{9} C_{03} + \frac{3}{9} C_{11} + \frac{2}{9} C_{21}$

$= \frac{4}{9}(24) + \frac{3}{9}(4) + \frac{2}{9}(4) = \frac{116}{9} = \$12.87/\text{period}$

(b) The six feasible stationary deterministic policies (that is, the policies where you never exceed the storage capacity) are

i	$d_i(R_1)$	$d_i(R_2)$	$d_i(R_3)$	$d_i(R_4)$	$d_i(R_5)$	$d_i(R_6)$
0	1	2	3	1	2	3
1	1	1	1	2	2	2
2	1	1	1	1	1	1.

The remaining 21 stationary deterministic policies are infeasible:

19.3-8(a) Minimize $4y_{11} + 4y_{21} + 8y_{31} + 3y_{12} + 7\ y_{32}$

subject to

$$y_{01} + y_{11} + y_{12} + y_{21} + y_{31} + y_{32} = 1$$
$$y_{01} - (3/8\, y_{01} + 1/2\, y_{11} + 5/8\, y_{21} + 3/4\, y_{31} + 3/8\, y_{12} + 5/8\, y_{32}) = 0$$
$$y_{11} + y_{12} - 1/4\,(y_{01} + y_{11} + y_{21} + y_{31} + y_{12} + y_{32}) = 0$$
$$y_{21} - (1/4\, y_{01} + 1/8\, y_{11} + 1/8\, y_{21} + 1/4\, y_{12} + 1/8\, y_{32}) = 0$$
$$y_{31} + y_{32} - (1/8\, y_{01} + 1/8\, y_{11} + 1/8\, y_{12}) = 0$$
$$y_{ik} \geq 0 \quad i = 0,1,2,3\ ,\ k = 1,2$$

(b) Simplex-method yields $y_{01} = 0.45$, $y_{12} = 0.25$, $y_{21} = 0.213$, $y_{32} = 0.087$ and other y_{ik}'s are zero. So, the optimal policy is R_4.

19.3-9(a)

Minimize $\frac{40}{3} y_{01} + \frac{56}{3} y_{02} + 24 y_{03} + 4 y_{11} + 19 y_{12} + 4 y_{21}$

subject to:

$$y_{01} + y_{02} + y_{03} + y_{11} + y_{12} + y_{21} = 1$$
$$y_{01} + y_{02} + y_{03} - (y_{01} + \tfrac{2}{3} y_{11} + \tfrac{1}{3} y_{21} + \tfrac{2}{3} y_{02} + \tfrac{1}{3} y_{12} + \tfrac{1}{3} y_{03}) = 0$$
$$y_{11} + y_{12} - (\tfrac{1}{3} y_{11} + \tfrac{1}{3} y_{21} + \tfrac{1}{3} y_{02} + \tfrac{1}{3} y_{12} + \tfrac{1}{3} y_{03}) = 0$$
$$y_{21} - (\tfrac{1}{3} y_{21} + \tfrac{1}{3} y_{12} + \tfrac{1}{3} y_{03}) = 0$$
$$y_{ik} \geq 0 \quad \text{for} \quad i = 0, 1, 2 \quad \text{and} \quad k = 1, 2, 3.$$

(b) Simplex-Method yields $y_{03} = 0.4444$, $y_{11} = 0.3333$, $y_{21} = 0.2222$, and $y_{01} = y_{02} = y_{12} = 0$. So, optimal policy is R_6.

19.4-1. Number of states: 3

Number of decisions: 2

Cost Matrix, C_{ik}: $\begin{bmatrix} 0 & 0 \\ -27 & -31 \\ -27 & -31 \end{bmatrix}$

$P_{ij}(1) = \begin{bmatrix} 0.5 & 0.5 & 0 \\ 0.3 & 0.5 & 0.2 \\ 0 & 0.6 & 0.4 \end{bmatrix}$ $P_{ij}(2) = \begin{bmatrix} 0.5 & 0.5 & 0 \\ 0.4 & 0.5 & 0.1 \\ 0 & 0.8 & 0.2 \end{bmatrix}$

Initial Policy:

$d_0(R_1) = 1$
$d_1(R_1) = 1$
$d_2(R_1) = 2$

Discount Factor = 1

19.4-1. (continued)

Iteration # 1

Value Determination:

$g(R_1) = 0 + 0.5v_0(R_1) + 0.5v_1(R_1) + 0v_2(R_1) - v_0(R_1)$
$g(R_1) = -27 + 0.3v_0(R_1) + 0.5v_1(R_1) + 0.2v_2(R_1) - v_1(R_1)$
$g(R_1) = -31 + 0v_0(R_1) + 0.8v_1(R_1) + 0.2v_2(R_1) - v_2(R_1)$

Solution of Value Determination Equations:

$g(R_1) = -18.8$
$v_0(R_1) = 52.84$
$v_1(R_1) = 15.27$
$v_2(R_1) = 0$

Policy Improvement:

State 0:
0 + 0.5(52.84) + 0.5(15.27) +(0) - (52.84) = -18.8
0 + 0.5(52.84) + 0.5(15.27) +(0) - (52.84) = -18.8

State 1:
-27 + 0.3(52.84) + 0.5(15.27) +(0) - (15.27) = -18.8
-31 + 0.4(52.84) + 0.5(15.27) +(0) - (15.27) = -17.5

State 2:
-27 + 0(52.84) + 0.6(15.27) +(0) - (0) = -17.8
-31 + 0(52.84) + 0.8(15.27) +(0) - (0) = -18.8

Optimal Policy:
$d_0(R_2) = 1$
$d_1(R_2) = 1$
$d_2(R_2) = 2$

$g(R_2) = -18.8$
$v_0(R_2) = 52.84$
$v_1(R_2) = 15.27$
$v_2(R_2) = 0$

19.4-2. Number of states = 2

Number of decisions = 5

Cost Matrix, C(ik):

0	4.5	5	----	----
----	----	----	50	9

Transition Matrix, p(ij)[1]:

$$\begin{bmatrix} 0.9 & 0.1 \\ 0 & 0 \end{bmatrix}$$

Transition Matrix, p(ij)[2]:

$$\begin{bmatrix} 0.98 & 0.02 \\ 0 & 0 \end{bmatrix}$$

Transition Matrix, p(ij)[3]:

$$\begin{bmatrix} 1 & 0 \\ 0 & 0 \end{bmatrix}$$

Transition Matrix, p(ij)[4]:

$$\begin{bmatrix} 0 & 0 \\ 1 & 0 \end{bmatrix}$$

Transition Matrix, p(ij)[5]:

$$\begin{bmatrix} 0 & 0 \\ 0 & 1 \end{bmatrix}$$

19.4-2. (continued)

Initial Policy:

d0(R1) = 1
d1(R1) = 4

Discount Factor = 1

ITERATION # 1

Value Determination:

```
g(R1) = 0    +  0.9v0(R1) +   0.1v1(R1) - v0(R1)
g(R1) = 50   +    1v0(R1) +     0v1(R1) - v1(R1)
```

Solution of Value Determination Equations:

```
g(R1)  = 4.545
v0(R1) = -45.5
v1(R1) = 0
```

Policy Improvement:

State 0:

```
0    + 0.9  (-45.5) + 0.1  (0) - (-45.5) = 4.545
4.5  + 0.98 (-45.5) + 0.02 (0) - (-45.5) = 5.409
5    + 1    (-45.5) + 0    (0) - (-45.5) = 5
---  + 0    (-45.5) + 0    (0) - (-45.5) = ---
---  + 0    (-45.5) + 0    (0) - (-45.5) = ---
```

State 1:

```
---  + 0    (-45.5) + 0    (0) - (0) = ---
---  + 0    (-45.5) + 0    (0) - (0) = ---
---  + 0    (-45.5) + 0    (0) - (0) = ---
50   + 1    (-45.5) + 0    (0) - (0) = 4.545
9    + 0    (-45.5) + 1    (0) - (0) = 9
```

Optimal Policy:

d0(R2) = 1
d1(R2) = 4

```
g(R1)  = 4.545
v0(R1) = -45.5
v1(R1) = 0
```

19.4-3.

Number of states: 2

Number of decisions: 2

Cost Matrix, C_{ik}: $\begin{bmatrix} -2 & -1 \\ -4 & -3 \end{bmatrix}$

$p_{ij}(2) = \begin{bmatrix} 0.5 & 0.5 \\ 0.25 & 0.75 \end{bmatrix}$ $p_{ij}(1) = \begin{bmatrix} 0.75 & 0.25 \\ 0.5 & 0.5 \end{bmatrix}$

Initial Policy:

$d_0(R_1) = 1$
$d_1(R_1) = 1$

Iteration # 1

Value Determination:

$g(R_1) = -2 + 0.75v_0(R_1) + 0.25v_1(R_1) - v_0(R_1)$
$g(R_1) = -4 + 0.5v_0(R_1) + 0.5v_1(R_1) - v_1(R_1)$

19.4-3. (continued)

Solution of Value Determination Equations:

$g(R_1) = -2.67$
$v_0(R_1) = 2.667$
$v_1(R_1) = 0$

Policy Improvement:

State 0:
-2 + 0.75(2.667) +(0) - (2.667) = -2.67
-1 + 0.5(2.667) +(0) - (2.667) = -2.33

State 1:
-4 + 0.5(2.667) +(0) - (0) = -2.67
-3 + 0.25(2.667) +(0) - (0) = -2.33

Optimal Policy:
$d_0(R_2) = 1$
$d_1(R_2) = 1$

$g(R_2) = -2.67$
$v_0(R_2) = 2.667$
$v_1(R_2) = 0$

19.4-4. Number of states = 2

Number of decisions = 2

Cost Matrix, C(ik):

$$\begin{bmatrix} 0 & 14 \\ 75 & 14 \end{bmatrix}$$

Transition Matrix, p(ij)[1]:

$$\begin{bmatrix} 0.125 & 0.875 \\ 0.125 & 0.875 \end{bmatrix}$$

Transition Matrix, p(ij)[2]:

$$\begin{bmatrix} 0.875 & 0.125 \\ 0.875 & 0.125 \end{bmatrix}$$

Initial Policy:

d0(R1) = 1
d1(R1) = 2

Discount Factor = 1

ITERATION # 1

Value Determination:

g(R1) = 0 +0.125v0(R1) + 0.875v1(R1) - v0(R1)
g(R1) = 14 +0.875v0(R1) + 0.125v1(R1) - v1(R1)

Solution of Value Determination Equations:
g(R1) = 7
v0(R1) = -8
v1(R1) = 0

Policy Improvement:

State 0:
0 + 0.125(-8) + 0.875(0) - (-8) = 7
14 + 0.875(-8) + 0.125(0) - (-8) = 15

19.4-4. (continued)

```
State 1:
75    + 0.125(   -8) + 0.875(0) - (0) = 74
14    + 0.875(   -8) + 0.125(0) - (0) = 7

Optimal Policy:
  d0(R2) = 1
  d1(R2) = 2

g(R1)  = 7
v0(R1) = -8
v1(R1) = 0
```

19.4-5

Number of states: 2

Number of decisions: 2

Cost Matrix, C_{ik}: $\begin{bmatrix} -0.12 & 0.292 \\ 0.5 & 0.417 \end{bmatrix}$

$p_{ij}(1) = \begin{bmatrix} 0.375 & 0.625 \\ 1 & 0 \end{bmatrix}$ $p_{ij}(2) = \begin{bmatrix} 0.875 & 0.125 \\ 1 & 0 \end{bmatrix}$

Initial Policy:

$d_0(R_1) = 1$
$d_1(R_1) = 1$

Iteration # 1

Value Determination:

$g(R_1) = -0.12+0.375v_0(R_1) + 0.625v_1(R_1) - v_0(R_1)$
$g(R_1) = 0.5 + 1v_0(R_1) + 0v_1(R_1) - v_1(R_1)$

Solution of Value Determination Equations:

$g(R_1) = 0.115$
$v_0(R_1) = -0.38$
$v_1(R_1) = 0$

Policy Improvement:

State 0:
-0.12+ 0.375(-0.38) +(0) - (-0.38) = 0.115
0.292+ 0.875(-0.38) +(0) - (-0.38) = 0.34

State 1:
0.5 + 1(-0.38) +(0) - (0) = 0.115
0.417+ 1(-0.38) +(0) - (0) = 0.032

New Policy:

$d_0(R_2) = 1$
$d_1(R_2) = 2$

Iteration # 2

Value Determination:

$g(R_2) = -0.12+0.375v_0(R_2) + 0.625v_1(R_2) - v_0(R_2)$
$g(R_2) = 0.417+ 1v_0(R_2) + 0v_1(R_2) - v_1(R_2)$

Solution of Value Determination Equations:

19.4-5 (continued)

$g(R_2) = 0.083$
$v_0(R_2) = -0.33$
$v_1(R_2) = 0$

Policy Improvement:

State 0:
-0.12+ 0.375(-0.33) +(0) - (-0.33) = 0.083
0.292+ 0.875(-0.33) +(0) - (-0.33) = 0.333

State 1:
0.5 + 1(-0.33) +(0) - (0) = 0.167
0.417+ 1(-0.33) +(0) - (0) = 0.083

New Policy:
$d_0(R_3) = 2$
$d_1(R_3) = 1$

Iteration # 3

Value Determination:

$g(R_3) = -0.12+0.375v_0(R_3) + 0.625v_1(R_3) - v_0(R_3)$
$g(R_3) = 0.5 + 1v_0(R_3) + 1v_1(R_3) - v_1(R_3)$

Solution of Value Determination Equations:

$g(R_3) = 0.115$
$v_0(R_3) = -0.38$
$v_1(R_3) = 0$

Policy Improvement:

State 0:
-0.12+ 0.375(-0.38) +(0) - (-0.38) = 0.115
0.292+ 0.875(-0.38) +(0) - (-0.38) = 0.34

State 1:
0.5 + 1(-0.38) +(0) - (0) = 0.115
0.417+ 1(-0.38) +(0) - (0) = 0.032

Optimal Policy:
$d_0(R_4) = 2$
$d_1(R_4) = 1$

$g(R_4) = 0.115$
$v_0(R_4) = -0.38$
$v_1(R_4) = 0$

19.4-6.

Number of states: 3

Number of decisions: 2

Cost Matrix, C_{ik}: $\begin{bmatrix} -20 & -9 \\ -6 & -3 \\ 18 & 8 \end{bmatrix}$

19.4-6. (continued)

$$p_{ij}(1) = \begin{bmatrix} 0.3 & 0.5 & 0.2 \\ 0.1 & 0.5 & 0.4 \\ 0.2 & 0.4 & 0.4 \end{bmatrix} \quad p_{ij}(2) = \begin{bmatrix} 0.3 & 0.5 & 0.2 \\ 0.1 & 0.5 & 0.4 \\ 0.2 & 0.4 & 0.4 \end{bmatrix}$$

Initial Policy:

$d_0(R_1) = 1$
$d_1(R_1) = 1$
$d_2(R_1) = 2$

Iteration # 1

Value Determination:

$$g(R_1) = -20 + 0.3v_0(R_1) + 0.5v_1(R_1) + 0.2v_2(R_1) - v_0(R_1)$$
$$g(R_1) = -6 + 0.1v_0(R_1) + 0.5v_1(R_1) + 0.4v_2(R_1) - v_1(R_1)$$
$$g(R_1) = 8 + 0.2v_0(R_1) + 0.4v_1(R_1) + 0.4v_2(R_1) - v_2(R_1)$$

Solution of Value Determination Equations:

$g(R_1) = -3.27$
$v_0(R_1) = -32.4$
$v_1(R_1) = -12$
$v_2(R_1) = 0$

Policy Improvement:

State 0:
-20 + 0.3(-32.4) + 0.5(-12) +(0) - (-32.4) = -3.27
-9 + 0.3(-32.4) + 0.5(-12) +(0) - (-32.4) = 7.732

State 1:
-6 + 0.1(-32.4) + 0.5(-12) +(0) - (-12) = -3.27
-3 + 0.1(-32.4) + 0.5(-12) +(0) - (-12) = -0.27

State 2:
18 + 0.2(-32.4) + 0.4(-12) +(0) - (0) = 6.732
8 + 0.2(-32.4) + 0.4(-12) +(0) - (0) = -3.27

Optimal Policy:

$d_0(R_2) = 1$
$d_1(R_2) = 1$
$d_2(R_2) = 2$

$g(R_2) = -3.27$
$v_0(R_2) = -32.4$
$v_1(R_2) = -12$
$v_2(R_2) = 0$

19.4-7. Number of states = 2

Number of decisions = 2

Cost Matrix, C(ik):

$$\begin{bmatrix} 0 & 0 \\ -1200 & -1200 \end{bmatrix}$$

Transition Matrix, p(ij)[1]:

$$\begin{bmatrix} 0.4 & 0.6 \\ 0.6 & 0.4 \end{bmatrix}$$

Transition Matrix, p(ij)[2]:

$$\begin{bmatrix} 0.5 & 0.5 \\ 0.4 & 0.6 \end{bmatrix}$$

19.4-7 (continued)

```
Initial Policy:

d0(R1) = 1                    Discount Factor = 1
d1(R1) = 1
ITERATION # 1

Value Determination:

g(R1) = 0     +  0.4v0(R1) +   0.6v1(R1) - v0(R1)
g(R1) = -1200+  0.6v0(R1) +   0.4v1(R1) - v1(R1)

Solution of Value Determination Equations:
g(R1)  = -600
v0(R1) = 1000
v1(R1) = 0

Policy Improvement:

State 0:
0     + 0.4   ( 1000) + 0.6   (0) - (1000 ) = -600
0     + 0.5   ( 1000) + 0.5   (0) - (1000 ) = -500

State 1:
-1200+ 0.6   ( 1000) + 0.4   (0) - (0) = -600
-1200+ 0.4   ( 1000) + 0.6   (0) - (0) = -800

New Policy:
  d0(R2) = 1
  d1(R2) = 2


ITERATION # 2

Value Determination:

g(R2) = 0     +  0.4v0(R2) +   0.6v1(R2) - v0(R2)
g(R2) = -1200+  0.4v0(R2) +   0.6v1(R2) - v1(R2)

Solution of Value Determination Equations:
g(R2)  = -720
v0(R2) = 1200
v1(R2) = 0

Policy Improvement:

State 0:
0     + 0.4   ( 1200) + 0.6   (0) - (1200 ) = -720
0     + 0.5   ( 1200) + 0.5   (0) - (1200 ) = -600

-1200+ 0.6   ( 1200) + 0.4   (0) - (0) = -480
-1200+ 0.4   ( 1200) + 0.6   (0) - (0) = -720

Optimal Policy:
  d0(R3) = 1
  d1(R3) = 2


g(R2)  = -720
v0(R2) = 1200
v1(R2) = 0
```

19.4-8

Markov Decision Processes Model:

Number of states: 4

Number of decisions: 2

Cost Matrix, C_{ik}: $\begin{bmatrix} 0 & --- \\ 4 & 3 \\ 4 & --- \\ 8 & 7 \end{bmatrix}$

19.4-8 (continued

$$p_{ij}(1) = \begin{bmatrix} 0.375 & 0.25 & 0.25 & 0.125 \\ 0.5 & 0.25 & 0.125 & 0.125 \\ 0.625 & 0.25 & 0.125 & 0 \\ 0.75 & 0.25 & 0 & 0 \end{bmatrix} \qquad p_{ij}(2) = \begin{bmatrix} 0 & 0 & 0 & 0 \\ 0.375 & 0.25 & 0.25 & 0.125 \\ 0 & 0 & 0 & 0 \\ 0.625 & 0.25 & 0.125 & 0 \end{bmatrix}$$

Initial Policy:

$d_0(R_1) = 1$
$d_1(R_1) = 2$
$d_2(R_1) = 1$
$d_3(R_1) = 2$

Iteration # 1

Value Determination:

$g(R_1) = 0 \quad +0.375v_0(R_1) + 0.25v_1(R_1) + 0.25v_2(R_1) + 0.125v_3(R_1) - v_0(R_1)$
$g(R_1) = 3 \quad +0.375v_0(R_1) + 0.25v_1(R_1) + 0.25v_2(R_1) + 0.125v_3(R_1) - v_1(R_1)$
$g(R_1) = 4 \quad +0.625v_0(R_1) + 0.25v_1(R_1) + 0.125v_2(R_1) + 0v_3(R_1) - v_2(R_1)$
$g(R_1) = 7 \quad +0.625v_0(R_1) + 0.25v_1(R_1) + 0.125v_2(R_1) + 0v_3(R_1) - v_3(R_1)$

Solution of Value Determination Equations:

$g(R_1) = 2.213$
$v_0(R_1) = -5.9$
$v_1(R_1) = -2.9$
$v_2(R_1) = -3$
$v_3(R_1) = 0$

Policy Improvement:

State 0:
```
0    + 0.375( -5.9) + 0.25( -2.9) + 0.25(   -3) +(0) - ( -5.9) = 2.213
---  +     0( -5.9) +    0( -2.9) +    0(   -3) +(0) - ( -5.9) = ---
```

State 1:
```
4    +   0.5( -5.9) + 0.25( -2.9) +0.125(   -3) +(0) - ( -2.9) = 2.85
3    + 0.375( -5.9) + 0.25( -2.9) + 0.25(   -3) +(0) - ( -2.9) = 2.213
```

State 2:
```
4    + 0.625( -5.9) + 0.25( -2.9) +0.125(   -3) +(0) - (   -3) = 2.213
---  +     0( -5.9) +    0( -2.9) +    0(   -3) +(0) - (   -3) = ---
```

State 3:
```
8    +  0.75( -5.9) + 0.25( -2.9) +    0(   -3) +(0) - (0) =     2.85
7    + 0.625( -5.9) + 0.25( -2.9) +0.125(   -3) +(0) - (0) =     2.213
```

Optimal Policy:

$d_0(R_2) = 1$
$d_1(R_2) = 2$
$d_2(R_2) = 1$
$d_3(R_2) = 2$

$g(R_2) = 2.213$
$v_0(R_2) = -5.9$
$v_1(R_2) = -2.9$
$v_2(R_2) = -3$
$v_3(R_2) = 0$

19.4-9

Markovian Decision Processes Model:

Number of states = 3

Number of decisions = 3

Cost Matrix, C(ik):

13.33	18.67	24
4	19	----
4	----	----

Transition Matrix, p(ij)[1]:

1	0	0
0.667	0.333	0
0.333	0.333	0.333

Transition Matrix, p(ij)[2]:

0.667	0.333	0
0.333	0.333	0.333
0	0	0

Transition Matrix, p(ij)[3]:

0.333	0.333	0.333
0	0	0
0	0	0

Initial Policy:

d0(R1) = 3
d1(R1) = 1
d2(R1) = 1

Discount Factor = 1

Average Cost Policy Improvement Algorithm:

ITERATION # 1

Value Determination:

```
g(R1) = 24    +0.333v0(R1) + 0.333v1(R1) + 0.333v2(R1) - v0(R1)
g(R1) = 4     +0.667v0(R1) + 0.333v1(R1) +       0v2(R1) - v1(R1)
g(R1) = 4     +0.333v0(R1) + 0.333v1(R1) + 0.333v2(R1) - v2(R1)
```

Solution of Value Determination Equations:

g(R1) = 12.89
v0(R1) = 20
v1(R1) = 6.667
v2(R1) = 0

Policy Improvement:

```
State 0:
13.33+ 1     (  20) + 0     (6.667) + 0     (0) - (20   ) = 13.33
18.67+ 0.667(  20) + 0.333(6.667) + 0     (0) - (20   ) = 14.22
24    + 0.333(  20) + 0.333(6.667) + 0.333(0) - (20   ) = 12.89

State 1:
4     + 0.667(  20) + 0.333(6.667) + 0     (0) - (6.667) = 12.89
19    + 0.333(  20) + 0.333(6.667) + 0.333(0) - (6.667) = 21.22
---   + 0     (  20) + 0     (6.667) + 0     (0) - (6.667) = ---

State 2:
4     + 0.333(  20) + 0.333(6.667) + 0.333(0) - (0) = 12.89
---   + 0     (  20) + 0     (6.667) + 0     (0) - (0) = ---
---   + 0     (  20) + 0     (6.667) + 0     (0) - (0) = ---
```

New Policy:

d0(R2) = 3
d1(R2) = 1
d2(R2) = 1

19.5-1. Let states 0, 1 and 2 denote \$600, \$800 and \$1000 offers, respectively, and let state 3 be that the car has already been sold (state ∞ of hint). Let decisions 1 and 2 be to reject and accept the offer, respectively.

$C_{01} = C_{11} = C_{21} = 60$, $C_{02} = -600$, $C_{12} = -800$ and $C_{22} = -1000$

19.5-1. (continued)

The transition probabilities are:

$$P(1) = \begin{pmatrix} 5/8 & 1/4 & 1/8 & 0 \\ 5/8 & 1/4 & 1/8 & 0 \\ 5/8 & 1/4 & 1/8 & 0 \\ 0 & 0 & 0 & 1 \end{pmatrix} \qquad P(2) = \begin{pmatrix} 0 & 0 & 0 & 1 \\ 0 & 0 & 0 & 1 \\ 0 & 0 & 0 & 1 \\ 0 & 0 & 0 & 1 \end{pmatrix}$$

Let the initial guess be: $\begin{pmatrix} \$600 \text{ offer : reject} \\ \$800 \text{ offer : accept} \\ \$1000 \text{ offer : accept} \end{pmatrix}$

The relevant system of equation is: $v_0 = 60 + .95(5/8\, v_0 + 1/4\, v_1 + 1/8\, v_2)$

$$V_1 = -800 + .95 V_3$$
$$V_2 = -1000 + .95 V_3$$
$$V_3 = .95 V_3$$

The solution is $(v_0, v_1, v_2, v_3) = (-7960/13, -800, -1000, 0)$

Policy improvement:

state 0 with decision 2: $-600 + .95 v_3 = -600 > v_0$

state 1 with decision 1: $60 + .95(5/8\, v_0 + 1/4\, v_1 + 1/8\, v_2) = -7960/13 > v_1$

state 2 with decision 1: $60 + .95(5/8\, v_0 + 1/4\, v_1 + 1/8\, v_2) = -7960/13 > v_2$

Hence, $\begin{pmatrix} \$600 \text{ offer: reject} \\ \$800 \text{ offer: accept} \\ \$1000 \text{ offer: accept} \end{pmatrix}$ is optimal.

19.5-2(a) Minimize $60(y_{01} + y_{11} + y_{21}) - 600 y_{02} - 800 y_{12} - 1000 y_{22}$

subject to $y_{01} + y_{02} - (.95)(5/8)(y_{01} + y_{11} + y_{21}) = 1/3$

$y_{11} + y_{12} - (.95)(1/4)(y_{01} + y_{11} + y_{21}) = 1/3$

$y_{21} + y_{22} - (.95)(1/8)(y_{01} + y_{11} + y_{21}) = 1/3$

$y_{ik} \geq 0 \quad i = 0,1,2 \quad k = 1,2.$

(b) The simplex-method yields $y_{01} = 0.81979$, $y_{12} = 0.5277$, $y_{22} = 0.43056$ and $y_{02} = y_{11} = y_{21} = 0$.

So, policy $\begin{pmatrix} 0:1 \\ 1:2 \\ 2:2 \end{pmatrix} = \begin{pmatrix} \$600: \text{reject} \\ \$800: \text{accept} \\ \$1000, \text{accept} \end{pmatrix}$ is optimal

19.5-3. $V_i^n = \min \begin{cases} 60 + .95(5/8\, V_0^{n-1} + 1/4\, V_1^{n-1} + 1/8\, V_2^{n-1}) & \text{for } k=1 \\ -(\text{offer}) & \text{for } k=2 \end{cases} \quad i = 0,1,2$

and $V_i^0 = 0$ for $i = 0,1,2$.

Iteration 1: $V_i^1 = \min\{60, -(\text{offer})\} = -(\text{offer})$ for $i = 0,1,2$

Iteration 2: $V_0^2 = \min\{-605, -600\} = -605$ with k = reject

$V_1^2 = \min\{-605, -800\} = -800$ with k = accept

$V_3^2 = \min\{-605, -1000\} = -1000$ with k = accept

Iteration 3: $V_0^3 = \min\{-607.97, -600\} = -607.97$ with k = reject

$V_1^3 = \min\{-607.97, -800\} = -800$ with k = accept

$V_2^3 = \min\{-607.97, -1000\} = -1000$ with k = accept

19.5-3. (continued)

The approximate optimal solution is $\begin{pmatrix} \$600 \text{ offer: reject} \\ \$800 \text{ offer: accept} \\ \$1000 \text{ offer: accept} \end{pmatrix}$

(which, by Problem 22, we know is in fact optimal).

19.5-4. Let states 0, 1 and 2 denote a selling price of \$10, \$20 and \$30, respectively, and let state 3 denote that the stock has already been sold. Let decisions 1 and 2 be to hold and sell the stock, respectively.

$C_{01} = C_{11} = C_{21} = 0$, $C_{02} = -10$, $C_{12} = -20$ and $C_{22} = -30$.

The transition probabilities are:

$$P(1) = \begin{pmatrix} 4/5 & 1/5 & 0 & 0 \\ 1/4 & 1/4 & 1/2 & 0 \\ 0 & 3/4 & 1/4 & 0 \\ 0 & 0 & 0 & 1 \end{pmatrix} \text{ and } P(2) = \begin{pmatrix} 0 & 0 & 0 & 1 \\ 0 & 0 & 0 & 1 \\ 0 & 0 & 0 & 1 \\ 0 & 0 & 0 & 1 \end{pmatrix}$$

Let the initial guess be $\begin{pmatrix} \$10: \text{hold} \\ \$20: \text{hold} \\ \$30: \text{sell} \end{pmatrix}$

The relevant system of equations is:

$$V_0 = 0 + .9(4/5 V_0 + 1/5 V_1)$$
$$V_1 = 0 + .9(1/4 V_0 + 1/4 V_1 + 1/2 V_2)$$
$$V_2 = -30 + .9 V_3$$
$$V_3 = 0 + .9 V_3$$

The solution is $(V_0, V_1, V_2, V_3) = (-4860/353, -7560/353, -30, 0)$

Policy improvement:

State 0 with decision 2: $-10 + .9 V_3 = -10 > V_0$

State 1 with decision 2: $-20 + .9 V_3 = -20 > V_0$

State 2 with decision 1: $0 + .9[3/4 V_1 + 1/4 V_2] = -21.21 > V_2$

Hence, $\begin{pmatrix} \$10: \text{hold} \\ \$20: \text{hold} \\ \$30: \text{sell} \end{pmatrix}$ is optimal.

19.5-5. (a) Minimize $-10 Y_{02} - 20 Y_{12} - 30 Y_{22}$

subject to

$$Y_{01} + Y_{02} - (.9)(4/5 Y_{01} + 1/4 Y_{11}) = 1/3$$
$$Y_{11} + Y_{12} - (.9)(1/5 Y_{01} + 1/4 Y_{11} + 3/4 Y_{21}) = 1/3$$
$$Y_{21} + Y_{22} - (.9)(1/2 Y_{11} + 1/4 Y_{21}) = 1/3$$
$$Y_{ik} \geq 0 \quad i = 0, 1, 2, \quad K = 1, 2$$

(b) The simplex method yields: $Y_{01} = 1.96059$ $Y_{11} = 0.95851$, $Y_{22} = 0.76463$

So, the optimal policy is $\begin{pmatrix} 0: 1 \\ 1: 1 \\ 2: 2 \end{pmatrix} = \begin{pmatrix} \$10: \text{hold} \\ \$20: \text{hold} \\ \$30: \text{sell} \end{pmatrix}$

19.5-6. $V_0^n = \min \begin{cases} .9(4/5\, V_0^{n-1} + 1/5\, V_1^{n-1}) & \text{for } k=1 \\ -10 & \text{for } k=2 \end{cases}$

$V_1^n = \min \begin{cases} .9(1/4\, V_0^{n-1} + 1/4\, V_1^{n-1} + 1/2\, V_2^{n-1}) & \text{for } k=1 \\ -20 & \text{for } k=2 \end{cases}$

$V_2^n = \min \begin{cases} .9(3/4\, V_1^{n-1} + 1/4\, V_2^{n-1}) & \text{for } k=1 \\ -30 & \text{for } k=2 \end{cases}$

and $V_i^0 = 0$ for $i = 0, 1, 2$.

Iteration 1: $V_0^1 = \min\{0, -10\} = -10$ with $k=2$
$V_1^1 = \min\{0, -20\} = -20$ with $k=2$
$V_2^1 = \min\{0, -30\} = -30$ with $k=2$

Iteration 2: $V_0^2 = \min\{-10.8, -10\} = -10.8$ with $k=1$
$V_1^2 = \min\{-20.25, -20\} = -20.25$ with $k=1$
$V_2 = \min\{-20.25, -30\} = -30$ with $k=2$

Iteration 3: $V_0^3 = \min\{-11.42, -10\} = -11.42$ with $k=1$
$V_1^3 = \min\{-20.49, -20\} = -20.49$ with $k=1$
$V_2^3 = \min\{-20.42, -30\} = -30$ with $k=2$

So the indicated approximation to the optimal solution is
($10 : hold, $20 : hold, $30 : sell), which happens also to be optimal.

19.5-7 (a) Let state 0 = chemical 0 produced this month; 1 = chemical 1 produced this month.
decision 1 = use process A next month; 2 = use process B next month

The four stationary deterministic policies are:

i	$d_i(R_1)$	$d_i(R_2)$	$d_i(R_3)$	$d_i(R_4)$
0	1	1	2	2
1	1	2	1	2

(b) Markovian Decision Processes Model:

Number of states = 2

Number of decisions = 2

Cost Matrix, C(ik):

28	26
37	24

Transition Matrix, p(ij)[2]:

0.2	0.8
0.3	0.7

Transition Matrix, p(ij)[1]:

0.2	0.8
0.3	0.7

Initial Policy:

d0(R1) = 2
d1(R1) = 2

Discounted Cost Policy Improvement Algorithm:

Discount Factor = 0.5

ITERATION # 1

Value Determination:

g(R1) = 26 + (0.5) [0.2V0(R1) + 0.8V1(R1)]
g(R1) = 24 + (0.5) [0.3V0(R1) + 0.7V1(R1)]

Solution of Value Determination Equations:
V1(R1) = 50.48
V2(R1) = 48.57

19.5-9. (continued)

Policy Improvement:

State 0:
```
28    + (0.5) [0.2   (50.48) + 0.8   (48.57) ] - 52.48
26    + (0.5) [0.2   (50.48) + 0.8   (48.57) ] - 50.48
```

State 1:
```
37    + (0.5) [0.3   (50.48) + 0.7   (48.57) ] - 61.57
24    + (0.5) [0.3   (50.48) + 0.7   (48.57) ] - 48.57
```

Optimal Policy:
```
d0(R2) - 2          V0(R1) - 50.48
d1(R2) - 2          V1(R1) - 48.57
```


19.5-8 (a) Minimize $28y_{01} + 26y_{02} + 46y_{11} + 22y_{12}$

Subject to:

$$y_{01} + y_{02} - \frac{1}{2}\left(\frac{1}{5}y_{01} + \frac{3}{10}y_{11} + \frac{1}{5}y_{02} + \frac{3}{10}y_{12}\right) = \frac{1}{2}$$

$$y_{11} + y_{12} - \frac{1}{2}\left(\frac{4}{5}y_{01} + \frac{7}{10}y_{11} + \frac{4}{5}y_{02} + \frac{7}{10}y_{12}\right) = \frac{1}{2}$$

$$y_{01}, y_{02}, y_{11}, y_{12} \geq 0$$

(b) Simplex method yields: $y_{02} = 0.7619$, $y_{12} = 1.2381$, $y_{01} = y_{11} = 0$.

So, policy $\begin{pmatrix} 0:2 \\ 1:2 \end{pmatrix} = \begin{pmatrix} \text{chemical 0: process B} \\ \text{chemical 1: process B} \end{pmatrix}$ is optimal.

19.5-9.

Markovian Decision Processes Model: Number of states - 2   Number of decisions - 2

Cost Matrix, C(ik):
```
|¯ 28    26  ¯|
|_ 37    24  _|
```

Transition Matrix, p(ij)[1]:
```
|¯ 0.2   0.8 ¯|
|_ 0.3   0.7 _|
```

Transition Matrix, p(ij)[2]:
```
|¯ 0.2   0.8 ¯|
|_ 0.3   0.7 _|
```

Initial Policy:
```
d0(R1) - 1
d1(R1) - 2          Discount Factor = 0.5
```

Method of Successive Approximations:

Initial V(j):
```
V(0) - 0
V(1) - 0
```

ITERATION # 1

State 0:
```
28    + (0.5) [0.2  (    0) + 0.8  (    0) ] - 28
26    + (0.5) [0.2  (    0) + 0.8  (    0) ] - 26
```

State 1:
```
37    + (0.5) [0.3  (    0) + 0.7  (    0) ] - 37
24    + (0.5) [0.3  (    0) + 0.7  (    0) ] - 24
```

New Policy and New V(j):
```
d0(R2) - 2,          V(0) - 26
d1(R2) - 2,          V(1) - 24
```

19.5-9. (continued)

ITERATION # 2

State 0:
```
28    + (0.5) [0.2  (   26) + 0.8  (   24) ] = 40.2
26    + (0.5) [0.2  (   26) + 0.8  (   24) ] = 38.2
```

State 1:
```
37    + (0.5) [0.3  (   26) + 0.7  (   24) ] = 49.3
24    + (0.5) [0.3  (   26) + 0.7  (   24) ] = 36.3
```

New Policy and New V(j):
```
  d0(R3) = 2,          V(0) = 38.2
  d1(R3) = 2,          V(1) = 36.3
```

19.5-10.

Markovian Decision Processes Model: Number of states = 2

Number of decisions = 2

Cost Matrix, C(ik):
```
 _            _
|  28     26   |
|_ 37     24  _|
```

Transition Matrix, p(ij)[1]:
```
 _            _
|  0.2    0.8  |
|_ 0.3    0.7 _|
```

Transition Matrix, p(ij)[2]:
```
 _            _
|  0.2    0.8  |
|_ 0.3    0.7 _|
```

Initial Policy:

d0(R1) = 1
d1(R1) = 2

Discount Factor = 0.5

Method of Successive Approximations:

Initial V(j):
```
  V(0) = 0
  V(1) = 0
```

ITERATION # 1

State 0:
```
28    + (0.5) [0.2  (    0) + 0.8  (    0) ] = 28
26    + (0.5) [0.2  (    0) + 0.8  (    0) ] = 26
```

State 1:
```
37    + (0.5) [0.3  (    0) + 0.7  (    0) ] = 37
24    + (0.5) [0.3  (    0) + 0.7  (    0) ] = 24
```

New Policy and New V(j):
```
  d0(R2) = 2,          V(0) = 26
  d1(R2) = 2,          V(1) = 24
```

ITERATION # 2

State 0:
```
28    + (0.5) [0.2  (   26) + 0.8  (   24) ] = 40.2
26    + (0.5) [0.2  (   26) + 0.8  (   24) ] = 38.2
```

State 1:
```
37    + (0.5) [0.3  (   26) + 0.7  (   24) ] = 49.3
24    + (0.5) [0.3  (   26) + 0.7  (   24) ] = 36.3
```

New Policy and New V(j):
```
  d0(R3) = 2,          V(0) = 38.2
  d1(R3) = 2,          V(1) = 36.3
```

ITERATION # 3

19.5-10. (continued)

```
State 0:
28    + (0.5) [0.2  ( 38.2) + 0.8  ( 36.3) ] = 46.34
26    + (0.5) [0.2  ( 38.2) + 0.8  ( 36.3) ] = 44.34

State 1:
37    + (0.5) [0.3  ( 38.2) + 0.7  ( 36.3) ] = 55.43
24    + (0.5) [0.3  ( 38.2) + 0.7  ( 36.3) ] = 42.43

New Policy and New V(j):
  d0(R4) = 2,            V(0) = 44.34
  d1(R4) = 2,            V(1) = 42.43
```

The optimal solution is, therefore, to use process B in all periods, regardless of the chemical produced.

19.5-11.

$$V_0^n = \min \begin{cases} 0 + .90(7/8\, V_1^{n-1} + 1/16\, V_2^{n-1} + 1/16\, V_3^{n-1}) & \text{for } k=1 \\ 4000 + .90\, V_1^{n-1} & \text{for } k=2 \\ 6000 + .90\, V_0^{n-1} & \text{for } k=3 \end{cases}$$

$$V_1^n = \min \begin{cases} 1000 + .90\,(3/4\, V_1^{n-1} + 1/8\, V_2^{n-1} + 1/8\, V_3^{n-1}) & \text{for } k=1 \\ 4000 + .90\, V_1^{n-1} & \text{for } k=2 \\ 6000 + .90\, V_0^{n-1} & \text{for } k=3 \end{cases}$$

$$V_2^n = \min \begin{cases} 3000 + .90\,(1/2\, V_2^{n-1} + 1/2\, V_3^{n-1}) & \text{for } k=1 \\ 4000 + .90\, V_1^{n-1} & \text{for } k=2 \\ 6000 + .90\, V_0^{n-1} & \text{for } k=3 \end{cases}$$

$$V_3^n = 6000 + .90\, V_0^{n-1} \qquad \text{for } k=3$$

and $V_0^0 = V_1^0 = V_2^0 = V_3^0 = 0$

Iteration 1: $V_0^1 = \min\{0, 4000, 6000\} = 0$ when $k=1$

$V_1^1 = \min\{1000, 4000, 6000\} = 1000$ when $k=1$

$V_2^1 = \min\{3000, 4000, 6000\} = 3000$ when $k=1$

$V_3^1 = 6000$ when $k=3$

Iteration 2: $V_0^2 = \min\{1293.75, 4900, 6000\} = 1293.75$ when $k=1$

$V_1^2 = \min\{2687.5, 4900, 6000\} = 2687.5$ when $k=1$

$V_2^2 = \min\{7050, 4900, 6000\} = 4900$ when $k=2$

$V_3^2 = 6000$ when $k=3$

Iteration 3: $V_0^3 = \min\{2729.53, 6418.75, 7164.38\} = 2729.53$ when $k=1$

$V_1^3 = \min\{4040.31, 6418.75, 7164.38\} = 4040.31$ when $k=1$

$V_2^3 = \min\{7905, 6418.75, 7164.38\} = 6418.75$ when $k=2$

$V_3^3 = 7164.38$ when $k=3$

Iteration 4: $V_0^4 = \min\{3945.80, 7636.28, 8456.58\} = 3945.80$ when $k=1$

$V_1^4 = \min\{5255.31, 7636.28, 8456.58\} = 5255.31$ when $k=1$

$V_2^4 = \min\{9112.41, 7636.28, 8456.58\} = 7636.28$ when $k=2$

$V_3^4 = 8456.58$ when $k=3$

19.5-11. *(continued)*

So the optimal policy is:

in periods 1,2,3: $\begin{pmatrix} 0\text{: leave alone} \\ 1\text{: leave alone} \\ 2\text{: overhaul} \\ 3\text{: replace} \end{pmatrix}$ and in period 4: $\begin{pmatrix} 0\text{: leave alone} \\ 1\text{: leave alone} \\ 2\text{: leave alone} \\ 3\text{: replace} \end{pmatrix}$

Chapter 20: Decision Analysis

20.2-1. a) Payoff Table: (in thousands of dollars)

Action \ State of Nature	θ_1 1000 sold	θ_2 10,000 sold
a_1 (sell rights)	800	800
a_2 (build computers)	0	5400
Prior probability	0.5	0.5

b) For a_1: $E[p(a_1, \theta)] = 0.5(800) + 0.5(800) = 800$ thousand

For a_2: $E[p(a_2, \theta)] = 0.5(0) + 0.5(5400) = 2700$ thousand

The optimal action under Bayes decision rule is a_2 (build comp's)

20.2-2. a) Payoff Table:

Action \ State of Nature	θ_1 High Interest	θ_2 Medium Interest	θ_3 Low Interest
a_1 (Plan 1)	220	170	110
a_2 (Plan 2)	200	180	150
Prior probability	0.6	0.3	0.1

b) Optimal (minimax) action is a_2 (value = 110)

c) Optimal (max likelihood) action is a_1 (value = 220)

d) For a_1: $E[p(a_1, \theta)] = 0.6(220) + 0.3(170) + 0.1(110) = 194$

For a_2: $E[p(a_2, \theta)] = 0.6(200) + 0.3(180) + 0.1(150) = 189$

So the optimal (Bayes) action is a_1, Plan 1.

20.2-3. a) Clearly, it does not make sense to stock more than 13 or less than 10 cases for tomorrow, so actions range from stocking 10 to stocking 13 cases.

Payoff Table:

Action \ State of Nature	θ_1 10 cases "sold"	θ_2 11 cases "sold"	θ_3 12 cases "sold"	θ_4 13 cases "sold"
a_1 (10 cases stocked)	50	50	50	50
a_2 (11 " ")	47	55	55	55
a_3 (12 " ")	44	52	60	60
a_4 (13 " ")	41	49	57	65
Prior probability	0.2	0.4	0.3	0.1

(Note that "sold" could mean that fewer are actually sold, if fewer had been stocked)

b) Optimal (minimax) action is a_1 (stock 10 cases)

c) Optimal (max likelihood) action is a_2 (stock 11 cases)

d) For a_1: $E[p(a_1,\theta)] = 0.2(50)+0.4(50)+0.3(50)+0.1(50) = 50$

For a_2: $E[p(a_2,\theta)] = 0.2(47)+0.4(55)+0.3(55)+0.1(55) = 53.4$

For a_3: $E[p(a_3,\theta)] = 0.2(44)+0.4(52)+0.3(60)+0.1(60) = 53.6$

For a_4: $E[p(a_4,\theta)] = 0.2(41)+0.4(49)+0.3(57)+0.1(65) = 51.4$

So the optimal (Bayes) action is a_3 (stock 12 cases).

20.2-4. The prior distribution is $P\{\theta=\theta_1\} = 2/3$, $P\{\theta=\theta_2\} = 1/3$.

For a_1: $-E[p(a_1,\theta)] = 2/3(1.155\times10^7) + 1/3(1.414\times10^7) = 1.241\times10^7$

For a_2: $-E[p(a_2,\theta)] = 2/3(1.012\times10^7) + 1/3(1.207\times10^7) = 1.077\times10^7$

For a_3: $-E[p(a_3,\theta)] = 2/3(1.047\times10^7) + 1/3(1.135\times10^7) = 1.076\times10^7$

Since these are expected <u>negative</u> payoffs, the optimal (Bayes) action is a_3 (order 25).

20.2-5. a) Optimal (maximin) action is a_1 or a_3 (both have values of -10).

b) Optimal (max likelihood) action is a_2

c) For a_1: $E[p(a_1,\theta)] = .1(30)+.5(5)+.4(-10) = 1.5$

For a_2: $E[p(a_2,\theta)] = .1(40)+.5(10)+.4(-30) = -3$

For a_3: $E[p(a_3,\theta)] = .1(-10)+.5(0)+.4(15) = 5$

The optimal (Bayes) action is a_3, expected payoff is 5.

20.2-5. d) If the choice of investment can be postponed, it is clear that the best choice would be a_i if E_i is the prediction made. So the expected payoff would be:

$$\text{Expected payoff} = .1(40)+.5(10)+.4(15)=15$$

20.2-6. Payoff Table: (in thousands of dollars)

Action \ State of Nature	θ_1 Dry	θ_2 Moderate	θ_3 Damp
a_1 (Crop 1)	20	35	40
a_2 (Crop 2)	22.5	30	45
a_3 (Crop 3)	30	25	25
a_4 (Crop 4)	20	20	20

a) For a_1: $E[p(a_1,\theta)] = .3(20)+.5(35)+.2(40) = 31.5$ thousand

For a_2: $E[p(a_2,\theta)] = .3(22.5)+.5(30)+.2(45) = 30.75$ "

For a_3: $E[p(a_3,\theta)] = .3(30)+.5(25)+.2(25) = 26.5$ "

For a_4: $E[p(a_4,\theta)] = .3(20)+.5(20)+.2(20) = 20$ "

The optimal (Bayes) action is a_1

b) The optimal (maximin) action is a_3.

c) The difference in expected revenues between a_1 and a_3 is $E[p(a_1,\theta)] - E[p(a_3,\theta)] = 5$ thousand dollars

20.2-7. For a_1: $E[p(a_1,\theta)] = .4(2x)+.2(50)+.4(10) = 14+.8x$

For a_2: $E[p(a_2,\theta)] = .4(25)+.2(40)+.4(90) = 54$

For a_3: $E[p(a_3,\theta)] = .4(35)+.2(3x)+.4(30) = 26+.6x$

At $x=50$, the optimal action is a_3 with expected payoff 56.

At $x=75$, the optimal action is a_1 with expected payoff 74.

The maximum amount that should be spent to increase x to 75 is 18.

20.3-1. a) $EVPI = [.5(800)+.5(5400)] - 2700 = 400$ thousand dollars

b)

$P(\theta=\theta_i)$	0.5	0.5				Posterior Distribution of θ	
	$P(S=s\mid\theta=\theta_i)$		$P(S=s\mid\theta=\theta_i)$		$P(S=s)$	$P(S=s\mid\theta=\theta_i)/P(S=s)$	
	θ_1	θ_2	θ_1	θ_2	= Sum	θ_1	θ_2
$S=1000$ sold	2/3	1/3	1/3	1/6	1/2	2/3	1/3
$S=10{,}000$ sold	1/3	2/3	1/6	1/3	1/2	1/3	2/3

20.3-1. c) Expected payoffs if S=1000 sold:

For a_1: $E[p(a_1, \theta | S=1000)] = \frac{2}{3}(800) + \frac{1}{3}(800) = 800$ thousand

For a_2: $E[p(a_2, \theta | S=1000)] = \frac{2}{3}(0) + \frac{1}{3}(5400) = 1800$ "

If S=10,000 sold:

for a_1: $E[p(a_1, \theta | S=10{,}000)] = \frac{1}{3}(800) + \frac{2}{3}(800) = 800$ thousand

For a_2: $E[p(a_2, \theta | S=10{,}000)] = \frac{1}{3}(0) + \frac{2}{3}(5400) = 3600$ "

So, in both cases, the optimal policy is a_2 (to build computers)

d) $EVE = [.5(1800) + .5(3600)] - 2700 = 0$

So performing the market research is not worthwhile.

20.3-2. a) $$P(\theta = \theta_1 | \text{predict } \theta_1) = \frac{P(\text{predict } \theta_1 | \theta = \theta_1)\, P(\theta = \theta_1)}{P(\text{pred. } \theta_1 | \theta = \theta_1) P(\theta = \theta_1) + P(\text{pred } \theta_1 | \theta = \theta_2) P(\theta = \theta_2)}$$

$$= \frac{(0.6)(0.4)}{(0.6)(0.4) + (0.2)(0.6)} = 2/3$$

$$P(\theta = \theta_2 | \text{predict } \theta_2) = \frac{(0.8)(0.6)}{(0.8)(0.6) + (0.4)(0.4)} = \frac{3}{4}$$

$P(\theta = \theta_2 | \text{predict } \theta_1) = 1/3$, $P(\theta = \theta_1 | \text{predict } \theta_2) = \frac{1}{4}$

The OR courseware supports these calculations.

b) Without research:

For a_1: $E[p(a_1, \theta)] = 0.4(400) + 0.6(-100) = 100$

for a_2: $E[p(a_2, \theta)] = 0.4(0) + 0.6(100) = 60$

So optimal is a_1, with exp. payoff 100.

With research:

If predict θ_1:

For a_1: $E[p(a_1, \theta | \text{pred. } \theta_1)] = \frac{2}{3}(400) + \frac{1}{3}(-100) = 233.333$

For a_2: $E[p(a_2, \theta | \text{pred. } \theta_1)] = \frac{2}{3}(0) + \frac{1}{3}(100) = 33.333$

If predict θ_2:

For a_1: $E[p(a_1, \theta | \text{pred } \theta_2)] = \frac{1}{4}(400) + \frac{3}{4}(-100) = 25$

For a_2: $E[p(a_2, \theta | \text{pred } \theta_2)] = \frac{1}{4}(0) + \frac{3}{4}(100) = 75$

So optimal to take action a_i if predict θ_i.

$P(\text{predict } \theta_1) = P(\text{pred. } \theta_1 | \theta = \theta_1) P(\theta = \theta_1) + P(\text{pred } \theta_1 | \theta = \theta_2) P(\theta = \theta_2)$

$= (0.6)(0.4) + (0.2)(0.6) = 0.36$

$P(\text{predict } \theta_2) = (0.8)(0.6) + (0.4)(0.4) = 0.64$

So, $EVE = [(0.36)(233.333) + (0.64)(75)] - 100 = 32$

Therefore, it is better not to do research. Exp. payoff = 100.

20.3-3. a) Payoff Table:

Action \ State of Nature	θ_1 Fair coin	θ_2 2-headed coin
a_1 (guess fair)	5	-5
a_2 (guess 2-head)	-5	5
Prior probabilities	0.5	0.5

b) Neither option is better. Both give expected payoffs of \$0.

c) $EVPI = [(0.5)5 + 0.5(5)] - 0 = \$5$

d) $$P(\text{fair} \mid \text{flip tail}) = \frac{P(\text{flip tail} \mid \text{fair})P(\text{fair})}{P(\text{flip tail} \mid \text{fair})P(\text{fair}) + P(\text{flip tail} \mid \text{2-head})P(\text{2-head})}$$

$$= \frac{(0.5)(0.5)}{(0.5)(0.5) + 0(0.5)} = 1$$

So $P(\text{2-head} \mid \text{flip tail}) = 0$

$$P(\text{fair} \mid \text{flip head}) = \frac{P(\text{flip head} \mid \text{fair})P(\text{fair})}{P(\text{flip head} \mid \text{fair})P(\text{fair}) + P(\text{flip head} \mid \text{2-head})P(\text{2-head})}$$

$$= \frac{(0.5)(0.5)}{(0.5)(0.5) + 1(0.5)} = \frac{1}{3}$$

$P(\text{2-head} \mid \text{flip head}) = \frac{2}{3}$

e)

k	θ_1	θ_2
$P_\theta(k)$	0.5	0.5

$Q_{X|\theta=k}(x)$

x \ k	θ_1	θ_2
X_1	0.5	0
X_2	0.5	1

$h_{\theta|X=x}(k)$

x \ k	θ_1	θ_2
X_1	1	0
X_2	0.333	0.667

f) If flip tail:

for a_1: $E[p(a_1, \theta \mid \text{flip tail})] = 1(5) + 0(-5) = 5$

for a_2: $E[p(a_2, \theta \mid \text{flip tail})] = 1(-5) + 0(5) = -5$

If flip head:

for a_1: $E[p(a_1, \theta \mid \text{flip head})] = \frac{1}{3}(5) + \frac{2}{3}(-5) = -\frac{5}{3}$

for a_2: $E[p(a_2, \theta \mid \text{flip head})] = \frac{1}{3}(-5) + \frac{2}{3}(5) = \frac{5}{3}$

So if tail occurs, guess fair coin; if head occurs, guess 2-headed coin.

g) $P(\text{flip tail}) = P(\text{flip tail} \mid \text{fair})P(\text{fair}) + P(\text{flip tail} \mid \text{2-head})P(\text{2-head})$

$= (0.5)(0.5) + 0(0.5) = 0.25$

$P(\text{flip head}) = 0.75$

So, $EVE = [(0.75)\frac{5}{3} + (0.25)5] - 0 = \$2.5$

The most you should be willing to pay would be \$2.50.

20.3-4. a) $EVPI = \left[(\tfrac{2}{3})(-1.012\times10^7)+(\tfrac{1}{3})(-1.135\times10^7)\right]-(-1.076\times10^7) = 230{,}000$

b) $$P(\theta=21 \mid 30 \text{ spares req.}) = \frac{P(30 \text{ spares req.} \mid \theta=21)P(\theta=21)}{P(30 \text{ spares req} \mid \theta=21)P(\theta=21)+P(30 \text{ spares req} \mid \theta=24)P(\theta=24)}$$

$$= \frac{(0.013)(\tfrac{2}{3})}{(0.013)(\tfrac{2}{3})+(0.036)(\tfrac{1}{3})} = .419$$

$P(\theta=24 \mid 30 \text{ spares req}) = .581$

For a_1: $E[p(a_1,\theta \mid 30 \text{ spares req})] = .419(-1.155\times10^7)+.581(-1.414\times10^7) = -1.305\times10^7$

For a_2: $E[p(a_2,\theta \mid 30 \text{ spares req})] = .419(-1.012\times10^7)+.581(-1.207\times10^7) = -1.125\times10^7$

For a_3: $E[p(a_3,\theta \mid 30 \text{ spares req})] = .419(-1.047\times10^7)+.581(-1.135\times10^7) = -1.098\times10^7$

So optimal action is a_3 (order 25).

20.3-5. a) Payoff Table: (in thousands of dollars)

Action \ State of Nature	θ_1 Poor	θ_2 Average	θ_3 Good rating
a_1 (extend credit)	-15	10	20
a_2 (don't extend credit)	0	0	0
prior probabilities	0.2	0.5	0.3

b) $E[p(a_1,\theta)] = 0.2(-15)+0.5(10)+0.3(20) = 8$ thousand dollars.

$E[p(a_2,\theta)] = 0$

So optimal action is a_1 (extend credit).

c) $EVPI = [0.2(0)+0.5(10)+0.3(20)] - 8 = 3$ thousand dollars

d) Prior Distribution:

k	θ_1	θ_2	θ_3
$P_\Theta(k)$	0.2	0.5	0.3

$Q_{X|\Theta=k}(x)$

x \ k	θ_1	θ_2	θ_3
X_1	0.5	0.4	0.2
X_2	0.4	0.5	0.4
X_3	0.1	0.1	0.4

Posterior Distribution:

$h_{\Theta|X=x}(k)$

x \ k	θ_1	θ_2	θ_3
X_1	0.278	0.556	0.167
X_2	0.178	0.556	0.267
X_3	0.105	0.263	0.632

20.3-5. e) If credit evaluation shows:

Poor: $E[p(a_1,\theta \mid \text{poor eval})] = 0.2778(-15) + 0.5556(10) + 0.1667(20) = 4.72$

$E[p(a_2,\theta \mid \text{poor eval})] = 0$

Fair: $E[p(a_1,\theta \mid \text{fair eval})] = 0.1778(-15) + 0.5556(10) + 0.2667(20) = 8.22$

$E[p(a_2,\theta \mid \text{fair eval})] = 0$

Good: $E[p(a_1,\theta \mid \text{good eval})] = 0.1053(-15) + 0.2632(10) + 0.6316(20) = 13.68$

$E[p(a_2,\theta \mid \text{good eval})] = 0$

So, in all cases, it is optimal to extend credit (action a_1).

f) EVE = 0 (we know this since the optimal policies remain the same).
So, it is not worthwhile to use the credit-rating organization.

20.3-6. a) $E[p(\text{screen},\theta)] = (0.8)(-1500) + (0.2)(-1500) = -1500$

$E[p(\text{don't screen},\theta)] = 0.8(-750) + 0.2(-3750) = -1350$

So the optimal action is a_2 (don't screen).

b) $EVPI = [(-750)(0.8) + (-1500)(0.2)] - (-1350) = 450$.

c) $P(p=0.05 \mid \text{defective}) = \dfrac{P(\text{defect} \mid p=0.05)P(p=0.05)}{P(\text{defect} \mid p=0.05)P(p=0.05) + P(\text{defect} \mid p=0.25)P(p=0.25)}$

$= \dfrac{(0.05)(0.8)}{(0.05)(0.8) + (0.25)(0.2)} = 0.444$

$P(p=0.25 \mid \text{defective}) = 0.556$

$P(p=0.05 \mid \text{non defective}) = \dfrac{(0.95)(0.8)}{(0.95)(0.8) + (0.75)(0.2)} = 0.835$

$P(p=0.25 \mid \text{non-defective}) = 0.165$

d) If defective found:

$E[p(\text{screen},\theta \mid \text{defective})] = 0.444(-1500) + 0.556(-1500) = -1500$

$E[p(\text{non-screen},\theta \mid \text{defect})] = 0.444(-750) + 0.556(-3750) = -2418$

If non-defective found:

$E[p(\text{screen},\theta \mid \text{non-defective})] = -1500$

$E[p(\text{non-screen},\theta \mid \text{non-defect})] = 0.835(-750) + 0.165(-3750) = -1245$

So optimal policy w/ experimentation is to screen if defective is found, and not screen if non-defective is found.

e) $P(\text{defective}) = (0.05)(0.8) + (0.25)(0.2) = 0.09$

$P(\text{non-defective}) = 0.91$

$EVE = [(0.09)(-1500) + (0.91)(-1245)] - (-1350) = 82.05$

Since the cost of the inspection is \$125 > \$82.05, the single item is not worthwhile inspecting.

20.3-7. a) $E[p(a_1,\theta)] = 0.2(4) + 0 + 0 = 0.8$

$E[p(a_2,\theta)] = 0 + 0.5(2) + 0 = 1.0$

$E[p(a_3,\theta)] = 0.2(3) + 0 + 0.3(1) = 0.9$

The optimal action is a_2.

b) $EVPI = [0.2(4) + 0.5(2) + 0.3(1)] - 1.0 = 1.1$.

20.3-8. a) $E[p(a_1,\theta)] = 0.5(50) + 0.3(100) + 0.2(-100) = 35$

$E[p(a_2,\theta)] = 0 + 0.3(10) + 0.2(-10) = 1$

$E[p(a_3,\theta)] = 0.5(20) + 0.3(40) + 0.2(-40) = 14$

The optimal (Bayes) action is a_1.

b) $EVPI = [0.5(50) + 0.3(100) + 0.2(-10)] - 35 = 18$.

20.3-9. a) $E[p(a_1,\theta)] = 0.2(-100) + 0.3(10) + 0.5(100) = 33$

$E[p(a_2,\theta)] = 0.2(-10) + 0.3(20) + 0.5(50) = 29$

$E[p(a_3,\theta)] = 0.2(10) + 0.3(10) + 0.5(60) = 35$

The optimal (Bayes) action is a_3. Expected payoff $= 35$.

b) If θ_1 occurs for certain, optimal is a_3 w/ payoff 10.

If θ_1 for certain does <u>not</u> occur, then $P(\theta=\theta_2) = \frac{0.3}{0.3+0.5} = \frac{3}{8}$

so $E[p(a_1,\theta|\theta\neq\theta_1)] = 10(\frac{3}{8}) + (100)\frac{5}{8} = 66.25$

$E[p(a_2,\theta|\theta\neq\theta_1)] = 20(3/8) + (50)5/8 = 38.75$

$E[p(a_3,\theta|\theta\neq\theta_1)] = 10(3/8) + (60)5/8 = 41.25$

and optimal is a_1 w/ expected payoff 66.25.

Expected payoff w/ this info $= 0.2(10) + 0.8(66.25) = 55$

and the max amount you should pay for this info

is $55 - 35 = 20$.

c) If θ_2 occurs for certain, a_2 is optimal with payoff 20.

If not,

$P(\theta=\theta_1) = \frac{2}{7}$, $P(\theta=\theta_3) = \frac{5}{7}$

$E[p(a_1,\theta|\theta\neq\theta_2)] = \frac{2}{7}(-100) + \frac{5}{7}(100) = 42.857$

$E[p(a_2,\theta|\theta\neq\theta_2)] = \frac{2}{7}(-10) + \frac{5}{7}(50) = 32.857$

$E[p(a_3,\theta|\theta\neq\theta_2)] = \frac{2}{7}(10) + \frac{5}{7}(60) = 45.714$

Optimal is a_3 with expected payoff 45.714

Maximum you should pay for the information is:

$$EVE = [0.3(20) + 0.7(45.714)] - 35 = 3$$

20.3-9. d) If θ_3 occurs for certain, a_1 is optimal with payoff 100.

If not,

$$P(\theta=\theta_1)=\frac{2}{5}\ ,\quad P(\theta=\theta_2)=\frac{3}{5}$$

$$E[p(a_1,\theta|\theta\neq\theta_3)]=\frac{2}{5}(-100)+\frac{3}{5}(10)=-34$$

$$E[p(a_2,\theta|\theta\neq\theta_3)]=\frac{2}{5}(-10)+\frac{3}{5}(20)=8$$

$$E[p(a_3,\theta|\theta\neq\theta_3)]=\frac{2}{5}(10)+\frac{3}{5}(10)=10$$

Optimal a_3 with expected payoff 10.

Maximum you should pay for the information is:

$$EVE=[0.5(100)+0.5(10)]-35=20$$

e) Maximum amount you should pay for perfect information is:

$$EVPI=[0.2(10)+0.3(20)+0.5(100)]-35=23.$$

f) Maximum amount you should pay for testing is 23.

20.3-10. a) $E[p(a_1,\theta)]=0.6(0)+0.4(-1)=-0.4$

$E[p(a_2,\theta)]=0.6(-1)+0.4(0)=-0.6$

Optimal action is a_1 (say coin 1 is tossed)

b) If outcome is heads (H):

$$P(\text{coin }1|H)=\frac{P(H|\text{coin}1)P(\text{coin}1)}{P(H|\text{coin}1)P(\text{coin}1)+P(H|\text{coin}2)P(\text{coin}2)}$$

$$=\frac{0.3(0.6)}{0.3(0.6)+0.6(0.4)}=\frac{3}{7}$$

$$P(\text{coin }2|H)=\frac{4}{7}$$

$$E[p(a_1,\theta|H)]=\frac{3}{7}(0)+\frac{4}{7}(-1)=-\frac{4}{7}$$

$$E[p(a_2,\theta|H)]=\frac{3}{7}(-1)+\frac{4}{7}(0)=-\frac{3}{7}$$

Optimal action is a_2.

If outcome is tails (T):

$$P(\text{coin }1|T)=\frac{0.7(0.6)}{0.7(0.6)+(0.4)(0.4)}=.7241\ ,\quad P(\text{coin }2|T)=.2759$$

$$E[p(a_1,\theta|T)]=.7241(0)+.2759(-1)=-.2759$$

$$E[p(a_2,\theta|T)]=.7241(-1)+.2759(0)=-.7241$$

Optimal action is a_1.

20.3-11. a)

a \ θ	0	1	2	3	4	5
a_1	-0.40	-0.40	-0.40	-0.40	-0.40	-0.40
a_2	1.60	-0.40	-0.40	-0.40	-0.40	-0.40
a_3	0.60	0.40	0.20	0.00	-0.20	-0.40

b) $E[p(a_1,\theta)] = -0.40$

$E[p(a_2,\theta)] = \frac{1}{6}(1.60) + \frac{5}{6}(-0.40) = -0.067$

$E[p(a_3,\theta)] = \frac{1}{6}(0.60) + \frac{1}{6}(0.40) + \dots + \frac{1}{6}(-0.40) = 0.10$

Optimal action is a_3 (sell film for \$1).

c)

$P(\theta=\theta_i)$	1/6	1/6	1/6	1/6	1/6	1/6														
	$P(S=s \mid \theta=\theta_i)$						$P(S=s \mid \theta=\theta_i)$						$P(S=s)$	Posterior Dist of θ: $P(S=s \mid \theta=\theta_i)/P(S=s)$					
	θ_1	θ_2	θ_3	θ_4	θ_5	θ_6	θ_1	θ_2	θ_3	θ_4	θ_5	θ_6	= sum	θ_1	θ_2	θ_3	θ_4	θ_5	θ_6
S = good	1	4/5	3/5	2/5	1/5	0	1/6	2/15	1/10	1/15	1/30	0	1/2	1/3	4/15	1/5	2/15	1/15	0
S = bad	0	1/5	2/5	3/5	4/5	1	0	1/30	1/15	1/10	2/15	1/6	1/2	0	1/15	2/15	1/5	4/15	1/3

d) If test = good:

$E[p(a_1,\theta \mid good)] = -0.40$

$E[p(a_2,\theta \mid good)] = \frac{1}{3}(1.60) + \frac{2}{3}(-0.40) = 0.267$

$E[p(a_3,\theta \mid good)] = \frac{1}{3}(0.60) + \frac{4}{15}(0.40) + \frac{1}{5}(0.20) + 0 + \frac{1}{15}(-0.20) + 0 = 0.333$

If test = bad:

$E[p(a_1,\theta \mid bad)] = -0.40$

$E[p(a_2,\theta \mid bad)] = 0(1.60) + 1(-0.40) = -0.40$

$E[p(a_3,\theta \mid bad)] = 0 + \frac{1}{15}(0.40) + \frac{2}{15}(0.20) + 0 + \frac{4}{15}(-0.20) + \frac{1}{3}(-0.40) = -0.133$

In <u>both</u> cases, the optimal action is a_2 (sell film for \$1).

The expected payoff is $\frac{1}{2}(0.333) + \frac{1}{2}(-0.133) = 0.10$.

20.3-12. a)
Payoff Table:

Action \ State of Nature	θ_1 coin 1	θ_2 coin 2
a_1 (predict 0 H's)	4	36
a_2 (predict 1 H)	32	48
a_3 (predict 2 H's)	64	16
prior probabilities	0.5	0.5

$E[p(a_1, \theta)] = \frac{1}{2}(4) + \frac{1}{2}(36) = \$20$

$E[p(a_2, \theta)] = \frac{1}{2}(32) + \frac{1}{2}(48) = \$40$

$E[p(a_3, \theta)] = \frac{1}{2}(64) + \frac{1}{2}(16) = \$40$

Optimal action is a_2 or a_3 (both have expected payoff \$40)

b) Prior Distribution:

k	θ_1	θ_2
$P_\theta(k)$	0.5	0.5

$Q_{X|\theta=k}(x)$

x \ k	θ_1	θ_2
X_1	0.8	0.4
X_2	0.2	0.6

Posterior Distribution:

$h_{\theta|X=x}(k)$

x \ k	θ_1	θ_2
X_1	0.667	0.333
X_2	0.25	0.75

c) If toss heads (H):

$E[p(a_1, \theta | H)] = 0.667(4) + 0.333(36) = 14.67$

$E[p(a_2, \theta | H)] = 0.667(32) + 0.333(48) = 37.33$

$E[p(a_3, \theta | H)] = 0.667(64) + 0.333(16) = 48$

Optimal action is a_3 (predict 2 H's)

If toss tails (T):

$E[p(a_1, \theta | T)] = 0.25(4) + 0.75(36) = 28$

$E[p(a_2, \theta | T)] = 0.25(32) + 0.75(48) = 44$

$E[p(a_3, \theta | T)] = 0.25(64) + 0.75(16) = 28$

optimal action is a_2 (predict 1 H)

$P(H) = 0.6$, $P(T) = 0.4$

Expected payoff $= 0.6(48) + 0.4(44) = \$46.40$

d) EVE $= 46.4 - 40 = \$6.40$

20.3-13. a) Let states θ_1, θ_2 be product successful, unsuccessful, resp. and actions a_1, a_2 be marketing, not marketing, resp.

$E[p(a_1,\theta)] = \frac{2}{3}(1{,}500{,}000) + \frac{1}{3}(-1{,}800{,}000) = \$400{,}000$

$E[p(a_2,\theta)] = 0$

Optimal action is a_1 (market new product).

b) $EVPI = [\frac{2}{3}(1{,}500{,}000) + \frac{1}{3}(0)] - \$400{,}000 = \$600{,}000$

c) $$P(\theta_1 \mid \text{predict success}) = \frac{P(\text{predict success} \mid \theta_1)P(\theta_1)}{P(\text{pred. succ.} \mid \theta_1)P(\theta_1) + P(\text{pred. succ.} \mid \theta_2)P(\theta_2)}$$

$$= \frac{0.8(2/3)}{0.8(2/3) + 0.3(1/3)} = 0.8421$$

$P(\theta_2 \mid \text{pred. succ.}) = 0.1579$

$$P(\theta_1 \mid \text{pred. no succ.}) = \frac{0.2(2/3)}{0.2(2/3) + 0.7(1/3)} = 0.3636$$

$P(\theta_2 \mid \text{pred. no succ.}) = 0.6364$

d) Prior Distribution:

k	θ_1	θ_2
$P_\theta(k)$	0.667	0.333

$Q_{X\mid\theta=k}(x)$

x \ k	θ_1	θ_2
X_1	0.8	0.3
X_2	0.2	0.7

Posterior Distribution:

$h_{\theta\mid X=x}(k)$

x \ k	θ_1	θ_2
X_1	0.842	0.158
X_2	0.364	0.636

e) $E[p(a_1,\theta \mid \text{pred. succ.})] = 0.8421(1{,}500{,}000) + 0.1579(-1{,}800{,}000) = \$979{,}000$

$E[p(a_2,\theta \mid \text{pred. succ.})] = 0$

$E[p(a_1,\theta \mid \text{pred. no succ.})] = .3636(1{,}500{,}000) + .6364(-1{,}800{,}000) = -\$600{,}000$

$E[p(a_2,\theta \mid \text{pred. no succ.})] = 0$

Optimal a_1 if pred. success, a_2 if not.

$P(\text{pred. success}) = P(\text{pred. succ.} \mid \theta_1)P(\theta_1) + P(\text{pred. succ.} \mid \theta_2)P(\theta_2)$
$= 0.8(2/3) + (0.2)1/3 = 0.6$

Expected payoff given info $= 0.6(979{,}000) + 0.4(0) = \$587{,}000$

So $EVE = 587{,}000 - 400{,}000 = \$187{,}000$

Cost of survey $= \$300{,}000 > \$187{,}000$

So optimal strategy is: Do not conduct survey, market product.

20.3-14. Let X = amount of fine. ("non-user" = non-user of drugs)

E[value of fines] (per person) = $X\,P(\text{test positive})$

E[value of payment to athletes] = $1 \cdot P(\text{test negative}) + 100\,P(\text{test pos} \,\&\, \text{non-user})$

$P(\text{test pos.} \,\&\, \text{non-user}) = P(\text{test pos.} \mid \text{non-user})\,P(\text{non-user})$

$= 0.05\,(.9) = 0.045$

$P(\text{test pos.}) = P(\text{test pos.} \mid \text{non-user})\,P(\text{non-user}) + P(\text{test pos.} \mid \text{user})\,P(\text{user})$

$= 0.05\,(0.9) + (0.95)(0.1) = 0.14$

So $0.14\,X = 0.86 + 100(0.045) = 5.36$

or $X = \$38.29$

20.4-1. a) (in millions of dollars)

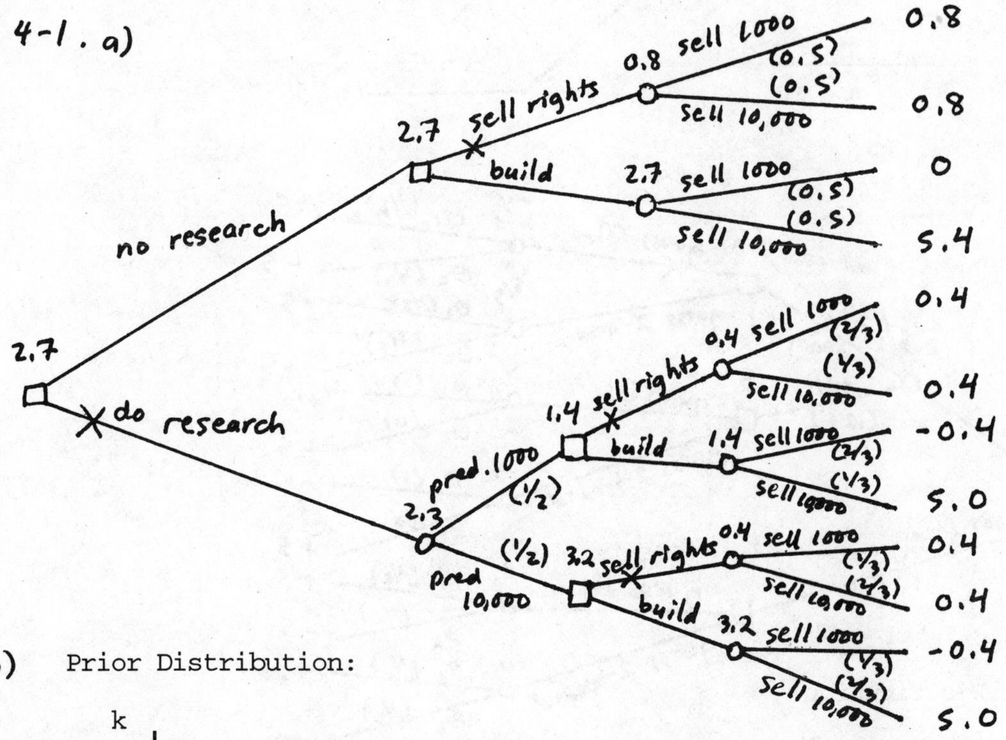

b) Prior Distribution:

k	θ_1	θ_2
$P_\theta(k)$	0.5	0.5

$Q_{X\mid\theta=k}(x)$

x \ k	θ_1	θ_2
X_1	0.667	0.333
X_2	0.333	0.667

Posterior Distribution:

$h_{\theta\mid X=x}(k)$

x \ k	θ_1	θ_2
X_1	0.667	0.333
X_2	0.333	0.667

c) See (a). The optimal policy is to do no research, but build the computers.

20.4-2.

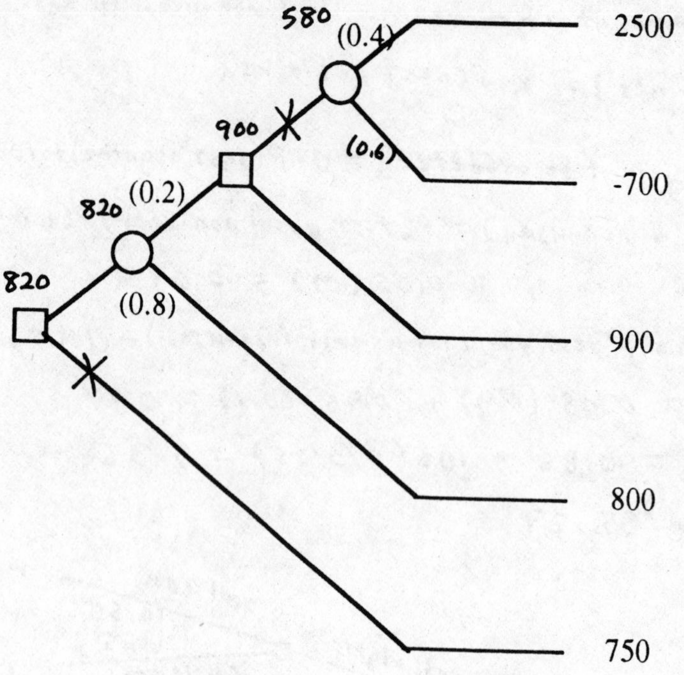

20.4-3. a)

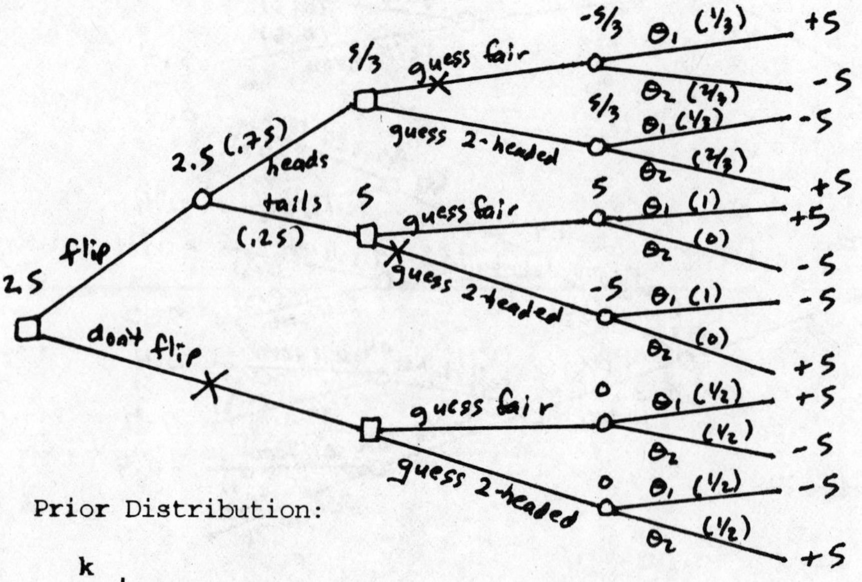

b) Prior Distribution:

k	θ_1	θ_2
$P_\Theta(k)$	0.5	0.5

$Q_{X|\Theta=k}(x)$

x \ k	θ_1	θ_2
X_1	0.5	0
X_2	0.5	1

Posterior Distribution:

$h_{\Theta|X=x}(k)$

x \ k	θ_1	θ_2
X_1	1	0
X_2	0.333	0.667

c) See (a). The optimal policy is to flip the coin and guess that it is fair if it comes up tails, and 2-headed if it comes up heads.

20.4-4. a) Payoff Table: (in millions of dollars)

Action \ State of Nature	θ_1 winning season	θ_2 losing season
a_1 (campaign)	3	-2
a_2 (don't campaign)	0	0
Prior probabilities	0.6	0.4

$E[p(a_1, \theta)] = 0.6(3) + 0.4(-2) = 1$ million ← optimal action

$E[p(a_2, \theta)] = 0$

$EVPI = [0.6(3) + 0.4(0)] - 1 = 0.8$ million

Thus, the university should be willing to pay up to \$800,000 for perfect information.

b) If the scout predicts a:

winning season:

$$P(w \mid \text{predict } w) = \frac{P(\text{pred. } w \mid w)\,P(w)}{P(\text{pred. } w \mid w)P(w) + P(\text{pred } w \mid L)\,P(L)} = \frac{3/4\,(0.6)}{3/4(0.6) + \frac{1}{4}(0.4)} = 0.8182$$

$P(L \mid \text{pred. } w) = 0.1818$

losing season:

$$P(w \mid \text{pred. } L) = \frac{1/4\,(0.6)}{1/4(0.6) + 3/4(0.4)} = 0.3333$$

$P(L \mid \text{pred. } L) = 0.6667$

c)

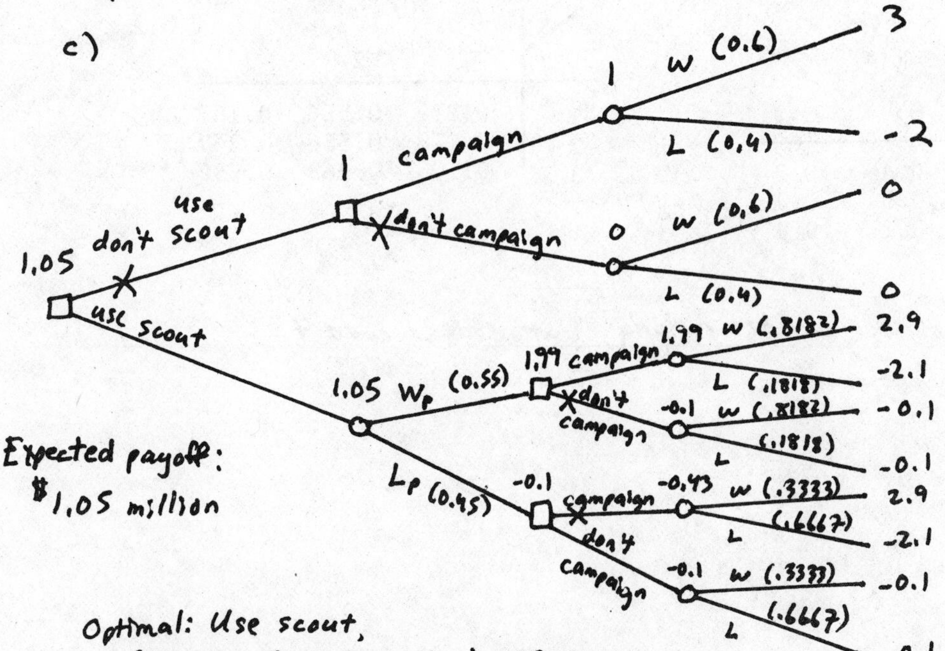

Expected payoff: \$1.05 million

Optimal: Use scout,
Campaign if predict winning season
Don't campaign if predict losing season.

20.4-5. a)

(in thousands of dollars)

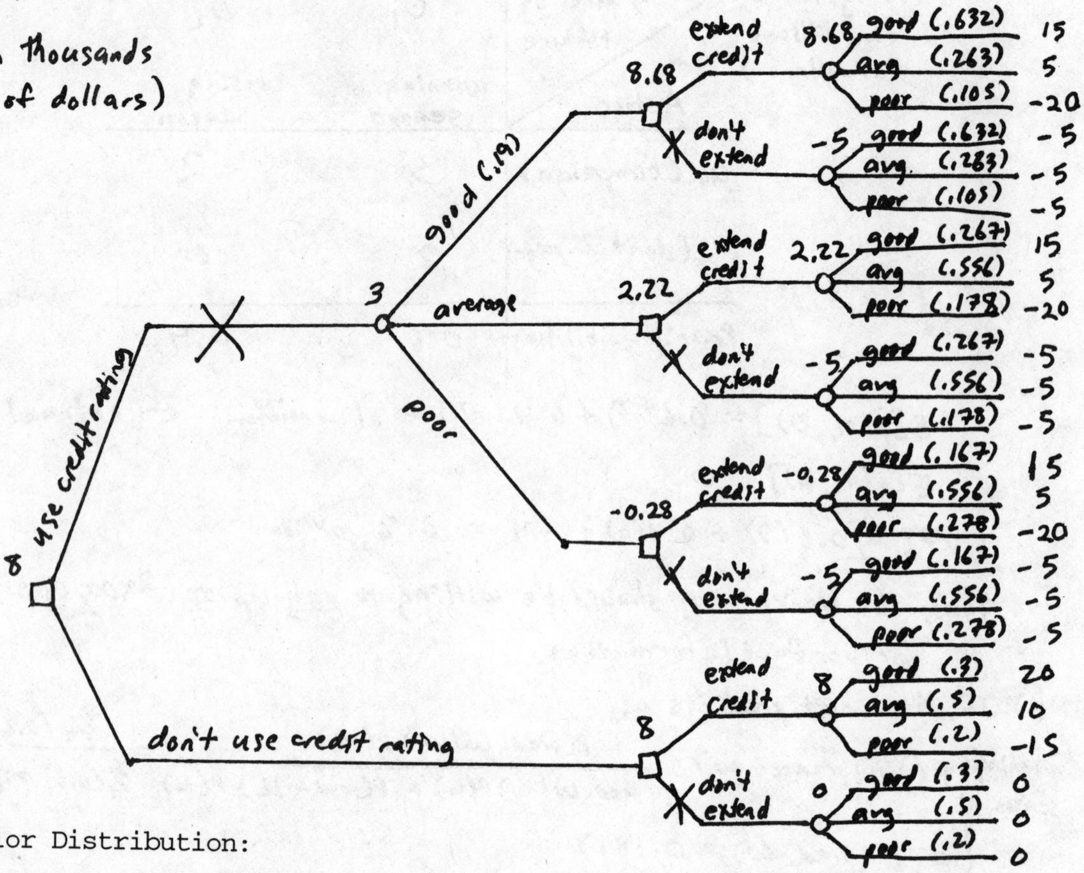

b) Prior Distribution:

k	θ_1	θ_2	θ_3
$P_\Theta(k)$	0.2	0.5	0.3

$Q_{X|\Theta=k}(x)$

x \ k	θ_1	θ_2	θ_3
x_1	0.5	0.4	0.2
x_2	0.4	0.5	0.4
x_3	0.1	0.1	0.4

Posterior Distribution:

$h_{\Theta|X=x}(k)$

x \ k	θ_1	θ_2	θ_3
x_1	0.278	0.556	0.167
x_2	0.178	0.556	0.267
x_3	0.105	0.263	0.632

c) Optimal to not use credit rating, but extend credit. (See (a)).

20.4-6. a)

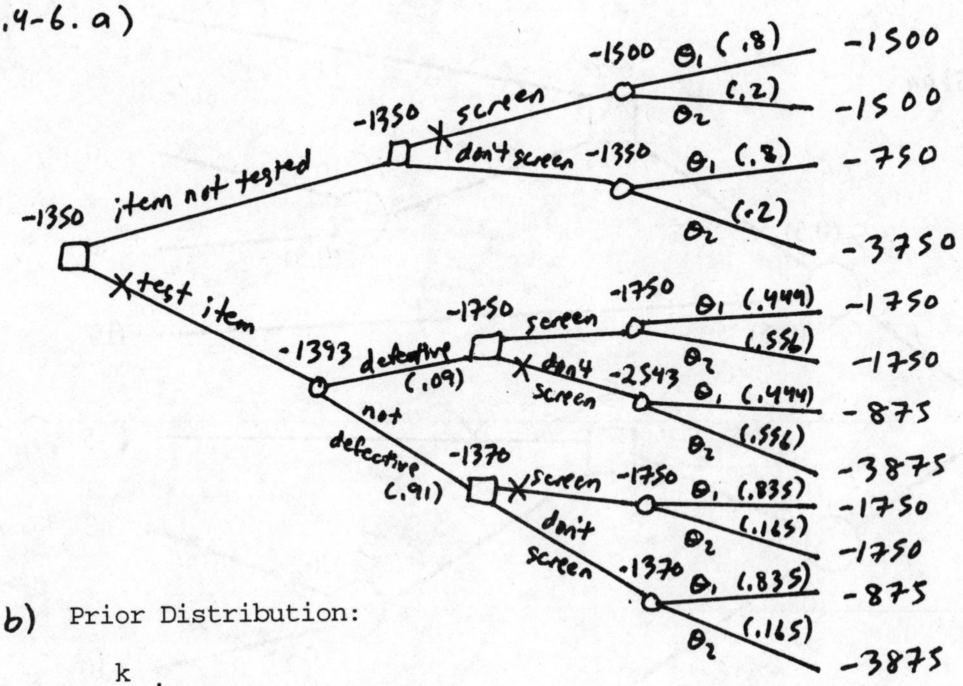

b) Prior Distribution:

k	θ_1	θ_2
$P_\theta(k)$	0.8	0.2

$Q_{X|\theta=k}(x)$

x \ k	θ_1	θ_2
X_1	0.95	0.75
X_2	0.05	0.25

Posterior Distribution:

$h_{\theta|X=x}(k)$

x \ k	θ_1	θ_2
X_1	0.835	0.165
X_2	0.444	0.556

c) See (a). Optimal is not to test item and not to screen.

20.4-7. a)

Bayesian:

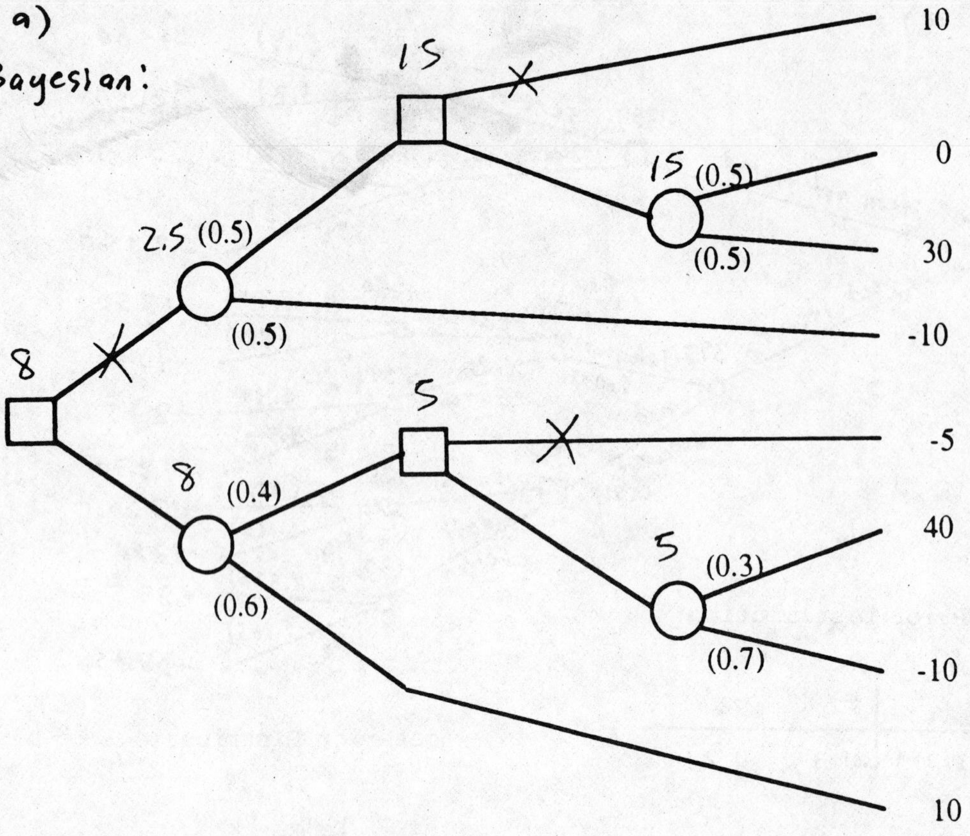

b)

Maximin:

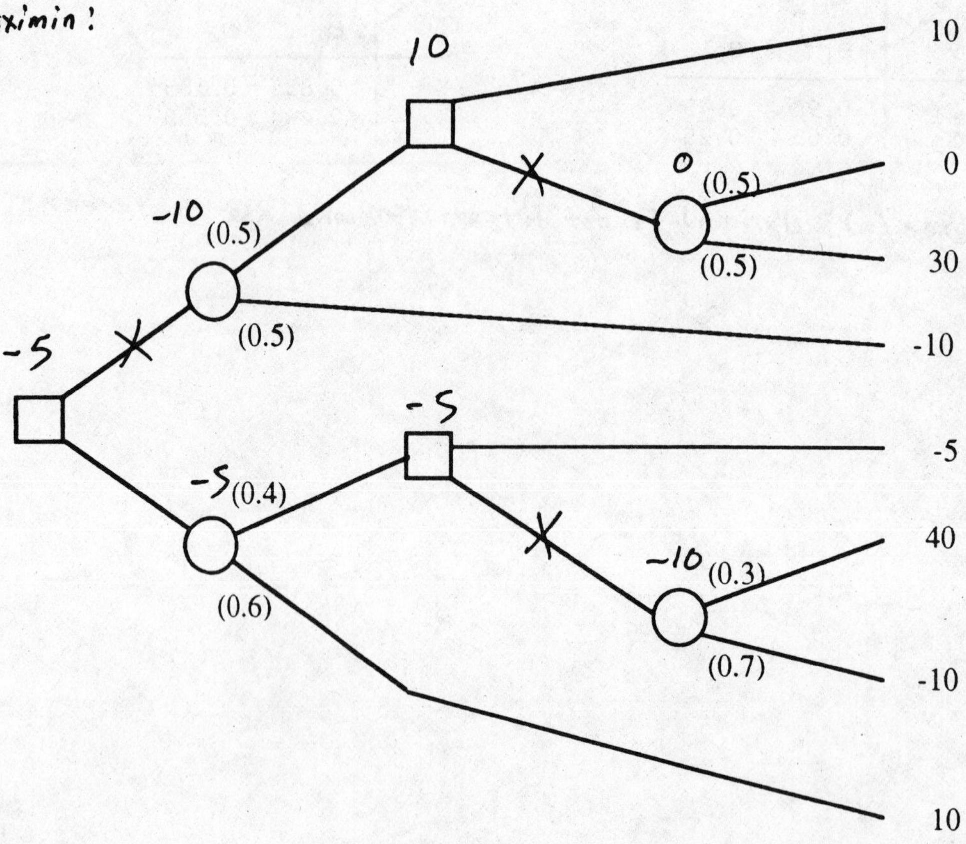

20.4-8. a)

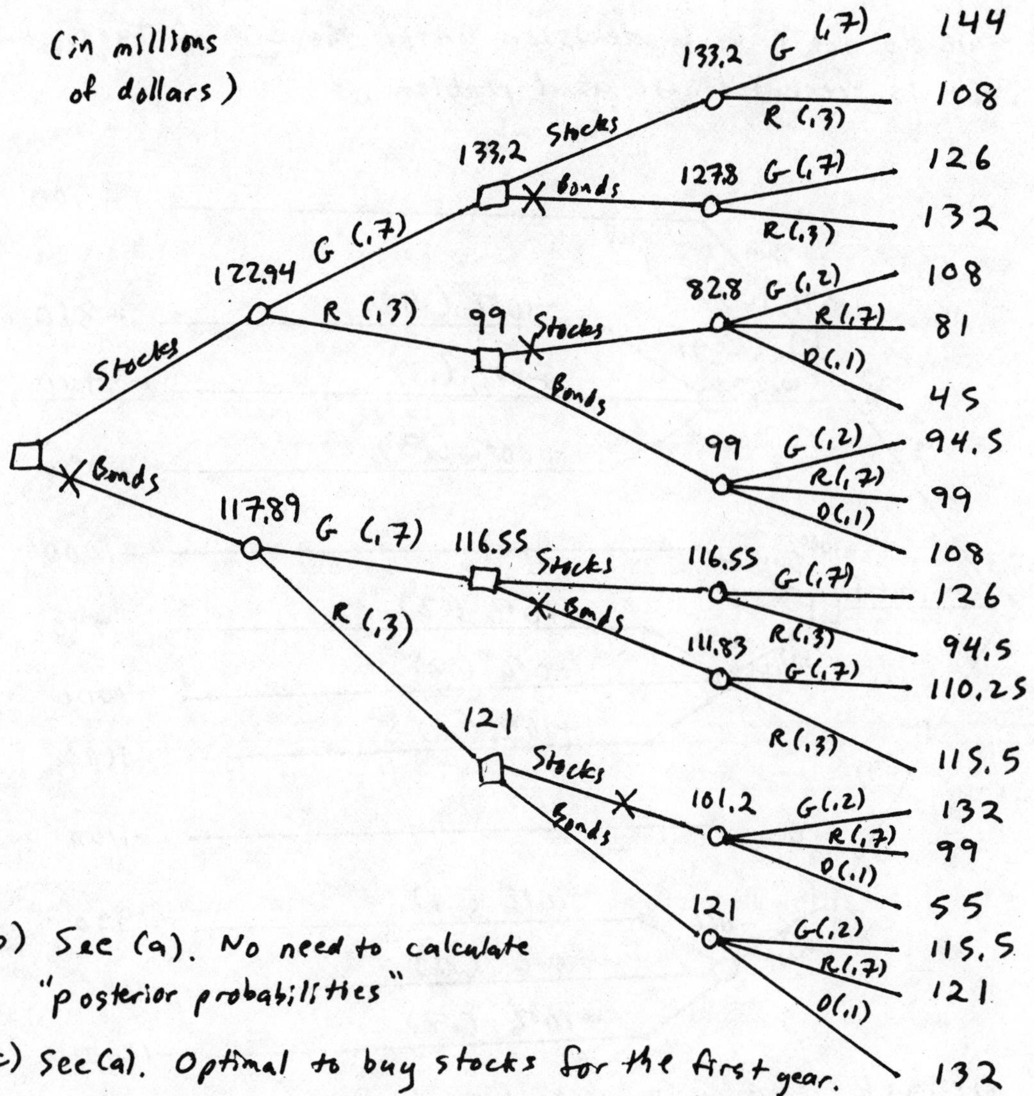

b) See (a). No need to calculate "posterior probabilities"

c) See (a). Optimal to buy stocks for the first year. If growth, continue investing in stocks, otherwise invest in bonds for second year.

20.4-9. This could be thought of as 3 different problems since we do not have a decision until the <u>end</u> of Tues., but it is presented here as 1 problem:

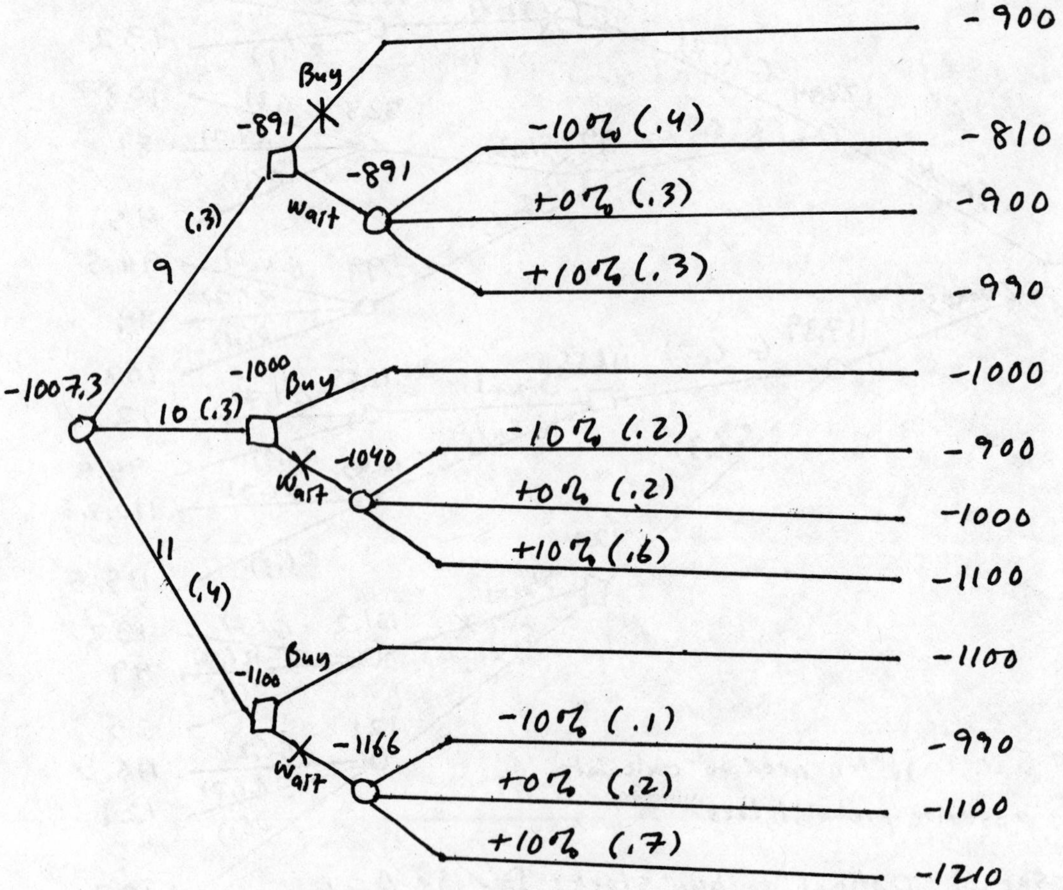

Optimal to Wait if price drops to 9, else Buy.

20.4-10. a)

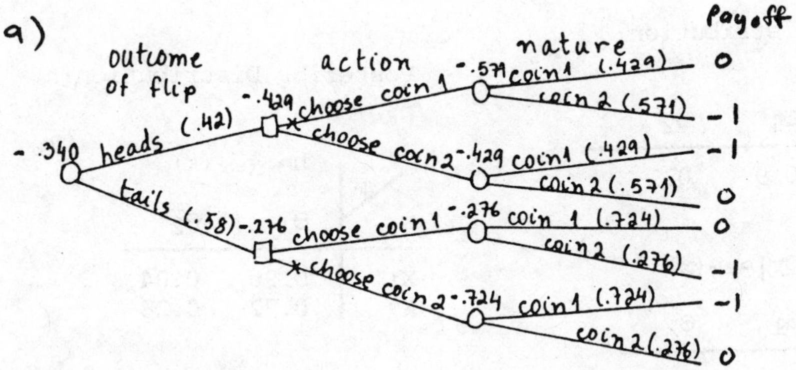

b) Prior Distribution:

k	θ_1	θ_2
$P_\Theta(k)$	0.6	0.4

$Q_{X|\Theta=k}(x)$

x \ k	θ_1	θ_2
X_1	0.3	0.6
X_2	0.7	0.4

Posterior Distribution:

$h_{\Theta|X=x}(k)$

x \ k	θ_1	θ_2
X_1	0.429	0.571
X_2	0.724	0.276

c) See (a). Optimal to choose coin 1 if tails is flipped and coin 2 if heads is flipped

20.4-11. a)

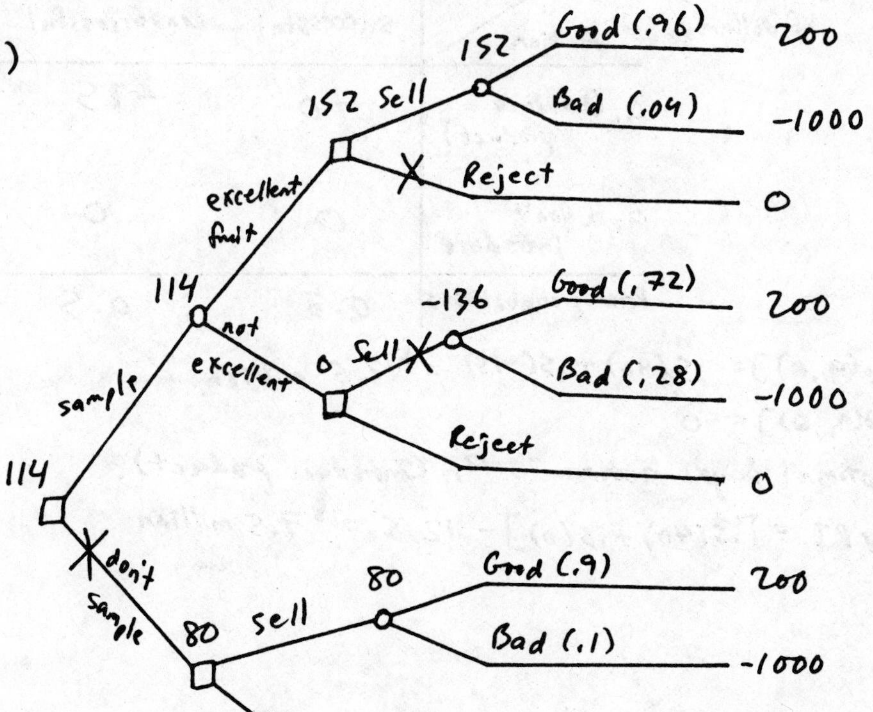

20.4-11. b) Prior Distribution:

k	θ_1	θ_2
$P_\Theta(k)$	0.9	0.1

$Q_{X|\Theta=k}(x)$

x \ k	θ_1	θ_2
X_1	0.8	0.3
X_2	0.2	0.7

Posterior Distribution:

$h_{\Theta|X=x}(k)$

x \ k	θ_1	θ_2
X_1	0.96	0.04
X_2	0.72	0.28

c) See (a). Optimal policy is to sample and sell if the fruit sampled is excellent, but reject if it is not.

d) EVE = 114 − 80 = \$34

e) EVPI = [.9(200) + .1(0)] − 80 = \$100

f) It would be worth 100 − 34 = \$66 to have "perfect information" compared to sampling.

20.4-12. a) Payoff Table (in millions of dollars)

Action \ State of Nature	θ_1 successful	θ_2 unsuccessful
a_1 (Introduce product)	40	−15
a_2 (Don't introduce	0	0
Prior probabilities	0.5	0.5

$E[p(a_1,\theta)] = .5(40) + .5(-15) = \$12.5$ million.

$E[p(a_2,\theta)] = 0$

Optimal Bayes action is a_1 (Introduce product).

b) EVPI = [.5(40) + .5(0)] − 12.5 = \$7.5 million

20.4-12. c)

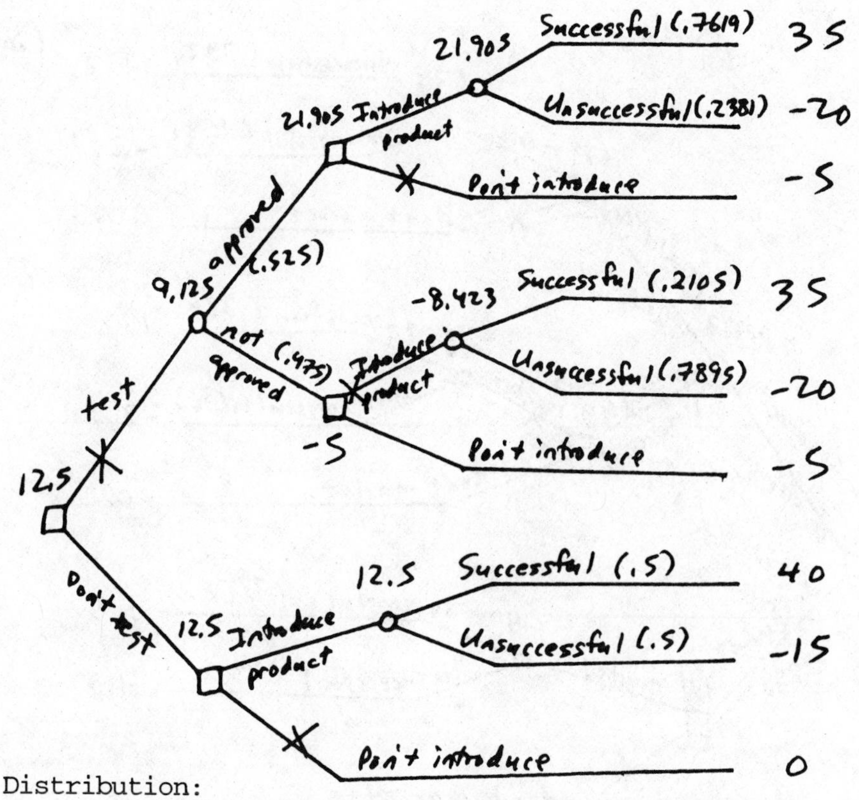

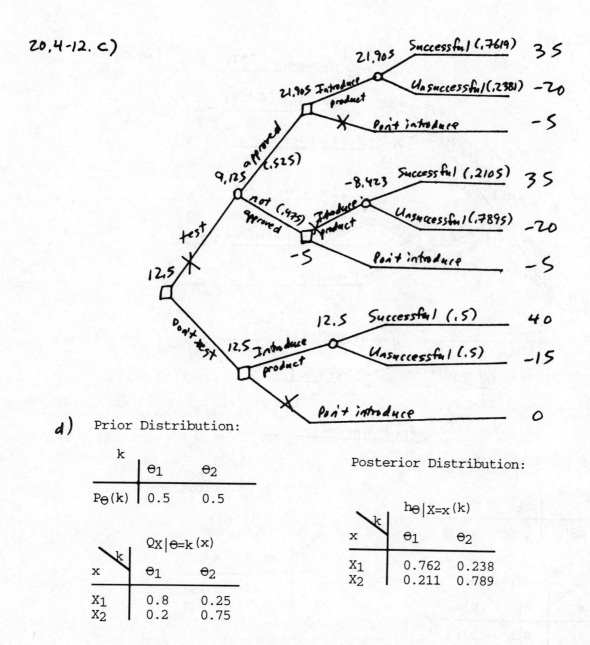

d) Prior Distribution:

k	θ_1	θ_2
$P_\theta(k)$	0.5	0.5

$Q_{X\mid\theta=k}(x)$

x \ k	θ_1	θ_2
X_1	0.8	0.25
X_2	0.2	0.75

Posterior Distribution:

$h_{\theta\mid X=x}(k)$

x \ k	θ_1	θ_2
X_1	0.762	0.238
X_2	0.211	0.789

e) See (a). Optimal is not to test, but introduce the new product.

20.4-13. a)

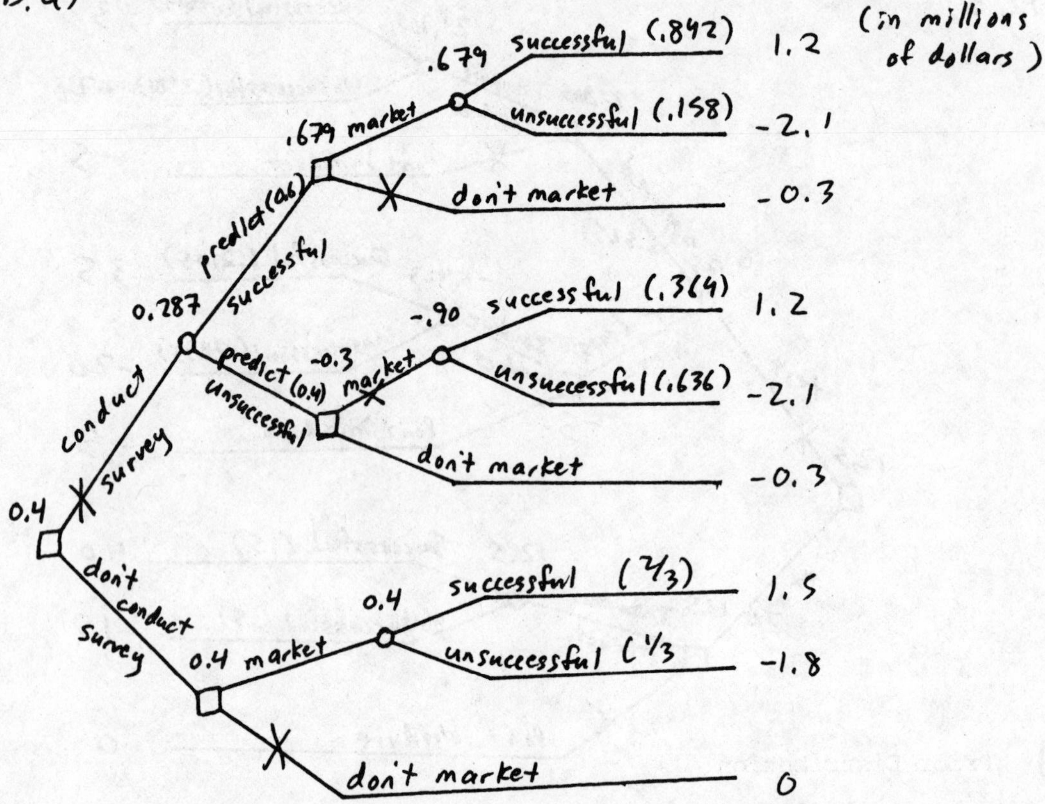

b)

Prior Distribution:

k	θ_1	θ_2
$P_\theta(k)$	0.667	0.333

$Q_{X|\theta=k}(x)$

x \ k	θ_1	θ_2
X_1	0.8	0.3
X_2	0.2	0.7

Posterior Distribution:

$h_{\theta|X=x}(k)$

x \ k	θ_1	θ_2
X_1	0.842	0.158
X_2	0.364	0.636

c) See (a). Optimal Policy is to not conduct a survey, but to market the new product.

20.4-14. a)+b)

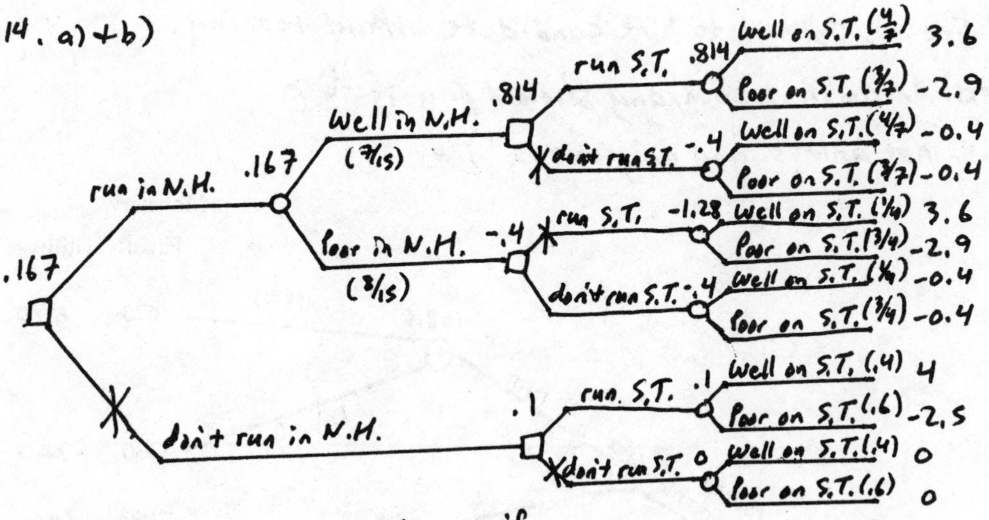

Optimal to run in N.H. and if candidate does well, then run in S.T. primaries, else don't run in S.T. primaries.

20.4-15. a)

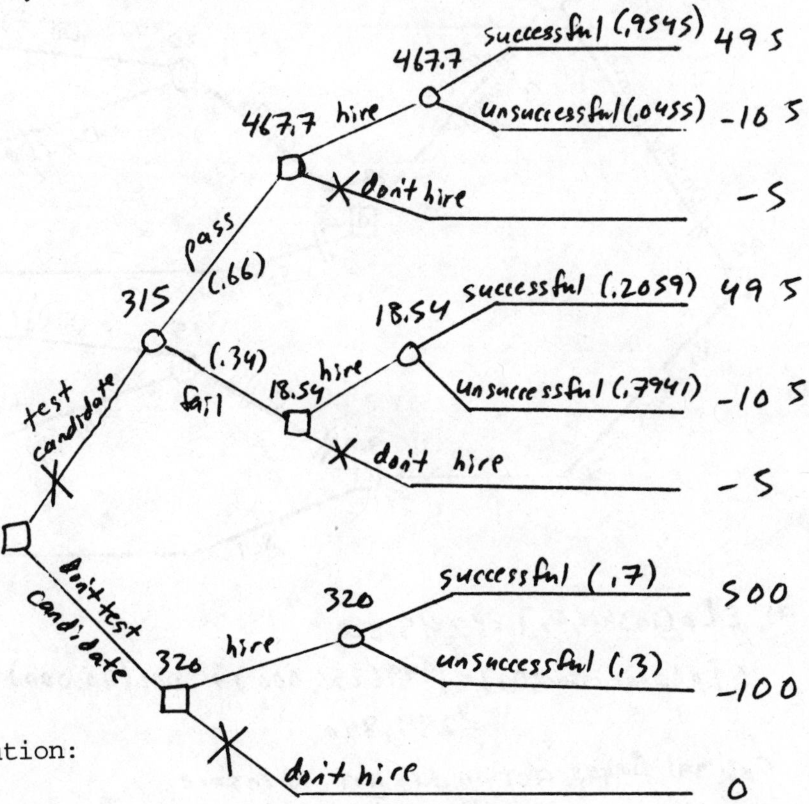

b) Prior Distribution:

k	θ_1	θ_2
$P_\Theta(k)$	0.7	0.3

$Q_{X|\Theta=k}(x)$

x \ k	θ_1	θ_2
X_1	0.9	0.1
X_2	0.1	0.9

Posterior Distribution:

$h_{\Theta|X=x}(k)$

x \ k	θ_1	θ_2
X_1	0.955	0.045
X_2	0.206	0.794

20.4-15. c) See (a). Optimal to hire candidate without testing.

d) Maximum amount company should pay is \$0.
(i.e. "not unless you pay me...")

20.5-1.

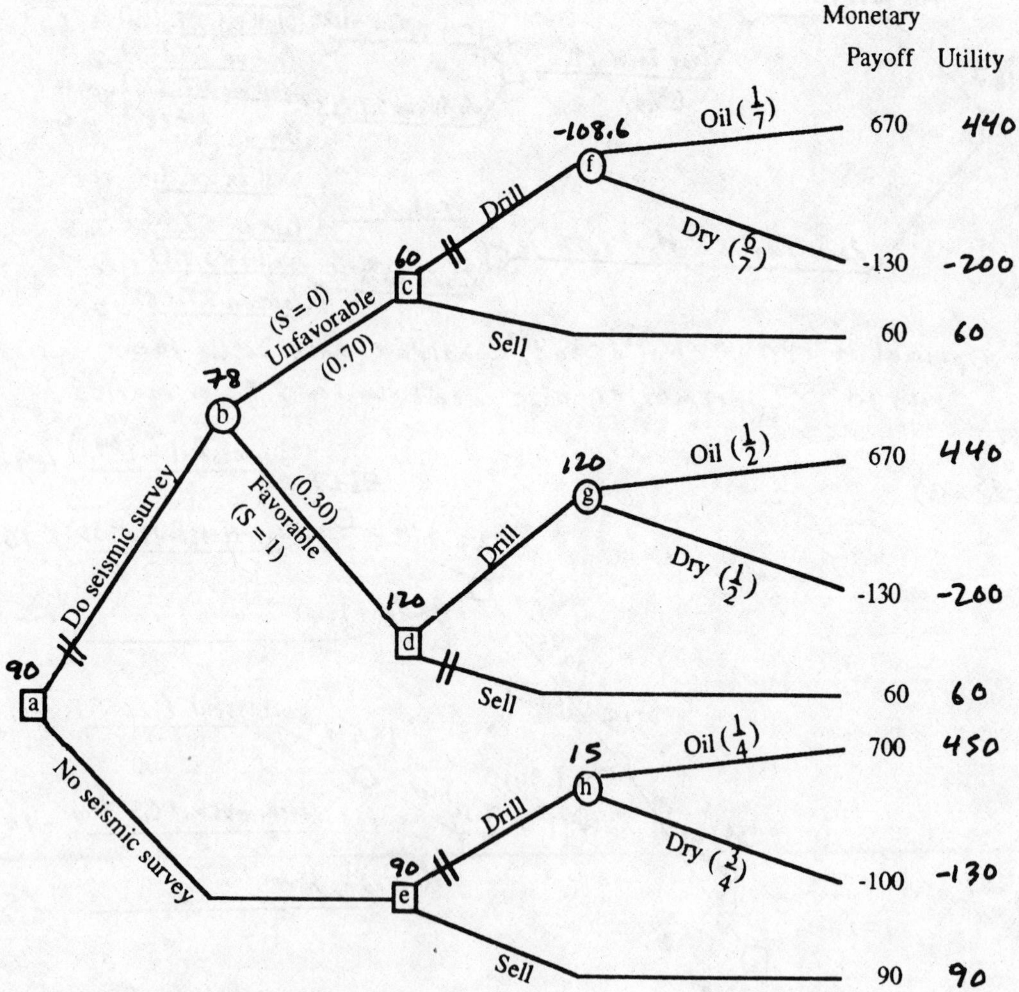

20.5-2. a) $E[p(\text{insure}, \theta)] = \$249,820$

$E[p(\text{don't insure}, \theta)] = .999(250,000) + .001(90,000)$
$= \$249,840$

Optimal Bayes action is <u>not</u> to insure.

b) $U(250,000 - 180) = \sqrt{249,820} = 499.820$

$E[\text{utility of not insuring}] = .999\,U(250,000) + .001\,U(90,000)$
$= .999(500) + .001(300)$
$= 499.800$

Optimal action is to take insurance.

20.5-3.

(Expected) utility of \$19 $= U(19) = \sqrt{25} = 5$

Expected utility of gamble $= .3\,U(10) + .7\,U(30)$

$= .3\sqrt{16} + .7\sqrt{36} = 5.4$

Optimal to take gamble.

20.5-4.

Expected utility of $a_1 = p\,U(25) + (1-p)\,U(30) = 5p + 6(1-p) = 6 - p$

Expected utility of $a_2 = p\,U(100) = 10p$

Expected utility of $a_3 = (1-p)\,U(49) = 7 - 7p$

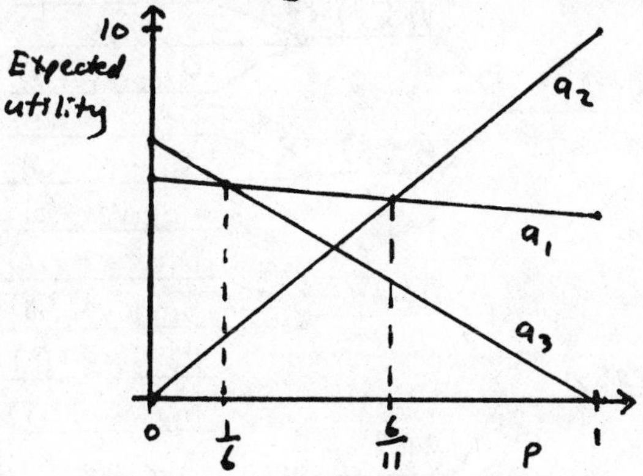

We see from the graph that a_1 maximizes expected utility when $\frac{1}{6} \le p \le \frac{6}{11}$. So the largest value of p for which choosing action a_1 maximizes expected utility is $p^* = \frac{6}{11}$.

20.5-5.

Prior Distribution:

	Theta1	Theta2
P(k)	0.5	0.5

Q(X|Theta=k)[x]

x \ k	Theta1	Theta2
1	0.8	0.2
2	0.2	0.8

Posterior Distribution:

h(Theta|X=x)[k]

x \ k	Theta1	Theta2
1	0.8	0.2
2	0.2	0.8

(Though it seems odd that the patient would have a utility of −1 or −2 since one would think dying (utility 0) is the worst possible, we will solve the problem as stated, with negative utilities)

20.5-5. (cont')

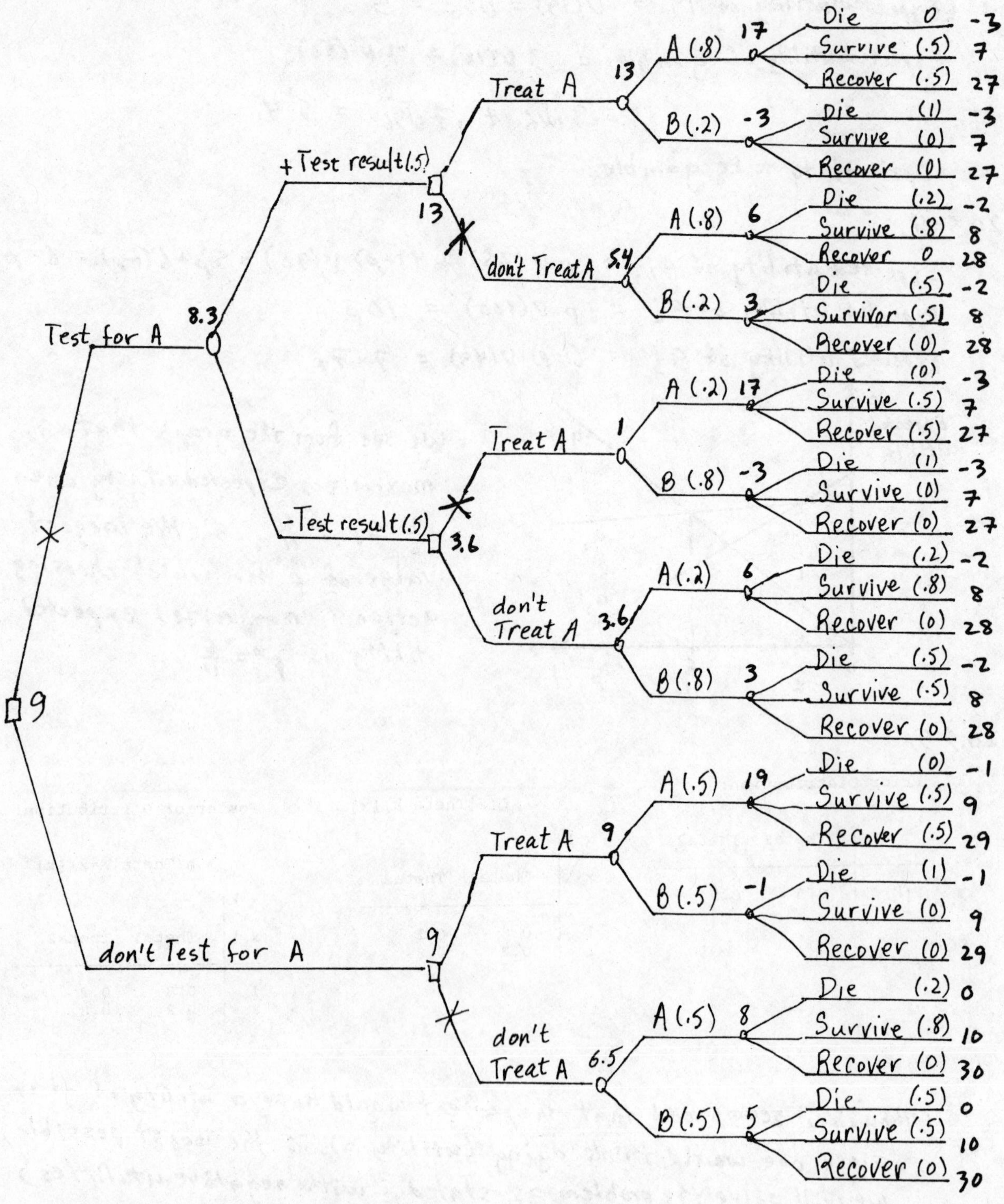

Thus, the patient's utility is maximized (at a value of 9 - slightly below that of surviving with poor health) by not testing for disease A, but immediately undergoing the treatment for disease A.

20.5-6.

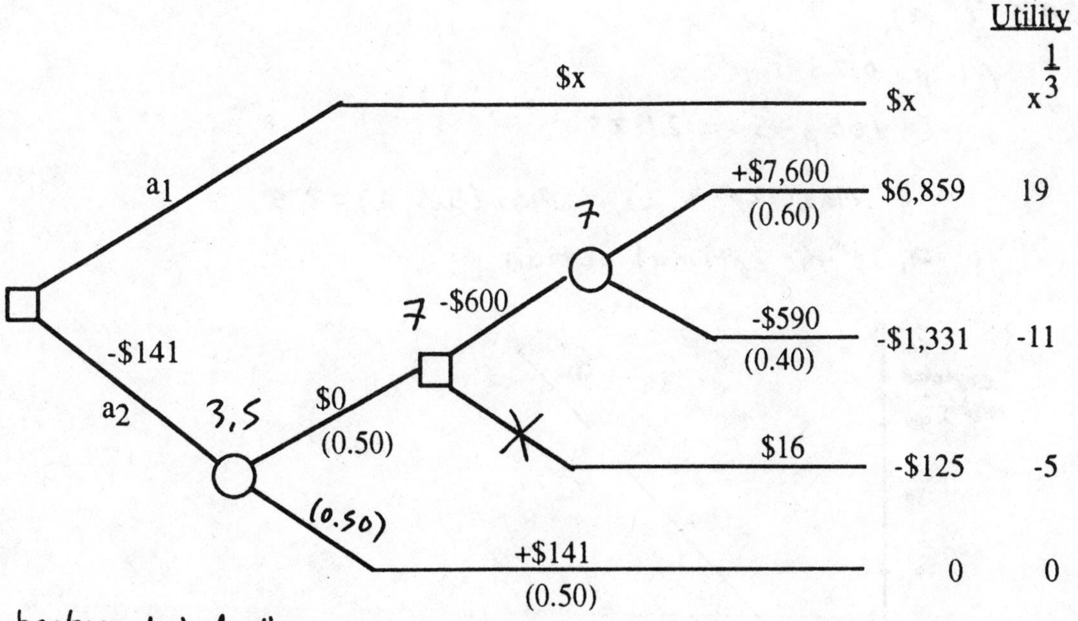

From backward induction, we see that:

$$U(x) = 3.5$$

must hold for the decision maker to be indifferent between a_1 and a_2.

So, $x^{1/3} = 3.5$ or $x = \$42.88$.

20.5-7.

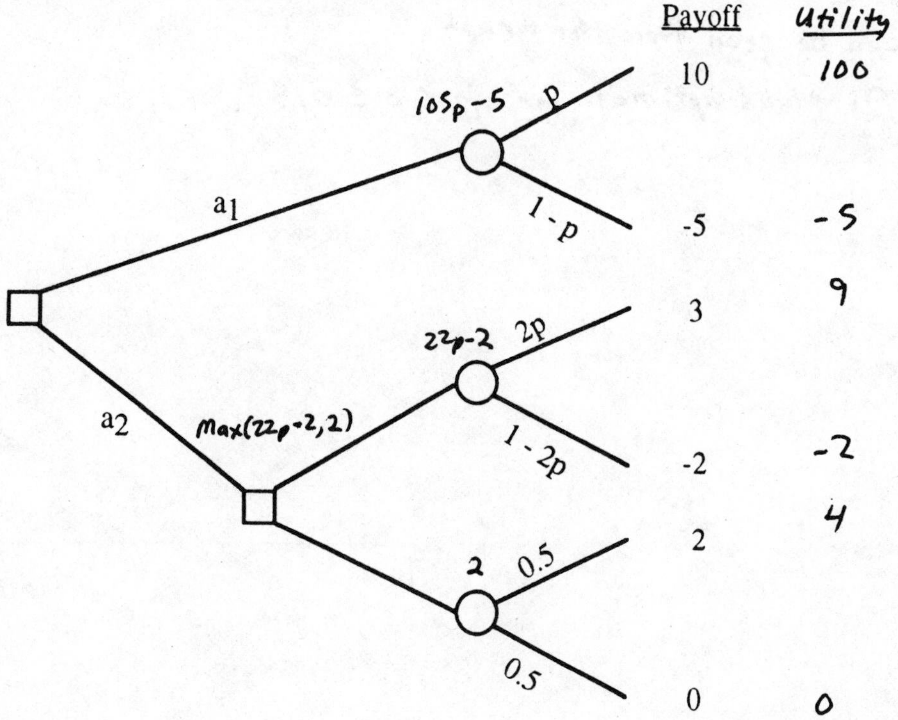

20.5-7. a)

At $p = 0.25$

$$105p - 5 = 21.25$$

and $\max(22p-2, 2) = \max(3.5, 2) = 3.5$

So a_1 is the optimal action.

b)

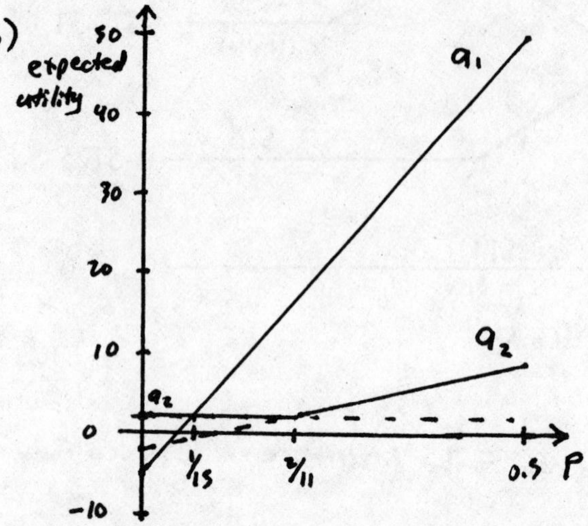

As can be seen from the graph,

a_1 stays optimal for $\frac{1}{15} \le p \le 0.5$.

Chapter 21
Simulation

21.1-1.

(a) Assigning the numbers 0,1,2,3,4 to heads and 5,6,7,8,9 to tails the sequence is: HHHTT

(b) Disregarding 0,7,8,9 and letting 1,2,3,4,5,6 correspond to the throw of a die the sequence is 5,2,4

(c) Assigning 0,1,2,3 to green, 4 to yellow and 5,6,7,8,9 to red, the sequence is Red, Green, Yellow, Red, Red

21.1-2.

To determine tomorrow's weather, look at a 3-digit random number r from Table 23.1.
If today is rainy and $000 \le r \le 599$, tomorrow will be rainy.
If today is rainy and $600 \le r \le 999$, tomorrow will be clear.
If today is clear and $000 \le r \le 799$, tomorrow will be clear.
If today is clear and $800 \le r \le 999$, tomorrow will be rainy.

n	Weather on day n	r	Weather on day n+1
0	clear	096	clear
1	clear	569	clear
2	clear	665	clear
3	clear	764	clear
4	clear	842	rainy
5	rainy	492	rainy
6	rainy	224	rainy
7	rainy	950	clear
8	clear	610	clear
9	clear	145	clear
10	clear	484	clear

21.1-3. (skipped)

21.1-4.

(a) Arrival time ~ exp(1/2 per minute)
Departure time ~ exp(1/6 per minute)
Time until next arrival is given by $x = -12 \ln(1-r)$
Time until next departure is given by $x = -6 \ln(1-r)$

Time (in minutes)	customers in system	r for arrival	r for departure	Minutes until next Arrival	Minutes until next Departure
0	0	.096	—	1.211	—
1.211	1	.596	.665	10.100	6.562
7.773	0	—	—	3.538	
11.311	1	.764	.842	17.327	11.071
22.382	0				

(b) $P\{\text{arrival in six-minute period}\} = 1 - e^{-\frac{5}{10}} = .393$
$P\{\text{departure in six-minute period}\} = 1 - e^{-1} = .632$

So, $0 \le r_a \le .392$ means there was an arrival
and $0 \le r_d \le .631$ means there was a departure

21.1-4 (continued)

(b)

Time (in minutes)	Customers in system	r_a	r_d	Arrival?	Departure?
0	0	.096	—	yes	—
6	1	.569	.665	no	no
12	1	.764	.842	no	no
18	1	.492	.224	no	yes
24	0	.950	—	no	—
30	0	.610	—	no	—
36	0	.145	—	yes	—
42	1	.484	.552	no	yes
48	0	.350	—	yes	—

c) Distr. of interarrival times: Exponential Mean = 0.2
Distr. of service times: Exponential Mean = 0.1

Current Time	Number of Customers in Queue	Customer Being Served	Next Arrival	Next Service Completion
0	0	Yes	0.4674	0.01815
0.01815	0	No	0.4674	---
0.4674	0	Yes	1.35969	0.76469
0.76469	0	No	1.35969	---
1.35969	0	Yes	1.37764	1.38405
1.37764	1	Yes	1.59748	1.38405
1.38405	0	Yes	1.59748	1.40728
1.40728	0	No	1.59748	---
1.59748	0	Yes	1.81374	1.9353
1.81374	1	Yes	2.07844	1.9353
1.9353	0	Yes	2.07844	2.09178
2.07844	1	Yes	2.09584	2.09178
2.09178	0	Yes	2.09584	2.09842
2.09584	1	Yes	2.3323	2.09842
2.09842	0	Yes	2.3323	2.26042
2.26042	0	No	2.3323	---
2.3323	0	Yes	2.33589	2.33749
2.33589	1	Yes	2.35022	2.33749
2.33749	0	Yes	2.35022	2.34943
2.34943	0	No	2.35022	---
2.35022	0	Yes	2.42298	2.40413
2.40413	0	No	2.42298	---
2.42298	0	Yes	2.42362	2.54099
2.42362	1	Yes	2.55037	2.54099
2.54099	0	Yes	2.55037	2.61055
2.55037	1	Yes	2.74492	2.61055
2.61055	0	Yes	2.74492	2.64271
2.64271	0	No	2.74492	---
2.74492	0	Yes	3.31753	2.80169
2.80169	0	No	3.31753	---
3.31753	0	Yes	3.32939	3.42686
3.32939	1	Yes	3.42362	3.42686
3.42362	2	Yes	3.89049	3.42686
3.42686	1	Yes	3.89049	3.65956
3.65956	0	Yes	3.89049	3.74341
3.74341	0	No	3.89049	---

21.1-4. c) (continued)

The results from the simulation run are as follows:

Average number waiting to begin service: 0.237795

Average number waiting or in service: 0.753969

Average: 0.04015 0.15169

d)

Results from simulation run:

Total run time simulated: 37.93445
Total number of arrivals: 177
Number of cycles completed: 100

	Point Estimate	95% Confidence Interval
L	0.702483	0.483296 to 0.92167
L_q	0.2733	0.127095 to 0.419504
W	0.151411	0.117119 to 0.185703
W_q	0.058906	0.032465 to 0.085348
P_0	0.570817	0.484536 to 0.657098
P_1	0.251102	0.208719 to 0.293486
P_2	0.112689	0.068119 to 0.157259
P_3	0.039876	0.012996 to 0.066756
P_4	0.021204	-0.00308 to 0.04549
P_5	0.004312	-0.00405 to 0.012674
P_6	0	0 to 0
P_7	0	0 to 0
P_8	0	0 to 0
P_9	0	0 to 0
P_{10}	0	0 to 0

e)

$\lambda = 5$

$\mu = 10$

$s = 1$

$L = 1$

$L_q = 0.5$

$W = 0.2$

$W_q = 0.1$

$P(\mathcal{W} > t) = 1$, where $t = 0$

$P(\mathcal{W}_q > t) = 0.5$, where $t = 0$

$P_0 = 0.5$
$P_1 = 0.25$
$P_2 = 0.125$
$P_3 = 0.0625$
$P_4 = 0.03125$
$P_5 = 0.01562$
$P_6 = 0.00781$
$P_7 = 0.00391$
$P_8 = 0.00195$
$P_9 = 0.00098$
$P_{10} = 0.00049$
$P_{11} = 0.00024$
$P_{12} = 0.00012$
$P_{13} = 0.00006$
$P_{14} = 0.00003$
$P_{15} = 0.00002$
$P_{16} = 8e-6$
$P_{17} = 4e-6$
$P_{18} = 2e-6$
$P_{19} = 1e-6$
$P_{20} = 5e-7$

21.1-4. (continued). L, L_q, W, W_q all fall out of the confidence interval.

P_0, P_1, P_2, P_3, P_4 are in the intervals. $P_i, i \geq 5$ are not.

21.1-5. Distr. of interarrival times: Translated Exp. Min = 0.5 Mean = 1
Distr. of service times: Erlang Mean = 1.5 k = 4

Current Time	Number of Customers in Queue	Customer Being Served Server 1	Customer Being Served Server 2	Next Arrival	Next Service Completion Server 1	Next Service Completion Server 2
0	0	Yes	No	1.6685	3.00911	---
1.6685	0	Yes	Yes	2.2903	3.00911	4.06113
2.2903	1	Yes	Yes	3.45204	3.00911	4.06113
3.00911	0	Yes	Yes	3.45204	4.31305	4.06113
3.45204	1	Yes	Yes	3.99204	4.31305	4.06113
3.99204	2	Yes	Yes	5.08213	4.31305	4.06113
4.06113	1	Yes	Yes	5.08213	4.31305	4.82208
4.31305	0	Yes	Yes	5.08213	7.01408	4.82208
4.82208	0	Yes	No	5.08213	7.01408	---
5.08213	0	Yes	Yes	5.80875	7.01408	6.56763
5.80875	1	Yes	Yes	6.42612	7.01408	6.56763
6.42612	2	Yes	Yes	8.45996	7.01408	6.56763
6.56763	1	Yes	Yes	8.45996	7.01408	7.793
7.01408	0	Yes	Yes	8.45996	9.25094	7.793
7.793	0	Yes	No	8.45996	9.25094	---
8.45996	0	Yes	Yes	8.45996	9.25094	8.95073
8.45996	1	Yes	Yes	9.01185	9.25094	8.95073
8.95073	0	Yes	Yes	9.01185	9.25094	10.3732
9.01185	1	Yes	Yes	10.7538	9.25094	10.3732
9.25094	0	Yes	Yes	10.7538	11.0051	10.3732
10.3732	0	Yes	No	10.7538	11.0051	---
10.7538	0	Yes	Yes	11.8319	11.0051	11.9901
11.0051	0	No	Yes	11.8319	---	11.9901
11.8319	0	Yes	Yes	12.5131	13.3238	11.9901
11.9901	0	Yes	No	12.5131	13.3238	---
12.5131	0	Yes	Yes	15.8697	13.3238	14.986
13.3238	0	No	Yes	15.8697	---	14.986
14.986	0	No	No	15.8697	---	---
15.8697	0	Yes	No	18.1124	16.8485	---
16.8485	0	No	No	18.1124	---	---
18.1124	0	Yes	No	19.0569	18.8949	---
18.1124	0	Yes	No	19.0569	18.8949	---
18.8949	0	No	No	19.0569	---	---
19.0569	0	Yes	No	19.8234	21.8863	---
19.8234	0	Yes	Yes	20.7688	21.8863	21.3164
20.7688	0	Yes	Yes	---	21.8863	21.3164

The results from the simulation run are as follows:

Average number waiting to begin service: 0.186891

Average number waiting or in service: 1.522408

Average: 0.18669 1.87597

21.1-6.

Priority Class 1 (higher priority) customers

Distr. of interarrival times:	Uniform	Min = 1	Max = 3
Distr. of service times:	Erlang	Mean = 1.5	k = 4

Priority Class 2 (lower priority) customers

Distr. of interarrival times:	Translated Exp.	Min = 0.5	Mean = 1
Distr. of service times:	Erlang	Mean = 1.5	k = 4

Current Time	# of Customers in Line Class 1	Class 2	Class of Customer Being Served Server 1	Server 2	Next Arrival Class 1	Class 2	Next Service Completion Server 1	Server 2
0	0	0	1	idle	1.19323	0.59076	4.05587	---
0.59076	0	0	1	2	1.19323	1.98438	4.05587	1.75598
1.19323	1	0	1	2	4.03947	1.98438	4.05587	1.75598
1.75598	0	0	1	1	4.03947	2.57211	4.05587	2.6547
2.57211	0	1	1	1	4.03947	4.35852	4.05587	2.6547
2.6547	0	0	1	2	4.03947	4.35852	4.05587	5.02524
4.03947	1	0	1	2	6.60605	4.35852	4.05587	5.02524
4.05587	0	0	1	2	6.60605	4.35852	6.31076	5.02524
4.35852	0	1	1	2	6.60605	5.60471	6.31076	5.02524
5.02524	0	0	1	2	6.60605	5.60471	6.31076	6.5263
5.60471	0	1	1	2	6.60605	6.32351	6.31076	6.5263
6.31076	0	0	2	2	6.60605	6.32351	7.80267	6.5263
6.32351	0	1	2	2	6.60605	7.67972	7.80267	6.5263
6.5263	0	0	2	2	6.60605	7.67972	7.80267	7.41307
6.60605	1	0	2	2	7.66733	7.67972	7.80267	7.41307
7.66733	2	0	2	2	9.48954	7.67972	7.80267	7.41307
7.41307	1	0	2	1	9.48954	7.67972	7.80267	8.0084
7.67972	1	1	2	1	9.48954	8.7606	7.80267	8.0084
7.80267	0	1	1	1	9.48954	8.7606	9.39632	8.0084
8.0084	0	0	1	2	9.48954	8.7606	9.39632	10.085
8.7606	0	1	1	2	9.48954	9.54627	9.39632	10.085
9.39632	0	0	2	2	9.48954	9.54627	11.8025	10.085
9.48954	1	0	2	2	11.0103	9.54627	11.8025	10.085
9.54627	1	1	2	2	11.0103	10.484	11.8025	10.085
10.085	0	1	2	1	11.0103	10.484	11.8025	10.6113
10.484	0	2	2	1	11.0103	11.2066	11.8025	10.6113
10.6113	0	1	2	2	11.0103	11.2066	11.8025	11.1199
11.0103	1	1	2	2	13.2226	11.2066	11.8025	11.1199
11.1199	0	1	2	1	13.2226	11.2066	11.8025	12.4916
11.2066	0	2	2	1	13.2226	11.804	11.8025	12.4916
11.804	0	3	2	1	13.2226	12.6438	11.8025	12.4916
11.8025	0	2	2	1	13.2226	12.6438	13.5255	12.4916
12.4916	0	1	2	2	13.2226	12.6438	13.5255	13.1055
12.6438	0	2	2	2	13.2226	13.1919	13.5255	13.1055
13.1055	0	1	2	2	13.2226	13.1919	13.5255	14.1874
13.1919	0	2	2	2	13.2226	14.1007	13.5255	14.1874
13.2226	1	2	2	2	15.2685	14.1007	13.5255	14.1874
13.5255	0	2	1	2	15.2685	14.1007	15.9147	14.1874

The results from the simulation run are as follows:

Class 1 customers:

Average number waiting to begin service: 0.209215

Average number waiting or in service: 1.007613

Average: 1.07381 2.59826

21.1-6. (continued)

Class 2 customers:

Average number waiting to begin service: 1.406468

Average number waiting or in service: 2.575706

Average: 0.38188 1.91684

21.1-7. Simulation Model:

Number of Servers: 2

Number of Priority Classes: 1

Distr. of interarrival times: Exponential Mean = 1
Distr. of service times: Exponential Mean = 1.5

Current Time	Number of Customers in Queue	Customer Being Served Server 1	Customer Being Served Server 2	Next Arrival	Next Service Completion Server 1	Next Service Completion Server 2
0	0	Yes	No	2.33701	0.27229	---
0.27229	0	No	No	2.33701	---	---
2.33701	0	Yes	No	2.60386	3.1414	---
2.60386	0	Yes	Yes	2.84746	3.1414	5.05512
2.84746	1	Yes	Yes	4.16722	3.1414	5.05512
3.1414	0	Yes	Yes	5.04597	4.76339	5.05512
4.76339	0	No	Yes	5.04597	---	5.05512
5.04597	0	Yes	Yes	6.61075	5.1765	5.05512
5.05512	0	Yes	No	6.61075	5.1765	---
5.1765	0	No	No	6.61075	---	---
6.61075	0	Yes	No	6.70434	8.25208	---
6.70434	0	Yes	Yes	6.75625	8.25208	11.153
6.75625	1	Yes	Yes	6.83624	8.25208	11.153
6.83624	2	Yes	Yes	9.0816	8.25208	11.153
8.25208	1	Yes	Yes	9.0816	10.8429	11.153
9.0816	2	Yes	Yes	10.2618	10.8429	11.153
10.2618	3	Yes	Yes	10.7651	10.8429	11.153
10.7651	4	Yes	Yes	11.2782	10.8429	11.153
10.8429	3	Yes	Yes	11.2782	11.7913	11.153
11.153	2	Yes	Yes	11.2782	11.7913	11.7613
11.2782	3	Yes	Yes	11.3375	11.7913	11.7613
11.3375	4	Yes	Yes	12.1104	11.7913	11.7613
11.7613	3	Yes	Yes	12.1104	11.7913	14.6103
11.7913	2	Yes	Yes	12.1104	14.0018	14.6103
12.1104	3	Yes	Yes	12.6641	14.0018	14.6103
12.6641	4	Yes	Yes	13.2024	14.0018	14.6103
13.2024	5	Yes	Yes	13.315	14.0018	14.6103
13.315	6	Yes	Yes	13.7682	14.0018	14.6103
13.7682	7	Yes	Yes	14.4399	14.0018	14.6103
14.0018	6	Yes	Yes	14.4399	15.7706	14.6103
14.4399	7	Yes	Yes	14.6746	15.7706	14.6103
14.6103	6	Yes	Yes	14.6746	15.7706	15.2742
14.6746	7	Yes	Yes	16.6616	15.7706	15.2742
15.2742	6	Yes	Yes	16.6616	15.7706	16.506
15.7706	5	Yes	Yes	16.6616	16.9501	16.506
16.506	4	Yes	Yes	16.6616	16.9501	21.0422

Current Time	Number of Customers in Queue	Customer Being Served Server 1	Server 2	Next Arrival	Next Service Completion Server 1	Server 2
16.6616	5	Yes	Yes	16.9059	16.9501	21.0422
16.9059	6	Yes	Yes	17.3022	16.9501	21.0422
16.9501	5	Yes	Yes	17.3022	16.9819	21.0422
16.9819	4	Yes	Yes	17.3022	20.5198	21.0422
17.3022	5	Yes	Yes	18.5906	20.5198	21.0422
18.5906	6	Yes	Yes	19.3884	20.5198	21.0422
19.3884	7	Yes	Yes	20.4609	20.5198	21.0422

21.1-8

Priority Class 1 (higher priority) customers
Distr. of interarrival times: Uniform Min = 20 Max = 30
Distr. of service times: Erlang Mean = 10 k = 4

Priority Class 2 (lower priority) customers
Distr. of interarrival times: Constant Value= 15
Distr. of service times: Exponential Mean = 5

Current Time	# of Customers in Line Class 1	Class 2	Class of Customer Being Served	Next Arrival Class 1	Class 2	Next Service Completion
0	0	0	1	20.9662	15	20.0607
15	0	1	1	20.9662	30	20.0607
20.0607	0	0	2	20.9662	30	36.9517
20.9662	1	0	2	43.6283	30	36.9517
30	1	1	2	43.6283	45	36.9517
36.9517	0	1	1	43.6283	45	40.041
40.041	0	0	2	43.6283	45	42.7364
42.7364	0	0	idle	43.6283	45	---
43.6283	0	0	1	69.6736	45	51.8887
45	0	1	1	69.6736	60	51.8887
51.8887	0	0	2	69.6736	60	61.6421
60	0	1	2	69.6736	75	61.6421
61.6421	0	0	2	69.6736	75	67.8873
67.8873	0	0	idle	69.6736	75	---
69.6736	0	0	1	94.7821	75	78.2757
75	0	1	1	94.7821	90	78.2757
78.2757	0	1	1	94.7821	90	98.8656
90	0	2	1	94.7821	105	98.8656
94.7821	1	2	1	122.615	105	98.8656
98.8656	0	2	1	122.615	105	109.77
105	0	3	1	122.615	120	109.77
109.77	0	2	2	122.615	120	111.814
111.814	0	1	2	122.615	120	117.919
117.919	0	1	1	122.615	120	122.161
120	0	2	1	122.615	135	122.161
122.161	0	1	2	122.615	135	127.739
122.615	1	1	2	145.231	135	127.739
127.739	0	1	1	145.231	135	146.108
135	0	2	1	145.231	150	146.108
145.231	1	2	1	168.028	150	146.108
146.108	0	2	1	168.028	150	152.401
150	0	3	1	168.028	165	152.401

21.1-8. (continued) (a)

Current Time	# of Customers in Line Class 1	Class 2	Class of Customer Being Served	Next Arrival Class 1	Class 2	Next Service Completion
152.401	0	3	1	168.028	165	156.619
156.619	0	2	2	168.028	165	163.511
163.511	0	1	2	168.028	165	172.04
165	0	2	2	168.028	180	172.04
168.028	1	2	2	196.952	180	172.04
172.04	0	2	1	196.952	180	192.609
180	0	3	1	196.952	195	192.609

(b) Results from simulation run:

Total run time simulated: 4737.519
Total number of arrivals: 505
Number of cycles completed: 100

Class 1:	Point Estimate	95% Confidence Interval
L	0.525567	0.473622 to 0.577512
L_q	0.089231	0.05789 to 0.120572
W	13.17398	11.93489 to 14.41307
W_q	2.236681	1.46041 to 3.012953
P_0	0.491242	0.448542 to 0.533942
P_1	0.49195	0.456924 to 0.526975
P_2	0.016809	0.005008 to 0.028609
P_3	0	0 to 0
P_4	0	0 to 0
P_5	0	0 to 0
P_6	0	0 to 0
P_7	0	0 to 0
P_8	0	0 to 0
P_9	0	0 to 0
P_{10}	0	0 to 0

Class 2:	Point Estimate	95% Confidence Interval
L	0.864216	0.67604 to 1.052392
L_q	0.551634	0.38184 to 0.721427
W	12.99759	10.16305 to 15.83212
W_q	8.296429	5.738414 to 10.85444
P_0	0.414273	0.351616 to 0.476929
P_1	0.388948	0.34859 to 0.429305
P_2	0.141112	0.102318 to 0.179906
P_3	0.036135	0.008536 to 0.063734
P_4	0.013023	0.000071 to 0.025975
P_5	0.006509	-0.00265 to 0.015671
P_6	0	0 to 0
P_7	0	0 to 0
P_8	0	0 to 0
P_9	0	0 to 0
P_{10}	0	0 to 0

21.2-1.

(a)

n	x_n	x_n+3	$\frac{x_n+3}{10}$	x_{n+1}
0	2	5	5/10	5
1	5	8	8/10	8
2	8	11	1 1/10	1
3	1	4	4/10	4
4	4	7	7/10	7
5	7	10	1	0
6	0	3	3/10	3
7	3	6	6/10	6
8	6	9	9/10	9
9	9	12	1 2/10	2

(b)

n	x_n	$5x_n+1$	$\frac{5x_n+1}{8}$	x_{n+1}
0	1	6	6/8	6
1	6	31	3 7/8	7
2	7	36	4 4/8	4
3	4	21	2 5/8	5
4	5	26	3 2/8	2
5	2	11	1 3/8	3
6	3	16	2	0
7	0	1	1/8	1

(c)

n	x_n	$61x_n+27$	$\frac{61x_n+27}{100}$	x_{n+1}
0	10	637	6 37/100	37
1	37	2284	22 84/100	84
2	84	5151	51 51/100	51
3	51	3138	31 38/100	38
4	38	2345	23 45/100	45

21.2-2. (a) $U_{n+1} = \dfrac{X_{n+1}+\frac{1}{2}}{10}$ $n=0,\cdots,9$

(b) $U_{n+1} = \dfrac{X_{n+1}+\frac{1}{2}}{8}$ $n=0,\cdots,7$

(c) $U_{n+1} = \dfrac{X_{n+1}+\frac{1}{2}}{100}$ $n=0,\cdots,99$

21.2-3.

n	x_n	$41x_n+33$	$\frac{41x_n+33}{100}$	x_{n+1}
0	48	2001	20 1/100	01
1	01	74	74/100	74
2	74	3067	30 67/100	67
3	67	2780	27 80/100	80
4	80	3313	33 13/100	13

21.2-4.

n	x_n	$201x_n+503$	$\frac{201x_n+503}{1000}$	x_{n+1}
0	485	97988	97 988/1000	988
1	988	199091	199 91/1000	091
2	91	18794	18 794/1000	794

21.2-5.

(a)

n	x_n	$13x_n+15$	$\frac{13x_n+15}{32}$	x_{n+1}
0	14	197	6 5/32	5
1	5	80	2 16/32	16
2	16	223	6 31/32	31
3	31	418	13 2/32	2
4	2	41	1 9/32	9

(b) Use $U_{n+1} = \dfrac{X_{n+1}+\frac{1}{2}}{32}$, we get

(0.1719, 0.5156, 0.9844, 0.0781, 0.2696)

21.2-6. (a) $X_1=7,\ X_2=10,\ X_3=5,\ X_4=9,\ X_5=11,\ X_6=12,\ X_7=6,\ X_8=3$
$X_9=8,\ X_{10}=4,\ X_{11}=2,\ X_{12}=1$

(b) Each integer appears only once in part (a)

(c) $X_{13}, X_{14}, \ldots$ will repeat X_1 to X_{12} with cycle length 12.

21.2-7.

$r = Pr\{X \le x\} = \int_{-10}^{x} \frac{dt}{50} = \frac{x+10}{50} \Rightarrow x = 50r - 10$

r	x = 50r − 10
.096	−5.20
.569	18.45
.665	23.25
.764	28.20
.842	32.10

21.2-8

(a) $r = Pr\{X \le x\} = \int_0^x 2t\,dt = x^2 \Rightarrow x = \sqrt{r}$

(b)

r	$x = \sqrt{r}$
.096	.310
.569	.754
.665	.815
.764	.874
.842	.918

21.2-9. $F(x) = x^2 \Rightarrow x = \sqrt{r} \Rightarrow r = x^2$

Then

r	x
0.0081	0.09
0.4096	0.64
0.2401	0.49

21.2-10. (a) $r = Pr\{X \le x\} = \int_{25}^{x} \frac{dt}{50} = \frac{x-25}{50} \Rightarrow x = 50r + 25$

r	x = 50r+25
.096	29.80
.569	53.45
.665	58.25

(b) $r = Pr\{X \le x\} = \int_{-1}^{x} \frac{(t+1)^3}{4}\,dt = \frac{(x+1)^4}{16} \Rightarrow x = 2r^{1/4} - 1$

r	$x = 2r^{1/4} - 1$
.096	0.113
.569	0.737
.665	0.806

(c) $r = Pr\{X \le x\} = \int_{40}^{x} \frac{(t-40)}{200}\,dt = \frac{(x-40)^2}{400} \Rightarrow x = 20(2+\sqrt{r})$

r	$x = 20(2+\sqrt{r})$
.096	46.197
.569	55.086
.665	56.310

21.2-11. (a) To determine whether $X=0$ or X is distributed uniformly between −5 and 15, look at a 3 digit random number from table 23.1.
$000 \le r \le 499 \Rightarrow X = 0$
$500 \le r \le 999 \Rightarrow X$ is uniformly distributed
If $X=0$, nothing else need be done.

21.2-11. (a) (continued)

If $X \sim U(-5,15)$, then use the next 3-digit random number as a decimal to generate X as follows:

$$r = Pr\{X \le x\} = \int_{-5}^{x} \frac{dt}{20} = \frac{x+5}{20} \Rightarrow x = 20r - 5$$

r	(from table 23.1)
096	$\Rightarrow x_1 = 0$
569	$\Rightarrow x_2 \sim U(-5,15)$
.665	$\Rightarrow x_2 = 20(.665) - 5 = 8.3$
764	$\Rightarrow x_3 \sim U(-5,15)$
.842	$\Rightarrow x_3 = 20(.842) - 5 = 11.84$

Hence, the sequence is (0, 8.3, 11.84)

(b) $Pr\{1 \le x \le 2\} = \int_1^2 (t-1)\,dt = \frac{1}{2}$

$Pr\{2 \le x \le 3\} = \int_2^3 (3-t)\,dt = \frac{1}{2}$

So for $0 \le r \le 1/2$, $r = \int_1^x (t-1)\,dt = \frac{(x-1)^2}{2} \Rightarrow x = \sqrt{2r} + 1$

and for $1/2 \le r \le 1$, $r = 1/2 + \int_2^x (3-t)\,dt = \frac{1}{2} - \frac{(3-x)^2}{2} \Rightarrow x = 3 - \sqrt{2-2r}$

r	$x = \begin{cases} \sqrt{2r}+1 & \text{when } 0 \le r^2 \le 1/2 \\ 3-\sqrt{2-2r} & \text{when } 1/2 \le r \le 1 \end{cases}$
.096	1.438
.569	2.072
.665	2.181

(c) Let Z be a Bernoulli random variable with $p = 1/3$; that is, $Pr\{Z=1\} = 1/3$ and $Pr\{Z=0\} = 2/3$. Then X is a random variable denoting the number of trials until the Bernoulli random variable takes on the value 1.

Let $000 \le r \le 332$ denote $Z = 1$
and $333 \le r \le 999$ denote $Z = 0$

r	Z	X
096	1	1
569	0	
665	0	
764	0	
842	0	
492	0	
224	1	6
950	0	
610	0	
145	1	3

Hence, the sequence is 1, 6, 3

21.2-12.

$$F(x) = \begin{cases} \frac{1}{8}x & 0 \le x < 2 \\ \frac{3}{4} & x = 2 \\ \frac{3}{4} + \frac{1}{4}(x-2) & 2 < x \le 3 \end{cases}$$

$$\Rightarrow x_i = F^{-1}(u_i) = \begin{cases} 8u_i & 0 \le u_i < \frac{1}{4} \\ 2 & \frac{1}{4} \le u_i \le \frac{3}{4} \\ 4u_i - 1 & \frac{3}{4} < u_i \le 1 \end{cases}$$

So, when $u = \{\frac{3}{4}, \frac{1}{2}, \frac{1}{4}, \frac{7}{8}\}$, $x = \{2, 2, 2, \frac{5}{4}\}$ with average $= \frac{29}{16}$

21.2-13. $r = P_r\{X \le x\} = P_r\{\frac{X-1}{2} \le \frac{x-1}{2}\} = 1 - \Phi(\frac{x-1}{2})$

$\Rightarrow x = 2\Phi^{-1}(1-r)+1$

r	$\Phi^{-1}(1-r)$	x
.096	1.308	3.616
.569	−0.175	0.650
.665	−0.425	0.150
.764	−0.719	−0.438
.842	−1.001	−1.002
.492	0.02	1.04
.224	0.762	2.524
.950	−1.645	−2.290
.610	−0.280	0.440
.145	1.059	3.118

Average = 0.7808

21.2-14.

r_i^1	r_i^2	r_i^3
.096	.764	.224
.569	.842	.950
.665	.492	.610

$\sum_{i=1}^{3} r_i^k$	$x_k = 20(\sum_{i=1}^{3} r_i^k) - 20$
1.330	6.6
2.098	22.0
1.784	15.7

(b) We pick first three uniform random numbers in 2-13.
Since $X = 5\Phi^{-1}(1-r) + 10$, we get

$X_1 = 16.54,\ X_2 = 9.125,\ X_3 = 7.875$

21.2-15 (a)

r_i^1	r_i^2	r_i^3	r_i^4
.096	.764	.224	.145
.569	.842	.950	.484
.665	.492	.610	.552

$\sum_{i=1}^{3} r_i^k$	$x_k = 2(\sum_{i=1}^{3} r_i^k) - 3$
1.330	−.340
2.098	1.196
1.784	.568
1.181	−.638

Let Z_i (for $i=1,2$) denote the chi-square observations.
Then $Z_1 = x_1^2 + x_2^2 = 1.546$
$Z_2 = x_3^2 + x_4^2 = 0.730$

(b)

r	$\Phi^{-1}(1-r) = x$
0.096	1.304
0.569	−0.175
0.665	−0.425
0.764	−0.719

21.2-15. (c) $Y = X_1^2 + X_2^2$

From (a), $Y_1 = 1.546$, $Y_2 = 0.7297$

From (b), $Y_1 = 1.731$, $Y_2 = 0.6946$

21.2-16. (a)

r	$x = -4 \ln(1-r)$
.096	.404
.569	3.367

(b)

r_1	r_2	$x = -2 \ln[(1-r_1)(1-r_2)]$
.096	.569	1.885
.665	.764	5.075

(c)

r_i^1	r_i^2	$\sum_{i=1}^{6} r_i^n$	$x_n = 4(\sum_{i=1}^{6} r_i^n) - 8$
.096	.224	3.428	5.71
.569	.950	2.965	3.860
.665	.610		
.764	.145		
.842	.484		
.492	.552		

21.2-17.

r	$x_n = -1 \ln(1-r)$
.096	.101
.569	.842
.665	1.094
.764	1.444

Hence, the Erlang observation is $\sum_{n=1}^{4} x_n = 3.481$

21.2-18 (a) $X = \{1, 8, 11, 10, 5, 12, 15, 14, 9, 0, 3, 2, 13, 4, 7, 6, 1\}$

(b) $X = \{1, 8, 5, 9, 0, 3, 2, 4, 7, 6\}$

(c) No. Since the numbers above are not independent of each other. The change we could make is to use a vastly larger modulo in (a) and get last digits of those integers.

(d) $X = \{0, 5, 7, 6, 3, 7, 9, 9, 5, 0\}$

(e) No. Some numbers (like 4) never gains a probability to appear in the sequence. We can use a vastly larger modulo and then apply (d) to alleviate the problem.

21.2-19. (a) True. Both r_i and $1-r_i$ are uniformly distributed

(b) False: Numerically, $\prod r_i \neq \prod (1-r_i) \Rightarrow \sum x_i \neq \sum y_i$

(c) True. Erlang distribution is sum of exponential distributions.

21.2-20. (a) Not valid. Since $Pr\{\frac{8}{8} \le r_i < \frac{9}{8}\} = 0$ and r_i wouldn't reach 8.

Mordify it as $\frac{n-1}{8} \le r_i < \frac{n}{8}$

(b) Valid. when $\frac{n-1}{8} \le r_i < \frac{n}{8}$, $n \le 1+8r_i < n+1$.

21.2-20 (c) Not Valid. $X = \{4, 3, 6, 5, 0, 7, 2, 1\}$ It doesn't cover 8.

Adjustment. Let $X' = X + 1$.

21.2-21

r_1	X	r_2	f(x)	Accept?
.096	.192	.569	.192	no
.665	1.330	.764	.670	no
.842	1.684	.492	.316	no
.224	.448	.950	.448	no
.610	1.220	.145	.780	yes
.484	.968	.552	.968	yes
.350	.700	.590	.700	yes

So, the three samples from the triangular distribution are 1.220, .968 and .700.

21.2-22

Let $x = 10r_1 + 10$

r_1	x	r_2	f(x)	Accept?
.096	10.96	.569	.0192	no
.665	16.65	.764	.1350	no
.842	18.42	.492	.1684	no
.224	12.24	.950	.0448	no
.610	16.10	.145	.1220	no
.484	14.84	.552	.0968	no
.350	13.50	.590	.0700	no
.430	14.30	.041	.0860	yes
.802	18.02	.471	.1604	no
.255	12.55	.799	.0510	no
.608	16.08	.577	.1216	no
.347	13.47	.933	.0694	no
.581	15.81	.173	.1162	no
.603	16.03	.040	.1206	yes
.605	16.05	.842	.1210	no
.720	17.20	.449	.1440	no
.076	10.76	.407	.0152	no
.202	12.02	.963	.0404	no
.412	14.12	.369	.0824	no
.976	19.76	.171	.1952	yes

So the three samples from the given distribution are 14.30, 16.03 and 19.76.

21.2-23. (a) Let 1,2,3,4,5,6 represent the faces of a die and ignore the digits 0,7,8,9 (See next page for the chart)

(b) $\frac{\bar{x} - .493}{\left(\frac{0.5}{\sqrt{n}}\right)} \sim N(0,1) \Rightarrow Pr\left\{\frac{\bar{x} - .493}{\left(\frac{0.5}{\sqrt{n}}\right)} \leq 1.64\right\} = .95$

So $Pr\left\{\bar{x} \leq \frac{.82}{\sqrt{n}} + .493\right\} = .95$

Let $\frac{.82}{\sqrt{n}} + .493 = .5$. Solving for n gives $\sqrt{n} = 117$ or $n = 13,689$.

21.2-23 (a) (continued)

Sequence required from Table 23.1 to get two numbers between 1 and 6	Sum of dice	Result
0, 9, ⑥, ⑤	11	Win
⑥, 9, ⑥	12	Loss
⑥, ⑤	11	Win
7, ⑥, ④	10	
8, ④, ②	6	
④, 9, ②	6	
②, ②	4	
④, 9, ⑤	9	
0, ⑥, ①	7	Loss
0, ①, ④	5	
⑤, ④	9	
8, ④, ⑤	9	
⑤, ②	7	Loss

So the sequence is Win, Loss, Win, Loss, Loss

21.2-24. We decide on size of risk by

$$\text{size} = \begin{cases} 0 & \text{if } 0 \le u < 0.7 \\ 1 & \text{if } 0.7 \le u < 0.9 \\ 2 & \text{if } 0.9 \le u < 1 \end{cases}$$

run 1

u	size
0.096	0
0.569	0
0.665	0
0.764	1

run 2

u	size
.492	0
.224	0
.950	2
.610	0

Size of loss by

$$x = \begin{cases} (20u)^2 & \text{if } 0 \le u < \frac{1}{2} \\ 200u & \text{if } u \ge \frac{1}{2} \end{cases}$$

u	x
.842	164.4

	x
.145	8.41
.484	91.09

$$\text{Total loss} = \sum_{i=1}^{4} I_{(\text{size}>0)} \sum_{j=1}^{\text{size}} x_{ij}.$$ Two simulation runs give us 164.4 and 99.5. Actually, 100 runs give us 145.

21.2-25. Since number of employees incurring medical expenses (#) has a binomial distribution, with $p = 0.9$ and $n = 3$,

$$P\{\# = 0\} = C_3^0\, 0.1^3 = 0.001,$$
$$P\{\# = 1\} = C_3^1\, 0.9 \cdot 0.1^2 = 0.027$$
$$P\{\# = 2\} = C_3^2 \cdot 0.9^2 \cdot 0.1 = 0.243$$
$$P\{\# = 3\} = C_3^3\, 0.9^3 = 0.729$$

Let $P_0 = 0$, $P_1 = 0.001$, $P_2 = 0.028$, $P_3 = 0.271$, $P_4 = 1$

In simulation, $\# = i$ if $P_i \le u < P_{i+1}$

So, $0.01 \Rightarrow \# = 1$, $0.20 \Rightarrow \# = 2$

Also, total amount $= \begin{cases} 100 & \text{if } 0 \le u < 0.9 \\ 10{,}000 & \text{if } 0.9 \le u < 1 \end{cases}$

So, only 0.95 causes actual payment from the insurance company

21.2-25 (continued)

So, the total payment is 5000$.

21.3-1. (a) $r = Pr\{X \le x\} = \int_1^x \frac{dt}{t^2} = 1 - \frac{1}{x} \Rightarrow x = \frac{1}{1-r}$

r	$x = \frac{1}{1-r}$
.096	1.106
.569	2.320
.665	2.985
.764	4.237
.842	6.329
.492	1.969
.224	1.289
.950	20.000
.610	2.564
.145	1.170

sum = 43.969 $\Rightarrow \hat{\mu} = \frac{43.969}{10} = 4.3969$

(b) For stratum 1, $r' = 0.0 + 0.6r$
stratum 2, $r' = 0.6 + 0.3r$
stratum 3, $r' = 0.9 + 0.1r$

Stratum	r	r'	$x = \frac{1}{1-r'}$	Sampling Weight	$\frac{x}{w}$
	.096	.058	1.062		2.124
	.569	.341	1.517		3.034
1	.665	.399	1.664	1/2	3.328
	.764	.829	5.848		5.848
	.842	.853	6.803		6.803
2	.492	.748	3.968	1	3.968
	.224	.922	12.821		3.205
	.950	.995	200.000		50.000
	.610	.961	25.641		6.410
3	.145	.915	11.765	4	2.941
					sum: 87.661

$\hat{\mu} = 87.661/10 = 8.7661$

(c) $r' = 1 - r \Rightarrow x' = \frac{1}{1-r'} = \frac{1}{r}$

r	$x = \frac{1}{1-r}$	$x' = \frac{1}{r}$
.096	1.106	10.417
.569	2.320	1.757
.665	2.985	1.504
.764	4.237	1.309
.842	6.329	1.188
.492	1.969	2.033
.224	1.289	4.464
.950	20.000	1.053
.610	2.564	1.639
.145	1.170	6.897
Sum	43.969	32.261
$\hat{\mu}$	4.3969	3.2261

$\hat{\mu} = \frac{4.3969 + 3.2261}{2} = 3.8115$

21.3-2.

Stratum	x	x^2	w	$\frac{x}{w}$	$\frac{x^2}{w}$
	8	64		80/18	640/18
	5	25		50/18	250/18
	1	1		10/18	10/18
	6	36		60/18	360/18
	3	9		30/18	90/18
1	7	49	18/10	70/18	490/18
	3	9		60/18	180/18
	5	25		100/18	500/18
2	2	4	9/10	40/18	80/18
3	2	4	3/10	120/18	240/18
			Sum:	620/18	2840/18

21.3-2 (continued)

Hence, $\hat{\mu} = \frac{620/18}{10} = 3^2/9$ and $E[\hat{x^2}] = \frac{2840/18}{10} = 17\,3/9$

21-3-3 (a) Let $X = \begin{cases} 0 & \text{if } 0.1 \le r_i < 1 \\ 100r_i + 5 & \text{if } 0 \le r_i < 0.1 \end{cases}$

r_i	0.096	0.665	0.842	0.224	0.610
x	14.5	0	0	0	0

Then, Average = EX = 2.9

(b)

stratum	r	r^*	X	W	$\frac{X}{W}$	
1	0.096	0.0864	0	$\frac{2}{9}$	0	← $r^* = 0.9r$
	0.665	0.9665	11.65		1.46	
	0.842	0.9842	13.42		1.68	
	0.224	0.9224	7.24		0.905	← $r^* = 0.9 + 0.1r$, $X = (r^* - 0.9) \times 100 + 0.5$
2	0.610	0.9610	11.10	8	1.39	
				sum	5.435	

Thus, $\hat{EX} = \frac{5.435}{5} = 1.08$

21-3.4. (a) $EX_{large} = \int_{2000}^{20,000} \frac{1}{18,000} x\,dx = 11,000$, $EX_{small} = \int_0^{2000} \frac{1}{2000} x\,dx = 1,000$

So, mean = 0.4 × 1000 + 0.2 × 11,000 = 2,600 \$

(b) Let $X = \begin{cases} 0 & \text{if } 0 \le r_i < 0.4 \\ \frac{r_i - 0.4}{4} \times 20,000 & \text{if } 0.4 \le r_i < 0.8 \\ 2000 + \frac{r_i - 0.8}{2} \times 180,000 & \text{if } 0.8 \le r_i < 1 \end{cases}$

r_i	0.096	0.665	0.842	0.224	0.610	0.569	0.764	0.492	0.950	0.145
x	0	1325	14780	0	1050	845	1820	460	15,500	0

So, mean = (1325 + 14780 + 1050 + 845 + 1820 + 460 + 15500) / 10 = 3678 \$.

(c)

stratum	r	r^*	X	W	$\frac{X}{W}$	
1	0.096	0.0384	0	0.25	0	← $r^* = r \cdot 0.4$
	0.569	0.6276	1138	0.75	1446	
	0.665	0.666	1330	0.75	1772	← $r^* = 0.4 + 0.4r$, $X = (r^* - 0.4) \times 5000$
2	0.764	0.7056	1528	0.75	2036	
3						

21.3.4. (continued)

	r	r*	x	w	$\frac{x}{w}$
stratum 3	.842	0.9684	17156	3	5718
	.492	0.8984	10656	3	3552
	.224	0.8446	6014	3	2005
	.950	0.9900	19100	3	6366
	.610	0.9220	12980	3	4327
	.145	0.8290	4610	3	1537
				sum	28629

So, sample mean = 28629/10 = 2862.9

21.3-5.

$$F(x) = \int_{-\infty}^{x} f(y)\,dy = \begin{cases} 0 & x < -1 \\ \frac{1}{2}(x+1)^2 & -1 \le x < 0 \\ 1-\frac{1}{2}(1-x)^2 & 0 \le x < 1 \\ 1 & x \ge 1 \end{cases}$$

$$\Rightarrow x = \begin{cases} \sqrt{2r} - 1 & \text{if } 0 \le r < \frac{1}{2} \\ 1-\sqrt{2(1-r)} & \text{if } \frac{1}{2} \le r < 1 \end{cases}$$

r	x	1-r	x
0.096	-0.5618	0.904	0.5618
0.569	0.0716	0.431	-0.0716

So, sample mean = 0

21.3-6.

$$F(x) = \int_{-\infty}^{x} f(y)\,dy = \begin{cases} 0 & x < -1 \\ \frac{x^3+1}{2} & -1 \le x < 1 \\ 1 & x \ge 1 \end{cases}$$

$$\Rightarrow x = \sqrt[3]{2u-1}$$

r	x	1-r	x
0.096	-0.9314	0.904	0.9314
0.569	0.5168	0.431	-0.5168

Then, sample mean = 0

21.3-7. (a) $F(x) = \int_{-\infty}^{x} f(y)\,dy = \begin{cases} 0 & x<0 \\ 0.4x & 0 \le x < 1 \\ 0.6x - 0.2 & 1 \le x \le 2 \\ 1 & x > 2 \end{cases}$

$\Rightarrow \quad x = F^{-1}(r) = \begin{cases} \dfrac{r}{0.4} & 0 \le r < 0.4 \\ \dfrac{r+0.2}{0.6} & 0.4 \le r < 1 \end{cases}$

r_1	x	r_2	x	r_3	x
.096	.24	.764	1.61	.224	.56
.569	1.28	.842	1.74	.950	1.91
.665	1.44	.492	1.15	.610	1.35
sum	2.96	sum	4.50	sum	3.82
$\hat{EX}$	0.99		1.5		1.27

(b) We just need add colums with $1-r_i$

$1-r_1$	x	$1-r_2$	x	$1-r_3$	x
.904	1.84	.236	.59	.776	1.63
.431	1.05	.158	.395	.050	0.125
.335	0.84	.508	1.18	.390	0.95
sum	3.73	sum	2.003	sum	2.705

So, $\hat{EX_1} = \dfrac{2.96+3.73}{6} = 1.115$

$\hat{EX_2} = \dfrac{4.50+2.003}{6} = 1.084$

$\hat{EX_3} = \dfrac{3.82+2.705}{6} = 1.0875$

21.3-8 (a) $P\{X=k\} = \begin{cases} .125 & k=0 \\ .375 & k=1 \\ .375 & k=2 \\ .125 & k=3 \end{cases}$

$\Rightarrow \quad X = \begin{cases} 0 & 0 \le r < .125 \\ 1 & .125 \le r < .5 \\ 2 & .5 \le r < .875 \\ 3 & .875 \le r < 1 \end{cases}$

r	X	1-r	X
.096	0	.904	3
.569	2	.431	1
.665	2	.335	1

$\dfrac{0+2+2}{3} = 1.33 =$ sample mean

(b) Sample mean $= \dfrac{4+5}{6} = 1.5$

21.3-8. (c) Let $X = \begin{cases} \text{head} & 0 \le r < \frac{1}{2} \\ \text{tail} & \frac{1}{2} \le r < 1 \end{cases}$

$r_1 = \{.096\ .569\ .665\} \Rightarrow X_1 = 1$, $r_2 = \{.764\ .842\ .492\} \Rightarrow X_2 = 1$

$r_3 = \{.224\ .950\ .610\} \Rightarrow X_3 = 1$ So, sample mean $= \frac{3}{3} = 1$

(d) We also have $r_1^* = \{.904\ .431\ .335\} \Rightarrow X_1^* = 2$,

$r_2^* = \{.236\ .158\ .508\} \Rightarrow X_2^* = 2$,

$r_3^* = \{.776\ .050\ .390\} \Rightarrow X_3^* = 2$,

Sample mean $= \frac{3+6}{3} = 3$

21.3-9. (a) For the shaft radius, $r_s = \int_1^s 400e^{-400(t-1)}\,dt = 1 - e^{-400(s-1)}$

so the shaft radius is given by $s = 1 + \frac{\ln(1-r_s)}{-400}$

For the bushing radius, $r_b = \int_1^b 100\,dt = 100(b-1)$

so the bushing radius is given by $b = 1 + \frac{r_b}{100}$

r_s	$s = 1 + \frac{\ln(1-r_s)}{-400}$	r_b	$b = 1 + \frac{r_b}{100}$	Interference? ($s > b$?)
.096	1.000252	.569	1.00569	no
.665	1.002734	.764	1.00764	no
.842	1.004613	.492	1.00492	no
.224	1.000634	.950	1.00950	no
.610	1.002354	.145	1.00145	yes
.484	1.001654	.552	1.00552	no
.350	1.001077	.590	1.00590	no
.430	1.001405	.041	1.00041	yes
.802	1.004048	.471	1.00471	no
.255	1.000736	.799	1.00799	no

Estimated probability of interference = 1/5

(b)

Stratum	Portion of Distribution	Stratum Random Number	Sample Size	Sample Weight
1	$0 \le F(b) \le 0.2$	$r_b' = .2r_b$	6	1/3
2	$0.2 \le F(b) \le 0.6$	$r_b' = .2 + .4r_b$	2	1/2
3	$0.6 \le F(b) \le 1.0$	$r_b' = .6 + .4r_b$	2	1/2

Stratum	r_s	$s = 1 + \frac{\ln(1-r_s)}{-400}$	r_b	r_b'	$b = 1 + \frac{r_b'}{100}$	Interference Weight
	.096	1.000252	.569	.114	1.00114	0
	.665	1.002734	.764	.153	1.00153	1/3
	.842	1.004613	.492	.098	1.00098	1/3
	.224	1.000634	.950	.190	1.00190	0
	.610	1.002354	.145	.029	1.00029	1/3
1	.484	1.001654	.552	.110	1.00110	1/3
	.350	1.001077	.590	.436	1.00436	0
2	.430	1.001405	.041	.216	1.00216	0
	.802	1.004048	.471	.788	1.00788	0
3	.255	1.000736	.799	.920	1.00920	0

Estimated probability of interference = 4/30 = 2/15

21.3-4 (c) (continued)

r_s	$s = 1 + \frac{\ln(1-r_s)}{-400}$	r_b	$b = 1 + \frac{r_b}{100}$	Interference? $s > b$?	$s' = 1 + \frac{\ln r_s}{-400}$	$b' = 1 + \frac{1-r_b}{100}$	Interference? $s' > b'$?
.096	1.000252	.569	1.00569	no	1.005859	1.00431	yes
.665	1.002734	.764	1.00764	no	1.001020	1.00236	no
.842	1.004613	.492	1.00492	no	1.000430	1.00508	no
.224	1.000634	.950	1.00950	no	1.003740	1.00050	yes
.610	1.002354	.145	1.00145	yes	1.001236	1.00855	no
.484	1.001654	.552	1.00552	no	1.001814	1.00448	no
.350	1.001077	.590	1.00590	no	1.002625	1.00410	no
.430	1.001405	.041	1.00041	yes	1.002110	1.00959	no
.802	1.004048	.471	1.00471	no	1.000552	1.00529	yes
.255	1.000736	.799	1.00799	no	1.003416	1.00201	yes

Estimated Probability of interference $= \frac{1}{2}\left(\frac{1}{5} + \frac{2}{5}\right) = 3/10$

Summarizing,

Method:	Monte Carlo	Stratified Sampling	Complementary
Pr{interference}:	1/5	2/15	3/10

21.4-1. (a)

$y_1 = 0+5+4 = 9$; $z_1 = 3$
$y_2 = 0+2 = 2$; $z_2 = 2$
$y_3 = 0+3+1+6 = 10$; $z_3 = 4$
$\bar{y} = 21/3 = 7$; $\bar{z} = 9/3 = 3$
So $Est[W_q] = 7/3 = 2\ 1/3$
$s_{11}^2 = (81+4+100)/2 - (9+2+10)^2/6 = 19$
$s_{22}^2 = (9+4+16)/2 - (3+2+4)^2/6 = 1$
$s_{12}^2 = (27+4+40)/2 - (21)(9)/6 = 4$
$s^2 = 19 - 2(7/3)4 + (7/3)^2 = 5.778 \Rightarrow s = 2.404$
$1 - 2\alpha = .90 \Rightarrow \alpha = .05 \Rightarrow K_\alpha = 1.645$
So $Pr\{1.572 \le W_q \le 3.094\} = .90$

(b)

$y_1 = 0+3+2 = 5$; $z_1 = 3$
$y_2 = 0+3+1+5 = 9$; $z_2 = 4$
$y_3 = 0$; $z_3 = 1$
$y_4 = 0+2+4 = 6$; $z_4 = 3$
$y_5 = 0+3+5+2 = 10$; $z_5 = 4$
$\bar{y} = 30/5 = 6$; $\bar{z} = 15/5 = 3$
So $Est[W_q] = 6/3 = 2$

$s_{11}^2 = (25+81+36+100)/4 - (10+6+0+9+5)^2/20 = 15\frac{1}{2}$
$s_{22}^2 = (9+16+1+9+16)/4 - (3+4+1+3+4)^2/20 = 1\frac{1}{2}$
$s_{12}^2 = (15+36+0+18+40)/4 - (30)(15)/20 = 4\frac{3}{4}$
$s^2 = 15\frac{1}{2} - (2)(2)(4\ 3/4) + (2)^2(1\frac{1}{2}) = 2\frac{1}{2} \Rightarrow s = 1.581$
$1 - 2\alpha = .90 \Rightarrow \alpha = .05 \Rightarrow K_\alpha = 1.645$
So $Pr\{1.612 \le W_q \le 2.388\} = .90$

21.4-2. When a service completion occurs, t minutes have passed since the last arrival, where $0 \le t \le 25$. The time until the next arrival is uniformly distributed from $\bar{t}$ to $25 - t$ where $\bar{t} = \max\{0, 5-t\}$. Thus, the probabilistic structure of when future arrivals will occur is <u>dependent</u> on the previous history, so this cannot be a regeneration point.

21.4-3. For any new tube, the time of the next failure is given by (current time + 1000 + 1000r) where r is a random number from Table 16.1.
At each shutdown, 1 hour is added to the time of the next failure for all tubes when simulating the status quo and 2 hours are added when simulating the proposal.

21.4-3. (Continued)

(a)

Time	r_1	r_2	r_3	r_4	Time of failure of tube 1	tube 2	tube 3	tube 4
0	.096	.569	.665	.764	1096	1569	1665	1764
1096	.842	—	—	—	2939	1570	1666	1765
1570	—	.492	—	—	2940	3063	1667	1766
1667	—	—	.224	—	2941	3064	2892	1767
1767	—	—	—	.950	2942	3065	2893	3718
2893	—	—	.610	—	2943	3066	4504	3719
2943	.145	—	—	—	4089	3067	4505	3720
3067	—	.484	—	—	4090	4552	4506	3721
3721	—	—	—	.552	4091	4553	4507	5274
4091	.350	—	—	—	5442	4554	4508	5275
4508	—	—	.590	—	5443	4555	6099	5276
4555	—	.430	—	—	5444	5986	6100	5277
5000	—	—	—	—	5444	5986	6100	5277

Estimated cost of status quo = 11 × \$120 = \$1320

Simulation of proposal:

Time	r_1	r_2	r_3	r_4	First tube to fail	time of failure
0	.096	.569	.665	.764	Tube 1	1096
1096	.842	.492	.224	.950	Tube 3	2322
2322	.610	.145	.484	.552	Tube 2	3469
3469	.350	.590	.430	.041	Tube 4	4512
4512	.802	.471	.255	.799	Tube 3	5769

Estimated cost of proposal = 4 × \$280 = \$1120

(b) Based on the simulations in part (a), the proposal should be accepted.

(c) For the proposed policy, each shutdown is a regeneration point because all tubes are replaced, and the process begins anew. For the status quo, the process never repeats itself because tubes are replaced one at a time.

(d)

cycle	Cycle Cost	Cycle length
1	\$280	1096
2	\$280	1226
3	\$280	1147
4	\$280	1043

$\bar{Y} = \$280 \qquad \bar{Z} = 1128$

$\text{Est}\{\text{cost/hour}\} = \$280/1128 = \$.2482$

$s_{11}^2 = (4 \times 280^2)/3 - (4 \times 280)^2/12 = 0$

$s_{22}^2 = (1096^2 + 1226^2 + 1147^2 + 1043^2)/3 - (1096+1226+1147+1043)^2/12$
$= 6071\,1/3$

$s_{12}^2 = 280 \times (1096+1226+1147+1043)/3 - 4 \times 280 \times (1096+1226+1147+1043)/12 = 0$

$s^2 = 0 - 2(.2482)(0) + (.2482)^2\, 6071\,1/3 = 374.10 \Rightarrow s = 19.34$

$1 - 2\alpha = .95 \Rightarrow \alpha = .025 \Rightarrow K_\alpha = 1.96$

$\Pr\{.2314 \le \text{cost/hour} \le .2650\} = .95$

21.4-4. (a) Run ORcourseware, we find

Distr. of interarrival times: Exponential Mean = 1.25
Distr. of service times: Exponential Mean = 1

	Point Estimate	95% Confidence Interval
L	4.109331	2.994014 to 5.224649
L_q	3.257527	2.203887 to 4.311167
W	5.11555	3.966628 to 6.264472
W_q	4.055171	2.933367 to 5.176976

(ii)

Distr. of interarrival times: Exponential Mean = 1.25
Distr. of service times: Erlang Mean = 1

21.4-4. (a) (continued)

	Point Estimate	95% Confidence Interval
L	2.465036	1.809107 to 3.120965
L_q	1.689561	1.093446 to 2.285676
W	3.242192	2.514277 to 3.970107
W_q	2.222231	1.527775 to 2.916688

(iii)

Distr. of interarrival times: Exponential Mean = 1.25
Distr. of service times: Constant Value= 1

	Point Estimate	95% Confidence Interval
L	2.066726	1.577832 to 2.555621
L_q	1.283938	0.839383 to 1.728492
W	2.64021	2.15363 to 3.126789
W_q	1.64021	1.15363 to 2.126789

So, $L_{q_2}/L_{q_1} = 1.6895/3.2575 = 0.52$

$L_{q_3}/L_{q_1} = 1.2839/3.2575 = 0.39$

(b) $L_q = \frac{\lambda^2\sigma^2+\rho^2}{2(1-\rho)}$, $L=\rho+L_q$, $W_q = \frac{L_q}{\lambda}$, $W = W_q + \frac{1}{\mu}$

(i) $L_{q_1} = \frac{0.64+0.64}{2\times 0.2} = 3.2$. $L_1 = 4$, $W_{q_1} = 4$, $W_1 = 5$

$L_{q_2} = \frac{0.64\times 0.25+0.64}{2\times 0.2} = 2$, $L_2 = 2.8$, $W_{q_2} = 2.5$, $W_2 = 3.5$

$L_{q_3} = \frac{0.64}{2\times 0.2} = 1.6$, $L_3 = 2.4$, $W_{q_3} = 2$, $W_3 = 3$

$L_{q_2}/L_{q_1} = 0.675$, $L_{q_3}/L_{q_1} = \frac{1.6}{3.2} = 0.5$

They all fall into 95% confidence intervals in (a).

21.4-5. Simulation Model:

Number of Servers: 2

Number of Priority Classes: 1

(i) Distr. of interarrival times: Exponential Mean = 0.625
Distr. of service times: Exponential Mean = 1

	Point Estimate	95% Confidence Interval
L	3.75003	2.843399 to 4.65666
L_q	2.198599	1.43651 to 2.960687
W	2.44113	1.92064 to 2.96162
W_q	1.431206	0.974273 to 1.888139

Distr. of interarrival times: Exponential Mean = 0.625
Distr. of service times: Erlang Mean = 1 k = 4

21.4-5. (continued)

	Point Estimate	95% Confidence Interval
L	3.085615	2.17746 to 3.99377
L_q	1.566264	0.762409 to 2.370119
W	2.046083	1.533526 to 2.558641
W_q	1.038595	0.550251 to 1.52694

(iii) Distr. of interarrival times: Exponential Mean = 0.625
Distr. of service times: Constant Value= 1

	Point Estimate	95% Confidence Interval
L	3.079994	2.3983 to 3.761687
L_q	1.519155	0.912034 to 2.126275
W	1.973294	1.626453 to 2.320134
W_q	0.973294	0.626453 to 1.320134

$L_{q_2}/L_{q_1} = 1.5662/2.1986 = 0.71$

$L_{q_3}/L_{q_1} = 1.5192/2.1986 = 0.69$

21.4-6. (i)

Distr. of interarrival times: Exponential Mean = 1
Distr. of service times: Exponential Mean = 0.8

	Point Estimate	95% Confidence Interval
L	4.109331	2.994014 to 5.224649
L_q	3.257527	2.203887 to 4.311167
W	4.09244	3.173303 to 5.011578
W_q	3.244137	2.346694 to 4.141581

(ii)

Distr. of interarrival times: Erlang Mean = 1
Distr. of service times: Exponential Mean = 0.8

	Point Estimate	95% Confidence Interval
L	2.427619	1.524316 to 3.330922
L_q	1.622541	0.807787 to 2.437295
W	2.500685	1.603934 to 3.397436
W_q	1.671377	0.854627 to 2.488126

(iii)

Distr. of interarrival times: Constant Value= 1
Distr. of service times: Exponential Mean = 0.8

	Point Estimate	95% Confidence Interval
L	2.547256	0.844499 to 4.250014
L_q	1.775653	0.170737 to 3.380569
W	2.547256	0.844499 to 4.250014
W_q	1.775653	0.170737 to 3.380569

$L_{q_2}/L_{q_1} = 1.6225/3.2575 = 0.50$

$L_{q_3}/L_{q_1} = 1.7756/3.2575 = 0.55$

21.4-7. (a)

Simulation Model:

Number of Servers: 2

Number of Priority Classes: 1

Distr. of interarrival times:	Exponential	Mean = 0.1111	
Distr. of service times:	Erlang	Mean = 0.2	k = 8

Results from simulation run:

Total run time simulated: 114.1685
Total number of arrivals: 1000
Number of cycles completed: 54

	Point Estimate	95% Confidence Interval
L	4.490582	3.574486 to 5.406679
L_q	2.724198	1.886388 to 3.562008
W	0.514125	0.427138 to 0.601111
W_q	0.311892	0.226637 to 0.397147

Exact Value $W = 0.683$, $W_q = 0.483$.
So, W falls outside the 95% confidence Interval generated above.

(b) Number of Servers: 2

Number of Priority Classes: 3

Priority Class 1 (highest priority) customers

Distr. of interarrival times:	Exponential	Mean = 1	
Distr. of service times:	Erlang	Mean = 0.2	k = 8

Priority Class 2 customers

Distr. of interarrival times:	Exponential	Mean = 0.3333	
Distr. of service times:	Erlang	Mean = 0.2	k = 8

Priority Class 3 (lowest priority) customers

Distr. of interarrival times:	Exponential	Mean = 0.2	
Distr. of service times:	Erlang	Mean = 0.2	k = 8

Results from simulation run:

Total run time simulated: 110.1993
Total number of arrivals: 1000
Number of cycles completed: 2

Class 1:	Point Estimate	95% Confidence Interval
L	0.211238	0.194652 to 0.227824
L_q	0.035491	0.034597 to 0.036385
W	0.266104	0.26302 to 0.269187
W_q	0.044709	0.039554 to 0.049864

21-4.7. (continued) (b)

Class 2:		Point Estimate	95% Confidence Interval
	L	0.88549	0.863184 to 0.907795
	L_q	0.279815	0.272767 to 0.286864
	W	0.287321	0.287321 to 0.287321
	W_q	0.090794	NAN(001) to NAN(001)

Class 3:		Point Estimate	95% Confidence Interval
	L	2.490976	2.428227 to 2.553724
	L_q	1.556251	1.517049 to 1.595454
	W	0.544341	0.544341 to 0.544341
	W_q	0.34008	0.34008 to 0.34008

Obviously, $W_{q_1} = 0.045 < 0.2$, $W_{q_2} = 0.09 < 0.4$, $W_{q_3} = 0.34 < 1$

The proposal meets management's goal.

Case Problem

Simulation of proposal 1:

Number of Servers: 3

Number of Priority Classes: 2

Priority Class 1 (higher priority) customers
Distr. of interarrival times: Exponential Mean = 0.5
Distr. of service times: Erlang Mean = 0.4167 k = 8

Priority Class 2 (lower priority) customers
Distr. of interarrival times: Uniform Min = 0.3333 Max = 0.6667
Distr. of service times: Translated Exp. Min = 0.1667 Mean = 0.3333

Results from simulation run:

Total run time simulated: 253.6297
Total number of arrivals: 1000
Number of cycles completed: 85

Class 1:		Point Estimate	95% Confidence Interval
	L	0.862937	0.782734 to 0.94314
	L_q	0.04306	0.025391 to 0.060729
	W	0.444128	0.428785 to 0.459472
	W_q	0.022162	0.01373 to 0.030593

Class 2:		Point Estimate	95% Confidence Interval
	L	0.676477	0.647687 to 0.705267
	L_q	0.021484	0.012534 to 0.030434
	W	0.339164	0.324319 to 0.35401
	W_q	0.010771	0.006264 to 0.015279

Case Problem (continued)

Total cost $= 30 + 200 \times 0.86 + 100 \times 0.67 = 269$ \$/per hour ①

Simulation of proposal 2:

Number of Servers: 2

Number of Priority Classes: 2

Priority Class 1 (higher priority) customers

Distr. of interarrival times:	Constant	Value= 0.5
Distr. of service times:	Erlang	Mean = 0.4167 k = 8

Priority Class 2 (lower priority) customers

Distr. of interarrival times:	Uniform	Min = 0.3333 Max = 0.6667
Distr. of service times:	Translated Exp.	Min = 0.1667 Mean = 0.3333

Results from simulation run:

Total run time simulated: 222
Total number of arrivals: 886
Number of cycles completed: 100

Class 1:		Point Estimate	95% Confidence Interval
	L	0.904803	0.861793 to 0.947814
	L_q	0.056091	0.039472 to 0.072709
	W	0.452402	0.430897 to 0.473907
	W_q	0.028045	0.019736 to 0.036354

Class 2:		Point Estimate	95% Confidence Interval
	L	0.693584	0.65009 to 0.737079
	L_q	0.052679	0.034883 to 0.070475
	W	0.349151	0.327875 to 0.370428
	W_q	0.026519	0.01758 to 0.035458

Total cost $= 40 + 200 \times 0.9048 + 100 \times 0.6935 = 299$ \$/per hour ②

Simulation of proposal 2:

Number of Servers: 2

Number of Priority Classes: 2

Priority Class 1 (higher priority) customers

Distr. of interarrival times:	Exponential	Mean = 0.5
Distr. of service times:	Erlang	Mean = 0.4167 k = 8

Priority Class 2 (lower priority) customers

Distr. of interarrival times:	Constant	Value= 0.5
Distr. of service times:	Translated Exp.	Min = 0.1667 Mean = 0.3333

Class 1:		Point Estimate	95% Confidence Interval
	L	1.067351	0.776656 to 1.358046
	L_q	0.288288	0.077474 to 0.499103
	W	0.569219	0.462558 to 0.675879
	W_q	0.153744	0.053218 to 0.25427

Case Problem : (continued)

Class 2:	Point Estimate	95% Confidence Interval
L	1.252638	0.797306 to 1.707971
L_q	0.570227	0.125552 to 1.014901
W	0.627216	0.400044 to 0.854387
W_q	0.285521	0.063234 to 0.507809

Total cost = 20 + 200 × 1.067 + 100 × 1.252 = 357 $ / per hour ③

Compare ① with ② and ③, proposal 1 is obviously the best. From tests Any other combination of the three proposals will generate higher cost than 1. So, 1 should be adopted.